T0405582

International Perspectives on
Sign Language Translator and
Interpreter Education

Interpreter Education Series

CYNTHIA B. ROY, SERIES EDITOR

JEMINA NAPIER, STACEY WEBB, AND ROBERT ADAM, *Editors*

International Perspectives on Sign Language Translator and Interpreter Education

Second Edition

GALLAUDET UNIVERSITY PRESS
Washington, DC

Gallaudet University Press
gupress.gallaudet.edu

Gallaudet University Press is located on the
traditional territories of Nacotchtank and Piscataway.

© 2025 by Gallaudet University
All rights reserved. Published 2025
Printed in the United States of America

ISBN: 978-1-954622-42-5 (casebound)
ISBN: 978-1-954622-43-2 (ebook)

Library of Congress Cataloging-in-Publication Data
Names: Napier, Jemina, editor.
Title: International perspectives on sign language translator and interpreter education /
    edited by Jemina Napier, Stacey Webb, and Robert Adam.
Description: Second edition. | Washington, DC : Gallaudet University Press, 2024. |
    Series: Interpreter education; volume 14 | Includes bibliographical references and index. |
    Summary: "This volume is a much-needed update to the 2009 book International
    Perspectives on Sign Language Interpreter Education. The second edition expands on
    countries included in the first edition, plus additional countries to give a wider
    global perspective"-- Provided by publisher.
Identifiers: LCCN 2024031444 (print) | LCCN 2024031445 (ebook) |
    ISBN 9781954622425 (hardcover) | ISBN 9781954622432 (ebook)
Subjects: LCSH: Interpreters for deaf people.
Classification: LCC HV2402.I58 2024 (print) | LCC HV2402 (ebook) |
    DDC 419--dc23/eng/20241010
LC record available at https://lccn.loc.gov/2024031444
LC ebook record available at https://lccn.loc.gov/2024031445

∞ This paper meets the requirements of ANSI/NISO Z39.48–1992 (Permanence of Paper).

Cover description: Top third of the cover is dark gray, with white and orange text reading "International Perspectives on Sign Language Translator and Interpreter Education. Second Edition. Jemina Napier, Stacey Webb, and Robert Adam, Editors." Rest of cover is a geometric rectangular pattern in a gradient of different colors, from dull and muted colors on the edges to bright colors in the middle.

Cover design by Tracy Cox.

While the authors have made every effort to provide accurate internet addresses and other contact information at the time of publication, neither the publisher nor the authors assume any responsibility for errors or changes that occur after publication. Furthermore, the publisher does not have any control over and does not assume any responsibility for third-party websites or their content.

We dedicate this book to our families, friends, and colleagues who have tirelessly supported us through the journey of bringing together this volume on global sign language translator and interpreter education.

SIGNED CHAPTER SUMMARIES

The QR code at the beginning of each chapter links to a signed chapter summary. Please scan or click the QR code to view the video. The videos can also be accessed by visiting the Gallaudet University Press YouTube channel under the playlist for this title.

CONTENTS

EDITORIAL ADVISORY BOARD

ACKNOWLEDGMENTS

We acknowledge the efforts of all the contributors to this volume and their patience during the length of time that it took to bring the finished volume to fruition. The editorial process was impacted by a confluence of many events, personal and professional, as well as the inevitable delays caused by the COVID-19 pandemic and the need for all of us to focus our efforts elsewhere. But we strongly believe that it was worth the tenacity and diligence in the end!

ABBREVIATIONS

Key Concepts

CEFR—Common European Framework of Reference for Languages
CoE—code of ethics
CPD—continuing professional development
DI—deaf interpreter
DT—deaf translator
DTIs—deaf translators and interpreters
ECTS—European Credit Transfer and Accumulation System
EDI—equality, diversity, and inclusion
EIPA—Educational Interpreter Performance Assessment (USA)
EUMASLI—European Master in Sign Language Interpreting
GDP—gross domestic product
HEIs—higher education institutions
IIP—Interpreter Internship Program (Canada)
NGO—nongovernment organization
NoS—National Occupational Standards (UK)
RPL—recognition of prior learning
SOTL—Scholarship of Teaching and Learning
SE—Special Education
SLI—sign language interpreting
SLTI—sign language translation and interpreting
SLT—sign language translation
T&I—translation and interpreting
UNCRPD—United Nations Convention on the Rights of
Persons With Disabilities
VET—vocational education and training
VRI—video remote interpreting
VRS—video relay services

Sign Languages

AdaSL—Adamorobe Sign Language
ASL—American Sign Language
Auslan—Australian Sign Language
BASL—Black American Sign Language
BSL—British Sign Language
CSL—Chinese Sign Language
CzSL—Czech Sign Language
DGS—German Sign Language
FinSL—Finnish Sign Language
FinSSL—Finland-Swedish Sign Language
GSL—Ghanaian Sign Language
IS—International Sign
ISL—Irish Sign Language
ISLs—Indigenous Sign Languages (Canada)
JSL—Japanese Sign Language
KosSL—Kosovo Sign Language
KSL—Kenyan Sign Language
Libras—Brazilian Sign Language
LSFB—French Belgian Sign Language
LSQ—Langue des Signes Quebecoise (Canada)
LSM—Mexican Sign Language
MSL—Maritime Sign Language (Canada)
NmG—Signed Dutch
NSL—Nanabin Sign Language
NTS—Norwegian Sign Language
NZSL—New Zealand Sign Language
ÖGS—Austrian Sign Language
RSL—Russian Sign Language
SASL—South African Sign Language
STS—Swedish Sign Language
UgSL—Ugandan Sign Language
USL—Ukrainian Sign Language
VGT—Flemish Sign Language (Belgium, Flanders)

Organizations or Systems Mentioned in Chapters

AAD[1]—Albanian Association of the Deaf
AAD[2]—(former) Australian Association of the Deaf

Abrates—Brazilian Association of Translators and Interpreters
AGSLI—Association of Ghanaian Sign Language Interpreters
AIIC—International Association of Conference Interpreters
AIT—National Association of Interpreters and Translators of Mexico
AIT-LS—National Association of Interpreters and Translators of Sign Language in Mexico
ANILS—(former) National Association of Sign Language Interpreters (Mexico)
APCI—Association of Police and Court Interpreters (UK)
AQF—Australian Qualifications Framework
ASLI—Association of Sign Language Interpreters UK
ASLIA—(former) Australian Sign Language Interpreters Association
ASLITA—Australian Sign Language Interpreters & Translators Association
ASLTA—American Sign Language Teachers Association
ATA—American Translators Association
ATIP-B.C—Baja California's Translator and Interpreter Association (Mexico)
AUSIT—Australian Institute for Interpreters and Translators
AVLIC—(former) Association of Visual Language Interpreters of Canada
BASLIN—(former) Black and Asian Sign Language Interpreters Network (UK)
BDA—British Deaf Association
BEI—Board of Evaluation of Interpreters (USA)
BKVT—Belgian Chamber of Translators and Interpreters
BEI—Board of Evaluation of Interpreters (Texas, USA)
BVDT—Association of Interpreters for the Deaf (Belgium, Flanders)
BVGT—Association of Flemish Sign Language Interpreters (Belgium, Flanders)
CAB—Flemish Communication Assistance Agency for the Deaf
CACDP—(former) Council for the Advancement of Communication with Deaf People (UK)
CAD-ASC—Canadian Association of the Deaf-Association des Sourds du Canada
CAK—Communications Authority of Kenya
CALI—Center for Atypical Language Interpreting (USA)
CASLI[1]—Canadian Association of Sign Language Interpreters
CASLI[2]—Center of the Assessment of Sign Language Interpreters (USA)
CCIE—Commission on Collegiate Interpreter Education (USA)
CDPF—China Disabled People's Federation
CDS—Center for Deaf Studies at Trinity College Dublin (Ireland)
CESLIS—Center for Sign Language Interpreting Services (Kenya)
CHS—Canadian Hearing Society
CIDP—Catholic Institute for Deaf People (Ireland)
CIOL—Chartered Institute of Linguistics (UK)
CISLI—Council of Irish Sign Language Interpreters
CIT—Conference of Interpreter Trainers (USA)

CIUTI—Conférence Internationale Permanente d'Instituts Universitaires de Traducteurs et Interprètes

CLIA—Canadian Language Industry Association

CMIC—Mexican College of Conference Interpreters

CNAD—Chinese National Association of the Deaf

CONADIS—National Council for the Development and Inclusion of People with Disabilities (Mexico)

CONOCER—Committee on Regulations and Labor Certification (Mexico)

CRTC—Canadian Radio and Telecommunications Commission

CSTZJ—Czech Society of Sign Language Interpreters

CTI—Center for Translation and Interpretation (Kenya)

CVRS—Canadian Video Relay Services

DANIDA—Danish International Development and Cooperation Agency

DDA—Deaf Development Association (Uganda)

DDL—Danish Deaf Association

Deaf Aotearoa (formerly the New Zealand Association of the Deaf, NZAD)

Deaf Australia (formerly the Australian Association of the Deaf, AAD

DeafSA—Deaf Federation of South Africa

DIN—Deaf Interpreter Network (UK)

Doof Vlaanderen—Deaf Flanders (Belgium)

DWEB—(former) Deaf Welfare Examination Board (UK)

ECML—European Center for Modern Languages

efsli—European Forum of Sign Language Interpreters

ENPSIT—European Network for Public Service Interpreting & Translation

EST—European Society for Translation Studies

EU—European Union

EUD—European Union of the Deaf

EULITA—European Legal Interpreters and Translators Association

FAD—Finnish Association of the Deaf

FEBRAPILS—National Federation of Sign Language Translators and Interpreters (Brazil)

FENEIS—National Federation of Deaf (Brazil)

Fevlado—(former) Federation of Flemish Deaf Clubs (Belgium, Flanders)

FSDB—Swedish Association for Deafblind people

GATI—Ghana Association of Translators and Interpreters

GESDO—sign language interpreter education program in Linz, Upper Austria

GIL—Ghana Institute of Languages

GILLBT—Ghana Institute of Linguistics, Literacy and Bible Translation

GNAD—Ghana National Association of the Deaf

HRF—Swedish organization for the hard of hearing

IASLI—(former) Irish Association of Sign Language Interpreters

IDS—Irish Deaf Society
IEP—Interpreter Education Program (USA/Canada)
IIP—Interpreter Internship Program (Canada)
IJC—International Court of Justice
IOCN—Interpreters of Colour Network (UK)
IRIS—Irish Remote Interpreting Service
ITAT—Institut für Theoretische und Angewandte Translationswissenschaft
(Department of Translation Studies at the University of Graz, Austria)
ITI—Institute of Translation and Interpreting (UK)
ITIA—Irish Translators' and Interpreters' Association
JASLI—Japanese Association of Sign Language Interpreters
JFD—Japanese Federation of the Deaf
KAD—Kosovar Association of the Deaf
KASLI—Kosovar Association of Sign Language Interpreters
KCCA—Kampala City Council Authorities (Uganda)
Kela—Social Insurance Institution of Finland (provision of sign language
interpreters)
KICD—Kenya Institute of Curriculum Development
KNAD—Kenya National Association of the Deaf
KNEC—Kenya National Examination Council
Komora—Czech Chamber of Sign Language Interpreters
KSLIA—Kenya Sign Language Interpreters Association
KSLRP—Kenyan Sign Language Research Project
LEMDA—London Ethnic Minority Deaf Association
LVT—Pavlovsk College for the Deaf (Russia)
Mano a Mano—Organization of Trilingual (ASL-Spanish-English) interpreters
MBSLIN—Muslim BSL Interpreters Network
MYH—Swedish National Agency for Higher Vocational Education
NAATI—National Accreditation Authority for Translators and Interpreters
(Australia)
NABS—National Auslan Interpreter Booking and Payment System (Australia)
NAD—National Association of the Deaf (USA)
NAJIT—National Association of Judiciary Interpreters (USA)
NAOBI—National Alliance of Black Interpreters (USA)
NASLI—National Association of Sign Language Interpreters (Ghana)
Nav—Norwegian Labour and Welfare Organization
NAVEKADOS—(former) National Federation of Catholic
Deaf-Mutes (Belgium, Flanders)
NCIEC—(former) National Consortium of Interpreter Education Centers (USA)
NDI—National Deaf Interpreters (USA)
NDIS—National Disability Insurance Scheme (Australia)

NDF—Norwegian National Association of the Deaf
NDWI—National Deaf Women of Ireland
NIEC—(former) National Interpreter Education Center (USA)
NRASLI—National Research Association for Sign Language Interpretation (Japan)
NRCPD—National Registers for Communication Professionals working with Deaf People (UK)
NRPSI—National Register of Public Service Interpreters (UK)
NTID—National Technical Institute for the Deaf (USA)
NUBSLI—National Union of British Sign Language Interpreters
NZSTI—New Zealand Society of Translators and Interpreters
OECD—Organization for Economic, Cooperation and Development
ÖGSDV—Austrian Sign Language Interpreters and Translators Association
OMT—Mexican Organization of Translators
OSEP—Office of Special Education Programs (USA)
OTZJ—Organization of Sign Language Interpreters (Czech Republic)
PANSALB—Pan South African Language Board
Pevnost—Czech Sign Language Center
RASLI—Russian Association of Sign Language Interpreters
RBSLI—Regulatory Body of British Sign Language Interpreters & Translators
RID—Registry of Interpreters for the Deaf (USA)
RISLI—Register of Irish Sign Language Interpreters
RNID—Royal National Institute for the Deaf (UK)
RSA—Rehabilitation Services Administration (USA)
RSLP—Regional Sign Language Project (Uganda)
RTO—Registered Training Organizations (Australia)
SALPC—South African Language Practitioners' Council
SALPC Act—South African Language Practitioners' Council Act
SAQA—South African Qualifications Authority
SASLI—(former) Scottish Association of Sign Language Interpreters
SATI—South African Translators Institute
SCOSLI—Scottish Collaborative of Sign Language Interpreters
SDR—Swedish Deaf Association
SKTL—Association of Finnish Translators and Interpreters
SLAC—Sign Language Acquisition Corpus (Ireland/Sweden)
SLIANZ—Sign Language Interpreters Association of New Zealand
SLIAO—Apprenticeship in Sign Language Interpreting Associates Ottawa Inc. (Canada)
SLIC—Sign Language Interpreting Committee (China)
SLICE—Sign Language Interpreter Certificate Examination (Japan)

SLIS—Sign Language Interpreting Service (Ireland)
SLN—AIIC Sign Language Network
SNN—Union of the Deaf and Hard of Hearing in the Czech Republic
SRLPDC—Scottish Register for Language Professionals Working With the Deaf Community
STAR Ghana Foundation—national center for active citizenship and philanthropy
STTF—Swedish Sign Language Interpreters Association
SVT—Finnish Association of Sign Language Interpreters
TAFEs—Technical & Further Education colleges (Australia)
Tenuto—Independent CPD training for SLIs in Flanders (Belgium)
TÖI—Institute for Interpreting and Translation Studies (Stockholm University, Sweden)
Tolkeforbunde—Norwegian Association of Interpreters
TTYR—Tulkkitoiminnan yhteistyöryhmä cooperative interpreting service (Finland)
UBOS—Ugandan Bureau of Statistics
UN—United Nations
UNAD—Ugandan Association of the Deaf
UNASLI—Uganda National Association of Sign Language Interpreters
UNDP—United Nations Development Program
UNESCO—United Nations Educational, Scientific, and Cultural Organization
UTOG—Ukrainian Deaf Organisation
VGTC—Flemish Sign Language Center (Flanders, Belgium)
Viittomakielen keskus—The Sign Language Center (Finland)
VLP—Visual Language Professionals (UK)
VOG—The All-Russian Federation of the Deaf
WASLI—World Association of Sign Language Interpreters
WFD—World Federation of the Deaf

STACEY WEBB, JEMINA NAPIER, AND
ROBERT ADAM

Sign Language Translation and Interpreting Education Two Decades On

An Introduction to the Volume

How Did We Get Here?

> Good teachers possess a capacity for connectedness. They are able to weave a complex web of connections among themselves, their subjects, and their students so that students can learn to weave a world for themselves. (Palmer, 1998, p. 36)

In 2004, Jemina published an article that provided a comparison of sign language interpreting (SLI) training, education, and assessment in the United Kingdom, the United States of America (United States), and Australia, where it was clear that the systems were very different despite having the same overarching goal of ensuring quality and professional standards for the training, regulation, and monitoring of SLI practice (Napier, 2004). Much has changed in these three countries and worldwide since that time.

The 2004 article provided the impetus for the edited volume titled *International Perspectives on Sign Language Interpreter Education*, which was published in 2009 as part of the Interpreting Education series by Gallaudet University Press. That volume gave an overview of the development and current state of play of SLI education, training, assessment, and certification in 15 countries. Almost two decades later, we believe that it is timely to present this second edition of the volume by updating existing chapters and adding new chapters to highlight the changes in SLI education across the world, to take stock of the professionalization of SLI and the emergence of sign language translation (SLT) as professional practice in many countries, and to reflect on the changing nature of the sign language translation and interpreting (SLTI) profession to include more deaf translators and interpreters (DTIs). This second volume, with a new editorial team whose members work together now but hail from different countries and have taken a variety of pathways into the profession and SLTI education, provides an

1

opportunity to reflect on the changing nature of SLTI and the way we teach, given that one size does not fit all:

> Some journeys are direct, and some are circuitous, some are heroic and some are fearful and muddled. But every journey, honestly undertaken, stands a chance of taking us toward the place where our deep gladness meets the world's deep need. (Palmer, 1999, p. 36)

As people and professionals, as interpreters, translators, and educators alike, we are all on a journey. Although this journey can feel like a solo one, we assure you that you are not alone. In fact, there are people all around the world who have traveled before you, are currently traveling with you, or will follow in your footsteps.

If you are reading this volume, it suggests that you have an interest in SLTI education and the SLTI profession and have committed to working with deaf communities and the next generation of SLTI practitioners. If no one has directly said "thank you" for your efforts, accept our appreciation for what you do and for the contributions you have made and will continue to make in our field.

Although this volume focuses on SLTI education in 22 countries worldwide, we have asked each author to contextualize SLTI in the broader context of the translation and interpreting profession and educational systems relative to their own country. In that sense, we envisage that this volume will also be useful for educators, practitioners, and researchers in the broader field of translation and interpreting studies.

It is increasingly recognized that it is important to state your positionality as an interpreting researcher (Hale & Napier, 2013; Mellinger, 2020; Tiselius, 2019; Wurm & Napier, 2017), and we suggest that there should be a similar expectation for interpreter educators. Before you travel the world with us, we want to share with you highlights of our own journeys that have brought us to this point in editing this volume together.

WHO ARE WE?

Stacey is hearing and was born and raised in the United States. Unlike Robert and Jemina, Stacey does not have any deaf family members and is a new signer (De Meulder, 2018). Stacey was born in San Diego, California, and lived in several different places in the United States. As of the writing of this book, she lives in Scotland and has worked at Heriot-Watt University since 2014, teaching and researching SLTI in the same programs as Robert and Jemina.

California was one of the first U.S. states to offer American Sign Language (ASL) to high school students. At 14 years of age, Stacey began taking classes both at her high school and a local community college. Signing quickly became part of her everyday life. She made deaf friends, and she went to every deaf event she could find, from bowling and coffee nights to driving 2 hours away to meet up with the hundreds of deaf people at "the Block," where signers would meet at a shopping mall and block foot traffic because there were so many people crammed into one place.

After completing all available ASL classes, Stacey enrolled in an interpreting program at the same community college. In 2004, she completed two associate's degrees (one in liberal arts/teaching and the other in interpreting) and headed to California State University, Northridge (CSUN), to enroll in a Deaf Studies bachelor of arts program to further her education. It was this same year that she got her first paid job as an interpreter and began freelancing and working in higher education settings. She became a certified interpreter with the Registry of Interpreters for the Deaf in 2006.

One year before starting at CSUN, Stacey was on the CSUN campus to attend an interpreter symposium at which Anna Witter-Merithew (coauthor of a chapter in this volume on the United States) was presenting on the "readiness-to-work" gap. Later, as a CSUN student, Stacey set up an event called "Support the Gap," a one-day conference aimed at bridging this gap and bringing new interpreters and seasoned interpreters together. Eventually, the same phenomenon influenced the topic of her doctoral degree (Webb, 2017).

Upon graduation, Stacey moved from the West Coast to the East Coast. She accepted a position at a university to work as the deaf and hard of hearing services coordinator. It was a challenging position because she saw very quickly how budgets and university cost-cutting measures impacted the services that deaf students could have on campus. These experiences contributed to her interest in higher education systems and university politics. She also actively worked as an interpreter in Washington, DC, and the metropolitan area.

Stacey moved to Nashville, Tennessee, where she continued interpreting and began her teaching career. She gained teaching experience through casual contracts, instructing practical and theoretical interpreting courses in both in-person and online formats. Stacey participated in the Etna Project,[1] a group of professional interpreters who meet periodically for discussions and reflection on their interpreting work. Betty Colonomos, the project leader, told Stacey, "Don't become another educator who doesn't understand how people learn." This advice prompted Stacey to enroll in a postgraduate program focused on adult education at Colorado State University, which provided her with a foundation in teaching and learning principles that have significantly enhanced her teaching practices.

Stacey's doctoral research led her to Heriot-Watt University, where she was introduced to the British deaf community and British Sign Language (BSL) and where she obtained a doctorate focusing on interpreter educators' experiences and well-being, as well as the readiness-to-work gap. Stacey is now a registered sign language interpreter in the United Kingdom. Since becoming a tenured assistant professor at Heriot-Watt, Stacey has played a key role in shaping and instructing the undergraduate BSL/English interpreting/translation program. She is passionate about facilitating early student engagement with deaf communities and creating hands-on learning opportunities by fostering collaboration among students and various professions. These connections have led to her being invited as a lecturer to train other professionals, such as nursing, midwifery, social work, and education students, who might work with interpreters and deaf people. In 2022, she decided to take a career break from higher education. During this period, she reflected on her role as an interpreter educator and researcher in higher education, reaffirming her commitment to the field. She returned to Heriot-Watt in 2023 equipped with new skills, fresh perspectives, and a renewed sense of purpose to make a meaningful impact in her work.

Jemina is hearing and was born and raised in England in a multigenerational mixed deaf–hearing family in which everybody could sign, so she is a heritage signer who grew up bilingual in BSL and English. She was exposed to other sign languages from an early age through international deaf tennis competitions that her parents participated in and deaf events they attended, so she, also from an early age, could use both one-handed and two-handed fingerspelling.

Jemina fell into interpreting by accident. Although she had done language bro-kering[2] for her parents and other family members, it had never occurred to her that mediating communication was something that she could do for a job. In the United Kingdom, a register for interpreters was just starting to be established when she was a teenager, and when she passed her Stage 3 "Advanced" BSL exam, her name was automatically put on the register as a trainee. Her first paid interpreting assignment was at the age of 17.

Universities were not offering degrees in SLI at that time, so Jemina opted to study sociology, which has served as a bedrock for the nature of research that she does now. While studying, she continued to work as an interpreter. As soon as she graduated in 1994, she began to interpret full time and was offered an in-house community interpreter position within a deaf social services team. Later, in 1995, she passed the qualification in the United Kingdom to become a registered sign language interpreter. She became a freelance interpreter working in conference, political, and media settings, and also specializing in mental health interpreting. In 1996, she enrolled in a master of arts program in BSL/English interpreting in the Deaf Studies Research Unit at Durham University. It was through this program that she discovered a love for linguistics. While completing this program, she began coordinating a course at the City Literary Institute in London that was designed to train and prepare interpreters, already registered as trainees, to become qualified registered sign language interpreters.

On completion of her MA, Jemina was awarded a scholarship to move to Australia in 1998 to obtain a PhD in linguistics. There, she focused on the analysis of sign language interpreters' linguistic coping strategies (Napier, 2002, 2016). She learned Australian Sign Language (Auslan) and became accredited as a professional Auslan/English interpreter in 1998. Her teaching career took off in Australia, as she began to deliver continuing professional development (CPD) training all over the country and then was invited to contribute to teaching on an Auslan/English interpreting community college course, teaching to entry level (what used to be known as paraprofessional level; see the Australia chapter in this volume).

After completing her PhD in 2001, Jemina established the first university SLI training program in Australia in 2002—the postgraduate program in Auslan/English interpreting at Macquarie University, which continues to be delivered in distance/ blended mode and is targeted at working interpreters who are seeking to obtain professional-level accreditation (now referred to as certification). Her passion for research on SLI and the application of research to SLI practice and pedagogy continued to grow. She undertook a master's degree in higher and professional education to better understand pedagogy and assessment in delivering university and professional courses and began publishing her own research and writing more about SLI pedagogy and the need for evidence-based teaching. In addition to the first edition of this volume (Napier, 2009), Jemina has coedited a volume on SLI education in the digital age (Ehrlich & Napier, 2015), and she was the inaugural editor of the *International Journal of Interpreter Education* and still serves on the editorial board. Jemina sees clear links between SLTI practice, research, and teaching, and much of her research is applied, so it directly benefits the education of students and CPD for working interpreters.

In 2013, Jemina moved to Edinburgh, Scotland, to take up a professorship (personal chair) at Heriot-Watt University. In this position, she has contributed to the undergraduate teaching program for BSL/English interpreting students and the European Master in Sign Language Interpreting (EUMASLI) and has supervised PhD students on a range of SLTI topics. While Jemina has worked full time in academia, she has always had one foot in the interpreting world. She continues to practice as an interpreter, primarily for conference and media settings in BSL and International Sign (IS).[3]

Robert is deaf and was born and raised in Australia, where he lived, studied, and worked as a Deaf Studies and Auslan academic and as manager of a statewide SLI service. In 2003, he moved to the United Kingdom to work at the City Literary Institute in London as coordinator of a teacher training course for BSL tutors, and from there he took on sign language researcher and teaching fellow roles, respectively, at City University and then University College London, respectively, before he joined the team at Heriot-Watt University in 2020.

Robert is a *heritage signer* (Napier, 2021) and has been exposed to many different signed languages from an early age. His parents, sister, and aunt are all deaf. His grandmothers were hearing but also fluent in Auslan and Irish Sign Language (ISL). This meant that, as a child, he used both one-handed and two-handed fingerspelling signed systems and grew up multilingually.

Robert often functioned as a language broker, as he would help his parents and aunt with written English by producing Auslan translations. Sometimes he would draft his own sick notes and have his mum sign them. You could say that he was destined to pursue a career in interpreting and translation. Robert remembers a poster at the Deaf club that advertised a deafblind interpreter training course with the Victorian Deaf Society (now Expression Australia). He and some friends registered because they thought it would be fun, and this led to his first paid job working as a deafblind interpreter.

Over the years he worked as an interpreter in Australia, doing mainly intralingual interpreting work, mostly in mental health and courtroom settings. Robert taught for the first Diploma of Interpreting in Melbourne when it was launched in 1990, and like many interpreter educators, he found that it is the practical interpreting experiences that can truly enrich student learning experience.

Although the use of IS has become more widespread in recent years, Robert's first exposure to IS was in 1989 at the Asia/Pacific Conference and Football Championships, hosted in Melbourne; he encountered IS again in Japan in 1990 at the World Federation of the Deaf (WFD) Conference. He now admits that at the time he did not understand everything, but this initial exposure was the beginning of a successful career working as an IS interpreter and translator. Just under a decade later, he was involved with organizing the 1999 World Congress of the WFD in Brisbane, and he found himself brokering between the Australian Organizing Committee and deaf international visitors. This was his first exposure to working in international settings and also an opportunity to see how it was possible to work in different languages and contexts and to bring people together.

Since then, Robert has interpreted at the Deaflympics, WFD congresses, academic conferences, high-level meetings, and university seminars. He is grateful to the Association of Sign Language Interpreters UK and then-Chair Christopher Stone, who set a precedent for hiring deaf interpreters at their annual conferences and annual general meetings. Robert's educational experiences have run parallel to all of the aforementioned practical interpreting experiences. Unlike interpreters today, many of whom enter education programs to graduate and start their practice, Robert was working as an interpreter and even educating interpreters while he studied for his bachelor of education in teaching languages other than English and then a BA in linguistics, followed by a MA degree in applied linguistics; and later a PhD in cognitive, perceptual, and behavioral sciences, looking at unimodal bilingualism in deaf communities (Adam, 2017).

When working on his PhD, Robert also became interested in researching and documenting the work of DTIs (Adam, Carty, & Stone, 2011; Adam et al., 2014a) and also in SLTI research and education more generally, leading to other important outputs (e.g., Stone et al., 2022). Some of his early articles arose from collaborations with other deaf IS interpreters, Julia Klintberg, Senan Dunne, Juan Carlos Druetta, and Markus Aro, who were able to share similar experiences of this career pathway and became valued friends and colleagues in IS interpreting settings (see Adam et al., 2014b). More than 30 years on, Robert continues to work in an ever-evolving profession as an interpreter in a variety of settings: as a deaf intralingual (or "relay") interpreter, as an ASL/BSL interpreter, and in many contexts in which IS is used. Robert also often thinks of the prescience of the two people who organized that first course in the Deaf Club all those years ago (Teresa Cumpston Bird and Carla Anderson) and their foresight in ensuring that deaf practitioners had the opportunity for training.

Who Are You?

So that's us.
Who are you?
What is your story?
What brought you to the profession of SLTI and specifically SLTI education?

We hope that you have taken some time to answer or reflect on these questions. Just as each chapter of this book shares the journey of SLTI education within a specific country, we have asked each author to share their story with you. The positionality statements from each author vary slightly, as we asked them to share what they felt most comfortable imparting about their journey specifically in relation to SLTI and SLTI education. We hope that by doing this it allows you to connect with the authors and the context in which they are working.

We also want to celebrate your individual journey: the risks you have taken, the hurdles overcome, the learning curves, and many successful milestones you have achieved. They have all helped SLTI education and the profession of interpreting within your country, and beyond, move forward.

Before giving an overview of the structure and content of the book and discussing some conventions we have established, first we give consideration to the international political and societal context that situates this volume, followed by a theoretical overview of how and why approaches to teaching SLTI might be disparate and have evolved over time—and how this evolution is positioned in the broader translation and interpreting pedagogy landscape.

THE INTERNATIONAL POLITICAL AND SOCIETAL CONTEXT

As we consider the contributions to this volume on SLTI, it is important to acknowledge the global political and societal context in which the SLTI profession and education operate. Globally, we have seen a massive shift in attitudes toward racism, colorism, sexism, ableism, and exclusion from political processes, with a reframing of the importance of diversity and inclusion in society, including in the academic world (Asumah & Nagel, 2024). Increasing numbers of countries have some form of equality or anti-discrimination legislation, which provide support mechanisms for people with protected characteristics to feel safe and able to participate in society without discrimination. However, there are also many countries where oppression and discrimination of marginalized groups continue, and some protected characteristics are still criminalized (e.g., homosexuality).

Initially proposed as a black feminist theory to consider how the intersections among gender, race, and color can impact black women's lives (Crenshaw, 1989), *intersectionality* has become a popular and widely cited social justice theoretical framework for analyzing sameness and difference among people. The focus of the theory is on how people experience marginalization, power, inequality, and oppression in the context of their complex overlapping identities and characteristics and how these affect their lived experiences, the choices they make in life, and the options they have available to them (Cho, Crenshaw, & McCall, 2013). The initial theory has been further evolved (Chan, Erby, & Fird, 2017), so an "expanded-intersectionality" (Bagga-Gupta, 2017) now recognizes that other identity categories are also salient and are not necessarily easy to separate (Gunnarsson, 2015)—for example, disability, language minority status, sexuality, and other characteristics in addition to race, gender, and color.

Deaf people have benefited from this political, theoretical, and societal shift. Their protected characteristics are often acknowledged under the banner of disability legislation and policies, so in this case their sign language rights are synonymous with disability rights (Murray et al., 2018). Nevertheless, there has been a groundswell of recognition for the rights of deaf people to use sign languages as a human right, resulting in more than 77 countries (at the time of writing) having officially recognized their national sign language in the form of a sign language law or act (De Meulder et al., 2019), with many others recognizing sign languages through language policies, general language legislation, or constitutions (WFD, 2023); some have more than one form of recognition. Of the 22 countries featured in this volume, eight have a sign language law or act, 18 have some form of official sign language recognition, and six acknowledge the national sign language in their constitution. Furthermore, there is increasing focus on how the experiences of deaf people as sign language users intersect with their other characteristics, such as color, race, disability, gender, sexuality, etc. (see for example Chapple et al., 2021;

Dunn & Anderson, 2019; Emery & Iyer, 2022; Kusters, 2019; Miller & Clark, 2020; Murray et al., 2020; Napier, 2024; Obasi, 2022; Smith-Warshaw & Crume, 2020; Wu & Grant, 2020).

Inevitably, as with the wider population of nonsigning hearing people, deaf signers' experiences are influenced by the part of the world in which they live, what was previously often referred to as living in "developing" or "developed" countries. The concept of "development" is now contested, as it is often positioned as a goal for countries through a white, Western lens where the perception is that a process of development will make a country "better" (Willis, 2020) (i.e., countries should aspire to be more like Western countries in terms of infrastructure, economy, etc.). Geographers, development studies researchers, politicians, and others have begun to refer more often to countries in the "Global North" and "Global South" to map country variations in a different way, with a focus on alternative philosophies of development, and to have dialogue about local and regional development within and between the Global North and South (Pike et al., 2014). For example, countries previously categorized as developed, like Australia, are situated geographically in the Global South. It could be argued, however, that this has just created different development boundary lines (Solarz, 2019).

Either way, it is clear that the experiences of deaf people are affected by where they live; whether their country recognizes their sign language; whether access to information and services in sign languages is valued and whether it is funded; whether SLI is accepted as a social institution (De Meulder & Haualand, 2021); whether SLI and SLT are regarded as legitimate professions that require interpreters and translators to be trained and paid; and whether infrastructure is available to support the development of SLTI as a profession and the establishment of training. In this context, McCartney (2017) argues that SLI should be considered a social justice profession because the existence of the profession makes a difference to deaf people's lives. As such, any consideration of the evolution of SLTI education must be placed within this wider political, societal, and social justice landscape. We cannot expect that SLTI education will be homogenous worldwide, and even if the SLTI profession and education systems are well evolved, there could still be significant variations, as they will need to operate within and align with the local cultural and political milieu.

THE EVOLUTION OF SLTI EDUCATION AND TRAINING

Globally, the understanding of SLTI interpreter education varies because it is dependent on the stage of professionalization in each national context. As you will see through the chapters of this book, SLTI has strong roots in deaf communities, and the original sign language translators and interpreters have always been either people with direct ties to deaf communities or deaf people themselves. Thus, those traditionally providing these services accepted a civic duty in offering a service for the public good or to support their own communities. In countries where sign language is not yet recognized as an official language or where the profession of translation and interpreting lacks status, this SLTI work might still be perceived as a civic duty. Therefore, in this context, if training is provided to those who are serving as interpreters, it is on a very short-term, ad hoc basis, and in some cases it does not exist at all (Napier & Goswell, 2013, in press).

Alternatively, where progress has been made and SLTI has advanced as a profession, education and training have evolved into more formalized education systems. However, the types of formal education remain variable and might be offered at vocational, undergraduate, and postgraduate levels. It is important to note that this process of professionalization also means that (hearing) sign language interpreters have to legitimize their involvement in the SLTI field (Friedner, 2018). Professionalization also lends itself to marketization, as it means that now that interpreters are more educated, they hold qualifications and join professional membership organizations and, consequently, essentially compete for business.

In the same way that SLTI has shifted in some countries from being merely a civic responsibility to one of a job market, formalized educational opportunities have also moved away from being focused on serving the public to increasingly aligning with globalization, marketplace forces, and neoliberal marketization ideology[4] (Connell, 2013; Frake, 2008; Holmes & Lindsay, 2018). Whereas colleges and universities were once places where young people came to develop themselves personally, socially, emotionally, and mentally, these institutions now adhere to a global model of higher education that is influenced by economic and political movements and general shifts in capitalism that promote neoliberal approaches to education, which requires them to operate as business enterprises valuing consumers, competition, and profit. With its focus on economic efficiency, competition, and individual responsibility, a neoliberalist ideology results in the commodification of education (Balan, 2023).

Given the various political and economic challenges of recent years (e.g., Brexit, the 2008 financial crisis, the post-2008 recession, changes of government administration, international conflicts, the current cost-of-living crisis), higher education has been impacted greatly, and the educational focus has become more centered on workforce readiness and employability. Although these shifts in university systems and structures are certainly context specific, it should be noted that neoliberal transitions and interventions that are shifting universities to focus on the marketplace are a global phenomenon (Connell, 2013; Frake, 2008; Holmes & Lindsay, 2018).

Given that the development of SLTI education is a response to workforce needs and to the push to professionalize interpreters, it makes sense that SLTI education programs are increasingly validated as suitable college and university program offerings. As a result, in many countries, SLTI education is now situated within the higher education system (Webb, 2017; Webb & Best, 2020; Webb & Napier, 2015). The higher education system can be understood firstly as an aggregate of formal entities (e.g., the higher education system in a specific country) and secondly as representing the specific population engaged with postsecondary educational activities (e.g., controllers, organizers, workers, and consumers) (Clark, 1983). Tierney (1999) explains how demographics, economics, and even political conditions influence the higher education system. SLTI education is also considered part of the profession of interpreting system and in many contexts is thus situated within the higher education system (Webb & Best, 2020; Webb & Napier, 2015), so one can see how the two systems overlap. Therefore, the factors explained by Tierney that impact higher education systems will also impact SLTI education, and in turn, what happens within SLTI education will influence what happens within the SLTI profession.

Although employability and workforce readiness are the new focus of higher education institutions (HEIs), there have been many criticisms questioning the ability of HEIs to meet these objectives (Abelha et al., 2020; Long et al., 2018). Employers across a range of sectors report being disappointed with graduates' level of performance when they do enter the workforce (Abelha et al., 2020). Such reports have also been specifically linked to graduates of SLTI education. Deaf people, SLI educators, and graduates themselves have all expressed concerns about the knowledge and skill deficiencies of sign language interpreters upon graduation from SLI education programs (Napier, 2009; Witter-Merithew & Johnson, 2005). Thus, although HEIs allege that they continue to honor the public interest, such changes and the adoption of neoliberal values have led many to challenge these claims (Lynch, 2006).

Webb (2017) argues that the consequences of marketization have impacted SLTI education to the point that if the profession wants to further professionalize, it will need a more cooperative approach in which key stakeholders return to the table and identify ways that they can navigate the future. As the need for qualified sign language translators and interpreters has and will continue to rise (Lesson et al., 2014; Napier & Leeson, 2016), so too will the expectations of stakeholders about the skills and abilities of working translators and interpreters, particularly in countries where deaf people have advanced educationally and professionally (Hall et al., 2016). Expectations have also changed with regard to the diversity of translators and interpreters to better represent different intersectional characteristics (Napier et al., 2022; Obasi, 2013; Parkins-Maliko, 2022; Sikder, 2019) and to thus more closely reflect diversities in deaf communities. However, scholars suggest that the current state of SLTI education is not able to keep up (Lesson et al., 2014; Webb, 2017).

In fact, many of the challenges of SLTI education, described in the first edition of this volume and in Webb's (2017) study, are direct consequences of marketization and the cost-saving practices of neoliberalism. Further examples of these challenges specifically relate to working within the confines of HEIs. For example,

Webb (2017) found that because of restricted workload models, educators struggle to find time to further develop and strengthen curricula, and they report needing more classroom resources to support teaching activities. She also reports that they find it difficult to locate and organize resources when they do exist, as well as to develop them when they do not. Educators describe a complex mix of roles and contracts, and it appears that many educators feel isolated, working part time or on hourly contracts. Financial constraints have further impacted by limiting invest-ment in program resources and staff development. There are indications that SLTI educators do not have enough opportunities to engage with research and further develop themselves professionally. Depending on the level of professionalization and where interpreter education is situated, you could be facing some of these same challenges in your own country.

Certainly, some countries do not yet offer formalized SLTI education within HEIs. As such, it is important to consider how other powerful external factors, such as demographics, economics, and even political conditions, influence operating higher education systems (c.f. Tierny, 1999). Additionally, deaf community expecta-tions will also have an influence over other systems (e.g., organizations, charities). Therefore, when SLTI education is provided on an ad hoc basis—for example, a deaf organizational charity offering classes—this training will also be influenced by these external factors, particularly in deciding key course aspects, such as when, how, how long, and to whom.

So, the next questions we have for you are:

What is the context in which you are working?
What are you juggling?
And most importantly, how are you doing?

It is worthwhile thinking about the context in which you are operating, because as you navigate this volume you will have a baseline for comparison. It is also impor-tant to recognize the landscape in which you are working and to be realistic about what changes might be possible given the local conditions.

We have a feeling that you, like us, have a lot on your plate. We understand and are aware of many of the stressors you are under and believe that the authors in this volume can also relate to your experiences. Nevertheless, we suspect that even under all the pressure, with everything you are juggling, you are still managing the demands in front of you. At the same time, if you are like us, or anything like the participants in Webb's (2017) doctoral research, we imagine you can relate to the feeling of having too much to do with not enough time or resources to do it.

As SLTI educators, we juggle the various demands of and tensions between the educational system, the SLTI profession, deaf communities, and our personal lives, and we move constantly between the various roles we hold, such as parent, friend, volunteer, athlete, etc. To say the least, it can be hard to stay balanced; right when you feel that you have managed to figure out the best position, something happens that requires a re-focus, and you do your best to reposition without falling over.

This illustrates the balancing act that many of us find ourselves in. The difficulty in striking a balance relates to the various identities, roles, and responsibilities that we hold. Day et al. (2006, p. 601) describe "identity" as one's unique "sense of purpose, self-efficacy, motivation and commitment." In other words, why do we do what we do, and where do we get the confidence, determination, and feeling of responsibility to stay committed to doing it? Billot (2010) explains identities as being intrinsically bound to values, beliefs, and practices; it is our sense of purpose that will impact how our identities develop, as well as how we position ourselves in the workplace.

Scholars today emphasize that we cannot explore identity as a single construct and that people are multilayered and complex beings that cannot easily be placed into a single box. Hence, intersectionality has been used as a framework to understand people's lived experiences. In relation to higher education, some scholars have explored intersections between educators' personal characteristics, such as race, ethnicity, nationality, gender, age, marital status, and caregiving roles, in relation to their experiences at work (Chan, Erby, & Ford, 2017). Other scholars have explored how professional characteristics, such as rank, contract type, administrative/leadership roles, teaching styles, and interests, can affect their perceptions of themselves and their colleagues, as well as how they make sense of their experiences within the workplace (Gillespie et al., 2001; Rosewell & Ashwin, 2019; Winterm et al., 2000).

Certainly, like all educators, SLTI educators have personal and professional characteristics that will impact our overall work experiences. Additionally, many of us hold dual (or even multiple) professional identities, as in addition to being educators, we are often also professional interpreters or translators. A dual professional role is not unique to SLTI educators. In fact, many educators are connected to a professional domain (Billiot, 2010). This dual professional identity and multiple roles within each can lead to what is known as role conflict and role strain, which can have a negative impact on well-being and job performance (Schaufeli et al., 2009). In a nutshell, there can be various incompatible demands, expectations, and values across and between professional roles. For example, as a professional interpreter, you want the profession to be filled with highly qualified people who are collegiate and have professional integrity; as a deaf person, you want the profession to be filled with highly qualified people who deliver services at a professional standard; as an educator, you are confined to the structures of the institution and must work within system walls. For example, undergraduate classes could be limited to 3 hours per week regardless of learning outcomes, the specific subject, or discipline.

You know that students need more contact hours to develop their (sign) language skills, and they need more exposure to various deaf signers, but with your educator hat on you know that there is no more time in the workload to add another class, and there is no money to pay additional external staffing costs. Thus, conflict.

So, this leads us to more questions for you to ponder. As we reflected on what brought you to interpreter education, we now ask you: Why are you an interpreter educator? What keeps you juggling the roles (if you do) of interpreter, deaf services user, and educator? What keeps you motivated to continue with these professional roles?

We reflected on this question, too. Not only do we have a strong passion for teaching and making a difference in individual lives as we see students have those remarkable "a-ha" moments, but at the end of the day, we do this work knowing that we are seeking to improve the quality of SLTI provision for deaf communities.

We hope that when modeling partnership practices between deaf and hearing educators, we can influence how deaf and hearing people work together, and DTIs will be seen as equal to their hearing interpreter counterparts. Ultimately, we believe that the more research that is done on SLTI, the better educational opportunities students will have, which will lead to more qualified interpreters working toward creating a more equitable and accessible world.

As described in the first edition of this volume and reiterated throughout the next several chapters, the SLTI profession has evolved directly from deaf communities, as interpreting services were provided by deaf peoples' family members and friends and by local clergy and social workers (Cokely, 2005; Scott-Gibson, 1992). In many countries, this is still the case. Consequently, deaf people were the ones who vetted and selected those who would deliver interpreting services. Today, in many national contexts, higher education has taken over the vetting process by using sign language as a "cash cow" that belies deaf people's interests (Robinson & Henner, 2018). However, valuing deaf people and their communities remains an integral component of SLTI education, and educators not only remain connected to deaf people because they are friends or family, but they are also encouraging students to interact and build relationships with deaf people and become active members of their respective deaf communities, particularly through principles of service learning (Shaw, 2013).

Moreover, increasingly, SLTI educators, researchers, and students are deaf themselves and therefore are already members of deaf community groups. These connections certainly have had an influence on the SLTI educator identity and how we see ourselves as members of the community while also teaching those who will become part of it. Involvement from deaf educators and researchers has also reframed the values of the SLTI profession, how to educate practitioners, and what research needs to be done (Haualand et al., 2023).

Webb's (2017) research suggests that it is these personal, identity-forming connections that give interpreter educators their purpose, motivation, and sense of personal and professional responsibility to carry out their work. When relating the former suggestion to Roberts and Davenport's (2002) report on job engagement, we can see how SLTI educators' connections to the deaf community are integral to our work. Roberts and Davenport's research reveals that when people personally identify with their work, they are more likely to be motivated and engaged with it. Thus, if interpreter educators have connections to deaf people, they will potentially have a sense of personal and professional responsibility, which also serves as a motivating factor. Therefore, even when challenges arise, SLTI educators do their best to stay balanced, manage their demands, and remain diligently working, with the aim of improving interpreter education and ensuring graduates are ready to work.

However, even with this high level of motivation, the day-in-and-day-out is still challenging; at times you probably feel tired and on the brink of burning out. You are juggling the many tasks that come with your professional roles, while also trying to be true to yourself and do right by a community of people. You likely have seen how your multifaceted identities entwined with your personal values have created an internal struggle as you navigate your personal and professional worlds. Such demands can lead to various levels of role strain and role conflict and truly have an impact on educator well-being (Gmelch et al., 1986; Idris, 2011; Whitehead, 2015). The difficulty here is that when well-being is negatively affected, it can also adversely affect job performance (Bakker & Demerouti, 2014), which can affect student learning and therefore also have an impact on SLTI graduates' levels of work-readiness (Webb, 2017).

Considering the state of the world in terms of shifts toward neoliberalism, we expect that many of these challenges continue and, in some cases, have worsened. However, we also believe that we remain motivated to weather the storms in order to educate future translators and interpreters, with deaf communities' participation and access at the forefront of our minds. It was this feeling of personal and professional responsibility that served as a buffer in preventing burnout for many of the interpreter educator participants in Webb's (2017) study. She reported how it was this feeling that pushed them to sacrifice their personal time and money to maximize teaching and learning successes.

Maybe you can relate? We do.

This Volume

This book includes insights from 22 countries across the globe, including Austria, Australia, Belgium, Brazil, Canada, China, Czech Republic, Finland, Ghana, Ireland, Japan, Kenya, Kosovo, Mexico, New Zealand, Norway, Russia, South Africa, Sweden, the United Kingdom, Uganda, and the United States.

We approached all the authors from the previous 2009 volume and also put out a call for other SLTI educators to contribute a chapter on their country, directly approaching people through our networks wherever possible. We also targeted countries that were not featured in the first volume (which had 15 chapters) to try and increase the representation from all over the world, especially from the continents of Africa, Asia, and South America and from Eastern Europe. We had contact with potential authors from 34 countries.

Unfortunately, one group of previous coauthors was not in a position to update their chapter (Fiji), and not everyone we approached for a new chapter could provide one in the end. Still, we were able to add many new chapters from countries that were not featured in the 2009 volume (namely Belgium, China, Czech Republic, Ghana, Kenya, Mexico, Norway, Russia, South Africa, and Uganda), and the previous Scotland-only chapter has now been expanded to the whole of the United Kingdom. The 2009 version also included a chapter from the Netherlands, the authors of which felt that this time around there was not enough significant change to be reported, so the information provided in the 2009 chapter remains relevant and is still considered a valuable resource.

Sadly, both coauthors of the Russia chapter passed away after submitting the first version of the chapter. We value the efforts of both Tatiana Davidenko and Anna Komorova in their initial overview of the Russian context for this volume, and we acknowledge their passings as a loss to the deaf and SLI communities, across Transcaucasia and globally. We appreciate the support from Bencie Woll and Valera Vinogradova for attending to the final revisions of the chapter on the basis of their experiences of working with Tatiana and Anna and other sign language teachers and interpreters in Russia.

The volume is structured with country chapters listed alphabetically. Although this new volume includes representation from many parts of the world, we recognize there is limited representation from across Africa, Asia, Eastern Europe, and Transcaucasia, and specifically there is no representation from the Middle East, despite our best efforts. We hope that in future iterations of this volume, there will be increased representation. In the meantime, we refer readers to the *Routledge Handbook of Sign Language Translation and Interpreting* (Stone et al., 2022), which features chapters on SLI in Africa (Parkins-Maliko, 2022), Asia (Sze et al., 2022), the Arab world (Semreen, 2022), East Africa (Busingye & Nantongo, 2022), and South America (Pinheiro & Stumpf, 2022), as well as some entries dedicated to the discussion of SLTI education (e.g., Sheridan & Lynch, 2022).

Each chapter in this volume is coauthored by deaf and hearing interpreter educators. These authors share their positionality and journey into SLTI education at the beginning of each chapter, just as we have. They then introduce you to the country by providing you with an overview of translation and interpreting within their respective country, including the development and status of the broader translation and interpreting profession and education and how SLTI is situated next to and within in these systems. The authors provide an outline of the professionalization of SLTI to highlight important historical influences and where the country sits today in terms of current professional associations and organizations, certifications and qualifications for interpreters, and regulation and legislation that apply to working interpreters and translators. The focus then shifts to SLTI education specifically, again with a historical overview, but with a specific focus on where SLTI education is at today in each country.

This format explores various educational pathways and program types, who the educators are, and the various challenges that they face working in SLTI education. Authors reflect on student readiness; discuss the relationships between deaf people and SLTI educational institutions and their students; highlight any research that has developed in the country around SLTI education, training, and assessment; and reflect on impacts of the COVID-19 pandemic on SLTI education. Finally, each chapter explores the road ahead, possible developments, and changes foreseen, as well as highlighting projects that specifically address the future of SLTI education.

As you read each chapter, please note that although we have outlined what we, the editors, have requested the authors discuss, not all countries are at the same stage of SLTI professionalization, which impacts how much information can be shared about each of these areas. In some cases, there may be limited to no information available. This also means that chapters will vary in length and in the extent to which they are able to formally provide references to support their statements. In some cases, their chapter might be the first opportunity to tell their country's story.

Where relevant, chapters discuss the advent of SLT practice and training/qualifications, although not all countries can evidence this development yet. We distinguish between translation and interpreting as follows: *Translation* is an activity in which a translator works from a set text into a text in recorded form (either written or signed), which is reviewed and edited until the final product is published (typically translations of website content, leaflets, information booklets, government information, storybooks, etc.). *Interpreting* is live, in real time, and contemporaneous, and it typically occurs between spoken and signed language or between two sign languages. Deaf interpreters can also work in a hybrid form, where they read from speech-to-text autocue or captions to provide real-time interpreting into sign language.

SLT practices are now increasingly being recognized as separate from SLI, and some countries are introducing separate training and qualifications (the United Kingdom, for example, has a separate qualification for deaf translators). However, in many countries, SLT is still emerging as a recognized practice and is still subsumed under SLI. Wherever possible, we have encouraged authors to discuss SLT as well as SLI.

One last point as editors is that we are very conscious of the fact that we asked authors to make their contributions in written English, which for the majority of the authors is not their first or preferred language. Through the editorial process we have made suggestions for ease of reading, but wherever possible, we have left the "voice" of the authors intact, which means that the text might not always read as would be expected idiomatically in English. We ask that readers keep this in mind.

Conventions

Before we conclude, we would like to establish a few conventions we have used throughout this volume:

1. Following the new wave of Deaf Studies, we are not using the D/deaf convention. We refer to deaf signers and signing deaf communities to recognize the intersectional nature of deaf identities and do not ascribe any judgment about being culturally deaf (see Kusters et al., 2017). However, we do recognize that not all countries have adopted this change and are still using the older convention because they are still at the stage of advocating for sign language rights and the recognition of deaf communities as linguistic and cultural minority groups. For them, using the uppercase convention of "Deaf" might still be important.
2. We are not using the term *Coda* to refer to children of deaf adults. Instead, we have adopted the term suggested by Napier (2021), *heritage signers*, to refer to hearing or deaf people who have grown up using a sign language at home with deaf parents or *people from deaf families*, such as with partners or extended family members who use sign language regularly with those family members.
3. For key interpreting concepts, we avoid using the term *sign-to-voice*, focusing on names of languages or signed/spoken language interpreting (see Haualand & Nilsson, 2020).
4. Terminology is not consistent across countries. You will read about *certification*, *accreditation*, *registration*, *qualification*, *state authorized*, etc. We have left these according to country, but each term essentially refers to the route to being recognized as a qualified, professional sign language translator or interpreter, including the types of training courses, whether ad hoc, intensive, community organization run, vocational/academic, and types of postsecondary colleges (folk high school, community college, university, applied sciences universities, etc.).

Considering the points discussed, we encourage you to reflect on the language and conventions used in your own context. To aid your understanding, we have included an index of key concepts, abbreviations for sign languages, and abbreviations for organizations and systems. Additionally, our authors have been tasked with elucidating any country-specific terminology within their respective chapters, enhancing accessibility for all readers.

We trust you will find this journey through the global landscape of SLTI education enlightening and engaging. We look forward to reconnecting with you on the other side of this exploration.

NOTES

1. See https://visitbmc.com/index.php/etna-project/about-etna-project.
2. *Language brokering* is the term used to describe the informal interpreting carried out by children in migrant or deaf families (Orellana, 2009; Napier, 2021).
3. IS is a translingual practice that relies on and produces mutual moral orientation among signers who do not use the same sign language, bringing sign languages into contact by borrowing lexical signs from different national sign languages (De Meulder et al., 2019; Green, 2014; Quinto-Pozos & Adam, 2015). There is increasing discussion about whether IS should be considered as a language in formal contexts, such as conferences and high-level meetings, because of the development of more established lexicon (Rathmann & Müller de Quadros, 2022).
4. Market ideology refers to managing the political economy in such a way to achieve appropriate welfare outcomes by offering choice and competition, which extends from the business/industry sector to public services; an aligned concept, neoliberalism, promotes economic efficiency, competition, rationalization, individualism, utilitarianism, a belief in progress and a laissez-faire policy of minimum governmental interference in the economic affairs of individuals and society (Wensley, 2009).

REFERENCES

Adam, R. (2017). *Unimodal bilingualism in the Deaf community: Language contact between two sign languages in Australia and the United Kingdom.* Unpublished doctoral dissertation, University College London.

Adam, R., Carty, B., & Stone, C. (2011). Ghostwriting: Deaf translators within the Deaf community. *Babel, 57,* 375–393.

Adam, R., Stone, C., Collins, S. D. & Metzger, M. (2014a). (Eds.). *Deaf interpreters at work: International insights.* Gallaudet University Press.

Adam, R., Aro, M., Druetta, J. C., Dunne, S., & af Klintberg, J. (2014b). Deaf interpreters: An introduction. In R. Adam, C. Stone, S. D. Collins, & M. Metzger (Eds.), *Deaf interpreters at work: International insights* (pp. 1–18). Gallaudet University Press.

Asumah, S. N., & Nagel, M. (2024). *Reframing diversity and inclusive leadership: Race, gender and institutional change.* State University of New York Press.

Bagga-Gupta, S. (2017). Center-staging language and identity research from Earthrise positions: Contextualizing performances in open spaces. In S. Bagga-Gupta, A. L. Hansen, & J. Feilberg (Eds.), *Identity revisited and reimagined: Empirical and theoretical contributions on embodied communication across time and space* (pp. 65–102). Springer.

Balan, A. (2023). Neoliberalism, privatisation and marketisation: The implications for legal education in England and Wales. *Cogent Education, 10*(2), 1–15. https://doi.org/10.1080/2331186X.2023.2284548

Billot, J. (2010). The imagined and the real: Identifying the tensions for academic identity. *Higher Education Research & Development, 29*(6), 709–721.

Busingye, B., & Nantongo, P. S. (2022). The state of sign language translation and interpreting in the East African community. In C. Stone, R. Adam, C. Rathmann, & R. Müller de Quadros (Eds.), *Routledge handbook of sign language translation & interpreting* (pp. 519–535). Routledge.

Chan, C. D., Erby, A. N. & Ford, D. J. (2017). Intersectionality in practice: Moving a social justice paradigm to action in higher education. In J. M. Johnson & G. Javier (Eds.), *Queer people of color in higher education* (pp. 9–29). Information Age Publishing.

Chapple R., Bridwell B., & Gray K. (2021). Exploring intersectional identity in Black Deaf women: The complexity of the lived experience in college. *Affilia, 36*(4), 571–592.

Cho, S., Crenshaw, K., & McCall, L. (2013). Toward a field of intersectionality studies: Theory, applications, and praxis. *Signs: Journal of Women in Culture and Society, 38*(4), 785–810.

Clark, B. (1983). *The higher education system.* University of California Press.

Cokely, D. (2005). Shifting positionality: A critical examination of the turning point in the relationship of interpreters and the Deaf community. In M. Marschark, R. Peterson, & E. A. Winston (Eds.), *Interpreting and interpreting education: Directions for research and practice* (pp. 3–28). Oxford University Press.

Connell, R. (2013). The neoliberal cascade and education: An essay on the market agenda and its consequences. *Critical Studies in Education, 54*(2), 99–112.

Crenshaw, K. (1989). Demarginalizing the intersection of race and sex: A black feminist critique of antidiscrimination doctrine, feminist theory and antiracist politics. *University of Chicago Legal Forum, 1*, 139–167.

Day, C., Kington, A., Stobart, G., & Sammons, P. (2006). The personal and professional selves of teachers: Stable and unstable identities. *British Educational Research Journal, 32*(4), 601–616.

De Meulder, M. (2018) "So, why do you sign?" Deaf and hearing new signers, their motivation, and revitalisation policies for sign languages. *Applied Linguistics Review, 10*(4), 705–724.

De Meulder, M., & Haualand, H. (2021). Sign language interpreting services: A quick fix for inclusion? *Translation and Interpreting Studies. The Journal of the American Translation and Interpreting Studies Association, 16*(1), 19–40.

De Meulder, M., Kusters, A., Moriarty, E., & Murray, J. J. (2019). Describe, don't prescribe. The practice and politics of translanguaging in the context of deaf signers. *Journal of Multilingual and Multicultural Development, 40*(10), 892–906.

De Meulder, M., Murray, J., & McKee, R. (2019). (Eds.). *The legal recognition of sign languages: Advocacy and outcomes around the world.* Multilingual Matters.

Dunn, L. M., & Anderson, G. B. (2020). Examining the intersectionality of deaf identity, race/ethnicity and diversity through a Black Deaf lens. In I. Leigh & C. O'Brien (Eds.), *Deaf identities: Exploring new frontiers* (pp. 279–304). Oxford University Press.

Ehrlich, S., & Napier, J. (2015). (Eds.). *Interpreter education in the digital age: Innovation, access, and change.* Interpreter Education Series, Vol. 8. Gallaudet University Press.

Emery, S., & Iyer, S. (2022). Deaf migration through an intersectionality lens. *Disability & Society, 37*(1), 89–110.

Frake, M. (2008). Quality education and the marketplace: An exploration of neoliberalism and its impact on higher education. *Brock Education Journal, 18*(1). https://doi.org/10.26522/brocked.v18i1.110

Friedner, M. (2018). Negotiating legitimacy in American Sign Language interpreting education: Uneasy belonging in a community of practice. *Disability Studies Quarterly*, *38*(1). https://doi.og/10.18061/dsq.v38i1.5836

Gillespie, N. A., Walsh, M., Winefield, A. H., Dua, J., & Stough, C. (2001). Occupational stress in universities: Staff perceptions of the causes, consequences and moderators of stress. *Work & Stress*, *15*(1), 53–72.

Gmelch, W. H., Wilke, P. K., & Lovrich, N. P. (1986). Dimensions of stress among university faculty: Factor-analytic results from a national study. *Research in Higher Education*, *24*(3), 266–286.

Green, E. M. (2014). Building the Tower of Babel: International Sign, linguistic commensuration, and moral orientation. *Language in Society*, *43*(4), 445–465.

Gunnarsson, L. (2015). Why we keep separating the 'inseparable': Dialecticizing intersectionality. *The European Journal of Women's Studies*, *24*(2), 1–14. https://doi.org/10.1177/1350506815577114

Hale, S., & Napier, J. (2013). *Research methods in interpreting: A practical resource*. Bloomsbury Publishing.

Hall, W., Holcomb, T., & Elliott, M. (2016). Using popular education with the oppressor class: Suggestions for sign language interpreter education. *Critical Education*, *7*(13). http://ojs.library.ubc.ca/index.php/criticaled/article/view/186129

Haualand, H., De Meulder, M., & Napier, J. (2023). Unpacking sign language interpreting as a social institution: The missing macro perspective? Introduction to special issue on 'Unpacking sign language interpreting.' *Journal of Translation & Interpreting Studies*, *17*(3), 351–358.

Holmes, C., & Lindsay, D. (2018). "Do you want fries with that?": The McDonaldization of university education—Some critical reflections on nursing higher education. *SAGE Open*, *8*(3). https://doi.org/10.1177/2158244018787229

Idris, M. K., 2011. Over time effects of role stress on psychological strain among Malaysian public university academics. *International Journal of Business and Social Science*, *2*(9), 154–161.

Kusters, A. (2019): Boarding Mumbai trains: The mutual shaping of intersectionality and mobility. *Mobilities*, *14*(6), 841–858. https://doi.org/10.1080/17450101.2019.1622850

Leeson, L., Wurm, S. and Vermeerbergen, M. (Eds.). (2014). *Signed language interpreting: preparation, practice and performance*. Routledge.

Leigh, I. & O'Brien, C. (2020). (Eds.). *Deaf identities: Exploring new frontiers*. Oxford University Press.

Lynch, K. (2006). Neo-liberalism and marketisation: The implications for higher education. *European Educational Research Journal*, *5*(1), 1–17.

Long, W. R., Barnes, L., Williams, A., & Northcote, M. (n.d.). *Are they ready? Accounting academics' perspectives of the preparedness of new student cohorts*. European Accounting Association Congress.

McCartney, J. L. (2017). Sign language interpreting as a social justice profession. *Caribbean Curriculum*, *25*, 79–96.

Mellinger, C. (2020). Positionality in public service interpreting research. *FITISPos International Journal*, *7*(1), 92–109.

Miller, C. A., & Clark, K. A. (2020). Deaf and Queer at the intersections: Deaf LGBTQ people and communities. In I. Leigh & C. O'Brien (Eds.), *Deaf identities: Exploring new frontiers* (pp. 305–335). Oxford University Press.

Murray, J., De Meulder, M., & le Maire, D. (2018). An education in sign language as a human right? The sensory exception in the legislative history and ongoing interpretation of Article 24 of the UN Convention on the Rights of Persons With Disabilities. *Human Rights Quarterly, 40*(1), 37–60.

Murray, J., Snoddon, K., De Meulder, K., & Underwood, K. (2020). Intersectional inclusion for deaf learners: Moving beyond General Comment No. 4 on Article 24 of the United Nations Convention on the Rights of Persons With Disabilities. *International Journal of Inclusive Education, 24*(7), 691–705.

Napier, J. (2002). *Sign language interpreting: Linguistic coping strategies.* Douglas McLean.

Napier, J. (2004). Sign language interpreter training, testing and accreditation: An international comparison. *American Annals of the Deaf, 149*(4), 350–359.

Napier, J. (Ed.). (2009). *International perspectives on signed language interpreter education.* Gallaudet University Press.

Napier, J. (2016). *Linguistic coping strategies in sign language interpreting* (2nd ed.). Gallaudet University Press.

Napier, J. (2021). *Sign language brokering in deaf-hearing families.* Palgrave.

Napier, J. (2024). Do deaf women feel safe on campus? A case study of one UK university. *Humanity & Society.* https://doi.org/10.1177/016059.762412321

Napier, J., & Goswell, D. (2013). Sign language interpreting profession. In C. A. Chapelle (Ed.), *The encyclopedia of applied linguistics.* Wiley-Blackwell. https://doi.org/10.1002/978140 5198431.wbeal1009

Napier, J., & Goswell, D. (in press). Signed language interpreting profession. In C. A. Chapelle (Ed.), *The encyclopedia of applied linguistics* (2nd ed.). Wiley-Blackwell.

Napier, J., & Leeson, L. (2016). *Sign language in action.* Palgrave Macmillan.

Napier, J., Skinner, R., Adam, R., Stone, C., Pratt, S., Hinton, D. P., & Obasi, C. (2022). Representation and diversity in the sign language translation & interpreting profession in the United Kingdom. *Interpreting and Society: An Interdisciplinary Journal, 2*(2), 119–130.

Obasi, C. (2013). Race and ethnicity in sign language interpreter education, training and practice. *Race Ethnicity and Education, 16*(1), 103–120.

Obasi, C. (2022). Identity, language and culture: Using Africanist Sista-hood and Deaf cultural discourse in research with minority social workers. *Qualitative Research, 22*(3), 353–368.

Orellana, M. (2009) *Translating childhoods: Immigrant youth, language and culture.* Rutgers University Press.

Palmer, P. P. (1999). *Let your life speak: Listening for the voice of vocation.* John Wiley & Sons.

Parkins-Maliko, N. (2022). Intersectionality of the sign language interpreter identity: An African perspective. In C. Stone, R. Adam, C. Rathmann, & R. Müller de Quadros (Eds.), *Routledge handbook of sign language translation & interpreting* (pp. 124–145). Routledge.

Pike, A., Rodríguez-Pose, A., & Tomaney, J. (2014). Local and regional development in the Global North and South. *Progress in Development Studies, 14*(1), 21–30.

Pinheiro, K. L., & Stumpf, M. R. (2022). The trajectory of the deaf interpreter and translator of International Sign Language: Lessons from Juan Carlos Druetta in South America. In C. Stone, R. Adam, R. M. de Quadros, & C. Rathmann (Eds.), *The Routledge handbook of sign language translation and interpreting* (pp. 267–282). Routledge.

Quinto-Pozos, D., & Adam, R. (2015). Sign languages in contact. In A. Schembri & C. Lucas (Eds.), *Sociolinguistics and deaf communities* (pp. 29–60). Cambridge University Press.

Rathmann, C., & Müller de Quadros, R. (2022). *International Sign Language: Sociolinguistic aspects*. Editora Arara Azul, Brazil.

Rosewell, K., & Ashwin, P. (2019). Academics' perceptions of what it means to be an academic. *Studies in Higher Education, 44*(12), 2374–2384.

Roberts, D. R., & Davenport, T. O. (2002). Job engagement: Why it's important and how to improve it. *Employment Relations Today, 29*(3), 21–29.

Robinson, O., & Henner, J. (2018). Authentic voices, authentic encounters: Cripping the university through American Sign Language. *Disability Studies Quarterly, 38*(4), 1–20.

Schaufeli, W. B., Bakker, A. B., & Van Rhenen, W. (2009). How changes in job demands and resources predict burnout, work engagement, and sickness absenteeism. *Journal of Organizational Behavior, 30*(7), 893–917.

Scott-Gibson, L. (1992). Sign language interpreting: An emerging profession. In S. Gregory & G. Hartley (Eds.), *Constructing deafness* (pp. 253–258). Open University Press.

Semreen, S. (2022). The state of sign language interpreting and interpreters in the Arab world: An exploratory study. In C. Stone, R. Adam, R. M. de Quadros, & C. Rathmann (Eds.), *The Routledge handbook of sign language translation and interpreting* (pp. 501–518). Routledge.

Shaw, S. (2013). *Service learning in interpreter education: Strategies for extending student involvement in the deaf community*. Gallaudet University Press.

Sheridan, S., & Lynch, T. (2022). Translation as a pedagogical tool. In C. Stone, R. Adam, R. M. de Quadros, & C. Rathmann (Eds.), *The Routledge handbook of sign language translation and interpreting* (pp. 181–192). Routledge.

Sikder, A. (2019). Power down. *Newsli: Magazine of the Association of Sign Language Interpreters UK, 109*, 8–12.

Smith-Warshaw, J., & Crume, P. (2020). Exploring the intersectionality of Deaf and Latinx cultures through service-learning. *American Annals of the Deaf, 165*(1), 20–51.

Solarz, M. W. (2019). *The global north-south atlas: Mapping global change*. Routledge.

Stone, C., Adam, R., Müller de Quadros, R., & Rathmann, C. (2022). *The Routledge handbook of sign language translation and interpreting*. Routledge.

Sze, F., Wong, F., Yi Lo, C. C., Chew, S., Sun, R., & Yanai, Y. (2022). Sign language interpretation training, testing and accreditation in Asia. In C. Stone, R. Adam, R. M. de Quadros, & C. Rathmann (Eds.), *The Routledge handbook of sign language translation and interpreting* (pp. 456–484). Routledge.

Tierney, W. G. (1988). Organizational culture in higher education: Defining the essentials. *Journal of Higher Education, 59*(1), 2–21.

Tiselius, E. (2019). The (un-)ethical interpreting researcher: Ethics, voice and discretionary power in interpreting research. *Perspectives, 27*(5), 747–760.

Webb, S., & Napier, J. (2015). Job demands and resources: An exploration of sign language interpreter educators' experiences. *International Journal of Interpreter Education, 7*(1), 23–50.

Webb, S. (2017). *Job demands, job resources, wellbeing and student outcomes: A study of sign language interpreter educators' perceptions*. Unpublished doctoral dissertation, Heriot-Watt University.

Webb, S., & Best, B. A. (2020). The most important cog in the system: A case for legislative change to drive professionalization. *Journal of Interpretation, 28*(1), Article 6. https://digitalcommons.unf.edu/joi/vol28/iss1/6

Wensley, R. (2009). Market ideology, globalization and neoliberalism. In P. Maclaran, B. Stern, & M. Saren (Eds.), *The SAGE handbook of marketing theory*. Sage. https://doi.org/10.4135/9781446222454

World Federation of the Deaf (2023). *The legislation of sign languages*. https://wfdeaf.org/news/the-legal-recognition-of-national-sign-languages/

Whitehead, P. S. (2015). *Role ambiguity, role strain, job dissatisfaction, and difficulty transitioning into academia among nursing faculty*. Unpublished doctoral dissertation, Walden University.

Willis, K. (2014). Development: Geographical perspectives on a contested concept. *Geography, 99*(2), 60–66.

Winter, R., Taylor, T. & Sarros, J. (2000). Trouble at mill: Quality of academic worklife issues within a comprehensive Australian university. *Studies in Higher Education, 25*(3), 279–294.

Witter-Merithew, A., & Johnson, L. J. (2005). *Toward competent practice: Conversations with stakeholders*. Registry of Interpreters for the Deaf.

Wu, C., & Grant, N. (2020). Intersectionality—beyond the individual: A look into cultural identity development of deaf and hard-of-hearing children of multicultural "hearing" families. In I. Leigh & C. O'Brien (Eds.), *Deaf identities: Exploring new frontiers* (pp. 226–253). Oxford University Press.

Wurm, S., & Napier, J. (2017). Rebalancing power: Participatory research methods in interpreting studies. *Translation & Interpreting, 9*, 102–20.

KAREN BONTEMPO, PATRICIA LEVITZKE-GRAY,
ROBERT ADAM, STEPHANIE LINDER, AND
JEMINA NAPIER

1

Revisiting Interpreting Down Under

Sign Language Translator and Interpreter Education and Training in Australia

Australia is a geographically vast country, populated by 26 million people,[1] who reside mostly in urban areas and along the coastal fringes. Although English is the de facto national language of Australia, there is diverse linguistic representation within the nation. The population includes indigenous people who speak 150 different Aboriginal languages (ABS, 2016)[2] and use a range of local sign languages (Green et al., 2022), and there is a considerable immigrant population speaking more than 300 languages, resulting in 20% of Australians speaking a language other than English at home.

Nevertheless, even today, descendants of the English-speaking British settlers who colonized the continent to set up a penal colony starting in 1788, and migrants from English-speaking countries, particularly the United Kingdom, make up most of the Australian population. These British settlers also brought British Sign Language (BSL) and Irish Sign Language (ISL) with them (Adam, 2016; Carty, 2018; Flynn, 1984), cementing the origins of Australian Sign Language (Auslan), despite the existing presence of indigenous sign languages in Australia. The best estimate of the number of deaf people who use Auslan (rather than "Auslan users" in a broader sense) remains somewhat dated, in the absence of clear Australian census data on the number of deaf people who use Auslan,[3] but it has previously been considered to be approximately 6,500 people (Johnston,

Where the information has not changed, some of the text from the original chapter on Australia (Bontempo & Levitzke-Gray, 2009) in the first edition of the *International Perspectives on Sign Language Interpreter Education* volume (Napier, 2009) features in this chapter in the second volume.

2004). Data from the 2021 Census, however, puts the number of people who use Auslan at home closer to 16,242,[4] but this figure also includes hearing people.

WHO ARE WE?

As noted by Hamachek (1999, p. 209), "Consciously, we teach what we know; unconsciously, we teach who we are." The person cannot be separated from the professional, yet this is not often acknowledged in professional rhetoric. Palmer (2007, p. 18) argues that a potentially dangerous flaw in teachers is the "split of personhood from practice" if educators distance themselves from their subject and their students. Indeed, the type of educator we are is the type of person we are. Robert and Jemina have already revealed themselves in the introductory chapter to this volume, outlining their journey into interpreter education and training and a myriad of other expert endeavors. Our positionality is important. So, who are we?

With no deaf family, Karen is hearing and can be considered a new signer (De Meulder, 2018). After some informal exposure to sign language in her teenage years, Karen's real introduction to Auslan was at age 19. Studying a double major in psychology and linguistics at university in Perth, Western Australia (WA), in the late 1980s, Karen started learning Auslan at the local deaf club and by mixing with the deaf community. She quickly progressed to studying interpreting and working in a deaf school, while completing her university degree.

Upon graduation from her interpreter training program, she moved to London, England, where she worked as a teacher in a deaf school. She returned to Perth to work full time for the WA Deaf Society in the early 1990s, where she advocated for a clear delineation of the roles of interpreter and community worker within the organization; she later became a freelance interpreter, interpreter educator, and a researcher in the field of interpreting. Karen's experience as an interpreter stretches across medical, legal, educational, political, and conference interpreting, with a special interest in Auslan-to-English interpreting work, and coworking with deaf interpreters, in particular. She continues to work as an examiner for the National Accreditation Authority for Translators and Interpreters (NAATI), a role she has held for more than two decades, and she has served on the executive of the Auslan interpreters association, ASLIA, at both state and national level for several years, including a term as the national president.

Karen's doctoral research focused primarily on aptitude for Auslan interpreting, providing her with opportunity to meld her interests in psychology, language, education and interpreting. While still immensely enjoying dabbling in interpreting, as well as maintaining her passion for interpreter education, training and mentoring opportunities, Karen has undertaken a career shift in recent years. Her main focus these days is curriculum leadership in language teaching programs in schools, and she closely collaborates with deaf instructors operating in this context.

Patricia (or Patti) is a fourth-generation proud deaf woman, born to a deaf mother and a hearing father, both from multigenerational mixed deaf–hearing families in which everyone signed. The Levitzke family hosted gatherings of deaf people in the early 1900s at their family bakery and home. These meetings were the origins of what later became the WA Deaf Society. The Levitzke legacy is impressive, with deaf and hearing family members working across the deaf community in various ways over the years, even to today, in significant roles. Patti's grandmother Dot Shaw was one of the driving forces behind the national deaf advocacy group, the Australian Association of the Deaf (AAD, now known as Deaf Australia). Her aunts, uncles, cousins, nieces, and nephews are all heritage signers and many of her family members are interpreters. Patti attended deaf schools throughout her childhood, and thus began her introduction to interpreting, in many ways. She became the language broker in the classroom for her peers, who did not understand their less than sign-proficient teachers.

Later, Patti and her partner, also from a multigenerational deaf family from Adelaide, South Australia (SA), had two deaf children. Advocating for her own children and navigating the education sector on their behalf led her further into her journey to formally becoming an interpreter and an educator. She completed a series of qualifications in human services, education, and interpreting, started training interpreters, and Patti became actively involved in ASLIA. She has been a board member of the WA Association of the Deaf, the state branch of Deaf Australia, for over 30 years.

Patti was the first deaf person in Australia to be awarded NAATI recognition as a deaf interpreter (DI) and she later worked closely with NAATI to design aspects of testing materials and structures for DI assessment and certification. Her work as a DI ranges from health care settings to legal settings, immigration, conference interpreting at national and international level, and the whole gamut of "slice-of-life" situations in which interpreters might have the opportunity to work. While her passion for interpreting has not waned, her availability has lessened. In recent years, Patti's commitment to education and training led her to take on the key role of language consultant and instructor in a large-scale Auslan second-language teaching program in one of the top secondary schools in WA while continuing to occasionally work as an interpreter and as an interpreter educator.

Stephanie Linder (or Stef as she prefers to be called) is a deaf, second-generation native signer of Auslan and a lifelong member of the deaf community. She has played various roles within the Australian deaf community, serving as a practitioner and educator in the field of sign language, translation, and interpreting (SLTI). With more than 20 years of extensive work in the deaf sector and interpreting space in Australia, she has shifted her professional and personal focus to the International Development Cooperation field. In this field, Stef can leverage her interpreting and educational experience.

Currently based in Copenhagen, Stephanie travels regularly and extensively. She has contributed to several research projects, including an investigation of how beginner errors can enhance the teaching of Auslan as a second language, exploring how deaf signers access health care information, developing evidence-based English into Auslan translation standards and production guidelines, and creating the Auslan Medical Signbank and Auslan Corpus. She is a recent graduate of the European Master of Sign Language Interpreting (EUMASLI), and her research examined the processes and product of interpreters' work in media settings.

As noted earlier, Jemina Napier and Robert Adam's positionality statements can be seen in the introduction to this volume. They both currently work at Heriot-Watt University, where they teach in undergraduate and postgraduate education programs and conduct research on sign language translation and interpreting practices and pedagogy. They have been (and continue to be) involved in various advisory groups, boards, and networks at the national and international levels that influence the development of the profession and training/education. They were both very involved in the Australian SLTI scene.

Jemina was an academic at Macquarie University in Sydney, where she established the first postgraduate program for Auslan interpreters, and was greatly involved with ASLIA as a board member and also as president. She practiced as an Auslan/English interpreter regularly and offered continuous professional development training through ASLIA branches. Jemina kickstarted the first systematic research on sign language interpreting (SLI) in Australia after she completed her doctorate on linguistic coping strategies of sign language interpreters in 2002.

Robert started work as a DI in deafblind settings before moving on to conference interpreting between IS and Auslan and working as a DI in legal, medical, and mental health settings, as well as coordinating the interpreting service at the Deaf Society of NSW (now Deaf Connect). He was a board member of the state branches of the AAD in Victoria and NSW, and for 15 years, he was a board member and then president of the AAD. Both Jemina and Robert were examiners for NAATI. Significantly, they wrote one of their first published peer-reviewed journal articles together, which was a comparison of Auslan and BSL interpreting, where they looked at the different features of the sign language interpreted product in both Australia and the United Kingdom using the same source text (Napier & Adam, 2002).

Kottler et al. (2005) speak of the "passionately committed" educator. We would consider ourselves to each have a sincere and deep love for teaching and learning. We all had different journeys that led us to arrive at this point in our careers as language teachers, researchers, interpreters, and interpreter educators. Our experiences have shaped our work in immeasurable ways, and hopefully they provide some additional context for you as you read our chapter.

Contextualization: Translation and Interpreting in Australia

The community interpreting sector in Australia (Hale, 2007), often referred to elsewhere as public service interpreting (De Pedro Ricoy et al., 2009), forged the path for professional recognition and regulation of interpreting practitioners in the nation. In 1977, the Australian government, recognizing a need to evaluate and determine standards for community interpreters and translators, established NAATI, a public, not-for-profit company jointly owned by the Commonwealth, state, and territory governments. The impetus for forming NAATI was to test the skill level and proficiency of people who were fluent in the spoken languages of migrant communities in Australia and were already performing the role of a community interpreter in various settings (Flynn, 1996). Their work was able to be legitimized by their accreditation as an interpreter, or as a translator, as meeting a benchmark standard when they were certified by NAATI.

Sign language interpreters were accepted for assessment and accreditation by NAATI in 1982, well before any national legislation or policy had even acknowledged sign language as the language of deaf Australians. Thus, the inclusion of SLI in a national interpreting testing regime by NAATI at that point in time was quite remarkable. Although the original focus at the time of its inception was on assessing and accrediting interpreters to work in migrant community languages, NAATI has evolved to certify entry-level interpreters in 65 languages, including 14 Aboriginal and Torres Strait Islander languages, as well as Auslan.[5] Auslan interpreting and translating credentials are now available across a wide range of options within the NAATI certification system.

Professionalization of SLI in Australia

Not unlike some other countries, the SLI profession in Australia has its origins in the arrival of the early teachers of the deaf and missionaries (referred to as *missioners*) who immigrated to Australia from Britain from the 19th century onward. Although the use of sign languages in indigenous communities before the invasion and colonization of the continent is acknowledged (Green et al., 2022), the stories of Betty Steel (Branson & Miller, 1995) and John Carmichael (Carty, 2000), as well as Sr. Mary Gabriel Hogan, a deaf Irish nun (Fitzgerald, 1999), also tell us that sign languages were introduced to Australia by the early settlers and potentially by convicts. Deaf society organizations were established around the nation, initially by ex-pupils of the first schools for deaf children in the late 19th century (Burchett, 1964; Flynn, 1999) and later by deaf people and missioners. Deaf societies initially employed these missioners, along with welfare officers and community workers, to perform the role of interpreter, often interchangeably with other duties (Flynn, 1999; Ozolins & Bridge, 1999). The role of interpreter would also often be filled by hearing heritage signers, hearing teachers of deaf people, other family members of deaf people, or members of the wider community who could sign (Napier et al., 2018), a practice that continued until the early 1980s.

However, a number of social and political factors in the 1980s and the 1990s, including the introduction of favorable government policies with regard to multiculturalism and the passing of federal discrimination legislation, resulted in increased access and opportunity for deaf people and had a significant impact on the interpreting profession in Australia (Napier, 2004; Napier et al., 2006; Ozolins & Bridge, 1999).

The introduction of standardized national testing of SLI in 1982, formal interpreter training in Australia from 1986 onward, and the establishment of an Auslan interpreting association in 1991 further established the SLI field in Australia (Flynn, 1996). Although these pioneer efforts were pivotal in prompting the professionalization of SLI in the nation, it should be acknowledged that these initiatives focused only on Auslan, the sign language introduced to Australia, and did not account for developing any capacity for recognition, training, or interpreting in any Aboriginal or Torres Strait Islander sign languages.

By the 1990s, the role of Auslan interpreter was more clearly delineated from that of other staff positions in organizations working with deaf communities, such as in the Deaf Societies around Australia. At this time also, generic interpreting agencies, which historically had provided exclusively spoken language interpreting services, started to include Auslan interpreters on their interpreter registers.

Current Professional Associations and Organizations

Deaf people in Australia are represented by a national organization of and for deaf people, Deaf Australia (formerly AAD), which was founded in 1986.[6] Before that, there had been previous attempts to establish a national organization, but neither the Australasian Deaf and Dumb Association in 1903 nor the Australian Association for the Advancement of the Deaf (AAAD) in 1932 (Carty, 2004) was successful, and often they were not led by deaf people. Deaf people were "represented" on a national basis by the Australian Federation of Deaf Societies, which was a federation of the deaf service providers in each of the six states. These service providers often had some deaf staff or some deaf board members, but at the time there was not significant deaf leadership in key roles in these organizations, indicating that deaf representation on a national level was not always authentic or driven by deaf-led organizations. These Deaf Societies have since evolved into two main service providers in Australia, Deaf Connect and Expression Australia, with other smaller providers also claiming space in this area. These organizations today are deaf-led but service focused, and interpreting is typically only one aspect of a wide range of services they provide for local deaf communities in each state and territory.

Deaf Australia, however, is not a service provider but instead is an active advocacy organization representing the Australian deaf community. It has branches in each state, which generally run on a voluntary basis, supporting their local communities and taking an interest in issues of concern, such as the quality and availability of interpreting services.

A national professional translators and interpreters' association, the Australian Institute of Interpreters and Translators (AUSIT), has existed in Australia since 1987. AUSIT has nearly 1,200 members, who are predominantly spoken language interpreters and translators, with fewer than 20 Auslan/English interpreters registered as current members.[7] Auslan interpreters are eligible to join AUSIT and other state-based spoken language interpreter associations, but they do so infrequently.

An Auslan interpreters' association emerged at the state level in 1983 when an informal meeting was held by welfare officers during the National Deafness Conference in Sydney. The national body of ASLIA[8] was established in Adelaide in 1991 and became incorporated in 1992. Branches already existed in various forms in most states, so a national executive was formed, relationships between states and the national body were formalized, and ASLIA became an increasingly strong force in the interpreting field (Ozolins & Bridge, 1999). However, the increasing workload demands on a voluntary association at both the state and national levels led to discussions around how ASLIA could increase efficiencies, which flagged a need to revise aspects of the constitution and to increase relevance, particularly in relation to serving the needs and interests of deaf translators and interpreters.

In 2023, ASLIA members voted to close the association and state branches as an incorporated body and to legally change ASLIA to a Company Limited by Guarantee. A more inclusive and sustainable constitution, a different organizational and legal structure, and a name change were proposed, specifically to incorporate reference to translators. The name change to ASLITA and a new constitution were accepted by members at a special meeting in August 2023. Nearly 500 Auslan interpreters representing all levels of NAATI certification are represented by this professional association at present.

Regulation/Legislation for SLTI Work

In Australia, there is no direct legislation, nor are there regulations, applicable to working as an interpreter or translator, although there is an implicit assumption in many government and professional sectors that interpreters and translators hold NAATI certification. In some jurisdictions, there is a specific government policy that stipulates that credentials or interpreting qualifications must be held. While not legislated, realistically in many contexts and domains across the nation, it would not be possible to gain work as an interpreter or translator without holding NAATI certification. Policy recommendations by various organizations or authorities might also stipulate an expected level of certification for practicing in a particular field of work, such as in legal settings. This is not always applied universally, however; indeed, there are some settings in which NAATI certification expectations are rarely adopted, such as in education, although this varies notably from state to state in Australia and even at the school or institution level within states and territories.

Auslan was first recognized as a community language in the National Languages Policy (Lo Bianco, 1987). The first Auslan dictionary was published in 1989 (Johnston, 1989), offering further legitimacy and authority to the language. The second National Languages Policy document recognized that "signing deaf people constitute a group like any other non–English-speaking language group in Australia, with a distinct sub-culture recognised by shared history, social life and sense of identity, united and symbolised by fluency in Auslan, the principal means of communication within the Australian Deaf Community" (Dawkins, 1992).

This was followed by the proclamation of the Disability Discrimination Act (1992) by the Commonwealth Government of Australia, which makes discrimination on the basis of disability unlawful and promotes equal rights, equal opportunity, and equal access for people with disability. The Human Rights Commission is the government agency responsible for liaising "with governments, the private sector and civil society to help individuals and organizations understand their rights and meet their legal responsibilities."[9] There have been successful complaints under the Act, which resulted in national initiatives for deaf people in Australia, such as the establishment of the National Relay Service, a government-funded telecommunications service provider for deaf or hard-of-hearing people, among others.

Sign Language Interpreter Education in Australia

Training of sign language interpreters originally took place in-house at Deaf Societies around Australia, both formally and informally, with short courses and training opportunities, professional development sessions, and mentoring of interpreters taking place in these organizations. By the mid-1980s, education and training largely shifted to the Technical and Further Education (TAFE) sector, as part-time courses emerged, first in Perth and followed by Sydney, Adelaide, and Melbourne. The first full-time TAFE course was submitted for accreditation by the TAFE Board of Victoria in 1985, and it later ran at Richmond College of TAFE, with candidates gaining a Certificate of Applied Social Science—Interpreting: Deaf/Hearing Impaired. This 2-year full-time course was discontinued in the late 1980s and replaced by alternative qualifications in line with the Australian Qualifications Framework (AQF), initially at the Certificate of Interpreting level and later at the

Diploma and Advanced Diploma levels at TAFE, as specific and tailored training packages were developed for interpreters.

A growing body of research (Madden, 1995, 2005; Napier, 2002a, 2002b; Ozolins & Bridge, 1999), along with changing demands from the deaf community, resulted in a call for further professionalization of the Auslan interpreting field in the late 1990s and early 2000s. The first Australian postgraduate university program for Auslan interpreters was established at Macquarie University, Sydney, in 2002, and it remains the only university program of its kind in Australia. There is only one person in a full-time role in academia in the SLI area in Australia, and this was also the case when the Australian chapter was published in the previous volume.

During 2002–2016, a significant body of research was published on SLI, led primarily by Jemina Napier while she lived in Australia, but also in collaboration with many other deaf and hearing scholars and interpreters. Research touched on (socio)linguistic aspects of interpreting (Goswell, 2011; Napier, 2002; Napier & Barker, 2004a, 2004b; Wang & Napier, 2014, 2016); access to healthcare information (Major et al., 2011; Major, at al., 2012; Major & Napier, 2012; Napier & Kidd, 2013; Napier et al., 2014); video remote interpreting (VRI) in courts (Napier, 2011, 2013; Napier & Leneham, 2011); the feasibility of interpreting for deaf jurors in court (Napier, 2011, 2012, 2013; Napier & McEwin, 2015; Napier & Spencer, 2008); cooperation between interpreters and deaf people (Napier et al., 2008; Napier & Rohan, 2007); interpreter personality and emotional stability (Bontempo et al., 2011, 2014); and techniques for educating sign language interpreters (Goswell, 2012; Napier, 2005, 2006, 2010; Major et al., 2012). A textbook on SLI was also coauthored specifically for the Australian and New Zealand contexts (Napier, et al., 2006) and was later updated (Napier et al., 2010) and then generalized because of demand for use of the textbook in other parts of the world (Napier et al., 2018).

Where We Are Today: Current Educational Pathways

Today there are multiple pathways to gaining NAATI certification, and all options involve an element of training and education before undertaking a NAATI interpreting examination process.[10] This has been the case since 2018, after a change to NAATI policy, and it is a significant shift in credentialing practice from the early days of NAATI, when interpreters could gain accreditation by direct testing without any formal training requirements. Despite being able to opt for direct testing before 2018, most Auslan interpreters elected to undertake interpreter training and education programs before NAATI testing, with 63.6% of Auslan interpreter respondents to one study indicating that they had completed entry-level interpreter training (Bontempo, 2005).

The NAATI certification system requires candidates to address prerequisites for eligibility (which vary depending on pathways); to successfully complete the certification test; and, if awarded certification, to meet recertification requirements every 3 years to demonstrate they are actively maintaining their skills, currency, and knowledge in the industry in order to retain their credentials.

A panel of examiners appointed by NAATI serves as an expert group on Auslan interpreting and translation. The Auslan panel is comprised of deaf and hearing people who have native or near-native competence in the languages under assessment; current NAATI certification; extensive professional experience in interpreting or translation; tertiary qualifications in translating, interpreting, Auslan, linguistics, or a related discipline; and the ability to demonstrate a history of ethical conduct and capacity for teamwork. Examiners are appointed by NAATI upon formal application from interested parties, who must list their credentials and experience suited to service as an interpreter or translator examiner. The Auslan panel helps maintain and set the standards for interpreting and translating practices in the field, develop appropriate test material for candidates, and mark translation and interpreting certification tests on a national scale. Obtaining NAATI certification is considered the gold standard for interpreting and translating in all examinable spoken and signed community languages used throughout the nation.

Since 2018, the NAATI certification system has broadened its scope considerably for Auslan interpreting practitioners. This includes approval of a conference-level credential in Auslan/English interpreting and specializations in legal or health domains, for example.[11] Developments in certification also include a recently approved credential as a recognized practicing translator from written English into Auslan—a credential for which only deaf practitioners are eligible, and a specialized skill for which formal recognition is considered a leading development worldwide. Although NAATI certifications are available to hearing Auslan interpreters across the spectrum of standard credentials available and issued by NAATI to a broad range of spoken language interpreters, not all standard credentials are currently available to deaf practitioners. Work continues to be undertaken in this space to widen the net with regard to NAATI credentialing for DIs in other recent specializations approved for hearing Auslan interpreting practitioners, such as conference interpreting, for example, where DIs are increasingly being employed in Australia (and have been for some time in international contexts).

Recertification with NAATI requires practitioners to apply for renewal of their interpreting or translating credential every 3 years. This can be completed online via compilation and submission of a log book, after having completed work practice criteria (a minimum number of assignments and ongoing work practice evidence is expected for different credentials) and after having met specific professional development criteria (a total of 120 professional development points must be accrued over a 3-year period), covering three categories: skills development and knowledge; industry engagement, including an ethics subcategory; and maintenance of language skills.[12]

Supply and Demand Issues

Australia continues to face a challenge in that demand for interpreters outstrips supply, a problem that was initially identified 20 years ago in a government-commissioned report on interpreter supply in 2004 (Orima, 2004). This means that certified provisional interpreters typically do not have trouble in obtaining interpreting work in the current market, sometimes in complex situations, and have little employment-related incentive to upgrade to the higher level of certification, despite the provisional certification level being an entry level of practice and intended for general conversation and noncomplex interpreting purposes only.

In most spoken languages tested by NAATI, certified provisional interpreters do not typically undertake demanding interpreting work, and they are expected to proceed to the certified interpreter level of accreditation. The exception to this is spoken languages of limited diffusion that have emerged recently in Australia.

Bontempo and Napier (2007) evaluated the disparity between the levels of NAATI accreditation in sign language interpreters by examining the self-reported skill gaps and perceived degree of competence identified by paraprofessionals (former nomenclature for what would now be considered a certified provisional interpreter) and professional-level (certified interpreter) Auslan interpreters in a research study. They found a significant difference in the perceived competence and skill gaps identified by practitioners according to their level of NAATI credential. As might be expected, interpreters holding a higher-level credential reported fewer skill gaps and significantly higher levels of competence overall than did provisionally certified interpreters. Such evidence illustrates the need to provide certified provisional practitioners with suitable training opportunities and systems to encourage and support them in achieving the higher interpreter level of practice and certification to further professionalize the SLI field in Australia.

An interesting development that has further impacted the supply-and-demand issue in the Auslan interpreting field arose from the legislation of the National Disability Insurance Scheme (NDIS) in 2013 and its rollout around the nation to full effect between 2016 and 2020 in each state and territory. The NDIS provides individualized government funding support to Australian citizens who are deaf and under the age of 65 years, allowing them to develop personalized plans for identified access and participation needs, such as interpreting requirements, Auslan courses (including lessons in the home for deaf children and their hearing family members, for example), accommodation and independent living support, deafness awareness training, the purchase of assistive technology, and so on. The NDIS gives agency to deaf people to manage their own plans in deciding their personal support requirements, in consultation with an NDIS planner.

Note that the availability of the NDIS does not diminish the responsibility of education providers, employers, government departments, hospitals, etc., to provide appropriate access and opportunities to deaf people. The NDIS is aimed more at increasing access to and participation in society at a personal level. This means that deaf people can determine what they require each year to access the wider community on an equitable basis, such as predicting and receiving an allocation in their plan for interpreting-related costs for attending family functions and important celebrations, such as weddings, and being able to communicate and engage with nonsigning hearing family members.

The NDIS has therefore led to a significant increase in demand for Auslan interpreting and translating services and related supports, and thus there has been a rise in demand for unqualified practitioners performing interpreting-type tasks to address a gap in the market and meet demand. These workers are often referred to as communication support workers in NDIS planning terms, or communication guides. They effectively function as pseudo-interpreters in less formal situations (such as at social/family functions) than those in which NAATI-credentialed interpreters typically work, but their funding allocation value in an NDIS plan is also less than the cost of a NAATI-credentialed interpreter or translator. An astute plan manager concerned about cost might therefore opt to appoint a communication guide rather than an interpreter on occasion for certain assignments. This means that the demand and need for interpreters have increased because of the scope of assignments becoming broader—and also deeper—in general, but it also creates an issue that the quality of communication services provided might now differ. In addition, if communication guide fees are considerably lower than interpreter fees and if interpreters feel as though they are missing out on some employment opportunities, interpreters could be asked to provide lower rates and conditions than those previously established in the interpreting sector. Furthermore, because of price point considerations and availability, provisionally certified interpreters, who are less experienced and less skilled practitioners than certified interpreters, might take on assignments beyond their knowledge and skill set. Because of demand considerations, interpreters at all levels of certification have also been able to set their prices when working freelance, sometimes unrealistically—meaning that some practitioners could charge fees that are not commensurate with their level of skill and credential, largely because the market demand is high and supply is restricted.

Programs

A number of TAFE colleges, as well as their vocational education and training (VET) equivalents around the nation, known as registered training organizations

(RTOs), provide language acquisition classes for Auslan learners and also conduct entry-level Auslan interpreter training courses. TAFE colleges and RTOs deliver VET programs at award levels below higher education university degree programs and with a heavy focus on practical skills and work readiness. VET courses include vocational competency courses in areas such as plumbing, information technology, youth work, aged care support work, and so on. Interpreter training courses at the Diploma level fall under the remit of VET courses. Private RTO Diploma of Interpreting courses can be expensive, depending on the provider, but TAFE courses in particular are often offered at a fraction of the cost of university studies because of government subsidies provided to TAFE colleges.

A national standard for the VET sector exists in Australia, founded on competency-based training philosophies, and built into national training packages. Courses are divided into units based on the packaging rules for the award, which are further segmented into a range of specific learning outcomes of practical performance and content knowledge elements, aligned with standards set by industry. The qualification training package also dictates assessment guidelines and expectations. Signed and spoken language interpreting courses at the college and RTO levels in Australia therefore are consistent in relation to expected exit competencies. Nonetheless, variation is reported "on the ground" in terms of operational factors and logistics, such as student recruitment processes, course admission screening processes, course delivery, actual details of content and material used, sequence of delivery, assessment tools, qualifications, quality and expertise of teaching personnel, availability of suitable resources, equipment, and so on (Bontempo and Napier, 2007; 2009).

The Auslan courses for language acquisition purposes are delivered at the Certificate II, III, and IV levels, in line with the AQF for languages, and also at the Diploma of Auslan level in some states and territories, which takes approximately 2 years full time or 4 years part time to complete. Recognition of prior learning is available, with unit exemption and placement testing available where applicable. The national Diploma of Interpreting is available upon completion of language acquisition studies or demonstration of equivalent language experience, and it generally requires successful admission screening for interpreter course entry and meeting various prerequisites. The course is conducted part time over 1 year or 18 months in most locations and under most conditions of delivery, although this varies across states and training organizations, with at least one TAFE course provider opting for a 6-month full-time course delivery for the Diploma of Interpreting in recent years. In recent years, the Diploma of Interpreting has been delivered in both face-to-face and online remote learning modes, or in a form of blended delivery, particularly after the pandemic. The majority of part-time programs typically involve a commitment two nights a week, and some weekend blocks.

A further qualification, the Advanced Diploma of Interpreting, has previously been conducted on just a few occasions, in Perth, WA, and in Melbourne, Victoria.

Some of the Diploma of Interpreting courses have enrolled deaf practitioners alongside hearing peers, whereas others have run separate courses with a deaf-only cohort or made selected units available to deaf students, rather than the full qualification, in order to meet NAATI test eligibility requirements for minimum formal training standards. The highest level of interpreting qualification available in Australia at present for Auslan interpreters is the Graduate Diploma of Auslan/English Interpreting at Macquarie University in Sydney, Australia. Course units allow for advanced study in legal and health domains and in conference interpreting, helpful in contributing to an interpreter's skill set, enabling them to potentially achieve a higher level NAATI credential. However, this degree is not currently available to deaf practitioners.

The AQF provides a national structure for the uniformity of all courses of study and qualifications issued in Australia—in schools, VET institutions, and higher education settings. The Diploma and Advanced Diploma available in the SLI field are VET-level qualifications only, and universities do not usually offer them unless they are universities with a technical institute affiliation.

Having a national VET structured training package that is the same for both signed and spoken language interpreters has its advantages and disadvantages. For example, courses have a strong community interpreting focus, as this is applicable to spoken language interpreting; however, educational interpreting receives limited attention in the training package, as it not in the usual domain of work for spoken language interpreters, yet it is a significant area of occupational demand for Auslan interpreters (Bontempo & Hutchinson, 2011; Judd et al., 2013). Similarly, the training package does not account for the rapid increase in work opportunities for Auslan interpreters in VRI contexts in recent years in Australia.

A significant concern with VET training packages is that changes to the training package potentially exclude deaf practitioners from engaging in the Diploma of Interpreting. Unit specifications for assessment, for example, might be written to require demonstration of capacity to work between signed and spoken language, rather than between two sign languages or between Auslan and written English. These exclusions have varied over the years, with some versions of the training packages and assessment specifications suited to deaf candidates in interpreting programs, whereas other versions of the training package have not allowed for accurate and appropriate assessment of deaf practitioners' skills under the performance element requirements of the package. Invariably, the training package has been written, as have various revisions and iterations of it, with hearing spoken language interpreters as the primary intended recipients of the VET course, rather than Auslan interpreters and deaf practitioners. Training package rules are not flexible, so modifying assessments in such a way that they are not compliant with the package requirements is not permitted.

Educator Demands and Resources

Unlike countries such as the United States of America, the United Kingdom, and New Zealand, it is not possible for an Auslan interpreter in Australia to become qualified through undergraduate study at university, although one postgraduate course exists at Macquarie University in Sydney for hearing Auslan interpreters with a minimum of 2 years' work experience in the field. It has been established that there is a significant demand for interpreters and a limited supply of competent Auslan interpreting practitioners in Australia, and existing interpreter education programs and training options do not appear to meet industry needs (Bontempo & Levitzke-Gray, 2009).

Anecdotal evidence demonstrates that retention rates are not high in Auslan courses over time and that there is also attrition from interpreting programs and upon entry to the profession. No research has been conducted to identify the retention and attrition issues, although we speculate that interpreter education courses are geared toward second language learners of sign language and thus are not tailored to the needs of people who already sign fluently, such as deaf students and heritage signers. It is also difficult to definitively ascertain what skills can be evaluated on entry to interpreter training programs that might be predictors of success for interpreting students (Bontempo & Napier, 2009).

An additional concern is that there are very few indigenous Australian sign language interpreters entering training programs and working in the profession, and there are even fewer working as interpreter educators. There are only a very few experienced indigenous DIs working in Far North Queensland, despite the specialized nature of interpreting work with deaf people who are Aboriginal or Torres Strait Islander (O'Reilly, 2005).

Not unlike the international scene, the SLI profession in Australia is dominated by women, at 83% of the practitioner population (Bontempo & Napier, 2007). This is reflected in the composition of Auslan classes and interpreter training programs, which typically include fewer male students. Similarly, there are fewer men working as Auslan teachers or as interpreter educators in the SLI field in Australia. Research and strategies to address recruitment, retention, attrition, and the racial and gender diversity issues in the sector have not been undertaken in Australia to date, unlike those that have been conducted in the United Kingdom, for example, which have been very informative in exploring how to improve and target diversity gaps (Napier et al., 2022).

Interpreter education programs do not run regularly on a face-to-face basis in all states and territories of Australia. Those that do conduct courses invariably run only one program per year or every 2 years, typically in a metropolitan city location. Programs often do not have enough students with the appropriate prerequisite skills at the time of intake to justify course costs, and therefore courses do not run every year, or programs are obliged to accept students who are inadequately skilled at the time of course entry in order to meet the minimum numbers stipulated by the VET course provider. Despite the existence of a national training package both for Auslan courses and for the Diploma of Interpreting, student skills and competence at the time of course exit vary, and the "readiness-to-work" gap is reported to be an issue in Australia, as it is elsewhere (Bontempo & Napier, 2007; Patrie, 1994).

A survey of interpreter educators by ASLIA in 2006 determined that a Diploma of Interpreting (Auslan) course ran in only four out of eight capital cities in that year and that retention of students was around 70% (ASLIA, 2006). Anecdotal evidence suggests that most novice practitioners and students obtain employment either before or during their interpreting studies, meaning that successful course completion does not result in increased numbers of available interpreters at the end of the academic year. Unfortunately, because of the lack of NAATI-certified Auslan interpreters available to work, a supply-and-demand consequence has arisen, whereby a large number of "signers" performing interpreting duties are able to gain employment in Australia, mostly in education settings, particularly on the east coast and in regional and remote areas where interpreters are less available. This problem has been further exacerbated by the rise of the 'communication support worker' or 'communication guide' since the advent of the NDIS, as previously discussed.

A key issue related to the developments in Australia with regard to interpreter education courses and programs of Auslan study at TAFE colleges, RTOs, and universities, including the more recent flexible-delivery-mode programs, is Cokely's (2005) reference to the "academic institutionalization" of sign language teaching and interpreter training. Although there are many favorable and positive aspects to formalized language acquisition and interpreter education opportunities, such courses, the college personnel, and the students themselves should not lose *connectedness* with local deaf communities (Hall et al., 2016).

Anecdotally at least, the ties between language and interpreting courses and the deaf community have diminished significantly in Australia, with social and political changes and the closure of the traditional deaf clubs in many states of Australia. Even if they are keen to connect with local deaf people, students do not have easy access to the diversity of the deaf community anymore, which potentially affects their acquisition of linguistic and cultural norms outside the artificial classroom environment. Nevertheless, the role of the deaf community in determining interpreting quality (Allsop & Stone, 2007), interpreting preferences and compatibility (Bontempo & Napier, 2007) remains very powerful. Creating networks and rekindling or nourishing existing ties between courses and the deaf community are imperative for Auslan students, interpreter course students, and practicing interpreters in Australia today.

Deaf Translators and Interpreters in Australia

As in other places around the world, the numbers of deaf people working professionally as DIs and deaf translators is on the increase (Adam et al., 2014). It is acknowledged, however, they have taken part in brokering activities within and around deaf communities in Australia for many years (Adam et al., 2011). Deaf people have undertaken interpreting, translating, and language brokering as a part of a reciprocal activity as members of the deaf community, and this activity often started while at school, brokering for fellow schoolmates and classroom teachers and helping with drafting written notes and letters. There are television and newspaper reports of deaf people doing this, such as an article in the *Melbourne Age* on July 14, 1980, about John McRae interpreting for Peter Jurgenstein, a professional deaf Australian Rules football player (see Figure 1).

Figure 1. John McRae interprets for Peter Jurgenstein, a professional deaf Australian Rules football player.

Source: M. Fiddian, "Fingers fly for the big man," *The Age* (Melbourne), July 14, 1980.

Historically, however, the role of the deaf practitioner in Australia has been that of a team interpreter (Napier, McKee, & Goswell, 2018), frequently interpreting for:

- users of a foreign sign language;
- linguistically or socially isolated deaf people who have limited sign language proficiency or an idiosyncratic signing style (perhaps because of minimal exposure to the deaf community, mental health issues, language deprivation, a very poor education, or the presence of a cognitive disability);
- deafblind people;
- situations in which trust or issues of cultural sensitivity and comfort are paramount (for example, trauma counseling); and
- IS users at conferences/events.

The NAATI website further notes that deaf people can become Certified Provisional Deaf Interpreters[13] to work between nonconventional sign languages (NCSL) and Auslan, typically working with clients who:

- have sensory or cognitive disabilities,
- have recently migrated to Australia and are more familiar with foreign sign languages,
- are educationally or linguistically disadvantaged, or
- have limited conventional Auslan.

These two explanations of DIs and their clientele offer a narrower view of the scope of practice of the deaf practitioner than is reality, and according to Egnatovich (1999), hearing interpreters might believe that DIs are there only for deaf people with minimal language skills or whenever they need them. The definition of NCSL and how it applies to a deaf client leans toward being quite restrictive, and it could be perceived as ableist terminology. NCSL is not able to be clearly defined nor is it consistently applied as a concept. The descriptor is open to wide interpretation, flexible assignment, and labeling concerns. This poses some risk in the assessment, application, and determinations of deaf people, and it raises legitimate questions about how this could be approached in interpreting practice and assessment. This definition also suggests that DIs are effectively required to do some of the most challenging work in the SLI profession without appropriate acknowledgment (i.e., not as certified interpreters, only as recognized or provisional interpreters), and DIs still have only intermittent or limited access to formal training opportunities. Notably, DIs still do not have access to university-level interpreting studies or to the full suite of NAATI certification system credentials.

In ASLIA's (2018) policy document on DIs,[14] the second sentence reinforces the forementioned hegemony: "In cases where the 'standard' Auslan<>English interpreter skill-set is insufficient for the demands or for cultural safety reasons, more specialised assistance is required to bridge the communication gap." Language such as this in documents such as this reinforce the notion that DIs are assigned only when the client does not use "standard" Auslan that can be understood by a hearing Auslan<>English interpreter. In other words, DIs are assigned only when the hearing interpreter is unable to work alone.

In recent years, however, the understanding and appreciation of the role and skills of DIs (and deaf translators) have shifted somewhat in Australia, with increasing value placed on the important extralinguistic knowledge and cultural skills a deaf interpreter brings to all interpreted events. Indeed, in the current era, deaf practitioners around the world work in many domains, ranging from broadcast media events to United Nations and parliamentary sessions, education settings, community events, entertainment settings such as music concerts, the political sphere, and special occasions such as weddings, as well as the usual domains of community interpreting work, like police, legal, hospital, and allied health care settings. Australian interpreting service providers, practitioners, and associations are slowly embracing this broader understanding of the work of DIs and the team approach, which is a considerable shift from earlier views of domains of practice and clientele and expands work opportunities between deaf–hearing interpreters in Australia. In fact, critical work was carried out to establish evidence-based Auslan translation standards for website translations (Hodge et al., 2015), and at the time of writing, funding has been secured for a follow-on project to update the standards.

Since the late 1990s, courses for deaf practitioners have been conducted in an ad hoc manner in several states, often by state Deaf society organizations or ASLIA branches. Training has ranged from weekend workshops to courses of several weeks' duration, to the first 1-year Diploma of Interpreting course in Perth, WA, in 2001. The diploma was directly equivalent and comparable to the Diploma of Interpreting undertaken by Auslan/English interpreters around the nation at that time, although it was adapted to suit the work context of deaf practitioners. The course emphasized consecutive rather than simultaneous interpreting techniques and was delivered directly in Auslan by hearing and deaf interpreter educators. The course was conducted with a cohort of deaf students only. Since that time, some formal Diploma of Interpreting courses have started to include deaf students, often in mixed classes with hearing students. These have run with varying degrees of success.

Alternative part-time study courses have run from time to time around Australia for deaf practitioners, but no recognized standard curriculum is in use for these short courses, and they do not result in any actual qualification. NAATI will accept them as evidence of training for the purposes of being able to sit the Certified Provisional Deaf Interpreter examination, however. No formal teaching resources, such as footage of deaf practitioners working in real-life settings, existed for use in early deaf practitioner training programs in Australia. Interpreter educators on deaf practitioner course programs to date have often been hearing people who have depended on the inclusion of deaf guests who are foreign signers or deafblind (for example, visits by experienced deaf practitioners who are able to demonstrate and model effective interpreting practices and talk about their experiences), as well as creatively developing or adapting existing Auslan interpreter training material for classroom use and practice.

ASLIA state branches afford deaf practitioners full membership status and entitlements if they have completed training or hold certification. Deaf practitioners also often access professional development activities conducted by ASLIA and others, including workshops run by AUSIT, for example. They participate alongside hearing interpreter peers, or on their own as participants in events tailored specifically for deaf practitioners, although these are far less common. Many of these initiatives have occurred only in the past few years.

A major impetus behind the move to formally certify deaf practitioners was the Deaf Relay Interpreter Certification Project that began in 2006 when the National Auslan Interpreter Booking and Payment System (NABS) medical interpreting service funded ASLIA to develop and administer a national certification process for deaf practitioners (Bontempo et al., 2014). This was in recognition of the variability of training, the lack of standardized testing available across the nation, and the requirement for NABS to employ certified interpreters in medical settings under the conditions of their contract with the federal government. Deaf people already holding an AQF qualification from TAFE were exempt from testing, but all other potential and practicing DIs were strongly encouraged to undertake the test if they intended to continue to work or to seek future work with NABS or other employers.

A test was developed and rolled out in 2007, similar in structure, format, and content to the Auslan paraprofessional-level/certified provisional NAATI video test of the time, with adaptations to suit the work context. The test included various cultural and ethical questions for the candidates and also contained two dialogues for interpreting in the consecutive mode. The test dialogues focused on assessing a candidate's capacity to work with deaf people who were not fluent Auslan users. Challenges were raised by the testing process. The nature of video testing allowed for standardization of test content and presentation but meant that the test was highly artificial. Deaf practitioners usually work in an organic manner within an interpreting team, and the nature of testing by prerecorded video could suppress some of the natural and logical strategies a deaf practitioner might use in real life. However, the alternative of national live testing of candidates was not viable in a country the size of Australia, though it was carefully considered by ASLIA at the time of product development.

Notably, although there was deaf input into this process and the project, deaf practitioners did not lead the project. A theme raised by some deaf candidates participating in the ASLIA/NABS test, and also expressed by the project personnel (Bontempo et al., 2014), was the need for quality training rather than just the introduction of a testing system. Test candidates also indicated the concomitant effect on status and recognition of the deaf practitioner certification standard, given that at the time it could potentially be achieved without the candidate having completed any form of training in interpreting. This process was followed by the announcement of Deaf Interpreter Recognition by NAATI in 2013, and NAATI has introduced further certification options for deaf practitioners since then.

With regard to work opportunities for DIs in Australia, although this is slowly evolving and increasing, the majority of the work to date has tended to be with specific populations (Bontempo et al., 2014) or online translation (Hodge & Goswell, 2021). Issues with regard to employment include the lower status of deaf practitioners (Morgan & Adam, 2012) and the reticence of service users to employ and pay for what is sometimes viewed as an unnecessary, supernumerary interpreter. To exacerbate the problem, there is little research on deaf interpreting/translation in Australia from which to draw data, although this is a growing area of exploration and interest outside of Australia (see, for example, Forestal, 2005; Tester, 2021).

A cultural and ideological change on the part of service providers, and Auslan interpreters as well, might be required to further increase employment opportunities for deaf practitioners. Education of service users could also be required in order to increase the involvement of deaf practitioners in interpreted settings. In growing the DI profession, it might be useful to think laterally about the value and skills of a competent deaf practitioner and how such a practitioner could effectively work in team situations in some circumstances where Auslan interpreters presently work alone. For example, working in inclusive education settings with primary school–aged children might be of enormous benefit to deaf children. In addition, there has been increased demand for translation of written text to signed language in recent years (for example, translations of legislation or translations of open captions on DVD footage). This is a specialized domain highly suited to deaf practitioners (Boudreault, 2005) and has been supported by a new translation credential developed by NAATI exclusively for DIs.

IMPACT OF THE COVID-19 PANDEMIC

The worldwide impact of the COVID-19 pandemic was initially experienced somewhat differently in Australia. Having the benefit of being a large island nation, with its geographic location away from early hotspots of virus transmission through international airports and travel routes overseas (Chokshi et al., 2021), Australia was in a unique position of being able to close international borders to nonresidents for 2 years between March 2020 and February 2022. Further domestic border closures across the states, lockdowns, and quarantining of returning residents, among other restrictions, all significantly contained outbreaks as they occurred and provided time to implement vaccination programs in Australia before borders, both domestic and international, were opened again. This time afforded a great deal of protection to vulnerable groups, and as a result, Australia fared significantly better, even a year after opening borders, when mortality rates and population sizes were compared with other countries (Bennett, 2023).

Given the border closures, the generally broad acceptance of lockdowns, and the low tolerance for outbreaks in the community, many Australians effectively lived in a parallel universe to that of many other countries in the world during various periods of time during the pandemic. Residents of some Australian states, such as WA, were able to move around very freely and live life relatively normally during the 2-year border closure, whereas other states on the east coast of the nation, such as Victoria, were subject to extended lockdowns as outbreaks occurred, often because of breaches in quarantine. This variability on a domestic level did lead to some differences in interpreting practices and interpreter training during the pandemic in Australia, and it certainly meant that our exposure, response, and position regarding interpreting and interpreter education and training were markedly different around the country, as well as in comparison with other nations.

No research or data on the impact of the pandemic on Auslan interpreting have been collected. Nevertheless, it is clear from anecdotal evidence that, as was the case elsewhere around the world, the deaf community and interpreters were required to pivot to varying degrees during periods of working from home or periods of restrictions. Some interpreters experienced financial impacts and dramatic changes to their work, with novel challenges presented by a downturn in the extent and nature of interpreting work available during periods of lockdown, quickly evolving working conditions, and requirements for social distancing and personal protective equipment. Meanwhile, some other interpreters were far less affected during this period, depending largely on where they lived.

Deaf people and interpreters in states experiencing greater COVID-19 impact and lockdowns rapidly became more proficient at using video remote interpreting technology and video conferencing software and changing their work and communication practices than did those in less affected states. With regard to interpreter training courses, many institutions quickly adopted a hybrid model of partially online, partially face-to-face teaching (the latter during periods of no restrictions during the 2 years of border closures), as this format allowed for rapid switching between modes of delivery during outbreaks, if needed. For the first time in Australian history, it meant that entry-level interpreter training programs could enroll students across state borders for online course components, providing some opportunity for cross-fertilization of skills, knowledge, and trainer expertise.

One benefit that did arise during this time was the increased access and opportunity to engage with quality professional learning, as interpreters around Australia were able to virtually participate in professional development courses and online workshops and conferences, including those taking place interstate or overseas.

In addition, deaf professionals and presenters were able to widen their prospective collaborators and audiences. Local interpreters—both deaf and hearing—were able to gain experience interpreting remotely in high-level forums in which they might not ordinarily have been employed to work because of the cost-prohibitive nature of flying an interpreter, or a deaf presenter, from Australia to the United States or Europe for face-to-face work opportunities. This new flexibility with regard to teaching and learning options and employment scope and opportunities were positive outcomes that arose from the challenges of the pandemic.

A negative of the increased working from home and online learning was, of course, the significant social isolation and psychological impact faced by many during this period. No studies of the stress, well-being, and occupational health impacts of the shift in conditions from on-site to online work on the deaf community or interpreters in Australia have been conducted to date. It is likely, however, that the increased demands on interpreters, including the trend toward working alone for longer periods of time, different teaming dynamics if working with a colleague virtually versus in-situ, and environmental considerations, to name just a few (for example, having to manage the technology requirements while turn-taking during a complex interpreting assignment via video creates additional cognitive and practical demands), have taken a toll on practitioners. Flexibilities afforded in working conditions during the pandemic, such as a single interpreter interpreting a press conference without a team member present with whom to switch, might be expected by some employers to continue during non-crisis periods. Such conditions were in response at the time to a critical need to urgently respond and to provide information in sign language in the early days of the pandemic, but they were not in line with the guidelines set by ASLITA for safe occupational practices for interpreters. This creates some potential for tension moving forward, should employers expect the same conditions from interpreters on an ongoing basis.

As was the case in a number of parts of the world (as mentioned in several of the chapters in this volume), the profile of SLI increased on television and in live online updates during the pandemic, with the appearance of interpreters during the often daily broadcasts from the Australian prime minister and state premiers. This undoubtedly had some awareness-raising benefits and created increased interest in learning Auslan among the wider community. From an interpreting perspective, though, the media interpreting provided was inconsistent in implementation and quality, with some states managing this much more effectively than others. Policies and practices in each jurisdiction varied considerably with regard to the use of a variety of suitable practitioners, including DIs; in other countries, this area of work was quite often done predominantly by DIs. The training in Australia to prepare interpreters for broadcast interpreting was relatively limited before the pandemic. Only a small pool of practitioners had previously had some exposure and experience with broadcast interpreting, having interpreted press conferences and updates

about natural disasters, and some practitioners had attended a short national training course on media interpreting.

A postpandemic concern has been that interpreters have since disappeared
from our television screens. Progress made in lobbying for access during various
crises has not resulted in sustainable and ongoing practices of Auslan-inclusive
information dissemination in Australia. ASLITA and Deaf Australia worked
together during the pandemic to ensure that consistent and accurate information
was provided to the media and to governments about interpreting standards and
technical requirements, and this collaboration will likely be ongoing, as advocacy continues to be needed to implement more consistent, quality broadcast
interpreting.

Indeed, more training, but also skill assessment, of interpreters doing VRI and
working in broadcast contexts would be welcome. Although we are not suggesting
that VRI be normalized, as it does not readily replace on-site interpreting, the dramatic shift to VRI conditions still has not swung back fully to face-to-face work in
some states, and this type of work does require a different skill set that is not formally taught at present and is effectively untested in Australia. The knowledge and
skills necessary for this type of work, as well as for media interpreting, should attract
greater attention in interpreter education courses moving forward.

The Road Ahead

The contemporary Australian context for SLTI certification, education, and training, along with the impact of the pandemic, have been described and discussed. The
increased recognition of the value of DIs has been notable in recent years. Undoubtedly, the greatest challenges in regard to SLTI education and training continue to
be the allocation and availability of resources—human, financial, and physical—in
response to a changing interpreting landscape in Australia and acknowledgment of
the importance of authentic and meaningful engagement with deaf practitioners
and deaf communities around the country.

Australia has a relatively small group of hearing, and not very ethnically diverse,
interpreters and interpreter educators. There are few interpreter education programs, limited training resources and materials, only one postgraduate university-level interpreter education program that is not available to deaf practitioners,
just one academic working full time specifically in interpreter education, limited
support for researchers of interpreting, and insufficient sign language interpreters certified at the highest interpreter levels of certification. The standard of training and opportunity to participate for deaf practitioners vary across the nation and
remain largely unfunded and unrecognized, and they frequently are not led by deaf
practitioners themselves.

Opportunities to expand research horizons and higher education courses should be embraced moving forward, as there has been a significant lull in research output in recent years in Australia. However, there is an increased willingness and an appetite for greater collaboration between deaf and hearing interpreters in Australia, which is very positive. The ever-changing and improving technologies for teaching and learning interpreting, and for our work as interpreters presents new opportunities, and these developments and evolutions in the field bode well for the future of the profession "Down Under."

Notes

1. See https://www.abs.gov.au/statistics/people/population/national-state-and-territory-population/latest-release
2. See https://www.abs.gov.au/census/find-census-data
3. See https://deafaustralia.org.au/media-release-census-2021/
4. See https://www.abs.gov.au/statistics/people/people-and-communities/cultural-diversity-census/2021
5. See https://www.naati.com.au/wp-content/uploads/2023/10/NAATI_Annual-Report_2022-23.pdf
6. See https://deafaustralia.org.au/history-and-achievements/
7. See https://ausit.org/find-an-interpreter/
8. See www.aslia.com.au
9. See https://humanrights.gov.au/our-work/disability-rights/about-disability-rights
10. See https://www.naati.com.au/information-guides/certification-pathways/auslan-pathways/
11. See https://www.naati.com.au/certification/
12. See https://www.naati.com.au/practitioners/recertification/
13. See https://www.naati.com.au/certification/cpdi/
14. See https://aslia.com.au/wp-content/uploads/1-Deaf-Interpreter-Policy-and-Guidelines.pdf

References

Adam, R. (2016). *Unimodal bilingualism in the Deaf community: Language contact between two sign languages in Australia and the United Kingdom.* Unpublished doctoral dissertation, University College London.

Adam, R., Aro, M., Druetta, J. C., Dunne, S., & af Klintberg, J. (2014). Deaf interpreters: An introduction. In R. Adam, C. Stone, S. D. Collins, & M. Metzger (Eds.), *Deaf interpreters at work: International Insights* (pp. 1–18). Gallaudet University Press.

Adam, R., Carty, B., & Stone, C. (2011). Ghost writing: Deaf translators within the deaf community. *Babel, 57*(3), 375–393.

Allsop, L., & Stone, C. (2007). *Collective notions of quality.* Paper presented at the SASLI Conference, Edinburgh, Scotland.

Australian Sign Language Interpreters Association. (2006). *State reports on interpreter education and training.* Paper presented at the Second ASLIA National Interpreter Trainers' Workshop, Perth, Western Australia.

Bennett C. M. (2023). COVID-19 in Australia: How did a country that fought so hard for extra time end up so ill prepared? *BMJ, 380,* 469. https://doi.org/10.1136/bmj.p469

Bontempo, K. (2005). *A survey of Auslan interpreters' perceptions of competence.* Unpublished manuscript, Macquarie University, Australia.

Bontempo, K., Goswell, D., Levitzke-Gray, P., Napier, J. & Warby, L. (2014). Testing times: Towards the professionalization of Deaf interpreters in Australia. In R. Adam, C. Stone, S. Collins, & M. Metzger (Eds). *Deaf interpreters at work: International insights* (pp. 51–89). Washington DC: Gallaudet University Press.

Bontempo, K., & Hutchinson, B. (2011). Striving for an 'A' grade: A case study of performance management of interpreters. *International Journal of Interpreter Education, 3*(1), Article 6.

Bontempo, K., & Napier, J. (2007). Mind the gap! A skills analysis of sign language interpreters. *The Sign Language Translator and Interpreter, 1,* 275–299.

Bontempo, K., & Napier, J. (2009) Getting it right from the start: Program admission testing of signed language interpreters. In C. Angelelli & H. E. Jacobson (Eds.) *Testing and Assessment in Translation and Interpreting* (pp. 247–295). John Benjamins.

Bontempo, K., & Napier, J. (2011). Emotional stability as a predictor for interpreter competence: A consideration in determining aptitude for interpreting. *Interpreting, 13*(1), 85–105.

Bontempo, K., Napier, J., Hayes, L., & Brashear, V. (2014). Does personality matter? An international study of sign language interpreter disposition. *International Journal of Translation and Interpreting Research. 6,* 23–46.

Boudreault, P. (2005). Deaf interpreters. In T. Janzen (Ed.), *Topics in signed language interpreting* (pp. 323–356). John Benjamins.

Branson, J., & Miller, D. (1995). *The story of Betty Steel: Deaf convict and pioneer.* Deafness Resources Australia.

Burchett, J. H. (1964). *Utmost for the highest.* Hall's Bookstore.

Carty, B. (2000). John Carmichael: Australian deaf pioneer. *Deaf History Journal, 3*(3), 24–36.

Carty, B. (2004). *Managing their own affairs: the Australian Deaf community during the 1920s and 1930s.* Unpublished doctoral dissertation, Griffith University.

Carty, B. (2018). *Managing their own affairs: The Australian Deaf community in the 1920s and 1930s.* Gallaudet University Press.

Chokshi, A., DallaPiazza, M., Zhang, W. W., & Sifri. Z. (2021). Proximity to international airports and early transmission of COVID-19 in the United States: An epidemiological assessment of the geographic distribution of 490,000 cases. *Travel Medicine and Infectious Disease.* 40:102004. https://doi.org/10.1016/j.tmaid.2021.102004

Cokely, D. (2005). Shifting positionality: A critical examination of the turning point in the relationship of interpreters and the deaf community. In M. Marshcark, R. Peterson, & E. Winston (Eds.), *Interpreting and interpreter education: From research to practice* (pp. 3–28). Oxford University Press.

Dawkins, J. (1992). *Australia's language: The Australian Language and Literacy Policy.* Australian Government Publishing Office.

De Meulder, M. (2018) "So, why do you sign?" Deaf and hearing new signers, their motivation, and revitalisation policies for sign languages. *Applied Linguistics Review, 10*(4), 705–724.

De Pedro R., Perez, I., & Wilson, C. (Eds.). (2009). *Interpreting and translating in public service settings. Policy, practice, pedagogy.* St. Jerome.

Egnatovitch, R. J. (1999). Certified Deaf Interpreter WHY? *RID Views, 16*(10), 1–2.

Fitzgerald, S. (1999). *Open minds, open hearts : Stories of the Australian Catholic deaf community.* CCOD.

Flynn, J. W. (1984). *No longer by gaslight. The first 100 years of the Adult Deaf Society of Victoria.* Adult Deaf Society of Victoria.

Flynn, J. W. (1996, May 22–26). *Reflections on sign language interpreting. Hobart, Australia: Australian Federation of Deaf Societies.* Paper presented at the National Deafness Conference, Hobart, Tasmania.

Flynn, J. W. (1999). *Some aspects of the development of post-school organizations of and for Deaf people in Australia.* Master's thesis, LaTrobe University, Melbourne.

Forestal, E. (2005). The emerging professionals: Deaf interpreters and their views and experiences of training. In M. Marsharck, R. Peterson, E. A. Winston, & P. Sapere (Eds.), *Sign language interpreting and interpreter education: Directions for research and practice.* (pp. 235–258). Oxford University Press.

Goswell, D. (2011). Being there: Role shift in English to Auslan interpreting. In L. Leeson, S. Wurm, & M. Vermeerbergen (Eds.), *Signed language interpreting: Preparation, practice and performance* (pp. 61–86). St. Jerome.

Goswell, D. (2012). Do you see what I see? Using ELAN for self-analysis and reflection. *International Journal of Interpreter Education, 4*(1), 72–81.

Green, J., Hodge, G., & Kelly, B. F. (2022). Two decades of sign language and gesture research in Australia: 2000–2020. *Language Documentation & Conservation, 16,* 32–78.

Hale, S. (2007). *Community interpreting.* Palgrave Macmillan.

Hamachek, D. (1999). Effective teachers: What do they do, how they do it, and the importance of self-knowledge. In R. P. Lipka & T. M. Brinthaupt (Eds.), *The role of self in teacher development* (pp. 189–224). State University of New York Press.

Hall, W. C., Holcomb, T. K., & Elliott, M. (2016). Using popular education with the oppressor class: Suggestions for sign language interpreter education. *Critical Education, 7*(13).

Haualand, H., & Allen, C. (2009). *Deaf people and human rights.* https://www.rasit.org/files/Deaf-People-and-Human-Rights-Report.pdf

Hodge, G., & Goswell, D. (2023). Deaf signing diversity and signed language translations. *Applied Linguistics Review, 4*(5), 1045–1083.

Hodge, G., Gowell, D., Whynot, L., Linder, S., & Clark, C. (2015). *What standards? The need for evidence-based Auslan translation standards and production guidelines.* ACCAN. https://accan.org.au/files/Grants/ACCAN_AuslanTranslationProject_FullReport-accessible.pdf

Johnston, T. (1989). *Auslan dictionary: a dictionary of the sign language of the Australian deaf community.* Deafness Resources Australia.

Johnston, T. (2004). W(h)ither the deaf community? Population, genetics, and the future of Australian Sign Language. *American Annals of the Deaf, 148*(5), 358–375.

Judd, J., Lewis, T. & Bontempo, K. (2013). Making mentoring matter: A case study in mentoring educational interpreters. In E. A. Winston & R. Lee (Eds). *Mentoring in sign language interpreting* (pp. 161–179). RID Press.

Kottler, J. A., Zehm, S. J. & Kottler, E. (2005). *On being a teacher: The human dimension.* Corwin Press.

Lo Bianco, J. (1987). *National Policy on Languages.* Australian Government Publishing Service.

Madden, M. (1995). The prevalence of occupational overuse syndrome among Australian sign language interpreters. *Journal of Occupational Health and Safety, 11,* 257–263.

Madden, M. (2005). The prevalence of occupational overuse syndrome in signed language interpreters in Australia—What a pain! In M. Metzger & E. Fleetwood (Eds.), *Attitudes, innuendo, and regulators: Challenges of interpretation* (Vol. 2, pp. 3–70). Gallaudet University Press.

Major, G., & Napier, J. (2012). Interpreting and knowledge mediation in the healthcare setting: What do we really mean by 'accuracy'? In V. Montalt & M. Shuttleworth (Eds.), *Linguistica antiverpiesa: Translation & knowledge mediation in medical and health settings* (pp. 207–226). Artesius University College.

Major, G., Napier, J., & Stubbe, M. (2012). 'What happens truly, not text book!': Using authentic interactions in discourse training for healthcare interpreters. Invited manuscript in K. Malcolm & L. Swabey (Eds.), *In our hands: Educating healthcare interpreters* (pp. 27–53). Gallaudet University Press.

Major, G., Napier, J., Ferrara, L., & Johnston, T. (2012). Exploring lexical gaps in Australian Sign Language for the purposes of health communication. *Communication & Medicine, 9*(1), 37–47.

Morgan, P., & Adam, R. (2012). Deaf interpreters in mental health settings—Some reflections and thoughts for deaf interpreter education. In B. Nicodemus & M. Metzger (Eds.), *Investigations in healthcare interpreting* (pp. 190–208). Gallaudet University Press.

Napier, J. (2002). University intepreting: Linguistic issues for considerations. *Journal of Deaf Studies and Deaf Education, 7*(4), 281–301. https://doi.org/10.1093/deafed/7.4.281

Napier, J. (2002c). *Sign language interpreting: Linguistic coping strategies.* Douglas McLean.

Napier, J. (2004). Sign language interpreter training, testing, and accreditation: An international comparison. *American Annals of the Deaf, 149,* 350–359.

Napier, J. (2005). Teaching interpreters to identify omission potential. In C. Roy (Ed.), *Advances in teaching sign language interpreters* (pp.123–137). Gallaudet University Press.

Napier, J. (2006). Effectively teaching discourse to sign language interpreting students. *Language, Culture and Curriculum, 19*(3), 252–265.

Napier, J. (2010). A case study of the use of storytelling as a pedagogical tool for teaching interpreting students. *The Interpreter & Translator Trainer, 10*(1), 1–32.

Napier, J. (2011). Here or there? An assessment of video remote signed language interpreter-mediated interaction in court. In S. Braun & J. L. Taylor (Eds.), *Videoconference and remote interpreting in criminal proceedings* (pp. 145–185). University of Surrey. http://www.videoconference-interpreting.net/BraunTaylor2011.html

Napier, J. (2012). Exploring themes in stakeholder perspectives of video remote interpreting in court. In C. J. Kellett (Ed.), *Interpreting across genres: Multiple research perspectives* (pp. 219–254). EUT Edizioni Universtà di Trieste.

Napier, J. (2013). "You get that vibe": A pragmatic analysis of clarification and communicative accommodation in legal video remote interpreting. In L. Meurant, A. Sinte, M. Van Herreweghe, & M. Vermeerbergen (Eds.), *Sign language research uses and practices: Crossing views on theoretical and applied sign language linguistics* (pp. 85–110). De Gruyter Mouton and Ishara Press.

Napier, J., & Adam, R. (2002). A comparative linguistic analysis of Auslan and BSL interpreting. *Deaf Worlds, 18*(1), 22–31.

Napier, J., & Barker, R. (2004). Accessing university education: Perceptions, preferences and expectations for interpreting by deaf students. *Journal of Deaf Studies and Deaf Education*, *9*(2), 228–238.

Napier., J. & Barker, R. (2004). Sign language interpreting: The relationship between meta-linguistic awareness and the production of interpreting omissions. *Sign Language Studies*, *4*(4), 369–393.

Napier, J., & Kidd, M. (2013). English literacy as a barrier to healthcare information for deaf people who use Auslan. *Australian Family Physician*, *42*(12), 896–899.

Napier, J., & Leneham, M. (2011). "It was difficult to manage the communication": Testing the feasibility of video remote signed language interpreting in courts in NSW, Australia. *Journal of Interpretation*, 53–62.

Napier, J., & McEwin, A. (2015). Do deaf people have the right to serve as jurors in Australia? *Alternative Law Journal*, *40*(1), 23–27.

Napier, J., & Rohan, M. (2007). An invitation to dance: Deaf consumers' perceptions of signed language interpreters and interpreting. In M. Metzger & E. Fleetwood (Eds.), *Translation, sociolinguistic, and consumer issues in interpreting* (pp. 159–203). Gallaudet University Press.

Napier, J., & Spencer, D. (2008). Guilty or not guilty? An investigation of deaf jurors' access to court proceedings via sign language interpreting. In D. Russell & S. Hale (Eds.), *Interpreting in legal settings* (pp. 71–122). Gallaudet University Press.

Napier, J., Carmichael, A., & Wiltshire, A. (2008). Look-Pause-Nod: A linguistic case study of a Deaf professional and interpreters working together. In P. C. Hauser, K. L. Finch, & A. B. Hauser (Eds.), *Deaf professionals and designated interpreters: A new paradigm* (pp. 22–42). Gallaudet University Press.

Napier, J., Major, G., & Ferrara, L. (2011). Medical Signbank: A cure-all for the aches and pains of medical sign language interpreting? In L. Leeson, S. Wurm & M. Vermeerbergen (Eds.), *Signed language interpreting: Preparation, practice and performance* (pp. 110–137). St Jerome.

Napier, J., McKee, R., & Goswell, D. (2006). *Sign language interpreting: Theory & practice in Australia and New Zealand*. Federation Press.

Napier, J., McKee, R., & Goswell, D. (2010). *Sign language interpreting: Theory & practice in Australia and New Zealand* (2nd ed.). Federation Press.

Napier, J., McKee, R., & Goswell, D. (2018). *Sign language interpreting: Theory & practice in Australia and New Zealand* (3rd ed.). Federation Press.

Napier, J., Sabolcec, J., Hodgetts, J., Linder, S., Mundy, G., Turcinov, M., & Warby, L. (2014). Direct, translated or interpreter-mediated? A qualitative study of access to preventative and on-going healthcare information for Australian Deaf people. In B. Nicodemus & M. Metzger (Eds.), *Investigations in healthcare interpreting* (pp. 51–89). Gallaudet University Press.

Napier, J., Skinner, R., Adam, R., Stone, C., Pratt, S., Hinton, D. P., & Obasi, C. (2022). Representation and diversity in the sign language translation and interpreting profession in the United Kingdom. *Interpreting and Society: An Interdisciplinary Journal*, *2*(2), 119–130.

O'Reilly, S. (2005). *Indigenous sign language and culture: The interpreting and access needs of Deaf people who are Aboriginal and/or Torres Strait Islander in Far North Queensland*. ASLIA National.

ORIMA Research. (2004). *A report on the supply and demand for Auslan interpreters across Australia*. https://web.archive.org.au/awa/20060209053526mp_/http://pandora.nla.gov.

au/pan/55566/20060209-0000/www.facs.gov.au/disability/auslan_report/Auslan_Interpreter_Report_with_Attachments.pdf

Ozolins, U., & Bridge, M. (1999). *Sign language interpreting in Australia*. Language Australia.

Palmer, P. J. (2007). *The courage to teach: Exploring the inner landscape of a teacher's life*. Jossey-Bass.

Patrie, C. (1994). *The readiness to work gap.* Paper presented at "Mapping our course: A collaborative venture." Proceedings of the 10th national convention of the Conference of Interpreter Trainers, Washington, DC.

Tester, C. A. (2021). *Intralingual interpreting in the courtroom: An ethnographic study of Deaf interpreters' perceptions of their role and positioning.* Unpublished doctoral dissertation, Heriot-Watt University, Edinburgh.

Wang, L., & Napier, J. (2014). Measuring bilingual working memory capacity of professional Auslan/English interpreters: A comparison of two scoring methods. *The Interpreters' Newsletter, 19*, 45–62.

Wang, J., & Napier, J. (2016). Directionality in signed language interpreting. *Meta, 60*(3), 518–541.

2

From Integration to Fragmentation to Cooperation

Sign Language Translator and Interpreter Education in Austria

As a descendant of the Habsburg monarchy, Austria has a long tradition as a plurilingual and pluricultural space. Bringing together many nationalities and approximately 12 languages, the Habsburg Empire required multifaceted forms of translation and interpreting in its administration, in its courts, and in communication with other empires, while noninstitutional translation and interpreting practices were carried out daily in numerous institutional and private settings (Wolf, 2015). Today, Austria is a relatively small country located in the southern part of Central Europe, with an area of 83,881.71 km² (Statistik Austria, 2018). It borders Switzerland and Liechtenstein to the west, Germany and the Czech Republic to the north, Slovakia to the northeast, Hungary to the east, and Slovenia and Italy to the south. It consists of nine federal provinces. On January 1, 2024, Austria had a population of 9,159,993 people (Statistik Austria, 2023). Austria is home to six autochthonous language minorities who are protected by law, including Burgenland Croats, Slovenes, Hungarians, Czechs, Slovaks, and Roma. In 2005, the Austrian Constitution was amended to include a clause in Section 8: "Austrian Sign Language is recognized as an independent language. The laws shall determine the details" [our translation] (BGBl. I Nr. 81/2005). Although this passage does not reveal anything about the right to assistance from interpreters, the recognition of Austrian Sign Language (*Österreichische Gebärdensprache* [ÖGS]) nevertheless was an important step toward greater inclusion for the 9,000 to 12,000 deaf people in Austria.[1]

WHO WE ARE

Christian and Nadja met in 1994 at the Department of Translation Studies at the University of Graz in a job interview. Christian is deaf and was born in Graz, the capital of the southern Austrian federal state of Styria. He is a deaf heritage signer who was raised in a multigenerational deaf family, and he grew up using ÖGS. Although he grew up with ÖGS in his family life, among family acquaintances, and in deaf clubs, his school years at hearing schools were very demanding. Because deaf people could not rely on interpreting services at that time (there were very few hearing heritage signers occasionally interpreting on an ad hoc basis), he under-stood virtually nothing in class and had to be tutored privately, especially in math-ematics and foreign languages. He was very ambitious and learned German to an excellent level. After his graduation from high school, Christian's dream was to work as a teacher for deaf children, but unfortunately this did not come to pass, as at the time of his graduation in the early 1990s the legal situation was such that it was impossible for him to attend and complete teacher-training college. Therefore, he started studying psychology, which he enjoyed very much, until he managed to get a position at the university.

Before meeting Christian, Nadja, who was raised bilingually in German and Serbian, had been working as a research assistant at the Department of Translation Studies at the University of Graz for a few years. She had studied linguistics and Slavic studies and was a literary translator. After the head of her department saw sign language interpreting (SLI) on Slovenian television, he felt a responsibility to bring SLI to the university, with the long-term goal of providing sign language inter-preter education in Austria, and Nadja took on the task of developing the course. This fortunate coincidence ultimately led to the implementation of SLI education at the Department of Translation Studies 12 years later, in 2002.

Before the full implementation of SLI education at the university, contacts were made with a deaf association, the first SLI courses were offered, and the first con-ference dedicated to sign language took place. Nadja started to write her doctoral dissertation during this time, conducting a survey of people who interpreted more or less regularly for deaf people in Austria. Together with the hearing linguistics stu-dent Karin Hofstätter, Nadja went in search of young deaf people, visited deaf clubs, and gradually learned ÖGS. In 1994, Christian was employed at the department, and Nadja completed her doctoral studies.

Soon, we began to participate in international projects. We traveled around Europe, learned a lot, and finally were able to offer two 1-year part-time courses, one for hearing sign language interpreters and one for deaf ÖGS teachers. National projects in the field of deaf studies, awareness raising, ÖGS teaching and learning, and ÖGS lexicography followed. Christian had meanwhile begun to study linguis-tics, and Karin supported him as an interpreter as well as she could. Although Nadja also enjoyed interpreting, she gave up this passion to devote herself to the organization of projects and to research. Moreover, she was responsible not only for ÖGS but also for other research fields at her department.

Christian started teaching ÖGS at our department in 1994. As there were no other ÖGS instructors with a linguistics background available in Austria for quite some time, he toured the country teaching ÖGS grammar. Soon, he started to hold lectures and workshops on ÖGS, sign language linguistics, didactics, deaf culture, and deaf sociology, both in Austria and abroad.

After several applications and numerous discussions with the authorities, ÖGS was finally granted approval as the 12th language in our curriculum, and SLI education commenced as a full program in 2002. In the meantime, Christian and Karin had produced extensive ÖGS teaching and learning materials. They actively contributed to the further development of the bachelor of arts (BA) and master of arts (MA) degree programs, and they initiated joint projects. As coordinators of the sign language translation and interpreting (SLTI) programs, they were responsible for selecting competent lecturers for the programs. Their commitment has contributed significantly to increasing the quality of ÖGS teaching and SLTI education. When Karin retired in 2021, Christian took over the coordination of the SLTI department. After having taught in the BA program for many years since 2018, he has become more interested in teaching translation courses for the MA program.

While Christian completed his linguistics degree on negation in ÖGS, Nadja went through a "habilitation" (postdoctoral degree) process and received the highest university degree after a doctorate (PhD), qualifying for professorship in 2017. In her habilitation thesis, she investigated the history of SLI in Austria and the construction of a professional self.

CONTEXTUALIZATION: TRANSLATION AND INTERPRETING IN AUSTRIA

Translator and interpreter education in Austrian universities commenced during the Second World War. As translation and interpreting (T&I) began to expand as a professional field, several academic programs were founded throughout Europe. The University of Vienna began training translators and conference interpreters in 1943; the Universities of Graz and Innsbruck launched their courses in 1946 (Wilss, 1999). Until the early 1970s, T&I programs focused exclusively on practical training. Graduates received an advanced diploma for either translation (*Diplomübersetzer*) or interpreting (*Diplomdolmetscher*), neither of which counted as a full academic degree. After the Austrian university reform in 1971, the academic status of T&I education was "upgraded" with the introduction of a 4-year "diploma study" (*Diplomstudium*). However, it was not until 1988 that each of the three universities offered full tenure for one professor of translation studies, as well as posts for young researchers, so that research activities could start to develop (Leikauf, 1997).

The European Bologna Declaration of June 1999 put a series of reforms in motion to standardize academic qualifications across the board and create a European Higher Education Area by 2010. In the course of the Bologna Process, previous "diploma studies" were replaced by the BA/MA structure. In Austria, it usually takes 3 years to earn a BA degree and another 2 years for an MA degree. Although during the first decades that the programs were offered, interpreter education focused on conference interpreting and interpreting in business settings, the Department of Translation Studies at the University of Graz (*Institut für Theoretische und Angewandte Translationswissenschaft* [ITAT]) started gradually introducing SLI and community interpreting in teaching and research in the early 1990s (Stachl-Peier, 2021). Today, social responsibility has become a central issue in the education of translators and interpreters in Austria, alongside the imparting of practical skills and scientific knowledge and methods (Kadrić & Kaindl, 2016).

Until the mid-1990s, SLI in Austria was performed by people who had not received any relevant education. As most of them had little to no contact with other sign language interpreters, there was no sense of community, connectedness, or commonality. A comprehensive study of the history and development of SLI in Austria revealed highly diverse mindsets, attitudes, behaviors, competencies, and ethics. Some interpreters were deeply rooted in deaf culture, whereas others had learned ÖGS as an "exotic" hobby or in the context of their main occupation. Some were assisting their deaf "protégés," offering advice and support; others were exercising a position of power in the deaf community. Some worked for free, giving up possibilities of professional development and neglecting their private lives; for others, interpreting was nothing more than an opportunity for earning some additional money (Grbić, 2023).

As noted in other chapters in this volume, as a consequence of growing discontent among a handful of interpreters and some deaf people, SLI in Austria underwent a rapid process of change in the 1990s. Interpreters started to meet on a regular basis, attended further training courses, founded an interpreters' association, developed an accreditation system, and started to work systematically toward defining the parameters of their profession. Much of the work toward these ends was undertaken in cooperation with the Department of Translation Studies in Graz, which in 2002 included ÖGS among the languages on offer in their new BA and MA programs.

Today, the status of sign language interpreters and translators in Austria is equivalent to that of any other T&I profession, and the SLTI association is one of six translators' and interpreters' associations in Austria that are represented on a joint website.[2] This status grew out of a combination of a rapid professionalization process, academic education, lobbying and networking, and appropriate payment, among other factors.

PROFESSIONALIZATION OF SIGN LANGUAGE INTERPRETERS IN AUSTRIA

The professionalization process of sign language interpreters began in the early 1990s. However, before the rapid development the occupation underwent in only a few years, a look back at history shows that the gradual institutionalization actually commenced in the 19th century during the Habsburg Monarchy.

From Habitualized to Organized Interpreting in History

In Austria, as in other countries, hearing heritage signers, spouses, priests and pastors, teachers for the deaf, and social workers provided interpreting services before the onset of the first professionalization efforts. These historical interpreting activities encompassed "habitualized" as well as "organized" interpreting services, a typology introduced by Grbić (2023) in her examination of the construction of the SLI profession in Austria. Habitualized interpreting takes place ad hoc in everyday social interactions. It does not require any sort of formal establishment and has a weak social order. Organized interpreting practices, on the other hand, are established deliberately. They follow more standardized interactional and relational patterns and lead to social order and social control.

Organized SLI can be traced back to the beginning of the 19th century. As court interpreting had to be well organized in the pluricultural and plurilingual Habsburg Monarchy, both spoken language interpreting and SLI were regulated by law (Wolf, 2015; Grbić, 2023). Over more than 100 years, teachers for deaf children were appointed and listed as permanently sworn-in "court interpreters for the deaf-mute" (*Dolmetscher für Taubstumme*) in the court and state almanacs. After the establishment of the first deaf club in the Monarchy,[3] which was founded in 1865 in Vienna, the deaf community started to organize interpreting services autonomously, parallel to the heteronomously organized court interpreting services. It was not until the end of the 1920s, however, when the Viennese club opened a state-funded counseling center for the deaf community, that law courts increasingly and frequently appointed hearing heritage signers as permanently sworn-in interpreters for deaf people (Grbić, 2023).[4]

First Steps: A Sense of Belonging and Further Education

Beginning with a meeting in October 1989, a handful of interpreters and social workers for deaf people started to meet together. Feeling isolated and overstrained, they founded the Working Group of Social Workers and Interpreters for Deaf People (*Arge*)[5] with the intention of fostering mutual acquaintance, exchange, cooperation, and support. Soon, they began to cooperate with deaf associations and various institutions, among them the ITAT, which started to offer weekend workshops for interpreters upon request. In preparation for the World Congress of the World Federation of the Deaf in Vienna in 1995, a deeply committed group of ÖGS interpreters organized additional workshops with experienced colleagues from abroad. Feeling that the market was growing in accordance with the increasing requirements of part of the deaf community in Austria, who had started to call for professional interpreter provision, the Arge started to cooperate more intensively with the ITAT (Grbić, 2023).

After discussions with the Arge and the Austrian Deaf Association, the ITAT developed a two-term part-time course within the framework of an international project funded by the European Union and the Austrian Ministry of Social Affairs. The opportunity to cooperate with 13 institutions from nine European countries brought with it the advantage of being able to draw on other people's expertise and experiences. The first course was conducted between February 1997 and March 1998 and was attended by 24 practicing ÖGS interpreters from all over Austria. The course consisted of 12 modules, taught by deaf and hearing experts from Austria, Denmark, Germany, and the United Kingdom. As a result of high levels of interest, the course was conducted a second time from September 1999 to May 2000, again with 24 participants (for further details, see Grbić, 2001). Despite the different backgrounds and motives of the interpreters, these initial activities contributed significantly to the development of a feeling of connectedness and belonging to the occupation.

The Interpreters' Association and the Occupational Aptitude Examination

The idea of founding a sign language interpreters' association dates back to the first meetings of ÖGS interpreters and social workers for deaf people at the beginning of the 1990s, but the association did not come into effect until March 1998, when the first 24 participants graduated from ITAT's further training course (Keckeis, Pauser, & Gerstbach, 1998). The participants had used the weekend seminars for internal meetings and developed plans for the future of their work, which they started to perceive increasingly as an occupation in its own right. The development progressed quickly, thanks to the commitment of the board members.

In November 1998, only 8 months after its foundation, the association *Österreichischer Gebärdensprach-DolmetscherInnen-Verband* (ÖGSDV) started to conduct occupational aptitude examinations for ÖGS interpreters before a national board that consisted of representatives from the ÖGSDV and deaf associations, as well as one representative from the ITAT. This was carried out in accordance with the Austrian Ministry of Social Affairs, which published a directive on January 1, 1999, stating that only interpreters who had successfully passed this examination were considered qualified. From 2000 onward, only people who had successfully passed the examination were allowed to receive payment from the Austrian government for SLI services. The scope and content of the occupational aptitude examination have been changed several times in relation to changes in market requirements, education policy, interpreting tasks, and expected skills. At present, it comprises a written part and a spoken/signed part. The written part consists of an essay on SLI, a reflective analysis of an interpreting assignment, and a knowledge test; the spoken/signed part comprises a monologic interpretation from ÖGS into German, a monologic interpretation from German into ÖGS, a dialogic setting, and a self-evaluation of the candidate's overall interpreting performance.

Initially, all candidates were hearing and had received no relevant education in interpreting. From January 2008, the occupational aptitude examination was restricted to candidates who had at least attended the preparation course *Achtung-FertigLos* (AFL), initially consisting of 13 modules and offered by the ÖGSDV since 2006, whereas graduates of the University of Graz and those of the private interpreter training program *Fachausbildung Gebärdensprachdolmetschen* (GESDO) in Linz (see section titled "Interpreter Education in Linz") were recognized as having qualified on the basis of having completed their education. Graduates can gain voluntary membership by passing the oral/signed part of the examination. In view of the increasing demand for sign language translation (SLT), the association was renamed and became the Austrian Sign Language Interpreters' and Translators' Association (*Österreichischer Gebärdensprach-DolmetscherInnen- und -ÜbersetzerInnen-Verband*) in 2013. An adaptation of the examination for SLT and SLI has been offered continuously since 2014, and the first deaf candidates took the exam in the same year. Between November 1998 and July 2021, a total of 247 candidates took the exam before the national examining board, of whom 154 (62.35%) passed and 93 (37.65%) failed. After the introduction of the AFL seminar series, the rate of positive examinations increased, and the candidates who completed their studies at the ITAT in Graz had the highest pass rate (90.91%). In July 2021, the association listed 111 members.[6] Not all ÖGS interpreters and translators are members of the ÖGSDV, and some are (also) members of the Austrian Association of Certified Court Interpreters (*Österreichischer Verband der allgemein beeideten und gerichtlich zertifizierten Dolmetscher* [ÖVGD], founded in 1920) or *Universitas Austria*, the Austrian Translators' and Interpreters' Association (founded in 1954).

SIGN LANGUAGE TRANSLATOR AND INTERPRETER EDUCATION IN AUSTRIA

As mentioned previously, before being allowed to receive payment from state authorities, prospective sign language interpreters and translators have been obliged to either complete a formal education program or to pass the occupational aptitude examination since 2008. Until 2020, hearing candidates without formal education had to attend the preparatory course AchtungFertigLos (*AFL*), while the first deaf candidates had to demonstrate their aptitude for the examination either by providing a certificate from the *Logo!* course for deaf interpreters and translators in Salzburg, which started in 2013, or before that by presenting a certificate from abroad. In 2019, *AFL* and *Logo!* were merged under the new term *Modus*. Furthermore, in October 2020, a new 3-year BA program for ÖGS interpreters started at the Health University of Applied Sciences Tyrol in Innsbruck. The following section will provide a brief presentation of these different paths that can lead toward professional qualification.

SLTI Education in Graz: An Integrated Approach

The initial 5-year "diploma program" started in 2002 and involved the study of two out of 12 foreign languages on offer, one of which was ÖGS. Although ITAT had offered the first academic ÖGS course in 1990 and continuously worked towards expanding the offerings by introducing individual courses, the full-time study program did not commence until the autumn of 2002, because of a lack of additional funding from the Ministry of Science. In comparison to other European countries, Austria lagged behind in terms of the academic education of sign language interpreters. However, the advantages of such a lengthy development process included the opportunity to develop the necessary structures, to exchange know-how within international and national projects, to develop further training programs for sign language interpreters and teachers, to train prospective teaching staff, to develop teaching materials, and to compile dictionaries (see Grbić, Andree, & Grünbichler, 2004). A particular advantage was the chance to integrate ÖGS as the 12th language in a study program at a translation studies department with long-standing experience in T&I education. At the ITAT in Graz, spoken language and sign language students share the same curricula and attend the same general courses irrespective of their choice of language(s) and their wishes to become, for example, a community interpreter for Arabic, a conference interpreter for French and Spanish, a technical translator for Hungarian, or an ÖGS interpreter and translator. Such integration contributes to broadening the horizons of both students and staff with regard to praxis and research and has helped to reduce asymmetries between different T&I professions in Austria.

To explore the similarities and differences between studying two languages with different modalities, a longitudinal study using qualitative as well as quantitative methods was conducted from 2004 to 2008. The study focused on four topics: beginners' motivations (Andree & Grünbichler, 2005); language learning (Grünbichler & Andree, 2006); the transition phase between language learning and interpreter training (Andree & Grünbichler, 2007); and students' experiences in interpreting classes, as well as their expectations with regard to their future work as interpreters (Grünbichler & Andree, 2008).[7] Shaw, Grbić, and Franklin (2004) conducted a further study on the readiness to apply language skills to interpreting in the context of spoken language interpreting and SLI programs.

In 2008, the ITAT introduced a BA/MA structure in accordance with the EU Bologna Process, and the diploma degree was replaced by a BA program in transcultural communication (3 years of study) and two MA programs, one in translation and one in interpreting (a further 2 years of study). The most recent revision of the curricula was implemented in 2017. The curricula on offer still include a BA program in transcultural communication and an MA program in translation, while the two MA programs in conference interpreting and in translation and dialogue interpreting replaced the earlier MA in interpreting. In addition, several further study programs and certificates were introduced to enable students to expand their language portfolios.[8]

The BA program in transcultural communication prepares students for an MA in translation and/or interpreting. Prospective students have to prove a competence level according to the Common European Framework of Reference for Languages (CEFR)[9] of B2[10] in English and German as a foreign language and A2[11] for the other languages. In the BA program, students attend courses in their first language in addition to courses in one or two foreign languages. The courses include language and communication, basic translation, culture and civilization, and introductions to transcultural communication, linguistics, T&I studies, and T&I fields. While the first 2 years focus on language and culture, the third year is devoted to the transition from language learning to T&I, during which time students are introduced to multilingual communication skills, (contrastive) discourse analysis, and the basic principles of translating and interpreting. In the final semester, students are required to write a BA thesis.

Whereas in former MA curricula, ÖGS students had the opportunity to study either one or two foreign language(s), the MA program in Translation and Dialogue Interpreting is restricted to a single language. However, it is possible to obtain interpreting or translation certificates for additional languages. Applicants are required to have acquired knowledge of the chosen foreign language at CEFR level C1.[12] They start their MA studies with introductory courses in T&I techniques, followed by modules on various fields of translation (such as technical translation or society, literature, and culture) and interpreting (such as public service interpreting, lecture and liaison interpreting, or speech-to-text interpreting). Apart from practical education, which is language specific, students also attend lectures and seminars on T&I studies, research methodology, terminology, project management, ethics, and breathing and speech techniques. In the final year, they have to write an MA thesis pertaining to either translation or interpreting studies. Currently (2024), the curricula are being revised again to account for the changes in translation professions caused by digitalization.

Interpreter Education in Linz: An Initiative of the Deaf Association

As a result of an acute shortage of interpreters in the province Upper Austria, the regional Deaf Association started to develop a 3-year interpreter education program in the early 2000s. Representatives of both the ÖGSDV and the ITAT acted as advisors in the process of developing the program. The program GESDO is taught in Linz, the capital of Upper Austria. It is not affiliated with any traditional educational institution, and it is funded by the regional government. GESDO is aimed at students who are qualified for tertiary education. Applicants have to pass an entrance examination, but ÖGS competence is not required. The first 3-year course started in October 2003 with 15 participants. The first year of the program is devoted primarily to the acquisition of ÖGS and deaf culture. The development of interpreting competences starts in the second year. The course includes classes in ÖGS and German, deaf studies, linguistics, T&I studies, interpreting, professional issues such as roles and ethics, and breathing and speech techniques, among other topics. In the final year, students are required to write a final thesis pertaining to the field of T&I studies.

One particular asset of this program is the large proportion of time dedicated to practical work experience. The advantage of such a private initiative is that structures are not too rigid, and curriculum changes can be made quite easily during the course of the program. However, students do not receive a graduation diploma or a degree from an accredited higher educational institution after completing the program. Several attempts to transfer this private interpreter education program to a regional university for applied sciences unfortunately failed for several reasons: unclear responsibilities (University of Applied Sciences for Social Affairs vs. University of Applied Sciences for Health), allocation of study locations (regionally restricted or Austria-wide), and finally costs. Nevertheless, the program is officially recognized by the state and its authorities. While the ITAT offers its MA studies every year, in Linz, one cohort of students must finish their studies before a new group starts.

ÖGSDV Preparatory Course: In Search of More Interpreters

The ÖGSDV accreditation procedure was changed in 2008 to counteract a lack of training among sign language interpreters, who until then could take the professional aptitude examination without having completed any formal education.

For some time, the examination board was confronted with the problem that candidates without training often failed the examination. To solve this problem, the ÖGSDV developed and introduced a compulsory series of seminars, intended to serve as preparation for the accreditation examination. The seminars were aimed at candidates from all over Austria with a high proficiency in ÖGS, including hearing heritage signers. The Matura (qualification for tertiary education) was not mandatory until 2010. The series comprised 13 weekend seminars in the first round and 17 weekend seminars in the final round, which took place in different provinces. Topics included language and communication (ÖGS and German), interpreting and translation, professional issues (such as role, ethics, and cooperation with clients), T&I studies, and teamwork with deaf translators and interpreters (ÖGSDV, 2018). The first series of seminars started in June 2006, and the last series ended in 2020, when AFL was merged with Logo! to become Modus.

Logo! Broadening the Field for Deaf Interpreters and Translators

As a result of the fact that it was not possible to integrate deaf students into existing SLI programs, both for organizational reasons and because many deaf applicants did not have the necessary school certificates, the Deaf Association in Salzburg, together with the organization *Soziale Initiative Salzburg*, started to provide a 2-year training course for deaf interpreters and translators called "Logo!". The course was designed in accordance with the curriculum of the certificate course for deaf interpreters in Hamburg in cooperation with the Universities of Hamburg and Salzburg and the Austrian Association of the Deaf. The course was provided twice (from 2013 to 2015 and from 2016 to 2018) and was funded by the Austrian government. It consisted of 13 modules that included topics such as German, ÖGS, International Sign, memory training, translation, interpreting, professional issues and ethics, T&I studies, and translating and interpreting in teams (Logo!, n.d.).

Modus: Testing a New Integrated Approach

In the autumn of 2019, Modus,[13] a merger of AFL and Logo!, was launched as a university course for deaf and hearing interpreters and translators at the University of Salzburg. The course is organized by the University of Salzburg together with the Deaf Association in Salzburg and the organization Soziale Initiative Salzburg in cooperation with the Austrian Association of the Deaf and the ÖGSDV, and it is funded by the government. The course comprises 90 European Credit Transfer and Accumulation System (ECTS) credit points in five semesters.[14] Admission requirements include first-language (German or ÖGS) proficiency equal to at least the C1 level as defined by the CEFR and second-language (German or ÖGS) proficiency equal to at least the B2 level. Applicants do not need to provide school certificates or qualify for university entrance; it is sufficient to have completed compulsory schooling.[15] The course consists of 14 modules, including language and communication (German, ÖGS, International Sign), T&I on various levels and in various fields, professional issues, T&I studies, work placement, and a final module preparing the students for the professional aptitude examination. A written or signed final thesis is not required (Universität Salzburg, 2019).

Interpreter Education in the West: A Recent BA Program at the Health University of Applied Sciences Tyrol

The Western part of Austria long felt understaffed with regard to SLI services and had planned to develop its own regional training program for quite some time. The recent 3-year BA program with 180 ECTS credits started after an official accreditation process in October 2020 at the Health University of Applied Sciences Tyrol in Innsbruck and not at the regional Department for Translation Studies at the University of Innsbruck. The program is offered every 3 years. The application process involves a multi-stage admission procedure, and applicants must also demonstrate ÖGS skills at CEFR level A1. The curriculum comprises the following modules: ÖGS and German language; communication; linguistics; sociology and cultural competence; interpreting techniques; interpreting in various settings; research skills; and an introduction to health issues. In addition, students must complete 14.5 weeks of internships (fh gesundheit, 2023). In 2023, the first round of graduates completed their BA studies.

The Road Ahead

Whereas the first edition of this chapter (Grbić, 2009) focused on the integrated approach of interpreter education at the University of Graz, where spoken and signed language translators and interpreters study side by side, today's educational landscape is diverse and spread across a diverse range of institutional settings. This means that the SLTI community is facing new challenges. As the course descriptions have shown, the basic contents of the diverse curricula do not differ significantly between institutions. They do, however, differ with regard to entry requirements, scope, duration, degree, and institutional affiliation. This makes cooperation and student exchange even more challenging than it was in the time when Graz, Linz, and the ÖGSDV strove to establish at least some kind of cooperation and exchange. Lack of exchange might even lead, in a worst-case scenario, to a fragmentation of the social world of SLTI practitioners. On the other hand, the new programs provide fresh impetus, challenging existing institutions to rethink their long-standing structures and approaches.

A further challenge is the lack of formal preparation for ÖGS teachers and SLTI educators. Although basic sign language teacher-training programs have been provided by various institutions, many teachers are ill prepared to respond to the need for an increased number of learners at a higher level. Although the ITAT has provided further training workshops in the broader context of T&I pedagogy for their own staff, such workshops were not accessible to educators from other institutions. As there are very few ÖGS teachers and SLTI educators with long-standing experience in teaching who have both a solid theoretical background and experience in the T&I field, some of them have become peripatetic, giving lectures and seminars at various institutions. To overcome the shortage of ÖGS teachers, a five-semester part-time course was launched in April 2024 in Salzburg, organized by a consortium consisting of the Austrian Association of the Deaf, the University of Salzburg, the Salzburg University of Education, the Salzburg Association of the Deaf and the organization Soziale Initiative Salzburg (Kompetenzzentrum ÖGS 2024).

The sudden and unplanned movement to online teaching in response to the COVID-19 pandemic also posed a major challenge. Although at the beginning of the pandemic teachers had no experience with technical and didactical aspects of online teaching, their skills and proficiency in using various digital learning applications and tools have improved. The mandatory transition to online teaching was especially challenging for students in the first 2 years of our BA program in Graz, as these students were just beginning to learn the foundations of the language. Given the three-dimensional visual/spatial elements of sign languages, learning them through two-dimensional platforms has proved challenging for students. Students had problems observing and imitating the movements of the hands and the body, as well as facial expressions, and they continue to face difficulties in understanding and using space appropriately. Therefore, additional training sessions had to be provided for these students after the pandemic. Although there were many difficulties in the switch to online teaching, some tools also have shown their benefits, and staff in Graz provide a maximum of 20% of teaching online for classes that include students who have completed CEFR level B1 or B2 (e.g., students' presentations, discussions with external visitors, and translation assignments in the MA program).

With these challenges in mind, we should pay serious attention to the needs of the expanding landscape of SLTI education. We should focus not only on the importance of quality but also recognize the importance of a common goal—that is, reinforcing the cohesion of the ÖGS T&I community, which requires us to develop new appropriate measures based on our knowledge and experience. To achieve a sustainable consolidation of the field while allowing new dynamics to evolve, a network among all the educational institutions involved, including a representative of the ÖGSDV, started to meet on a regular basis in September 2020. It is hoped that the cooperation will continue to grow to ensure unity in diversity.

Notes

1. There are no reliable figures, and estimates range between 8,000 and 12,000. According to Hartl and Unger (2014, 38–9), working on the basis of a common estimate according to which one per thousand of the population was deaf and signing, the number of signing deaf people in Austria would have been around 8,400 in 2014 and around 9,000 in 2024, if calculated in relation to the population increase over the intervening time.
2. AIIC Österreich (AIIC Austria), Interessengemeinschaft von Übersetzerinnen und Übersetzern literarischer und wissenschaftlicher Werke (Austrian Association of Literary and Scientific Translators), Österreichischer Gebärdensprach-Dolmetscher:innen- und Übersetzer:innen-Verband (Austrian Sign Language Interpreters' and Translators' Association), Österreichischer Verband für Schriftdolmetschen (Austrian Speech-to-Text-Interpreters' Association), Österreichischer Verband der allgemein beeideten und gerichtlich zertifizierten Dolmetscher (Austrian Association of Sworn and Court Certified Interpreters), Universitas Austria Berufsverband für Dolmetschen und Übersetzen (Universitas Austria Interpreters' and Translators' Association).
3. The *Wiener Taubstummen-Unterstützungsverein* (Viennese Support Association for the Deaf-Mute) was founded in 1865 for the purpose of socializing, education, and mutual support and was restricted to men.
4. It was not until 1849 that one had to pass a language exam to be sworn in as a court interpreter. Until the late 20th century, sign language interpreters only had to provide confirmation that they were proficient in ÖGS.
5. *Arbeitsgemeinschaft der Sozialarbeiter und Dolmetscher für Gehörlose*, for short: *Arge*.
6. Figures provided by the association ÖGSDV.
7. The project was funded by the Anniversary Fund for the Promotion of Scientific Research and Teaching of the National Bank of Austria and the Austrian Ministry of Social Affairs.
8. The MA program in Conference Interpreting is currently offered only to spoken language students.
9. See CEFR: https://www.coe.int/en/web/common-european-framework-reference-languages.
10. *Independent* user B2: Can understand the main ideas of complex text on both concrete and abstract topics, including technical discussions in his/her field of specialization. Can interact with a degree of fluency and spontaneity that makes regular interaction with native speakers quite possible without strain for either party. Can produce clear, detailed text on a wide range of subjects and explain a viewpoint on a topical issue giving the advantages and disadvantages of various options.
11. *Basic* user A2: Can understand sentences and frequently used expressions related to areas of the most immediate relevance (e.g., very basic personal and family information, shopping, local geography, employment). Can communicate in simple and routine tasks

requiring a simple and direct exchange of information on familiar and routine matters. Can describe in simple terms aspects of his/her background, immediate environment, and matters in areas of immediate need.

12. *Proficient* user C1: Can understand a wide range of demanding, longer texts, and recognize implicit meaning. Can express himself/herself fluently and spontaneously without much obvious searching for expressions. Can use language flexibly and effectively for social, academic, and professional purposes. Can produce clear, well-structured, detailed text on complex subjects, showing controlled use of organizational patterns, connectors, and cohesive devices.

13. Universitätslehrgang Dolmetschen und Übersetzen für Österreichische Gebärdensprache, Deutsch und International Sign (University course in interpreting and translating for Austrian Sign Language, German and International Sign).

14. In comparison, the BA program in Transcultural Communication at the ITAT comprises 180 ECTS credit points in six semesters; the MA programs for translation and/or interpreting comprise 120 ECTS credit points in four semesters.

15. In Austria, there are 9 years of compulsory education in school. After that, all young persons must either continue school education or go into vocational training (Lehre) until the age of 18.

REFERENCES

Andree, B. & Grünbichler, S. (2005). Berufswunsch GebärdensprachdolmetscherIn? Eine Studie zu Vorstellungen, Zielen und Motivationen von Studienanfängerinnen in Österreich. *Das Zeichen, 19*(71), 352–59.

Andree, B. & Grünbichler, S. (2007). Das Studium Gebärdensprachdolmetschen am ITAT: Vom Spracherwerb zur Translation—Herausforderungen und Probleme aus Sicht der Lehrenden. *Das Zeichen, 21*(77), 480–88.

BGBl. I Nr. 81/2005. (2005, August). Änderung des Bundes-Verfassungsgesetzes vom 9. August.

fh gesundheit. (2023). Ihr Studium, Ihre Zukunft. Gebärdensprachdometschen. https://www.fhg-tirol.ac.at/data.cfm?vpath=pdf-dokumente/broschueren-bsc/fhg_gsd_bachelor_image folder_web_2023-08-01

Grbić, N. (2001). First steps on firmer ground: A project for the further training of sign language interpreters in Austria. In I. Mason (Ed.), *Triadic exchanges: Studies in dialogue interpreting* (pp. 149–172). St. Jerome.

Grbić, N. (2009). Sign language interpreter training in Austria: An integrated approach. In J. Napier (Ed.), *International perspectives on sign language interpreter education* (pp. 3–14). Gallaudet University Press.

Grbić, N. (2023). *Gebärdensprachdolmetschen als Beruf. Professionalisierung als Grenzziehungsarbeit. Eine historische Fallstudie in Österreich.* Transcript.

Grbić, N, Andree, B. & Grünbichler, S. (2004). *Zeichen setzen: Gebärdensprache als wissenschaftliche und gesellschaftspolitische Herausforderung.* ITAT.

Grünbichler, S. & Andree, B. (2006). Sprach- und Kulturkompetenz als Basis für das Dolmetschen. Eine Studie zum Spracherwerb und zur Sprachkompetenz von Studierenden im zweiten Studienjahr. *Das Zeichen, 20*(74), 464–471.

Grünbichler, S. & Andree, B. (2008). *Begleitforschung zum Studium Gebärdensprachdolmetschen. Eine quantitative Untersuchung zu Ausbildung und Wissenserwerb, dolmetschspezifischen Fragestellungen und beruflichen Vorstellungen von höhersemstrigen Studierenden an fünf Hochschulen im deutschsprachigen Raum*. Unpublished research report, University of Graz. https://static.uni-graz.at/fileadmin/gewi-institute/Translationswissenschaft/Gebaerdensprache/Forschungsprojekte/uedoawww_files_forschungsbericht_gruenbichler_andree_2008.pdf

Hartl, J. & Unger, M. (2014). Abschätzung der Bedarfslage an ÖGS-DolmetscherInnen in Primär-, Sekundär- und Tertiärbildung sowie in Bereichen des täglichen Lebens. Research report, Institute for Advanced Studies Vienna. https://irihs.ihs.ac.at/id/eprint/3024/

Kadrić, M. & Kaindl, K. (2016). Translation als zentrale Nebensache in einer globalisierten Welt—eine Einführung." In M. Kadrić & K. Kaindl (Eds.), *Berufsziel Übersetzen und Dolmetschen: Grundlagen, Ausbildung, Arbeitsfelder* (pp. 1–15). A. Francke.

Keckeis, E., Pauser, N. & Gerstbach, B. (1998). Der steinige Weg vom 'Gehörlosendolmetscher' zur Gebärdensprachdolmetscherin in Österreich. *Das Zeichen*, 12(45), 452–457.

Kompetenzzentrum ÖGS. (2024) Lehrgang „Gebärdensprachdozent:in". https://www.oegs.net/gesdoz/

Leikauf, G. (1997). Metamorphosen eines Dolmetschinstituts. 50 Jahre Übersetzer- und Dolmetscherausbildung an der Universität Graz." In N. Grbić & M. Wolf (Eds.), *Text – Kultur – Kommunikation. Translation als Forschungsaufgabe* (pp. 15–29). Stauffenburg.

Logo. (n.d.). "Modulbeschreibungen." Salzburg, Austria.

ÖGSDV – Österreichischer Gebärdensprach-DolmetscherInnen- und -ÜbersetzerInnen-Verband. (2018). AchtungFertigLos. Österreichweite Seminarreihe zur Vorbereitung auf die Berufseignungsprüfung zum/zur GebärdensprachdolmetscherIn. Vienna, Austria.

Shaw, S., Grbić, N., & Franklin, K. (2004). Applying language skills to interpretation: Student perspectives from signed and spoken language programs. *Interpreting*, 6(1), 69–100.

Stachl-Peier, U. (2021). Sign language interpreting and community interpreting—collaboration and mutual gains. In P. Šveda (Ed.), *Changing paradigms and approaches in interpreter training: Perspectives from central Europe* (pp. 64–84). Routledge.

Statistik Austria. (2018). *Statistisches Jahrbuch 2018*. Nielsen.

Statistik Austria. (2024). Bevölkerung zu Jahres-/Quartalsanfang. https://www.statistik.at/statistiken/bevoelkerung-und-soziales/bevoelkerung/bevoelkerungsstand/bevoelkerung-zu-jahres-/-quartalsanfang

Universität Salzburg. (2019). Curriculum für den Universitätslehrgang 'Dolmetschen und Übersetzen für Österreichische Gebärdensprache, Deutsch und International Sign' an der Universität Salzburg (Version 2019W). https://www.plus.ac.at/wp-content/uploads/mitteilungsblatt/U76p06vW5cCrJmiS_NYP5I85GrkPGzH7k.pdf

Wilss, W. (1999). *Translation and interpreting in the 20th century: Focus on German*. John Benjamins.

Wolf, M. (2015). *The Habsburg monarchy's many-languaged soul: Translating and interpreting, 1848–1918*. K. Sturge (Trans.). John Benjamins.

KAROLIEN GEBRUERS, KRISTY JONCKERS,
KRISTOF DE WEERDT, AND
MYRIAM VERMEERBERGEN

3

The Sign Language Interpreting Profession in Flanders, Belgium

Past, Present, and Future

This chapter reports on the history and the current situation of the sign language interpreting (SLI) profession in Flanders, the northern part of Belgium. Belgium is a federal constitutional monarchy with a rather complex institutional organization, evidenced by the fact that the country has six governments administering around 11.5 million people.[*] After a process of state reforms that have been implemented since the 1970s, Belgium now consists of three official regions: the Flemish Region in the north, the Walloon Region in the south, and the Brussels-Capital Region more or less in the middle of the country. These regions partly—though not entirely—overlap with the communities of which the country is composed: the Flemish community, the French community, and the small German community (in the Walloon Region). As official entities they are, for instance, responsible for education, culture, and language use in their respective communities.

Belgium has three official spoken languages: Dutch, which is spoken in Flanders and Brussels; French, which is spoken in Wallonia and Brussels; and German. In addition, the country has three sign languages recognized by the governments of each community: Flemish Sign Language (*Vlaamse Gebarentaal* [VGT],[1] recognized in 2006; see Vermeerbergen & Van Herreweghe, 2008), French-Belgian Sign Language (*la langue des signes de Belgique francophone* [LSFB], recognized in 2003; see Haesenne et al., 2008), and German Sign Language (*Deutsche Gebärdensprache* [DGS], recognized in 2019; see Doof Vlaanderen, 2019a). In 2003, the Flemish deaf community was estimated to include 6,000 deaf signers (Loots, et al., 2003), but

[*] See https://www.belgium.be/en/about_belgium.

there are no more recent numbers available. Describing the context and evolution of the SLI profession in the Walloon Region falls out of the scope of this chapter, as it has its own distinct history and development. However, for further reading, we highly recommend the paper of Haesenne et al. (2008) about the establishment of an academic training program, the work of De Meulder and Haesenne (2019) on the recognition of LSFB and VGT, and the publications of Gebruers and Haesenne (2021) and Hanquet and le Maire (2021) on co-interpreting at Belgian COVID-19 press briefings, including sections on training of LSFB/French interpreters.

The next section provides an overview of our own journeys to SLI and education, followed by a brief introduction to the general interpreting training and profession in Flanders. Next an overview is given of the education, training, and certification of deaf and hearing sign language interpreters.

Who Are We?

Karolien is a hearing white woman who grew up with a deaf cousin, so she was introduced to sign language at an early age. Because of this close connection, she enrolled in VGT courses and eventually became a Dutch/VGT interpreter in 2012. With a background in speech, language, and hearing sciences, Karolien initially combined her work as an audiologist, in which she worked with deaf people, with interpreting, until she transitioned to full-time interpreting in 2016. In 2019, she completed the European Master in Sign Language Interpreting (EUMASLI)[2] program, which further sparked her research and teaching interests. From 2012 to 2016, Karolien was involved in the interpreter training program in Mechelen, and then from 2018 to 2021, she was a lecturer at the university training in Antwerp. Karolien was part of the steering group of the deaf interpreter (DI) training that ran from January 2022 to June 2023. Since 2016, she has been involved in Tenuto, a nonprofit organization offering professional development training for sign language interpreters. Karolien is committed to lifelong learning and is passionate about engaging with the current and next generation of both deaf and hearing interpreters—hence, her contribution to this volume. Currently, she is working on a doctorate focusing on gender in the International Sign conference interpreting context, at Heriot-Watt University in Scotland, and is occasionally invited as a guest lecturer at the interpreter training program in Antwerp.

Kristy is a hearing woman who had no connections to deaf people or the deaf community while growing up. However, she has always had an interest in foreign languages, so in 2009, she enrolled in the Bachelor in Applied Language Studies at KU Leuven in Antwerp and studied Dutch, English, and VGT. Afterward, she successfully completed her master's in interpreting in Dutch, English, and VGT in 2013 and the postgraduate program in SLI in 2014. She has been working as a VGT/Dutch interpreter in several settings ever since.

Being passionate about continuous learning and development and gathering and sharing knowledge, Kristy also trained as a teacher at the University of Antwerp. From 2017 to 2023, she combined her interpreting work with a teaching position in the interpreting program in Mechelen. She found her way back to her alma mater in 2018 and has been teaching at KU Leuven in Antwerp in the bachelor, master, and postgraduate programs since then.

In 2023, Kristy took on the role of regional contact person for the Antwerp region in the VGT Interpreter Association, acting as a liaison between the interpreters working in the field (in Antwerp) and the national association, as well as gathering information and organizing opportunities for interpreters to get together.

Kristof was born deaf to deaf parents, and VGT is his native language. In 1999, he worked as a research assistant at the University of Ghent, contributing to the lexicographic research on VGT. Additionally, he participated in a project aimed at filling gaps in the lexicon. Starting in 2004, he worked as a VGT instructor in various vocational sign language interpreter training programs. Since 2010, he has been teaching sign language proficiency to undergraduate students and interpreting students in the master's degree program. Kristof was involved in international projects such as SignTeach and has engaged himself on a national level by, for example, creating children's stories through eBooks in VGT. In 2018, he conducted a study on the aspirations of DIs with regard to training in Flanders. He also served as the coordinator for a one-off training program for deaf VGT interpreters, which took place from January 2022 to June 2023.

Myriam is a hearing woman born in Belgium. While studying Germanic languages at the end of the 1980s, she developed an interest in signed language linguistics. Her first contacts with deaf people date back to that time. On the advice of her mentor and professor, De Vriendt, she applied for a doctoral scholarship from the Flanders Research Foundation. She worked on her dissertation, focused on the morphosyntax of VGT, from 1990 until 1996. This made her a pioneer in VGT linguistic research. In the absence of courses, she learned VGT through close contact with deaf signers. In 1997, Myriam cofounded the *Vlaams GebarentaalCentrum* (VGTC; Flemish Sign Language Center). In the same year, she started a postdoctoral research project on VGT and remained affiliated with the Research Foundation–Flanders as a postdoctoral research fellow until 2007. Since 2008, she has been working at KU Leuven, Antwerp Campus, where, together with deaf colleagues, she developed the first-ever Flemish academic program for sign language interpreters. As the then-president of VGTC, Myriam was involved in the path toward the recognition of VGT in 2006. From 2008 to 2016, she served as a member of the Advisory Committee on VGT, and she took on the role of vice-chair of this committee in 2020. She is a former board member of the Sign Language Linguistics Society and served three terms as an expert for the World Federation of the Deaf. Myriam has also been an external examiner for several international training courses, including

EUMASLI. Today, Myriam is still associated with the Antwerp Campus of the Faculty of Arts at KU Leuven and is also appointed extraordinary professor at the Department of Dutch and Afrikaans at the University of Stellenbosch, South Africa.

CONTEXTUALIZATION: TRANSLATION AND INTERPRETING IN FLANDERS, BELGIUM[3]

Flanders currently offers five academic interpreting programs, organized by four universities: Vrije Universiteit Brussel,[4] University of Antwerp, Ghent University, and KU Leuven. Each program consists of a 3-year Bachelor of Applied Language Studies (180 credits in the European Credit Transfer and Accumulation System [ECTS]) and a 1-year Master of Interpreting (60 ECTS credits). The universities are keen to develop a 2-year master's program, but this is hampered by the fact that the Flemish government only rarely allows master's programs of more than 60 ECTS credits. Therefore, two of the five universities now offer a postgraduate program in conference interpreting, constituting a fifth year of study. Only one university, the Antwerp Campus of KU Leuven, includes VGT in its program.

The current university programs (bachelor's and master's programs) originated from 4-year study programs—two candidatures and two licentiates—for translators and interpreters, which were organized by university colleges. These "two-cycle" programs at the academic level were, to a certain extent, similar to university programs. In 2004, as part of the European Bologna Process, the bachelor of arts/master of arts structure was introduced into higher education in Flanders. This meant that the two-cycle university college programs, including the translation and interpreting programs, had to start a process of academization. Moreover, each of these university colleges was required to affiliate itself with a Flemish university, which resulted in a complete integration of the interpreting programs into the universities in 2013.

The university interpreting programs offer mainly European languages, with a few exceptions such as Arabic. Naturally, though, Flanders also has a need for interpreters of other languages—languages for which initially only ad hoc interpreters who were not trained and had no form of recognition were available. Community interpreting and translation services were established at the end of the 20th century to bring some order to the provision of community interpreters. In 2004, the government ordered a central training and testing center for community interpreters to be set up. This center was integrated into the Flemish Agency for Integration and Civic Integration in 2015 and is still responsible for the certification of *social interpreters*.[5] It also offers a (limited) training program.

Certified community interpreters are used exclusively for communication between a non-native person and public services (e.g., in the context of employment, health care, social housing, etc.). For interpreters in a legal context, sworn court interpreters are employed. The government decided only recently, in 2017, that sworn court interpreters must have completed a formal program of study. KU Leuven has been offering a specific program for court translators and interpreters since 2000. Students can enroll in some of the courses as part of their Master of Interpreting program or follow the entire program as standalone training. The study program was accredited by the Federal Public Service for Justice in 2018, which means, among other things, that graduates are included in the national register of sworn translators and interpreters without further formalities.

Furthermore, translators and interpreters can join the Belgian Chamber of Translators and Interpreters (BKVT), a national professional association founded in 1955. The BKVT defends the interests of interpreters (and translators) with regard to, among others, the government, and also offers (relatively small-scale) continuing education. Belgian organizations and institutions often play a prominent role in European and global organizations that defend the interests of interpreters and translators internationally, such as the European Legal Interpreters and Translators Association (EULITA), the European Network for Public Service Interpreting and Translation (ENPSIT), and the Conférence Internationale Permanente d'Instituts Universitaires de Traducteurs et Interprètes (CIUTI).

Of course, in Brussels, Belgium's capital, conference interpreting is widespread, given the presence of the European institutions. One might expect that, given the multilingualism in Belgium, particularly in Brussels, there would also be clear regulations for the use of spoken language interpreters outside these institutions, but this is not the case. Legislation on the provision of spoken language interpreters is quite complex and domain specific. A discussion of this topic lies outside the scope of this chapter. As far as the development of the SLI profession in Flanders is concerned, it followed its own pathway, which we will explain in the following sections.

Professionalization of Sign Language Interpreters in Flanders[6]

Deaf clubs are among the oldest societies in Belgium. In 1936, the Belgian clubs decided to merge into a national federation called NAVEKADOS (the National Federation of Catholic Deaf-Mutes). Given the federal situation in Belgium described in the introduction to the chapter, NAVEKADOS split up into a Flemish and a Walloon federation. The Flemish umbrella organization of deaf clubs was called Fenedo at first (Federatie van de Nederlandstalige Dovenverenigingen; Federation of Dutch-language Deaf Clubs), which became Fevlado (Federatie van de Vlaamse Dovenorganisaties; Federation of Flemish Deaf Clubs) in 1986. In 2017, Fevlado was renamed Doof Vlaanderen (Deaf Flanders).[7]

The Flemish deaf association has played an important role in the professionalization of sign language interpreters. It initiated the establishment of the first officially recognized "Interpreting for the Deaf" program in Ghent in 1981. This program started out as a 3-year part-time vocational training offered in an adult education center and was limited to approximately 180 contact hours. Ten years later, the program was expanded to 280 teaching hours and spread over 4 years of vocational training. The establishment of an interpreting program was part of a broader initiative aimed at the development and promotion of Signed Dutch (Nederlands met Gebaren [NmG]). NmG combines the grammar of Dutch (i.e., following spoken Dutch word order) with "unified signs," of which many, though not all, are borrowed from VGT. In Ghent, students learned how to interpret between Dutch and NmG. Much attention was paid to learning how to produce the signs. The courses were given by deaf teachers who had not received official training.

It should be noted, though, that 2 years before the foundation of the interpreter training program in Ghent, another program was established in Mechelen. However, it took a long time for this program to become officially recognized. The founders of this program rejected the development and use of NmG and its unified signs. Instead, they chose to teach signs as expressed by deaf people, not realizing that "authentic signing" does not consist only of authentic signs but also of a specific grammar. The general understanding was that signers combined their signs with a simplified grammar of Dutch.

Some of the students, often hearing heritage signers, already had good signing skills before starting the program, but graduates who did not already know VGT struggled to understand VGT used by deaf signers and vice versa. As a result of emerging research on the grammar of VGT and an increasing awareness of VGT as a fully fledged language in the mid-1990s, both interpreter training programs moved away from NmG or "sign-supported Dutch" and started to include (initially mainly theoretical) information on the linguistics of VGT. This gradual change involved attempts to engage deaf signers as co-trainers. In Mechelen, for example, deaf signers were hired as (voluntary) teaching assistants. In Ghent, however, it was strongly felt that there was an urgent need for trained deaf teachers. As none were available given the overall lack of educational opportunities for deaf people, a system of on-the-job training was implemented. Furthermore, students were encouraged to engage with the deaf community and to practice their productive and especially their receptive language skills through interaction with deaf signers.

In 1983, the Flemish deaf association established the nonprofit Association of Interpreters for the Deaf (Beroepsvereniging voor Doventolken [BVDT])[8] in anticipation of the first group of interpreting graduates. The first qualified interpreters graduated in 1984, but, at the time, there was no legislation on the payment of professional sign language interpreters, nor was there much demand for their services. Moreover, the majority of students who attended the interpreter training program did not do so with the intention of working as interpreters. They did so because their profession required them to communicate with deaf people (e.g., as a teacher) or because they had deaf friends or family members.

The prevailing idea was that government involvement and funding were needed to create a network of professional interpreters, which is what happened in the early 1990s. In 1991, the Flemish deaf association, then known as Fevlado, founded the Flemish Communication Assistance Agency for the Deaf (Vlaams Communicatie Assistentie Bureau voor Doven [CAB]) to organize SLI services. Additionally, in 1994, the Flemish government adopted a decree related to establishing regulations by which the Flemish Fund for Social Integration for People With a Handicap could cover the cost of assistance from "interpreters for the deaf." As a result of this decree, deaf people were entitled to a limited number of government-funded interpreting hours in personal and employment settings. Flemish sign language interpreters were (and still are) required to register with CAB in order to officially start working and receive payment through this system of government-funded interpreting hours. Since 1996, government-funded interpreting hours have also been available in educational settings.

In 2008, 27 years after the start of the very first training program, an academic training program for sign language interpreters was established at Lessius University College in Antwerp (now part of KU Leuven) (see the next section) (Vermeerbergen & Russell, 2017). Around the same time, Tenuto was founded, an independent nonprofit organization aimed at providing continuous professional development (CPD) activities for sign language interpreters. Currently, the board consists of five hearing interpreters and three DIs who voluntarily engage in organizing CPD training. Notably, at present, graduated interpreters are not required to attend CPD training; there is no regulatory body that monitors interpreters' quality and development.

Similar to international developments (e.g., Napier & Leeson, 2015; Pollitt, 2000; Roy, 1993), the role of sign language interpreters in Flanders evolved from "helper" to "conduit" to "bilingual–bicultural professional" in the 1980s and 1990s (Van Herreweghe & Vermeerbergen, 2006). While these changes laid the foundations for the SLI profession, the professionalization process accelerated from the 2000s. Worldwide, the development of the SLI profession has always been closely related to sign language recognition and the advocacy work done by sign language communities (Napier, 2019). The recognition of VGT in 2006 and Belgium's ratification of the United Nations Convention on the Rights of Persons with Disabilities (UNCRPD) in 2009 are two examples of changes in legislation that had an impact on the VGT community and, as a consequence, on the interpreting profession. Advocacy work and legal actions of Doof Vlaanderen and deaf individuals, for instance, have also resulted in an increase in the number of government-funded interpreting hours and in increased availability of SLI in more varied settings and domains.

The professionalization of SLI was long hampered by the fact that most sign language interpreters were not full-time interpreters; that is, interpreting was their secondary occupation alongside a main occupation. Part of the reason for this was and is that the self-employed status in Flanders is not a very attractive one, although the low remuneration of sign language interpreters certainly plays a part as well. As a result, a substantial number of interpreters work as interpreters for only a couple of hours per month. The fact that the SLI profession in Flanders, as in many other countries (see Napier & Leeson, 2016, p. 215), is numerically female-dominated might be a contributing factor, too. The number of interpreters working full time has increased only very recently, probably in the past 5 to 10 years. In 2010, only 16 of the 80 interpreters participating in a survey indicated that they worked full time (Roodhooft, 2010). A questionnaire sent out by the interpreter association BVGT in 2019 showed that 42 out of 107 respondents worked full time as interpreters (BVGT, 2019). Recently, in part thanks to the efforts and social media presence of both the interpreter association BVGT and Tenuto, it has become clear that more and more sign language interpreters in Flanders are motivated to promote and elevate the profession, creating positive momentum. However, professionalization is also an individual matter, as every interpreter can instigate change by reflecting on the way in which the profession is represented (Gebruers, 2019).

Professionalization of Deaf Interpreters and Translators in Flanders

Another important international evolution is the increasing visibility of DIs. Adam et al. (2014, p. 16) propose the following definition for a DI: "Deaf professional who undertakes both inter- and intra-language interpreting, as well as translation from a written or a spoken to a sign language." We adopt this definition and refer to deaf professionals who work as interpreters and/or translators as DIs. Indeed, in Flanders, the most commonly used terms are *hearing interpreter* and *deaf interpreter*. As the interpreting profession develops, however, this terminology might evolve and move past stressing the audiological status of an interpreter (see De Meulder & Heyerick, 2013).

Although, as in many other countries, there have always been deaf people who worked as interpreters (for example, negotiating meaning between their peers and hearing teachers in deaf schools) (De Meulder & Heyerick, 2013; Leeson & Vermeerbergen, 2010), in Flanders, DIs have only recently become visible in mainstream society. The professionalization of DIs started around 2010. Initially, they worked mainly between VGT and another sign language at, for example, conferences, and occasionally in settings with deaf immigrants or deafblind people.

The demand for translations from Dutch (often in a written form) to VGT has been growing since the official recognition of VGT in 2006 (De Weerdt &

Vermeerbergen, 2018). Because of this evolution, in 2010, Fevlado (currently Doof Vlaanderen) established a translation service. In the same year, the association organized a short program for deaf translators/presenters, in which eight deaf people enrolled. Among other things, they learned how to translate Dutch texts from an autocue to VGT (Fevlado, 2010). In 2011, Visual Box, a deaf-led media company, was founded, providing increasing translation work for DIs. In 2012, DIs truly became visible when Karrewiet, the daily news for youngsters, included interpretation into VGT by DIs working between written Dutch and VGT using an autocue (see De Meulder & Heyerick, 2013, for an extensive account of interpreters on television). At present, translation work (e.g., for accessible websites in sign language) is conducted mainly by DIs.

The Advisory Committee on VGT[9] reports an increasing demand for DIs to work with, among others, deaf migrants (see Van Schil, 2016), deaf people with different language backgrounds, and deafblind people, and it stresses the need for an all-encompassing training that meets the needs of (future) DIs (Adviescommissie VGT, 2019). Furthermore, training programs for hearing interpreters should prepare their students to work in a mixed deaf/hearing interpreting team (De Meulder & Heyerick, 2013; Gebruers & Haesenne, 2021) and instill the notion of becoming advocates for DIs into interpreter students (Mathers, 2009).

SIGN LANGUAGE INTERPRETER EDUCATION IN FLANDERS

In this section, we will discuss the recent developments in and current situation of interpreter training for hearing interpreters as well as DIs, and we will briefly highlight how this was impacted by the COVID-19 pandemic.

Hearing Interpreters

It is clear that the professionalization of SLI in Flanders is mostly in line with Cokely's (2005) interpretation of the way SLI evolved as a profession in the United States. In Flanders, too, the deaf community was actively involved in setting up interpreter training. Additionally, the deaf association played a role in the establishment of the first professional body of sign language interpreters and in the foundation of the Flemish interpreting agency. However, in the process, the deaf community has had to surrender control significantly, especially when it comes to selecting who would become an interpreter. The profile of the students enrolling in SLI training programs in Flanders has changed, as well. In the past, students often enrolled in the program to acquire the necessary skills to communicate with deaf family members and friends or with deaf people with whom they worked (Heyerick & Vermeerbergen, 2012), whereas nowadays, the goal is primarily to become professional sign language interpreters.

As mentioned previously, there were two vocational SLI training programs in Flanders: one in Ghent and one in Mechelen. In September 2019, these programs became part of the university colleges, effectively making them undergraduate programs. The program in Mechelen became part of Artesis Plantijn (AP) University College, and the program in Ghent became part of Artevelde University College. Both now constitute part-time programs of 120 ECTS credits, spread out over 4 years.

In September 2020, the Flemish government decided that all future sign language interpreters would need to obtain a master's degree, which implied that the two vocational training programs will no longer be able to educate future interpreters. This decision is a result of a rather long-lasting debate about the level of training required for sign language interpreters. The Advisory Committee on VGT (2019), for example, advised that only training at an academic level should be provided for all future interpreters. Those in favor of academic training argued, among other things, that interpreters of spoken languages are also trained exclusively at the universities. Those who were not in favor of shutting down the two non-academic programs pointed out that there are currently too few interpreters available and claimed that this scarcity would increase if only one program remained. However, the shortage of available interpreters is not so much a result of (too) few interpreters graduating, but rather of the low number of graduates choosing to work as full-time interpreters, although, as already mentioned, this is slowly changing.

In 2008, a third SLI training program was founded at Lessius University College (now KU Leuven, Faculty of Arts, Antwerp Campus) through the inclusion of VGT as a language choice in its Bachelor of Applied Language Studies and Master of Interpreting (Vermeerbergen & Russell, 2017).[10] This SLI program is a full-time 4-year bachelor of arts/master of arts track (240 ECTS credits) followed by a 1-year part-time postgraduate program (24 ECTS credits).[11] In the bachelor's program, students study three languages: Dutch, as their first language, a second spoken language (French, German, or English), and VGT. During the master's program, students are trained to interpret between Dutch and VGT and between Dutch and their second spoken language. However, starting in 2023–2024, students can also opt for a master's degree in interpreting focusing on Dutch and only one "foreign" language, including VGT. Within the 1-year master's program, for which students are also required to write a thesis, there is little room for a work placement. Moreover, fairly soon after the start of the program, it became clear that 4 years of training was insufficient to properly prepare students for the professional field. It should be noted that students, in principle, do not (have to) know any VGT when they begin the bachelor's program. Furthermore, the program features a second foreign language, which also demands a significant amount of learning and teaching time from students and teaching staff—hence the establishment of a fifth year in the form of a part-time postgraduate program. In this final year, students focus mostly on simultaneous interpreting between Dutch and VGT. The program also includes an extensive work placement, during which students have the opportunity to develop their skills and become novice professional interpreters under the guidance of professional interpreters, who play an important role as mentors.

The VGT Group of KU Leuven (i.e., the teaching staff of VGT) includes both hearing and deaf staff members. In the bachelor's program, deaf colleagues teach sign language proficiency classes and subjects related to deaf culture and deaf communities. Courses on sign language linguistics are taught by hearing sign language linguists. The Master of Interpreting program and the postgraduate program employ five lecturers. The three hearing lecturers are active sign language interpreters and the two deaf lecturers are experienced DIs, one of whom graduated from the EUMASLI program. For most interpreting courses, a deaf and a hearing lecturer work together as a team. The (optional) course on VGT translation is taught by the deaf teachers.

The number of graduates of this academic program is still very limited. However, the fact that they often work full time as sign language interpreters, engage in the interpreter association, and become involved in teaching and research shows that academic SLI education contributes to the professionalization of the SLI profession. The very first doctoral research on SLI in Flanders was also carried out at KU Leuven by Isabelle Heyerick, who studied linguistic interpreting strategies of deaf and hearing interpreters working into VGT (Heyerick, 2021).

An important difference between SLI training and spoken language interpreting training is that spoken language interpreting students are able to practice their language proficiency by immersing themselves in the language and culture of the language in question by, for example, going abroad on an Erasmus+ exchange.[12] However, there is no equivalent place to which SLI students can travel (Napier, 2015). Naturally, the Flemish SLI training programs encourage their students to have as much contact as possible with VGT signers outside of the program, and they set up initiatives to this end. Both Mechelen and Ghent organized a language immersion weekend, during which first- and second-year students, lecturers, and deaf guests communicated solely in VGT. Students' sign language (communication) skills showed clear signs of improvement after such a weekend. At KU Leuven, students organize a monthly signing café, where students and deaf people gather informally. The Antwerp campus of KU Leuven also houses the VGTC, the center of expertise on VGT, enabling students to easily engage with hearing and deaf sign language researchers.

As is customary for interpreting programs with spoken languages, the SLI training of KU Leuven starts with exercises on consecutive interpreting, before switching to simultaneous interpreting. For a long time, the two part-time programs paid no attention to consecutive interpreting, but this changed over time. It should also be noted that the existing programs are mostly one-size-fits-all programs, with little room for specialization. However, KU Leuven does offer SLI students the possibility of including the specific module for court translators and interpreters in their individual study programs.

Because of the COVID-19 pandemic, all regular classes were canceled during the first lockdown in 2020 and replaced by remote online classes and exercises, which had a big impact on the students' well-being. The pandemic significantly affected both their lives as students and their learning possibilities. Physical classes were canceled—or limited after the situation was deemed to be safer again—and certain exercises normally part of the courses (e.g., interpreting in the community, interpreting guided tours) could no longer take place. Because the switch to online or blended learning was so abrupt, in the beginning, it was difficult to find the proper videoconference tools that suited the requirements. In addition, sign languages are three-dimensional languages, which makes communicating on screen more challenging for interpreter students. One of the biggest challenges for interpreter students seemed to be on the level of work placement, as they found it more difficult to achieve their goals, both in terms of honing their interpreting skills in different settings and reaching the number of required hours of practice. Deaf people seemed to be more hesitant to accept interns in online settings, for example, and several aspects of interpreting were more challenging to practice properly in an online setting. Furthermore, the interaction with the participants of an interpreted event, both hearing and deaf, is also very different between online and on-site events (see also De Meulder et al., 2021, for an extensive report on the impact of COVID-19 on sign language interpreters across the globe). Consequently, students might be more reluctant to step into working in the field immediately after completing their SLI training, as they might feel they have not had enough practice because of the limited work placement possibilities. On a positive note, the pandemic taught us, educators and interpreters, how to cope better with online education and online interpreting. In the future, more attention will be paid to remote interpreting in the SLI training program, as it has become part of the new normal.

DI Training

At the time of finalizing this chapter (September 2023), we can proudly attest that the first training program specifically for DIs in Flanders was recently completed. Before January 2022, there was no specific training program for DIs, and the existing SLI programs had not been adapted to meet the needs of DI students. In the past, though, some DIs have enrolled in individual courses at KU Leuven or in a few modules of the part-time vocational training in Mechelen.

The lack of training has made it challenging for both individuals and organizations to officially engage DIs and remunerate them for their work (De Weerdt & Vermeerbergen, 2018). DIs who have work experience but did not receive formal training cannot register with the interpreter service (CAB) because the Flemish government requires a diploma to do so. Before the dedicated DI training was established, only two DIs were registered with CAB. One DI graduated from the EUMASLI program in 2015; the other DI graduated from a program at the University of Mons[13] in Wallonia in 2017. The fact that Flemish DIs were looking for training opportunities outside of Flanders only illustrated the need for formal DI training.

In 2018, De Weerdt and Vermeerbergen conducted a survey to investigate the practices and, more importantly, the needs and aspirations of working DIs. Data were gathered from 12 participants via semi-structured interviews carried out by the third co-author of this chapter, who is a DI himself. Results showed that respondents worked both informally (e.g., for friends) and formally (e.g., television work), carried out translation as well as interpreting assignments, and undertook inter-language interpreting (e.g., International Sign/VGT) and intra-language interpreting (e.g., working with deafblind people). All DIs considered training to be very important. The question on what such training should look like elicited a range of responses, but, in sum, DIs in Flanders desired the establishment of an intensive training for working DIs on the one hand, and a full academic program for future candidates on the other hand. The participants stated that, overall, they would prefer to have a training program separate from hearing interpreter students, except for some specific courses. Furthermore, the majority of the respondents stated that training should be provided by deaf trainers (also from abroad). However, for some courses (e.g., sign language linguistics) hearing trainers would be accepted, as well.

Recently, Doof Vlaanderen (2019b) has been paying increasing attention to the topic of DIs by, for instance, organizing a conference and gathering DIs to discuss possible pathways for the future. In their memorandum,[14] the deaf association outlined the need for a continuing education course for DIs who are already working on the one hand, and an all-encompassing training for future DIs on the other hand. This idea is in line with the findings of De Weerdt and Vermeerbergen (2018). With the necessary qualifications, DIs can be officially recognized, which facilitates their professional engagement in the interpreting field. The memorandum of Doof Vlaanderen also emphasized the need for organizations and institutions to become aware of the added value of providing DIs (Doof Vlaanderen, 2019b).

Since March 13, 2020, daily, and later weekly, press conferences have been held by the national crisis center to inform Belgian citizens about the evolution of the crisis and by the Prime Minister to announce the COVID-19 measures in Belgium. Partly as a result of Doof Vlaanderen's advocacy work and earlier advice from the Advisory Committee on VGT, a team of deaf and hearing sign language interpreters, including the first co-author of this chapter, were responsible for providing SLI during these press conferences (see Gebruers & Haesenne, 2021; Gebruers, Vermeire, & Garitte, 2022, for an extensive account of this practice; and Rijckaert & Gebruers, 2022, for an account of how this practice was experienced by deaf people). The DIs took relay from the hearing interpreters, providing interpretation from spoken into sign language. As the press conferences were held in two spoken languages, Dutch and French, two interpreting teams were involved: one team working from Dutch into VGT and one team working from French into LSFB. The conferences were broadcast live, and the footage was used by multiple national television broadcasting companies. This kind of visibility and attention to DIs in the media (e.g., newspapers and television shows) was unprecedented in Flanders. It raised greater public and political awareness of DIs, which led to an increase of working opportunities for them (for example, at press briefings of the Flemish government, at the announcement of the public broadcaster VRT of its new CEO, and at press conferences about the floods in 2021, to name a few).

As outlined previously, different stakeholders aspired to set up a training program for DIs, but securing adequate funding remained a major challenge. However, in 2021, the Antwerp Campus of KU Leuven partnered up with Doof Vlaanderen, Visual Box, Tenuto, and BVGT and applied to the Advisory Committee on VGT[15] for a (limited) budget to organize a 1.5-year training for DIs who already had working experience. Fortunately, the budget was allocated, and a working group was established (including the first and third co-authors of this chapter and Carolien Doggen) to design a curriculum, which was partly based on the needs assessment survey conducted by De Weerdt and Vermeerbergen (2018) and good practices from abroad. The training ran from January 2022 to June 2023 and was both theory and practice based. The 160 hours of training encompassed modules such as VGT and Dutch linguistics, sign language proficiency, diversity within deaf communities, translating and interpreting techniques (with attention for specific target groups), codes of ethics, and work placement. The course was taught mainly by experienced deaf instructors/interpreters from Belgium and abroad and had a hybrid form, combining classroom teaching with online learning activities. In partnership with Tenuto, a workshop was organized to bring deaf and hearing interpreters together to exchange ideas, discuss challenges and opportunities, practice co-interpreting, and foster future collaborations. In March 2023, "Deaf Interpreters in the Picture" was organized to create a greater awareness within deaf communities in Flanders. Throughout the training, Visual Box shared information and created social media buzz about the work and the profession of DIs. In addition to establishing the DI training, KU Leuven and the Advisory Committee on VGT, with support from Doof Vlaanderen and BVGT, advocated for the recognition of DIs in order for them to register with the interpreter agency and to facilitate their consolidation within the field. In September 2023, 18 DIs officially graduated and received their certificates, along with the associated recognition.

Although a significant amount of the preparation work (i.e., lobbying, researching, advising) was done in the past, we believe the pandemic—and the good practices it brought about with regard to DIs—acted as a catalyst for the approval of the budget request and for actually providing training for experienced DIs. We look forward to what else the future might bring to the professionalization of deaf VGT interpreters.

The Road Ahead

We are living in interesting times when it comes to the development of the SLI profession in Flanders. The profession will be shaped by the ongoing self-empowerment of deaf people and by their changing preferences (Napier, 2011). Deaf people in Flanders have, for example, more access to higher education, which creates opportunities and challenges for the interpreters working in those educational settings. In 2018, Vermeerbergen and Van Herreweghe wrote that they expected the spontaneous standardization process of VGT to accelerate because of its greater use on television and on the Internet. It seems that VGT is experiencing particularly interesting times, with important societal changes related to its uses and practices resulting in rapid changes. Technology, for instance, is advancing rapidly, and the SLI profession needs to keep an open mind as to how these advances will have an impact (see De Meulder, 2022; Soetemans & Vermeerbergen, 2023).

SLI training programs face the challenge of keeping up with multiple developments in order to properly prepare their graduates for these practices. To date, there is no transition period in which new graduates can work alongside a more experienced interpreter mentor. Apart from the possibility of working with a co-interpreter and pairing up with a supportive buddy via Tenuto, there is no official mentoring scheme, so novice interpreters are simply thrown in the deep end. Moreover, there is currently no system to monitor sign language interpreters' quality, CPD training is not compulsory, and opportunities are scarce. It is clear that there is, and will increasingly be, a need for further professional development, such as training focusing on interpreting in different settings (e.g., medical settings), team interpreting, working with specific audiences (e.g., children, deafblind signers), and remote interpreting.

In addition, Flanders is clearly lagging behind its neighboring countries and even other regions within Belgium when it comes to interpreting fees and working conditions (see de Wit, 2016). The Advisory Committee on VGT states that in order to appeal to more interpreting students and graduates, the SLI profession has to become more attractive. One important way to achieve this is to improve the working conditions and remuneration of VGT/Dutch interpreters (Adviescommissie VGT, 2019; BVGT, 2019). At the moment of our writing this chapter, the competent authorities have shown willingness to tackle this issue in order to elevate the SLI profession.

In terms of training DIs, we are delighted that the first ad hoc training for working DIs took place in 2022–2023, and we hope this will be a stepping stone toward the establishment of a structural academic training program in which deaf people who aspire to become DIs can enroll. However, at the moment, we cannot foresee whether or when another training opportunity will take place. Educating both deaf and hearing interpreters about how to work together will be an important aspect of training and further education, as well.

To conclude, as (socio)linguistic research on VGT remains scarce, the resulting lack of documentation on VGT complicates the training and practice of sign language interpreters. We hope to see an increase in research on SLI from different perspectives, as this type of research not only helps us understand SLI education, but also feeds into it (see Turner, 2005; Best, 2015). Lastly, we expect to see more collaboration between SLI and spoken language interpreting researchers and educators, with both deaf and hearing scholars from disciplines other than interpreting studies.

Notes

1. The name for the sign language used in Flanders has changed from *Belgian Sign Language* to *Flemish Belgian Sign Language* to *Flemish Sign Language*.
2. See https://www.eumasli.eu.
3. We thank Professor Heidi Salaets and Professor Lieven Buysse for their valuable input for this section.
4. This is the Dutch-speaking University in Brussels (VUB); its French-speaking counterpart is the Université libre de Bruxelles (ULB). Both universities carry the same name, so to avoid confusion, we use the original Dutch name instead of an English translation of it.
5. Note that *social interpreters* (*sociaal tolken* in Dutch) is the term used in Flanders, which is comparable to *community interpreters*.
6. For a comprehensive historical account, see De Witte & Callewier (2008); Heyerick & Vermeerbergen (2012); Van Herreweghe & Van Nuffel (2000); and Van Herreweghe & Vermeerbergen (2006). The information included here is based on these publications.
7. The Walloon counterpart is Féderation Francophone des Sourds de Belgique (FFSB). In the East Cantons, there is Hörgeschädigte Ostbelgiens (HOB).
8. The interpreter association's name changed to VVTG (Vlaamse Vereniging Tolken Gebarentaal; Flemish Association of Sign Language Interpreters) in 2001 and to BVGT (Beroepsvereniging Vlaamse GebarentaalTolken; Association of Flemish Sign Language Interpreters) in 2009. See https://bvgt.be.
9. As a result of VGT recognition, the Advisory Committee was founded to advise the government on all VGT-related matters.

10. The University made grateful use of the experience of international colleagues and initiatives of the European Forum of Sign Language Interpreters (efsli) in developing a model curriculum and learning outcomes for an SLI program (efsli, 2013).
11. See https://www.kuleuven.be/opleidingen/master-tolken for more information on the curriculum in Dutch.
12. See https://erasmus-plus.ec.europa.eu/opportunities/opportunities-for-individuals/students/studying-abroad.
13. See http://applications.umons.ac.be/web/en/pde/2018-2019/cursus/5181.htm. Note that attendees of this training received a University Certificate in Interpreting in a Legal Context: Judicial Environment and Asylum Sector.
14. See https://www.doof.vlaanderen/lobbywerk/dossiers/memorandum.
15. The decree related to VGT makes it possible to financially support yearly projects that contribute to the societal anchoring of VGT. The Advisory Committee on VGT is responsible for reviewing project applications and advising the competent Minister, who makes the final decisions.

Rᴇꜰᴇʀᴇɴᴄᴇs

Adam, R., Aro, M., Druetta, S. D., and Klintberg, J. A. (2014). Deaf interpreters: An introduction. In R. Adam, C. Stone, S. D. Collins, & M. Metzger (Eds.), *Deaf interpreters at work: International insights* (pp. 1–18). Gallaudet University Press.

Adviescommissie VGT (2019, April 15). *Vijf prioritaire aanbevelingen van de Adviescommissie Vlaamse Gebarentaal voor de verkiezingen 2019-Addendum memorandum 2014-2019 [Five priority recommendations of the Flemish Sign Language Advisory Committee for the 2019 elections – Addendum memorandum 2014–2019].* http://www.adviesvgt.be/2-zorg-voor-meer-actieve-tolken-en-gesubsidieerde-tolkuren

Best, B. (2015). 'We are at another transition stage': An interview with Jemina Napier. *Newsli: The Magazine for the Association of Sign Language Interpreters in the United Kingdom, 91*, 13–17.

BVGT. (2019, October 15). *Op het kruispunt naar professionalisering—de weg naar een volwaardig statuut voor tolken VGT [At the crossroads of professionalization—The road to a full statute for VGT interpreters].* https://bvgt.be/sites/default/files/2019-10/Op%20het%20kruispunt%20van%20professionalisering%20-%20de%20weg%20naar%20een%20volwaardig%20statuut%20voor%20tolken%20VGT%20.pdf

Cokely, D. (2005). Shifting positionality: A critical examination of the turning point in the relationship of interpreters and the deaf community." In M. Marschark, R. Peterson & E. A. Winston (Eds.), *Sign language interpreting and interpreter education: Directions for research and practice* (pp. 3–28). Oxford University Press.

De Meulder, M. (2022). *Don't mention the machine—The #awkward future of human sign language interpreting.* Paper presented at the #awkward efsli conference, Manchester, UK. https://maartjedemeulder.be/slides/.

De Meulder, M., & Heyerick, I. (2013). (Deaf) interpreters on television: Challenging power and responsibility. In L. Meurant, A. Sinte, M. Van Herreweghe & M. Vermeerbergen (Eds.), *Sign language research, uses and practices: Crossing views on theoretical and applied sign language linguistics* (pp. 111–136). Mouton De Gruyter.

De Meulder, M., Pouliot, O., & Gebruers, K. (2021). *Remote Sign Language Interpreting in Times of COVID-19*. Unpublished research report. University of Applied Sciences Utrecht.

De Meulder, M. & Haesenne, T. (2019). A Belgian compromise? Recognising French-Belgian Sign Language and Flemish Sign Language. In M. De Meulder, J. J. Murray, & R. L. McKee (Eds.), *The legal recognition of sign languages: Advocacy and outcomes around the world* (pp. 284–300). Multilingual Matters.

De Weerdt, K., & Vermeerbergen, M. (2018, May). *Deaf interpreters in Flanders, Belgium: A long past, but a short history*. Paper presented at the International Conference on Non-Professional Interpreting, Stellenbosch, South Africa.

de Wit, M. (2016). *Sign language interpreting in Europe: 2016 edition*. Create Space.

De Witte, D., & Callewier, J. (2008). Tolken [interpreters]. In M. Vermeerbergen & M. Van Herreweghe (Eds.), *Wat geweest/gewenst is [What has been and what is desirable]* (pp. 219–247). Academia Press.

Doof Vlaanderen. (2019a, February 27). *Parlement van Duitstalige Gemeenschap erkent de Duitse Gebarentaal cultureel! Doof Vlaanderen feliciteert Hörgeschädigte Ostbelgiens en alle gebarentaligen in Oost-België! [The parliament of the German speaking community culturally recognises German Sign Language! Deaf Flanders congratulates Hörgeschädigte Ostbelgiens and alle sign language peoples in eastern Belgium!]* https://twitter.com/DoofVlaanderen/status/1100674726370967552.

Doof Vlaanderen. (2019b, May). *Memorandum verkiezingen 2019 [Memorandum elections 2019]* [Website]. https://www.doof.vlaanderen/sites/default/files/imce/memorandum_doof_vlaanderen.pdf.

European Forum of Sign Language Interpreters. (2013). *Learning outcomes for graduates of a three year sign language interpreting training program*. European Forum of Sign Language Interpreters.

Federation of Flemish Deaf Organisations. (2010). *Opleiding dove vertalers en presentatoren [Training deaf translators and presenters]* [Website]. http://www.fevlado.be/upload/content/file/Fevlado/Ledenblad_Dovennieuws/DN32010.pdf.

Gebruers, K. (2019). *Exploring the professional self: A study of Flemish sign language/Dutch interpreters in times of professionalization*. Unpublished Master's Thesis. Humak University of Applied Sciences, Helsinki, Finland. https://www.theseus.fi/handle/10024/227584.

Gebruers, K., Vermeire, L. & Garitte, J. (2022). 'Finally it was time to provide a deaf interpreter': A multiparty perspective on the provision of signed language interpreters during the COVID-19 press briefings in Belgium. In F. M. Federici & S. O'Brien (Eds.), *Translating Crisis (pp. 127–143)*. Bloomsbury.

Gebruers, K., & Haesenne, T. (2021). Providing co-interpreting teams of deaf and hearing signed language interpreters at Belgian COVID-19 press briefings: A silver lining? In G. A.M. De Clerck (Ed.), *UNCRPD Implementation in Europe - a deaf perspective: Article 9: Access to information and communication* (pp. 212–226). European Union of the Deaf.

Haesenne, T., Huvelle, D. & Kerres, P. (2008). One step forward, two steps back… Toward a new signed language interpreter training program in French-Speaking Belgium. *The Sign Language Translator and Interpreter, 2*(2), 259–278.

Hanquet, N., & le Maire, D. (2021). Co-interprétation sourd et entendant: L'union fait la force [Co-interpreting by deaf and hearing interpreters: Unity is strength]. *Traduire: Une autre perspective sur la traduction, 245*, 86–98.

Heyerick, I. (2021). *A descriptive study of linguistic interpreting strategies in Dutch-Flemish Sign Language Interpreting: Exploring interpreters' perspectives to understand the what, how and why.* (Unpublished doctoral dissertation). KU Leuven, Belgium. https://limo.libis.be/primo-explore/fulldisplay?docid=LIRIAS1989719&context=L&vid=KULeuven&search_scope=ALL_CONTENT&tab=all_content_tab&lang=en_US.

Heyerick, I. & Vermeerbergen, M. (2012). Sign language interpreting in educational settings in Flanders, Belgium. In L. Leeson & M. Vermeerbergen (Eds.), *Working with the Deaf community: Education, mental health and interpreting* (pp. 117–132). Interesource Group (Ireland) Limited.

Leeson, L., & Vermeerbergen, M. (2010). Sign language interpreting and translation. In Y. Gambier & L. van Doorslaer (Eds.), *Handbook of translation studies* (pp. 324–329). John Benjamins.

Loots, G., Devisé, I., Lichtert, G., Hoebrechts, N., Van De Ginste, C. & De Bruyne, I. (2003). *De gemeenschap van doven en slechthorenden in Vlaanderen. Communicatie, taal en verwachtingen omtrent maatschappelijke toegankelijkheid [The community of deaf and hard of hearing people in Flanders. Communication, language and expectations concerning societal accessibility].* Cultuur voor Doven.

Mathers, C. M. (2009). Modifying instruction in the deaf interpreting model. *International Journal of Interpreter Education, 1,* 68–76.

Napier, J. (2011). Signed language interpreting. In K. Windle & K. Malmkjaer (Eds.), *The Oxford handbook of translation studies (pp. 357–376).* Oxford University Press.

Napier, J. (2015). Comparing spoken and signed language interpreting. In H. Mikkelson & R. Jourdenais (Eds.), *Routledge handbook of interpreting studies* (pp. 129–143). Routledge.

Napier, J. (2019, April 9). *Is There Disruption in the Sign Language Interpreting Profession?* https://streetleverage.com/live_presentations/is-there-disruption-in-the-sign-language-interpreting-profession/.

Napier, J., & Leeson, L. (2015). Signed language interpreting. In F. Pöchhacker (Ed.), *Encyclopedia of interpreting studies (pp. 376–381).* Routledge.

Napier, J. & Leeson, L. (2016). *Sign language in action.* Palgrave Macmillan.

Pollitt, K. (2000). On babies, bathwater and approaches to interpreting. *Deaf Worlds: International Journal of Deaf Studies, 16(2),* 60–64.

Rijckaert, J., & Gebruers, K. (2022). A pandemic accompanied by an infodemic: How do deaf signers in Flanders make informed decisions? A preliminary small-scale study. In P. Blumczynski & S. Wilson (Eds.), *The languages of COVID-19: Translational and multilingual perspectives on global healthcare* (pp.179–196). Routledge.

Roodhooft, L. (2010). *A Survey Amongst Flemish SLIs Concerning Disproportionate Directionality in Interpreting: VGT-to-Dutch Interpretation versus Dutch-to- VGT Interpretation. What are the experiences/opinions of Flemish SL interpreters with regard to interpreting from their B language into their A language?* Unpublished paper. Humak University of Applied Sciences, EUMASLI, Module Research Methods.

Roy, C. B. (1993). The problem with definitions, descriptions, and the role metaphors of interpreters. *Journal of Interpretation, 6(1),* 127–154.

Soetemans, L. & Vermeerbergen, M. (2023). When (shared) space and time don't matter. Remote video-mediated (synchronous and asynchronous) communication in Flemish Sign Language. *IEEE International Conference on Acoustics, Speech, and Signal Processing Workshops proceedings* (pp. 1–4). https://doi.org/10.1109/ICASSPW59220.2023.10193316.

Turner, G. H. (2005). Toward real interpreting. In M. Marschark, R. Peterson & E. A. Winston (Eds), *Sign language interpreting and interpreter education: Directions for research and practice* (pp. 29–56).: Oxford University Press.

Van Herreweghe, M., & Van Nuffel, M. (2000). Sign (language) interpreting in Flanders, Belgium. *Journal of Interpretation*, *17*, 101–127.

Van Herreweghe, M., & Vermeerbergen, M. (2006). Deaf signers in Flanders and 25 years of community interpreting. In E. Hertog & B. Van der Veer (Eds.), *Taking stock: Research and methodology in community interpreting* (pp. 293–308). Linguistica Antverpiensia, New Series.

Van Schil, E. (2016). *Onderzoek naar de meerwaarde van (dove) gebarentaaltolken in de communicatie met dove allochtonen, asielzoekers en vluchtelingen [A study on the added value of (deaf) signed language interpreters in the communication with deaf immigrants, asylum seekers and refugees]*. (Unpublished Master's Thesis). KU Leuven, Belgium.

Vermeerbergen, M., & Russell, D. (2017). Interview with Dr. Myriam Vermeerbergen: Flemish Sign Language. *International Journal of Interpreter Education*, *9*(1), 61–66.

Vermeerbergen, M. & Van Herreweghe, M. (2008). De status van de Vlaamse Gebarentaal: van ondergronds bestaan tot culturele erkenning [The status of Flemish Sign Language: from an existence underground to a cultural recognition]. In M. Vermeerbergen & M. Van Herreweghe (Eds.), *Wat geweest/gewenst is. Organisaties van en voor Doven in Vlaanderen Bevraagd over 10 Thema's. [What has been, what is, and what is desirable. Organizations of and for deaf people in Flanders on 10 topics]* (pp. 1–23). Academia Press.

Vermeerbergen, M., & Van Herreweghe, M. (2018). Looking back while moving forward: The impact of societal and technological developments on Flemish Sign Language lexicographic practices. *International Journal of Lexicography*, *31*(2), 167–195.

MARIANNE ROSSI STUMPF AND
RONICE MÜLLER DE QUADROS

4

The Status of Sign Language Translator and Interpreter Education in Brazil

The Connection Between Research and Formal Education

Brazil is the fifth-largest populated country in the world, with significant ethnic and political complexity—a republic divided into 27 states. It has 230,000,000 inhabitants, of whom 8,000,000 are deaf or hard of hearing (INEP, 2010). Brazilian Portuguese is established as the official language by the national constitution, and Brazilian Sign Language (*Língua Brasileira de Sinais* [Libras]) is a national sign language recognized by law as a language of deaf communities in Brazil (Law 10.436/2002). The law is regulated by a decree that includes a language plan for Libras (Decree 5.626/2005). Libras is also referred to in several other laws and official documents, such as the accessibility law (Law 10.098/2000) and the National Educational Plan (instituted by Law 13.005/2014). All these official documents present language rights for deaf people with regard to Libras and bilingual education in Libras and Portuguese. These legal recognitions favor the implementation of language policies that include Libras as the official language of deaf people in Brazil.

With regard to sign language translation and interpreting (SLTI) education, Decree 5.626/2005 included formal education in these two areas as one of the specific goals to be reached. This had important consequences for the implementation of formal education for sign language translators and interpreters at technical and higher levels. In this chapter, the goal is to give an overview of this process in Brazil, especially highlighting the implementation of the training, which went hand in hand with the production of research in translation studies and sign language interpreting (SLI). First, we contextualize SLTI in Brazil. Then, we describe the professionalization of SLTI, which is also a consequence of formal education. Finally, we present details about the establishment of formal education for SLTI, which is consolidated today through legal recognition, and its relationship with establishing SLTI as an area of research.

WHO ARE WE?

Marianne Rossi Stumpf is deaf and a professor and researcher at the Federal University of Santa Catarina (UFSC), Brazil. She holds a doctorate in information technology in education from the Federal University of Rio Grande do Sul, which included research at the Université Paul Sabatier and the University of Paris 8 (2001–2005), as well as a postdoctorate from the Catholic University of Portugal in Lisbon (2013–2014), with support from the Brazilian federal agency for the support and evaluation of graduate education (*Coordenacao de Aperfeicoamento de Pessoal de Nivel Superior* [CAPES]). As a tenured professor of the postgraduate program in linguistics at UFSC, she is currently working on development of the SignWriting system, acquisition of writing, translation from Libras and Portuguese, and the sign-terms of a glossary linked to research projects involving Libras Documentation and Sign Bank. She leads the Advanced Research Group in Deaf Studies (GRUPES), registered with the Brazilian National Council for Scientific and Technological Development (*Conselho Nacional de Desenvolvimento Científico e Tecnológico* [CNPq]), in which her students participate. She is deputy director of the Center for Communication and Expression at UFSC (2021–2025). She has been a member of the advisory committee of the Anísio Teixeira National Institute of Educational Studies and Research (since 2014) for the national proficiency exam for university admission (*Exame Nacional do Ensino Médio* [Enem]) in Libras within the Ministry of Education.

Ronice Müller de Quadros is a hearing heritage signer and has been a professor and researcher at UFSC since 2002 and a researcher at CNPq (PQ1c), with investigations related to the study of sign languages since 2006. She holds a bachelor's degree in education, a master's degree (1995), and a doctorate (1999) in linguistics from Pontifícia Universidade Católica do Rio Grande do Sul. Her studies included an 18-month internship at the University of Connecticut (1997–1998) in which she researched the grammar and acquisition of Libras. She undertook research visiting at Gallaudet University and the University of Connecticut (2009–2010) related to bimodal bilingual development (children using Libras and Portuguese and children using American Sign Language [ASL] and English), which was funded by the U.S. National Institutes of Health and CNPq (2009–2014). She was a visiting researcher at Harvard University, where she researched bimodal bilingual languages (Libras and Portuguese and ASL and English) with funding from CNPq (2015–2016). She continues to work with bimodal bilingualism in hearing children of deaf adults, with funding from the U.S. National Science Foundation (2018–2021). Ronice is also coordinating the consolidation of the National Libras Corpus (http://libras.ufsc.br/), which includes several subprojects for the composition of the Libras documentation, with funding from CNPq (2018–2021) and the Ministry of Culture (2014–2018).

Contextualization: Translation and Interpreting in Brazil

In Brazil, formal education in languages happens at the university level. Language courses (referred to as *Letras)* aim to train professionals with solid linguistic and literary knowledge in a 4-year program for those who will teach language courses (*Letras Licenciatura*) and those who will work in translation/interpreting (*Letras Bachelors*). The country's higher education institutions offer degrees with different approaches that align with the needs of the region, which might include training in English, Spanish, and German, among others. In 2006, Libras was included as one of the languages available for Letras Licenciatura and, in 2008, for Letras Bacharelado. This means that any professional trained in Letras Libras carries a diploma equivalent to any other language.

In 2010, there was an important achievement in the area. SLTI was integrated into the Translation Studies Program at UFSC to graduate students with master's degrees and doctorates in this area. The translation and interpreting of Libras is considered part of the Translation Studies field, which includes all languages. In this way, the pair Libras and Portuguese is studied with the theoretical background of translation and interpreting studies, and researchers in this field started to produce knowledge in this area, impacting the training of these professionals. After this first achievement, two other Translation Studies programs from Brazil included sign language studies as part of their programs: the University of Brasilia (UnB) and the Federal University of Ceará (UFC).

Professionalization of SLTI in Brazil

Until the legal recognition of Libras in 2002, sign language interpreters worked as interpreters according to requests and the needs of deaf people. These interpreters had other main jobs and added the function of interpreter because they knew Libras and learned to interpret through experience in different contexts.

Training programs were built by the National Federation of Deaf Education and Integration (*Federação Nacional de Educação e Integração dos Surdos* [FENEIS]) in association with some universities, but these tentatively were very local, and they were offered only through short training courses. This resulted in an urgent need for training because interpreters were being requested in many formal contexts and needed more formal education (the first course was offered in 1997 by FENEIS with a duration of 80 hours). FENEIS also established an interpreting theme as part of its work agenda in 1988. Then, in 1992, the first version of the Ethical Statement of Sign Language Interpreters was established.

Law 10.436/2002 had an essential impact on the recognition of sign language interpreters in Brazil. Its regulation through the decree opened up the space for the formal education of this professional group. Also, sign language translators were recognized as having a distinct area of work.

The National Federation of Sign Language Translators and Interpreters (FEBRA-PILS) in Brazil, established in 2008, regulates these professions in collaboration with local associations across the whole country. One of its actions was restructuring the first version of the Ethical Statement of Sign Language Translators and Interpreters established previously by FENEIS. FEBRAPILS also represents interpreters and translators in government with regard to public policies and professional recognition and works closely with FENEIS. FEBRAPILS operates under three main pillars: 1) the initial and continued training of sign language translators and interpreters; 2) professionalization to reflect on the performance of sign language translators and interpreters in light of the code of conduct and ethics; and 3) the political engagement of sign language translators and interpreters to build collective knowledge in communities.

In this way, FEBRAPILS understands the critical nature of partnerships and the importance of working closely with deaf people to safeguard interpreting and translation services. FEBRAPILS also maintains a close relationship with the Brazilian Association of Translators and Interpreters (*Associação Brasileira de Tradutores e Intérpretes* [Abrates]). This partnership promotes the interaction of translation and interpreting professionals in the field, including those using Libras. That is, Libras is one of the languages overseen by Abrates, regardless of the difference in language modality.

The fact that we have qualified professionals makes it possible to hire professionals to work in sign language programs created nationwide. Even so, 4,438 professional interpreters work in mainstream schools but have no high-level training; these interpreters hold a provisional certification granting them the right to act as translators and interpreters. This certification was given to some sign language interpreters as a result of a strategy created by the government to qualify those who were already fluent in Libras, recognizing them as interpreters when there were no formal education opportunities, yet there was a clear need for interpreters. The government then created a certification that evaluated their sign language skills and their skills as sign language interpreters. Their tests were analyzed by a committee that included deaf professionals to evaluate their skills for being qualified independently of their educational background. This certification lasted for 10 years, from 2007 to 2017.

In 2008, when the first bachelor's degree for sign language translators and interpreters was established, the provisional certification was put on hold. However, this certification was a transitional step from having qualified interpreters without formal educational qualifications to having interpreters who would be recognized as qualified with higher-degree education. This was an interim measure the government created to offer sign language interpreters some form of recognition given that the formal education route was recently established.

Formal Education of Sign Language Translators and Interpreters in Brazil

Formal SLTI education in Brazil was established in 2008, just after the sign language teachers' education was established in 2006. The creation of a bachelor's degree, a 4-year course, impacted the professionalization of Libras translators and interpreters.

The first program established by UFSC was a special program financed by the government to meet a demand for the education of sign language interpreters in 15 states of the country, a course offered in parallel to Letras Libras Licenciatura, which is for sign language instructors and prioritizes deaf students. These two courses were an innovation in preparing content and materials in Libras (planning of evaluation activities, approval of video scripts, preparation of signed and written study notebooks). As such, the Letras Libras courses (Licenciatura and bachelor) have Libras as the language of instruction. In this sense, these courses represent a shift from the historically established logic, in which hearing and Portuguese perspectives organized formal education, to the perspective of deaf people, which reflects current linguistic policies. The first two offerings of these programs involved 1,300 students across 15 universities associated with UFSC, of whom 90% in the first class of Licenciatura (the course that trains sign language teachers) were deaf.

In Letras Libras, all the materials were made available in Libras. This means that the materials in Portuguese were translated into Libras. This requirement was established to guarantee the access of deaf students to this formal education when it was first made available in 2006, as it was focused on giving formal education to Libras teachers, with the prioritization of deaf instructors. Deaf translators who were experienced in the field led this translation process. Professors from translation studies were invited to give support to these translators. This opened the door for translation studies to discover the area of sign language translation (SLT) studies, a separate area of SLI studies.

The bachelor's level course (the course that trains SLTI practitioners) began with 450 students, almost all of whom were hearing with the aim of training translators and interpreters of Libras/Portuguese. We had a balanced number of deaf and hearing students in each course. For the Licenciatura (Libras teachers), almost all were deaf, whereas for the bachelor, almost all were hearing (sign language interpreters and translators). In this course, several Libras interpreters who already worked as professional interpreters enrolled in the program, as they to date had not yet been trained as interpreters. These first courses, which were special offerings with specific resources from the government, opened the door to establishing regular sign language programs across the country.

Training of deaf and hearing master's and doctoral graduates happened in parallel to the training at the undergraduate level. These qualified deaf and hearing persons actively participate in the decision-making and planning related to the issues in which deaf people are involved and the issues of the quality of translation and interpreting. Increasing educational opportunities have affected the professionalization of SLTI in Brazil. Sign language interpreters have become increasingly visible in different spaces of society, such as in education and the media.

We have trained researchers through the graduate programs in linguistics and translation studies, with specific research involving Libras, deaf education, interpreting, and translation. The formal education at higher levels at the university feeds back into the training of translators and interpreters across the country and gives visibility to SLTI. Also, it influences Libras language planning.

UFSC, the university that established these first sign language programs in Brazil, in 2014 had a Libras Department, with 29 tenured professors (17 deaf and 12 hearing professors) who work in the Letras Libras courses and the graduate programs in linguistics and translation studies. This university recognizes Libras as the first language of deaf people and offers its assessment tools in Libras. Today, Letras Libras programs are spread around the country. There are 40 Licenciatura Letras Libras courses (for sign language teachers) and eight bachelor's degrees (for sign language translators and interpreters). The universities are establishing their respective departments and building up faculty teams of deaf and hearing professors. This brings a deaf perspective to the training of professional Libras translators and interpreters. The students in the bachelor courses are mostly hearing people, which requires training with deep knowledge about deaf communities, in addition to the languages involved in SLTI practice. Given the access of deaf students to these courses, Libras is the main language of instruction to guarantee equal opportunity for these students.

Today, there are interpreters and translators in Brazil with formal education; however, there is not enough supply to meet demand. To date, there are approximately 650 professionals who have graduated from Letras Libras courses, and more than this number of professional interpreters of Libras and Portuguese are hired in public services, especially in federal public universities and public schools. Some of them have completed other kinds of training in technical-level or specialization courses (2 years offered at educational institutes or universities). Both hearing and deaf sign language interpreters are working mainly in the education setting, but Brazil is starting to see more qualified interpreters working in other contexts, as well. Deaf interpreters work primarily at international conferences as interpreters of Libras and International Sign Language[1] or ASL. There are also deaf translators working in call centers that provide deaf public access to banks and other commercial companies when deaf people need services.

SLTI Education Curriculum in Brazil

As for the Letras Libras course, at UFSC, for example, the bachelor's degree in Letras Libras requires completion of a curriculum that is organized over a minimum of eight periods (4 years), giving a total of at least 2,800 hours, fulfilled as follows: 600 hours in basic knowledge of the area (linguistics, literature, deaf studies, introduction to interpreting studies, introduction to translation studies); 1,200 hours in specific knowledge of the area; and 840 hours in knowledge of the area of translation and interpreting for the bachelor's degree (translation and interpreting studies, techniques, and practices).

The translation and interpreting knowledge covered in the curriculum of Letras Libras constitutes the core of subjects responsible for building the profile for the translator and interpreter of Libras and Portuguese, enabling the development of skills and abilities that guarantee professional performance. In these core subjects, theoretical discussions involved in the processes of translation and interpreting are promoted, and aspects of the professional ethics of the translator and interpreter are also discussed, as well as their role in the relationships between the linguistic communities involved. The cognitive, social, cultural, and linguistic processes involved in translation and interpreting are also analyzed, with special consideration of the effects of language modality (sign language in a visual–spatial modality and Portuguese language in an oral–auditory modality), as well as their written representations (signwriting for Libras and alphabetic writing for Portuguese).

The academic, scientific, and cultural activities covered in the curriculum of Letras Libras comprise academic activities that aim to develop interpersonal skills, including cooperation, communication, leadership, and critical thinking, with the goal of ensuring the development of competencies across the curriculum. These activities are configured around optional subjects, participation in seminars and lectures, scientific initiation activities of multidisciplinary projects, participation in events of an academic nature, and continued learning activities. The courses cover intercultural and linguistic aspects, translation studies, interpreting studies, and methodological and technical issues of translation and interpreting.

There are also 420 hours of mentoring in SLI and/or translation practice. In parallel to the course, the students must engage in 210 hours of academic–scientific–cultural activities that include conferences, workshops, and other activities related to their area, selecting the activities most relevant to their curriculum. Proficiency in Libras is required for students to enroll in this course; proficiency is determined through an entry assessment, the Libras test. Video technology is used to administer the assessment tool, in which applicants watch an initial video and then respond to the questions. All questions are asked in Libras and have multiple-choice answers (again, all produced in Libras). The main goal of this assessment is to evaluate the sign language proficiency of the candidate with regard to comprehension. If they pass the assessment, they are approved for enrollment and then start the classes, which are all delivered in Libras. The assignments are also generally produced in Libras.

A new curriculum was established in 2019 at UFSC, which includes more knowledge about deaf people, deaf communities, and translation studies applied to the context of sign language and spoken language and incorporates results of knowledge produced in the context of Translation and Interpreting Studies. The changes stem from the perception that technical training is not sufficient in the training of professional sign language translators and interpreters. The cultural base, especially related to deaf roots, is very important in the development of these professionals. This more subjective knowledge implies ways of deaf-centered teaching and learning and represents a significant challenge in the training of these professionals (Oliveira & Quadros, 2022). In the next section, we will return to this issue.

This UFSC Letras Libras program has served as a reference for the other programs established later with enforced programs from the government. At the time of writing, there are eight SLTI programs throughout the country: (1) UFSC, (2) Florianópolis, and (3) the Federal University of Rio Grande do Sul, Porto Alegre (south of the country); (4) the Federal University of São Carlos, São Paulo, (5) the Federal University of Rio de Janeiro, Rio de Janeiro, and (6) the Federal University of Espirito Santo, Vitória (southeast of the country); (7) the Federal University of Roraima, Boa Vista (north of the country); and (8) the Federal University of Goias, Goiânia (center area of the country). These universities are spread around the country. UFSC maintains two offering formats: an e-learning system and a face-to-face format. The e-learning system covers parts of the country that need education but do not have a university to train sign language translators and interpreters.

With formal education of SLTI having been available since 2008 and with advances in research (see next section), revisions to the curricula of the programs have been needed, as suggested through regular review processes. The review processes focused on the technical aspects and on issues in the training of sign language interpreters (Luchi, 2019; Martins, 2016; Martins & Nascimento, 2015; Rodrigues, 2013, 2018a, 2018b, 2019).

The reviews revealed that there was something very important missing from our program, because it was clear that deaf people were not happy with the graduating professionals. They recognized the graduates as being technically proficient, but did not understand the point of their work in the context of deaf people in society. This helped us realize that sign language translators and interpreters are somewhat unique among interpreters and translator practitioners generally. With spoken/written languages, interpreters and translators are called upon in fewer and more restricted circumstances. Deaf people, however, negotiate much of their lives via these professionals. This means that these professionals have a unique role. For Deaf people, it is not a choice; it is a necessity to work with sign language interpreters in everyday life. For this reason, there is a relationship between sign language translators and interpreters and deaf people that involves far more than the act of translation or interpreting.

Translation Studies and the SLTI Graduate Program: Research and Formal Education Connected

The Graduate Program in Translation Studies (PGET) at UFSC aims to train competent professionals to carry out research, translation practice, and theoretical teaching of translation independently of language pairs. The program has two lines of research: literary studies of translation and interpreting and linguistic studies of translation and interpreting. Since 2008, there have been researchers working on SLTI in this program. As mentioned previously, the number of researchers related to sign language has grown in the past 15 years (2008–2022). The fields of investigation into SLTI were established after the creation of the bachelor's degree in Libras. As a counterpart, the undergraduate course benefits from the development of such investigations. The graduate programs in linguistics and translation studies at UFSC approved the production of theses and dissertations produced entirely in Libras, and there are already two doctoral studies entirely in Libras: Machado (2018) and Pimenta (2019).

The master's and doctoral selection process for the Graduate Program in Translation Studies and the Graduate Program in Linguistics at UFSC can be undertaken by deaf candidates in Libras. The program hires a Libras/Portuguese translator and a video editing team with good knowledge of Libras to carry out translations into Libras (recorded on video) with the supervision of the deaf and fluent signer professors, adapting the questions when needed.

During the administration of the test in Libras, candidates are allocated to laboratories in which individual computers are available. Thus, deaf candidates can watch the video and answer questions in Libras. Deaf candidates answer the questions in sign language, film themselves recording the answers, and save the file on the computer they are using. At the end of the test, the supervisor saves all videos on a hard drive to start the correction process the next day. This type of process guarantees the possibility of admission of deaf people into the respective postgraduate programs and guarantees the opportunity for deaf people to apply for available places in the programs under conditions parallel to those of their hearing colleagues.

The principles adopted by this university are to guarantee the inclusion of deaf people through the use of their own language, Libras, as the Portuguese language cannot be an exclusion factor. This university is a reference point for other universities that have started to open up to research in SLTI studies. The main language policy incorporated into these programs is the following:

a. Deaf researchers have the right to access the programs through Libras.
b. Deaf researchers have the right to produce their knowledge in Libras.
c. In sign language studies classes, signing professors teach in Libras, with interpreters into Portuguese upon request.
d. Classes with professors that do not sign have interpreters working into Libras, upon request.
e. All professors can advise a student at the master's and doctorate levels; if the professor does not sign, interpreters are provided upon request.

After 2010, two other programs opened streams for sign language research: UFC and UnB. Subsequently, the three main programs at UFSC, UFC, and UnB have produced 58 researchers in SLT and 35 researchers in SLI. Also, there were 36 research studies focusing on SLT and SLI (Rodrigues & Christmann, 2023). Rodrigues and Christman present a synthesis of the specific studies of SLT and SLI in the context of these three programs from 2010 to 2022 (see Table 1).

From 2010, SLTI research has been consistently produced, with approximately 14 research projects concluded per year. The 129 completed dissertations thus far were produced by both deaf and hearing researchers. Rodrigues and Christmann

Table 1. Quantification of Theses and Dissertations Produced in Translation Studies at UFSC, UnB, and UFC from 2010 to 2022: Evolution of Sign Language Studies in Brazil

Programs	Research	General	Libras	% of Libras
PGET/UFSC	Dissertation	203	20	9.80%
PGET/UFSC	Thesis	304	67	18.40%
PSTRAD/UnB	Thesis	174	30	17.20%
POET/UFC	Thesis	83	12	14.40%
Totals		764	129	15.60%

(Rodrigues & Christmann, 2023, p. 11)

(2023) identified that deaf researchers produced 34.1% of the research (44 research projects completed). Also, they identified that 55.8 % (72 projects) were produced by women. With regard to intersectionality,[2] more than half of the deaf researchers were women (23 of the 44 research projects conducted by deaf researchers). As mentioned by Rodrigues and Christmann (2023, p. 15).[3]

> These data are relevant since highlighting the participation of women and deaf people in the production of research within the scope of ETILS, in postgraduate programs in Translation Studies, can significantly contribute to their visibility and recognition in the academic world, thus as well as valuing their contribution to the advances and enrichment of the field, going against misogynistic or ableist perspectives.

The evolution of the research on SLTI is having a positive impact on the formal education of these professionals. Since 2010, around 14 researchers per year complete a research study on SLTI (Rodrigues & Christmann, 2023).

Since 2010, SLT has gained prominence as we have advanced our experience in translating tests, national university entrance exams, teaching materials, official documents, glossaries, literature, and other materials. The development of translation practices in these contexts established this as a professional area of activity for sign language translators, with the involvement of many deaf professionals in addition to hearing persons. From these SLT practices, research on SLTI has increased, generating several important outputs and thus leading the way in this area. The following studies are a few examples.

Pinheiro (2020) conducted a study about deaf interpreters in Brazil. She found that they usually work as professionals between Libras and International Sign or ASL. Also, there are deaf sign language translators working from Portuguese written texts to Libras, especially for educational purposes. She identified that deaf translators are progressively occupying more professional spaces. Also, she identified that the SLTI programs omit specific educational needs for deaf students and proposed specific policies to apply to these programs.

Luchi (2019) analyzed all the curricula of the country's eight SLTI programs. He found that these programs focus on mostly technical issues. Conversely, the programs are missing specific training related to deaf studies.

Nogueira (2016) analyzed SLI in conference settings. Specifically, he analyzed the coworking of these professionals working in pairs or trials in the simultaneous translation from Libras to Portuguese in translation booths. He found much more collaboration among the professionals inside the booths because they were not in front of deaf signers in the conference space but were rather in a more restricted space, where they could use written notes, signing, and whispering to support the interpreting in the moment.

Martins (2013) conducted research with Libras interpreters in educational settings. She found that these interpreters were much more successful when they collaborated closely with teachers. The practical work included a strong communicative relationship between interpreters and teachers to achieve better interaction with deaf students in mainstream schools.

Souza (2014) researched hearing heritage signers as sign language interpreters. As a heritage signer himself, he analyzed how these professionals transitioned from their experiences of brokering (interpreting) at home to their work as professional interpreters.

Segala (2010) researched the translation work done from written Portuguese to Libras by deaf translators, focusing on the different effects of the language modalities—what he referred to as intermodality skills. As a deaf translator himself, his study contributed to the inclusion of Libras translation in the Translation Studies Program because he highlighted the complexity of doing this work when working with a visual language produced by the body, and he drew parallels with written Portuguese/Libras translation. Segala was the first researcher to focus an analysis on deaf translators working from written Portuguese to Libras.

Significant progress has also been made in the translation and interpreting processes present in conference contexts, as analyzed by Nogueira (2016), establishing simultaneous interpreting in booths and identifying elements that typify performance in the booth in the context of Libras conference interpreting practices from Libras (source language) to Portuguese (target language).

Researchers have also begun to focus on the different practices of simultaneous interpreting to map the challenges involved in these practices, especially the contexts of community interpreting, including the educational context (Martins, 2003, 2008).

Rodrigues (2013) conducted research analyzing the simultaneous interpreting process and considering psycholinguistic issues. He identified specific strategies developed by sign language interpreters to deal with information packaging in the interpreting process.

Santos (2013) mapped the SLI studies around the country from 1990 to 2010. She found that the research produced was related mainly to education settings. Still, she noted that in from 2005 to 2010, studies began to be more oriented to translation studies, showing the impact of formal SLTI education on research. She identified an apparent change in the focus of SLTI research from educational contexts and special education to linguistics and applied linguistics areas, especially bilingualism and translation studies.

Silva (2013) focused on the effects of the presence of sign language interpreters in classrooms, with consideration of the participation of deaf students in class interactions in mainstreaming contexts. She found that the classes require adjustments to guarantee the full participation of deaf students.

Krusser (2017) studied how design might interact with translation to facilitate the reading of Libras texts in videos by deaf students. Her research aligned translation studies with design studies, an interface that has been very important because of the visual modality of Libras.

Machado (2018) examined creative uses of sign language in organizing a Libras literary anthology. Her study was especially important because she had produced a dissertation in Libras, causing discomfort in the Translation Studies Program because her production needed to be accessed through simultaneous interpreting into Portuguese for nonsigning researchers. She also discussed the translation of Libras-based artistic productions into Portuguese. Müller de Quadros and Stumpf (2019) did work related to translation policies applied to sign language, raising the importance of deaf presence in this research context, as in any SLTI training.

Thus, it can be seen that research has advanced in the field of SLTI, strengthening the area of translation studies and interpreting studies.

The Road Ahead

For the future, the strong research development in SLTI studies take us into new spaces in terms of social achievements, cultural and linguistic gains, and the development of technologies. Also, the research feeds into language and educational policies to make true inclusion possible. The main aspects we wish to mark from our history in Brazil in the area of continuing development of SLTI studies and education are the following:

1. To increase the integration of SLTI research into translation and interpreting studies as complementary studies that contribute to these areas.
2. To review SLTI education, incorporating more information about the theories of Deafhood and Deaf Gain (Bauman & Murray, 2014; Ladd, 2003) and deaf awareness throughout the whole curriculum.
3. To review SLTI education, considering technological improvements, with revisions of the role of this kind of technology and the work done by human professionals.
4. To encourage deaf sign language interpreters and translators to lead research in the area.
5. To empower the relationships among sign language professionals, including deaf sign language interpreters and translators.

All these aspects must be incorporated into the curriculum of SLTI and education in a course like Letras Libras. The most important advance is the clear statement of identity and cultural aspects, including Deafhood, Deaf Gain, and deaf awareness into the curriculum as topics as important as the technical issues. The presence of deaf researchers also influences this move.

CONCLUSION

The purpose of this chapter was to present the situation of SLTI education in Brazil and the connection between research and formal education. The formal education of these professionals was established as a consequence of legal requirements. In 2008, the first university course was created, and in parallel, SLTI studies began to emerge, with an increase in the number of researchers in different topics, including deaf researchers.

The history of SLTI education in Brazil during the past 15 years since we published our chapter in the first volume on SLI education (Müller de Quadros & Stumpf, 2009) shows an impressive development, promulgated by language policies. This evolution impacts the training of these professionals, which is currently established in eight universities in different regions of Brazil.

Research into SLTI is growing and reaching different arenas. For new versions of the curriculum, the research has an impact, especially with respect to the perceptions of the field as integral to the wider field of translation and interpreting studies, as well as the perceptions of deaf people and their sign language. These changes impact the use of sign language as the language of communication among deaf people and the language to engage deaf people in society, which affects the roles of sign language translators and interpreters.

One important aspect is that the growth of research in SLTI has included deaf researchers. This guarantees a deaf perspective in the formal education of these professionals. Today in Brazil, SLTI areas represent a field of research in consolidation and a field of linguistic and gender diversity that includes the presence of deaf people.

ACKNOWLEDGMENTS

We thank the editors, Jemina Napier, Stacey Webb, and Robert Adam, for their detailed feedback, which contributed to making this publication about the experiences in Brazil accessible to the readers through this volume.

NOTES

1. See endnote in the Introduction chapter to this volume about the use of the terms *International Sign* and *International Sign Language*.
2. See the Introduction chapter in this volume for an overview of intersectionality theory.
3. Original translated from Portuguese into English by the authors.

REFERENCES

Bauman, H.-D. L., & Murray, J. J. (2014). *Deaf gain: Raising the stakes for human diversity.* University of Minnesota Press.

Krusser, R. (2017). *Design Editorial na tradução de português para Libras.* Tese de Doutorado. Programa de Pós-Graduação em Estudos da Tradução. Universidade Federal de Santa Catarina. Florianópolis.

INEP. (2010). Instituto Nacional de Estudos e Pesquisas Educacionais Anísio Teixeira. http://portal.mec.gov.br/component/tags/tag/32044-censo-da-educacao-superior#:~: text=Representantes%20de%202.625%20institui%C3%A7%C3%B5es%20de,partir %20de%2015%20de%20fevereiro

Ladd, P. (2003). *Understanding Deaf culture: In search of Deafhood.* Multilingual Matters.

Luchi, M. (2019). *A institucionalização de cursos superiores de formação de tradutores e intérpretes de Libras/Língua Portuguesa no Brasil no decênio 2005/2015: O que os cursos esperam de seus alunos?* Dissertação da tese da Universidade Federal de Santa Catarina, Florianópolis.

Machado, F. A. (2018). *Antologia da Poética em Língua de Sinais Brasileira.* Tese de Doutorado. Programa de Pós-Graduação em Estudos da Tradução. Universidade Federal de Santa Catarina, Florianópolis.

Martins, V. (2008). *Educação de surdos no paradoxo da inclusão com intérprete de língua de sinais: Relações de poder e (re) criações do sujeito.* Dissertação de Mestrado. Faculdade de Educação da Universidade Estadual de Campinas. UNICAMP, Campinas/SP, 2008.

Martins, V. (2016). Tradutor e intérprete de língua de sinais educacional: desafios da formação. *Belas Infiéis, 5*(1), 147–163.

Martins, V. (2013). *Posição-mestre: desdobramentos foucaultianos sobre a relação de ensino do intérprete de língua de sinais educacional.* Tese de doutorado defendida na Faculdade de Educação da Universidade Estadual de Campinas. UNICAMP, Campinas/SP.

Martins, V. & Nascimento, V. (2015). Da formação comunitária à formação universitária (e vice e versa): novo perfil dos tradutores e intérpretes de língua de sinais no contexto brasileiro. *Cadernos de Tradução, 35*(2).

Müller de Quadros, R. (2019) *Libras no Ensino superior.* São Paulo, Brazil: Editora Parábola.

Müller de Quadros, R., & Stumpf, M. R. (2009). Brazilian Sign Language interpreter education in Brazil: From voluntary work to formal distance learning. In J. Napier (Ed.), *International perspectives on sign language interpreter education* (pp. 221–247). Gallaudet University Press.

Müller de Quadros, R., & Stumpf, M. R. (2019). Recognizing Brazilian sign language: Legislation and outcomes. In M. De Meulder, J.J. Murray, & R. McKee (Eds.), *The legal recognition of sign languages: Advocacies and outcomes around the world* (pp. 238–267). Multilingual Matters. Blue Ridge Summit.

Müller de Quadros, R., Souza, S. X., & Segala, R. (2012). Brazilian Sign Language deaf-translation performance: Descriptive concepts and approaches to procedures led by deaf translator-actors. In M. Metzger & R. Müller de Quadros (Eds.), *Signed language interpreting in Brazil* (pp. 21–42). Gallaudet University Press.

Nogueira, T. C. (2016). *Intérpretes de Libras Português no contexto de conferência: uma descrição do trabalho em equipe e as formas de apoio na cabine.* Dissertação de Mestrado. Programa de Pós-Graduação em Estudos da Tradução. Universidade Federal de Santa Catarina, Florianópolis.

Oliveira, S. M., & Müller de Quadros, R. (2022). Translation policies for the education of sign language translators and interpreters in school environments. In C. Stone, R. Adam, C. Rathmann, & R. Müller de Quadros (Eds.), *The Routledge handbook of sign language translation and interpretation* (pp. 442–455). Routledge.

Pinheiro, K. L. (2020). *Políticas Linguísticas e suas implementações nas Instituições do Brasil: o tradutor e intérprete surdo intramodal e interlingual de Línguas de Sinais de Conferência.* Tese de Doutorado. Programa de Pós-Graduação em Estudos da Tradução. Universidade Federal de Santa Catarina, Florianópolis.

Rodrigues, C. (2013). *A interpretação para a língua de sinais Brasileira: efeitos de modalidade e processos inferenciais.* Tese de doutorado. Programa de Pós-Graduação em Estudos Linguísticos da Faculdade de Letras. Universidade Federal de Minas Gerais, Belo Horizonte.

Rodrigues, C. (2018a). Formação de intérpretes e tradutores de língua de sinais nas universidades federais brasileiras: constatações, desafios e propostas para o desenho curricular. *Revista Translatio, 15*, 197–222.

Rodrigues, C. (2018b). Competência em tradução e línguas de sinais: a modalidade gestual-visual e suas implicações para uma possível competência trajetória intermodal. *Múltiplos horizontes da tradução na América Latina, 57*(1), 287–318.

Santos, S. A. (2013). *A tradução/interpretação de língua de sinais no Brasil: uma análise das teses e dissertações de 1990 a 2010.* Tese (Doutorado em Estudos da Graduação) Universidade Federal de Santa Catarina, Florianópolis.

Segala, R. (2010). *Tradução intermodal e intersemiótica/interlinguística: Português escrito para a língua de sinais.* Universidade Federal de Santa Catarina, Florianópolis, Santa Catarina, Brazil.

Silva, A. M. da. (2013). *Análise da participação dos alunos surdos no discurso de sala de aula do mestrado na UFSC mediada por intérpretes.* Dissertação de mestrado. Universidade Federal de Santa Catarina. Programa de Pós-Graduação em Estudos da Tradução.

Souza, S. X. (2010). *Performances de tradução para a língua brasileira de sinais observadas no curso de Letras Libras* [Translation performances into Brazilian Sign Language observed in the Libras Language Studies Course]. (Unpublished Master's dissertation). Universidade Federal de Santa Catarina, Florianópolis, Santa Catarina, Brazil.

Souza, J. C. (2014). *Intérpretes Codas: Construção de identidades.* Dissertação (Mestrado em Tradução) – Centro de Comunicação e Expressão, Universidade Federal de Santa Catarina, Florianópolis.

DEBRA RUSSELL, JEANETTE NICHOLSON,
AND NIGEL HOWARD

5

The Winds of Change

Canadian Sign Language Interpreter
Education Programs

Canada is a country of contrasts, shaped by a number of factors: It is physically the second-largest country in the world, with 10 provinces and three territories; it has four and a half different time zones; and it takes 12 hours to fly from coast to coast, from Vancouver, British Columbia, to St. John's, Newfoundland. As a bilingual country of English and French, Canada has a long history of employing interpreters to deliver services in both official languages. Canada also has more than one signed language, and as of 2019, the Government of Canada, through the passing of Bill C-81, known as the Accessible Canada Act, recognized American Sign Language (ASL), *le langue des signes Quebecoise* (LSQ), and Indigenous Sign Languages (ISLs) as the sign languages used by deaf Canadians.

Malcolm and Howard (2009) also identify that Canada has a history of Maritime Sign Language (MSL), a unique blend of ASL and British Sign Language used by deaf people in New Brunswick, Nova Scotia, Prince Edward Island, and Newfoundland and Labrador. However, as of 2020, there are few signers who use MSL, and despite efforts to preserve the language, the vast majority of deaf people in those regions use ASL, with both ASL and LSQ used in New Brunswick. Recently, there have been attempts to revive MSL through the development of online videos and community courses. This loss of language is also a concern for LSQ users, and Boudreault (2019) has argued that LSQ is an endangered language and requires significant attention to preserve and foster its continued use in Quebec and certain parts of New Brunswick and Ontario.

Despite having such a large land mass, Canada has a relatively small population of 36 million. Unfortunately, Canada does not collect census data that allow us to know the population of deaf citizens. However, the Canadian Association of the Deaf–Association des Sourds du Canada (CAD-ASC) estimates there could be 500,000 deaf signers and more than 3.6 million hard of hearing people, some of whom might also be signers. With that background to our country's context, we next introduce ourselves and explore the ways in which interpreting has developed in Canada.

Who Are We?

As authors, we wish to acknowledge our positionality and how that influences our work. All of us are Canadian interpreters, researchers, and interpreter educators. Our backgrounds bring together signed language linguistics in ASL; education, interpreting, and psychology; specializations in legal, medical, and mental health; and remote video and video relay interpreting.

Debra first met deaf people when she was attending college. This led her on a journey of learning ASL and working with the deaf community. She became fluent in ASL and developed a deep appreciation and awareness of language diversity. At that time, Canada did not have formal interpreter education, so she credits her interpreter education as "coming from the deaf community, by the deaf community." She worked first as an employment counselor, providing support for deaf people in obtaining interviews, job orientation, and employment training. Those 2 years saw her work with the community to create a specialized unit for the deaf community that still exists today. More importantly, that experience exposed her to linguistic variation among deaf youth and adults from all walks of life and across the education spectrum. At the same time, Canadian interpreters were beginning to establish interpreter associations, and Debra was a founding member of the national Canadian association.

Debra then moved to a remote Indigenous community, Yellowknife, Northwest Territories, where she worked as a travel agent, a job that she obtained through the deaf network by being formally introduced by the superintendent at the Alberta School for the Deaf to a family in Yellowknife with a deaf child. With that opportunity, Debra had a chance to visit many of the northern communities, many of which had deaf residents, from the Dene in the McKenzie Delta to the Inuit in the eastern Arctic. This experience again offered her a window into language variation and perhaps the earliest glimpses by a nonnative person of what is now recognized as Inuit Sign Language.

Upon returning to Edmonton, Debra returned to school, earning a bachelor of education degree (BEd), while continuing to provide interpreting services on campus for deaf students in undergraduate, master, and doctoral programs and within the broader community. At that time, interpreter education programs (IEPs) were being formed across Canada, and upon graduation with her BEd, Debra began teaching in the program at Grant McEwan College. Life took Debra to Ontario and then back to Alberta; she interpreted in both provinces. She enrolled in a master of arts (MA) program in adult education and community development and then in the doctoral (PhD) program in education. As an interpreter educator and researcher, she maintains an active interpreting practice with a primary focus on legal and mental health settings. Her research agenda has included examining interpreting practices in legal settings, with specific attention to the ways in which interpreting can support or interfere with deaf people gaining full access to the legal system, as well as mediated education for deaf students and deaf interpreting.

Debra continues to deliver workshops and presentations to both signed and spoken language interpreters. She has also been shaped by her work at the national, regional, and international levels, given her involvement with the World Association of Sign Language Interpreters (WASLI). She has held leadership roles with the Canadian national organization representing sign language interpreters, known now as the Canadian Association of Sign Language Interpreters (CASLI), and has also served as the WASLI North American representative, followed by 8 years of service in the role of president. The privilege of teaching, learning, and traveling to more than 60 countries has shaped her lens about interpreter education, the human rights of deaf people, and the ways in which interpreters demonstrate allyship within the deaf community. Given an entire working career spent living and working in deaf communities, she also has a natural bias toward social justice for linguistic minorities.

When Jeanette was completing her fourth year of an honors bachelor of arts (BA) program, an opportunity to connect and volunteer with the deaf community in the local area became a life-changing experience. Instead of pursuing her intended career as an educator, Jeanette was encouraged by deaf community members to pivot and apply to an IEP. Jeanette was mentored by deaf leaders, studied ASL and interpreting, and was privileged to be invited back again and again into deaf space, exposed to the stories of connection and of oppression. After she completed her IEP and worked as an interpreter, her spark to become an educator rekindled, and a passion for mentoring and teaching was the impetus for her application for her master of science in interpreter pedagogy at the University of North Florida. Jeanette returned to teach in the same undergraduate interpreting program from which she had once graduated. Jeanette is interpreting, mentoring, developing curriculum, and teaching for a company that provides video relay services (VRS), video remote interpreting (VRI), and community interpreting in Canada. Jeanette continues to be inspired by the stories of the collective activism of deaf communities and strives to approach her work through an anti-oppressive lens. Jeanette is currently married to a deaf educator and interpreter and has a deaf son who is in their third year at Gallaudet University, Washington, DC.

Nigel, who is a deaf interpreter (DI) and interpreter educator, describes his journey as a confluence of several factors. Born and raised in Vancouver, British Columbia,

Nigel's first exposure to interpreting and language was when his high school hired an interpreter to work in Nigel's classes. Before that, he had not thought of language and culture in any significant way, but he marks that experience as a pivotal moment in which he recognized that the signs the interpreter used were not based on English and that in fact there were two languages that he was learning. Soon after that, Nigel had an opportunity to attend the Deaflympics to compete in the swimming events. This was a life-changing experience for him during which he met deaf people from around the world, all using their own national sign languages. From that point forward, Nigel became intensely interested in sign language and deaf culture. After completing his Bachelor degree with a major in psychology, he relocated to Toronto, where he was recruited into a training program for ASL instructors, which opened him up to the possibility of teaching ASL as a career.

When Nigel returned to British Columbia, he worked at the dormitory at a school with deaf students, often finding himself in the role of language mentor and cultural broker for the students who came from very diverse backgrounds. At the same time, he began teaching in the interpreting program at Douglas College, working with interpreter educators who encouraged him to begin providing interpreting services in legal, medical, and mental health settings, which then led him to teaching medical and legal interpreting. He taught for Douglas College in the Program of Sign Language Interpretation and in Child, Family, and Community Studies for 25 years, and he did graduate studies at Bristol University, where his understanding of Deafhood was enriched through the teaching of and friendship with Dr. Paddy Ladd.

Nigel is currently an adjunct professor both at the University of British Columbia and the University of Victoria in the Department of Linguistics. Nigel has been an interpreter for more than 25 years in various settings, such as medical, mental health, legal, theater, community, and conference/workshop settings, locally, nationally, and internationally, and has taught numerous workshops throughout the world. He is an Accredited International Sign Interpreter by the World Federation of the Deaf and WASLI. He is part of the United Nations team of International Sign interpreters and interprets on media.

CONTEXTUALIZATION: TRANSLATION AND INTERPRETING IN CANADA

In Canada, translation and interpreting are well developed in terms of conference-level interpreter education, beginning in 1936 when the University of Ottawa offered the first postsecondary education for translators and interpreters. This training was formalized in 1971 with the founding of the School of Translation and Interpretation. In the mid-1980s, this same school, under the leadership of Roda Roberts, collaborated with sign language interpreters and offered a 6-week summer institute that drew interpreters from across the country. The program had some combined classes with spoken language interpreters, and other classes were specific to the ASL/English or the LSQ/French cohort. They currently offer an online program for translation into French, along with two BA programs in French and English, as well as a trilingual option that includes Spanish. There are also two MA programs in conference interpreting and translation studies and a PhD in translation studies. In addition to the University of Ottawa, several other universities in Canada prepare translators at the undergraduate, graduate, and postdiploma levels. Glendon College at York University offers a master's degree in conference interpreting. Accreditation of spoken language interpreters is generally offered by the professional bodies representing interpreters and translators, and several provinces have protected titles, where only accredited interpreters can use the titles of "translator," "conference interpreter," "court interpreter," "community interpreter," and "medical interpreter."[1]

However, the landscape for community interpreters varies from short-term training for bilingual speakers, offered by professional associations and interpreting agencies, to 6-month programs offered by immigrant settlement agencies. The Canadian Language Industry Association (CLIA) works hard to promote the field of community interpreting. Various postsecondary institutions offer a standard program of 180 hours that provides the foundational training for interpreters working in medical, legal, domestic violence, and social service sectors. By contrast, the development of sign language interpreting (SLI) in Canada has resulted in much longer programs of study. We next describe the professionalization of SLI in Canada.

PROFESSIONALIZATION OF SIGN LANGUAGE INTERPRETERS IN CANADA

McDermid (2008) offers an excellent synopsis of the history of SLI in Canada. He cites Carbin (1996) in identifying that in 1860, the sister of the first deaf lawyer in North America provided interpreting services for him and their deaf brother in a legal context. Carbin (1996) describes several other examples of SLI in the late 1800s in legal and community settings, as well as religious settings. In contrast, Leahy (2016) examined archival records in the United States of America (United States) and United Kingdom to determine the historical path of interpreting in legal contexts. Leahy (2016) cites the British Archives at Kew in the United Kingdom, identifying a legal case from 1324 that records examples of deaf people using interpreters in the legal system. She also found a Canadian court case from Hamilton, Ontario, that took place in 1864, in which a deaf youth was sentenced to jail for the death of his infant sibling. What is not clear in the records is whether a sign language interpreter was used in the trial, in which the accused was viewed as an "idiot."

Canadian records reveal that a woman named Annie Byrne was appointed in the late 1800s to act as an interpreter and social worker for the Toronto Mission of the Deaf, a position she held for some 60 years (Carbin, 1996). Records of the Ontario Association of the Deaf show that two volunteer interpreters were thanked for working at the 1902 Ontario Association of the Deaf conference. Carbin (1996) describes that in that same time period, the principal at the Manitoba School for the Deaf was interpreting for field trips, as noted in the school yearbook; similarly, the superintendent at the Saskatchewan School for the Deaf interpreted for students attending the technical institute. It is also interesting to see that Carbin (1996) and Stratiy (1996) make specific mention of Isabel Crawford, born in 1865 to a missionary family that worked among the North American Indians [sic] (1883–1906). Isabel became deaf at the age of 16, and when she took on her first missionary assignment, she might have been one of the first DIs in North America, working with the Kiowa tribe in their interactions with others.

The past 100 years have seen tremendous growth and development of interpreting in Canada, including many sectors, such as public service, media, VRS, medical, legal, conference, and high-level political meetings. However, the growth of interpreting as a "profession" seems to have occurred in the late 1970s, when we observed interpreters across the country working in part-time and full-time roles, interpreting on television for daily or weekly interpreted news and the Government of Canada's daily Question Period.[2] The presence of interpreters on public media served to raise awareness of interpreting and sparked an interest in sign language classes, which were then taught largely by nondeaf people, many of whom were teachers of the deaf, had deaf family members, or were the earliest interpreters. In this same time period, we also saw interpreters being paid to work in community and legal settings.

In those early stages of interpreter development in Canada, DIs were also part of the landscape. This is consistent with the assertion of Stone (2009) and Adam et al. (2011) that deaf people have always functioned as language brokers, interpreters, and ghostwriters. As in many other countries, deaf teachers working at schools for the deaf or in college upgrading programs were often used as intermediary interpreters, bringing their bilingual and cultural expertise to bear on the assignment. The interpreters supported linguistic access either in tandem with a hearing interpreter or independently by using written language to communicate with the hearing person and forms of sign language and gesture to communicate with the deaf consumer. Several of these deaf teachers earned the Reverse Skills Certificate from the Registry of Interpreters for the Deaf (RID) and worked as intermediary interpreters, most often in legal and social service settings. Angela Stratiy (personal communication, March 13, 2020) recalls that she was awarded the Reverse Skills Certificate in 1977 after having taken some interpreting workshops in Winnipeg. We could not locate records of the interpreter associations that offered professional development during the late 1970s to 1980s to see whether there were specific offerings for DIs, but it seems that most of the DIs participated in the general workshops offered to nondeaf interpreters (A. Stratiy, personal communication, March 13, 2020).

During the late 1970s, Canadian interpreters formed the first national organization to represent interpreters, with support from the two national deaf organizations, the Canadian Cultural Society of the Deaf and the Canadian Association of the Deaf. Four women, Janice Hawkins, Louise Ford, Mary Butterfield, and Dottie Inkenbrandt, are largely credited with obtaining Government of Canada funding to host a founding meeting that was attended by interpreters from coast to coast. Janice, Louise, and Mary were all born to deaf families in which ASL was their first language. They were also some of the first interpreters to provide professional interpreting services, and they acted as our earliest interpreter educators. Dottie was an American interpreter who had relocated to Vancouver, and she was able to draw on her training from the United States to support interpreting development in Canada. The Association of Visual Language Interpreters of Canada (AVLIC) was founded in Winnipeg in November 1979 (Letourneau, 1990; Russell & Malcolm, 1992). At the time, there were provincial interpreter chapters affiliated with the RID in the United States, but the desire for a Canadian network of interpreters was strong, and the provincial organizations that existed at the time quickly became chapter-affiliated members of the Canadian national body. In 2018, AVLIC changed its name to CASLI, with a membership of approximately 1,000 active members, of whom 52 are DIs.

Employment Opportunities for Canadian Sign Language Interpreters

CASLI collects only basic demographic information on its members. However, what is clear from the many job postings that CASLI shares with its membership is that there is a great deal of employment opportunity across the country. Canadian interpreters continue to work in a range of settings, from public schools with one or more deaf students, to medical and mental health appointments, legal contexts, public service appointments, postsecondary classes, and religious settings. One area of employment that was not an option when Malcolm and Howard (2009) described the Canadian interpreting landscape is Canadian VRS and VRI. Although interpreters in Canada have provided VRS services for American deaf signers for more than a decade, other than an 18-month pilot test, there were no VRS services provided to deaf Canadians. This changed in 2016 when the Canadian Radio and Telecommunications Commission mandated the creation of a Canadian VRS to serve deaf customers in ASL/English and LSQ/French. This resulted in a major growth opportunity for interpreters based in cities such as Vancouver, Kelowna, Edmonton, Toronto, Ottawa, Montreal, and Halifax, where multiple service providers established call centers. Because Canada is a bilingual country, services must be provided in LSQ/French as well as ASL/English, with Francophone services taking place in call centers in Gatineau, Montreal, and Quebec City, which appears to be sufficient to meet the demand at the present time (B. Jenkins, personal communication, May 01, 2024).

Given the ongoing shortage of Canadian interpreters, an American company, Convo, is the primary provider of VRS for ASL-English interpreting and a Canadian company, Asign, provides additional sign language interpreting, and SIVET is the primary provider of LSQ-French interpreting and ISEP provides additional sign language interpreting in LSQ. Convo has also created two Canadian centers that employ Canadian interpreters in an attempt to provide the most linguistically and culturally appropriate service. This is because interpreters in the United States might not be familiar with Canadian sign language variation or the context that frames many calls to Canadian government programs, financial institutions, or Canadian legal services providers. Another challenge is that the quality of interpreting skills in the United States is different from that in Canada. Deaf Canadians report that American interpreters use a much stronger literal interpreting style, and many of the interpreters do not possess the expected level of skill for the ASL/English work. A positive and unique feature of the Canadian implementation of VRS is that one of the service companies Asign has been very intentional in recruiting and hiring deaf managers who are also DIs and have experience as interpreter educators. By having this talent pool within the centers, any calls that require the services of a deaf–hearing interpreter team can be handled quickly and efficiently. This model has resulted in Canadian callers expressing a great deal of satisfaction with the quality of interpreting (R. Whiting, personal communication, May 18, 2024). A key advocate for the Canadian Radio and Telecommunications Commission developments stated:

> After years of advocacy and hard work by deaf community members, it is fantastic that the SRV Canada VRS has been realized and the demand for sign language interpreters is growing. The concern is that the industry is growing too fast for the available resources. It would be nice to see "homegrown" Canadian interpreters for VRS services on a 24/7 basis. It would be wonderful if we had deaf interpreter training for VRS to bring on more options of available interpreters. I am satisfied with the quality of service provided by the Canadian interpreters but it is not clear to the community how to provide feedback after an experience with a particular interpreter. There needs to be quality assurance mechanisms built into the system so that interpreters have room to grow. Are the interpreters being taught the geographic sign language differences for a national service? Having to fingerspell local words is tedious. And finally, we do still need many interpreters for community, post-secondary, and medical appointments. (L. Kellett, Personal communication, May 01, 2024)

The above quote is an excellent reminder of the complexity of VRS work and the need to ensure that the service is of the highest quality, recognizing the different

ASL dialects and language variation among deaf people in Canada, while also not detracting from the need for face-to-face interpreting in community settings.

Many of the VRS companies are also equipped to offer VRI services within their centers, and again, this is a relatively new area of employment for Canadian interpreters. However, this is not a new area for United States–based companies, and increasingly, we find that these companies are marketing their VRI services to Canadian institutions, especially hospitals and courts, emphasizing the ease of booking, the "immediate access" available 24/7, and the diversity of spoken languages that can be provided in addition to ASL services. Although these American companies might appear to be a cost-effective solution, as the hospital is paying for only the minutes of service used versus a 2-hour minimum, the service providers are often very unfamiliar with Canadian sign language variation, similar to what was described in the VRS context. The risk of medical errors based on faulty interpreting rises with the use of VRI and interpreters that are not well prepared to serve Canadian patients. The other frequent challenge noted by deaf patients who have used the option of VRI is that hospital Wi-Fi can be very inconsistent, depending on the age of the hospital and the firewalls and securities used in hospital settings. This has prompted professional organizations to produce best-practice papers designed to educate health care and legal personnel about when VRI services might and might not be appropriate. There are mixed reactions to the use of VRI among the deaf community, especially in medical settings, and there are currently some deaf community members moving forward with human rights complaints after having been forced to use VRI that did not meet their needs, which appears to be in violation of the Canadian Human Rights legislation.

We also recognize that interpreters, especially those who are deaf, are developing new business opportunities in translation work. For example, the Canadian Museum for Human Rights in Winnipeg, Manitoba, has many of its exhibits and displays available with translation into International Sign, LSQ, and ASL. Passport Control in Vancouver also has adopted the convention of providing a digital overview of the customs process in ASL, LSQ, and International Sign. With the passing of Bill C-81, it is anticipated that more government services will transform their websites to include LSQ and ASL for information that is routinely available in French and English.

In times that are not national emergencies, the demand for co-interpreting teams varies from province to province. Only a handful of DIs work full time, and those who hold full-time positions are often hired within the education system or within interpreter referral agencies. Even though most hearing interpreters are receptive to having DIs working with them, there are still others who see themselves as capable of interpreting all of their assignments without the inclusion of a DI. DIs are frequently found working during immigration hearings, where typically the deaf person involved in the hearing does not possess Canadian ASL as their primary language or could present with limited communication abilities. DIs are also working frequently in medical settings, the legal system, and public media events.

Since the overview of the Canadian SLI profession and education was published in the first volume (Malcolm & Howard, 2009), we have also seen a particular aspect of professional practice emerge that is focused on providing designated interpreting services for deaf academics and deaf professionals. This goes hand in hand with deaf postsecondary students' being provided with SLI services for their advanced educational opportunities, be that in medical school or in PhD programs in education, linguistics, biology, or engineering. Given the specialized nature of a particular discipline, a designated interpreter who can develop a rapport with the professional and learn about the area of discipline is preferred to using a variety of contract interpreters who might know very little about the academic content and research agenda of the deaf professional. This also necessitates that interpreters ensure they are academically qualified for the work, which requires education beyond the IEP. However, this is a challenge in Canada, as there are few interpreters with graduate-level training or undergraduate degrees in other fields of study in addition to having interpreter education qualifications.

Currently, in the arts and cultural sector, there are interpreters working with theater companies to offer access to a range of programming options geared toward children and adults. It is less common for interpreters who are deaf to be hired in theater productions, and as more and more deaf artists emerge in Canada, there is tension surrounding interpreted theater when contrasted with deaf-led sign language theater. Some of the controversy stems from discussions of the deaf ecosystem and how to better support the development of deaf arts, as opposed to supporting hearing interpreters' private businesses. Although some of the interpreters do work with ASL coaches and deaf theater advisers, there are a great many more who do not involve the deaf community in decisions about which shows should be interpreted, how to best provide interpreting (i.e., zoned interpreting or shadow interpreting[3]), and how to market the accessible events in ways that can attract deaf theater patrons.

A significant world event that brought attention to Canadian DIs was the 2020 COVID-19 pandemic. In Canada, a significant number of the televised broadcasts, including municipal, provincial, and federal government briefings, were interpreted by deaf–hearing teams. This conscious choice of lobbying for DIs to be used during this time of extreme emergency for our country and the world drew on research completed by Russell, McLaughlin, and Demko (2017) for the Canadian Hearing Society that examined communication accessibility for deaf and hard of hearing citizens during times of emergencies. The Canadian Hearing Servcies released guidelines for broadcasters, stressing the preference of the deaf community for DIs.[4] The research study included the pilot samples of two broadcasts, one with a certified and well-respected hearing heritage signer interpreter from a deaf family and the other with a deaf–hearing team of interpreters. A Canadian panel of experts and an international panel of sign language linguists and sign language users confirmed that the DI was by far the most preferred option for interpreting, especially given the emergency information that was to be relayed in the broadcast. Despite the fact that both interpreters had ASL as a first language, the panel preferred the DI, stating that the DI provided the most linguistically accessible interpreting, managed the pace of information, and used sophisticated ASL strategies to manage content that needed to be prioritized and some information that needed to be omitted because of the pace.

Finally, a significant shift that has occurred since 2009 is the rising number of interpreter referral businesses that have emerged in every major city. Our earliest interpreting referral services were often embedded in organizations that offered a range of services to the deaf community, from employment support to equipment and technological resources, counseling, and literacy programs. Many of those agencies are now experiencing a great deal of competition from independent interpreter referral services. One of the most successful private agencies is a deaf-owned and -operated referral service that provides LSQ/French and LSQ/ASL interpreting and translation services. However, some Canadian companies working with spoken language interpreters have expanded their services to include ASL/English interpreting services. This is worrisome in that the majority of those agencies have no relationship with deaf communities or the professional organizations representing interpreters, and there are numerous examples of spoken language interpreting agencies hiring sign language interpreters who are not members of CASLI and might not be qualified for community work.

These changes to the employment landscape then have an impact on how we educate interpreters and the curriculum used to ensure graduates are familiar with these new areas of professional practice. We now turn our attention to the programs that are preparing interpreters for today's changing world.

SIGN LANGUAGE INTERPRETER EDUCATION IN CANADA

Our earliest sign language IEPs came about in the late 1970s, at the same time that interpreters were forming networks, creating provincial organizations, and establishing AVLIC. The first short-term interpreter program was delivered by Red River Community College in Winnipeg, with instruction provided by Janice Hawkins. At a similar time, Vancouver Community College delivered a paraprofessional program designed to train people to work with the deaf community, and many of the earliest interpreters in British Columbia completed that program before being hired as community interpreters. In the early 1980s, college-based IEPs of 1 year in length were established in British Columbia, Alberta, Ontario, Manitoba, and Nova Scotia. In 1999, the highest number of interpreting courses operating in Canada was eight

(Scully, 1999). All of the courses were hosted at colleges, and many of them evolved into a model of 1 year of deaf studies, which included a heavy emphasis on acquiring ASL and learning about deaf culture and community, followed by entrance into a 2-year interpreting program. All but one of the colleges have traditionally offered both the deaf studies and ASL/English interpreting program within the same college department; the exception occurs in British Columbia, where Vancouver Community College delivers the 10-month deaf studies program, and Douglas College offers the IEP. In 2020, Douglas College began to offer its own deaf studies program to allow for greater options for students considering interpreting as a career.

Angela Stratiy was the first deaf educator to become the chair of an IEP, followed by Phyllis Beaton Vasquez. It should be noted that from their inception, all of the Canadian interpreter programs employed deaf ASL and LSQ instructors, and this has remained a constant to the present time. This educational practice of having only deaf people teach ASL or LSQ began in the early 1980s and reflected a conscious decision to have those first-language users of ASL and LSQ, who also have the lived experience of being deaf, as the models of language and cultural transmission. Beginning in the 1980s, the Canadian Cultural Society of the Deaf and its provincial counterparts began delivering training and offering a certification system for sign language instructors, leading to sufficient numbers of highly qualified instructors. At the university level, institutions like the University of Manitoba, University of Alberta, and University of Ottawa have a 15-year history of offering ASL for credit, often within departments of linguistics or modern languages. The University of Victoria began offering ASL for credit some 10 years ago, and as at other universities, the popularity of the ASL classes surpasses that of many of the other spoken language classes offered. The number of ASL classes has expanded consistently across all of the Canadian institutions.

The earliest record of discussions about creating a program or a series of courses for deaf individuals interested in becoming DIs took place in Winnipeg in 1988 (Mitchell, Evans, & Spink-Mitchell, 1988). McDermid (2008) indicates that this activity was followed by a report in 1990 on the role and use of DIs by the Independent Interpreter Referral Services (IIRS) (Dubienski, 1990). The first Canadian deaf interpreting workshop took place in 1977 in Winnipeg before the community hosted RID certification exams.

As of 2020, there were six IEPs in Canada: Five were ASL/English interpreting programs, and the other is an LSQ/French interpreting program. Over the years, there were as many as eight programs, but three are no longer delivered because of lack of demand or quality of training provided (Scully, 1999). Douglas College delivered an ASL-English interpreting program until 2023–2024, prior to transitioning the program to Vancouver Community College (British Columbia). The other two programs are George Brown College (Ontario), and Nova Scotia Community College (Nova Scotia). The LSQ/French interpreter program is delivered by the University of Quebec at Montreal. Also, as of 2024, both Lakeland College (Alberta) and Red River College (Manitoba) are officially on hold and not currently taking students.

We approached all of the Canadian programs for an updated perspective, revealing some interesting changes that have occurred over the past 10 years. For example, Vancouver Community College is working on an applied degree and will be moving forward with an application to the Degree Quality Assurance Board. The training of interpreters is a particular challenge for Quebec, as historically, the training is a part-time postsecondary program that attracts small numbers of students. In 2019, the University of Quebec at Montreal expanded its previous certificate program in French/LSQ interpreting to an advanced program of 60 credits. Prospective students entering the program are required to demonstrate French and LSQ fluency on a number of assessments.

George Brown College in Toronto, Ontario, has elevated the previous 3-year diploma program to a BA degree in interpreting, the first in Canada. The other two ASL-English programs are diploma based, typically 2 years in length, with a prerequisite of having completed 1 year of deaf studies. One program, Red River College, had a joint program with the University of Manitoba, where students could graduate with a diploma in ASL/English interpreting, and if they choose, they could continue to complete an undergraduate degree in linguistics. This joint program has experienced a decrease in enrollment, and as a result the institutional partnership was dissolved.

Nova Scotia Community College continues to provide a program, but the number of graduates from this program remains very small, and the program has experienced challenges in recruiting qualified instructors. In some instances, instructors have been hired who might have community experience as interpreters but do not possess undergraduate degrees, let alone graduate degrees. This has been a concern for interpreters and deaf communities, as the quality of the interpreter graduate is often dependent on the quality of instruction, and some perceive such decisions as negatively impacting the program standards that have been historically high. These decisions are contrary to the demand for more highly qualified interpreters to work in all sectors, especially in public service settings at the provincial and federal government levels. With increased expectations for highly qualified interpreters, interpreter programs need to be raising their standards; adapting their prerequisites, the academic content that is taught, and the nature of the assessments; and examining carefully their succession plans for qualified instructors.

Each of the programs reports having a screening process that can include individual interviews, group activities with other prospective students, and references from deaf community members and interpreters. There are established prerequisites in terms of established grade point averages and ASL and English proficiency, and George Brown College also requires a math or science university course. George

Brown College is working on articulation agreements with the other programs to allow for advance entry to the program, recognizing the length of time spent in a 2-year interpreter program. This would allow students from other Canadian IEPs to enter Year 3 of the program if they have maintained a grade point average of 3.0 or higher. Such a move would be seen as a positive step forward for our profession, as it would increase the number of interpreters with an undergraduate degree in interpreting and result in a pool of interpreters ready to then pursue graduate studies should they desire to do so. Before acceptance, students would need to complete an introductory research course and two additional liberal studies courses, achieving a minimum of 65% in all three courses. Something that stood out for us while conducting the research for this chapter was that George Brown College was the only program that indicated that their program design was intentionally designed to meet the accreditation standards of the Commission on the Collegiate Interpreter Education (CCIE).

Although the numbers of graduates per year does not meet the growing demand for interpreters, especially since the implementation of a Canadian 24/7 VRS and the legislative passing of the Accessible Canada Act (Bill C-81), there are no plans to expand the number of IEPs. To deliver an effective interpreter program, qualified faculty must be recruited, and interpreter educators with master's or doctoral degrees are in short supply in Canada. Additionally, given the CCIE standard ratio of 16 students per class, interpreter programs are expensive to deliver, making them less attractive to some postsecondary institutions in the current culture of economic cuts to postsecondary education.

Each of the programs has developed its own curriculum, tailored to local/regional needs, but there is a great deal of similarity across the programs in terms of offering courses in discourse analysis, consecutive and simultaneous interpreting, ethical decision-making, service learning within the deaf community, and specialized knowledge to work with people who are deafblind. Recently, George Brown College has offered two courses on working with technology with a focus on remote video interpreting applications and a further course on working in VRS. Vancouver Community College offers two specialized courses that explore understanding the paradigm described as Deafhood. All of the programs report offering face-to-face classes and some blended courses that have both online components, some which are synchronous and some of which are asynchronous, and face-to-face instruction. The programs all require that students complete supervised practicum placements. In a review of the program websites, what is described is that all of the programs offer instruction to prepare the graduate for general community work. There is no opportunity to offer a specialization, such as health care or legal interpreting, as these are skill sets that require interpreting experience before specializing, and most interpreter students have limited experience with the deaf community before enrolling in an IEP. Douglas College has offered a post-diploma in medical interpreting, which was comprised of four additional courses, but this diploma is no longer delivered, as the demand for it has been declining.

There have been instances in which deaf interpreting students have completed IEPs; for example, Lakeland College graduated two DIs in 2010, and Douglas College has had a DI complete the program through Prior Learning Assessment Reviews, and more recently a deaf ASL/LSQ interpreter completed the full interpreter program. Although all the programs are open to deaf applicants, the recruitment of deaf students has not happened within any of the programs in any targeted way. This raises the question of how best to educate DIs in Canada.

Challenges for IEPs

Deaf Interpreting Training Options

There are two tracks that make it possible to become a DI in Canada. One is to meet the criteria set by AVLIC, now CASLI, for the Deaf Interpreter Membership Category. The criteria are similar to RID, in that members must have completed an IEP or have taken 100 hours of training in ethics, cognitive processes of interpreting, etc. This includes:

• 40 documented hours of work as a DI within the prior 4 years
• 20 documented hours of professional development specific to deaf interpreting within the prior 4 years
• 20 documented hours of professional development specific to the process of interpreting within the prior 4 years
• 20 documented hours of professional development specific to ethics within the prior 4 years

In addition, the applicant is required to produce two letters of support from the board of the affiliate chapter to which the applicant is applying to become a member and a letter of support from a deaf organization in good standing in the province where the applicant resides/works or a letter of support from an active CASLI member who has experience working with the applicant. The person is to be mentored by a professional interpreter (deaf) in varying situations. Discussions and evaluations take place in all three phases—before, during, and after assignment—in order to develop the critical reflection necessary for this practice profession.

Like any criteria, these criteria are neither perfect nor completely ideal. Revisions to the above criteria tend to take place during the national interpreters' conference, held every 2 years. The goal of constant revisions is to ensure reasonableness and fairness given the varying standards across the country and the evolution of our profession. For example, in British Columbia, it is expected that an interpreter does a minimum of 4 years of community interpreting and takes additional interpreter training focused on medical settings before being considered for the roster of interpreters who are qualified to work in medical situations. This process applies to both deaf and hearing interpreters. The criteria for specialized situations vary from province to province across Canada. A significant change has been that an Ontario interpreting service has also implemented a DI screening tool that requires CASLI membership as a prerequisite. The test involves interpreting video scenarios, and if successful, the candidate is then interviewed and assessed for ethical decision-making ability before placement on the roster.

The second option to become a DI is to enroll in an IEP. All of the programs indicate that they welcome applications from deaf people. Over the years, there has been debate about the need for a specialized DI education program, given that many DIs do not require some of the courses that hearing interpreters require, especially in terms of learning ASL and deaf culture and understanding the nature of deaf communities and deaf organizations. However, there are core components that all interpreters require, including understanding translation processes, cognitive processing, and interactional demands; consecutive and simultaneous interpreting; ethical decision-making; co-interpreting practices; working with technology; specialized topics, such as working with children or seniors; deafblind interpreting techniques; and planning for ongoing professional development.

For the two programs that have graduated DIs, one challenge is to ensure that there are at least two deaf students in the same cohort, in order to allow for some natural peer support. It can also be challenging for faculty to differentiate instruction in order to make assignments appropriate and realistic for the DI. There have been deaf students who started an IEP and left early. The reasons for leaving are as varied for deaf students as they are for hearing students, such as discovering that interpreting is not a career path that they wish to pursue, financial pressures to work while attempting to study full time, or personal reasons. However, another area of concern is the uncertainty of gainful employment as DIs in Canada on a full-time basis, and this is a reason that many deaf interpreting students do not apply to IEPs. The 2- to 4-year investment in taking an IEP is an expensive undertaking, especially if employment options are scarce. For many, working as a professional DI is an "additional" job to supplement income and often is performed from a sense of obligation to the community, to provide accessibility for a variety of segments within the deaf community, such as deafblind people and senior citizens.

What has not emerged in any comprehensive manner among the IEPs is a collaborative plan about how to provide this foundation of training if taking a full-time IEP is not desirable and how best to identify, recruit, and screen deaf students who have the greatest potential for success.

The Next Generation of Educators

A challenge identified by several programs is that their core faculty are approaching retirement age, and there is a very small cohort of emerging interpreter educators who possess graduate training and interpreting experience to replace the long-time educators. Malcolm (2018) identified this same challenge and put forth a call for action among the programs to encourage interpreters to pursue higher education and consider interpreter education as a career path. Succession planning and building capacity within the communities were cited as key issues facing three of ASL/English interpreting programs.

As described earlier in this chapter, there are significant concerns in some communities about SLI education programs that have employed faculty who do not possess undergraduate degrees, let alone graduate training, raising the question of how to continue to promote high standards and consistency among programs across the country.

Another challenge George Brown College identified is that to deliver a bachelor-level degree program, there must be at least one faculty member with a PhD, and all other faculty must have MA degrees. The reality is that there are very few educators in Canada with a PhD. Although there could be educators completing MA degrees, at the time of our writing this chapter, there is just one interpreter educator enrolled in a PhD program.

A further challenge that is layered within succession planning is how to ensure that there are sufficient deaf administrators embedded in our program structures that a deaf lens is placed on curriculum planning and learning activities. The lack of deaf faculty members in leadership roles can also lead to distance between the deaf community and IEPs, and although advisory committees that include deaf representation exist, that is not the place where curriculum decisions are made. Although deaf instructors are hired to teach ASL and work as lab instructors, not all programs have a sufficient cadre of deaf instructors in full-time or leadership roles.

Expensive Programming

For Canadian programs, the costs associated with being a student can be a financial barrier. This is a concern for George Brown College, in that the cost of living in the Greater Toronto Area is one of the highest in the country, and this is coupled with the fact that the program is now a degree, requiring 4 years of tuition payment. While the program at Vancouver Community College is located at Vancouver, the most expensive city in Canada, the college is committed to keeping the tuition low as they highly value the social contribution as and such do not see the program as operating at a loss (Barb Mykle-Hotzon, personal communication, May 18, 2024).

Attracting Diverse Learners

A challenge identified across the programs is that of attracting a student body that is more diverse. Traditionally, learners have been female and Caucasian, but the Canadian deaf community is multicultural and diverse, and intersectionality is a frequent conversation point. At the present time, only Douglas College reports having any interpreting students from Indigenous backgrounds. This is a huge gap, given the presence of deaf First Nations citizens living across Canada. How do programs attract students from diverse ethnic and cultural communities? For example, the deaf community in Toronto has a very large number of Asian community members, Toronto and Montreal have larger numbers from African and Caribbean countries, and Calgary and Alberta have larger numbers of Syrian, Ukrainian, and Afghani deaf community members. Given this diversity, how best do we document the diversity within the deaf community and then attempt to match that diversity within the recruitment and selection processes for IEPs? This is a challenge that will require collaboration among organizations representing deaf people, IEPs, and interpreter associations.

Attracting Student Numbers

Douglas College reported that in 2019 they suspended intake to the program because of insufficient numbers of qualified applicants. Red River College reported that when they operated the joint degree program, they had fewer than five students in some years, suggesting that the linguistics degree was less attractive to students. George Brown College reports that although there appear to be consistent levels of hearing student applications, they have far less interest in the program from deaf applicants. A further factor influencing the recruitment of potential students is the career profile of sign language interpreters. The estimated wages for sign language interpreters varies widely. For example, interpreting in the kindergarten–to–grade 12 education system in a rural environment pays considerably less than does work in urban sites, or when contrasted to freelance rates. In some cases, the hourly rate paid to interpreters has remained static for the past 15 years, while the cost of living continues to increase. These factors require a multifaceted and systemic approach to marketing the profession, advancing standards of practice, and looking at the entry point of sign language acquisition as a gateway to sparking an interest in interpreting.

Teaching Interpreting During a Pandemic

During the COVID-19 pandemic, all of the Canadian IEPs were faced with moving traditional face-to-face classes to online learning platforms. For programs that already offered some courses in a blended or fully online format, the transition was a smoother one. For other programs, students and faculty alike were challenged by learning how to manage skill-based interpreting classes through platforms like Zoom. Students who were completing their practicums often had fewer opportunities, as interpreters were also making the transition to online interpreting.

Students experienced several challenges, including the need to purchase technology, such as larger computer monitors to lessen the fatigue of watching ASL instructions online; increased costs for upgrading Internet packages suitable for spending hours accessing instruction via Zoom; juggling the responsibilities of parenting and managing children at home who were also learning to navigate online learning; and the stress of provincial government rule changes that resulted in schools opening for a period of time and then closing and moving back to online learning. For both faculty and students, not everyone was equipped with a space in their home environment that was suitable to teaching or learning. For faculty members, in addition to pivoting their classes to online formats, they also had to learn how to implement COVID-19 protocols, including reducing the number of students who could attend a face-to-face class, which impacted scheduling and classroom use; social distancing practices during practice activities such as role plays; and cleaning regimes required between classes. Colleges were also required to advise students when a person who had been on campus had tested positive for COVID-19 to determine whether others could have been accidently exposed to the virus.

As Canada emerges from the pandemic, there are a number of lessons to be learned for IEPs, and there are some valuable insights that could offer solutions to other challenges. For example, attracting diverse learners and making the programs accessible to students living outside of the geographic location of the program might be much easier if significant portions of the program were delivered in online formats. Some of the deaf ASL instructors have suggested that the online format supported the instruction and that their students actually performed better, perhaps because of having to attend to the visual environment in ways that were different and more focused than in the regular classroom. Online learning also means that programs are not limited to hiring faculty members who live in the communities near the programs, which can broaden the capacity of the program through recruitment of faculty with unique skills and experiences not found in local teachers.

IEP Quality

Although the previous section described approaches to the education of interpreters, we want to acknowledge that over the years, concerns have been expressed about the quality of sign language interpreters graduating from IEPs (McDermid, 2008; Palusci, 2003; Scully, 1999; Stratiy, 1995). In an effort to increase the skills and knowledge of recent graduates, internship and apprenticeship models have been implemented by some hiring bodies. One example of this is the Interpreter Internship Program (IIP) that is hosted by the Canadian Hearing Services in Ontario, the apprenticeship program offered by a company known as Asign, and the mentorship program offered by the New Brunswick Deaf and Hard of Hearing Society. We next describe these bridges from graduation from an IEP to professional practice.

Interpreter Internship Program

The IIP is funded by the Government of Ontario with the specific goal of supporting interpreter development in the area of health care. The program began shortly after the 1997 Supreme Court of Canada decision on Eldridge, a case concerning the availability of equal medical treatment for persons who are deaf. The delivery of adequate health care across the country is critical, and the adoption of the Canada Health Act in 1984 can be seen as an attempt to legislate this effect. During the early stages of the Eldridge[5] case, the Canada Health Act was cited as one of the pieces of faulty legislation. Provision of equal medical services to people who are deaf is the core of Eldridge *v.* British Columbia (Attorney General),[6] and the Supreme Court of Canada ruled unanimously in favor of the appellants, finding that Section 15 of the Charter had been violated. The decision led to updates of both the Hospital Insurance Act and the Medicare Protection Act to reflect the requirement to provide an interpreter for medical services for deaf and hard of hearing persons. The decision also led provinces to deliver medical interpreting services, and one concern about doing this was the training and qualifications of interpreters to work in medical contexts, as this is not part of the generalist curriculum of IEPs. On the basis of these factors, the Ontario Interpreting Services applied for funding to create an internship that would select four to eight interns who had graduated from an IEP and offer them 10 months of targeted instruction and support.

The IIP model has been thoughtfully constructed to include supervised assignments in which the intern works with an interpreter supervisor, integrating their language, interpreting, and interaction management skills in settings with genuine interlocutors engaged in authentic communicative interactions. IIP stresses that it operates on a model of shared responsibility, where interns take on increased responsibility to prepare for the interpretation and to provide the service. Supervisors use a range of strategies to support the intern during the assignment, from providing missed information to offering confirmation of correct information and taking over some aspects of the interpretation when appropriate. Each assignment is followed by a structured debriefing and detailed feedback, in order to enhance the learning for future assignments.

The approach taken to curriculum development suggest that interns are exposed to classroom work, individual work, one-to-one support and tutoring, assignment days, and finally, a longer placement. The curriculum has been created with problem-based learning in all aspects of language instruction, knowledge modules, interpreting instruction, and role plays.

The IIP is using all the best-practice approaches found in the literature, including problem-based learning, situated learning in authentic contexts, and working with language tutors and supervising interpreters who have significant experience to mentor the interns. The program has resulted in an additional 100 interpreters passing the in-house screening tool and joining the organization as staff or freelance interpreters.

Mentorship in New Brunswick

The success of the IIP has also spurred other agencies to consider their own in-house mentoring and apprenticeship programs. Another example of such a bridging program is offered by the New Brunswick Deaf and Hard of Hearing Society (NBDHHS), which obtained government funding to create a mentorship curriculum with a contracted pool of deaf and hearing interpreter educators. One intern is selected per year and is supported to work through the program modules with the contract educators and to gain real-world interpreting experience with the staff and freelance interpreters. The program has operated for the past few years and has been a creative option that has benefited the community by recruiting new interpreters to a province that has traditionally struggled to attract qualified interpreters.

Apprenticeship With Asign (formerly known as SLIAO)

The final example we have chosen to highlight is the apprenticeship model offered by Asign. This private company manages two VRS call centers across Canada with a number of interpreters providing service remotely and offers VRI as well as community interpreting services. As one of the fastest-growing SLI companies in Canada, it has expanded its support to employees by procuring an in-house interpreter educator and has developed an apprenticeship program for a recent graduate of an IEP with less than 5 years of interpreting experience. The model for the apprenticeship program is based on individual assessments and 12 modules consisting of practice experiences, teamed assignments with support from interpreters working in the community, and self-directed learning activities supported by the interpreter educator. After completing the first year of the SAP with intensive support from the interpreter educator and deaf managers in the centers, the apprentice has a strong foundation to work within the community and work remotely on video. Ongoing support from interpreters both in the community and in the call centers affords the nascent interpreter an abundance of opportunities to provide successful interpretations for deaf consumers, either in the community or using a video platform.

THE ROAD AHEAD

As we look to the future, we offer several recommendations that, if implemented, could lead our interpreter education in new directions.

Collaboration Among IEPs

The first is a call for collaboration among Canadian IEPs to develop a cross-institutional approach to curriculum resources. For example, an ASL corpus and other ASL-related resources that could be shared across the six programs would be useful in ensuring that graduates are able to see samples of the linguistic variation that exists in Canada. Each program has resources and materials that reflect language use in the province in which the program is hosted. Given the implementation of Canada-wide VRS and VRI options, there is a need for creativity in ensuring graduates are prepared to serve our diverse deaf community well. Another possible area of collaboration would be for more courses to be offered in blended or entirely online options, especially for the final year of the only interpreting degree program at George Brown College. This would allow interpreters from across Canada to access Year 3 or Year 4 of the program from their local communities, rather than restricting the program to those who are geographically based in the Greater Toronto Area. Having more interpreters with a BA in ASL/English interpreting, from multiple provinces, could enhance the numbers of interpreters who would be interested in pursuing graduate studies and moving into positions as the next generation of interpreter educators.

Linguistic Research

Although Canadian interpreter educators have and continue to be research contributors, there is a need for sociolinguistic research on the ISLs used in areas of Canada by our First Nations deaf community members. We also support the advice of Boudreault (2019) in stressing the need to preserve and strengthen LSQ as a language and then to use that research to inform the LSQ/French interpreting program. In a similar vein, MSL must be documented in more rigorous ways by ensuring that signers who still can use it are recorded and having deaf sign language linguists in Canada work with local deaf community members to analyze the corpus.

Interpreting and Translation Studies for Deaf Students

We also believe that there are incredible opportunities for the IEPs to collaborate with the professional association, CASLI, to develop a model of relevant interpreting and translation studies that would be attractive to deaf students. Given that ASL and LSQ translation contracts are increasingly becoming available for government-related information, museums, and so on, it would be useful to provide a core foundation of translation courses for the individuals or teams of translators performing this work. Similar to the ways in which postsecondary institutions develop post-diploma and postgraduate programs, the programs could choose to create one translation program and one interpreting program, delivered via summer residency requirements and blended formats, in order to have a sufficient pool of applicants and to support education that is linguistically and culturally designed to meet the needs of the participants.

Curriculum Renewal Processes

All of the programs are in a constant cycle of curriculum revitalization, but we note that not all of the programs offer courses in VRS and VRI work. Given how many recent graduates move into VRS work, this is an obvious gap. There is also very little emphasis within the curriculum on co-interpreting within deaf–hearing teams, and this is a pressing need not only for recent graduates and DIs, but also for working professionals who have limited formal training in co-interpreting. This need has been highlighted during the pandemic with interpreter teams working the public media broadcasts. Although Alberta provided specific training for deaf–hearing teams working emergency broadcasts months before the COVID-19 pandemic, this training has been absent in all of the other provinces, so interpreter teams are having to learn to work together while they are providing the service. Examining current contexts in which interpreters, both deaf and hearing, find themselves working and creating learning outcomes based on those current demands could strengthen the quality of interpreter graduates.

Professional Development: Whose Job Is It?

We also acknowledge that IEPs cannot teach everything, but once again, there are opportunities for professional associations representing interpreters and IEPs to collaborate on a structured and comprehensive professional development program for interpreters.

Diversity, Recruitment, and Retainment

Only one program reported having any students from a First Nations background, and although there is some ethnic and cultural diversity within the cohorts studying at the present time, is that diversity sufficient to match the changing face of the deaf community? Processes must be put in place by deaf national organizations, working with their provincial affiliated organizations to identify the diverse aspects of our communities in order to inform IEPs' approaches to recruiting from targeted communities. However, marketing and recruitment are only part of the equation, as we know that we have lost deaf students and others who might have been from other minority communities. How we retain students, especially those from minority communities, needs to be explored, and strategies need to be implemented that address the challenges experienced by our nontraditional learners.

Creating the Next Generation of Interpreter Educators

All of the programs in Canada are challenged to hire qualified interpreter educators, both deaf and hearing. This is a pressing issue for our field, for without academically and experientially qualified instructors, the quality of education offered to students will suffer. Some graduate programs in the United States offer a specialized program in teaching interpreter education, but this option can be cost prohibitive for many Canadians as it often means paying double tuition in U.S. dollars. Graduate programs in adult education are delivered by many Canadian universities, and these are solid options for educators, but these same programs do not have courses specific to teaching interpreting. This issue leads to opportunities for structured mentoring for potentially interested interpreters, so they can learn specific techniques that have worked well for teaching interpreting and translation, assessment of interpreting assignments, curriculum planning, and so on. However, a danger of mentoring is that the prospective interpreter educators view the techniques as "the" way to teach, passing along approaches that might no longer be effective for the current student populations.

Conclusion

This chapter has provided an overview of the state of SLI education in Canada at 15 years on from the prior report. There are many possibilities for navigating the winds of change while retaining the elements that have served Canadian IEPs well. The Canadian context is such that with such a small number of IEPs, educators can work collaboratively, building on the professional relationships that exist in our profession. It is by working with the deaf community in meaningful ways to anchor IEPs in the deaf community, as well as by collaborating with the interpreter community and professional organizations such as CASLI and its provincial affiliated organizations, that we can design a plan to educate interpreters for the coming years.

Acknowledgments

The authors thank the following interpreter educators who provided us with valuable information and insight: Barb Mykle Hotzon, Rick Zimmer, Terry Janzen, Corene Kennedy, Alice Delude, Sheila Johnston, and Lisa Kellett. Any errors of fact or representation are our own.

Notes

1. For a further description of accreditation practices, see https://atio.on.ca/
2. The Question Period occurs each day the House of Commons of Canada is in session. Members of the parliament can ask questions of government ministers (including the prime minister).

3. For the purposes of this chapter, *zone* or *shadow* interpretation is defined as when the interpreter or interpreters are each placed in one location on the stage, commonly far stage-right, far stage-left, or far up-stage to stay out of the way of the actors as they go through their blocking (Bolstad, 2019).
4. See https://www.chs.ca/aec/broadcasters/best-practice
5. Eldridge v. British Columbia (Attorney General), [1997] 3. S.C.R. 624)
6. For a more complete description of the Eldridge decision, see Russell (2019).

REFERENCES

Adam, R., Carty, B., & Stone, C. (2011). Ghostwriting: Deaf translators within the deaf community. *Babel*, *57*(4), 375–393.

Bolstad, N. (2019). The show must go on! But where?: The use of American Sign Language interpretation in the theater. Honors Senior Western Oregon University Theses/ Projects. https://digitalcommons.wou.edu/honors_theses/201

Boudreault, P. (2005). Deaf interpreters. In T. Janzen (Ed.), *Topics in signed language interpreting: Theory and practice* (pp. 323–355). John Benjamins Publishing.

Boudreault, P. (2019, July 24). *Mise en danger de la Langue des Signes: Une etude de cas de la Langue des Signes Quebecoise*. [Paper Presentation]. World Federation of the Deaf Congress, Paris, France.

Carbin, C. (1996). *Deaf heritage in Canada: A distinctive diverse and enduring culture*. McGraw-Hill Ryerson.

Eldridge v. British Columbia (Attorney General). (1997). 3. S.C.R. 624.

Leahy, A. (2016, January 1). The history of interpreting. *British Deaf News* (London).

Letourneau, R. W. (1990). AVLIC 1990. In S. MacFayden (Ed.), *AVLIC '90 gateway to the future: Papers from the AVLIC 1990 conference* (pp. 1–7). Association of Visual Language Interpreters of Canada.

Malcolm, K. (2017). Interpreter education in Canada: Where are we now? *AVLIC News 33*(2), 3–4.

Malcolm, K. (2018). Interpreter education: Call to action. *The AVLIC News*.

Malcolm, K., & Howard., N. (2009). Traveling the path of excellence in interpreter education: The Canadian experience. In J. Napier (Ed.), *International perspectives on interpreter education* (pp. 248–265). Gallaudet University Press.

McDermid, C. (2008). Brief history of Canadian ASL-English Interpreting: York University. (Eric Document Reproduction Service No. ED 502 281)

Paluci, S. (2003). Interpreters in the educational setting. *The AVLIC News*, *19*(32), 4–6.

Russell, D., & Malcolm, K. (1992). Interpreting in Canada. In J. Plant-Moeller (Ed.). *Expanding horizons: Proceedings of the Twelfth National Convention of the Registry of Interpreters for the Deaf* (pp. 23–36). RID Publications.

Russell, D. (2019). Internatiaonal perspectives and practices in health care interpreting with sign language interpreters: How does Canada compare? In M. Ji, M. Taibi, & I. Crezee (Eds.), *Multicultural health translation, interpreting and communication* (pp. 37–66). Routledge.

Russell, D., McLaughlin, J., & Demko, R. (2017). *Barrier-free emergency communication for deaf and hard of hearing people*. Canadian Hearing Society.

Scully, L. (1999). One plus three equals more. *The AVLIC News*, *15*(3), 5.

Stone, C. (2009). *Toward a deaf translation norm*. Gallaudet University Press.

Stratiy, A. (2005). Best practices in interpreting: A deaf community perspective. In T. Janzen (Ed.), *Topics in signed language interpreting: Theory and practice* (pp. 231–250). John Benjamins Publishing.

XIAOYAN XIAO, WEI LU, AND XIAO ZHAO

6

Sign Language Interpreter Education in China

Situated in southeastern Asia, China is the world's most populated country, with 1.41 billion people according to the latest census released in 2021.[1] Jacques (2009, p. 196) once commented that "China is, by the standards of every other country, a most peculiar animal." With 56 ethnic groups, China enjoys very rich linguistic diversity. Such diversity places pressure on communication between different linguistic groups and raises concerns in terms of the unity of the country. Therefore, since 1920, a standard version of Chinese, Mandarin Chinese (or *Putonghua*), belonging to the family of the northern dialects, has been promoted and used in schools, in the media, and on official occasions. Standardization has also been a key theme in minority language policy. Although promoting the use of a common language to hold China together is a practical solution, Guo (2004) points out that when initially implementing Putonghua, policymakers and speakers of numerous Chinese dialects had the misconception that Putonghua should replace dialects that were believed to be inferior to the standard Chinese language.

The emphasis placed on needing a standard language for all and the perceived inferiority of dialects have also been reflected throughout the contemporary history of Chinese deaf education and sign language interpreting (SLI) education. China is home to the world's largest deaf population, 20.04 million from the 2010 census[2] at the time of writing (specific data are not yet available from the 2021 census). In China, deaf people have long been viewed as disabled with a medical condition. The discussion of deafness as a cultural and linguistic identity has only recently entered the discourse (Gong, 2009; Zhao, 2015). A sympathetic attitude toward people with disabilities is deeply rooted in Chinese society, which has been influenced by Confucianism (Deng & Harris, 2008). In the Law of China on the Protection of Disabled Persons (1990),[3] disability is defined as a physical or mental "deficit." It is therefore based on the presence or absence of impairment, and there is a clear divide between those who are "normal" (nondisabled) and those who are "abnormal" (disabled). This conceptualization of deaf people is vividly reflected by a Chinese term that is widely used to refer to any kind of disability: 残疾 (read as *can ji*). 残 literally means "incomplete" and 疾 "illness" (Guo et al., 2005). Thus, the historic importance attached to having a standard language and the definition of deafness as disability have affected both how deaf signers perceive themselves and their language and how the education sector perceives what is the right education for the deaf people.

The first deaf school in China was founded in 1887 by an American missionary Annetta T. Mills (the Chefoo School), which encouraged the proliferation of deaf education and formation of deaf community in China during the following decades (Widmer, 2023; Wan, 2024). After the founding of the People's Republic of China in 1949, supportive policies were offered to deaf individuals, predominantly in the field of education. The Chinese government set up "schools for deaf-mutes" and implemented several laws and regulations, such as the Regulations on Education for Individuals With Disabilities. Around the early 1950s, 42 such schools existed, providing education to about 2,400 students (Lytle et al., 2005).

After the third National Conference on Civil Affairs in 1955, the Ministry of the Interior (later known as the Ministry of Civil Affairs) set up an agency that specialized in social welfare management. More attention was given to employment issues faced by disadvantaged groups. Under the guidance of local governments, deaf people who were capable of basic work were organized into "production groups" and participated in handicraft industry or other small-scale industrial production. Factories that provided job opportunities for disabled people became known as "social welfare factories" (Han, 2020). Apart from the limited salaries paid by welfare factories, deaf people also received extra monthly allowances for living expenses from local departments of civil affairs.

Government efforts to provide work and education resources to the deaf population inevitably encountered the need to solve the "problems" caused by Chinese Sign Language (CSL). The term CSL is used to refer to the quite different sign language systems used in China by different stakeholders. Although an increasing number of researchers, educators, and deaf people acknowledge that the indigenous CSL used by deaf signers should be regarded as the first language of Chinese signers, many (especially hearing educators of deaf children) believe that CSL is no more than a derivative and a visual form of the Chinese language, rather than a language in its own right (Zhang & Huang, 2013, p. 29). Standardizing CSL has been an important mission and has gained support not only from the authorities but also from deaf signers themselves (Xiao & Yu, 2009; Liu et al., 2013). Though mistakes have been made, for example, regarding signed Chinese as the standardized CSL (Shen, 2008), the situation has been improving. In 2019, four volumes of *The Dictionary of Chinese National Sign Language* containing more than 8,200 lexical items were published as a national effort to create a standardized lexicon of CSL. The title itself is an improvement over the previous lexical collection, which was misleadingly titled *The Chinese Sign Language* (1990). Currently, there is very limited research on the grammar of CSL, although a team of scholars from Shanghai have begun to explore CSL linguistics (e.g., Ni, 2007; Li, 2010; Lin, 2016).

Who Are We?

Xiaoyan Xiao is a professor from Xiamen University China. She has many years of experience training spoken language interpreters and teaching Chinese Sign Language with Deaf co-instructors. For the past 2 decades, her research interests have mainly focused on sign language interpreting and deaf studies. She has received a number of grants to investigate SLI and interpreter education in China and has published extensively on these themes.

Wei Lu is a deaf lecturer from Zhejiang Vocational College of Special Education China. He has a master's degree in SLI from Korea Nazarene University in South Korea. He is the only educator in the SLI program of his institute. He currently teaches International Sign, CSL for Specific Purposes, and Interpreting into CSL.

Xiao Zhao is an assistant professor from Xiamen University. She has a doctorate from Heriot-Watt University in the United Kingdom. Her current research interests include the social aspects of interpreting, both in the spoken and signed modes.

As a team composed of one deaf researcher and two hearing researchers, we bring unique perspectives to this research on SLI education in China. Our deaf researcher, Wei Lu, has firsthand experience with SLI and is a trainer and a deaf interpreter himself, providing us with an insider's perspective on the complexities and nuances of this field. On the other hand, our two hearing researchers, Xiaoyan Xiao, a pioneering researcher in China who has focused on investigating SLI and SLI education and has led reforms in SLI textbook development and testing in China, and Xiao Zhao, who has been carrying out research in SLI since 2011, bring a different perspective that is informed by their academic and professional experiences.

Being based in China, we are familiar with the local educational context and the role of sign language interpreters, especially the obstacles deaf people and SLI educators encounter within the Chinese society. The collaboration demonstrated by this chapter between deaf and hearing researchers confirms that diverse perspectives can coalesce into a comprehensive and nuanced understanding of SLI education in China. Our varied experiences, both personal and professional, enrich our approach and enable us to scrutinize the subject matter from multiple angles.

CONTEXTUALIZATION: TRANSLATION AND INTERPRETING IN CHINA

According to the Language Industry Report released by the Translator's Association of China 2020,[4] the output of language industry in China totaled RMB 38.4 billion (or USD 6 billion) in 2019 and RMB 36.6 billion (or USD 5.7 billion) in 2020 despite the impact of the pandemic. The top five languages in demand are English, Japanese, German, French, and Russian. The report also mentioned minority languages and languages (or dialects) for the Poverty Alleviation Campaign. However, there is no mention of sign language–related services, as language access for deaf people has remained within the work scope of the China Disabled People's Federation (CDPF) and CSL-related research is still housed mainly under the discipline of Special Education (SE).

The Chinese Ministry of Education listed interpreting as a compulsory course for all English majors across the country in 2000 to meet the increasing needs for international exchanges. In 2006 and 2007, respectively, the Bachelor of Translation and Interpreting (BTI) and the Master of Translation and Interpreting (MTI) programs were set up, as an endeavor to prepare skilled professionals for the cultural, social, and economic developments of the nation. By 2023, there are in total 316 MTI programs and 309 BTI programs[5] across the country, offering translation and interpreting programs between Mandarin Chinese and 11 other languages, namely English, French, Japanese, Russian, German, Spanish, Italian, Arabic, Korean, Thai, and Vietnamese.[6]

PROFESSIONALIZATION OF SIGN LANGUAGE INTERPRETERS IN CHINA

During the initial phase, after the founding of the People's Republic of China in 1949, federations for the disabled were established at both the national and local levels. People affiliated with those federations, without professional training and status, were regularly assigned interpreting tasks for deaf people (Guo & Zhang, 2007). It was not until 2007 that SLI was officially listed as a "new" profession by the Ministry of China Labor and Social Security.[7] However, currently there is no official registration system at the national level for sign language interpreters. In 2008, the Ministry published a National Occupational Standard Test for CSL Interpreters (Pilot Edition). This test consisted of three levels. Through 2017, more than 8,000 test takers were awarded certificates.[8] However, because of poor design and bitter complaints from deaf signers that certificate holders were not competent to interpret, the test was suspended in 2017. In March and May 2023, the Chinese National Association of the Deaf (CNAD) released new documents: *Specifications for Sign Language Translation (Part I: Interpreting Services)* and *Specifications for Assessing*

Chinese Sign Language Interpreters. Meanwhile, a new certification test for SLI is in preparation and due to be released in 2024.

Previous studies by Xiao's team (Xiao & Yu, 2009; Xiao & Li, 2013; Xiao et al., 2015; Xiao et al., 2018) give a glimpse into the status quo of SLI as a profession in China:

- The overwhelming majority (81%) of the interpreters reported working on a part-time basis.
- The rate of general satisfaction with SLI services among deaf signers is low.
- Topping the list of reasons for such dissatisfaction is the incomprehensibility of interpreters' signing.
- The majority of deaf viewers (76%) have difficulty comprehending the signed renditions of news programs, which are now available on more than 300 Chinese national and local television channels.[9]
- Interpreters report that their biggest challenge at work is difficulty in understanding deaf individuals' signing.
- There is a mismatch between where SLI is provided (e.g., conferences and television) and where deaf people most need SLI (e.g., hospitals).

China is currently witnessing an emerging trend of deaf interpreters, albeit in limited numbers. This scarcity can be attributed to the lack of SLI education programs in the country that accommodate deaf students. Consequently, aspirants, such as the deaf author of this article, are compelled to seek educational opportunities abroad in countries like South Korea to secure a diploma in SLI. Upon returning to China, these deaf interpreters normally work at international conferences. They often bridge the communication gap by interpreting between different sign languages or mediating between local variations of CSL and general CSL. This role becomes particularly critical in settings such as police stations. However, it is worth noting that, at present, there are no full-time employment opportunities specifically for deaf interpreters.

Sign Language Interpreter Education in China

Dilemmas observed in China's SLI market reflect problems in SLI education. The first post-secondary SLI program was established in Zhengzhou University of Technology (or ZUT) in 2004. Currently there are four SLI programs,[10] with the other three being the Nanjing Normal University of Special Education (2005–); Zhengzhou Normal University (2012–)[11] and Zhejiang Vocational College of Special Education (2015–). There is no standard curriculum design for this "new" major (Xiao et al., 2020). Thus, each program can refer only to the curriculum structure of SE to arrange courses (Wang, 2012). Because a large proportion of the courses focus on CSL acquisition, courses on interpreting skills and domain knowledge are a rather small proportion of the program (Han, 2013).

As of the 2020–2021 academic year, each of these programs enrolled approximately 30 students who had no prior knowledge of CSL. To date, only one hard of hearing student has been admitted into the Nanjing program in 2019. This student had no prior signing experience either. The 3-year and 4-year academic programs adopt distinct 2+1 and 3+1 structures, respectively. Under this scheme, students dedicate the initial 2 years (for 3-year programs) or 3 years (for 4-year programs) to on-campus study. The final year, however, is reserved for practical internships that provide field experience.

The majority of the instructors in these SLI programs are from an SE background. The ZUT program employs three deaf instructors who teach mainly CSL. The Nanjing program also employs three full-time deaf instructors who teach CSL, deaf culture, and some interpreting courses. The Zhejiang program employs one deaf instructor (i.e., the second author of the present paper) who teaches CSL, International Sign, and interpreting into CSL. The Zhengzhou Normal University program currently does not have deaf instructor in their SLI program, but there are deaf instructors in other programs who teaches CSL. In interviews we have conducted with educators, both hearing and deaf, it is clear that there is a lack of communication or coordination among them in designing course structure and content. The course leaders and lead educators of these programs all share an urgent need for teaching resources, especially CSL videos suited to different levels. Educators are struggling to find appropriate materials and have to source whatever is available. In a classroom observation by the first author, the educator teaching simultaneous interpreting was found to be using a Chinese/English interpreting textbook, using only the Chinese texts in the book as source texts. Other educators resort to newspaper reports or online personal video postings for teaching, though some programs have developed their own textbooks (e.g., Zhang & Ren, 2015; Bai, 2016; Fu, 2019). Nevertheless, resources are still very much limited.

Most of the educators report that they need further training on pedagogy and assessment to improve the teaching quality. The four program leaders also expressed a deep concern that because of the lack of employment opportunities for CSL interpreters, students lack motivation (see Gao, 2019), and the programs are under pressure to shut down. One of the Nanjing program educators commented that after the Nanjing program was promoted to being the only BTI program in China, students have more difficulty finding a job because SE schools, the biggest employer for SLI graduates (see Peng, 2020), are less willing to take their graduates because they do not hold a teacher's certificate.

According to a survey of recent graduates (n = 162, graduated between 2018 and 2020) of these programs (Peng, 2020), SE schools and rehabilitation agencies employ more than half of the graduates (33% and 21% of the graduates, respectively). Most of the graduates surveyed (76%) self-evaluated their level of signing as being intermediate[12] (able to understand or use CSL in daily life) or lower and are confident interpreting only for nontechnical everyday interactions or in SE classrooms. When asked whether they would like to pursue a master's degree in SLI (none available in China at the time of writing), the majority of participants responded in favor of doing so, with 48% answering with a definite "yes" and another 40% selecting "very likely."

Course leaders (e.g., Fu, 2017a) admit that the lack of practice courses in the current curricula has resulted in graduates not being ready for work upon graduation. This is also reflected in previous studies, which show that deaf signers attribute their dissatisfaction with interpreting quality to the interpreters' poor signing and interpreting skills, as well as their lack of subject knowledge and level of professionalism (Xiao et al., 2018).

All programs encourage students to engage with the deaf community on campus. One common advantage of all four of these programs is that the host institutions enroll a large number of deaf students who study art, bakery, or photography. For experienced teachers in these programs, they usually teach classes directly in CSL. For new teachers or contracted professionals, the programs provide SLI services in class, or when the demand cannot be met, resort to voice-to-text technology. Professional interpreters and senior SLI students are often hired to provide interpreting services. Apart from this, the large deaf cohort creates many opportunities for SLI on campus. University departments prefer to hire student assistants and volunteers majoring in SLI, and public event organizers also hire interpreters from the SLI major. SLI students are also encouraged to engage with the deaf community through mixed residence arrangements and other campus activities.

Research on SLI Education, Training, and Assessment

There is a small handful of published papers in China that discuss SLI education. Some papers introduce the practice of SLI programs in countries like the United States and South Korea (e.g., Bai, 2011; Meng, 2010; Xiao & Zhang, 2017a, 2017b, 2017c; Yin, 2018). Other authors discuss issues relating to the SLI curriculum and pedagogy (Bai, 2013; Fu, 2017a; Luo, 2017; Wang et al., 2019; Xu, 2013; Zhang et al., 2019). Fu (2017b) criticized the current CSL courses that focus on teaching individual vocabulary because of the lack of theoretical guidance on CSL linguistics and called for a change of perspective to align more with the teaching principles for second-language acquisition.

Building on the firsthand data collected from the Chinese SLI market and the four current SLI programs, Xiao et al. (2020) identified issues that required immediate resolution and proposed a Chinese model for SLI education that offers degrees full time or part time from associate level to doctorate, in both special education (current programs) and in translation studies (future programs).

To address the scarcity of suitable SLI teaching resources, a new set of CSL interpreting textbooks have been developed. These textbooks include basic SLI theories and provide relevant topics; the books have been carefully designed to ensure their level of difficulty is appropriate for the learner (Xiao, 2021, 2022).

The Road Ahead

The Chinese central government has been making efforts to increase accessibility for deaf persons as designated by the Accessibility Decree of the State Council which became law taking effect in 2023.[13] One of the most visible events is the provision of sign language–interpreted news programs. Police and courts are another area in which SLI services are guaranteed according to the Provisions on the Procedures for Handling Criminal Cases by Public Security Organizations.[14] It is not surprising that in the previous two nationwide surveys Xiao's team has conducted, the police and court settings were ranked as the first- and third-most needed areas of interpreting access (Xiao & Yu, 2009; Xiao et al., 2018).

In recent years, encouraging changes have been taking place in some cities to overcome deaf patients' difficulties in accessing medical services. The city of Shanghai took the lead in 2012 and has been providing SLI services in some of its hospitals. Since 2014 and 2017, respectively, financed by the local chapters of the CDPF, deaf people in Beijing[15] and in Xiamen[16] can request CSL interpreters to access public services, such as hospitals and banks.

The Sign Language Interpreting Committee (SLIC) of the CNAD was set up in 2018. Since 2019, SLIC has been hosting interpreting training crash courses for CSL interpreters selected from each of China's provinces, including the Tibet and Xinjiang autonomous regions. Another effort led by SLIC is the creation of a new national certification test to replace the previous test, which was suspended in 2017. The first author has been heavily involved in the designing and rolling out of the new test which has drawn on interpreting testing principles generally. We have referred to SLI tests administered by the Registry of Interpreters for the Deaf (RID) in the United States and the National Accreditation Authority for Translators and Interpreters (NAATI) in Australia and have taken into full consideration the realities of SLI in China. The new test scheme was trialed in 2021 and 2022. At the time of writing, a nationwide rollout is under planning.

With raised awareness of information accessibility in China, there is increased potential for paid sign language translation (SLT) work. In China, this type of work is only just beginning to gain recognition, even though translation is not new to deaf people, as many deaf people have shared and translated stories and commentaries, as well as provided sign language lessons online, adding Chinese captions to cater to a wider audience.[17] Another type of commonly seen SLT is signed songs,[18] which have been an unusually popular form of entertainment and performance for learners of CSL and the general public. Deaf translators have also been translating Chinese poetry into CSL (see Lin, 2021) in a competition hosted by the Shanghai Deaf Association in 2018. Additionally, a signed version of the "Three Gorges Museum Introduction" has recently been released,[19] signaling initial efforts to create information accessibility in culture and heritage domains like museums. Looking ahead, there is great potential for SLT in the marketplace, and according to the Accessibility Law of 2023, all government websites need be accessible for deaf and blind people. To the best of the authors' knowledge, no official website in China has a CSL window as of the time of writing this chapter.

In sum, with improvements in legislation and regulations and with increased public awareness of accessibility, China is yet to unleash its great potential as one of the world's largest SLI and SLT markets, if not *the* largest.

Notes

1. See http://www.stats.gov.cn/tjsj/zxfb/202105/t20210510_1817176.html
2. See http://www.stats.gov.cn/tjgz/tjdt/200612/t20061205_16908.html
3. See http://www.scio.gov.cn/32344/32345/32347/33466/xgzc33472/Document/1449134/1449134.htm
4. See https://mp.weixin.qq.com/s/zE1niXWOmS2UGZ96Exv6jw
5. See https://cnbti.gdufs.edu.cn/info/1006/1595.htm
6. See https://yz.chsi.com.cn/zsml/zyfx_search.jsp
7. See http://www.nptb.org/xwdetail.asp?id=50
8. Information from presentation by Guowei Yang at the Forum for Translation and Interpreting Education and Assessment, Xiamen, April 2–3, 2021.
9. See http://www.cdpf.org.cn/sjzx/tjgb/202004/t20200402_674393.shtml
10. A fifth program set up in 2011 in Yinhkou Vocational College was suspended since 2022 because of a disappointing employment rate among its graduates. Personal communication with the program leader. The timeline for the resumption of this program remains uncertain.
11. Zhengzhou Normal University program experienced a suspension between the years 2019 and 2022. The program resumed operation in fall 2023.
12. The original survey divides students into four levels: elementary, intermediate, advanced, and professional. At the elementary level, students are able to understand or use some basic vocabulary but might not understand or sign full sentences. At the intermediate level, students are able to understand or use CSL in daily life. At the advanced level, students are able to understand or use CSL in professional settings to some extent. At the professional level, students self-identify as being able to fully understand CSL and use CSL in professional settings fluently.
13. See http://www.gov.cn/gongbao/content/2012/content_2182743.htm; 中华人民共和国无障碍环境建设法__中国政府网 (www.gov.cn)
14. See http://www.gov.cn/gongbao/content/2013/content_2332778.htm
15. See http://www.cndcm.cn/html/shehui/todoctor/16302_1.html
16. See http://www.siming.gov.cn/xxgk/xwgg/jrsm/201708/t20170816_661990.htm
17. See for instance https://mp.weixin.qq.com/s/lhYWPsIML6p8vHAeCdNHXQ

18. See for instance https://mp.weixin.qq.com/s/tSHGq5GYe8LuZ2DM3oKA2w
19. See https://www.163.com/dy/article/GAONS8CA0541ES64.html

REFERENCES

Bai, R. (2011). A comparative study of Chinese and South Korean higher sign language translation education systems. *Journal of Zhongzhou University*, *28*(6), 96–98.

Bai, R. (2013). Exploring cooperation models for sign language interpreting major in universities. *Journal of Suihua University*, *33*(10), 5–10.

Bai, R. (2016). *Practical guidance on sign language interpreting*. Zhengzhou University Press.

Chinese National Association of the Deaf. (2010). *The Chinese sign language*. Huaxia Publishing House.

Chinese National Association of the Deaf. (2023a). *Specifications for sign language translation (Part I: Interpreting services)*. Huaxia Publishing House.

Chinese National Association of the Deaf. (2023b). *Specifications for Assessing Chinese Sign Language Interpreters*. Huaxia Publishing House.

Deng, M., & Harris, K. (2008). Meeting the needs of students with disabilities in general education classrooms in China. *Teacher Education and Special Education: The Journal of the Teacher Education Division of the Council for Exceptional Children*, *31*(3), 195–207.

Fu, M. (2017a). Construction of ladder practical teaching system for sign language translation major. *Experimental Technology and Management*, *34*(05), 165–169.

Fu, M. (2017b). *A study on the teaching reform of sign language teaching from the perspective of linguistics*. Hangzhou Normal University.

Fu, M. (2019). *Basics of sign language interpreting*. Zhengzhou University Press.

Gao, X. (2019). *Sign language interpreting students' motivations and expectations*. Xiamen University.

Gong, Q. (2009). Linguistic analysis of issues between sign language and Chinese in deaf education. *Chinese Journal of Special Education*, *105*(3), 63–67.

Guo, B., Bricout, J. C., & Huang, J. (2005). A common open space or a digital divide? A social model perspective on the online disability community in China. *Disability & Society*, *20*(1), 49–66.

Guo, H., & Zhang, N. (2007). The history and professionalization of sign language interpreting in America. *Journal of Zhongzhou University*, *2*, 74–77.

Guo, L. (2004). The relationship between Putonghua and Chinese dialects. In M. Zhou and H. Sun (Eds.), *Language policy in the People's Republic of China* (pp. 45–54). Springer.

Han, M. (2013). A study of the cultivation model of sign language interpreting talents in universities. *Journal of Nanjing Technical College of Special Education*, *4*, 25–29.

Jacques, M. (2009). *When China rules the world: The end of the Western world and the birth of a new global order*. Penguin.

Li, X. (2010). *Investigation into the classifier construction of Shanghai Sign Language* [Unpublished doctoral dissertation]. Fudan University.

Lin, H. (2016). *On the interrogative of Shanghai variety of Chinese Sign Language* [Unpublished doctoral dissertation]. Fudan University.

Lin, H. (2021). Translation or creation? A case study of signed Chinese poetry from the perspective of multimodality theory. *Journal of Specialized Translation*, *35*(1), 209–230.

Liu, Y., Gu, D., Cheng, L., & Wei, D. (2013). Survey of sign language use in China. *Applied Linguistics*, *2*, 35–41.

Luo, Q. (2017). Cultivating the training of sign language in the perspective of globalization. *Journal of Zhongzhou University, 34*(3), 112–116.

Lytle, R. R., Johnson, K. E., & Hui, Y. J. (2005). Deaf education in China: History, current issues, and emerging deaf voices. *American Annals of the Deaf, 150*(5), 457–469.

Meng, F. (2010). An enlightenment of the development of sign language translation major in American universities. *Journal of Zhongzhou University, 27*(2), 41–43.

Ni, L. (2007). *Research on the directions of verbs in Chinese Sign Language* [Unpublished doctoral dissertation]. Fudan University.

Peng, Y. (2020). *Sign language interpreter education in China: An integrated approach to curriculum*. Xiamen University.

Shen, Y. (2008). Problems of and thought on the diversification, standardization and language development of sign language: The standardization of Chinese sign language learning from CLSLR2 Conference in Netherlands. *Chinese Journal of Special Education (6)*, 34–40.

Wan, S. (2024). The formation of the Deaf community in China, 1887–1945. *Review of Disability Studies: An International Journal, 18/19*, 1–24.

Wang, F., Xu, H. & Sun, S. (2019). The importance of sign language textbooks to the teaching of sign language interpreting major. *Journal of Suihua University, 39* (7), 38–40.

Wang, X. (2012). Study on curriculum design of sign language interpreting in higher vocational colleges and universities. *Jiangxi Education, 12*, 18–19.

Widmer, E. (2023). Schooling the blind and deaf of China: Mary West Niles and Annetta Thompson Mills, and their legacies. *The Journal of American-East Asian Relations, 30*, 351–391.

Xiao, S., & Zhang, N. (2017a). Cultivation mechanism and enlightenment of sign language interpreters in Western countries I. *Modern Special Education, 17*, 71–73.

Xiao, S., & Zhang, N. (2017b). Cultivation mechanism and enlightenment of sign language interpreters in Western countries II. *Modern Special Education, 19*, 70–73.

Xiao, S., & Zhang, N. (2017c). Cultivation mechanism and enlightenment of sign language interpreters in Western countries III. *Modern Special Education, 21*, 69–70.

Xiao, X. (2021). *The coursebook of sign language interpreting: levels I*. Shanghai Foreign Language Education Press.

Xiao, X. (2022). *The coursebook of sign language interpreting: levels II-III*. Shanghai Foreign Language Education Press.

Xiao, X., & Li, F. (2013). Sign language interpreting on Chinese TV: A survey on user perspectives. *Perspectives: Studies in Translatology, 21*(1), 100–116.

Xiao, X., & Yu, R. (2009). Survey on sign language interpreting in China. *Interpreting, 11*(2), 137–163.

Xiao, X., Gao, X. & Zhao, X. (2018). Survey on sign language interpreting in mainland China: The status quo, problems and solutions. *Chinese Translators Journal, 6*, 66–72.

Xiao, X., & Han, C. (2022). A Comparative Judgment Approach to assessing Chinese sign language interpreting, *Language Testing, 39*(2), 289–312.

Xiao, X., Peng, Y. & Deng, Y. (2020). Sign language interpreter education: In search of a Chinese model. *Journal of Foreign Languages, 43*, 98–106.

Xiao, X., Chen, X. & Palmer, J. (2015). Chinese viewers' comprehension of signed language interpreting on television: An experimental study. *Interpreting, 17*, 91–117.

Xu, J. (2013). First exploration on "studio" teaching mode for sign language interpreting specialty in higher vocational schools. *Vocational and Technical Education, 34*(5), 35–37.

Yin, Y. (2018). The development of sign language policy and education in Republic of Korea and its enlightenment. *Language Policy & Language Education*, *42*, 56–61.

Zhang, F., Yuan, X. & Lu, W. (2019). Design of teaching situation in the practical teaching of sign language from the perspective of embodied cognition. *Research and Exploration in Laboratory*, *5*, 260–264.

Zhang, N., & Huang, L. (2013). Two views of sign language. *Modern Special Education*, *1*, 29–30.

Zhang, N., & Ren, H. (2015). *Introduction to sign language interpreting*. Zhengzhou University Press.

Zhao, X. (2015). *Constructing linguistic identity and interpreting: A case study of sign language interpreting on Chinese television for high-profile political conferences* [Unpublished doctoral dissertation]. Heriot-Watt University.

NAĎA HYNKOVÁ DINGOVÁ, DENISA
LACHMANOVÁ, AND RADKA NOVÁKOVÁ

7

Czech Sign Language Interpreting

Development of the Profession in the 20th and 21st Centuries

The Czech Republic (also known as Czechia) is a landlocked state located in central Europe that borders Germany to the west, Poland to the northeast, Slovakia to the east, and Austria to the south.

It is a pluralist multiparty parliamentary representative democracy. The head of the state is the president, and the head of government is the prime minister. The parliament has legislative power, and it is bicameral (has two legislative chambers), consisting of the Chamber of Deputies and the Senate. The juridical power is divided into a four-level court system plus the Constitutional Court. The capital city is Prague. The Czech Republic covers an area of 78,866 square kilometers with 10.7 million inhabitants living in three historical territories (Bohemia, Moravia, and Czech Silesia). The current administrative division of the country is into 14 self-governing regions.

The official language is Czech, which is used by most of the population. However, many people use other languages, one of which is Czech Sign Language (CzSL). Under current legislation, which we will discuss later in relation to the professionalization of CzSL interpreting, members of so-called "traditional minorities" can use their languages for official purposes. For Czech deaf people, the presence of an interpreter during court hearings, police investigations, and most official hearings is a matter of course.

WHO ARE WE?

Naďa is hearing and was born and raised in the Czech Republic. She always answers the question about how she became an interpreter by saying that it happened by accident. She never ceases to be amazed by this, and she says that there is no such thing as a coincidence. She did not want to go to college; rather, she wanted to get married and have lots of children. Living peacefully in her native Cheb, she had a long-standing deaf acquaintance.

But Nad'a's environment pushed her to study. She looked for a field where she could just send an application and they would not accept her—and everyone would be happy that way. Her finger fell on the Drama Education for the Deaf program at the Janáček Academy of Music and Performing Arts in Brno. Only when she arrived did she find out that it was a course intended only for deaf people. Forty of them were having fun around her, all communicating in sign language, and she did not understand anything. She encountered sign language for the first time. For many classmates who had had bad experiences with hearing people, she was a pleasant surprise. She wanted to run away. The talent contests tested visual memory, movement and expression skills, and the art of dramatization. She gradually got used to the environment, and it started to seem very interesting to her. In the end, the program accepted her, but they had no idea how to deal with her. They were not prepared for a hearing student. Her acceptance was given on the condition that she learn to communicate with deaf classmates within a year; otherwise, she would be transferred to another course. In 2016, she completed her studies at the Janáček Academy of Music and Performing Arts in Brno.

As part of her studies, Nad'a completed an internship at the experimental kindergarten Pipan in Prague and decided that she did not want to teach young deaf children. When she was approached by the Television Club for the Deaf to interpret and write scripts, the option grew on her. She could not imagine doing anything else. She was comfortable with a certain level of depersonalization—that is, that she did not have to stand for herself but rather functioned as an intermediary.

Nad'a has interpreted in just about every arena, from schools to senior clubs, community interpreting, court interpreting, and more. She began interpreting at Charles University in Prague and later also taught future interpreters.

From 2001 to 2005, Nad'a was a deputy chairperson of the Czech Chamber of Interpreters in the Czech Republic, and from 2006 to 2011, she headed the organization. In 2004, she became a member of the expert commission on issues of interpreting for deaf people at the Association of Organizations of Deaf and Hard of Hearing in the Czech Republic. She also studied one semester of deaf studies at the University of Central Lancashire in Preston in the United Kingdom from 2011 to 2012. Several times, she also attended courses in British Sign Language at the University of Bristol in the United Kingdom and in American Sign Language at the Rochester Institute of Technology in the United States of America.

Since the COVID-19 pandemic, Nad'a has also been interpreting for television broadcast news on state television and interpreting television press conferences and in the Senate of the Czech Republic.

Denisa is hearing with no relationship to the deaf community. After completing grammar school in Prague, she had an idea that she would study at university in the field of speech therapy. In 2011, she visited the open house of the Faculty of Arts at Charles University in Prague, and she was charmed by two different institutes: the Institute of Phonetics and the Institute of Deaf Studies (IDS). She completed bachelor's degrees in both areas. Then she continued with her master's degree studies at the IDS, and she became more self-confident in communicating in CzSL.

In 2016, Denisa was offered work at the IDS as an interpreter. She enthusiastically agreed and has been an internal employee ever since. In 2017, she became a member of a team in the editorial department of news broadcasting in CzSL on Czech Television. She believes that the team of deaf editors with a deaf news presenter is the best environment in which to work. She also has experience in community interpreting. However, she prefers to interpret at conferences and educational seminars. During the COVID-19 pandemic, she interpreted television broadcasting news on state television. Then she went on maternity leave.

One of Denisa's most important career experiences was being a member of the team in the PRO-Sign Common European Framework of Reference (CEFR) for languages project linked to CzSL (2019–2022).[1] Two of the main outcomes of the project are the Framework of Reference for Sign Languages and the Reference Level Descriptors of CzSL for levels A1–B2. She would like other teams abroad to learn about this project and continue further international cooperation in this area.

Radka was born deaf into a deaf family in Prague. CzSL was the first language in which she communicated and the language in which she learned about the world from her parents. A powerful leader in the Czech Republic who is an expert in linguistics and translation, Radka loved mathematics and numbers in high school. However, the college introduced her to language and linguistics.

She was among the first students of deaf studies at Charles University in Prague in 1998. During her studies, in 2005, she completed a study visit at the Centre for Deaf Studies at the University of Bristol in the United Kingdom. In 2000, she also studied a 1-year internship at Gallaudet University in Washington, DC, in the United States.

In 2000, together with her deaf colleague Petr Vysuček, Radka founded the *Pevnost* (Czech Sign Language Center), an organization that provides CzSL courses to the public to the present day. The founding of the organization by deaf people themselves was a pioneering step in 2000.

From 2000 to 2008, Radka worked in news broadcasting in CzSL on the Czech state television as a news presenter. Then she changed her role, and she has been working as an editor until now. After completing her master's degree at the Faculty of Arts, she became an academic staff member; since 2003, she has been working in deaf studies.

Radka is also proud to be one of the team involved in the PRO-Sign CEFR in the project on CzSL (2019–2022). She provided the translation of the summary of the project in International Sign on the project webpage. She shares all her knowledge about CEFR and sign languages with her colleagues abroad and presents on this topic at international conferences.

CONTEXTUALIZATION: TRANSLATION AND INTERPRETING IN THE CZECH REPUBLIC

Professional translation and interpreting of CzSL have been hot topics over the past three decades, even though the first sign language interpreter was registered on the list of court interpreters in 1956. This step did not immediately lead to any significant changes in the systematic education of interpreters or to any enhancement of their working conditions. For a long period, deaf people and their language needs were not respected.

Transition to a Democratic Society and Establishment of a University Program

After the transition from the communist regime to a democratic society in the 1990s, the atmosphere in the former Czechoslovak Republic and later the Czech Republic became more open to various changes, including new attitudes toward deaf people. An important milestone was the year 1998. The first (and still the only) deaf studies program was launched in combination with the Czech language and literature program within the Institute of Czech Language and Theory of Communication at the Faculty of Arts, Charles University, in Prague.

With regard to education on the translation and interpreting of spoken languages, the Institute of Translation Studies was established in 1963 at the Faculty of Arts, Charles University, in Prague. It belongs to the European translation study program, which has a long history. The translation study programs in other European countries started after the Second World War. It is also a unique program in the Czech Republic focused on translation and interpreting education and offering bachelor's, master's, and doctor of philosophy (PhD) programs. The founders of this program were Prague linguistic experts. This was similar to the situation in the 1990s and the foundation of the IDS.

The academic environment has become a focal point and at the same time the driving force behind systematic research of sign language and its application in practice (applied linguistics). This important change was possible thanks to Professor Macurová. She was the leading figure in the first academic research on CzSL.

Laws and Self-Esteem Among Deaf People

The interpreting situation has always been shaped by the political situation, which is reflected in legal documents. In the area of interpreting for deaf people, several legal norms have been accepted, which influence the form and manner of provision of interpreting services for deaf people. Before 1998, the right of deaf people to have an interpreter (more precisely, an "interpreter for contacts with the deaf and dumb") was mentioned only in the Act on Experts and Interpreters (1967). The act of 1967 was not primarily intended to defend the rights of the deaf community.

The fundamental legal document that guarantees the right to communicate in CzSL is Act No. 155/1998 Coll., "On Communication Systems of Deaf and Deaf-blind Persons," as amended by Act No. 384/2008 Coll. In its first form, this act was adopted by the parliament of the Czech Republic in 1998. It was amended in the autumn of 2008 ("The Act on Communication Systems of Deaf and Deafblind People"), exactly 10 years later. The main aims of the amendment were to suppress the term *sign system* as much as possible and to include other communication forms, such as visualization of the spoken Czech language and its written record (speech-to-text reporting) among the means of communication of deaf people. The main goal was to ensure that deaf people were not discriminated against. In addition to sign language, other communication forms were added to address the communication barriers of people who do not use sign language, such as people who became deaf at a later age. Thanks to this act, deaf people and deafblind people have the right to freely choose the communication form or system that best fits their needs from the communication forms and systems listed in the act . Their choice must be fully respected so that they are entitled to be treated equally and to be active in all areas of society, including the exercising of their legal rights. This ensures that deaf people in the Czech Republic have the right to request interpreting in their chosen communication form/system and that their choice of communication form/system is respected. However, there have not yet been any implementation regulations added to this act, which complicates the fulfillment or satisfaction of the rights of deaf people in practice. This act is used by representatives of organizations that provide interpreting services for deaf people, representatives of schools for deaf children, and representatives of state administration offices involved in the creation of other laws.

The second very important law associated with the provision of interpreting services is Act No. 108/2006 Coll., "On Social Services," as amended. This act lists various types of social services and determines the types of facilities in which these services can be provided. According to this legislative standard, the majority of interpreting services are provided and paid for. It addresses primarily community interpreting—interpreting in situations such as dealing with authorities, the police, a doctor, or a bank.

Each of these two aforementioned laws determines the requirements for interpreting services (including professional and lifelong interpreter education, interpreting techniques, and quality control). Nevertheless, the profession of sign language interpreting (SLI) is not described as a profession in the catalog of occupations in the Czech Republic, which means that this profession does not formally exist. This complicates the matter significantly.

Furthermore, international laws, documents, and declarations that stressed the need to respect minorities and their right to use their language in education and social life were adopted for the Czech environment—for example, the Convention on the Rights of Persons With Disabilities, the Brussels Declaration, and the Resolution of the European Parliament on Sign Languages.

The first deaf people who were exposed to deaf studies gradually gained self-awareness and confidence. In addition, a new group was formed, called the Association of Deaf Educators and Deaf Lecturers (*Asociace neslyšících pedagogů a neslyšících lektorů* [ANEPL]; established April 16, 2016), which is for sign language teachers and deaf teachers in the Czech Republic. Some people felt very positive that change was coming, but deaf people were still being denied their language. Society strongly adhered to a medical model. For example, at the beginning of the 21st century, people (hearing heritage signers, people from the community, authorities from deaf organizations, users of signed Czech) questioned the abilities of deaf people to teach sign language. Deaf people were disadvantaged by their lack of access to education, which was nonexistent at that point. Instead of emphasizing the translation skills between CzSL and Czech, interpreters' exams tested sign language interpreters' social skills and knowledge of alternative substitutional communication systems.

PROFESSIONALIZATION OF SIGN LANGUAGE INTERPRETERS IN THE CZECH REPUBLIC

Professional interpreting has been recognized since 1956, when the first CzSL interpreter was registered on the list of court interpreters. No further advances were made throughout the 1960s. Unfortunately, no training programs for interpreters were launched, though such programs were being launched in other countries around the same time (e.g., in England, France, and Finland). It was not until the 1990s that a professional organization for CzSL interpreters was established. CzSL interpreters were gathered initially under the deaf association, the Union of the Deaf and Hard of Hearing in the Czech Republic (*Svaz neslyšících a nedoslýchavých v České republice* [SNN]).

In the mid-1990s, other organizations connecting sign language interpreters began to emerge. The first of these was the Czech Society of Sign Language Interpreters (*Česká společnost tlumočníků znakového jazyka* [CSTZJ]), established in 1995.

Later, in 1996, the Organization of Sign Language Interpreters (*Organizace tlu-močníků znakového jazyka* [OTZJ]) was introduced. Both these organizations were closely tied to the deaf association. Currently, they are no longer active.

Until another professional organization was established, hearing professionals and people not related to deaf people or sign language perceived deaf people through the medical model. They viewed themselves as superior to deaf people. Deaf people had to integrate into society with the help of an interpreter (i.e., a social worker), and they needed a unified sign system. The professional research on the sign system was the work of hearing people exclusively. Interpreting services for deaf people were considered as assistance, and the interpreters/social workers provided this assistance mostly in their free time. This attitude was influenced by the political situation in our country at that time and clearly without the involvement of deaf experts and other deaf stakeholders.

Influence From Abroad

One of the main hearing influencers involved in the changes that took place at the end of the 20th century is Vesta Dee Sauter, an American interpreter and a hearing heritage signer. She worked in the Czech Republic in the late 1990s as a religious missionary. She supported the Czech deaf community and their sign language. First, she encouraged deaf people not to be shy and to be proud of their sign language. She explained to deaf people that their language was equal to spoken language. She mentored deaf people on how to best teach CzSL, including useful and appropriate methods that are still used today. She was an ally who fought for hearing people to be respectful of deaf people, their views, and their experiences.

Additionally, Vesta mentored CzSL interpreters, especially in theater (and other types of art) interpreting and religious interpreting. Through her intense work with inexperienced sign language interpreters of CzSL and the whole Czech deaf community, she contributed to the current understanding of professional SLI in the Czech Republic. Among others, she cooperated with the IDS as a teacher of courses focused on deaf culture and deaf identity. Furthermore, she participated in the training of deaf sign language teachers and the creation of the first educational programs held by the professional organization of sign language interpreters.

Changes After 2000

After the year 2000, ideas about professional interpreter services from abroad started to appear on the Czech scene. The emphasis was placed on the strict division between two (separate) professions—the interpreter on one side and the social worker on the other side. The view of the role of interpreter as a "helper" was slowly shifting as interpreters, who were traditionally heritage signers, were advised to not assist their relatives so that they could remain neutral and objective when working as an interpreter, as the risk of losing objectivity might be higher for them. In addition to knowing sign language, theoretical knowledge of linguistics and translation studies was recognized as important for a professional interpreter to master. At the time, there was a lot of pressure on interpreters who were used to the former way of providing interpreting services. Those interpreters often preferred the role of a "helper." In this role, they gained power over deaf people to manipulate them easily. Some interpreters did not respect deaf people and often treated them as people without rights and with low abilities. Efforts have been made to develop new training programs for interpreters, as well as retraining. All these trends, however, have not been accepted positively by all interpreters. Many believed that mastering sign language skills and having experience with deaf family members were sufficient prerequisites for becoming an interpreter.

Thanks to new findings from linguistics research from the Faculty of Arts in the years 1996–2000, deaf people were gradually made aware of how valuable their language and culture were. They were introduced to public courses provided in CzSL and via professional interpreter services. New organizations came into existence that focused on these topics as well. First, Pevnost was established on May 25, 2000. The focus of this organization was teaching CzSL to the public. After some time, the training of interpreters was added as an additional goal for this organization. The second organization was the Czech Chamber of Sign Language Interpreters (*Česká komora tlumočníků znakového jazyka* [Komora]; established December 20, 2000). This is a professional organization training interpreters for deaf people, which brought a new perspective on interpreting, stressing primarily the quality of services provided.

The first major achievement came in 2000 with the creation of the Code of Ethics (CoE) written by Komora. The CoE determines the basic obligations and rights of its interpreters in the performance of their profession and connection therewith. The CoE applies in situations otherwise not regulated by law or other regulations. It has been created to fulfill clients' rights to full communication. The form of this CoE was subsequently revised in 2010.

From 2006 to 2011, Komora was also involved in international activities. In 2006, the annual meeting and conference of the European Forum of Sign Language Interpreters (efsli) was organized on its premises. In 2006 and 2008, Komora cooperated with efsli for the annual efsli Summer School, where participants learned to translate between English and their national sign languages. A year later, in 2009, Komora's representatives actively participated in the efsli annual meeting and had a presentation at the Conference in Talin. Moreover, the creation of a DVD titled *Preventing Burnout Syndrome in the Interpreting Profession* was published successfully. In 2010, Komora took part in the Eurosign Interpreter project,[2] cooperating with the University of Sussex (United Kingdom), the University of Hamburg (Germany), and the Dering Service de l'Emploi (France). The project aimed to enhance the skills of deaf sign language interpreters and create further possibilities for their application. Another important moment was in 2013, when Josefina Kalousova, a member of Komora, was elected to the efsli board.

CzSL interpreters are increasingly active in different professional organizations and expert boards, including those of spoken languages. Also, CzSL interpreters take part in various meetings with government organizations.

SIGN LANGUAGE INTERPRETER EDUCATION IN THE CZECH REPUBLIC

The education of sign language interpreters in the Czech Republic can be categorized into four areas: (1) education in deaf organizations, (2) education in professional organizations of interpreters, (3) academic education, and (4) education through a private agency.

Education in Deaf Organizations

The first training of interpreters for deaf people started to take place in deaf associations in the late 1950s. It was in the form of 2- to 4-week courses taking place every year. Thus, this was the first approach to training interpreters for interpreting with deaf people when it could not be studied at any university, and no professional organization had yet been established. The training gathered a group of around 20 interpreters who were users of the signed Czech system. The participants trained each other, checked new signed vocabulary, and discussed topics they were interested in. They obtained a certification of participation.

One of the most important achievements of a deaf organization was the establishment of the Pevnost Institute of the Deaf for Specialized Education on August 27, 2007. The Institute focused on teaching CzSL to doctors, nurses, police officers, and others who meet deaf people in various fields. One of the target groups was also CzSL interpreters. However, the Pevnost Institute no longer continued with the educational program after 2014. All activities and projects were handed over to the Pevnost Czech Sign Language Center, which was established on May 25, 2000, and offers various courses for interpreters, such as weekend courses, intensive summer and winter courses, and afternoon courses accredited by the Ministry of Labor and Social Affairs. Some courses are designed to focus on the general practice of grammar; others are dedicated to one topic, such as interpreting in driving school, mammography, or political topics; and some focus on interpreting for clients with limited communication skills. Both beginner interpreters and interpreters with longer experience attend these courses to practice their skills in CzSL.

A group consists of 8 to 12 people. After participating in the class or passing the final exam, interpreters obtain a certificate showing the number of successfully completed hours of education.

Deaf teachers in Pevnost gather regularly at seminars and participate in international projects focused on teaching hearing people and implementing the CEFR for languages into CzSL teaching and testing. For example, Pevnost was a successful organizer of the first international conference LESICO for Sign Language Teachers in 2013 in Prague.

Education in Professional Organizations of Interpreters

In the mid-1990s, professional SLI organizations began to appear, and interpreters were offered systematic education for the first time. The OTZJ, which is part of the Union of the Deaf and Hard of Hearing in the Czech Republic (*Svaz neslyšících a nedoslýchavých v*) provides sign language interpreters, interpreters' qualification courses, and training courses for the public. The interpreters were awarded accreditation of different levels, with Level I being the highest, which allowed interpreters to work in a court or police station. Level II enabled interpreters to interpret at doctor's appointments, and Level III was the lowest level, allowing interpreters to work only in daily routine situations. Although this on the surface appears to be a clear structure for awarding accreditation on the basis of skill, there was no document describing the competencies of the three levels of this accreditation. Additionally, there was no formal evaluation process, and the evaluation of interpreters depended on personal contacts and sympathy. The majority of the members of the examining board were hearing heritage signers. A minority of the members of the board were deaf signers who preferred the signed Czech system in their communication.

The first effort to provide systematic interpreter training was led by the project The Tree of Knowledge (2009–2011). It was supported by the Ministry of Labor and Social Affairs and aimed generally at educating social workers (no reference available). It was a nationwide accredited course organized by the SNN in cooperation with Komora, which provided it with content and a total of 14 lecturers. It was the first time that the biggest organization in the Czech Republic for deaf people cooperated with a professional organization for interpreters. Komora established the notion of sign language education and provided educated tutors. The course consisted of 12 weekend modules of 172 hours in total. After completing the course, the participants received a certificate. This certificate was given to them on the basis of regular attendance, a written test on the theory of interpreting, and an oral examination consisting of an interpretation from spoken Czech into CzSL and vice versa with the use of audio and video recordings. The examinations took place in front of a seven-member committee, which consisted of four representatives of Komora, one representative of the SNN, and two impartial deaf representatives who were experts in sign language. Since 2011, another similar course has not been available.

The Czech Society of Sign Language Interpreters (Česká společnost tlumočníků znakového jazyka [CSTZJ]; established 1996) did not have a separate training program for interpreters but has organized regular interpreting exams depending on the applicants' interest. These exams were usually preceded by the participation of the candidate in the weekly training (see OTZJ mentioned previously). Then the applicant was interviewed by a committee of interpreters and deaf people; he or she was asked several questions, mainly from the social field, and self-evaluated his or her own sign language translation. When the applicant passed the examination successfully, he or she received an interpreting certification of the relevant category I through III (according to the previously discussed system of categories). Although this certification was available, a certain risk was associated with the lifetime validity of any certification without appropriate continued professional development requirements in place. Interpreters within the CSTZJ were not distinguished from each other as sign language interpreters, interpreters of the signed Czech system, and lipspeakers, etc. Interpreters could take part in courses led by the deaf association in which they improved their lipspeaking skills. Unfortunately, no specialized methodology has been developed for this area. Since 2011, no activities of CSTZJ have been published (including no courses and no exams for interpreters having been organized). Today, CSTZJ does not carry out any activities. The name of the association is kept only in the database of the authorities.

Komora offered a Certification Training Program (Certifikovaný vzdělávací program [CVP]) during the period between 2004 and 2011. As part of the project, "Training of Lecturers and Creation of Teaching Materials for CzSL Interpreters, Transliterators[3] of Signed Czech, and Lipspeakers of Spoken Czech," in 2008, almost 80 different types of study materials (books, DVDs, etc.) were created. Since then, these materials have been serving as the basis for all interpreter training in the Czech Republic and Slovakia. The CVP arose from the need to provide a coherent system of SLI training that would guarantee a certain quality. It was based on the European Union's requirements for language education as set out in the CEFR. Thus, the CVP follows the standards of education in spoken languages. The required competence of the interpreter consists of language knowledge on the one hand and social, cultural, and general knowledge on the other hand. Dozens of interpreters participated in the CVP. Only 10 to 15 interpreters applied and passed the final exam.

The CVP was accessible not only to professionals in the field of hearing impairments[4] but also to the public. Seminars took place mostly on the weekends, and the language used during the seminars depended on the participants' preferences. The CVP distinguished three specializations: an interpreter of CzSL, a transliterator of signed Czech, and a visualizer (lipspeaker) of spoken Czech. Each specialization had a different length of study time. They differed also in the number of credit points to be earned in the curriculum and the number of hours of compulsory practice.

All students selected a pathway on the basis of their main interests and professional goals. Each pathway had a specific duration to take the student from start to completion. For example, becoming an interpreter required 2.5 years, becoming a transliterator of signed Czech required 1.5 years, and becoming a visualizer of spoken Czech required 1 year. The total length of study for all specializations could be extended by a maximum of 1 year.

In addition to seminars, the CVP students were also required to gain real-life experiences that aligned with their chosen pathway specialization (interpreter, transliterator, or lipspeaker). As such, students, often accompanied by their supervisors, attended assignments at which they served as the practice professional, supporting their learning and reflective practice.

After reaching the prescribed number of points/credits and completing the practice hours required by their specialization, students were then allowed to sit the final exam to demonstrate their theoretical knowledge and practical skills. The successful students gained a certificate that proved their proficiency. This certificate expired at the end of the following calendar year, and to renew it, all certified interpreters, transliterators, and lipspeakers had to take continuing professional development courses that equated to 50 credits, which were typically achieved by participating in seminars offered by Komora.

The CVP was a high-quality alternative to university education. However, because of an extensive administration and financial burden for the professional organization, the CVP has not been offered since 2012.

Since its establishment, Komora has been closely connected with the deaf community, primarily with Pevnost. During the first decade of Komora's existence, there were three main areas of interest and important activities. The first was raising awareness among deaf people about professional interpreters' services. The second focus was on the education of deaf interpreters. In CVP, hearing and deaf interpreters were studying together. A class titled "International Sign System for Deaf Participants" was opened. Third, cultural activities bringing hearing and deaf students together were introduced. Hearing and deaf interpreters collaborated for decades on theatrical plays, concerts, and events that were in the scope of interest of public media. Close cooperation and shared main values between the Faculty of Arts and Komora have been evident since the beginning. Because of these efforts, more and more people respect deaf people and their language. Also, the Czech deaf community is opening itself to others.

Aside from Komora, none of the professional organizations provide systematic SLI training or education anymore. Only Komora offers about five independent seminars every year, which are based on current topics and interpreters' needs. Some of them are accredited by the Ministry of Labour and Social Affairs or by the Ministry of Education. The participants obtain a certificate with the number of completed hours from each course.

ACADEMIC EDUCATION

Here we outline the academic SLI education that is available at three different institutions.

Charles University in Prague

Higher education is offered at the Faculty of Arts, Charles University, in Prague. The 3-year bachelor's degree in deaf studies at the IDS has been available since 1998. In 2013, the IDS split from the Institute of Czech Language and Theory of Communication, and the deaf studies program stood alone as an independent department. In the summer of 2023, the IDS transformed into the Institute of Czech and Deaf Studies (*Ústav bohemistiky pro cizince a komunikace neslyšících*).

To apply, candidates are required to have completed secondary school education with a school-leaving examination and to have completed a written entrance exam (at least 50% success rate; number admitted: 40 students). The program does not require applicants to have any knowledge of CzSL, but knowledge of English and other languages is considered an advantage. In the first year, all students attend the same general courses. In the second year, in the spring semester, students choose a compulsory specialization in addition to general subjects. In this semester, they must choose from three modules: interpreting and translation, pedagogy, and research. The study is completed with a state bachelor's examination. The graduates are prepared to work in different domains where they will support communication between deaf and hearing people. They are professionals with advanced knowledge of CzSL and are familiar with deaf culture, various modes of communication, and other particularities about the deaf community.

Students of the interpreting and translation module are taught a variety of subjects, including the status of the field of SLI in the Czech Republic and abroad, the concept of a professional interpreter versus different models of interpreting, the principles of interpreting, ethics, standards, and more. Furthermore, students acquire the skills necessary for working with a signed language (e.g., mental representation, visualization) and learn how to interpret bimodally from a linear language (spoken language) to a strongly visual language (sign language) and vice versa. The curriculum is divided into four semesters with compulsory and optional courses.

A graduate of the Czech/CzSL interpreting and translation module will have acquired the following knowledge:

- the theory of translation and interpreting,
- the theory of interpreting and translation with deaf people,
- the history of interpreting and translation with deaf people, focusing on the situation in our country,
- the techniques, models, and procedures used especially in community interpreting,
- basics of social work in relation to deaf people in the Czech Republic,
- the principles of interpreting and translation in the field of interpreting and translation for public administration and education,
- basics of the legal framework of the SLI profession and funding processes,
- secure knowledge of deaf interpreters' and translators' CoE (and of the modified versions of this code for different interpreting environments), and
- knowledge of interpreting and translation operational methods (cooperation in a team; organization, planning and preparation; implementation; reflection; materials, aids, and technology; cooperation with interpreting or translation authorities; mental hygiene, etc.).

An integral part of SLI academic education is 90 hours of authentic interpreting practice. Students are introduced to various situations (community interpreting, interpreting in education, individual interpreting in an organization, individual interpreting in appointments, interpreting for a larger number of clients).

Practice includes:

- observation in various interpreting situations under the guidance of experienced interpreters and a reflection of the situation: 30–40 hours;
- observation in organizations that provide interpreting for deaf people: 5–10 hours (including reflection); and
- self-interpreting under the guidance of experienced interpreters: 20–30 hours (including reflection).

At least 10% of the interpreting is supervised by one of the teachers, either with their direct participation in the interpreted situation or through video recordings. The program has been accredited until 2028, and no study fees are required from regular[5] students.

College in Hradec Králové

Since 2015, another academic option for studying SLI has been available. The 3-year Czech Sign Language Interpreting Program was established at the College in Hradec Králové (100 km east of Prague). Applicants are required to have full secondary or full secondary vocational education completed through a school-leaving examination; to fulfill personality requirements and demonstrate motivation, communication skills, and medical fitness; exhibit an appropriate level of general knowledge; demonstrate a basic orientation toward the deaf community and its culture; and demonstrate a basic orientation in issues of communication mediation with the majority society and deaf users of CzSL. Knowledge of CzSL is not obligatory. The list of subjects includes:

- History of Sign Language Interpretation,
- Introduction to the Interpreting Profession,
- Translation Theory and Practice,
- Sign Language Interpretation Theory,
- Interpreting Ethics, Current Interpreting Issues,
- Consecutive Interpreting, Simultaneous Interpreting,
- Interpreting for Deafblind People, and
- Team Interpreting, Interpreting Observation in Education.

The program is enriched by other subjects, such as Intralingual Cognitive Processing, Visual Communication, Introduction to the Study of the Deaf Community, Basics of Psychology, Fundamentals of Education, Deaf Pedagogy, Introduction to the Study of Ethics, and others. The study fee is 3000 CZK (120 euros, 130 USD) per year.

Masaryk University in Brno

In 2019, a 3-year BA degree program was established at the Faculty of Arts at Masaryk University in Brno (200 km southeast of Prague). The first students of the Czech Sign Language Interpreting Studies program began their studies in the fall semester of 2020. Because of the COVID-19 pandemic, all classes were shifted online. Unfortunately, this program has no longer continued enrolling new students since the academic year 2022–2023. Entrance examinations consisted of a study skills test (60%) and a motivation letter (maximum of 2,000 characters; 40%). After students complete their studies, graduates are expected to:

- understand natural languages as systems of rules,
- use linguistic terminology and standard theoretical approaches applicable in the field of modern linguistics,
- communicate at the CEFR B2 (intermediate) level of CzSL,
- analyze natural utterances in CzSL from a linguistic and sociolinguistic perspective,
- be well acquainted with the cultural and historical context of the deaf community in the Czech Republic and also partly in the world,
- have knowledge of appropriate legislation in the field of social services,
- have proper skills to translate between CzSL and Czech, and
- be aware of the ethical principles of the interpreting profession.

The compulsory practical training comprises 480 hours and can be divided into 430 hours of interpreting in organizations providing interpreting services and 50 hours in community organizations of the deaf.

The course Practical Training and Supervision in Social Work I includes at least 50 hours of observation and 100 hours of direct interpreting. Course II comprises 200 hours of direct interpreting. Regular students are not required to pay any study fees.

To summarize, all the programs mentioned are taught by hearing and deaf professionals in close cooperation. The IDS at the Faculty of Arts at Charles University in Prague has the highest-quality staff in terms of length of experience and the level of expertise in the field. Most interpreters with university education working as interpreters or teachers of future interpreters are graduates of this oldest study program.

EDUCATION THROUGH A PRIVATE AGENCY

The private agency EduCor—Education by Heart (*EduCor—vzdělávání srdcem*; established Fall 2022) offers SLI courses. The courses are held online with Czech and foreign lecturers and deaf and hearing experts. The topics include, for example, the CoE, interpreting dilemmas, and translation exercises. After passing the course, participants receive a certificate accredited by the Ministry of Labor and Social Affairs with confirmation of the completed hours. The agency cooperates with other deaf organizations, such as Pevnost.

THE IMPACT OF THE COVID-19 PANDEMIC

The COVID-19 pandemic has had many impacts on the provision and training of sign language interpreters. All the activities were shifted online. Because of the integration of new educational approaches, students were forced to learn more autonomously, and more time was asked of students to reflect on their interpreting performance in interpreting education. It also opened doors for students to develop their teamwork skills as they navigated assignments outside of the classroom. However, a less positive impact of COVID-19 was that the interpreter trainees missed in-person, face-to-face communication opportunities. It seems that on one hand, the theoretical side of the study is managed very well, and in some cases better than traditional face-to-face teaching, as online teaching instigated the creation of many new materials. Teachers were motivated to create many multimedia study materials, such as video tutorials. On the other hand, some interpreting practices, such as interpreting at places like the doctor's office, were replaced by remote (video) interpreting/translation, Zoom conferences, and online interpreting. These remote learning experiences are very different, and it is difficult to know how the lack of face-to-face development will impact sign language interpreters' professional practice, as online and face-to-face interactions require different approaches to working.

THE ROAD AHEAD

The development of sign language translation and interpreting has become stagnant in the Czech Republic, at the level of professional organizations, at the level of education in deaf organizations, and at the level of legislative support. Despite all efforts, there is still no master's degree available in Czech/CzSL interpreting. We firmly believe that this will change in the upcoming years. However, given the huge demand for quality interpreting services, great pressure can be expected to be placed on qualitative and quantitative change in the education of translators and interpreters.

The outcomes of the CEFR project linked to CzSL (as noted earlier) serve as reference material for future follow-up documents for sign language translation and interpreting education. The evaluation and testing process of interpreters will be designed according to the CEFR A1-B2 (proficient–intermediate) language levels. Steps will be taken to create a unified testing system in the Czech Republic. Also, research on teaching new interpreters is expected to be launched in the coming years.

The availability of training courses for interpreters has changed in recent years. Deaf community organizations and organizations of interpreters have begun to work together and cocreate educational programs. This move is very beneficial for both the deaf community and interpreters.

NOTES

1. See https://www.ecml.at/ECML-Programme/Programme2012-2015/ProSign/tabid/1752/Default.aspx
2. See https://www.plm.uw.edu.pl/eurosign-interpreter-2/
3. *Transliteration* (also known as *literal interpretation*) is the process by which spoken language is closely translated to signs. The signing fully follows the grammar and syntax of spoken language. This means the signs are produced in the word order of the Czech language. Hard-of-hearing people who do not use CzSL (e.g., people who lost hearing later in life) often prefer this kind of service because it supports lipreading.
4. The term *hearing impairment* is widely used in the Czech Republic. It is a general term used to include people who are deaf, people who are hard of hearing, and hearing people who lost their hearing at a later age. This term is also used in legislation.
5. A *regular* student in the Czech university system is classified as a student up to the age of 26 years with regular daily school attendance who can access university education for free.

8

Sign Language Interpreter Education in Finland

Situated in Northern Europe, Finland is a country of 130,559 square miles, approximately the size of Japan and Italy. Finland is a republic that elects a parliament of 200 representatives once every 4 years and a president once every 6 years. Having been independent since 1917, Finland has faced wars and grown from poverty to a wealthy country. Finland has been a member of the European Union since 1995 and began to use the euro as a currency in 1999 (InfoFinland, 2021).

Finland has always been multilingual, as it is situated between, and often governed by, Sweden and Russia, and thus has Swedish- and Russian-speaking populations. As the number of people speaking foreign languages is growing in Finland, the country is becoming more multilingual (Report of the Government on the Application of Language Legislation, 2017).

The population of Finland in 2018 was approximately 5.5 million, with 87.6% of the population speaking Finnish as their mother tongue. The other official national language is Swedish, with 5.2% of the population registered as speakers of Swedish (Statistics Finland, 2020). The Åland Islands region of Finland has Swedish as the sole official language (Åsub, 2020). In Northern Finland, Sámi people have the right to use their own language in public services (Sámi Language Act). The number of people who speak at least one of the three Sámi languages is approximately 2,000 (under 0.04% of the population), although the number of indigenous Sámi people is much higher. In addition, the Constitution of Finland mentions the rights of people who use the Roma language and people who use sign language. Other large languages are Russian (more than 84,000 speakers), Estonian (more than 49,000 speakers), and Arabic (more than 34,000 speakers) (Statistics Finland, 2020).

This chapter is partly based on, and is updated from, a chapter in the first edition of this volume: *Sign Language Interpreter Training in Finland* by Nisula and Manunen (2009).

In 1995, sign language was added to the Finnish Constitution. In 2015, the Sign Language Act was introduced, and it clearly mentions both Finnish Sign Language (FinSL) and Finland-Swedish Sign Language (FinSSL) (Sign Language Act). FinSSL is an endangered minority language, as it has only about 90 deaf signers who live mostly in the provinces of Ostrobothnia and Uusimaa. The last school for Finland-Swedish deaf children in Porvoo was closed in 1993, and the last training for FinSSL interpreters was delivered in 1990–1993 at Porvoo Folk High School (Andersson-Koski, 2015). Since 2015, however, there has been a positive shift in that the Finnish government has financed revitalization measures for FinSSL.

There is no exact number of FinSL users available, but it is estimated to be around 2,800 people (Rainò, 2021). Although it has been possible to register either FinSL or FinSSL as a native language[1] since 2008, few people actually do. The reason behind this remains a mystery; it might be because the majority of signers are bilingual (Rainò, 2021), but there is no research on the topic. The Ministry of Justice has developed an indicator tool for monitoring linguistic rights. The linguistic landscape is also documented in a report once during every government (i.e., every 4 years) (Report of the Government on the Application of Language Legislation, 2017).

Education in Finland is free and builds on a 9-year compulsory basic education that starts at the age of 7 years. After that, it is possible to attend vocational or general upper secondary education, both of which also open a path to higher education. Higher education is provided on a dual model by universities and universities of applied sciences (UASs). Generally, universities are regarded as more theory oriented, whereas UASs are more vocational. There are also numerous opportunities to attend adult education classes and lifelong learning initiatives (Ministry of Education and Culture, 2020).

WHO ARE WE?

Juha Manunen and Liisa Halkosaari have been working together in sign language interpreting (SLI) education for more than a decade. They are both senior lecturers at Humak University of Applied Sciences, with Juha working in Eastern Finland, in Kuopio, and Liisa in the southern capital of Helsinki.

Juha is deaf and was born in and lives in Eastern Finland. He is the only deaf person in his family and identifies as *viittomakielinen*, a FinSL user.[2] Juha found his way to the deaf community and culture through years in deaf schools. Juha has been working as an interpreter educator at Humak since 2001. He has been in a key position of teaching FinSL at Humak from the very beginning of his career. Juha started studying for a master of arts (MA) in FinSL while working and graduated in 2008 from the University of Jyväskylä. He also holds a qualification as a professional sign language teacher. Juha is not an interpreter himself and therefore likes to keep his teaching focus on language. However, experiences from teaching as well as from lifelong use of Finnish interpreting services in different contexts have given him a wide base to build on when doing, for example, assessments of interpreting. Juha is also generally interested in issues of SLI services.

Juha has always been interested in linguistics, languages, and cultures and has studied several languages. In addition to FinSL, Juha uses International Sign (IS) and FinSSL when working. He has been involved in teaching in the European Master in Sign Language Interpreting (EUMASLI) program since its establishment and in the revitalization project for FinSSL. The main part of his working hours goes to teaching and assessment of FinSL, deaf culture, and history, as well as interpreting, in the bachelor of arts (BA) program.

Juha has been using his enthusiasm for languages and linguistics by participating in different development projects: He has been involved in updating sign language teaching and evaluation in the BA curriculum in Humak. Juha was also a member of a cooperative group organized by the University of Jyväskylä in 2017–2019 for creating national skill level critique descriptions for FinSL.

Liisa is a hearing interpreter and interpreter educator. Her background is in the hearing community of the monolingual part of Western Finland. She started her journey with deaf communities in her early 20s when she started to study SLI with no background knowledge of sign languages.

She graduated from the BA program in interpreting at Diaconia University of Applied Sciences in 2002, realizing that this would be only the start of her journey. While working as an interpreter, she also applied to study FinSL at the University of Jyväskylä to deepen her language knowledge and skills. Liisa sees the community of signing students and staff (deaf and hearing) in Jyväskylä as crucial to her professional, ethical, linguistic, and attitudinal development. She also reflects back on her experiences in a religious environment at a young age, as well as her experiences in a queer minority, as having a significant role in her understanding of deaf linguistic minorities.

Liisa started in her current position at Humak in 2013, the same year she finished her MA in FinSL at Jyväskylä. Before that, she worked at Humak in different positions, including interpreting, teaching, and project work. While working, she studied for a qualification as a professional/vocational teacher (Haaga-Helia University of Applied Sciences in 2016).

During 2016–2023, Liisa's work included managing educational projects within the revitalization initiatives for FinSSL. Liisa is the study program director of EUMASLI at Humak, teaches interpreting and FinSL in the BA program, supervises theses, and develops digital learning environments. She is interested in linguistics, language attitudes, and power dynamics in linguistic groups. In 2023, she took a sabbatical year from Humak to work as a full-time interpreter.

CONTEXTUALIZATION: TRANSLATION AND INTERPRETING IN FINLAND

There are different paths to working as an interpreter or a translator in Finland. On a vocational level, there is a "further vocational qualification" for community interpreting (spoken languages) and two "specialist vocational qualifications": interpreting for people with speech impairments and court interpreting. For translators, there is an Authorized Translator's Examination, which is outside of the educational system (eRequirements, 2020; Finnish National Agency for Education, 2020).

Since 2011, it has been possible to obtain a BA in community interpreting at Diaconia University of Applied Sciences (Diak UAS), concentrating on more uncommon languages, like Somali, Arabic, and Farsi (Thurén, 2012). Both UASs providing SLI education, Humak University of Applied Sciences (Humak UAS) and Diak, have during recent years expanded their offerings to include educating interpreters for people with speech impairments. There are also two different MA programs for SLI.

For some major languages, education is available at the BA and MA levels at four different universities, with a variety of degree titles, such as "English Language and Translation" and "German: Multilingual Communication and Translation Studies" (Studyinfo, 2020). None of these universities, however, provides studies in sign languages (apart from sporadic courses).

The University of Jyväskylä is the only university in Finland offering the opportunity to study FinSL from the bachelor's level to the doctoral level. The Sign Language Center (*Viittomakielen keskus*) began its operations in early 2010 at the Department of Languages of the Faculty of Humanities. The activities of the Sign Language Center are based on a designated objective assigned by the Ministry of Education. The center is responsible for developing and coordinating research on sign language in Finland and also for providing education in sign language (Sign Language Center, 2020).

Because of European standards, there is now a register for legal interpreting, which also includes sign language interpreters (Finnish National Agency for Education, 2020). There is also a specialization program in legal interpreting, which is the first training for higher education students in Finland. The training responds to the growing need for high-quality interpreting and qualified legal interpreters in Finland. The training provides opportunities to apply to the register for legal interpreters (Diak, 2020; Finnish National Agency for Education, 2020).

The working life of interpreters (both spoken and sign language) is somewhat precarious; a lot of interpreters work as freelancers and have little opportunity to negotiate their salary. The same goes for translators, who have little power to decide the price to charge for their work (Language Experts, 2020). Generally, the government-paid services are priced through a competitive bidding system, which also has an impact. For example, in 2017, the bidding for both community interpreting (by the state agency Hansel) and interpreting for disabled people (including deaf signers) (by the state agency Kela) experienced significant challenges that raised many questions, and the process was criticized (Huusko, 2017; Rainò, 2020; Rainò & Vik, 2020).

While trade unions concentrate on the interests of their members, there is also the Association of Finnish Translators and Interpreters (*Suomen kääntäjien ja tulkkien liitto ry* [SKTL]), which was founded in 1955. SKTL aims to foster professionalism and quality in the field (SKTL, 2020).

Professionalization of SLI in Finland

SLI became a profession in Finland relatively rapidly at the end of the 1970s. The shift from SLI as volunteer work to SLI as a paid career made it relevant to establish a union, and the Finnish Association of Sign Language Interpreters (*Suomen Viittomakielen Tulkit ry* [SVT]) was set up in 1982 (Salmi & Laakso, 2005).

SLI services were first based on the Disabled Peoples Welfare Act of 1979. The number of funded hours per year for deaf people was 120 (double that for deafblind people), and the National Board of Social Welfare had a list of accepted interpreters (Hassinen & Lehtomäki, 1986). Since the establishment of the profession, the service has been financed by the state. However, it became a subjective right in 1994 as interpreting services were moved under the Services and Assistance for the Disabled Act (Salmi & Laakso, 2005). Deaf people have the right to use an interpreter in any life situation; interpreting is not restricted to health care or legal matters but is also available for social and leisure activities and for traveling abroad. All the costs of interpreting services are covered by the government (Act on Interpreting Services for Disabled People; Rainò & Vik, 2020).

In 1994, the *Kuurojen Liitto ry* (Finnish Association of the Deaf [FAD]), together with other associations (of interpreters, deafblind people, and hard of hearing people) formed a cooperative group called *Tulkkitoiminnan yhteistyöryhmä* (TTYR), which is a collaborating committee/working group of interpreting services. The group took on the responsibilities of updating the list of interpreters (which then became a register of interpreters) and of coordinating and leading discussions in the field of SLI. When applying to the register, interpreters commit to the code of ethics (Hynynen, Pyörre, & Roslöf, 2010). TTYR is a group still working today, with a focus on cooperation and with representatives from numerous associations and interpreter training units.

The ethics guidelines for interpreters were devised in the 1980s, and for many years, there was a separate code of ethics for SLI. The current code of ethics for community interpreters is not language specific and was ratified in 2013 (Language Experts, 2020; Services and Assistance for the Disabled Act; Thurén, 2012).

There was a constant shortage of interpreters in Finland until the 2010s. As local municipalities were the ones responsible for the services, there was some variation in skills and inequality in service provision, even though the updated Finnish Constitution in 1995 mentioned the rights of sign language peoples. When people have better access to society, this leads to a demand for more interpreting (Rainò, 2020; Topo et al., 2000).

Until early 2000, most interpreting work was done on a freelance basis, but there were some public service interpreting centers and in-house teams in schools with full-time interpreters. Over the subsequent 10 years, the number of interpreting agency businesses began to increase, while municipalities in two big areas started centralizing the purchasing of interpreting services. This was a result of a project aiming to develop the services. The first bid in 2005 was prepared with service users, municipalities, and service providers. Centralization made it more common for interpreters to be employed by a company that sells interpreting services or to start a company of their own. The previous struggle of freelancers to ensure that they got paid seemed to come to an end (Huusko, 2017; Rainò & Vik, 2020).

The centralization process, aiming for geographical equality, finally concluded in 2010, when the whole interpreting service for disabled people was moved under the Social Insurance Institution of Finland (*Kansaneläkelaitos* [Kela]). The service arranged by Kela is based on the Act on Interpreter Service for the Disabled. According to the law, people with hearing or speech impairments are entitled to a minimum of 180 hours of interpreter services per year; for deafblind people, the minimum is 360 hours (Kela, 2020a).

Where We Are Today: Change Is Inevitable

Even if the linguistic landscape has developed and deaf people are seen as a linguistic and cultural minority group, interpreting services are still a part of services for disabled people. The law is secondary, which means that interpreting is provided by Kela only if it is not organized by someone else. Other laws that mention or require organization of interpreting services include the Basic Education Act, the Administrative Procedure Act, and the Act on the Status and Rights of Patients (Kela, 2020a). In practice, this means that local municipalities are responsible for organizing interpreting in schools and in hospitals; police departments and other public services must provide service at some level in sign languages. None of the legislation sets any qualification standards for interpreters.

When Europe was faced with the refugee crisis in 2014–2015, a growing number of refugees applied for asylum in Finland. Among them were disabled people. The Finnish Immigration Service (Migri) had to arrange interviews with deaf refugees. The deaf refugees could not use FinSL, many of them were not able to read or write, and many did not know the sign language of their home country, either.

This created communication challenges (Sivunen, 2019). There was a need for deaf interpreters because they had translanguaging skills and the ability to modify their signing according to asylum seekers' needs or to use IS (FAD, 2020).

Deaf peoples' rights to interpreting services is promoted and monitored by FAD. The aforementioned cooperative TTYR also has an important role in monitoring interpreting services. Their aim is to enhance interpreting services and challenge any problematic issues within Kela's interpreting services (FAD, 2020). TTYR publishes its comments and other information on a Facebook page.

For Kela, taking responsibility for interpreting services has been a major change. It has raised a lot of discussion, criticism, and feelings of unfairness among the Finnish deaf community and FinSL interpreters. In 2017, there was a wave of activity among deaf community members. Some activists started a campaign called "Stop-Kela" to try and make a difference and to stop the bidding contest. The campaign shared stories on social media of unsuccessful organization of interpreting by Kela (Tupi, 2018). Since 2013, also on Facebook, the site Herää, Kelan tulkkauspalvelu![3] (Wake up, Kela's interpreting services!) is actively used by deaf people to highlight problems related to interpreting services provided by Kela. Deaf people have also used social media to seek out interpreters when Kela has not been able to arrange interpreting.

Nevertheless, the recent changes in the interpreting service are not only negative. Whenever necessary, deaf people can apply for additional interpreting hours with practically no restriction. Deaf people new to the service have the opportunity to be introduced to interpretation services by Kela, with the opportunity to choose interpreters, for example, for study or work.

From the beginning of 2019, after 37 years of promoting the interests of FinSL interpreters, SVT was incorporated with an association of translators, Käännösalan asiantuntijat ry (KAJ), to form a new association called Language Experts (Kieliasiantuntijat ry). Language Experts has almost 3,000 members working in the fields of translation, interpreting, multilingual communication, terminology, and language planning. The association is a member of a larger Finnish trade union called Akava Special Branches and also of international cooperative organizations, such as the World Association of Sign Language Interpreters (WASLI) and the European Legal Interpreters and Translators Association (EULITA) (Language Experts, 2020).

The register of interpreters was administered by the cooperative group TTYR until 2015. There was discussion previously of the problematic role of a nonofficial group monitoring interpreting services. Joining the register has always been voluntary, and it has had no official impact on whether someone works as an interpreter. There has been a minimum requirement of passing the final exam, agreed on by the interpreter training units and TTYR, but there has not been any monitoring of quality after an interpreter has joined the register. When the discussions on centralizing interpreting services began, TTYR made efforts to find a new solution for the register (Thurén, 2012). After Kela took over the services and started listing interpreters on its own register, TTYR decided to close the register for good in 2015 (Rainò & Vik, 2020).

Kela uses the same minimum requirements as those set previously by TTYR for working as a sign language interpreter. Interpreters are required to have graduated with a BA from an SLI training program and to pass the final exam (Rainò & Vik, 2020). An SLI student is required to have at least "good" skills (i.e., a grade of 3 on a scale of 0–5) on the final exam in order to be allowed to practice SLI professionally. The final exam usually consists of four parts: a monologue interpretation to Finnish and FinSL from video sources, a simulated dialogue interpretation on the field of social or health services, and a reflection on ethics.

All interpreters working with Kela must commit to following the code of ethics, which includes a promise to continually develop their professional skills. There is still no concrete continuous professional development requirement (e.g., hours to spend in education) to practice as an interpreter. Some companies have their own quality development programs, and they arrange courses and mentoring for their employees (see, e.g., Huhtinen, 2015).

There have been a few studies (many of them BA or MA theses) about working conditions and work-related well-being of interpreters from the 1990s to the 2020s (see, e.g., Martikainen, 2016). Changes in the business have had a remarkable effect on interpreters. Companies in the SLI field experienced a severe drop in income after 2013, as a result of changed employment practices around the bidding contest in 2013. This decreased the number of interpreters working full time on a monthly basis and increased the number of flexible contracts on an hourly basis. The latter practice does not support well-being at work (Huusko, 2017). The flexible form of contract is referred to as a "zero-hours contract" because in a worst-case scenario that is how many hours for which an interpreter is booked. According to a survey in 2018, only 26% of sign language interpreters have a full-time permanent job contract, whereas 60% have a flexible contract (Putkonen-Kankaanpää, 2019).

Interpreters have also expressed their concerns about the decreasing number of FinSL users, the effect of the Kela bidding system, and the oversupply of working interpreters (Raitio-Virtanen, 2013). There have been discussions about changing the bidding system to be more flexible and more customer oriented.

Sign Language Interpreter Education in Finland

SLI education has advanced from short courses organized by FAD in the 1970s to a bachelor's degree in a university of applied sciences since 1998. However, there has been no systematic detailed follow-up on changes in education in the past 20 years.

In January 1962, FAD provided the very first interpreter training course. There were 35 participants on the course, which occurred over a weekend. After that, it took 15 years until any formal training was provided again. In 1978, FAD established a training program of 170 hours for participants with varying skills in sign language. Participants in the training were, for example, professionals working with deaf people, hearing heritage signers, or people with deaf family members (Salmi & Laakso, 2005).

FAD continued to provide interpreter training until 1983, when the training was transferred to a folk high school in Turku. For the first 2 years of the offering, the course of full-time study lasted for 1 year. In 1986, interpreter training was deemed by the Ministry of Education to be a form of professional education. Therefore, the course was extended to last for 2 years and was also provided in Kuopio. Since 1986, there have not been any prerequisites for any level of sign language fluency before entry into interpreter training. Since 1988, the curriculum's duration of full-time study was 3 years (Salmi & Laakso, 2005).

In the 1990s, the politics of the educational structure changed in Finland. The first UASs were introduced at the end of the 1990s, with the total duration of studies limited to 3.5 to 4.5 years. Both the Turku and Kuopio training units founded their UASs and started a 3.5-year (soon 4-year) bachelor's degree for SLI (Rainò & Vik, 2020).

There was some criticism in the beginning: People perceived the theory and written assignments as getting too much focus while learning to sign got less attention. Even today, at times students or other stakeholders can be seen complaining about the amount of and emphasis on writing in SLI studies. However, one aspect emphasized in the curriculum is the internship, which means practical learning in the field with professional interpreters. UASs are even required to have a minimum of 30 European Credit Transfer and Accumulation System (ECTS) credits of practice or internship in their curricula (Universities of Applied Sciences Act).[4]

Where We Are Today

The current route to becoming a sign language interpreter in Finland is relatively straightforward: Graduate from a 4-year, 240-ECTS bachelor's degree program in interpreting at either Diak or Humak (both situated in Helsinki). Humak also had an SLI education program in Kuopio, but after a structural change in 2018, students at the Kuopio unit concentrated on intralingual interpreting with different methods, such as augmentative and alternative communication. A similar change had been made at Diak in 2011 (Rainò & Vik, 2020). Today, the Kuopio unit provides expertise in multimodal interaction and concentrates on linguistic accessibility. Strong pedagogical skills and expertise in interaction provide a basis for the development of interaction environments, situations, and practices. Graduates from this program can work in communication guidance and coaching roles, as well as working as interpreters (Humak, 2020). Even after these changes, the question remains: Are we educating too many interpreters? (Rainò, 2020). We will return to this question at the end of this chapter.

The program in the Helsinki unit at Humak has been open to both deaf and hearing interpreting students since its beginning in 2001. However, the number of deaf students has been quite low since the first group started in 2001, with six deaf students with hearing peers. By the end of 2020, there were altogether eight deaf students who had graduated from this program. Many of them are also actively working as sign language translators.

In Finland, it seems that sign language translation (SLT) is carried out mainly by deaf translators, most of them trained interpreters, as there is no specific education for translating (Halkosaari, 2021). An interview with deaf interpreters in 2016 revealed that they all[5] work with both interpreting and translation assignments (Paanala & Nurmi, 2016). There are no comprehensive studies or reports on SLT in Finland in general. It is worth mentioning that since the 1980s there have been more than 30 deaf interpreters (with training provided by the FAD) working with deafblind people (Rainò & Vik, 2020).

Graduating from a 4-year BA does not always require 4 years. The student has the option of applying for recognition of prior learning, which means accreditation of skills and competencies previously acquired through formal training, work, or other activities. For example, for interpreters with an older vocational degree, it is possible to achieve a BA in a shorter time, often in 2 years. These students typically work and study at the same time, and their studies are structured with more distance learning and less contact on campus.

Any bachelor's degree at a UAS consists of (1) basic and professional studies, (2) studies of free choice, (3) a professionalism-promoting internship, and (4) a BA thesis (Amendment of Universities of Applied Sciences). The extent of professional studies has naturally been the largest for interpreter students, two of the major topics being sign language and interpreting. There are also studies in spoken languages, interaction, translation, social sciences, accessibility, and deaf studies, to name but a few.

There are two options for an MA degree within the SLI field. One is the national 1.5-year (90 ECTS) Developing Interpreting Services program (organized jointly by Diak and Humak) that started within the field of SLI education but is now open also to community interpreters or interpreters for speech-impaired people who already have a bachelor's degree. For SLI, there is an international choice for an MA: the joint degree EUMASLI, which is organized by Humak University of Applied Sciences, Heriot-Watt University in Scotland, and Magdeburg-Stendahl University of Applied Sciences in Germany. Both of the MA programs aim to develop the profession—the national degree more on a structural level and EUMASLI with a focus on leadership, research on SLI, and interpreting in international settings (EUMASLI, 2021; Humak, 2021).

Currently, there is no path to a doctor of philosophy (PhD) degree in SLI, which we see as a major problem in developing the field both for the interpreting profession and for education programs. Obtaining a research degree is possible through other aligned programs, such as Applied Linguistics at the University of Jyväskylä or translation studies at the University of Helsinki. There are a couple of PhD students at the moment, but as of 2020, there have not yet been any doctoral dissertations on SLI in Finland.

The People: Educators, Students, and Stakeholders

In our experience, students today differ from those of 20 or even 10 years ago. This is no surprise because the world and society are ever changing. Our observations and informal discussions with teaching staff refer to a decrease in motivation and commitment among students. There is concern about the well-being of students, as many seem to be overwhelmed by the demands of the profession. The effects of both of these issues are seen in the high number of dropouts from the training programs. The demands escalate during the final exams in the final year, when students have to pass the interpreting exam with a level of "good" skills in order to graduate with a license to practice the profession.

Entering SLI education has always required an entrance examination. The entry requirements for higher education in Finland have been different for different programs, and not all of them have required entrance examination. However, the national requirements for entering higher education in Finland were renewed in 2020. Although an entrance examination can still be a part of the entry requirements, one's acceptance to a higher education program is more dependent on secondary education grades and certificates ("certificate selection"). The background of the reform is concerns about the high rejection rate; in Finland, two thirds of applicants were left without a place to study at the university level every year. In addition to that, the entrance examinations have been expensive, and they have been perceived to contribute to a delay in the start of studies (Ministry of Education and Culture, 2020).

Humak followed the renewal, and after reviewing the entrance examination for the SLI education program, we no longer organize an "entrance exam day" at the campuses, but different systems have been applied. Students still apply via the national joint application process. In 2020, Humak's students were selected by the common national entrance exam, but the applicants were required to complete a video pre-assignment to show ability in visual communication. In 2021 and 2022, applicants were required to join in an elective course with some obligatory tasks. In 2023, students were selected with no extra assignments, through the common national entrance exam and certificate selection.

To work as a senior lecturer at a UAS, there is a requirement of having a master's degree and qualification in teaching (Amendment of Universities of Applied Sciences). This has at times been a challenge in the hiring of deaf teachers. However, the legislation does enable some flexibility when a candidate is an expert in the field in question. Also, the number of deaf people finishing academic education has grown, especially in sign language teaching. Despite this growth, there are only four deaf interpreter educators in Finland at this time.

At Humak, the workload is shared with no specific concentration by hearing status. Teaching and other responsibilities are divided according to one's expertise. At times, there is a lack of a native language model, for which we try to compensate with language practice hours within the deaf community and by having deaf visitors and visiting lecturers.

There has been a change in the state financing system, which has also led to a change in our work. Compared to 10 years ago, one big change in our work is the increased amount of research, development, and innovation. As there is no institution responsible for basic research on SLI, there is a lack of continuous development in that area. However, there are multiple projects that provide different views on development. Two examples of projects Humak has been involved in are Developing Deaf Interpreting in Europe (an Erasmus+ project coordinated by the Danish Deaf Association) and Visual Sign News (financed by Google, in cooperation with the Albanian Deaf Association). We saw both of these projects as opportunities to contribute and gain knowledge.

One of the recent projects was a part of the revitalization program for FinSSL. The project *Lev i vårt språk* (Livs; Live in Our Language) was the first implemented government-funded project with the aim of strengthening the position of FinSSL. The aim of the first part of the project in 2015–2017 was to strengthen the identity of the language users and increase their cultural and linguistic knowledge. The second part of Project Livs, in 2018–2020, aimed to train interpreters in FinSSL (Livs, 2020). One of the specialties in the aforementioned interpreter training was the involvement of the sign language community in a very broad way, which was partly due to the lack of qualified trainers. However, it had a very positive impact on the results. Students were highly motivated, and they found a connection to the community, which will be a valuable part of revitalizing the language (Halkosaari, 2020).

Thus, there are challenges and changes but also hope and enthusiasm about participating in new innovations and developing the profession. In the next section, we look at the potential future of sign language translation and interpreting in Finland as well as some recent phenomena within the field.

The Road Ahead

A 2020 report (Rainò & Vik, 2020) discusses the future of SLI services, as well as the future needs of SLI education. Centralization of interpreting services has made it possible to monitor the statistics provided by Kela. In 2007, before the changes, it was estimated that the total costs of the service were around 10 million euros. In 2012, the costs were 31 million; in 2015, 42.5 million; and in 2019, 47.4 million. The number of working interpreters in 2007 was estimated to be less than 500, whereas in 2012 and 2019, it was approximated at 800 interpreters (Rainò & Vik, 2020; Statistical Database of Kela, 2020a).

The population of deaf people requiring interpreters has not changed much in the past years. Although the number of people entitled to SLI services is approximately 6,000 (in 2018 and 2019), only 3,400 use their right and actually book interpreters. However, a figure relevant to SLI is the number of service users using signed languages (this includes FinSL, FinSSL, and signed speech), which is 2,857 (Statistical Database of Kela, 2020a).

A study about the use of interpreting with children and youth using cochlear implants shows that the majority use spoken language and prefer intralingual interpreting techniques, such as speech-to-text interpreting (Martikainen & Rainò, 2014).

The question then arises of whether there are too many interpreters in Finland. Almost 800 interpreters work for 3,400 (potentially up to 6,000) deaf, hard of hearing, or low vision people. The number of interpreting hours provided by Kela in 2019 was approximately 511,000 hours. This would mean 639 hours for one interpreter per year—if the work was evenly shared. If we count a generous number of weeks for vacation, that would leave an interpreter with 15 hours of interpreting per week (Statistical Database of Kela, 2020a; see also Rainò, 2020; Rainò & Vik, 2020).

Rainò (2020) has conducted more detailed calculations on the statistics provided by Kela. She suggests that the right choice would be to decrease the number of sign language interpreters trained annually. Even though the UASs in Finland, both Diak and Humak, have adapted their SLI programs to respond to the change in interpreter users' needs, she suggests that the fundamental problem of training too many interpreters remains unresolved (Rainò, 2020). Education is also always dependent on, and affected by, the financing system. Because the state finances all programs and the major issue affecting the financing is the number of graduated students, the UASs are left with no realistic choices (Rainò & Vik, 2020). Decreasing the number of students would decrease financing, which again would make it hard to continue with the SLI education programs.

Not everyone sees the situation as negative, and the numbers do not give the full picture. It is, however, estimated that the needs for SLI will decrease or at least remain at current levels. In the light of these statistics, significant changes will occur during 2040–2070. The need to arrange services for elderly deaf people will increase the need for interpreters. The younger generation has higher levels of education and internationalization is growing, which will potentially increase the demand for interpreters capable of interpreting in different languages between different methods. Advances in technology bring more needs and opportunities, as the availability of interpreters will improve. As for interpreting for speech-impaired people, the need will expand because of a large group of potential users. Not all needs are identified, and not all people who are entitled to interpreting services are aware of their rights because the focus of the client organizations is not on the speech impairment but on the underlying condition or disability (Rainò & Vik, 2020).

Asylum-seeking people in Finland have found it difficult to communicate with the reception center staff because of a lack of a common understandable language. For this reason, a project, KUVAKO, was established, with the purpose of developing picture communication for everyday situations at reception centers. The project lasted 3 years (2017–2020). The aim was to compile and harmonize pictures previously used by reception centers and create new ones. The resources developed during the project will also be able to support interpreting. One of the outputs of the project is an easy-to-use picture-based mobile application that is accessible to everyone (KUVAKO, 2020).

SLT is a growing field because of accessibility guidelines. Recommendations and guidelines with regard to quality in SLT were published in 2015 (Sign Language Board, 2015). The Sign Language Board of the Institute for the Languages of Finland has also published and updated a quality assessment tool for signed documents, specifically to be used to evaluate the quality of a translation from a spoken/written language to a signed language (Sign Language Board, 2021). These guidelines and tools seem to be a reaction to the growing production of SLT, as more and more public services publish at least some information in FinSL and also FinSSL.

The worldwide COVID-19 pandemic caused a sudden exceptional situation in SLI service as people had to avoid meeting each other in the same space. Thus, Kela recommended using more video remote interpreting (VRI) if it was possible for both partners in the situation (Kela, 2020b). Experiences have been positive and useful for both interpreters and interpreting service users. However, VRI also brings challenges, such as functionality of the technology, audibility, and visibility, as well as the requirements and flexibility of all partners communicating at a distance (Jaamalainen & Manunen, 2020).

It seems that VRI will become a stronger service because of the perceived benefits. This means it should also have a more notable role in SLI education. Because of the growth of VRI, the professional code of ethics for interpreters needed to be updated (Language Experts, 2021) to add explicit information about, for example, an interpreter's skills with the technology and applications used to interpret for a video call.

In addition to the new openings in linguistic accessibility and technology, we are looking forward to going back to a more intensive connection to the deaf communities. The newly awakened awareness of FinSSL as being severely endangered has led to a joint effort by both deaf people and interpreters to save the language. This is our vision for the diverse community of FinSL, as well. We wish to see our SLI education with a big deaf heart.

Notes

1. The population data in Finland have included information on language since their inception and still use the term *äidinkieli*, which translates to either "mother tongue" or "native language."
2. In Finnish we use the term *viittomakielinen*, which does not fully translate to English. It refers to being a signer as an identity, comparable to nationality.
3. Herää, Kelan tulkkauspalvelu! https://www.facebook.com/groups/714799755206479
4. For more detailed history, see Nisula & Manunen (2009).
5. Four out of all five (at that time) active deaf interpreters were interviewed, and all four stated they do both interpreting and translation.

References

Act on interpreting services for the disabled people. (2010). [*Laki vammaisten henkilöiden tulkkauspalvelusta 133/2010*]. Ministry of Social Affairs and Health. https://www.finlex.fi/fi/laki/alkup/2010/20100133

Amendment of Universities of Applied Sciences [*Valtioneuvoston asetus ammattikorkeakouluista*]. (2014). Ministry of Education and Culture. https://www.finlex.fi/fi/laki/alkup/2014/20141129

Andersson-Koski, M. (2015). My own language—our culture. A survey of the situation of the Finland-Swedish Sign Language and the Deaf Finland-Swedish Sign Language users in Finland 2014–2015. [*Mitt eget språk— vår kultur. En kartläggning av situationen för det finlandssvenska teckenspråket och döva finlandssvenska teckenspråkiga i Finland 2014–2015*] (in Swedish only). Helsinki: Finlandssvenska teckenspråkiga r.f. http://www.dova.fi/wp-content/uploads/2015/07/PDF_Mitt_eget_sprak_var_kultur.pdf

Åsub – Statistics and Research Åland. (2020). https://www.asub.ax/sv

Diak. (2020). *Specialisation in court interpreting*. Diaconia University of Applied Sciences. https://www.diak.fi/en/for-continuing-learners/training-services/specialisation-studies/specialisation-in-court-interpreting

eRequirements. (2020). Finnish National Agency for Education. https://eperusteet.opintopolku.fi/#/en

EUMASLI (European Master in Sign Language Interpreting). (2021). https://www.eumasli.eu

FAD. (2020). Interpreting. [*Tulkkaus*]. Finnish Association of the Deaf. https://www.kuurojenliitto.fi/fi/viittomakielet-ja-viittomakieliset/tulkkaus

Finnish National Agency for Education. (2020). https://www.oph.fi/en

Finnish National Agency for Education. (2020). Register for legal interpreters. [*Oikeustulkkirekisteri*] (in Finnish only). https://www.oph.fi/fi/palvelut/oikeustulkkirekisteri

Halkosaari, L. (2020). The final report of project Live in Our Language. [*Lev i vårt språk - projektin loppuraportti*]. Helsinki, Finland: Humak University of Applied Sciences.

Halkosaari, L. (2021). When the translator gives a face to the text. [*Kun kääntäjä on tekstin kasvot*] (in Finnish only). *Kiekaus*, *1*, 8–10. Language Experts.

Hassinen, L., & Lehtomäki, E. (1986). *Interpreting services for the deaf and deaf-blind and deafened people in Finland*. Finnish Association of the Deaf.

Huhtinen, H. (2015). *Quality and professionality through evaluation of interpreting* [*Tulkkauksen arvioinnilla laatua ja ammatillisuutta*] [Video]. Sign Language Sector Cooperative. https://www.via-ok.net/blogi/tulkkauksen-arvioinnilla-laatua-ja-ammatillisuutta

Hynynen, H., Pyörre, S. & Roslöf, R. (2010). Life at hands: Professional picture of a sign language interpreter [*Elämä käsillä: viittomakielentulkin ammattikuva*] (in Finnish only). Diaconia University of Applied Sciences. http://urn.fi/URN:ISBN:978-952-493-101-4

InfoFinland – Finland in your own language. (2021). Information about Finland. https://www.infofinland.fi/en/information-about-finland

Jaamalainen, A-M., & Manunen, J. (2020). All at distance working! Experiences about the distance interpretation [*Kaikki etänä! – Kokemuksia etätulkkauksesta*]. *Language Experts*. https://kieliasiantuntijat.fi/kiekaus-kokemuksia-etatulkkauksesta/

Kela. (2020a). Interpreting Service for the Disabled. https://www.kela.fi/web/en/interpreter-service-for-the-disabled

Kela. (2020b). The effects of the coronavirus on the interpretation service for the disabled [*Koronaviruksen vaikutukset vammaisten tulkkauspalvelussa*]. https://www.kela.fi/-/koronaviruksen-vaikutukset-vammaisten-tulkkauspalvelussa

KUVAKO. (2020). Project KUVAKO [*KUVAKO-hanke*]. http://kuvako.humak.fi/

Language Experts. (2020). Salaries and fees [*Palkat ja palkkiot*]. *Language Experts*. https://kieliasiantuntijat.fi/fi/kieliasiantuntija-tyossa/palkat-ja-palkkiot/

Language Experts. (2021). The professional ethics code for interpreters was updated [*Tulkkien ammattieettistä säännöstöä päivitettiin*]. https://kieliasiantuntijat.fi/tulkkien-ammattieettista-saannostoa-paivitettiin

Livs. (2020). Live in our language [*Lev i vårt språk*]. http://livs.humak.fi/

Martikainen, L. (2016). Job satisfaction and job control of educators and interpreters working on a field of sign language interpreting [*Viittomakielen tulkkausalalla toimivien kouluttajien ja tulkkien työtyytyväisyys ja työnhallinta muutostilanteessa*]. [Master's thesis], University of Eastern Finland.

Martikainen, L., & Rainò, P. (2014). Language choices and the need for interpreting services for deaf children and young people with cochlear implants [*Sisäkorvaistutetta käyttävien lasten ja nuorten kuntoutus- ja tulkkauspalvelujen toteutuminen ja tarve tulevaisuudessa*] Sosiaali- ja terveysturvan selosteita 89/2014. Kelan tutkimusosasto. https://helda.helsinki.fi/handle/10138/144490

Ministry of Education and Culture. (2020). FAQs about the student admissions reform in higher education institutions. https://minedu.fi/en/faqs-about-student-admissions

Nisula, M., & Manunen, J. (2009). Sign language interpreter training in Finland. In J. Napier (Ed.), *International perspectives on sign language interpreter education* (pp. 15–34). Gallaudet University Press.

Paanala, A. & Nurmi, K-R. (2016). Deaf interpreters: Education, job description and co-operation with hearing interpreters [*Kuurot tulkit: koulutus, työnkuva ja yhteistyö kuulevien tulkkien kanssa*] (in Finnish only). BA thesis, University of Applied Sciences, Helsinki.

Putkonen-Kankaanpää, H. (2019). Survey for interpreters' employment and salary in 2018 [*Tulkkien työsuhde- ja ansiokysely 2018*]. Humanistisen ammattikorkeakoulun julkaisuja, 96. Humak University of Applied Sciences.

Rainò, P. (2020). *Too many sign language interpreters? Finland's education market and labour in numbers.* Unpublished manuscript.

Rainò, P. (2021). Sign language barometer 2020. Research report [*Viittomakielibarometri 2020. Tutkimusraportti.*]. Publications of the Ministry of Justice, reports and guidelines 2021:4. Ministry of Justice. https://julkaisut.valtioneuvosto.fi/handle/10024/162839

Rainò, P., & Vik, G-V. (2020). Prospects of public service interpreting. The educational needs and future prospects of community interpreting, sign language interpreting, speech-to-text interpreting, and interpreting for the speech and language impaired persons [*Tulkkausalan tulevaisuudennäkymät. Asioimistulkkauksen, viittomakielen- ja kirjoitustulkkauksen sekä puhevammaisten tulkkauksen koulutustarpeista ja alan tulevaisuudennäkymistä*]. Humak University of Applied Sciences. http://urn.fi/URN:NBN:fi-fe2020102185861

Raitio-Virtanen, S-M. (2013). Survey of sign language interpreter's considerations and expectations of the future of their work and how the field of sign language interpreting can benefit from the results [*Kartoitus viittomakielentulkkien ajatuksista ja odotuksista työnsä tulevaisuudesta ja sen tulosten hyödyntämisestä viittomakielen tulkkausalalla*] [Unpublished master's thesis]. Diaconia University of Applied Sciences, Helsinki. http://urn.fi/URN:NBN:fi:amk-2013060312546

Report of the Government on the Application of Language Legislation. (2017). Government publications 10/2017. http://urn.fi/URN:ISBN:978-952-287-476-4

Salmi, E., & Laakso, M. (2005). The history of the Finnish Sign Language users [*Maahan lämpimään - Suomen viittomakielisten historia*]. Finnish Association of the Deaf.

Sámi Language Act 1086/2003. Unofficial translation. Ministry of Justice. https://www.finlex.fi/en/laki/kaannokset/2003/en20031086.pdf

Services and Assistance for the Disabled Act 1987/380 (amendments 19.12.2008). Unauthorised translation from Finnish. Ministry of Social Affairs and Health. https://www.kumpuvuori.fi/wp-content/uploads/2018/04/Disability20Services20Act.pdf

Sign Language Act 359/2015. Translation from Finnish. Ministry of Justice. https://www.finlex.fi/en/laki/kaannokset/2015/en20150359.pdf

Sign Language Board. (2015). Enhancing quality in sign language translation. [*Laatua viittomakielelle kääntämiseen*] (in Finnish, FinSL and FinSSL only). Institute for the Languages of Finland. The Finnish Association of the Deaf. https://kuurojenliitto.fi/viittomakielten-lautakunta/

Sign Language Board. (2021). Quality assessment for material in sign language [*Viittomakielisen aineiston laadun arviointi*] (in Finnish only). Institute for the Languages of Finland. The Finnish Association of the Deaf. https://kuurojenliitto.fi/viittomakielten-lautakunta/

Sign Language Centre. (2020). University of Jyväskylä. https://www.jyu.fi

Sivunen, N. (2019). An ethnographic study of deaf refugees seeking asylum in Finland. *Societies, 9*(2), 1–16.

SKTL The Association of Finnish Translators and Interpreters. (2020). www.sktl.fi/in-english

Statistical database of Kela, Kelasto. (2020). https://www.kela.fi/kelasto

Statistics Finland. (2020). Population. https://www.stat.fi/index_en.html

Studyinfo. (2020). Finnish National Agency for Education & Ministry of Education and Culture. https://studyinfo.fi/wp2/en

The Constitution of Finland. (1999). (amendments up to 817/2018 included). Translation from Finnish. Ministry of Justice. https://www.finlex.fi/en/laki/kaannokset/1999/en19990731.pdf

Thurén, V. (2012). *Permission to translate: About authorizing and registering interpreters* [*Lupa tulkata—tulkkien auktorisoinnista ja rekisteröinnistä*] (in Finnish only). Humak University of Applied Sciences. http://urn.fi/URN:ISBN:978-952-456-130-3

Topo, P., Heiskanen, M-L., Rautavaara, A., Hannikainen-Ingman, K., & Saarikalle, K. & Tiilikainen, R. (2000). Interpreting services for the hearing and speech impaired. Implementation of the Disability Services Act [*Kuulo- ja puhevammaisten tulkkipalvelut. Vammaispalvelulain toteutuminen*] (in Finnish only). Sosiaali- ja terveysalan tutkimus- ja kehittämiskeskus (Stakes) raportteja 255. Stakes.

Tupi, E. (2018). The sign language civil activism case StopKela [*Viittomakielinen kansalaisaktivismi case stopKela*]. A Blog. Finnish Association of the Deaf. https://www.kuurojen liitto.fi/fi/blogi-listaus/viittomakielinen-kansalaisaktivismi-case-stopkela

Universities of Applied Sciences Act (2014). (amendments up to 563/2016 included). Translation from Finnish. Ministry of Education and Culture. https://www.finlex.fi/en/laki/kaannokset/2014/en20140932_20160563.pdf

TIMOTHY MAC HADJAH, DANIEL FOBI,
MARCO STANLEY NYARKO, AND
ELISA M. MARONEY

9

Reflecting on the Professionalization of Sign Language Interpreting in Ghana

Ghana is a small country in West Africa, comprised of approximately 92,000 square miles, with a population of approximately 28 million (Ghana Statistical Service, 2016). About 211,700 of the Ghanaian people have speech and hearing "impairments" (Ghana Census, 2010, as cited by Hadjah, 2016, p. 3). An estimated 30 to 81 indigenous languages are spoken in Ghana, along with at least three known sign languages: Ghanaian Sign Language (GSL), Adamorobe Sign Language (AdaSL), and Nanabin Sign Language (NSL; Hadjah, 2016; Nyst, 2010). AdaSL and NSL are considered as village sign languages in Ghana because their use among deaf people is limited to the geographic locations of two villages: Adamorobe in the Eastern Region and Nanabin in the Central Region. On the other hand, GSL is considered a de facto national language and the medium of instruction for deaf education in the country (Oppong & Fobi, 2019).

Historically, GSL is related to American Sign Language (ASL). In 1957, Andrew Jackson Foster, the first black deaf person to graduate from Gallaudet College, traveled to West Africa on a missionary trip and established the first school for the deaf in West Africa at Accra-Ghana, where he lived for 1 year, teaching at the school he established (Hairston & Smith, 1983; Oppong & Fobi, 2019). With the medium of instruction being Total Communication,[1] Foster presumably used ASL, which then permeated Ghanaian deaf education (Ilabor, 2010; Foster, 1975). The deaf school then became a hub for GSL emergence. As GSL has developed and spread, it has become the most commonly used form of sign language in Ghana (see Hadjah, 2016, for more about the current status of GSL).

179

WHO ARE WE?

Timothy Mac Hadjah is a sign language linguist currently pursuing a doctorate at Leiden University. Timothy's research journey has been deeply rooted in a personal connection with the deaf community in Ghana. This connection has evolved over the years and has significantly influenced his academic pursuits and career choices. His involvement in researching sign languages in Ghana stems from a profound familiarity with the region and an understanding of its rich cultural diversity. It has become imperative for him to delve deeper into the intricate signing systems within the Ghanaian deaf community. This endeavor goes beyond mere academic curiosity; it is driven by a genuine desire to facilitate effective communication, bridge gaps, and, most importantly, acknowledge and honor the diverse heritage of sign language variations within this community.

Timothy's journey into the world of sign languages began during his Basic Education/1st Cycle Education at Sarkodie M/A Primary/Junior High School in Koforidua, Eastern Region, Ghana. It was in this inclusive school setting that he first encountered the deaf community. This encounter sparked a profound fascination with sign language, with the underlying objective of fostering better understanding and inclusivity between the hearing and deaf communities in Ghana. Building on this passion, he completed his bachelor's degree in linguistics and philosophy in 2010. His dedication to sign language led him to engage deeply with the deaf community for field research, which culminated in the attainment of a master of arts (MA) degree in 2013 and a master of philosophy degree in 2016. However, his involvement with sign language and the deaf community extended far beyond the confines of academia. He voluntarily served as an interpreter for deaf people in church settings, striving to enhance their participation and inclusion. He also took on the role of a sign language interpreter at the University of Ghana, specifically within the Linguistics Department and the Office of Students with Special Needs (OSSN). His academic pursuits, practical experiences, and unwavering commitment to the deaf community have collectively shaped his interest in and dedication to the study of GSL.

Timothy firmly believes that understanding the diverse signing systems is essential not only for bridging communication gaps but also for honoring the unique linguistic traditions of this vibrant community. His positionality as a hearing signer deeply embedded within the deaf community in Ghana provides a unique perspective that enriches the comprehensive exploration presented in his research. It is his hope that his work will contribute to a greater understanding and appreciation of GSL and, in turn, foster increased inclusivity and recognition of the linguistic diversity within the Ghanaian deaf community.

Daniel (Dani) Fobi has more than 15 years of experience working as a hearing sign language interpreter. He grew up in a multilingual environment and speaks four languages. Dani's journey as an interpreter began with his involvement in the church and his undergraduate studies. As an undergraduate student, he had a colleague and housemate who was deaf, so anytime his interpreters were absent, Dani stepped in, which helped him understand deaf people. His interpreting skills also improved, since at the university he interpreted 16 courses in an academic year. At the same time, he supported interpreting at church, which gave him religious exposure to interpreting. Dani has worked as an interpreter in other contexts, including health, law court, basic school, and political platforms. Through this experience, he developed his knowledge of deaf people mainly through the interpreting lens and at the higher education level. He is currently a lecturer in deaf education and inclusive education, a sign language interpreter, and graduate programs coordinator at the University of Education, Winneba (UEW), Ghana. He is also a project officer and a visiting research fellow at the School of Education, University of Leeds, in the United Kingdom. His research interests are in early education for deaf children, inclusion for special needs individuals in various contexts, multimodal communication, and sign language interpreting. Dani is currently working to support scholarship in sub-Saharan Africa and building the academic and research capacity of researchers of the region by providing mentorship and professional development training to teachers.

Marco Stanley Nyarko is a deaf educator, sign language instructor, and interpreter trainer who has served both the international and national deaf community. Marco started learning sign language in 1995, 3 years after losing his hearing. Seeing the importance of sign language in deaf education, he developed a passion for sign language learning and research and assiduously participated in sign language programs. Marco has been actively involved in teaching sign language since 2005, when he was appointed as sign language tutor for Signs of Hope International Organization, a volunteer nongovernmental organization (NGO) based in the United States of America that offered volunteer services to deaf schools in Southern Ghana. For the best part of 3 years, Marco trained teachers in sign language in deaf schools to facilitate communication and teaching. In 2009, Marco participated in Educational Partnership for Africa Programs, an international program at the University of Central Lancashire (UCLan) in the United Kingdom, leading to the creation of the first sign language curriculum at the University of Ghana. In recognition of this effort, the Ghana National Association of the Deaf (GNAD) appointed Marco as sign language interpreting (SLI) trainer for the Association. Marco worked with GNAD, trained several national and local sign language interpreters, and engaged in sign language research work. Between 2017 and 2020, Marco served as a part-time lecturer in sign language at the University of Ghana, where he trained third- and fourth-year undergraduate students in the linguistic program. Currently, he works as a sign language lecturer at the College of Health Sciences, Kwame Nkrumah University of Science and Technology, Ghana.

Elisa Maroney began learning ASL when she was 20 years old at Oregon College of Education (now Western Oregon University). At the age of 22, she participated in a 1-year interpreter preparation program at Western Oregon State College (now Western Oregon University). The next year, she was a special undergraduate student at Gallaudet College (now University), living in the residence hall with deaf and deafblind roommates while taking general education classes with deaf students. At age 25, she participated in a 6-week interpreter training program at the National Technical Institute for the Deaf (NTID) at Rochester Institute of Technology. She then completed a bachelor of science degree in speech language pathology at the University of the District of Columbia. While working full-time at Gallaudet University, she completed a master's degree in linguistics there. Earning her doctorate in linguistics from the University of New Mexico, Elisa has been interpreting, teaching, and coordinating interpreter programs for more than 30 years. Currently, she is co-coordinator and a professor in the interpreting studies program at Western Oregon University. Elisa holds the National Interpreter Certificate, Ed: K–12 certification, along with Certificates of Interpretation and Transliteration from the Registry of Interpreters for the Deaf (RID), and Qualified Certification from the American Sign Language Teachers Association (ASLTA). She has served in many capacities in organizations supporting deaf children, adults, interpreters, and interpreter educators in the United States and abroad. In 2006, she was selected to as one of 13 commissioners on the Commission on Collegiate Interpreter Education (CCIE), joining the first accrediting body for interpreter education programs and the first group of commissioners. She served the CCIE as president from June 2011 to December 2013, followed by a 2-year term as immediate past president. She spent the 2015–2016 year on sabbatical leave teaching at the UEW. Since then, she has worked with deaf professionals, interpreters, and interpreter educators from the United States, Ghana, and Europe to develop interpreter education in Ghana, as well as to share their stories through presentations and publications.

CONTEXTUALIZATION: TRANSLATION AND INTERPRETING IN GHANA

Ghana is a multilingual West African country with an estimated 30 to 81 indigenous spoken languages (Bamgbose, 1991; Boadi, 1971; Dakubu, 1988; Grime, 1984; Lewis et al., 2014; Spencer, 1971). There is no consensus on the exact number of spoken languages in the country; this has been partly due to the lack of making a clear distinction between what should be constituted a dialect or a language (Obeng, 1997). With no *de jure* national language, English is the official language in the country (introduced as a foreign language by British colonial masters).

Ghana is a linguistically heterogeneous country where family members and friends served as nonprofessional interpreters in times past. Both English and Akan[2] have been the linguae francae in the country. As such, most interpreting services have centered on these languages. In 1992, the Ghana Association of Translators and Interpreters (GATI) was founded to professionalize their work. Within the first 25 years, the organization floundered, but in 2016, the association was relaunched (GATI, 2018–2020). Before the association's establishment, diploma programs in translation were ongoing in Ghana since 1964, when the School of Translation was established (Ghana Institute of Languages, 2020). In collaboration with the Ghana Institute of Languages (GIL), the University of Ghana in Legon offers a bachelor's in translation (GIL, 2020). The University of Ghana also offers a master's degree in conference interpreting and a master's degree in translation (University of Ghana, 2016). The language focus for these interpreting and translation courses at both GIL and the University of Ghana has been mainly on foreign languages, such as English, French, German, Russian, Arabic, Chinese, Portuguese, and Spanish. This does not come as a surprise since GIL was established to promote international relationships (GIL, 2020). As such, local languages have not been their focus.

The University of Ghana, Legon, offers a conference interpreter education program. It is a 24-month master's program for spoken language interpreters. The university has been in partnership with the Pan-African Consortium on Interpretation and Translation.

In Ghana, the Disability Act (Act 715, 2006) is the only legislation that advocates for the inclusion of persons with disabilities in all activities without discrimination. Although this act stipulates the various sanctions associated with discrimination against individuals on the basis of their disabilities, the law enforcers have yet to come to terms with ensuring that appropriate sanctions are given to those who breach the law. With regard to interpreting, there are no professional bodies that regulate interpreting activities; however, the Judicial Service of Ghana has an interpreter handbook that provides guidelines to professionalize interpreting services in the courtroom (*The Judiciary of Ghana: Interpreters' Handbook*, 2011). The handbook, which talks about interpreters' duties, responsibilities, work ethics, and education with regard to legal jargon, had Judicial Service interpreters as its target group rather than the general public. The Judicial Service is known to have permanent interpreters but none with skill in SLI.

PROFESSIONALIZATION OF SIGN LANGUAGE INTERPRETERS IN GHANA

There are many factors affecting the development of the SLI profession in Ghana (Adade et al., 2022). There is evidence to suggest that SLI services have existed in

Ghana (for deaf signers in the village of Adamorobe) before the emergence of GSL or even before Ghana gained independence in 1957 (see Kusters, 2014a; Miles, 2004). However, there are no historical records or traces of the professionalization of SLI in terms of registration or certification in the country (Oppong & Fobi, 2019). This could partly be due to cultural stereotypes of the past, in which deaf signers were alluded to as "societal misfits" (Nortey, 2009; Asmis, 1912, p.39) and deaf signers were not considered a linguistic minority group. Such cultural stereotypes and the fact that most well-known sign language interpreters in the past did not have any strong educational background for the work they did led to the notion of their work as a charitable service.

However, since the GNAD was established in 1968, there have been some groups of interpreters who have affiliated themselves with GNAD. This relationship with GNAD also brought interpreters together, and they formed an association in 2009, the Association of Ghanaian Sign Language Interpreters (AGSLI). The initial goal of forming AGSLI was to pursue an agenda to professionalize their work. Unfortunately, its management was weak, which gradually led to its dissolving into a dormant state. In 2015 and 2016, with sponsorship from the Star Ghana Foundation (Star Ghana)[3] and the Danish International Development Agency (DANIDA),[4] GNAD published a printed directory for all known sign language interpreters in the country. In the synopsis of the directory in 2016, GNAD portrayed SLI as a profession and outlined some key regulations and a code of ethics within which interpreters were expected to work. However, GNAD is unable to account for the professionalism of the interpreters listed in the directory. In 2018, a new sign language interpreters' association known as National Association of Sign Language Interpreters (NASLI)[5] was formed. NASLI was established in the Western Region of Ghana but was not popularly known until the 2020 COVID-19 crisis in the country, which called for the dissemination of information to members of the deaf community. NASLI is currently a vibrant interpreters association in the country.

As indicated previously, SLI in Ghana has existed as long as deaf communities have existed. Parents, siblings, relatives, and friends of deaf people served as interpreters even before formal education began for deaf people in Ghana in 1957 (Fobi, Fobi, Appau, & Oppong, in press). Because the majority of the interpreters did not understand sign language, they communicated through gestures, symbols, and icons of things for which they were interpreting. After Foster's introduction of formal education for deaf people in Ghana in 1957, there was a blend of ASL and the Ghanaian rudimental signs, which later evolved into GSL (Fobi & Oppong, 2019; Oppong & Fobi, 2019). Between 1957 and 1970, after schools had been established for deaf people, teachers of deaf and hard of hearing children served as interpreters in parent–teacher association (PTA) meetings and also for events in the communities that involved deaf individuals (Fobi et al., 2022).

As communities became more inclusive of deaf individuals, more teachers of deaf and hard of hearing children were recruited to interpret at events such as church gatherings and other related events. They were often church members who were not paid. However, incentives were given to those interpreters who visited the church from the outside and were not regular members of those churches. The churches that championed training for their members were the Church of Christ and the Jehovah's Witnesses (Fobi & Oppong, 2019). Currently, more churches and mosques in the country have joined in the training of sign language interpreters for their deaf members (Fobi et al., 2022). Because the exit point for the majority of deaf students is at the senior secondary level (Oppong & Fobi, 2019), the few deaf students who managed to get into tertiary education before the 21st century had to find their own means of coping with their education without any formal interpreting services provided. It was in 2006 that the UEW officially provided interpreters to three deaf students who enrolled in bachelor's degree programs at the UEW.

Ghana has approximately 15 schools for the deaf, and inclusive education was implemented officially in 2015 for first-cycle education (i.e., the first 9 years of education) and secondary-cycle education (i.e., secondary, vocational, or technical education; Oppong & Fobi, 2019). Organized interpreting services are only rarely available in inclusive schools (Oppong & Fobi, 2019). However, there are organized interpreting service provisions for deaf students at the tertiary level (Aseidu et al., 2018). There are about seven major public universities in the country, out of which the University of Ghana, the University of Cape Coast, and the UEW are known to have established offices with interpreters. The UEW has approximately 45,600 students, with the largest population of deaf students at about 50 in the 2014–2015 academic year (Oppong & Fobi, 2019). The UEW has employed upward of three full-time interpreters, five part-time interpreters, and two to eleven interns[6] during any given semester. They also have one to two recent graduates fulfilling their national service duty as sign language interpreters. National Service is a program for new university graduates to have practical experience while demonstrating their civic responsibility for Ghana.

Where We Are Today

GNAD is the principal representative organization that advocates for the deaf community in Ghana (Oppong & Fobi, 2019). A president and board members, all deaf, head the association. GNAD has branches in each of the previously recognized 10 regions of Ghana (i.e., Eastern, Western, Volta, Upper-East, Upper-West, Northern, Greater Accra, Central, Brong-Ahafo, & Ashanti Region).[7] All 10 branches are active and are responsible for recruiting and training interpreters to support their advocacy for deaf communities in Ghana. GNAD has been playing an active role in spreading the use of GSL to students in schools for deaf children, teachers of deaf and hard of hearing children, and parents of deaf children (Fobi & Oppong, 2019; Oppong & Fobi, 2019). GNAD has a permanent office in Accra from which it operates. It sometimes organizes workshops on the acquisition of GSL for teachers and students in schools for the deaf. Upon request, GNAD helps professional educators of deaf children to produce textbooks on sign language for deaf people and the general public in Ghana.

The Ghana Institute of Linguistics, Literacy, and Bible Translation (GILLBT) is a Christian NGO devoted solely to linguistic work in the country. Currently, GILLBT is working on a special project on research, education, and Bible translation into sign language for deaf people. Work has been started on translation of the New Testament. At the moment, GILLBT has about five deaf translators working as a team on Bible translation. We understand that the project might take some time to complete. One eminent challenge the project faces is variation in GSL and how to negotiate for the appropriate variants that might be suitable for the majority of deaf Ghanaians. It is hoped that the translation work, when complete, will be published online and in an app of the Deaf Bible Society[8] because of their partnership with GILLBT (C. A. Atimbange, personal communication, October 13, 2021). A follow-up investigation indicated that GILLBT has started publishing some of their work (the Book of Luke, New Testament) on the Deaf Bible Society website[9] and through their app.[10] Through partnerships and collaborations, the organization has translated the Christian Bible into many Ghanaian languages. With regard to linguistic work, GILLBT's main collaborators have been the University of Ghana and the Summer Institute of Linguistics based in the United States.

Before the GILLBT project, there had been previous Bible translation work in GSL. For example, between 2007 and 2009, cohorts of selected deaf Ghanaians were invited to Kenya to be trained in Christian leadership and Bible translation by DOOR-Africa Deaf Christian Leadership and Translation Program (A. Okeyre, personal communication, October 14, 2021). After the training, Biblical stories were translated into GSL and published in the Deaf Bible Society app. Apart from Bible translation, there is no known official sign language translation work in Ghana.

Outside the legal domain, organizations such as tertiary institutions, social welfare organizations, GNAD, and religious bodies set their codes of ethics to guide interpreters' practices within those contexts. Interpreters who work in tertiary institutions are often required to have a minimum of a bachelor's degree and excellent signing skills (usually assessed on the basis of recommendations from the deaf community or people who can communicate with deaf people). In other settings, interpreters are often recruited on the basis of their interest in sign language and their signing skills. In such settings, very little attention is paid to the qualifications of the interpreters. In all these settings, there is little supervision to ensure that interpreters adhere to their codes of ethics (which often do not exist); often, deaf signers assess the interpreters, and such reports are given to the department heads, who manage the interpreters.

There are a few occasions on which deaf people in Ghana are involved in direct or relay interpreting (Kusters, 2012; 2014a, 2014b). For example, there are instances in which foreign deaf researchers visit Ghana for field work and get assistance from relay interpreting by local deaf people. There is also direct interpreting by educated deaf people, who serve as interpreters mostly to handle disputes between deaf individuals and a member of the hearing community. Their intervention mainly helps resolve domestic issues because they are knowledgeable in the pragmatics and ethnography of communication for both the deaf and the hearing communities. Another instance in which deaf people might be engaged in SLI is during church gatherings (Kusters, 2014b). In these instances, the deaf interpreters are mostly bilingual in the sign languages of Ghana or knowledgeable in the English language to provide interpreting support. Even though deaf interpreters in Ghana are not trained for the job, there are other instances in which deaf people are engaged in interpreting services. They rely mostly on a hearing interpreter who might not possess sign language linguistic competencies. In situations such as conferences, deaf people with multilingual sign language abilities serve as interpreters and interpret foreign sign languages into GSL for the deaf Ghanaian audience. For example, on August 10, 2019, there was an international conference held at the University of Ghana. This conference brought deaf linguists from America, Europe, and different African countries. The conference also attracted the deaf community in Ghana. Because of the relationship of some researchers with deaf people from Adamorobe village, the conference was graced with monolingual sign language users of AdaSL. This created a situation for relay interpreting by multilingual deaf individuals. The presenters had different sign language linguistic backgrounds, and as such, the service of a deaf interpreter with multilingual sign language competency was engaged. More research on the contributions of deaf interpreters in Ghana is needed, as well as development of interpreter preparation opportunities for deaf people to become interpreters.

Within the tertiary context, deaf people support their interpreters in instances in which hearing interpreters are unable to make meaning for deaf students who are often not familiar with or are new to learning through interpreters. In such cases, deaf students who understand what hearing interpreters interpret mediate (broker) to their colleagues in GSL. In some instances, hearing interpreters are unable to comprehend what some deaf students sign when they interact with lecturers in the classrooms. Their deaf colleagues (classmates) interpret to the hearing interpreters before these interpreters can relay the information to hearing lecturers and students. Though not documented, anecdotal evidence suggests similar interpreting occurs in various settings, including courts, hospitals, and other social gatherings.

Profile of Interpreters and Interpreting Work

Maroney et al. (2020) surveyed 13 sign language interpreters in Ghana and found that the interpreters they surveyed reported that they were multilingual, with sign language as one of their working languages. Many of the survey respondents reported that they used a number of spoken languages, including English, Ga, Twi, and Fanti, as well as GSL. They tended to work between GSL and a spoken language (English and/or an indigenous spoken language).

Of the 13 interpreters, one interpreter had a master's degree, two had bachelor's degrees, three had diplomas (indicating completion of higher education in technical, vocational, and liberal arts disciplines that do not result in bachelor's degrees), and seven were students in their third year of sign language coursework in tertiary institutions. All but three of the Ghanaian interpreters were affiliated with a university. Only one was employed as a full-time interpreter; two were beginning their 1-year compulsory national service as interpreters, and seven were beginning their internships as interpreters. Three were community interpreters, unaffiliated with a university.

Similar to other parts of the world, the settings in which interpreters work include church/religious settings, educational institutions, community settings, social events, conferences, courts, political campaigns, and police stations.

The 13 interpreters said that in their current practice as sign language interpreters, their employment might be full time or part time. The only interpreters who were paid as professionals for their work were at the tertiary level. Others performed voluntary interpreting services as National Service interpreters, student interns, and volunteers; none of these were professionally trained. National Service in Ghana refers to a 1-year service obligation of recent graduates of tertiary institutions; they receive a small stipend for their service.

Although the sample size was small, and the data collection was limited to the Central Region, these preliminary results indicate that interpreters working in Ghana are confronted by challenges and achievements familiar to other countries throughout the world where SLI is at different stages of professional development.

SIGN LANGUAGE INTERPRETER EDUCATION IN GHANA

With regard to SLI education, often undergraduate students trained in the Education for the Hearing Impaired of the Department of Special Education are given some training in interpreting to support deaf students at the UEW. There is also a 1-year diploma program at the University of Cape Coast (UCC) for interpreters. The GSL Interpretation Program started in July 2017, hosted by UCC and organized by GNAD with funding support from DANIDA. Currently, the Department of Education and Psychology at UCC has incorporated a sandwich session (a short session that occurs between traditional semesters) diploma program in GSL interpreting.

In addition to the diploma program at the UCC, there are short-term interpreter training opportunities offered throughout the country and at the UEW. The diploma program in GSL at UCC under the Department of Education and Psychology is intended to be a two–sandwich semester course for participants who have some communicative knowledge and proficiency in GSL (University of Cape Coast, 2020) but will be organized into three sandwich sessions for successful applicants who do not meet specific criteria, for example, competency in GSL. The university has also indicated publicly that they will involve GNAD in their interview and assessment process in admitting potential students. With this gesture, there is reason to believe that potential deaf applicants can be involved in the program because some deaf people were among the first cohort of students trained in 2017. The premier program at UCC commenced with visiting professional deaf lecturers from Africa and Europe.

The Diploma Course at the UCC

The diploma course for GNAD interpreters began as a result of a partnership between GNAD and the UCC. The course was approved within 6 months in 2017, and an announcement was made for interpreters to apply. Twenty-seven interpreters were admitted to the course as the first cohort. In 2018, a second cohort made up of 26 interpreters was added to increase the number of professional interpreters.

There were three lecturers for the course at UCC. The first was a lecturer from Uganda, who works in applied sign language linguistics; he was selected to lead the course. The second lecturer was a native GSL signer who held a bachelor's degree in special education. His role was to offer the practical aspects of the course, while the Ugandan lecturer offered the theoretical aspects. The third lecturer, a deaf Ghanaian, was an experienced trainer who had previously received informal education on GSL documentation and development from the Deaf Education Project Ghana in 2009. In addition, he served as a GSL teacher and advocate for many years (J. Amuah, personal communication, December 22, 2020). As such, he was a suitable candidate to assist with the training. He taught history and deaf education in Ghana as part of the course.

GNAD Interpreter Training Program

GNAD occasionally, depending on availability of funds, embarks on short-term training programs for the general public. In such training, GNAD typically invites professional educators to provide instruction. Participants are given a certificate of participation after successfully taking the training (R. F. Manso, personal communication, April 22, 2019). Such short-term, standardized training is vital to most interpreters in Ghana because the majority of them have learned sign language from family members, friends, and churches or at private institutions with quasi-certification.[11]

The first record of GNAD providing a series of SLI training is from 2003 (GNAD Newsletter, 2003, 2009, 2010). One notable interpreter training, an Interpreters Training Workshop for the district and national interpreters, was conducted from August 23, 2009, to September 5, 2009. The facilitators of the workshop were a senior lecturer from South Africa and an instructor from Ghana, who is a hearing heritage signer. The 2-week workshop was offered as a refresher for interpreters who have been interpreting for many years but lacked current professional skills. The workshop was funded by DANIDA and the United Nations Educational, Scientific, and Cultural Organization (UNESCO).

In most interpreter training organized by GNAD, regional leaders of GNAD select two interpreters from each of the then 10 regions of Ghana on the basis of how often these interpreters offer services to the deaf community. The refresher course became an annual event where new interpreters were included with the previous group until the program ended in 2013. In 2015, GNAD, under the DANIDA project, again organized assessment for interpreters leading to the selection of interpreters who would participate in the diploma course at the UCC.

Short-Term Interpreter Training

The short-term annual training opportunities at the UEW are cofacilitated by Ghanaian interpreters along with a group of faculty and students from Western Oregon University, as well as one British Sign Language (BSL)/English interpreter from Edinburgh, Scotland. This program is infused with the demand–control schema and observation–supervision,[12] with an emphasis on developing a community of practice for interpreters in Ghana.

Most of the training opportunities are face-to-face, but there has been at least one distance program offered by two Western Oregon University faculty using M-learning[13] on the Canvas platform (Darden & Maroney, 2018). This modular program was 8 weeks in duration. Half of the participants were from the United States, and the other half were from Ghana. All were working interpreters. The demand–control schema and supervision concepts were explored and practiced. The interpreter educators provided this at no cost to the participants.

As mentioned earlier, there is one formal SLI education program in Ghana at the UCC. Students attend what is called a "sandwich" session in the summer. This session is an 8-week semester for the first year when the program starts and 10 weeks for the second semester. Students are in class from 8:00 a.m. to 5:00 p.m. each working day during the semester while on campus. During the academic year, students participate in both theoretical and practical work to improve their interpreting skills. The two-semester course is a face-to-face program in which students come into contact with tutors and lecturers.

There is no training program for educators of interpreting or translation in Ghana. There are doctoral students (including one of the authors of this chapter) studying in related disciplines who might be able to teach interpreting. The current trainers are language instructors or members of the deaf community, or they are coming from outside of Ghana.

Interpreting Services During COVID-19

Access to interpreting services during the COVID-19 pandemic was largely through the presidential briefings and daily media briefings by the Ministry of Health. On March 12, 2020, the first confirmed cases of COVID-19 were recorded in Ghana. According to the Minister of Health, these two cases were imported from Turkey and Norway (Agyeman-Manu, 2020). The demand for SLI in media briefings began shortly after the President began his regular media briefings (Edwards, Nyarko, & Akrasi-Sarpong, forthcoming). This was because in the first briefing, interpreters were absent, and the deaf community advocated through various social media platforms, insisting "Bring Our Interpreters Back." The government of Ghana accepted this and acted swiftly to bring on interpreters in the subsequent media briefings (Swanwick et al., 2020). Also, because schools were on break, the Ghana Education Service (GES), in collaboration with other state agencies and the media, facilitated learning for students on television. In most of these television programs, there were interpreters who interpreted for deaf students at the various levels and for the various lessons (Swanwick et al., 2020). This service paved the way for deaf individuals to access information on the COVID-19 pandemic in Ghana. In different places in the world, sign languages are seen as disaster entertainment; some interpreters have become social media celebrities (Hou & Octavian, 2020), and others have become "pandemic stars" (Brown, 2020).

Although deaf individuals in Ghana could access information on the pandemic, information was limited to the presidential and Ministry of Health media briefings, with minimal access to other information, such as the advertisements on COVID-19. GNAD in collaboration with Star Ghana and DANIDA reproduced some of these COVID-19 adverts in GSL and shared the information on social media, on platforms such as WhatsApp, Facebook, and Instagram.

The Road Ahead

Graduate and undergraduate programs in interpreting studies were proposed at the UEW in 2014 and 2016, respectively. To date, there has been no movement forward on these degrees.

Several Ghanaians, deaf and hearing, are currently pursuing higher education both at home and abroad in the areas of sign language linguistics, deaf education, and SLI. This seems promising for the future of interpreter education in Ghana because one of the main challenges observed is interpreter educator availability in the country. There have also been several calls for and a government commitment to create accessibility for deaf citizens in the country (Hadjah, 2016). For example, the Parliament of Ghana has recently agreed to engage a sign language interpreter as part of the reforms in the House. One can, however, observe that awareness is gradually being created about the need for professional interpreters in all sections of society, including health care, education, and the legal system (e.g., police, court, and Parliament).

The University of Ghana, Legon, is developing a public service interpreter education program that will include pathways for SLI. The UCC in collaboration with GNAD is providing a diploma program for interpreters, and the UEW, in collaboration with Western Oregon University, continues to offer short-term training and has plans to start undergraduate and graduate programs in SLI and a graduate program in deaf education.

Concluding Remarks

SLI in Ghana has undergone a series of transitions since its inception. Although there have been some challenges associated with these transitions, considerable success has been achieved in SLI and for deaf people. At the moment, there is a lack of synergy between the various institutions in their quest to promote best practices for interpreters and SLI education. Therefore, the various stakeholders must make concerted efforts. Available expertise and resources need to be pulled together to support interpreters and also to help bridge the communication gap that exists between the deaf community and hearing people. Government and other law enforcement agencies in the country should show their commitment by ensuring that succinct laws are put in place to support communication for deaf people and to make certain that those laws and regulations are adhered to in the country. The nation should also work toward the standardization of interpreting through a professional code of ethics in all settings in which interpreting is required.

Notes

1. *Total Communication* is an educational philosophy that combines several different methods of communication, primarily signing and speaking simultaneously.
2. A Kwa language belonging to the branch of the Niger-Congo language family spoken in Ghana and Ivory Coast.
3. See https://www.star-ghana.org

4. DANIDA is the overarching term for the organization under the Ministry of Foreign Affairs of Denmark, which is responsible for Denmark's international development cooperation.
5. See https://www.naslig.org
6. Students who, as part of their bachelor's or diploma training, are required to do one semester teaching or interpreting.
7. In 2019, the 10 administrative regions in the country were increased to 16 regions, with the addition of Bono-East, Ahafo, Savannah, North-East, Western-North, and Oti Region.
8. The Deaf Bible Society is a nongovernmental organization based in the United States devoted to spreading the message in the Bible to all deaf people in the world through sign language.
9. See https://www.deafbiblesociety.com
10. See https://apps.apple.com/nl/app/deaf-bible/id567788508?l=en
11. Certificate obtained from an unaccredited school or course of study.
12. Dean and Pollard (2013) have developed a work analysis framework that provides guidance for interpreters when making ethical and effective decisions. Demands are the challenges the interpreter faces, and controls are the resources the interpreter uses to mitigate the challenges.
13. *M-Learning* or *mobile learning* is receiving an education via the Internet and one's own personal devices, such as a mobile telephone or a tablet.

References

Adade, R., Appau, O., Mprah, W. K., Fobi, D. Marfo, P. S., & Atta-Osei, G. (2022). Factors influencing sign language interpretation service in Ghana: The interpreters' perspective. *Journal of Interpretation, 30*(1), Article 1. https://digitalcommons.unf.edu/joi/vol30/iss1/1

Asiedu, M. A., Hadjah, M. T., & Tei-Doe O. I. (2018). Tertiary education for persons with disability: The role of the Office of Students with Special Needs at the University of Ghana. *Ghana Journal on Disability, 1*, 85–103.

Asmis, W. (1912). Law and policy: Relating to the natives of the Gold Coast and Nigeria. *Journal of the Royal African Society, 12*(45), 17–51.

Bamgbose, A. (1991). *Language and the nation: The language question in Sub-Saharan Africa*. Edinburgh University Press.

Boadi, L. A. (1971). Education and the role of English in Ghana. In J. Spencer (Ed.), *The English language in West Africa* (pp. 49–65). Longman Group.

Brown, R. L. (2020, August 30). How 2 sign language interpreters became unlikely pandemic stars. National Public Radio. https://www.kisu.org/npr-coronavirus-updates/2020-08-30/how-two-sign-language-interpreters-became-unlikely-pandemic-stars

Dakubu, M.-E. K. (1988). *The languages of Ghana*. Kegan Paul International for the International African Institute.

Darden, V. & Maroney, E. (2018). "Craving to hear from you": An exploration of M-learning in global interpreter education. *Translation & Interpreting Studies, 13*(3), 442–464.

Data Productions Unit, Ghana Statistical Service. (2016). *Populations projections summary, 2010–2016.* http://www.statsghana.gov.gh/docfiles/2010phc/Projected%20population%20by%20sex%202010%20-%202016.pdf

Dean, R. K., & Pollard, R. Q. (2013). *The Demand-Control Schema: Interpreting as a practice profession*. CreateSpace Independent Publishing Platform.

Fobi, D., Fobi, J., Appau, O., & Oppong, A. M. (2022). Interpreting in Ghana. In E. Maroney & Y. N. Offei (Eds.), *Signed languages, interpreting, and the deaf community in Ghana*. https://openoregon.pressbooks.pub/ghanaiandeaf/

Fobi, D., & Oppong, A. M. (2019). Communication approaches for educating deaf and hard of hearing (DHH) children in Ghana: Historical and contemporary issues. *Deafness & Education International*, *21*(4), 195–209.

Foster, A. (1975). *The social aspect of deafness: School years*. Keynote presentation at the Seventh World Congress of the Deaf, Washington, DC.

Ghana Association of Translators and Interpreters. (2018–2020). *History of GATI*. http://gatigh.org/pages/about_history.html

Ghana Institute of Languages. (2020). *About us: Our history and background*. http://gil.edu.gh/about.html

GNAD Newsletter. (2003). Bi-Annual publication of the Ghana National Association of the Deaf. Issue No. 5.

GNAD Newsletter. (2009). Bi-Annual publication of the Ghana National Association of the Deaf. Issue No. 13.

GNAD Newsletter. (2010). Bi-Annual publication of the Ghana National Association of the Deaf. Issue No. 14.

Grimes, B. (1984). *Ethnologue: Languages of the world*. Wycliffe Bible Translators.

Hadjah, T. M. (2016). *Number marking in Ghanaian Sign Language* [Unpublished master's dissertation]. University of Ghana.

Hairston, E., & Smith, L. (1983). *Black and deaf in America: Are we that different*. T.J. Publishers.

Hou, L., & Robinson, O. (2020). Sign languages as disaster entertainment. *Anthropology News*, *10*. https://www.anthropology-news.org/articles/sign-languages-as-disaster-entertainment/

Judiciary of Ghana. (2011). *Interpreters handbook*. http://www.jtighana.org/downloads/publications/Interpretershandbook.pdf

Kusters, A. (2012). Being a deaf white anthropologist in Adamorobe: Some ethical and methodological issues. In U. Zeshan & C. de Vos (Eds.), *Sign languages in village communities: Anthropological and linguistic insights* (pp. 27–52). De Gruyter Mouton.

Kusters, A. (2014a). Deaf sociality and the deaf Lutheran church in Adamorobe, Ghana. *Sign language Studies*, *14*(4), 466–487.

Kusters, A. (2014b). Language ideologies in the shared signing community of Adamorobe. *Language in Society*, *43*(2), 139–158.

Lewis, M. P., Gary F. S, & Charles D. F. (2014). (Eds.). *Ethnologue: Languages of the world*, 17th ed. SIL International. https://www.ethnologue.com/country/GH?ip_login_no_cache=%85%96%F9%9D%E7%23%C7%08&cache

Maroney, E., Fobi, D., Puhlman, B., & Buadee, C. M. (2020). Interpreting in Ghana. In D. Hunt & E. Shaw (Eds.), *The Second International Symposium on Signed Language Interpretation and Translation Research* (pp. 20–35). Gallaudet University Press.

Miles, M. (2004). Locating deaf people, gesture and sign in African histories, 1450s–1950s, *Disability & Society*, *19*(5), 531–545.

Nortey, D. A. (2009). *Barriers to social participation for the deaf and hard of hearing in Ghana*. Master's thesis, The University of Bergen.

Nyst, V. (2010). Sign languages in West Africa. In D. Brentari (Ed.), *Sign languages: A Cambridge language survey* (pp. 405–432). Cambridge University Press.

Obeng, S. (1997). An analysis of the linguistic situation in Ghana. *African Languages and Cultures, 10*(1), 63–81.

Oppong, A. M., & Fobi, D. (2019). Deaf education in Ghana. In H. Knoors, M. Brons & M. Marschark (Eds.), *Deaf education beyond the western world* (pp. 53–72). Oxford University Press.

Pan African Masters Consortium in Interpretation and Translation. (2017). *Universities.* https://pamcit.unon.org/universities-0

Spencer, J. (1971). West Africa and the English language. In J. Spencer (Ed.), *The English language in West Africa* (pp. 1–34). Longman Group.

University of Ghana, Legon. (2016). *Graduate academic programmes.* http://admission.ug.edu.gh/applying/postgraduate/graduate-academic-programmes

University of Cape Coast. (2020). *Sandwich admissions (undergraduate).* https://ucc.edu.gh/admission-notices/sandwich-admissions-undergraduate

University of Ghana, Legon. (2014). *MA Conference Interpreting.* https://www.ug.edu.gh/french/admissions/ma-conference-interpreting

SARAH SHERIDAN, TERESA LYNCH,
AND LORRAINE LEESON

10

Sign Language Interpreting in Ireland

This chapter documents the development of sign language interpreting (SLI) education and research in Ireland. In 1994, the first cohort of interpreters graduated with a diploma in Irish Sign Language (ISL)/English Interpreting.[1] The funding for this initial training was provided by the European Union. State funding commenced in 2001, marking the establishment of the Centre for Deaf Studies (CDS) at Trinity College Dublin (TCD). These landmark outcomes were the result of sustained lobbying by the Irish deaf community and allies. As we will see, several intermittent steps led to the formation of the CDS, including increased levels of societal and political awareness of ISL and recognition of the Irish deaf community.

Ireland has two official languages recognized in the Constitution of Ireland (1937):[2] Irish is the first official language of Ireland, while English is the second language of the state. In practice, English is pervasive and is the de facto working language. ISL does not have constitutional recognition. However, the Irish Sign Language Act of 2017 (henceforth the ISL Act) protects individuals whose preferred language is ISL. The passing of the ISL Act on December 24, 2017, was a momentous occasion that followed the culmination of more than three decades of politicization by the Irish deaf community (Conama, 2019). Moreover, the ISL Act espouses the right to linguistic and cultural autonomy and access to public services through ISL:

> The State recognises the right of Irish Sign Language users to use Irish Sign Language as their native language and the corresponding duty on all public bodies to provide Irish Sign Language users with free interpretation when availing of or seeking to access statutory entitlements and services. (ISL Act 2017; Section 3[1])

The ISL Act was formally commenced in December 2020, 3 years after the act's adoption. There are regulations written into the act that facilitate monitoring of progress, with a 3-year post-commencement review due to take place in 2023. However, a number of critical developments have followed from commencement of the act, including an interpreter registration process, with details to follow.

Before the ISL Act, ISL was mentioned explicitly in just one piece of legislation: the Education Act (1988). There, it was referenced in a section on support services. However, citizens of Northern Ireland (which forms part of the United Kingdom [UK] of Great Britain and Northern Ireland) who use ISL and/or British Sign Language (BSL) were afforded recognition under the auspices of the Good Friday Agreement,[3] which was ratified by both the government of the UK and the government of the Republic of Ireland. This came into effect on December 2, 1999.[1] More recently (March 7, 2018), the United Nations Convention on the Rights of Persons with Disabilities (UNCRPD) was ratified in Ireland. Ireland signed the convention in March 2007 yet was the last European Union member state to ratify it. Therefore, its implementation is a work in progress.[4]

According to the Irish Census 2016,[5] 4,226 persons in the Republic of Ireland use ISL in the home. Leeson and Saeed (2012) suggest that on the island of Ireland (including Northern Ireland), this figure could rise to 65,000 when second (or subsequent) language users are included. This includes family and friends of deaf people, as well as those who undertake classroom learning of ISL. This echoes estimations that have been put forward in other contexts when the absolute numbers of sign language users in a region are considered to be higher than official statistics (De Meulder, 2018). One of the challenges we face is the lack of robust data around such figures, and in particular, disaggregated figures that will allow us to clearly see how many deaf signers are based in a given territory. The lack of robust data impedes language planning (Leeson & van den Bogaerde, 2020).

The economic context of a country influences investment in education and research. Ireland has experienced a turbulent decade in this regard. Leeson and Lynch (2009) commented on the buoyant "Celtic Tiger" economy during that period, as there had been unprecedented economic growth in the 1990s and 2000s. This took a remarkable turn in 2008, as the country fell into a downward spiral of economic decline, culminating in a bailout from the International Monetary Fund (Bielenberg, 2018) that had significant consequences. Locally, it led to funding from the Irish Ministry for Education for a taught master's of arts (MA) program at the CDS being halted, while government funding that was to support an ambitious cross-Ireland roll-out of a 4-year blended learning bachelor of arts (BA) in deaf studies, which included a pathway in SLI, was cut by more than 70%. This meant that our plans for engagement with partner universities in the south of the country (Cork) and the mid-west (Limerick/Tipperary) could not be implemented. Instead, we moved forward with a traditional face-to-face (F2F) bachelor program in Dublin.

Although the economy stabilized, and continued growth was forecast ahead of the COVID-19 pandemic in 2020–2021, Irish investment in higher education remains firmly toward the bottom end of the scale in comparison with other countries within the Organization for Economic Cooperation and Development (OECD), with 0.26% of gross domestic product (GDP) invested in research and development (the OECD average is 0.51% of GDP; Government of Ireland, 2018). This context makes it challenging to propose new programs or secure Irish governmental research funding. Despite this context, we have secured funding from European sources that has allowed us to move forward in other ways.

Ireland is a culturally and linguistically diverse country. The Irish Census 2016 illustrates this point, showing that 11.6% of the population comprises non–Irish nationals.[6] This trend of inward migration is relatively new. With regard to population change, in 1987, the number of "immigrants" per thousand of the population amounted to 17.2. In 2019, figures suggest an increase to 88.6 per thousand.[7] No data are available on the number of inward deaf migrants, a point that requires investigation to ensure necessary supports are in place.

WHO ARE WE?

Sarah is hearing and was born and raised in Dublin, Ireland. She does not have any deaf family members, but she developed an early interest in ISL as a result of having deaf signing neighbors. When Sarah went on to secure her first job, she worked alongside a deaf man who sparked her interest in formally learning ISL. This was the catalyst for the beginning of her ISL learning journey, and she began attending ISL evening classes in 1999. Over time, she became aware of the CDS at TCD and decided to leave her career in banking to train as an interpreter. At that time, a degree program was not offered in Ireland, so Sarah completed two diplomas, one in deaf studies and one in ISL/English interpreting. Her freelance interpreting career commenced in 2007, and she simultaneously worked on a full-time master's degree in intercultural studies at Dublin City University (DCU).

Sarah is registered as an interpreter with the Register of Irish Sign Language Interpreters (RISLI), and over the past 16 years, she has interpreted in a variety of settings, specializing in medical and mental health interpreting with a particular interest in maternity care. She served on the committee of the Council of Irish Sign Language Interpreters (CISLI) from 2011 to 2013 and the Board of the Sign Language Interpreting Service (SLIS) from 2013 to 2016. Since 2019, she has been a member of the Deaf Education Partnership Group.

Since joining TCD as an assistant professor in 2011, Sarah has taught at both the undergraduate and postgraduate levels and delivered continuous professional development (CPD) training to practicing sign language interpreters, most recently contributing to the inaugural Irish Deaf Interpreter training program. She has also served as an external examiner for the undergraduate and postgraduate SLI programs at the University of Wolverhampton in the United Kingdom.

From a research perspective, Sarah completed her doctor of philosophy (PhD) in 2019 on the topic of sign language learning anxiety. More broadly, her research explores aspects related to identity, social justice, the psychology of language learning, and SLI workplace well-being. Her most recent publication (Sheridan & O'Donnell, 2023) documents the experiences of Irish-based sign language interpreters working during the COVID-19 pandemic, where she puts forward recommendations to promote SLI workplace well-being and career longevity.

Sarah's research has been informed by, and informs, her teaching. She endeavors to find solutions to longstanding language learning issues—for example, reducing language learning anxiety and promoting positive psychology in language learning spaces. Two years ago, she developed a postgraduate elective module, "Psychology of Language Learning," and she enjoys creating and adapting modules with research findings and her professional experience in mind. She has a background in course design, and along with Lorraine Leeson, she developed a postgraduate diploma in sign language interpreting. Sarah is passionate about continually developing her pedagogical practice. She undertook a postgraduate diploma in educational studies (TCD, 2015) and a postgraduate certificate in workplace wellness (2021) and has completed several teaching-related short courses, most recently receiving a Digital Badge in Universal Design for Teaching and Learning from the National Forum and Trinity-Inclusive Curriculum Project.

As director of equality, diversity, and inclusion (EDI) at Trinity's School of Linguistic, Speech, and Communication Sciences, Sarah champions inclusive education to create welcoming classrooms and social spaces for all students and staff. She continues to advocate for inclusive policies and curricula, equitable processes, and accessible events, and she will support initiatives to enhance a diverse teaching and learning community at the School.

Teresa was born deaf, the youngest in a family that was hearing apart from one deaf brother. Although communication with much of her family was difficult, Teresa's brother attended the St. Joseph's School for Deaf Boys and signed with her when he was at home. Because she was lucky enough to have her deaf brother as a role model, ISL became Teresa's first language.

During Teresa's time at St. Mary's School for Deaf Girls, the use of signing was prohibited. Students were taught only through ineffective methods of lipreading and speech. Consequently, students' general level of educational attainment was poor. Teresa was not encouraged to complete her Leaving Certificate (the final examination for school leavers in Ireland). Instead, she left school early and spent several years working for an airline. At the same time, Teresa became involved in the Irish deaf community. She joined committees and groups, such as the Dublin Deaf Association. Notably, after years of membership and service on various committees,

Teresa became the first female chairperson of the Irish Deaf Society (IDS). Through her involvement with the deaf community, Teresa became more consciously aware of the barriers and discrimination that deaf people face every day, and her interest in advocacy and activism was ignited.

For decades, the Irish deaf community never used any official name to describe their method of communication. Even among deaf people themselves, signing was not conceptualized as a full language. Teresa came to feel that this was not accurate she recognized that the language they used was rich and complex. In 1988, Teresa gave a presentation at the IDS's first congress, where she addressed Ireland's deaf community for the first time on the topic of "What is ISL?" To Teresa and others, it was clear that ISL was deserving of greater understanding, recognition, and status. After 30 full years of advocating and campaigning, Teresa was proud to see ISL recognized by the Irish government as Ireland's third official language in 2017.

In 1993, Teresa and her husband moved to the United States of America, where she joined a cohort of students who would become the first qualified deaf interpreters (DIs) in the United States. This group was trained by MJ Bienvenu (deaf) and Betty Colonomos (hearing heritage signer). Subsequently, Teresa became one of the first students to study in the newly established Department of Deaf Studies at Gallaudet University. When Teresa learned that her family would be expanding, she withdrew from Gallaudet. After the birth of her son in 1995, the family of three returned to Ireland.

Back in Ireland, Teresa worked as a DI and also took a position with the IDS, where she became the first deaf person to be appointed as supervisor to a staff of 24. In 2001, she received a diploma in community management from the National College of Ireland. In 2003, she began studying for her diploma at the CDS in TCD and qualified as an ISL teacher. During this time, Teresa was also heavily involved with the National Deaf Women of Ireland (NDWI), organizing workshops across Ireland and translating information for the deaf community on topics such as domestic violence.

Beginning in 2009, Teresa taught ISL and interpreting at CDS and published many research papers in collaboration with deaf and hearing colleagues. In 2011, she began a Master degree in Deafhood Studies at Bristol University, which she completed with a thesis discussing the professionalization of DIs in Ireland.

In 2019, Teresa and Lorraine Leeson were granted funding by the Citizens' Information Board and by SLIS to design and set up a 1-year program to train DIs in Ireland. This course was run by the CDS at TCD. Because of the COVID-19 pandemic, it was conducted entirely online; nevertheless, it was still an enormous success, and out of 24 original participants, 23 graduated to become qualified DIs.

In recent years, Teresa has been active in the deaf community and in the world of interpreting. She was the chairperson of NDWI from 2011 to 2019 and was a member of the NDWI focus group who created and revised ISL vocabulary relating to domestic abuse and gender-based violence (GBV). The outputs are aimed specifically at providing improved communication with deaf refugees and immigrants who do not know ISL. Teresa's contribution to glossary-building also included significant contributions to the IDS subcommittee tasked with creating COVID-related signs for use by interpreters during daily televised Health Service Executive briefings, ensuring the Irish deaf community's adequate access to information throughout the pandemic.

In 2021, Teresa was awarded Woman of the Year by NDWI. Teresa was heavily involved in the creation of RISLI and currently sits on the RISLI Panel. Teresa continues to teach ISL and interpreting at the CDS, as well as working actively as a DI. Her areas of interest with regard to interpreting include legal and medical settings.

Lorraine grew up in a hearing family in Cabra, a Dublin locale steeped in Irish deaf history and where many deaf people lived because of the close proximity to two major deaf schools. As a result, she had an early introduction to the Irish deaf community. Having studied childcare on leaving school, she took a class in sign language and then worked as a houseparent in St. Joseph's School for Deaf Boys. In 1992, the IDS, TCD, and the University of Bristol secured funding to run the first ISL/English interpreter training program alongside an ISL teacher training pathway, and Lorraine was selected as a student. This meant studying between the UK and Ireland and being exposed to deaf and hearing people using a range of different sign languages. While at Bristol University, Lorraine developed a keen interest in sign linguistics, which prompted her to continue studying. She completed a master's degree and then a PhD in linguistics, focusing on describing aspects of the grammar of ISL. Although she had hoped to focus her PhD on interpreting, she took the advice of Daniel Gile, a leading interpreting studies scholar, who told her that before one can explore how someone interprets between ISL and English, someone needs to describe more of the grammar of ISL. Among her many publications, she has authored a volume on ISL (with John Saeed; 2012) and continues to work with colleagues from across the world to explore further how sign languages work, to apply questions from interpreting education and practice, and to drive forward pan-European work on the teaching and learning of sign languages.

Lorraine also went on to complete a postgraduate program in women's studies (2007), which has informed her ongoing work around gender equality and the transgenerational nature of gendered signing. Across her studies, Lorraine continued to work as an interpreter, initially as the IDS's first in-house interpreter, and then as a freelance interpreter, with opportunities to work at international meetings and conferences. She developed a particular interest in interpreting in legal contexts, which, over time, has also intersected with significant work around domestic violence, sexual violence, and GBV.

Lorraine subsequently went on to work as course director for the University College Cork–Cork Deaf Enterprises–Bristol University ISL/English interpreting and ISL teaching (European Union–funded) program from 1997 to 1999. Across 2000–2001, Lorraine split her time between Brussels (Belgium) and Bristol (UK). In Brussels, she worked for the European Union of the Deaf (EUD), learning a lot about the politics of representation and mechanisms for raising awareness of sign languages on the pan-European agenda from talented EUD leaders like Helga Stevens, Liisa Kauppinen, Johan Wesemann, Knud Søndergard, Markku Jokinen, and Lars-Åke Wikström (among others). In Bristol, she lectured part time on the BSL/English Interpreting degree program and had the privilege of sharing an office (and many great conversations) with the legendary Paddy Ladd.

In 2001, after decades of lobbying on the part of the IDS and allies, the Irish government confirmed funding for the CDS at TCD Lorraine was appointed as the founding director. In this role, she worked closely with deaf and hearing colleagues to establish undergraduate programs in interpreting, deaf studies, and ISL teaching, as well as opening opportunities for postgraduate work to the PhD level.

Another opportunity to travel arose in 2013, when Lorraine had the great honor of serving as the Julian and Virginia Cornell Distinguished Visiting Professor to Swarthmore College in Pennsylvania (United States) for the academic year 2013–2014. While there, she had the opportunity to formally take American Sign Language (ASL) classes, to deliver some course content for Gallaudet University, and to further develop connections with interpreter educators and linguists in North America.

While we all grappled with the challenges that COVID-19 brought, there were also some incredible opportunities. During 2020–2021, Lorraine worked closely with Teresa Lynch to develop and roll out a DI education program funded by the state's Citizen Information Board. She also had the opportunity to co-delivered on the University of Malta's first SLI education program, designed and coordinated by Marie Alexander and Alison Vere. This presented a remarkable opportunity to co-teach online with presidents past and current of the World Association of Sign Language Interpreters (WASLI): Debra Russell and Christopher Stone.

Lorraine's research work has informed public discussion, political debate, and policy implementation in Ireland and at the European level, including the ISL Act (2017) and the establishment of RISLI (2020). She is a RISLI-registered interpreter and serves as a member of the RISLI Panel.

In recent years, Lorraine's work at the university has broadened to look at issues of research integrity and EDI. She currently serves as the associate vice provost (vice president) for EDI at TCD but continues to work with intention on issues that particularly affect access and participation via interpreting.

Contextualization: Translation and Interpreting in Ireland

There are limited education pathways for spoken language interpreters in Ireland. The Association of Translators and Interpreters Ireland (ATII)[8] (formerly the Irish Translators' and Interpreters' Association) reports that currently, no accredited spoken language community interpreting program is available in Ireland. Previously, a one-semester community interpreting course was delivered at DCU, leading to a graduate certificate in community interpreting. DCU also previously delivered conference interpreting training. Both courses are now defunct. Currently, DCU offers an optional community interpreting module in the MA program in translation studies and offers some training in the final year of their bachelor's degree in applied language and translation studies. The National University of Ireland (NUI) in Galway provides the only dedicated course in conference interpreting, which is the master's degree in conference interpreting. As it stands, Irish, English, French, Spanish, Italian, and German are languages offered in the program. Those wishing to pursue postgraduate studies in interpreting may also apply to the European Master in Conference Interpreting, which is hosted by 16 universities in conjunction with the European Commission and the European Parliament.[9] In 2023, the University of Limerick ran a short course, "Communication and Interpreting in the Irish Healthcare System," which attracted both spoken and signed language interpreters.

There is a strong translation community in Ireland. Master's degree programs in translation studies are offered at DCU, University College Cork, and the NUI in Galway. In addition, a specialized postgraduate program in literary translation is delivered by TCD, while DCU offers a Master of Science (MSc) in Translation Technology.

From the above discussion, we see that the lack of fully devoted translation and interpreting (T&I) programs at the undergraduate level is an issue. Trinity's CDS remains the only dedicated community interpreter training hub in Ireland. However, despite the lack of accredited programs generally, we see from the work of the ATII that there is a thriving T&I community. Membership in ATII is predicated on qualification; the lowest point of entry requires a Level 7 qualification on the Irish National Framework of Qualifications (associate membership; normally a diploma or 3-year degree program). To become a professional member, an in-house examination is required in addition to a minimum of 3 years' relevant professional experience. Furthermore, ATII offers an additional examination to register as a certified legal translator. To qualify to take this examination, the translator must be able to provide evidence of at least

5 years' documented translation experience. Although the ATII is predominantly a spoken language interpreter and translation association, student and associate memberships are open to signed language interpreters. Professional membership and legal translator certification are currently not available to ISL interpreters. However, there are other avenues open to sign language interpreters in Ireland, which we will go on to discuss. In the next section, we turn to consider the changing landscape of SLI regulation in Ireland.

PROFESSIONALIZATION OF SIGN LANGUAGE INTERPRETERS IN IRELAND

Leeson and Lynch (2009) offer a comprehensive overview of the birth of the interpreting profession in Ireland, which coincides with key milestones in SLI education (summarized in the next section). In 1994, after completion of the first SLI education program, there was demand for an interpreting agency to be established. A working group comprising deaf people, interpreters, service providers, and ISL teachers set out to regulate the emerging profession. After extensive negotiation, the first SLI agency, the state-supported Irish Sign Link, was established.

Another important development occurred in 1994 with the establishment of the Irish Association of Sign Language Interpreters (IASLI), which was affiliated to the European Forum of Sign Language Interpreters (efsli). IASLI set out to uphold the standards of deaf and hearing interpreters and ensure that the necessary safeguards were put in place to protect the Irish deaf community. However, because of funding constraints, absence of staff or office space, and lack of consensus on the way forward, IASLI was disbanded in 2007. After the disbanding of IASLI, there was no professional body representing sign language interpreters until CISLI was formed in May 2011. CISLI partners with efsli, the ITIA, and WASLI, as well as the deaf-led national organization IDS. Since its inception, CISLI has endeavored to advance the profession and encourages best practice in the following ways[10]:

- Serving as the national representative body for professional ISL interpreters in Ireland
- Working in close partnership with Irish deaf-led organizations for the future benefit of deaf people in Ireland who use signed languages and the profession of interpreters whose working languages include a signed language
- Supporting the development of CISLI regional committees to advance the profession of interpreting in their regions
- Supporting and collaborating with programs designed to facilitate the education and training of ISL interpreters
- Providing support for professional development and for a national forum for discussion of issues pertinent to the field of interpreting

- Upholding and promoting the CISLI's Code of Ethics and Guidelines for Professional Conduct
- Recognizing the importance of evaluation of interpreters in Ireland whose working languages include a signed language
- Developing, providing, and promoting the dispute resolution process for CISLI members and the individuals they serve.

The current professional associations and organizations that ISL interpreters may join include CISLI, the ATII, and the Association of Sign Language Interpreters UK (ASLI), which has a regional grouping in Northern Ireland (ASLI-NI). ASLI-NI is not in our jurisdiction (Northern Ireland is part of the United Kingdom), but some interpreters work cross-border between the Republic of Ireland and Northern Ireland and may be members of both CISLI and ASLI, with the potential to become members of the register of interpreters in both jurisdictions. CISLI has run continuous CPD events since its establishment, with the scope for this to increase given that since January 2021, interpreters who are members of RISLI are obligated to complete a set number of hours of CPD annually. CDS is also very active in the realm of public engagement and in delivering CPD events. Additionally, CPD has been delivered and/or supported by private and state-funded SLI agencies in Ireland.

Following on from the ISL Act, the state-funded SLIS was mandated by the government to establish a national register and provide quality assurance with regard to interpreting provision. This is also an integral feature of the National Disability Inclusion Strategy 2017–2021, supported by the Department of Justice and Equality. Public services are now permitted to work only with ISL interpreters listed on the national register. Details related to the registration scheme process, code of conduct, the membership and operation of the registration panel, and a CPD system, have now been agreed upon, informed by a review of international best practices (Leeson & Venturi, 2017).

Before the passing of the ISL Act in 2017, there was no statutory regulation or legislation that governed the profession of SLI in Ireland. A noteworthy point is that the clear majority of sign language interpreters in Ireland are freelance practitioners, but in recent years, there have been significant moves toward the employment of interpreters. Employers now include the national Houses of the Oireachtas (parliament), which recently employed two full-time sign language interpreters, while other bodies have hired ISL interpreters on a permanent or contract basis—for example, Reach Deaf Services, DCU, TCD, and the Monaghan-Cavan Education and Training Board. SLIS is also an employer of interpreters contracted to work for the Irish Remote Interpreting Service (IRIS).

The position of DIs has also been carefully considered in light of these changes. DIs are an important part of the interpreting ecosystem and the Irish interpreting community. Their importance has been acknowledged, evidenced by the active

engagement of DIs as members of CISLI, and made increasingly visible via their registration under the SLIS accreditation schemes and their inclusion in the interpreting
registration processes that will follow from the ISL Act 2017 (Leeson & Venturi,
2017). Anecdotally, we know that demand for DIs and deaf translators is increasing.
Although, until recently, most DIs have not accessed formal training (though the
Bachelor in Deaf Studies interpreting pathway is open to them), most have engaged
in nonaccredited CPD tailored to DIs. A prime example of this was training offered
under the auspices of the Justisigns Project, led by CDS (2013–2016).[11] The aim of
this CPD training was to support those who sought to work as DIs in legal settings. As
noted earlier, following from the commencement of the ISL Act in 2020, one of the
measures funded was a short program for DIs that ran from 2020 to 2021. We return
to the accreditation opportunities for DIs in the next section.

Issues With the Supply of Sign Language Interpreters

SLIS has expressed concerns that the national capacity is less than 12,000 SLI
days per year, insufficient to meet the current demands of service providers and
deaf citizens. Although RISLI has 112 members (as of May 2024),[12] SLIS estimates
that only 75 ISL interpreters are active. Fewer than half (44%) report working
full time, with most working about 3.5 days per week (SLIS, 2017). Although there
are no data that explore this in more detail, it is important to note that the profession of SLI in Ireland is still relatively young and overwhelmingly female, so these
figures might reflect work–life balance considerations. Furthermore, demand could
vary in different parts of the country, and full-time work might not be available in
all areas. As a result, interpreters might take on other work and will not always be
available to travel/interpret. The combination of such factors results in the extreme
marginalization of the Irish deaf community, particularly in rural communities
(McGilloway, 2021; Oireachtas, 2016). Building capacity in this sector will help
create employment for and social inclusion of deaf people and help meet objectives
set out in the National Skills Strategy 2025.

   The critical issue is that there is a growing demand for sign language and accessible services. SLIS is exploring a Sign Language Service Strategic Framework
to Increase the Availability and Quality of Sign Language Interpreting in Ireland
(August 2019); work is ongoing and remains a priority for all stakeholders.

Research on SLI in Ireland

Trilingual interpreting contexts have been receiving increased attention internationally in recent years (see, for example, McKee & Awheto, 2010; Quinto-Pozos
et al., 2010; Treviño & Quinto-Pozos, 2018). In Ireland, Leeson et al. (2018) looked
at how experienced interpreters handle code-switching between Irish and English

in the source language text to ISL, while Cichocka (2021) completed a small survey on trilingual capacity in the European context.

Interpreting in tertiary education has received attention in the Irish context (Leeson, 2012; Leeson & Foley-Cave, 2007; McGrotty & Sheridan, 2019). McGrotty and Sheridan's (2019) results indicate that deaf students prioritize the need for quality interpreting over full access, regardless of perceived skill level. However, the perceived skill level of the interpreter requires more attention, as respondents did not state what criteria they specifically use to evaluate quality. An important finding is that students place a high value on the level of trust they establish with their interpreter(s). This trust is established by maintaining an effective working relationship and desire for interpreters to act in a benevolent manner. This includes the need for direct communication with the student (to inform them of important information, such as being absent or late) and adjustment of interpreting style to align with the needs of the student. Another important aspect is the need for subject-specific terminology to be well managed by the interpreter (see also Leeson, 2012; Leeson & Foley-Cave, 2007).

Other work has included analysis of the journey from interpreter education to professional practice (Sheridan & Lynch, 2022), including student identity formation and renegotiation (Sheridan, 2021) and key transitional phases of freelance interpreters' careers (Venturi, 2020). Venturi identified a range of gaps that need to be addressed by several stakeholders (educators, professional associations, interpreting agencies, interpreters as individuals). Interpreter work in emergency settings is also a theme that has been explored (e.g., Leeson, 2019) and is now securing much greater attention as a result of the COVID-19 pandemic.

Engagement in a range of European-funded projects across the past decade has led to analysis of interpreting in a range of professional settings and supported evidence-based development of teaching resources around workplace interpreting (Napier et al., 2020; Sheikh et al., 2021), legal interpreting (Leeson et al., 2017, 2020, 2022; Napier et al., 2022); health care interpreting (Leeson et al., 2014), and interpreting in the contexts of domestic violence, sexual violence, and GBV (Cabeza-Pereiro et al., 2022; Napier et al., 2024). These projects have all facilitated examination of the Irish context as part of the wider European landscape and allowed us to more clearly benchmark developments and identify gaps.

SIGN LANGUAGE INTERPRETER EDUCATION IN IRELAND

In Ireland, education for sign language interpreters commenced in 1992. The initial program was funded by the European Commission's Horizon program and led by Bristol University in partnership with the IDS and TCD. It was a 2-year, full-time course, hosted by Bristol University, resulting in a Diploma in Deaf Studies (Interpreting). In parallel, a 1-year full-time program ran, which led to a Certificate in Deaf Studies (Teaching). Subsequently, in 1994, the (then) National Association for Deaf People (NAD; now Chime), in collaboration with the United Kingdom's Royal National Institute for the Deaf (RNID), established a 6-month, self-directed learning program. This was specifically aimed at those who were already working as interpreters in the field. In 1998, a second round of EU Horizon funding made it possible for Cork Deaf Enterprises, Bristol University, and NUI Cork (now University College Cork) to offer the Diploma in Deaf Studies (interpreting) and a certificate program (teaching). Because of funding constraints, this program was delivered over an 18-month duration, but the structure mirrored the original TCD–Bristol collaboration. The deaf candidates from this cohort, taking the teaching pathway, were among the first to complete the Bachelor in Deaf Studies at Bristol University.

Despite this progress, there was a need to establish an Irish base for SLI education to ensure stability and further grow the pool of available interpreters. This came to fruition in 2001, when the then Minister for Education and Science announced funding for a 5-year period to establish the CDS at TCD. This remains the home for Deaf Studies in Ireland today.

CDS initially offered three 2-year diploma programs that led to the Diploma in ISL/English Interpreting, ISL Teaching, or Deaf Studies. Funding under the government's Strategic Innovation Fund, round II (SIF II), allowed for a move to the Bachelor in Deaf Studies, which commenced in 2009. However, as noted earlier, we had to scale back on our original ambitions because of funding cutbacks that stemmed from the recession. This 4-year, full-time honors degree is mapped to Level 8 in the Irish National Framework of Qualifications (NFQ), allowing graduates with appropriate grades access to Level 9 postgraduate programs. The first graduates from the Bachelor in Deaf Studies program (interpreting pathway) graduated in 2013.

In addition to the CDS programs outlined previously, another pathway to interpreting exists: the Signature National Vocational Qualification (NVQ) Level 6 program. Signature approves training centers, assesses the required components, and verifies that standards have been met. In Ireland, a limited number of sign language interpreters have accessed this route (Leeson & Venturi, 2017). CDS remains the primary pathway to qualification as an ISL/English interpreter in Ireland.

There is currently no postgraduate pathway in Ireland for those wishing to pursue further SLI studies. On one occasion (2012–2013), Queen's University Belfast accepted students with ISL/English and BSL/English backgrounds into their MA in Interpreting (Leeson & Venturi, 2017), and will again in fall 2024. Other potential pathways include the European Master in Sign Language Interpreting (EUMASLI), but only one ISL interpreter has completed in this international study program to date.[13] Nevertheless, we note that several sign language interpreters have completed postgraduate studies in a range of other domains (e.g., ethics, intercultural studies, equality studies, linguistics, education, counseling). Table 1 provides an indicative overview of numbers of ISL/English interpreters in both the Republic of Ireland and Northern Ireland and their level of training.

Table 1. Trained/Registered Interpreters in Ireland, 1992–2023

Training Institution/ Registering Body	Time Frame	Level of Training	Graduates
Trinity College Dublin and Bristol University	1992–1994	2 years full time leading to a Diploma in Deaf Studies (Interpreting)	9
NUI Cork and Bristol University	1998–1999	2 years full time leading to a Diploma in Deaf Studies (Interpreting)	10
Trinity College Dublin Centre for Deaf Studies (CDS)	2003–2019	2 years full time leading to a Diploma in Irish Sign Language/English Interpreting	60
Trinity College Dublin Centre for Deaf Studies (CDS)	2013–2023	4 years full time leading to a Bachelor in Deaf Studies (Irish Sign Language/ English Interpreting)	82
Royal National Institute for the Deaf (RNID)/ National Association for the Deaf (NAD†)	1994	6-month training period— no formal qualification	13*
Signature CSL, Galway	2016	NVQ Level 6	4
Signature, Northern Ireland	Unknown	Various levels of qualification held, but not NRCPD registered	3
NRCPD	Unknown	NRCPD registered	1
Queens University Belfast	2013–present	NVQ Level 9	1
Subtotal			*165*
*Less overlap**			*Total 120–129 for overlapping students = ?*
Total			156

* Some overlap (*n* = 9) as some RNID/NAD candidates later completed further training at CDS.
† NAD has since changed its name twice—first to DeafHear.ie, and more recently to Chime.

Note. Adapted and updated from Leeson and Venturi, 2017.

Current Considerations on the Delivery of the Bachelor's Degree in Deaf Studies

The CDS teaching team comprises deaf and hearing professionals (four deaf members and two hearing members of staff in full-time or part-time contracts, with additional occasional teaching delivered on a supplementary basis). ISL is taught by deaf colleagues, and interpreting modules are delivered by both deaf and hearing staff. A range of additional modules are common to all students in the first 2 years of the degree program, with the exception of elective modules that can be selected from offerings from across the university (e.g., Criminal Law, language modules, Film Studies). As a result of a university-wide restructuring of undergraduate programs, degree content has been modified quite significantly in recent years. However, following from efsli's documentation around core content required in European degree-level interpreter education pathways (Leeson & Calle, 2013), we maintain emphasis on core modules, which include sign linguistics, language acquisition, and ethics, as well as modules related to working with deaf communities. At the beginning of Year 3, and having met entry requirements for their preferred route, students move to a specialist pathway (ISL teaching, deaf studies, or interpreting). In Years 3 and 4, the curriculum relates predominantly to their chosen pathway. Across these third and fourth years, students continue to attend ISL classes and must complete a practicum component for 12 weeks, where they shadow and work alongside professional interpreters. Our revised degree structure also facilitates the possibility of undertaking a placement abroad—for example, under the European Union's Erasmus+ program.[14]

Demand for participation in SLI education has fluctuated over the past 20 years, though we have noted a small increase in numbers applying and gaining entry in the past few years, which could be a knock-on effect of increased visibility of ISL in the media. The majority of students (school leavers) enter through the national points-based system, the Central Applications Office. For mature students and those applying through specific access avenues like the Trinity Access Program (TAP), which supports populations with lower progression rates into higher education, a separate entry route is in place, which entails one-on-one interviews. Although we have regularly been asked to consider offering our program on a part-time or blended distance-learning approach, given resourcing issues, we have not been in a position to do this to date. Therefore, those with family or employment commitments or who reside outside of Dublin might not be able to embark on 4 years of full-time study. This point will be returned to when we discuss the implications of teaching during COVID-19.

We are committed to exploring alternative pathways via a range of funding mechanisms—for example, via a phased, blended conversion course in SLI for those who already possess a primary degree and know ISL to the B2 (intermediate) level of the Common European Framework of Reference (CEFR) for Languages (Council of

Europe, 2001; Leeson & van den Bogaerde, 2019; Leeson et al., 2016; Leeson & Calle, 2013; e.g., teachers in deaf schools, hearing heritage signers). However, given our earlier discussion on investment in higher education in Ireland, funding opportunities are scarce and are highly competitive.

DI Training

O'Connell and Lynch (2020) reported on the lack of training programs in universities targeted at DIs, noting this has implications for professional development and skill enhancement. Their study specifically investigates the lived experiences of DIs in Ireland through the lens of a phenomenological framework. In doing so, they offer insights into the emergence of the profession and the key role of pioneering DIs. While outlining important milestones in the Irish context, O'Connell and Lynch (2020) also raised critical issues related to DI professionalization, noting the proportionally low percentage of DIs in the field in comparison with hearing counterparts. Further questions are raised about how DIs view themselves as professionals and issues that influence their motivation to work in this field. Research findings indicate that disadvantages exist for DIs, primarily as a result of insufficient professional training opportunities and the absence of formal qualifications (O'Connell & Lynch, 2020).

Although CDS programs are open to prospective DIs, to date, no deaf candidate who has completed the bachelor's degree in deaf studies has selected the interpreting pathway. However, we are hopeful that with increasing awareness, registration processes, increasing demand, and consequent employment opportunity for DIs, we will see this change. Until recently, there were five DIs working regularly in the field, three of whom came through the Justisigns Project DI CPD training offered by CDS (2013–2016). Following from the adoption of the ISL Act (2017), and in preparation for the establishment of the RISLI, SLIS secured a small sum from the Citizens Information Board (CIB) to support the delivery of a training pathway for DIs that would allow those who successfully complete the program to register with RISLI. CDS was awarded the tender to develop and deliver the training, which comprised four modules: An Introduction to Interpreting—Theory and Practice; Introduction to Deaf Interpreting; Sign Language in Action; and An Introduction to Ethics for Deaf Interpreters. Although the original intention was to deliver this program in a F2F manner, COVID-19 restrictions led to this becoming a fully online, remote endeavor. Because of demand, we recruited 24 students instead of our intended 12. This final cohort was chosen on the basis of both fluency in ISL and prior experience working as DIs. In addition, each successful candidate submitted a compelling outline of their reasons for wanting to participate in the training. We sought to ensure that we had a good gender balance, that there was a good geographic distribution of candidates selected, and that we factored in age range.

There is increasing awareness about the need for DIs in specific settings and the skills required in these contexts. In tandem, demand for translation work is also increasing, particularly in relation to public health matters (e.g., COVID-19 information[15]) and political information (e.g., in the lead up to elections). Sign language translation (SLT) is recognized as a specific skill separate from interpreting. However, although elements of translation were covered in the aforementioned DI CPD course, intensive training is not currently provided. The majority of SLT work is predominantly carried out by deaf translators, and the volume of work is likely to increase as we enter the era following official ISL recognition. Furthermore, a significant number of the DI student cohort has expressed a desire to pursue translation as a career pathway rather than interpreting.

It is worth noting that although the field of T&I internationally has seen the emergence of interpreting from under the broader banner of "translation," it could be that in the ISL context, we will see a reverse approach. That is, although the ISL Act makes explicit reference to interpreting and the need for regulation of the SLI profession, it is silent with respect to SLT and translators. This is an issue that the IDS's Cross-Community Group, which is monitoring implementation of the ISL Act, has noted.

Pedagogical Research

Internationally, there is significant lack of empirical evidence to underpin the training and assessment of second (or subsequent) language learners learning a language expressed in a new modality (M2L2 learners), including interpreters (Chen-Pichler, 2012; Haug, 2017; Haug et al., 2019; Leeson et al., 2019; Leeson et al., 2022). In response, there have been several developments in the field of applied sign linguistics from researchers based in Ireland, often in collaboration with colleagues internationally.

One key area that we have engaged with relates to the teaching, learning, and assessment of sign languages in second-language learning contexts. Working with the Council of Europe and the European Centre for Modern Languages (ECML), we have led pan-European work on aligning sign language teaching and assessment to the CEFR for Languages (Council of Europe, 2001). Indeed, the *ProSign* project produced the ECML's first adaptation of the CEFR for sign languages (Leeson et al., 2016), drawing on earlier, local work in a small number of European countries (e.g., France, the Netherlands, Ireland, Germany, Sweden; Leeson & van den Bogaerde, 2019).[16] Drawing on this work, efsli published a series of learning outcomes, including CEFR-aligned expectations for language competency in the working languages of graduating interpreters (Leeson & Calle, 2013; Leeson & Bowen, 2013). In 2020, the Council of Europe published a modality-inclusive CEFR (Council of Europe, 2020), giving equal visibility and status to descriptors of language competency in spoken and signed languages (Leeson & van den Bogaerde, 2019), another important milestone that supports raising awareness of sign languages and, by implication, sign language teaching and learning, including in the education of sign language interpreters.

Another strand of work relates to the use of corpora to inform teaching practice. Until recently, international emphasis was focused predominantly on the creation and analysis of L1 sign language corpora. In turn, these materials often featured in the classroom (Leeson, 2008; Cresdee & Johnston, 2014; Mesch & Wallin, 2008). Nevertheless, there remained an absence of L2 corpora that tracked the progression and milestones of learners of a signed language (Leeson et al., 2019). Thus, the Sign Language Acquisition Corpus (SLAC) commenced in 2013 as a cross-linguistic venture between the CDS and the Sign Language Department, Stockholm University, Sweden. The aim of SLAC was to develop a corpus of data from adult learners of ISL or Swedish Sign Language (STS) as a second or subsequent language, many of whom proceed to becoming sign language interpreters. Leeson et al. (2020) have carried out an initial analysis of M2L2 (second-modality second-language) learners' fingerspelling competency in ISL based on a subset of data extracted from SLAC. Nicodemus et al. (2017) also looked at how advanced L2M2 users (that is, sign language interpreters from different countries: Australia, United States, UK, and Ireland) use fingerspelling when interpreting. This study had a cross-linguistic sample of interpreters, including four ISL/English interpreters who provided an ISL version of President Obama's first inaugural address. A body of work is also under way on a corpus comprising spoken and sign language interpretations of English-language source texts that explores, among other things, how interpreters' own experiences and knowledge base are evidenced in their target-language outputs (e.g., Janzen et al., in press; Leeson et al., 2015). These studies point the way to gaps in practical knowledge that we then fold into our interpreter education curriculum.

An emerging area of focus is the challenges faced by M2L2 learners in the classroom. Sheridan (2019) adopted a Grounded Theory methodological framework to explore the main concern of novice learners and how they process or resolve the identified concern. Sheridan found that learning to accommodate the performative aspects of a signed language and the physicality of the language were key issues for new learners. Participants—many of whom aspire to be interpreters—comment that there is nowhere to hide in the classroom, and for some, this induces mild to significant anxiety reactions. On a positive note, Sheridan found that this discomfort dissipates for most learners as they progress through the first year of study (see also Grehan & Leeson, 2020). The study highlights that further research is required in the area of learner well-being and positive psychology in the sign language classroom. Tangentially, Sheridan (2021) discusses how M2L2 learners' language ideologies evolve as they become invested in the language and the community. As such, they view themselves as allies after this acculturation process. Such work aligns with work on the positionality of interpreters (Cokely, 2005) and helps to deepen our understanding of how the status of languages intersects with attitudes to languages and to the ways in which interpreters see and perform their work.

Despite such studies, Leeson and Sheridan (2019) point out that evidence-based classroom research is slow to emerge. This prevents innovative research methodologies developing from classroom contexts. In turn, this gap has the potential to hold back interpreter education, as educators often await robust findings to inform their practice.

TEACHING DURING THE COVID-19 PANDEMIC

In March 2020, the COVID-19 pandemic took hold in Ireland along with the rest of the world, and as the university moved online with only a weekend's notice, adaptations had to be made instantly to facilitate the move to teaching online. The Blackboard virtual learning environment had previously been available to us for the purpose of uploading lecture notes and materials, but we had to adjust to using it in a very different way (e.g., live online classes, navigating and learning how to use Zoom). Although content did not change substantially, we were cognizant of screen fatigue and the complexity of learning sign language and interpreting from a two-dimensional screen rather than a three-dimensional classroom space. As we were approaching the end of the 2019–2020 academic year, rapport had already been established with students, and this helped. Commencing a new academic year in September 2021, lecturers were more comfortable with navigating the technical demands of being online, and some modules were redesigned (activities rather than content) to better fit a synchronous online format. This included the use of a range of features available through Blackboard and Zoom, such as the use of whiteboards, polls, and breakout groups, as well as preparing some prerecorded content for theory-based modules. We were fortunate that face-to-face classes were possible for undergraduate students taking practical sign language and interpreting modules from September to December 2021, but we continued with a hybrid format (live face-to-face and live online) for students who could not travel or were not permitted to attend because of COVID-19 restrictions. This also allowed classes to be recorded for students for self-study review. We returned to fully online classes from January 2021 as we entered into a 5-month national lockdown period, which brought us to the end of our academic year and through our examination period. The intention was to have as much face-to-face teaching as possible for the 2021–2022 academic year, but hybrid arrangements were in place for some larger classes while social distancing rules applied (until the end of October 2021).

As noted earlier, DI CPD training has been delivered fully online because of logistical considerations, including national lockdowns and associated COVID-19 regulations. The most difficult element of teaching during COVID-19 was engaging with new cohorts, such as our first-year students and the DI cohort, especially with regard to working to build rapport. Class sizes were larger for these groups, particularly the DI group (*n* = 24). We constantly had to monitor whether students were receiving the same individual attention as they would in a typical classroom. We were also mindful that students might wish to make a point and at times could be overlooked or missed if teachers or classmates did not have the opportunity to pin their screens. We therefore developed a countdown system in which students signed "5-4-3-2-1" before expressing their point. The use of multiple screens for PowerPoint presentations and students was taxing for lecturers to monitor, and with time, a process that left only the presenting parties online, with other students turning their cameras on only to raise a question or give feedback, helped to manage "emboxed discourse"[17] fatigue.

Moving forward, we are open and receptive to the possibilities that online and blended teaching modes can bring, particularly for students based outside of Dublin, who could prefer remote learning and who for various reasons might not be in a position to travel or relocate. We are cognizant of class sizes; fewer than 15 students seems optimal for practical online classes. Breaks and class duration are important points to consider, and policies might need to be updated rather than mirroring standard teaching policies and practices in the face-to-face space. We endeavor to adapt our curricula and pedagogical approach in this evolving landscape.

THE ROAD AHEAD

Ireland has faced many challenges across the past 15 years since the 2009 Ireland chapter was published, and these have affected SLI education. Hard-won funding opportunities were lost because of recession-driven funding cuts, yet we persevered and weathered the storm. Today, the ISL Act has commenced, and this brings the promise of significant change and additional stability to the field. We have a legal basis for a register of interpreters, for CPD requirements, and for recognition of DIs. Implementation of the act will also bring increased demand for interpreters because of increased obligations on public services, promised investment in a government-funded "access to work" interpreting fund, and a pilot voucher system that opened up funding for interpreting in hitherto unfunded social and familial settings (pilot concluded in November 2021; the voucher system was relaunched in late 2023).

At CDS, we continue to engage in research that supports our teaching and practice. For example, in 2020, we embarked on a European Commission funded Erasmus+ project, Justisigns 2, which sought to develop evidence-based training for interpreters working in GBV contexts in partnership with key stakeholders, including police forces and rape crisis centers (Cabeza-Pereiro et al., 2022; Napier et al.,

2023).[18] We respond to opportunities that will allow for widening participation in interpreter education, and we seek to maximize digital learning opportunities to help us bridge the urban–rural divide. As our teaching team ages, another important consideration is capacity building going forward. We are very conscious of our need to strategically map our goals for the coming decade and beyond, while remaining responsive to the changing social, economic, and legal ecosystem in which we operate. Although teaching during the COVID-19 pandemic was arduous, our greatest challenges remain financial investment to support the developments we are committed to seeing happen, capacity building, and succession planning.

NOTES

1. We note that there were people interpreting in Ireland before this point, but this marked the beginning of formal interpreter education in Ireland.
2. See: http://www.irishstatutebook.ie/eli/cons/en/html
3. See: https://www.gov.uk/government/publications/the-belfast-agreement
4. See: https://www.ihrec.ie/crpd/ ISL translation provided.
5. Source: https://www.cso.ie/en/releasesandpublications/ep/p-cp9hdc/p8hdc/p9tod/
6. See: https://www.cso.ie/en/releasesandpublications/ep/p-cp7md/p7md/p7anii/
7. See: https://www.cso.ie/en/releasesandpublications/er/pme/populationandmigration estimatesapril2019/
8. See: https://www.atii.ie/about/about-atii/
9. See: https://www.emcinterpreting.org
10. See: https://cisli.ie/home/aims/
11. See: http://www.justisigns.com/JUSTISIGNS_Project/About.html
12. See: https://risli.ie/interpreters/directory-of-interpreters/
13. See: https://www.eumasli.eu
14. See: https://ec.europa.eu/programs/erasmus-plus/opportunities/traineeships-students_en
15. See: https://www.hse.ie/eng/services/covid-19-resources-and-translations/covid-19-irish-sign-language-resources/
16. See: https://www.ecml.at/Thematicareas/SignedLanguages/ProSign/tabid/4273/language/en-GB/Default.aspx
17. See: https://twitter.com/jahochcam/status/1298028954788528128?s=20
18. See: https://justisigns2.com

REFERENCES

Bielenberg, K. (2018, March 17). Hell at the gates: How the financial crash hit Ireland. *The Independent*.

Cabeza-Pereiro, C., Casado-Neira, D., Conway, B., Clark, L., Del-Pozo-Trivaño, M., Flanagan, J., Freir, C., et al. (2022). *Silent harm. A training manual for service providers and interpreters who work with deaf, refugee, and migrant women and girls who have experienced gender-based violence*. Interesource Group (Ireland) Limited.

Chen-Pichler, D. (2012). Acquisition. In R. Pfau, M. Steinbach, & B. Woll (Eds.), *Sign language: An international handbook* (pp. 647–686). De Gruyter Mouton.

Chen-Pichler, D., & Koulidobrova, E. (2016). Acquisition of sign language as a second language (L2). In M. Marschark & P. C. Spencer (Eds.), *The Oxford handbook of deaf studies, language, and education*. Oxford University Press.

Cichocka, E. (2021). *Multilingual interpreting in Europe*. Unpublished research paper submitted in part-fulfillment of the Bachelor in Deaf Studies. Trinity College Dublin.

Conama, J. B. (2019). "Ah, that's not necessary, you can read English instead": An analysis of state language policy concerning Irish Sign Language and its effects. In J. Murray, R. L. McKee & M. De Meulder (Eds.), *The legal recognition of sign languages: Advocacy and outcomes around the world* (pp. 19–35). Multilingual Matters.

Council of Europe. (2001). *Common European framework of reference for languages: Learning, teaching, assessment*. Press Syndicate of the University of Cambridge.

Cokely, D. (2005). Shifting positionality: A critical examination of the turning point in the relationship of interpreters and the deaf community. In M. Marschark, R. Peterson, & E. Winston (Eds.), *Sign language interpreting and interpreter education: Directions for research and practice* (pp. 3–28). Oxford University Press.

Cresdee, D., & Johnston, T. (2014). Using corpus-based research to inform the teaching of Auslan (Australian Sign Language) as a second language. In D. McKee, R.S. Rosen, & R. McKee (Eds.), *Teaching and learning of signed language: International perspectives* (pp. 85–110). Palgrave MacMillan.

De Meulder, M. (2018). "So, why do you sign?" Deaf and hearing new signers, their motivation, and revitalisation policies for sign languages. *Applied Linguistics Review*, *10*(4), 705–724.

Government of Ireland. (2018). *The research and development budget (R&D) 2017–2018*. Dublin: Government of Ireland. https://enterprise.gov.ie/en/publications/the-r-d-budget-2017-2018.html

Grehan, C., & Leeson, L. (2020). Bridging the gap: The European Language Portfolio and L2 Irish Sign Languages Learners at A2-B1 level. *Teanga*, *11*, 100–119.

Haug, T. (2017). *Development and evaluation of two vocabulary tests for adult learners of Swiss German Sign Language*. [Unpublished master's dissertation]. Lancaster University.

Haug, T., Ebling, S., Boyes-Braem, P., Tissi, K. & Sidler-Miserez, S. (2019). Sign language learning and assessment in German Switzerland: Exploring the potential of vocabulary size rests for Swiss German Sign Language. *Language Education and Assessment 2*(1), 20–40.

Janzen, T., Leeson, L., & Shaffer, B. (In press). *Simultaneous interpreters' gestures as a window on conceptual alignment*. Parallèles.

Leeson, L. (2012). Interpreters in tertiary education. In L. Leeson & M. Vermeerbergen (Eds.), *Working with the Deaf community: Mental health, education and interpreting* (pp. 1–35). Interesource Group Publishing.

Leeson, L. (2019). Ophelia, Emma, and the beast from the east: Effortful engaging and the provision of sign language interpreting in emergencies. *Disaster Prevention and Management*, *29*(2), 187–199.

Leeson, L., & Bowen, S. (2013). *Assessment guidelines for sign language interpreting training program*. European Forum of Sign Language Interpreters.

Leeson, L., & Calle, L. (2013). *Learning outcomes for graduates of a three-year sign language interpreting training program*. European Forum of Sign Language Interpreters.

Leeson, L., Fenlon, J., Mesch, J., Sheridan, S., & Grehan, C. (2019). Use of corpora in L1 and L2/Ln sign language pedagogy. In R. Rosen, (Ed.), *Routledge handbook of sign language pedagogy*. Routledge.

Leeson, L., Flynn, S., Lynch, T., & Sheikh, H. (2020). You have the right to remain signing: A snapshot of the Irish justice system and deaf signers. *Teanga*, *11*, 142–173.

Leeson, L., & Foley-Cave, S. (2007). Deep and meaningful conversation: Challenging interpreter impartiality in the semantics and pragmatics classroom. In M. Metzger, & E. Fleetwood (Eds.), *Translation, sociolinguistic, and consumer issues in interpreting* (pp. 39–73). Gallaudet University Press.

Leeson, L., Janzen, T., & Shaffer, B. (2015, July). *I SEE what you mean: Visual conceptualization in spoken and signed language interpreters*. Paper presented at the International Cognitive Linguistics Conference (ICLC) 13. University of Northumbria, Newcastle.

Leeson, L., & Lynch, T. (2009). Three leaps of faith and four giant steps: Developing interpreter training in Ireland. In J. Napier (Ed.), *International perspectives on sign language interpreter education* (pp. 35–56). Gallaudet University Press.

Leeson, L., Muller de Quadros, R., & Rossi Stumpf, M. (2022). Applied uses of sign language corpora. In J. Fenlon & J. Hochgesang (Eds.), *Sign language corpora* (pp. 128–157). Gallaudet University Press.

Leeson, L., Napier, J., Haug, T., Lynch, T., & Sheikh, H. (2021). Access to justice for deaf signers. In G. De Clerck (Ed.), *UNCRPD implementation in Europe - a deaf perspective: Article 9: Access to information and communication* (pp.161–175). European Union of the Deaf.

Leeson, L., Napier, J., Skinner, R., Lynch, T., Venturi, L., & Sheikh, H. (2017). Conducting research with deaf sign language users. In J. McKinley & H. Rose (Eds.), *Doing research in applied linguistics: Realities, dilemmas and solutions* (pp. 134–145). Routledge.

Leeson, L., & Saeed, J. I. (2012). *Irish Sign Language: A cognitive linguistic account*.: Edinburgh University Press.

Leeson, L., Sheikh, A. A., Rozanes, I., Grehan, C., & Matthews, P. A. (2014). Critical care required: Access to interpreted healthcare in Ireland. In M. Metzger & B. Nicodemus (Eds.), *Investigations in healthcare interpreting* (pp. 185–233). Gallaudet University Press.

Leeson, L., & Sheridan, S. (2019). Sign language interpreting. In M. Baker & G. Saldanha (Eds.), *Routledge encyclopedia of translation studies* (2nd ed.). Routledge.

Leeson, L., Sheridan, S., Cannon, K., Murphy, T., Newman, H., & Veldheer, H. (2020). Hands in motion: Learning to fingerspell in Irish Sign Language (ISL). *Teanga*, *11*, 120–141.

Leeson, L., Stewart, M., Ferrara, C., Bostock, I., Nilsson, P., & Cooper, M. (2018). "A President for all of the Irish": Performing Irishness in an interpreted Inaugural Presidential Speech. In C. Stone & L. Leeson (Eds.), *Interpreting and the politics of recognition* (pp. 37–64). Routledge.

Leeson, L., & van den Bogaerde, B. (2019). Sign languages. In D. Newby, F. Heyworth, & M. Cavalli (Eds.), *Changing contexts, evolving competences: 25 years of inspiring innovation in language education.* (pp. 100–107). Council of Europe.

Leeson, L., & Van den Bogaerde, B. (2020). (What we don't know about) Sign languages in higher education in Europe: Mapping policy and practice to an analytical framework. *Sociolinguistica*, *34*(1), 31–56.

Leeson, L., van den Bogaerde, B., Rathmann, C., & Haug, T. (2016). *Sign languages and the common European framework of reference for languages. Common reference level descriptors*. European Centre for Modern Languages.

Leeson, L., & Venturi, L. (2017). *A review of literature and international practice on national and voluntary registers for sign language interpreters*. http://www.citizensinformationboard.ie/

downloads/social_policy/SLIS_TCD_Review_of_National_Registers_of_Sign_Lan guage_Interpreters_March_2017.pdf

McGilloway, C. (2021, August 18). *Physical violence and sexual violence.* [Webinar]. Justisigns 2 & National Deaf Women of Ireland. Webinar.

McGrotty, C., & Sheridan, S. (2019). Irish Sign Language interpreting in higher education in Ireland: The experience of deaf students. *REACH Journal of Special Needs Education in Ireland, 32*(2), 72–83.

McKee, R. & Awheto, S. (2010). Constructing roles in a Māori Deaf trilingual context. In R. McKee & J. Davis (Eds.), *Interpreting in multilingual, multicultural contexts* (pp. 85–118). Gallaudet University Press?.

Mesch, J., & Wallin, L. (2008). Use of sign language materials in teaching. In O. Crasborn, E. Efthimiou, T. Hanke, E. Thoutenhofd, & I. Zwitserlood (Eds.), *Proceedings of the 3rd workshop on the representation and processing of sign languages: Construction and exploitation of sign language corpora [Language Resources and Evaluation Conference (LREC)].* (pp. 134–137 European Language Resources Association (ELRA).

Napier, J., Cameron, A., Leeson, L., Conama, J. B., Rathmann, C., Peters, C., & Sheikh, H. (2020). *DESIGNS: Creating Employment for Deaf Signers in Europe.* [Unpublished research report]. Centre for Deaf Studies, Trinity College Dublin.

Napier, J., Skinner, R., Turner, G. H., Leeson, L., Lynch, T., Sheikh, H., Vermeerbergen, M., et al. (2022). Justisigns: Developing research-based training resources on sign language interpreting in police settings in Europe. In J. Brunson (Ed.), *Teaching legal interpreting.* Gallaudet University Press.

Napier, J., Leeson, L., Del-Pozo-Triviño, M., Casado-Neira, D., Sheikh, H., Harold, G., Clark, L., et al. (2023). *Silent harm: Gender-based violence in the EU—A review of service provision for victims.* CDS/SLSCS Monograph Series No. 6. Trinity College Dublin.

Napier, J., Clark, L., Leeson, L., & Quigley, L. (2024). "I faced so many barriers": Access to support for deaf female survivors of domestic violence in the UK. *Just. Journal of Language Rights and Minorities, 3*(1). https://doi.org/10.1007/1-4020-8039-5_3

Nicodemus, B., Swabey, L., Leeson, L., Napier, J., Petitta, G., & Taylor, M. M. (2017). A cross-linguistic analysis of fingerspelling production by sign language interpreters. *Sign Language Studies, 17*(2), 143–171.

O'Connell, N. P., & Lynch, T. (2020). Deaf interpreters' perception of themselves as professionals in Ireland: A phenomenological study. *Journal of Interpretation, 28*(2), Article 4. https://digitalcommons.unf.edu/joi/vol28/iss2/4

Oireachtas (2016, September 28). Joint Committee on Justice and Equality. Irish Sign Language: Irish Deaf Society. https://data.oireachtas.ie/ie/oireachtas/debateRecord/joint_committee_on_justice_and_equality/2016-09-28/debate/mul@/main.pdf

Quinto-Pozos, D., Casanova de Canales, K., & Treviño, R. (2010). Trilingual video relay service (VRS) interpreting in the United States. In R. McKee & J. Davis (Eds.), *Interpreting in multilingual, multicultural contexts* (pp. 28–54). Gallaudet University.

Sheikh, H., Napier, J., Cameron, A., Leeson, L., Rathmann, C., Peters, C., Conama, J. B., & Moiselle, R. (2021). Supporting access to employment for deaf signers through research-informed training resources: the DESIGNS project. In G. De Clerck (Ed.), *UNCRPD Implementation in Europe—A deaf perspective: Article 9: Access to information and communication.* (pp. 179–193). European Union of the Deaf.

Sheridan, S. (2019). *Composing the L2-M2 self: A grounded theory study on the concerns of adult Irish Sign Language learners.* Unpublished doctoral dissertation, Trinity College Dublin.

Sheridan, S. (2021). Re-visioning the deaf community: The journey to developing a mixed-modality multilingual identity. *The Language Learning Journal, 49*(4), 452–465.

Sheridan, S., & Lynch, T. (2022). Translation as a pedagogical tool. In *The Routledge Handbook of Sign Language Translation and Interpreting* (pp. 181–192). Routledge.

Sheridan, S., & O'Donnell, J. (2023). Irish sign language interpreter workplace wellness during COVID-19: Looking back and moving forward. *Journal of Interpretation, 31*(1), Article 1.

Sign Language Interpreting Services. (2017). *SLIS position paper: A national skill shortage in sign language interpreting.* SLIS.

Treviño, R., & Quinto-Pozos, D. (2018). Name pronunciation strategies of ASL-Spanish-English trilingual interpreters during mock video relay service calls. *Translation and Interpreting Studies, 13*(1), 71–86.

Venturi, L. (2020). *Mentoring for Irish Sign Language interpreters: A grounded theory approach.* [Master's thesis]. Trinity College Dublin (University of Dublin).

11

Sign Language Interpreter Education in Japan

Its Unique Background and Future Challenges

Japan is a small island country in Far East Asia. It is comprised of four main islands divided into 47 prefectures. A large proportion of Japanese society is ethnically, culturally, and linguistically homogenous. In fact, it is so taken for granted that the entire population communicates in the Japanese language that there is no law designating Japanese to be the national language of the country. Japan is economically and politically relatively stable, but the country is confronted with the problem of a rapidly aging society and decreasing birth rate. According to the government statistics, 341,000 people hold hearing disability certificates, of whom 25% of those less than 65 years of age use sign language or sign language interpreting (SLI) for daily communication (Oka, 2022, p. 59).

WHO ARE WE?

Harumi Kimura is deaf and has been teaching Japanese Sign Language (JSL) at the College of the National Rehabilitation Center for Persons With Disabilities, Japan, since 1999. She also appears regularly on television as one of the deaf newscasters on NHK Sign Language News 845. Harumi studied at the Yamaguchi Prefectural School for the Deaf (Shimonoseki Branch School) and received her bachelor's degree from the Japan College of Social Work. She received her master's degree from Hitotsubashi University, Graduate School of Language and Society.

Harumi began her career as a civil officer at the Setagaya City Office (1989–1991). She later became the instructor on the NHK TV educational program *Sign Language for Everyone* (1991–1994), and the newscaster for NHK *Weekly Sign Language News for Children* (1999–2001). She has been on the board of directors of

Meisei Gakuen School for the Deaf since 2007. Harumi is the author of many books on the Japanese deaf community and JSL, such as *Dreams That the Deaf Embrace* (2012), *The Deep Chasm Between Japanese Sign Language and Signed Japanese* (2011), *The World of the Deaf* (2009), *Japanese Sign Language and Deaf Culture: The Deaf Are Strangers* (2007), and *An Introduction to Sign Language* (1995). Her website is http://www.kimura-harumi.com/.

Noriko Miyazawa is a Japanese hearing heritage signer, sign language interpreter, and educator of sign language interpreters. She has been engaged in interpreter education since 1991. As a board member of the National Research Association for Sign Language Interpretation (NRASLI) in Japan, she has been committed to breaking social barriers confronting deaf signers and improving the status of sign language interpreters since 1988.

CONTEXTUALIZATION: TRANSLATION AND INTERPRETING IN JAPAN

Professional translation and interpreting in Japan developed in the fields of international politics and economy. Spoken language interpreting grew out of a need arising after the end of World War II for communication during the International Military Tribunal for the Far East (also known as the Tokyo War Crimes Tribunal), for communication with the occupation army, and for communication support with those who began participating in international conferences. Those who interpreted during this postwar period did not receive any formal interpreter training. Formal interpreter training in Japan was established to supply interpreters for the Tokyo Olympics held in 1964. Interpreter agencies were set up and began providing interpreter training out of a need to recruit interpreters for their own agencies. In the Japanese domestic community, even the politicians believed without doubt that "Japan is a monolingual country" and never even considered the need for translating and interpreting in domestic activities within the country.

PROFESSIONALIZATION OF SLI IN JAPAN

It was in the context of the perception of Japan as a monolingual country that, in 1945, the Japanese Federation of the Deaf (JFD) started advocating for awareness that there are deaf people in Japan who do not understand Japanese and that welfare specialists who could sign were needed in social welfare offices throughout the country. Because of this initial stance on the part of JFD, when SLI in Japan actually began to develop, it grew within the framework of social welfare. It should also be noted that 1945 was still many years before the International Year of Disabled Persons, and the concept of welfare for persons with disabilities had not yet taken root in Japan.

Initially, the provision of interpreting between Japanese and JSL was accounted for in the Law for the Welfare of People With Physical Disabilities (Law No.283, Article 4-2) of 1949, which specifies the welfare services that should be provided to persons with disabilities. For those people who cannot communicate in spoken languages because of being deaf, the law specifies that SLI services should be provided. This law was later updated in 2005 as the Act on Comprehensive Support for Persons With Disabilities (Articles 77-7 and 78), specifying the services that should be provided to individuals with disabilities and services that should be provided to the communities in which disabled people reside. SLI is therefore designated as a service, not merely for individuals with disabilities, but for the community at large. The law specifies the need for cities and towns to provide SLI services and for prefectures to train hearing persons to become sign language interpreters.

It was from the 1960s that the so-called "sign language circles" began to be established by hearing people in different parts of the country. These are groups or clubs established by hearing people as a place to converse in sign language with deaf people of the neighborhood and to brush up their signing skills. The very first sign language circle was started by a student studying to become a nurse. One of the patients to whom she was assigned was a deaf person. Finding it hard to communicate with the patient, she called on her friends, and with the help of the deaf organization, established *Mimizuku*, the first sign language circle. It was also about this time that a movie called *Happiness of Us Alone*, which was about the hardships experienced by a deaf couple, became a hit and aroused a strong interest in sign language in Japanese society.

In response to such trends, the Ministry of Health and Welfare established the Project to Train Sign Language Volunteers in 1970. This was the initial stage of the Japanese system whereby government funds were allocated to train sign language interpreters within each community, but the content of the training program was limited to the level of training hearing people to become "volunteer helpers" for deaf people. In 1988, the Project to Train Sign Language Interpreters was begun, differentiating between classes for volunteers, centering mainly on teaching basic sign language, and more advanced classes for interpreter training. This project was begun in response to petitions by the JFD to the Ministry of Health and Welfare for a formal training of interpreters.

Although Japan now has a standard curriculum for interpreter training, and although there are different levels of certification, the concept that sign language interpreters are "helpers for the deaf" still prevails to this day. As such, interpreters are primarily working in the social welfare field, which consequently hinders the development of SLI as a specialized profession. The number of hours of training provided through the established training system is very limited (90 hours in total), and the level of proficiency of interpreters who have completed the course and who are working in the community depends greatly on the skills of each individual acquired over years on the job. In the meantime, however, increasing numbers of deaf people are advancing into professional fields, and the need for sign language interpreters with accompanying professional skills is increasing. There are now deaf professionals in a range of fields, including science, engineering, architecture, and economics, who require highly skilled sign language interpreters when they attend meetings and conferences. The established system of supplying "helpers" for the deaf in their daily life activities in the community cannot meet this need for professional interpreters.

Current Professional Associations and Organizations

Japan has two organizations of sign language interpreters. The Japanese Association of Sign Language Interpreters (JASLI) was established in 1992. Only sign language interpreters who pass the Sign Language Interpreter Certificate Examination (SLICE) are eligible to register for membership. Currently, there are approximately 2,500 members. JASLI hosts training sessions for skill improvement, publishes training materials, and also hosts a Sign Language Conference every year in June.

The other organization is NRASLI, established in 1974. There is no certification requirement to become a member. Anyone who is interested in sign language, SLI, or issues related to the deaf community can join as a member. Most of its members are either sign language interpreters or those studying to become interpreters. Currently, there are approximately 10,500 members. NRASLI has branches in all 47 prefectures of the country, and each branch conducts many local activities. NRASLI hosts training sessions on the SLI system, as well as on how sign language interpreters should conduct themselves during assignments. It also compiles and publishes materials for educating interpreters. Every year, in August, it cohosts the national Research Conference on Sign Language Interpretation, together with the JFD. Every 5 years (since 1990), NRASLI conducts a nationwide survey on the working conditions and health conditions of those who are employed as sign language interpreters, and findings are published as the *Report on the Working Conditions and Health Conditions of Those Employed as Sign Language Interpreters*. It also conducts an annual demographic survey of sign language interpreters throughout the country.

Japan has two certification systems for sign language interpreters. The SLICE was begun in 1989. Those who pass this examination become nationally certified sign language interpreters. Currently, the only job requiring this accreditation is interpreting for televised broadcasting of the candidates' political views during elections. Although not stipulated by law, interpreting in court is also assigned mainly to those with SLICE accreditation. For most other SLI assignments, this national accreditation is not required. The SLICE is held once per year. There is no prerequisite for those taking the examination except that they must be 20 years of age or more. The examination is held once every year in five locations across the country. A written examination is held in May to test knowledge on four subjects: basic knowledge about welfare for persons with disabilities, basic knowledge about persons with hearing disabilities, knowledge about how sign language interpreters should conduct themselves in different situations, and Japanese language proficiency. A test of interpreting skills is held in September (signed-to-spoken simultaneous interpreting of two video clips, each one about 2 minutes long, and voice-to-sign simultaneous interpreting of two audio recordings, also about 2 minutes each). As of March 29, 2024, there are 4,194 nationally certified sign language interpreters, all of whom are hearing interpreters.

The Ministry of Health, Labour, and Welfare Ordinance No. 96 (March 31, 2009), the Ordinance on the Examination and Certification of the Knowledge and Skills of Sign Language Interpreters, states the purpose and significance of the SLICE and specifies the conditions for the selection of organizations to which the execution of the examination can be consigned. Currently, the Information and Culture Center for the Deaf is consigned by the Minister of Health, Labour, and Welfare to execute the SLICE examination.

The other certification is the National Unified Sign Language Interpreter Test. Those who pass this test are recognized as sign language interpreters, having the skills to work as interpreters in the community. The test is held once every year in December. Those who have completed the Courses to Train Sign Language Interpreters program or who exhibit the same level of skills and knowledge are eligible to take the test. Many local prefectures and cities use this National Unified Sign Language Interpreter Test as the graduation exam for the training course and as the examination of proficiency to be registered as a sign language interpreter for the local interpreter referral system administered by the local government. Other prefectures and cities do not use the Unified Test but conduct their own original tests of proficiency. Those who pass such local examinations are also considered sign language interpreters.

The National Unified Sign Language Interpreter Test consists of a written test (basic knowledge of SLI and Japanese language proficiency) and a test of interpreting skills, in which the examinee interprets a short dialogue between a deaf and hearing person (or persons) shown in a video clip. When the two examinations are compared, the written test for SLICE is more difficult than the Unified Test. Most of the questions for the Unified Test are taken directly from the standardized Sign Language Interpreter Curriculum textbooks.

Sign Language Interpreter Education in Japan

In 1970, the Ministry of Health and Welfare introduced the Courses to Teach Sign Language Volunteers program in many prefectures and cities of Japan as a first step toward the establishment of an SLI system. In the initial stages, these classes simply taught basic conversational-level sign language, but they eventually began to train people who were interested in becoming interpreters.

In 1988, the Ministry of Health and Welfare established the Courses to Train Sign Language Interpreters. This project was begun in response to petitions by JFD to the Ministry of Health and Welfare for the formal establishment of government-funded SLI training courses. The actual manner in which to execute both the Courses to Train Sign Language Volunteers and Courses to Train Sign Language Interpreters was left up to the discretion of each prefecture, and the teachers and trainers were mostly deaf members of the local deaf associations.

After a while, JFD and the SLI organizations began to realize the need for more professional sign language interpreters. In response to this need, the SLICE commenced in 1989. In the following year, 1990, the Sign Language Interpreter Division was established within the College of the National Rehabilitation Center for Persons With Disabilities (under the authority of the Ministry of Health, Labour, and Welfare). Since then, several specialized schools and colleges have established SLI education programs, but because of the lack of applicants, most have had to shut down. Currently, the only educational institutions conducting SLI education are the College of the National Rehabilitation Center for Persons With Disabilities and Gunma University.

Because of the history of SLI education in Japan, even today, the largest number of interpreters are trained in the Courses to Train Sign Language Interpreters administered by local prefectural, and municipal administrations throughout Japan as a project under the jurisdiction of the Ministry of Health, Labour, and Welfare. Although not many in number, there are interpreters who went through the Sign Language Interpreter Training Program at the College of the National Rehabilitation Center for Persons With Disabilities. Gunma University has only recently started its courses to train sign language interpreters and has yet to show results.

The Courses to Train Sign Language Interpreters are held in numerous prefectures and municipalities throughout the country. Those who wish to take the course must show that they have acquired basic knowledge of sign language by taking the Courses to Train Sign Language Volunteers, by participating in sign language circles, or by taking private sign language lessons. After completion of the course, the students take the National Unified Sign Language Interpreter Test. Those who pass this test can become members of the registry of interpreters of their local town or city administration. Deaf people living in the local area can request interpreting by these registered interpreters free of charge.

The Courses to Train Sign Language Interpreters all use a standardized curriculum and syllabus developed by the National Center of Sign Language Education affiliated with the JFD. As a rule, the instructors need to complete the Course for Sign Language Interpreter Trainers. It is advised that local classes be taught by a pair of hearing and deaf instructors, but in many communities, there are classes that are taught by only hearing instructors. The Course for Sign Language Interpreter Trainers only gives instruction on how the syllabus should be taught and does not include professional studies on linguistics, second-language acquisition theory, or interpreting theory.

These local Sign Language Interpreter Training Courses provide 90 hours of training divided into a basics course, an applied course, and a practical skills course. The classes are taught once a week for between an hour and half and two hours, and the students complete the course in 2–3 years. The curriculum consists of practical skills training (interpreting practice in both language directions, JSL < > Japanese), case studies, role plays, basic knowledge about interpreting, and deaf cultural theories.

After completing the course, the students take the Unified Sign Language Interpreter Test, but very few pass the test on their first try after completing the training course. Many pass the test 2–3 years after the completion of the training course. Even when they pass the test, they are still not proficient enough to take on interpreting assignments on their own. This entire training system is operated in conjunction with the local deaf associations so that the opinions and preferences of the deaf associations have a large influence on the selection of instructors and other matters pertaining to the administration of the course. The instructors are not employed full time, so it is hard to find people who are willing to take on the task. There is no in-service training for instructors, and there is no assessment system for class management or for teaching ability.

The second type of interpreter training in Japan is the Sign Language Interpreter Training at the College of the National Rehabilitation Center for Persons With Disabilities. All students take the SLICE and the Unified Sign Language Interpreter Test before they graduate from the college. As the majority of people who want to become sign language interpreters receive their training in the local community courses, students graduating from the training program in the college must pass the Unified Sign Language Interpreter Test to be accredited and accepted into the community interpreter referral scheme operated by the local administrations. Also, students studying in the training program in the college are encouraged to take part in events hosted by the deaf organizations in the communities in which they live. As part of the curriculum, they work as volunteer staff members at large events held by deaf organizations.

The college has its own original curriculum and syllabus modeled after the advanced interpreter education programs of other countries of the world. It is a 2-year course of a total of 2,400 hours covering the teaching of JSL, sign language translation, and interpreting skills and theories. The basic course (260 hours) includes introductions to linguistics, anthropology, sociology, psychology, Japan's social welfare system, Japan's legal system, Japan's medical system, and information literacy. The teaching of JSL and practical interpreting skills takes up a total of

1,390 hours. Interpretation theories and knowledge about hearing disabilities are taught over a total of 270 hours, and 480 hours are devoted to fieldwork and graduation research.

The faculty consists of four full-time instructors and many external lecturers. JSL is taught by deaf instructors using the direct method of instruction (natural approach, communicative approach). Translation/interpreting skills from Japanese to JSL are taught by deaf teachers, and translation/interpreting skills from JSL to Japanese are taught by hearing teachers. Case studies and interpreting practice are taught by a joint team of hearing and deaf teachers. The college places importance on the Immersion Program so that as far as possible, even classes on theories of interpreting are taught by deaf teachers in JSL. All the instructors and external lecturers have knowledge of linguistics and second-language acquisition theories.

Those students who successfully complete the 2-year course at the college have the right to transfer to the bachelor of arts course of the Japan College of Social Work from their junior year (there is a transfer eligibility examination). At the Japan College of Social Work, the students can take one of the bachelor of arts courses in fields such as social work and mental health to become certified social workers and mental health workers. This will enable them to become accredited sign language interpreters with specialized knowledge of and accreditation in social welfare and service provision.

A relatively new undertaking is the Sign Language Supporter Training Project Office, funded by the Nippon Foundation and initiated in 2017 in the Education Department of Gunma University. The course offers 120 hours of JSL training as part of the University's liberal arts education and 90 hours of sign language interpreter education as a professional education course. The curriculum, developed by the university, is formally approved by the Ministry of Health, Labour, and Welfare and JFD as meeting the requirements of SLI education. Therefore, students graduating from the course are eligible to take the National Sign Language Interpreter Test. Beginning in 2023, Gunma University has also started a Japanese Sign Language Practical Skills Development Program, which offers a formal certificate of completion to those successfully completing the course. This is an online evening course, which enables those who are working in the daytime to apply. As it is an online course, students from any part of the country can take the course, so consequently, the course might help to solve the issue of the disparity of skills existing among different parts of the country.

In Japan, there are very few established courses in higher education institutions (HEIs) focused on educating professionals in different fields to acquire JSL skills. Likewise, because of the low status of the SLI profession, there are very few HEIs aimed at educating interpreters to become professionals with proficiency in linguistic communication skills and interpreting skills. As Gunma University's program is housed in the Education Department, those majoring in Special Education and aspiring to become teachers in deaf schools are educated with the same curriculum as those aspiring to become sign language interpreters. Gunma University incorporates such methodologies as translanguaging, enabling students to make full use of their L1 understanding to understand the difference with JSL as an L2 language, and a task-based approach, enabling students to experience and understand language use in many different situations.[1]

Currently, Japan does not have any organization or referral system for deaf interpreters (DIs). As evidenced in other countries such as Australia and the United Kingdom (Adam Carty & Stone, 2011; Napier, 2021), in Japan too, many deaf people have the experience of brokering for other deaf people by translating between Japanese text and JSL. The need for DIs is evident, but many still think that interpreting is a job for hearing people. This has hindered the development of a Deaf Interpreter Referral System in Japan. A few parts of Japan, such as Okinawa Prefecture, have started their own system of providing a team of deaf and hearing interpreters to requests in the local community. They are receiving positive feedback from the clients about the quality of the interpreting because of the "deaf translation norm" (Stone, 2009).

In response to such needs, a private organization (NPO Japan Sign Language Teachers Center) has started offering a course for training deaf people to become interpreters and training hearing interpreters to work as feeders (pivot interpreters) in deaf–hearing interpreting teams. One instructor is a Registry of Interpreters for the Deaf (RID)–certified DI. Other instructors are those who have experience training hearing people to become interpreters. The course offers 35 classes (52.5 hours) covering interpreting theory and practical skills training. Those who complete the course are assigned to interpret for lectures, meetings, presentations, and more, and they gradually gain experience. Deaf people come from all over the country to take the course. For the 2020–2021 school year, the course was conducted online because of the spread of COVID-19. Although DIs are still not widely recognized by society, DIs interpreted on NHK television for the Opening and Closing Ceremonies of the Tokyo Olympics and Paralympics held in 2021. This had a big impact on society. Many deaf people throughout the country commented that the interpretation was easy to understand. This might pave the way for increased use of DIs in many new areas.

INFLUENCE OF COVID-19

Because of the outbreak of COVID-19, many educational institutions could not hold on-site classes during the 2020 and 2021 school years (beginning in April and ending in March). This affected the community sign language courses as well, and many prefectures closed the courses during the 2020 school year. Some community classes experimented with online teaching via Zoom and other platforms. However, some students were not familiar with these online systems, and some did not have the equipment and environment for online learning, which created a gap between those who could access the online courses and those who could not. When we consider the fact that some prefectures offer courses in only one location and many students travel quite a long distance to take the course, it might be worth considering the establishment of a hybrid system that uses both on-site and online teaching even after the pandemic as a way to increase the number of students.

The College of the National Rehabilitation Center for Persons With Disabilities also had to close down soon after the start of the new school year in April 2020. It began online lessons, but first-year students learning JSL for the first time had difficulty acquiring the spatial elements of sign language. After resuming classes at school, the teachers had to correct many expressive errors in signing. Together with online classes, the college used Google Classroom for sharing course materials with the students. The flipped classroom[2] approach was an effective method whereby the students would first do the assigned task on their own and then hold online discussions on what they studied. To participate in online classes, the students had to familiarize themselves with the use of equipment and applications. This turned out to be a good practice to prepare students for online SLI assignments.

THE ROAD AHEAD

As stated earlier in this chapter, the teaching of JSL and JSL/Japanese interpreters began as a community-based social welfare project, and this system continues to this day. However, the need for SLI is rapidly growing beyond the needs within the deaf community. New needs for interpreting are increasing in HEIs, in the business world, and in other professional areas. It is becoming evident that the training of volunteer sign language "helpers" cannot meet the emerging needs for more professional interpreters. Even among the nationally certified sign language interpreters, only a handful are capable of handling high-level academic and conference interpreting, as many of them have not experienced university education themselves. Most of them are graduates of the Sign Language Interpreter Training at the College of the National Rehabilitation Center for Persons With Disabilities. Interpreters trained in the community courses are still focused on community interpreting.

Moreover, the sign language interpreters currently working in the communities throughout Japan are aging. Those who were trained as volunteers and who supported the SLI system over many years are now in their 60s and 70s, but young interpreters are not coming through the pathways to replace them. This is a clear threat to the continuation of the SLI profession itself. There is a critical need to increase the number of interpreters, especially those of a younger generation. However, given the current system of providing once-a-week classes in the community and the difficulty of earning a living as a sign language interpreter due to the low payment rates, the profession is not attractive enough to make young people want to become interpreters. Unless we shift from community-based training to a more formal education in HEIs, Japan's SLI profession is at risk of extinction.

A study titled "Structural Problems of Sign Language Interpretation Systems in Japan: A Field Survey of Kanazawa-shi, Kyoto-shi, and Nakano-ku" (Sakamoto et al., 2011) notes that requests from the deaf community for SLI are heavily concentrated on interpreting in hospitals, social activities, and schools and that the same clients are using the services repeatedly. In other words, services to deaf individuals are disproportionately concentrated in terms of both contexts and users. SLI services are paid out of public funds, and deaf individuals receive services for free. The fee paid to sign language interpreters is decided by the local administration, and in most cases, it is far below the amount needed to sustain a living. This low fee discourages many young people from entering the profession. Those who are currently working as interpreters typically have a different main job to sustain their living expenses and are only working part time as interpreters. To solve such issues, Sakamoto, Sato, and Watanabe (2011) propose (1) the establishment of a standardized evaluation and accreditation of interpreters throughout the country; (2) the dividing of the certification of interpreters into different professional fields, such as education, legal, medical, etc., and the dividing of the certification into different levels, such as levels 1–3; and (3) the payment of interpreters depending on the certified level.

The Sakamoto et al. (2011) report also proposes that further study is needed on whether the level of proficiency of the interpreters and ease of use of the public referral system affects the number of requests for interpreting, which varies from location to location, as well as why some deaf people do not use the public SLI referral system. If the reason is that the system is focused on providing interpreting in the community and does not allow for provision of interpreters in HEIs and in the workplace, this could mean that deaf people are greatly disadvantaged in developing and demonstrating their skills in society.

Conclusion

SLI training in Japan began approximately 50 years ago as a social welfare project. When the training courses were first started, there were no experts on SLI education, and research on sign linguistics was still in its early stages, so courses were not based on any sound scientific theories. Over the years, Japan has gradually learned from the examples of other countries and has been making minor changes in the SLI system.

However, the need for SLI has been expanding beyond the established community interpreting field into broader, more specialized fields. New methods of SLI are also being introduced, such a video relay services (VRS) and video remote interpreting (VRI). Therefore, there is an urgent need for sign language interpreters with expertise in specialized fields and technological skills, as well. There are also areas in which collaboration between hearing interpreters and DIs is essential. However, a training, accreditation, and referral system for DIs is still not available. We need to begin by raising awareness of the importance of DIs.

The training of sign language interpreters conducted in communities throughout Japan is still operated as part of the country's social welfare project. Although the government funding for this nationwide project is decreasing from year to year, it is still considered to be a stable project, as it is operated by government funding. However, if we are to further develop the SLI profession, we need to establish a high-level, specialized, formal SLI education program in HEIs. We have to keep striving to realize this goal.

ACKNOWLEDGMENTS

This chapter on Japan has been translated from Japanese to English and its contents revised by Machiko Takagi, an interpreter and interpreter educator, and Norie Oka, a linguist and educator.

NOTES

1. See Gumma University website https://sign.hess.gunma-u.ac.jp/project/future.html
2. A flipped classroom is an instructional strategy and a type of blended learning, which aims to increase student engagement and learning by having pupils complete readings at home and work on live problem-solving during class time.

REFERENCES

Adam, R., Carty, B., & Stone, C. (2011). Ghostwriting: Deaf translators within the Deaf community. *Babel*, 57(4), 375–393.

Gumma University Sign Language Supporter Training Project Office website. https://sign.hess.gunma-u.ac.jp/project/future.html

Ministry of Health, Labour, & Welfare. (2009). Ordinance on the examination and certification of the knowledge and skills of sign language interpreters. Ordinance No. 96. https://www.mhlw.go.jp/web/t_doc?dataId=83ab0582&dataType=0&pageNo=1

Ministry of Health, Labour, & Welfare. (2022). The 128th meeting of the social security council disability division, Document No. 3. https://www.mhlw.go.jp/content/12601000/000932566.pdf

Napier, J. (2021). *Sign language brokering in deaf-hearing families*. Palgrave.

Oka, N. (2022). Japanese Sign Language; A language of the deaf community. In J. C. Maher (Ed.), *Language communities in Japan* (pp. 59–67). Oxford University Press.

Sakamoto N., Sato H., & Watanabe, A. (2011). Structural problems of sign language interpretation systems in Japan: A field survey of Kanazawa-shi, Kyoto-shi, and Nakano-ku. *Core Ethics*, 7, 131–140.

Stone, C. (2009). *Toward a Deaf translation norm.* Gallaudet University Press.

Takeda, K. & Matsushita, K. (2021). Conference interpreting in Japan. *The Routledge handbook of conference interpreting* (pp. 150–158). Routledge.

Takada, E., & Koide, S. (2009). Training of sign language interpreters in Japan: Achievements and challenges. In J. Napier (Ed.), *International perspectives on sign language interpreter education* (pp. 190–199). Gallaudet University Press.

Tsuruma, I., & Yokkaichi, A. (2013). Wagakuni ni okeru shuwa tsuyakusha yosei jigyo no jittai to kadai (A survey on current situation of training for sign language interpreters in Japan). *Interpreting and Translation Studies (Journal of the Japan Association for Interpreting and Translation Studies), 13,* 97–114.

JEFWA G. MWERI, LEONIDA T. KAULA, AND
WASHINGTON AKARANGA

12

Kenya Sign Language Interpreter Education a Decade On (2009–2019)
The Highs and Lows

This chapter examines the Kenyan Sign Language (KSL) interpreting scene between 2009 and 2019. The chapter provides a brief overview of the history of KSL and KSL interpreting by delving into the Kenyan linguistic and cultural arena to give readers insight into sign language interpreter education in Kenya. The chapter also traces the most significant developments during this 10-year period, which include but are not limited to the promulgation of the Kenyan Constitution (2010) and the effects felt thereafter and their role on SLI training; the amended Disability Act (2015); and the requirement by the Communications Authority of Kenya that all news aired on television must have KSL interpreting. Some of the questions the chapter will deal with include: What new programs have emerged since, and what is the current state of the old ones? Who are the people involved in these programs, both as students and trainers? The chapter will also examine current research on KSL and KSL interpreting. Although positive progress has been made, several challenges have also been encountered. We examine some of these challenges, such as the infiltration of foreign sign languages; the lack of well-trained personnel to teach KSL interpreting, which leads to a focus on teaching lexical items, less concentration on teaching KSL grammar and interpreting theories and practice, and a lack of focus on KSL proficiency; availability of facilities; and the COVID-19 pandemic and its effects on interpreter training programs. The chapter concludes by looking at the way forward, which includes the establishment of recognized training programs and the testing, grading, certification, and licensing of KSL interpreters.

The Kenyan Context

Kenya is a country located in the East African region and has the following neighbors: Ethiopia to the north, Somalia to the northeast, Tanzania to the south, Uganda to the west, South Sudan to the northwest, and it also borders the Indian Ocean to the southeast. Kenya is currently estimated to have a population of approximately 54 million people. Kenya is a country with linguistic and cultural diversity. It is estimated that Kenya has about 47 different ethnic groups. According to Mweri (2009, p.161), "apart from this linguistic diversity resulting from these native languages, the Kenyan linguistic scene also records the existence of several 'foreign' languages, including English, French, Japanese, Hindustan, and Arabic which can be seen as Kenya Languages in their own right." Thus, Kenya is a highly multilingual society. Okombo (1994), quoted in Mweri (2009, p. 161), asserts:

> The current language situation in Kenya, as in most of Africa, is that some kind of diglossia already exists, involving the selective use of an ethnic language (Kiswahili/first language) in one set of circumstances and the use of one official often foreign language (English) in another set. The 2010 Constitution bestowed Kiswahili as Kenya's official language alongside English apart from being the national language.

It is important to be cognizant of the fact that the classification of languages in Kenya has always been based mainly on spoken languages, and KSL was never considered. However, this situation was remedied after the (2010) Kenyan Constitution recognized KSL as one of the Kenyan indigenous languages for deaf Kenyans and also as a language of Parliament. Article 7, Section 3, states that the State shall "(a) promote and protect the diversity of language of the people of Kenya; and (b) promote the development and use of indigenous languages, Kenyan Sign Language, Braille and other communication formats and technologies accessible to persons with disabilities."

On the other hand, Section 120 states, "(1) The official languages of Parliament shall be Kiswahili, English and Kenyan Sign Language, and the business of Parliament may be conducted in English, Kiswahili and Kenyan Sign Language." This therefore means that the government of Kenya is obliged by law to promote and protect KSL as an indigenous language of Kenya and also help in the development and promotion of KSL interpreting, as Article 54 (d) of the Kenyan Constitution asserts: "A person with any disability is entitled—(d) To use Sign Language, Braille or other appropriate means of communication. . . ."

The recognition of KSL in the Kenya Constitution (2010) is one of most celebrated highs in the period under review.

Since the 2009 publication of the chapter "Sign Language Interpreter Training in Kenya" (Okomo et al., 2009) in the first edition of this volume, a lot has happened. One inevitable development over this period of time is of course an increase in the number of people who are deaf in Kenya. In 2009, we estimated that there were about 800,000 Kenyans who were deaf, using statistics from the Kenya Campaign on Disability and HIV and AIDS advocacy proposal. Ten years later, the exact number of persons who are deaf in Kenya is still not clear. As of the national census in 2019, the total population of Kenya was estimated at 47,564,296. From this figure, we can extrapolate the population of persons who are deaf. Ten percent of any population comprises persons with one form of disability or another. Given this fact, then approximately 4,800,000 Kenyans fall under this category. This therefore gives us approximately 1,300,000 Kenyans who are deaf at different levels. The aforementioned national census did not provide any specific statistics on persons with disabilities. If we go by the previously mentioned figure of roughly 1,300,000 persons who are deaf, then it basically means that the need for interpreters and the consumption of SLI services has also increased substantially over the years.

Who Are We?

Jefwa G. Mweri is a hearing senior lecturer at the University of Nairobi (UON) Department of Kiswahili and the director of the Kenyan Sign Language Research Project (KSLRP) at the UON. The project was established in 1991. Jefwa is a teacher by profession and a linguist by training and has more than 30 years of university teaching experience. He has also done extensive research and published articles in referred journals and chapters in books on KSL interpreting, sociolinguistic and grammatical issues in KSL, and health issues affecting people who are deaf. His research interests are mainly KSL discourse analysis, language and health care, language and communication, and the education of people who are deaf in Kenya and worldwide. Jefwa has been involved in many activities, such as training interpreters, teaching KSL, creating HIV and AIDS awareness among the deaf community, producing KSL educational materials, and conducting research on KSL.

Leonida Tausi Kaula, hearing, has been interpreting for more than 20 years and is the immediate past president of the Kenyan Sign Language Interpreters Association (KSLIA). She holds a master's degree in interpreting from the UON and is currently pursuing a doctor of philosophy (PhD) degree at the same university. Her interpreting experience includes a variety of settings, including education, conferences, and television. She has been interpreting the parliamentary proceedings of the Parliament of Kenya on the national broadcaster for the past 9 years. In addition to interpreting, Leonida is a lecturer at the Technical University of Kenya (TUK) and also teaches a component of interpreting at the KSLRP at the UON. Through the Center for Sign Language Interpreting Services (CESLIS), an interpreting agency, she has organized professional development initiatives aimed at equipping interpreters with necessary skills to enhance their competence. She has achieved this goal by periodically organizing and conducting themed interpreter training sessions, mentoring upcoming interpreters, and creating awareness of SLI.

Washington Akaranga, Deaf, is a senior researcher at the KSLRP. He has been involved with the project since its inception in 1991, and he is one of the five people who are deaf in the project. He has a wealth of experience in KSL training and research, having been involved in the initial research that eventually produced the first KSL dictionary. His involvement in the production of KSL educational support materials has been invaluable. Washington is also the coordinator of all KSL training programs, under which the interpreter training falls. He has contributed immensely to the KSL interpreter training program, having himself been a beneficiary of SLI training under the Regional Sign Language Project (RSLP) supported by the Danish Association of the Deaf in 1996. He has also coauthored numerous articles on KSL and KSL interpreting.

CONTEXTUALIZATION: TRANSLATION AND INTERPRETING IN KENYA

The Center for Translation and Interpretation (CTI) at the UON entered into collaboration with the United Nations to launch CTI in November 2010. The center offers postgraduate degrees at the doctoral and master's levels in both translation and interpreting (T&I). The programs were established with a view to fill the gap occasioned by the scarcity of qualified professional translators and interpreters from the African continent.

The center, being one of its kind in the Eastern and Central African region, is committed to providing quality training, research, and practice in T&I. The CTI ensures that it produces translators and interpreters who are well-equipped to compete for jobs in the international market on an equal footing. Both T&I have been taught since, and CTI has produced translators and interpreters of various languages, including but not limited to French, Kiswahili, German, Arabic, Spanish, and Portuguese. CTI is open to, and accommodates, students from the entire African region.

Although CTI focuses on spoken languages, it has the potential to also train KSL interpreters. A case in point are the projects that some of the students have completed. In 2014, a master of arts (MA) student researched *A Comparative Analysis of Challenges Associated With English and Kiswahili Source Texts in Kenyan Sign Language Interpretation: A Case Study of KTN [Kenya Television Network] News*. Another student studying in 2021 worked on a project about deaf people in Kenya and explored "The Quality of Intralingual Live Subtitles and Their Role in Inclusivity: A Comparative Assessment of Citizen TV and BBC News Broadcasts."

Professionalization of SLI in Kenya

The history of SLI in Kenya is intrinsically linked to deaf education. It goes back to 1958, when the first schools and units for the deaf were established in Kenya. Two units for the deaf were started by the Aga Khan Foundation in Nairobi and Mombasa. Before that, SLI was not a considered a profession as such, but like the history of interpreting in other countries, SLI as a form of linguistic exchange did occur. Teachers in the schools, for instance, would learn some KSL, and in turn, they would transfer information from hearing to deaf children and vice versa. The 1960s saw the establishment of more schools—for instance, the schools for the deaf in Mumias and Nyangoma that were established by Catholic missionaries. It was not until the early 1980s that KSL started to gain prominence. During the same period, specifically 1982, the Swedish Deaf Association (SDR) initiated the building of Machakos School for the Deaf to pilot teaching deaf children using sign language as a medium of instruction. This initiative also saw the recruitment of some teachers who went through a 2-month crash course in sign language and how to use it in the teaching of deaf students. However, it is important to note that at this point the training was in Signed Exact English (SEE) and not the natural KSL.

In 1987, the Kenya National Association of the Deaf (KNAD) was established and registered under the Societies Act as an umbrella body to advocate for the rights of people who are deaf in Kenya. This was done with assistance from the SDR. The association between KNAD and SDR saw intensified training in KSL. Many hearing people were trained in KSL, and this is the cohort that represents the first generation of KSL trained interpreters. One important fact to point out here is that the SDR put emphasis on KSL development and did not insist on the teaching of Swedish Sign Language (STS), a fact that positively impacted the growth and development of KSL.

The Origins and Role of the KSLRP

A public lecture at the UON organized by KNAD and the Swedish volunteers working at KNAD on sign language and the need for universities to be involved in sign language research resulted in the establishment of the KSLRP in 1991. The project based at the UON is still in existence and has been the center of KSL interpreter training over the past 30 years.

The broad objective of KSLRP has been to collect, analyze, and publicize information about KSL. KSLRP provides factual information that can be used for the betterment of the lives of deaf people in Kenya. As such, KSLRP has played a pioneering role in the development of the SLI profession in Kenya. In performing this role, KSLRP is engaged in different activities such as research, training, and production of materials, among many others. Research in KSL conducted by KSLRP staff over the years has enabled the language to gain recognition in Kenya and else-where. Because of this, today, as pointed out earlier, KSL is recognized in the Ken-yan Constitution (2010) as an indigenous language and a language of parliament.

KSLRP staff have also been able to do extensive research in KSL, and its staff members have been able to disseminate some of the findings by writing papers and presentations in international forums. KSLRP also engages in raising awareness of or sensitivity with regard to issues such as HIV and AIDS, disability in general, and the issues of deafness and people who are deaf in Kenya, in particular through various sensitization workshops and seminars. KSLRP staff have also been engaged in the production of educational support materials used in schools for deaf children in Kenya, as well as other materials that are used by the general populace interested in understanding the deaf and learning KSL.

The Inception of KSLIA

Another significant occurrence that influenced the direction of KSL interpreter training happened in the 1990s, when the United States of America Peace Corps (an American volunteer organization) introduced a deaf education program that placed volunteer teachers in Kenyan schools for the deaf. Some of the volunteer teachers were deaf, and therefore, the Peace Corps program relied heavily on interpreters to carry out its pre-service training. Interpreters were needed to facilitate communi-cation between the instructors and the deaf volunteers. The organization invested in one or two interpreters from the United States to work with local interpreters to build their capacity. In 1999, a strong group of American deaf volunteers advocated for funding to build the capacity of local interpreters. Consequently, in September 2000, the Peace Corps organized an interpreter workshop. The 1-week workshop involved two American Sign Language (ASL) interpreters, three deaf Americans as facilitators, and 10 KSL interpreters as participants. The main resolution of the workshop was to establish an interpreters' association. On October 22, 2001, the KSLIA was finally registered (Kaula, 2015).

Legislation That Has Assisted the Growth of KSL Interpreting on Television

Legislation passed by the Kenyan Parliament has been instrumental in giving SLI and sign language interpreters their rightful status. Some of this legislation precedes 2009, such as the 2003 Act for Persons With Disability, which provided several rights and privileges to deaf people, such as the reservation of employment opportunities in the public sector and catering to the communication needs of deaf people in learning institutions. The act further required television stations to provide SLI or captioning during news and other educational programs. This law was later amended after 2009, after the proposed Persons With Disabilities (Amendment) Act of 2015 was discussed in Parliament. These proposed amendments have had a major impact on KSL interpreting. For instance, Section 28A of this amended act (1) recognizes KSL as the official language of deaf people and (2) places KSL on a footing equivalent to English and Kiswahili. Furthermore, Section 21A (1) and (2) require any public institution offering services to citizens to provide qualified sign language interpreters and ensure that information is disseminated to the public about the availability of sign language interpreters for the deaf. The proposed amendments originated in 2013 and had the effect of influencing the direction of SLI on television, as the same year saw the onset of KSL interpreting of news on national television.

Three television stations, namely the national broadcaster Kenya Broadcasting Corporation (KBC) and two privately owned television stations, the Kenya Television Network (KTN) and the Good News Broadcasting System (GBS), employed interpreters to interpret the news for deaf viewers. The inception of KSL interpreting on television was further solidified in 2016 by a directive from the Communications Authority of Kenya (CAK), a regulatory authority for the communication sector in Kenya that was established in 1999 by the Kenya Information and Communications Act (1998) with the mandate of facilitating the development of the information and communications sectors, including broadcasting, multimedia, telecommunications, electronic commerce, and postal and courier services. The CAK directive required that all television stations have news bulletins interpreted into KSL. Consequently, from July 1, 2016, sign language interpreters are now contracted to interpret news for deaf viewers. Today, Kenya has more than 50 television stations (some of which broadcast in local dialects or languages), most of which provide interpreting for news bulletins. The rules from the CAK, however, require all media houses to ensure they have 100% signing during news and events of national importance, as well as for all emergency announcements. Thus far, the rules are mostly followed for television news interpreting (save for the national broadcaster, KBC, which endeavors to have interpreters during events of national importance). The advent of COVID-19 in late 2019 also increased the demand for interpreting, as critical information was regularly being disseminated by the government. For example, all Ministry of Health daily briefings had in-person interpreting. This was monumental for KSL users, as historically, the Ministry of Health and other ministries have not provided KSL interpreting for most major announcements, including national holidays.

Given that the Kenyan Constitution (2010) has officially recognized sign language, and Article 120 (i) stipulates that the official languages of parliament shall be Kiswahili, English, and KSL and that the business of parliament may be conducted in English, Kiswahili, and KSL, as a consequence, the Kenyan parliament has contracted sign language interpreters to interpret on television during its parliamentary proceedings. Similarly, public and private entities and non governmental organizations use SLI services in meetings, public forums, seminars, and workshops.

After the promulgation of the 2010 constitution, Kenya now operates on a two-tier system of government comprising the national government and the county governments. The county governments, 47 of them, also operate county assemblies. One county government nominated a deaf member of the county assembly during the first 5 years of the implementation of the devolved government, which resulted in the employment of a KSL interpreter in that county. A few other counties have employed interpreters to ease communication when deaf persons seek services at the county offices.

Growth of Interpreting in Tertiary Institutions

A few tertiary institutions have contracted sign language interpreters for their deaf students. For instance, the UON during this period has had about 10 deaf students pursuing various degree programs at different times. Some of these students have since graduated; two of them graduated with a bachelor of science (BSc) in engineering in December 2019.

Data from the disability desk at the dean of students office indicate that at time of writing, two persons who are deaf are enrolled in PhD programs. One is pursuing a PhD in political science and the other a PhD in business administration. One graduate student is pursuing a master's degree in human rights, while two other students are pursuing bachelor of arts degrees (one in political science and one in law).

This is a major improvement in the education of people who are deaf and also in the field of interpreting because the UON has had to hire interpreters for the ever-increasing number of students who are deaf. Each student is normally assigned a sign language interpreter to provide interpreting during lectures. Furthermore, a few other tertiary institutions have contracted sign language interpreters for their deaf students. The United States International University–Africa is a private University in Kenya that has been admitting learners who are deaf (so far four, pursuing different courses) and also provide interpreting services for them. To date, three interpreters have been hired.

The KSLIA database also reveals that there are a number of interpreters interpreting for deaf students in higher education institutions. For example, Kenyatta University enrolled four persons who are deaf: two pursuing bachelor's degrees in commerce and special education, one a diploma, and the fourth a master's degree in public policy and administration. With this enrollment of students who are deaf, three interpreters were hired. Maseno University has three interpreters who provide services to students who are deaf and are enrolled in the institution. These are but a few examples of the achievements that people who are deaf in Kenya have been able to realize over the years. This high enrollment and its attendant employment of KSL interpreters have been unprecedented in the history of deaf education in Kenya. It is not an occurrence that would have been envisaged in 2009.

Sign Language Interpreter Education in Kenya

Through its other mandate of training, KSLRP has over the years trained more than 10,000 hearing people in KSL. These are hearing people from all walks of life. Some have gone on to become sign language interpreters. KSLRP is the only institution that trains KSL interpreters and certifies them. Similarly, KSLRP has trained professionals such as nurses, police officers, social workers, and staff from the Kenya Medical Training College (KMTC) and many other organizations to further our goal of reaching out and empowering deaf people through KSL. This includes staff from various government departments, with sponsorship from the National Council for Persons With Disabilities (NCPWD). KSLRP also engages stakeholders in the education sector on the challenges for deaf children at school. This is done through seminars and workshops of stakeholders and through collaboration with the Kenya Society of Deaf Children to advocate for the rights of deaf children.

Training remains one of the most important functions at KSLRP. Project staff have trained interested hearing people in basic KSL and advanced KSL. The Advanced KSL training has a component of interpreting that introduces learners to principles of interpreting, as they continue to acquire more vocabulary and KSL grammar. Thereafter, students go for a 3-month industrial attachment to get firsthand experience in signing and interpreting. The KSLRP's training program, which is the pioneering program in KSL training, is targeted mainly at teaching KSL to interested hearing people and, in some cases, people who became deaf later in life to enable them to access KSL interpreting.

The birth of KSLRP in 1991 later led to the start of a Regional Sign Language Project (RSLP), which was an offshoot of a proposal for an interpreter training program presented to the Danish Deaf Association (DANIDA) by the late Okoth Okombo, who was then director of KSLRP. According to Kaula (2015), from Okombo's proposal, a RSLP involving a partnership between the Deaf Associations of Kenya, Uganda, Tanzania, and Zambia was born. This RSLP was launched in 1996. However, it was not until 1997 that DANIDA funded the first SLI training (Phase 1), which involved Kenya, Uganda, Tanzania, and Zambia.

Initially, the training involved six people (three hearing and three deaf) who underwent a 4-month crash program in SLI training in Denmark at the Center for Sign Language and Sign-Supported Communication. The three hearing persons involved were already practicing interpreters, while the deaf persons were sign language instructors in their respective countries. The six were trained as Trainers of Trainers (TOTs) in SLI.

In Phase 2, each of the deaf associations of the four participating countries were again required to recruit three deaf sign language instructors and three practicing interpreters to undergo a 2-year training program in SLI. The Kenyan participants were picked from different organizations, from KSLRP, KNAD, and a church for

deaf people in Nairobi. The training was conducted by Danish interpreter trainers together with the team of TOTs who had previously undergone training in
Denmark. Within the 2-year period, all the trainees converged five times for 6 weeks
fulltime for residential training. After each 6-week period, the teams returned to
their respective countries for practical experience with supervision by the trainers.
At the end of the 2-year training in the year 2000, Kenya had three trained interpreters and three deaf KSL instructors who were expected to continue training
interpreters. One trained interpreter/TOT was absorbed into KSLRP to assist with
its training program as a component of interpreting was added to the KSL program.
The other two trained interpreters continued practicing interpreting: One (now
deceased) worked as a freelance interpreter, while the other was later employed by
the judiciary to interpret court cases involving deaf persons.

As pointed out earlier, the UON through the KSLRP is the pioneering institution in KSL and SLI training. The KSLRP also works in close cooperation with the
Center for Translation and Interpreting at UON. The KSLRP uses a curriculum that
has been considered acceptable since 1991 and is based on the KSL syllabus for the
elementary, intermediate, and advanced stages. The training pays specific attention
to the development of signing and observation skills in the students. The training is
divided into three main parts: Part 1, Basic KSL (3 months; 96 hours), combines the
elementary and intermediate stages, during which students are expected to develop
fluency in KSL. Part 2, Advanced KSL (3 months; 96 hours), introduces the learner
to principles of interpreting, which then would help the learners increase their
awareness and ability to interpret KSL into both spoken English and Kiswahili.
Part 3, Attachment/Practicum (3 months; 480 hours; full time), requires learners
to go on a 3-month full-time attachment/practicum at a deaf organization after the
advanced course. The purpose of this attachment is to further expose learners to the
Kenyan deaf community and culture in a practical way and provide them an opportunity to practice KSL with its native users. The 3 months of attachment greatly
enhances their communication ability in KSL and their interpreting skills.

Institutions Offering KSL Training

Since 2009, the colleges and universities offering one form of sign language course
or another has increased drastically. The more KSL becomes popular as it is being
used to interpret news, the more hearing non-signers want to learn the language.
A Google search of colleges and universities offering a certificate in KSL reveals
that about 15 colleges and more than five universities are currently offering some
form of KSL training. What all these institutions have in common is that they do
not use a standardized curriculum. Each institution uses a form of curriculum they
have developed. This leaves the teaching of KSL prone to abuse because some colleges teach foreign sign languages or a mixture of KSL with foreign sign languages

while purporting to be teaching KSL. The other issue this scenario presents is the difficulty of certification. Each institution issues their own certificate. Some certificates are recognized, whereas others are not.

Most of these institutions also have no capacity to teach SLI because the staff do not have the necessary qualifications. Thus, most training basically focuses on teaching signed lexical items. Moreover, there is a mistaken belief that any deaf person can teach KSL. There is also a widespread misconception that on learning basic KSL, one can become an interpreter, which has led to the infiltration of the field with "half-baked" KSL interpreters. This has led to compromising the quality of SLI services. Faith-based organizations have also infiltrated this field, some offering KSL classes in churches or mosques without using qualified personnel. There are also increased numbers of churches providing "KSL interpreting" for their church services for deaf congregants.

Another pre-2019 effort on the development of SLI curriculum was in 2008, when a stakeholders' workshop was held, supported by Deaf Aid Kenya, which developed a 2-year curriculum for a diploma in KSL interpreting. The curriculum was approved by the Kenya Institute of Curriculum Development (KICD), a body tasked with developing curricula. Exams for this curriculum were to be administered by the Kenya National Examination Council (KNEC). However, to date, no institution has implemented this curriculum. Nevertheless, this was a major milestone in improvingthe potential for SLI training.

Since 2018, efforts have been underway to table a KSL bill in the national assembly. However, there is some ongoing controversy about this, with one group led by KNAD drafting their own bill, and one member of the Senate drafting her own bill, which was presented to the Senate in 2019. The KNAD initiative was supported by Mobility International USA (MIUSA) and involved public participation through stakeholders' involvement. There is a need for close cooperation among all those intending to table bills on KSL. Stakeholder involvement should be paramount, and deaf stakeholders should be at the forefront in this.

THE ROAD AHEAD

The future of KSL interpreting and interpreter training is bright. All indications are that SLI training will grow in leaps and bounds going forward. However, this can happen only if certain measures are put in place to guide KSL interpreter training. There is a need for a harmonized curriculum that colleges offering KSL should follow. Although the situation for universities might be slightly different because they offer Senate-approved courses, a national body that would test and certify all interpreters would be a welcome addition. This requires political goodwill on the part of the government. The various bills being drafted and presented to the parliament can go a long way to help in this, as long as there is a clear understanding of the purpose and that the best interests of deaf Kenyans are at the forefront.

Nonetheless, there are also challenges ahead for SLI education in Kenya. Although the number of people interested in KSL and those being trained has risen tremendously, one of the main challenges is a lack of agreement on who should be considered as a qualified interpreter. Qualifications are not well defined. Training institutions also have no set prerequisite criteria for their training programs. It seems that interest is the main qualification for whoever wants to learn KSL. Similarly, organizations that engage interpreters on a full-time or part-time basis most of the time do not engage professionals or the KSLIA to interview for them but rather go for anybody who can sign. Furthermore, there seems to be no consideration of one's competence in English and Kiswahili (the official languages in Kenya) or which interpreters work from English or Kiswahili into KSL and vice versa.

The varied skills and limited competence of interpreters have definitely lowered the standards of KSL interpreting. A case in point is a petition by members of the deaf community presented to the steering committee on the implementation of the Building Bridges Initiative, a taskforce established by the Kenyan president and the opposition leader in 2019 that was tasked with evaluating national challenges. Concerns were raised about "the quality of sign language interpretation on Kenyan television stations in Kenya." According to the Building Bridges Initiative letter addressed to the chairman of the Kenya Media Association, "the community informed the task force many a time the quality of sign language interpretation was substandard and even incompetent to the level that the deaf community did not understand the message in the broadcast." This is an issue of quality control that has been made difficult by the lack of a regulatory body to ensure the quality of interpretation.

Proper training is a mirage in most of the colleges and universities at which KSL is offered because most of the time, qualified instructors are not available. Thus, for the majority of KSL classes, only KSL lexical items are taught. Very few instructors have a linguistic background, which means that teaching of KSL grammar is a tall order in itself; teaching principles of interpreting, theories, and practice is even more arduous. There is, therefore, a lack of focus on KSL proficiency, with the emphasis instead being on teaching vocabulary most of the time. Students who complete such training cannot by any stretch of imagination claim to be interpreters. Nevertheless, some of them end up interpreting in various situations.

Related to this is the challenge of nonexistent specialized training. Most training offered in Kenya is what we might call generalized training, and none of the programs really focus on any specialized fields. A KSL interpreter is likely to interpret in all sorts of situations, which raises the question of efficacy. How effective is such an interpreter when they do broadcast, medical, educational, legal, social interpreting, etc., given that the discourse used in all these situations is different and the contexts are also different?

There is also the challenge of people who mean well but are either ignorant or lack the capacity to consult stakeholders and especially specialists in this field (impostors). A case in point is one nominated senator in the Kenyan Parliament who introduced the proposed KSL bill (2019). This bill has several positive aspects, like the section that is intended to regulate SLI in Kenya. This is something to celebrate because it is what KSLIA has been working to achieve. However, the bill also had a lot of misinformation that emanates from pure ignorance—for instance, the intended introduction of SEE through the back door by christening it Kenyan Signed English (KSE). The bill said in defining KSE that it "means manually coded English involving producing signs which correspond to an English word in an English sentence in English word order designed to facilitate communication between the deaf and hearing community." Ironically, and in a contradictory way, the bill defines KSL as the "sign language predominantly used in Kenya by the deaf community." What is even more worrying is that in the Constitution of Kenya (2010), the supreme law of the land does not mention KSE anywhere.

The KNAD, KSLIA, and other stakeholders presented comprehensive proposals on the KSL bill (2019) during a public consultation forum. It is, however, unclear whether the proposals will be taken into consideration by the time the final bill could be passed. The bill will have to go through a long process of first, second, and third readings in Parliament, and given these kinds of processes, it is impossible to determine the time it will take before it is finally passed.

Although the use of deaf interpreters (DIs) for enhanced communication has been encouraged by the World Federation of the Deaf, to date, there are no DIs in Kenya. Kenyan society at large also does not understand the idea of DIs. To date, deaf people have not formally been involved with SLI. In our view, even if understood, it is likely to only be frowned upon by hearing people and also perceived as expensive, as most entities already contracting hearing interpreters find it expensive.

Another vexatious challenge is the issue of remuneration of KSL interpreters. There seems to be a misunderstanding of the role of a KSL interpreter, and therefore, there is no set standard for their payment for services offered. According to an August 2019 circular from the Salaries and Remuneration Commission, a government body whose mandate is to review remuneration and benefits of the public service (all government employees), KSL interpreters are somehow grouped as personal guides for deaf people, and therefore, their remuneration is determined as such. In this context, a KSL interpreter attached to a deaf government employee is to be paid a monthly stipend of Ksh. 20,000 (the equivalent of $135 USD at the current exchange rate), which is extremely low. The payment is not remitted directly to the interpreter, but rather paid to the deaf person who then pays the interpreter, reinforcing the lack of professional recognition of interpreters. The issue of poor remuneration has been a recurring challenge, with no solution in sight. Interpreters are generally compensated the same regardless of qualifications, skill, and experience.

The lack of a well-established training curriculum and certification and standard licensing procedures has led to an unclear process of contracting KSL interpreters. The response to the growing demand for KSL interpreters is met mostly through referrals. Interpreters are known by reputation and are referred for jobs by word of mouth. In most cases, interpreters are engaged for work without any qualifications being demanded of them save for knowledge of sign language. Currently, there is no certification process to ensure licensing of interpreters in Kenya. It is common to find individuals with very minimal sign language skills interpreting in high-level assignments that require experienced interpreters. Furthermore, practicing interpreters are at different levels of skill, some with several years of experience and others with minimal skills and no experience at all. Employers are unable to distinguish these levels, as there is no system for licensing interpreters according to qualifications, skill, and experience.

The 2010 constitutional amendments in Kenya presented a unique opportunity for positive change and progress in many fields, including the field of KSL interpreting. If the government pledges fidelity to the Constitution of 2010, many of the challenges discussed earlier can find resolution. This will also open the doors that will enable us to address the challenges faced by deaf people, interpreters, and other stakeholders. The selection of the National Dialogue Committee, which is trying to find areas to be amended 10 years on, is also a moment that presents a hopeful chance for these groups to voice their concerns and recommendations. A collaborative effort involving deaf people, interpreters, and other stakeholders holds great promise for a more inclusive and equitable future for all Kenyan citizens. We together can work toward a new constitutional dispensation that is more inclusive and responsive to the needs of all citizens, and deaf people and interpreters in particular, ensuring a brighter future for Kenya in the field of KSL interpreting.

ACKNOWLEDGMENTS

This chapter is dedicated to the memory of Okoth Okombo, who was a leader in KSL teaching and KSL interpreter training and the lead author of the first chapter on SLI education in Kenya (Okomo, Mweri,& Akaranga, 2009).

REFERENCES

Kaula, L.T. (2015). The legislation of Kenyan Sign Language and its impact on the signlanguage interpreting profession in Kenya. In I. Heyerick & S. Ehrlich (Eds.), *Proceedings of the World Association of Sign Language Interpreters Conference, Human Rights: Where do interpreters fit in?* (pp. 22–25). World Association of Sign Language Interpreters.

Kenya National Bureau of Statistics (2019). Kenya Population and Housing Census Results. https://www.knbs.or.ke/2019-kenya-population-and-housing-census-reports/

Kenyan Sign Language Research Project. (1997). *Kenyan Sign Language syllabus for Elementary (Stage 1), Intermediate (Stage II), and Advanced (Stage III) stages*. Kenyan Sign Language Research Project.

Mweri, J. G. (2009). Structural borrowing: The case of Kenyan Sign Language (KSL) and Kiswahili Contact Signing. *Journal of Language, Technology & Entrepreneurship in Africa, 1*(2), 160–174.

Okombo, O. (1994). Kenyan Sign Language: Some attitudinal and cognitive issues in the evolution of a language community. In I. Alilgren & K. Hyltenstam (Eds.), *Bilingualism in deaf education* (pp. 37–54). Signum.

Okombo, O., Mweri, J. G., & Akaranga, W. (2009). Sign language interpreter training in Kenya. In J. Napier (Ed), *International perspectives on sign language interpreter education.* Gallaudet University Press.

Republic of Kenya. (2003). The Persons With Disabilities Act.

Republic of Kenya. (2010). Constitution of the Republic of Kenya.

Republic of Kenya. (2015). The Proposed Persons With Disabilities (Amendment) Act.

Republic of Kenya. (2019). The Kenyan Sign Language Bill. Kenya Gazette Supplement No. 128 (Senate Bills No. 15). Nairobi, Kenya: Government Printers.

SELMAN HOTI, ROBERT ADAM, AND
ARTTU LIIKAMAA

13

Beginnings of the Sign Language Interpreter Training Program in Kosovo

This chapter gives an overview of the interpreter training program in the Republic of Kosovo, which was launched in 2005 with funding from the Finnish Association of the Deaf (FAD) and the Ministry for Foreign Affairs of Finland. It will also detail the input of the local interpreter trainer; interpreter trainer advisers from Australia, the United Kingdom, and Finland; and international guest interpreter trainers from Canada, Australia, Ireland, England, and Scotland. It will summarize how Kosovo has developed the interpreter training program, starting from nothing and progressing to a system that includes an advanced curriculum for a vocational interpreter training program, certification of the sign language instructor and sign language interpreter trainers, government legislation that recognizes the profession of sign language interpreting (SLI), and implementation of payment system for SLI services.

The Kosovo Context

Kosovo is located in the Balkans region of Europe, and its neighboring countries are Serbia, Montenegro, Macedonia, and Albania. Kosovo's recent history is characterized by a war in which approximately one million Albanians were forced by Yugoslavian soldiers and paramilitaries out of Kosovo. The war ended after NATO strikes in 1999, when the genocide also ended.

According to the 2011 census, the first census conducted after the 2008 declaration of independence, the population of Kosovo reached 1.8 million (Kosovo Statistics Agency). Population density is close to 200 per square kilometer, one of the highest in Europe. Kosovo also has the youngest population in Europe: Half of its population is under the age of 25 years. The majority of the population is composed of ethnic Albanians, while the largest minority is Serbian. According to the Kosovo Statistics Agency Census in 2011, around 92.9% of the population are ethnic Albanians, whereas the Serbian population accounted for 1.5%, Bosnians 1.6%, and others 3.7% (Roma, Ashkalia, and Egyptians).[1] The official languages of Kosovo are Albanian and Serbian. However, in the cities that have a concentration of at least 5% of the total population who use a particular language, that language can become an official language within that municipality. *Gjuha e Shenjave Kosovare* (Kosovo Sign Language [KosSL]) was informally recognized in 2010 through a decision by the prime minister.

On February 17, 2008, the Kosovo Assembly declared the independence of Kosovo. Since then, more than 100 countries have recognized Kosovo, and it has joined numerous international organizations. In October 2008, Serbia sought an advisory opinion from the International Court of Justice (ICJ) on the legality of Kosovo's declaration of independence under international law. The ICJ released an advisory opinion in July 2010 affirming that Kosovo's declaration of independence did not violate the general principle of international law.

WHO ARE WE?

Selman Hoti is a hearing heritage signer who was born and raised in Kosovo and is an interpreter and interpreter trainer with the Kosovar Association of the Deaf (KAD) and the Albanian National Association of the Deaf (ANAD). He has worked for KAD since July 2004. He works as an interpreter on the Kosovar television signed news and was a board member of the World Association of Sign Language Interpreters (WASLI) representing the Balkan region from 2007 to 2015.

Robert Adam's detailed positionality statement as a deaf academic, interpreter, translator, and educator can be seen in the Introduction chapter. He is currently associate professor in the Department of Languages and Intercultural Studies at Heriot-Watt University and was previously a teaching fellow at the Deafness Cognition and Language Center (DCAL) at University College London. During his time at DCAL, he was also an adviser to the Kosovar interpreter training program. As an adviser, he was involved in establishing the KosSL interpreter accreditation panel, setting up their first interpreter assessments, and providing training to new panel members, as well as providing training on how to organize the new KosSL dictionary using linguistic principles. He also wrote the guidance for using the KosSL dictionary.

Arttu Liikamaa is a deaf lecturer in the SLI training program at Humak University of Applied Sciences. He has a master of arts (MA) degree in Finnish Sign Language (FinSL) from the University of Jyväskylä. He has worked for the FAD as a linguistic and pedagogical adviser for development cooperation projects in the Balkan region, in cooperation with the AAD and the KAD, during the years 2009–2020.

Contextualization: Translation and Interpreting in Kosovo

Kosovar institutions apply a system of multilingual legislation in which extensive language rights of different communities are safeguarded through both the legislative framework and international instruments. The legal framework requires primary legislation to be published in five languages (Albanian, Serbian, Turkish, Bosnian, and English).[2] On the basis of Articles 2.3 and 2.4 of the Law on the Uses of Languages, a language traditionally spoken or spoken by 3% of the population can be recognized as a "language in official use." Users of such languages can receive services and obtain documents in their languages only through individual requests. In Kosovo, there are no universities or colleges that provide SLI education programs. However, the Faculty of Philology in the University of Prishtina offers a 4-year course with two majors combined, including Albanian Language and Literature, English Language and Literature, German Language and Literature, French Language and Literature, and Turkish Language and Literature. There is also a MA-level degree in Translation and Interpretation.

Translation and interpreting in Kosovo before the 1999 war was practiced by only a few talented and experienced practitioners; after the war, however, because of a sudden, extraordinary need for translation, these skills have been practiced for "those who are in need and those who do it indeed" (Kajradagu & Krasniqi, 2020, p. 94). Also, there is no national body or agency that accredits translators or interpreters in Kosovo. The Kosovo Prosecutorial Council is the only institution that certifies translators, including sign language interpreters for the judicial system. The regulation defines the engagement and sets fees for translators and interpreters in the judicial system. After the war, with the heavy presence of the United Nations Mission in Kosovo, there was a sharp rise in the requirement for spoken language interpreters, many of whom were employed without any formal interpreter training.

Professionalization of SLI in Kosovo

The professionalization of SLI in Kosovo has been a slow development. In early 2001, a survey of the deaf community in Kosovo was conducted by FAD. That survey revealed that there were no trained interpreters in Kosovo. Despite this situation, there was one interpreter who had deaf parents who was working at the University of Prishtina, and there was another interpreter working at the Prishtina Deaf Club. At the same time, a seminar was held with representatives from the deaf community, during which they identified priorities of and for the deaf community.

On the basis of these priorities, a funding application was submitted to FAD with three main objectives, which were as follows:

1. Organizational training to build the capacity of the deaf community and their clubs to have a functioning and representative umbrella organization for the Kosovar deaf community;
2. Basic-level interpreter training to begin to provide equal opportunities for deaf citizens and enable them to have greater independence in Kosovo; and
3. Sign language work to increase the status of KosSL by producing information and training related to sign language.

The Kosovar project successfully received funding to implement these three main objectives. The project team consisted of Colin Allen, organizational adviser (Australia), Ramadan Gashi, Deaf liaison officer (Kosovo), Sheena Walters, interpreter trainer, (Australia), and Selman Hoti, local interpreter trainer. The team carried out another survey of the 12 deaf clubs in Kosovo (The Organizational Training Project for the Kosovar Deaf Community, Report on the Evaluation of the Status of 12 Clubs and Interpreters in Kosovo, October to November 2004, in Pristina, Kosovo). One part of this survey sought to collect information about SLI in Kosovo and to investigate the viability of conducting a basic-level interpreter training program.

KosSL was officially recognized by the Government of the Republic of Kosovo (GRK) prime minister. This recognition was the result of advocacy efforts by the deaf community, facilitated by the Working Group for Kosovar Sign Language Recognition. This working group consisted of international experts, including Liisa Kauppinen, former president of the World Federation of the Deaf (WFD), as well as representatives from the Kosovo deaf community and the government. This was followed by approval in 2014 of Regulation of Government of the Republic of Kosovo GRK No. 15/2014[3] by the Kosovo government on the provision of services in sign languages in the Republic of Kosovo. The purpose of the regulation is to define rules and procedures on providing SLI services for the deaf community in Kosovo. This regulation applies to all public institutions at the local and national levels, and the UN Convention on the Rights of Persons With Disabilities,[4] which was adopted in 2006, influenced the development of this regulation as well. The service started in 2016, and deaf people now receive professional SLI for their interactions in public services, and this is paid for by the GRK. This service is limited to the public sector, so KAD has continued to lobby the government to renew the regulation to also include SLI services in the private sector, and so far the GRK has established a working group to develop the concept note on the Sign Language Law.

In parallel to these developments, the project established an Interpreter Working Group that worked in close liaison with the KAD. The Interpreter Working Group consisted of four interpreter students, a deaf administrator, two project interpreters, and the international interpreter trainer adviser. The working group created policies and guidelines for both interpreters and the community.

To date, the Interpreter Working Group has published three pertinent documents: a Code of Professional Conduct, guidelines on working conditions, and a printed brochure for hearing people on "How to Work with a Sign Language Interpreter." The working group also developed statutes for the establishment of the Kosovar Association of Sign Language Interpreters (KASLI) with the aim of developing the SLI profession. In 2008, KASLI was established, and now KASLI is a full member of the European Forum of Sign Language Interpreters (efsli). Although Kosovo has seen great development since the original survey in 2001, the SLI profession still can be considered as semiprofessional and has a long way to go. Thus far, the professional standards for sign language interpreters have been developed by interpreter trainer and ratified by the National Qualification Agency. These standards are based on four main functions: (i) linguistic, cultural and interaction competencies, (ii) facilitation of communication between hearing and deaf community in various settings, (iii) adherence to the code of professional conduct and ethics during interpreting, and (iv) ensuring their own well-being and working conditions. Efforts are currently underway to accredit the curriculum for SLI training at the university level, specifically within the realm of applied science.

Sign Language Interpreter Education in Kosovo

Although ad hoc versions of SLI training existed during the ex-Yugoslavia era (up until 1998), through which sign language interpreters were certified after attending weekend courses, there was a need for a systematic training program. The project team asked clubs to invite people with signing skills and who were interested in being involved to a basic-level interpreter training program. The project team evaluated the applicants' signing skills and noted all their contact details. The project team met prospective interpreting students at six of the 12 deaf clubs around Kosovo and interviewed 19 people. Eleven women and eight men were interviewed, and of those, 14 people fulfilled the criteria for acceptance into the first basic-level interpreter training.

The aim of the basic-level training was to have professional interpreters working within the community after the completion of the program. Because of the fact that the interpreter training program did not provide students with sign language classes, there was a requirement for prospective candidates to already have fluent KosSL skills. The prerequisite of fluency in sign language typically meant that these candidates were hearing heritage signers. Another important point in the selection of students was their willingness and ability to travel to attend training modules.

A total of 14 out of 19 applicants satisfied the sign language competency and willingness-to-travel criteria and were invited to attend the training sessions. A meeting was then held to discuss the aims of the training program. All applicants were not expected to find accommodation, transport, or meals during training sessions; they just had to be willing to travel to and from the venue on training days.

First Year of Training

This first year of training provided basic information about interpreting, languages, and deaf studies. As each module was taught over 2 days, the first day of each module often focused on theory, and the second day of training was more practical in nature and included deaf community members. As most of the students in the first cohort were already fluent signers, the practical exercises revolved around different interpreting settings. Deaf individuals were invited from different provinces and with varying signing styles.

Second Year of Interpreter Training: Advanced Interpreter Training Program, 2006

For the second round of the basic-level interpreter training in 2006, the project attempted to attract a wider variety of potential applicants. This included advertising the course on university notice boards. More than 30 individuals expressed interest, and from this group, only 10 were successful. Of those 10 successful applicants, five were male and five were female. Of this group, only two had deaf parents. Of note is that during the 2 years the interpreter training program was offered, we have successfully managed to increase the numbers of males and non-native sign language users in the program. A slightly different approach was used in the selection process to screen potential candidates for each course, and this saw the establishment of a panel composed of local deaf people.

With 14 students in the program, 11 successfully completed the basic-level interpreter training program and moved into the second year of the training, the advanced interpreter training program. The project then organized a 5-day intensive interpreter training program with a visiting teacher from Australia.[5] The 10 students from the advanced interpreting training program were in attendance, as well as two interpreters from Serbia and one from Albania. Table 1 provides details of the 2006 advanced-level interpreter training content.

The intensive interpreter training program was developed in consultation between project staff and the trainer, with reference to previous modules/content already covered from local and international trainers, while also addressing the students' signing skills. This was the first time in the history of interpreters in Kosovo that hearing trainee interpreters were trained by an international

Table 1. Intensive Training Program

Day	Topic
Day 1	Interpreting context
Day 2	The interpreter
Day 3	The interpreting process
Day 4	Interpreting environment
Day 5	Interpreting evaluation

interpreter educator and provided with theory relating to the interpreting profession. It was also a unique opportunity for the local interpreter trainer to co-teach with and get feedback from a professional educator and to have the opportunity to reinforce previous knowledge taught during previous modules for the students. Support was also given to the local trainer on giving feedback to and evaluating students, supporting the local trainer on teaching strategies.

Final Year of the Interpreter Training Program

A total of 10 out of 14 students successfully passed the second year and were eligible to attend the final year of the interpreter training program. In the third year of training, the local trainer and trainer adviser developed a student handbook, which provided students with detailed information about the final year of interpreter training program. The student handbook included a mission statement, beginning program and dates, module descriptions, classes, punctuality and attendance requirements, trainer contact details, resource facilities, placement details, general rules and regulations at the project office, general information about assessment procedures, what is expected from students, essential skills, a sample marking sheet for KosSL, a sample interpreting test marking record, and an interpreter feedback form.

Program Requirements

Attendance is an essential requirement of students in the interpreter training program. Students in the basic-level interpreter training program were expected to attend 75% of classes. Those students who did not attend the required classes were asked to leave the program, and they did not receive a certificate at the end of the program. In the advanced interpreter training program and in the final year, students were required to attend 90% of classes. The attendance requirement was nonnegotiable, and students were asked to attend classes regularly to attain the objectives associated with each module.

After each module, a questionnaire was given to students to gather feedback on such things as venue, facilities, and teaching style. However, there was also an assessment form that the teacher would fill in to evaluate the development of each student's skills. Also, in the fifth class in each program, students were individually filmed. A feedback document listing a range of comments was sent to each student individually. Topics covered general knowledge about interpreting, general knowledge about signs, deaf culture, ethics, and recommendations for improvement. These evaluations were developed by the local trainer and international adviser with involvement and input from local deaf people.

Questionnaires were developed (approximately 10–12 questions, depending on the topics), and students completed this small piece of evaluation at the beginning of the next training module to review their learning in the prior module. This was a very beneficial exercise and assisted the trainers in understanding how much the students could comprehend of the most recent topic taught. If a number of students scored poorly, the trainers would regroup and go over the material again to ensure the students could take in the information and then apply this to practical activities.

In the third year, students were required to do continuous assessment, formal assessment, and written assessments:

1. Continuous assessment: A percentage of the final mark for a given course was awarded through coursework completed during the program. Coursework was intended to give students a means of evaluating their own progress in relation to the overall demands of the program of study. Coursework also included the completion of coursework assignments, reports or in-class presentations, or placements or practical language tasks. Where suitable, these showed evidence of reading and research at the appropriate level.
2. Formal assessment: This included written tests or language performance tests. Instructions relating to the language(s) of the test were given before the examination period. Generally, language tests were held in KosSL.

Resources

There is a dearth of interpreting resources in the Albanian language because most interpreting resources are written and published in English. The local trainer translated all the training resources into two languages: Albanian and English (when required). Because of few resources being readily available in Albanian, students were unable to use the books at the project office library or resources from the internet. For those few students who have English skills, the office library was open during working hours. Also, the project office offered students the use of facilities for access to, for example, the internet or the camera for their signing assignments.

Accreditation and Certification

In 2012, Selman Hoti (the local trainer), with the support of the Robert Adam (adviser for local trainers and a certified deaf interpreter), worked closely to establish an accreditation panel, which consisted of five members, of whom three (deaf community representative [deaf person], sign language researcher [deaf person], and experienced sign language interpreter [hearing person]) were evaluators and two, both deaf, were observers (member of the KAD board of directors and international adviser). This panel received training before the first round of assessment so that the evaluators would be able to conduct the process without the international advisers having to be involved, as it was felt that this had to be conducted entirely by local people in order to remain valid. The assessment process took place in 2012 and 2015. Of 30 students, 16 passed the assessment and received a certificate as a KosSL interpreter. The assessment tasks for the process were as follows:

1. Short conversation, two questions on community and interpreting: worth 10% (7.5% required to pass)
2. Interpreting of a 5-minute conversation (doctor's appointment): worth 30% (22.5% required to pass)
3. Interpreting of a 5-minute conversation (job interview): worth 30% (22.5% required to pass)
4. Videotape of previous interpreting activity: worth 30% (22.5% required to pass) or translation of signed presentation into written Albanian: worth 30% (22.5% required to pass)

A score sheet previously prepared by Selman Hoti and Susan Emerson was used to assess the candidates. Susan Emerson previously held the position of interpreter/ interpreter trainer adviser during the early days of the project and played a pivotal role in the training program. Her responsibilities included working in close collaboration with local interpreter trainers, actively contributing to the formulation and enhancement of training materials, and fostering valuable connections with international guest trainers and organizations, and this expertise during her time in Kosovo was invaluable.

After completion of the program, students were given a certificate of attendance. The certificate of attendance included the module topics and the hours/classes attended.

New SLI Training Curriculum

A new sign language interpreter training curriculum was developed by Selman Hoti (local trainer) and Arttu Liikamaa (FAD pedagogical adviser). The curriculum was originally prepared for the university level, but after scanning the possibilities (human resources), the government and KAD with the support of FAD decided that this program should be accredited at an applied science level. So far, the government has established a working group (including KAD and expertise from Finland) to develop SLI standards and this new curriculum and to accredit this training program through the Kosovo National Qualification Agency.

This curriculum is worth a total of 120 credits, equivalent to 2 full academic years, and is mapped onto the European Credit Transfer and Accumulation System (ECTS).[6] One credit corresponds to 25 hours, with approximately 10 contact hours and 15 hours of independent study. This training program, the structure of which can be seen in Table 2, consists of two main sections, with 60 credits for studying KosSL and 60 credits for studying SLI. To become a high-quality and professional interpreter, it is recommended that students take the training program over 4 years. Learning a new language requires time, and therefore studying KosSL provides a maximum of 20 credits per year.

In the first year, students study the basics of KosSL and achieve competence in KosSL skills at around the A2 (basic) level of the Common European Framework of Reference for Languages (CEFR).[7] Students also explore the profession of SLI.

In the second year, students develop their comprehension and production skills in KosSL and their awareness of the linguistic structure of KosSL. They begin translation and interpreting studies. The focus is more on translation than on interpreting because the study of interpreting requires strong skills in KosSL, and at this point, students have mastered only the basics.

Table 2. Interpreter Training Program Curriculum

1st year	Sign language 1 (10 credits)	Sign Language 2 (10 credits)	Interpreting 1 (10 credits)
2nd year	Sign Language 3 (10 credits)	Interpreting 2 (10 credits)	Sign Language 4 (10 credits)
3rd year	Interpreting 3 (10 credits)	Sign Language 5 (10 credits)	Interpreting 4 (10 credits)
4th year	Interpreting 5 (10 credits)	Sign language 6 (10 credits)	Interpreting 6 (10 credits)

In the third year, students study interpreting and translation in improvised settings. Students also explore the work of an interpreter in real interpreting settings. In terms of their KosSL skills, students aim to achieve the CEFR B1 (intermediate) level.

In the fourth year, students strengthen their interpreting skills in authentic interpreting settings with support from mentors. Upon successful completion of the training program, the student will have achieved a proficiency in KosSL that is equivalent to B2 (high intermediate) level, along with the tools necessary for lifelong learning of sign language skills and professional development. An interpreter might work in one or more of several settings, and these include educational settings and community settings. They might also work in the unit that provides SLI or in a freelance capacity.

Through extensive training, accreditation initiatives, and active community engagement, the interpreter training program in Kosovo has successfully cultivated proficient interpreters and established the groundwork for SLI services across diverse sectors. To perpetuate this achievement, KAD, in collaboration with FAD and the Humak University of Applied Sciences, has validated and certified the competencies of sign language instructors and sign language interpreter trainers. This academic endeavor underscores their commitment to ensuring the highest standards of education and professional development in the field of SLI.

Deaf Interpreters and Educators

Deaf people are also eligible to study the KosSL interpreter curriculum. Sign language modules 1–6 can be used as the basis for teaching KosSL to teachers of children, parents of children, and other interested persons.

KAD also has developed the training program for deaf adults to become sign language instructors. The training program, the content of which can be seen in Table 3, is for deaf adult people who use KosSL. The training program is 60 credits,

Table 3. Sign Language Content

Deaf culture (8 credits)	Sign language (8 credits)	Introduction to teaching (8 credits)
Teaching practice 1 (5 credits)	Teaching practice 2 5 credits	Teaching practice 3 (5 credits)
Teaching practice 4 (5 credits)	Teaching practice 5 (5 credits)	Teaching practice 6 (5 credits)
Albanian language (6 credits)		

equivalent to one academic year according to the ECTS. One credit is 25 hours, with approximately 10 contact hours and 15 hours of independent study.

This training program began in 2013, and 15 deaf adults have passed and became sign language instructors. Sign language instructors teach KosSL primarily to hearing people.

THE ROAD AHEAD

One of the major challenges in delivering the SLI training program in Kosovo was the lack of knowledge within the community about the demands and requirements of modern professional interpreter training, such as the length of training and elements involved. This is because people were more familiar with their experience of the former Yugoslavia interpreter training system, where after a 1-week interpreting "program," trainee interpreters were "certified" to work as "professional" interpreters. Also, some members of the community could not see the necessity of formal training because some trainee interpreters were already bilingual (i.e., heritage signers).

For Robert Adam, this was a unique experience in that he was able see the process before sign language recognition by the GRK and before the establishment of SLI training. For him, it was a pleasure to work with a group of people with deep involvement with the deaf community who were very keen to develop their knowledge and skills. The interpreter accreditation process that he worked on with Selman Hoti, with involvement from sign language researchers Drita Toprlak and Nebih Cakaj, became a recognized process that was acknowledged by interpreters, the deaf community, and the government, and it was a privilege for him to be a part of this process. In addition, for Arttu Liikamaa, it was a pleasure and honor for him to work with the KAD and see closely how the association's genuine deaf community–based work has grown over the years from the beginning and brought valuable local human resources for years to come. As a representative of the FAD, he points out that this sustainable development process requires a long-term international development cooperation and an active partner on the local level, as KAD has been. The Kosovar Sign Language Interpreter training model, which progressed from nothing to an advanced level, is a good example for other development projects in countries in the Balkan region, as well as around the world, and formed the basis of the *Manual for Sign Language Work Within Development Cooperation*, which was a joint collaboration of the FAD, WFD, Albanian National Association of the Deaf, and KAD.[8]

ACKNOWLEDGMENTS

The authors acknowledge the extensive work of key people involved as international advisers and trainers in the early days of the project, including Colin Allen, Sheena Walters, and Susan Emerson, whose work laid the foundations for the ongoing work in Kosovo.

NOTES

1. These estimates could underrepresent Serbs, Roma, and some other ethnic minorities because they are based on the 2011 Kosovo National Census, which excluded northern Kosovo and was partially boycotted by the Serb and Roma communities in southern Kosovo.
2. See Article 5 (4) of the Law on the Use of Languages.
3. See https://gzk.rks-gov.net/ActDetail.aspx?ActID=10363
4. See https://www.un.org/development/desa/disabilities/convention-on-the-rights-of-persons-with-disabilities.html
5. Professor Jemina Napier, who was then at Macquarie University in Sydney, but now is at Heriot-Watt University, Scotland
6. See http://ec.europa.eu/education/lifelong-learning-policy/ects_en.htm
7. See http://www.coe.int/t/dg4/linguistic/cadre1_en.asp
8. See www.slwmanual.info

REFERENCES

Finnish Association of the Deaf (2001). *The situational analysis of the deaf community of Kosovo.* The Organizational Training Project for the Kosovar Deaf community: Report on the evaluation of the status of 12 Deaf clubs and interpreters in Kosovo, October-November 2004, Pristina, Kosovo.

Kajragdiu, L., & Krasniqi, S. (2020). Written and oral translation challenges and solutions in Kosovo. *Homeros 3*(2), 91–96.

Kosovar Association of the Deaf (2007). *Student handbook: Advanced basic level interpreter training program.* Pristine, Kosovo: The Organizational Training and Sign Language Development Project for the 11 Regional Deaf clubs in Kosovo, March 2006.

Kosovar Association of the Deaf (2005). *Basic level interpreter training program.* Pristine, Kosovo: The Organizational Training and Sign Language Development Project for the 11 Regional Deaf clubs in Kosovo, March 2005.

SERGIO PEÑA, ALEJANDRA ÁLVAREZ, AND
JOSÉ LUÍS MAGAÑA-CABRERA

14

From a Bumpy Road to a Smoother Highway

The Past, Present, and Future of Sign Language Interpreting in Mexico

Mexico is well known for being a grand mosaic of a multicultural and multilingual society. The Mexican deaf community is part of that mosaic because they have fought for the rightful recognition of their language and culture. The existence of the Mexican deaf community is as old as the many indigenous communities in the country. It is well known in Mexico that among pre-Hispanic cultures, people with disabilities, including deaf people, were considered to possess a unique bond with the gods (Alfaro, 2019). Also, records dating from the 16th century have been found, stating that during the Spanish colonization, the Franciscans communicated with deaf people using some sort of sign language (Cruz-Aldrete, 2008).

Besides these records, there is not much information about the deaf community in Mexico, at least until the end of the 19th century. Deaf people eventually met in schools, at sporting events, in local parks, and even in small diners. They created clubs and continued to meet and mingle with each other, and thus they began to create a community with their own values, customs, and sign language, named *lengua de señas Mexicana* (Mexican Sign Language, or LSM).

Some individuals in the Mexican community have always in some way or another mediated communication between deaf and hearing people, namely sign language interpreters. In this chapter, we provide an overview of how these people have come to be recognized as sign language interpreters, what challenges the sign language interpreting (SLI) field has experienced in Mexico, current developments in the field with regard to the work and the profession, and what the future holds for the SLI field in Mexico.

Who Are We?

Sergio Peña is hearing and has a bachelor's degree in liberal studies with a special-ization in linguistics and bilingual education from San Diego State University. He is a certified American Sign Language (ASL) interpreter with the Registry of Inter-preters for the Deaf (RID) in the United States and an LSM < > Spanish certified interpreter, as well as a certified trainer and certified rater by the Comisión de Nor-matividad y Certificación Laboral (Commission for Regulations and Labor Certi-fications, CONOCER). ASL, English, LSM, and Spanish have been his working languages for more than 30 years. He is a speaker, trainer, writer, and teacher in the multilingual field of interpreting and translating in the United States, Mexico, and other countries in Latin America and the Caribbean. He was part of the task force that developed the original and most recent LSM < > Spanish national interpreter certification in Mexico (EC0085 and EC1319).

Alejandra Álvarez is deaf and bilingual (LSM and written Spanish) and holds a bachelor's degree in pedagogy from Universidad Nacional Autónoma de México (National Autonomous University of Mexico, UNAM). She is an LSM teacher at the Centro de Lenguas de la Facultad de Estudios Superior–Aragón, a multidisciplinary academic entity of UNAM. She is also the active technical secretariat of Movimiento en la Defensa de Educacion Bilingüe para Sordo (Movement in Defense of Bilingual Education for the Deaf). Alejandra is a con-sultant for Mejora Educativa en el Modelo de Educación Bilingüe (Educational Improvement in Bilingual Education Model for Deaf Children) in the Office of Special Education and Inclusiveness of Mexico City and an activist who fights for inclusion and advocates access to communication through the use of com-petent LSM < > Spanish interpreters. As a deaf interpreter (DI), she fights and advocates for the professionalization of both hearing and deaf sign language interpreters. She also is an active member of Asociación de Intérpretes y Traduc-tores de la República Mexicana, A.C. (the National Association of Interpreters and Translators of Mexico, AIT).

José Luís Magaña-Cabrera is a hearing Spanish < > English translator and a cer-tified LSM < > Spanish interpreter with more than 20 years of experience in confer-ence, educational, and legal settings. He cowrote the published book *Lo que hace a un intérprete SER INTÉRPRETE* (*What Makes an Interpreter Be an INTERPRETER?*) with Sergio Peña, the first book of its kind in Mexico and other Latin American countries. He has a bachelor's degree in pedagogy and a specialized diploma in translation pedagogy and didactics from UNAM. He has collaborated nationally and internationally with different universities, government agencies, and nongov-ernmental organizations (NGOs) in the development of sign language and spoken native language interpreting training programs. He was part of the task force that developed the most recent LSM < > Spanish national interpreter certification in

Mexico (EC1319) and is now involved in training interpreters from Mexico, the United States, Cuba, and Costa Rica.

Contextualization: Translation and Interpreting in Mexico

It is important to acknowledge the field of spoken language interpreting in Mexico. By 1982, spoken language conference interpreting was an established profession, but stakeholders still needed to organize, create a professional network, and create discussion forums among experts to help agree on what would be the work settings in general and how professional development would be accomplished in the field. Sergio Alarcón, a young interpreter in the 1980s, decided to organize a conference with new, experienced, and well-known interpreter colleagues. Interpreters such as Italia Morayta,[1] a seasoned interpreter who pioneered the field of spoken language interpreting in Mexico, attended this conference. This was a key event in Mexico's early efforts to bring the nation's spoken language interpreters together to build an organized group of stakeholders. This event was the cornerstone and the beginning of what later came to be known as the Colegio Mexicano de Intérpretes de Conferencia de México, A.C. (Mexican College of Conference Interpreters, CMIC), a not-for-profit organization of conference interpreters.[2] For the past four decades, this member-driven organization of conference interpreters has empowered the field with annual national conferences, professional papers, bulletins, webpages, training, and shared experience discussions. The CMIC has a code of ethics that governs the professional conduct of its members; this code is highly respected among practitioners nationwide, regardless of their membership status.

In the past few years, CMIC has had both deaf and hearing sign language interpreters involved in presenting and giving workshops on SLI in their national conferences. In addition to member organizations, many universities and technical schools have contributed to the spoken language interpreting field by offering academic courses, degrees, and professional formation with interpreter training and preparation programs. The CMIC, schools, universities, and other similar organizations continue to nurture programs in the interpreting field. Mexico has bachelor of arts, master of arts, and doctor of philosophy programs in the field of translation and interpreting (T&I) in many spoken/written languages.

Although other state T&I associations, such as the Asociación de Traductores e Intérpretes de Baja California (Baja California's Translator and Interpreter Association, ATIP-BC),[3] have included SLI members, CMIC has not only included SLI members but has also invited them to participate in their events more often since 2012. During 2020 and 2021, the Orgnaización Mexicana de Traductores (Mexican Organization of Translators, OMT) also contributed to the dissemination of information about SLI by inviting LSM interpreters to present workshops at their annual conferences.

Professionalization of SLI in Mexico

There are few records on the history of SLI in Mexico. On November 28, 1867, under the presidency of Benito Juarez, the first national school for the deaf, Escuela Nacional de Sordomudos (National School for the Deaf-Mute) was officially established in Mexico City. This school-based institution brought together deaf people from different parts of the country. Eduardo Huet, a deaf French teacher who came from Brazil, was appointed by the president as the director of the school. Because of this, the school used a combination of Brazilian, French, and autochthonous (local) sign languages as the main source of teaching. Hundreds of deaf children benefited from this institution. It is this school that was to become the center of the deaf community in Mexico.

During this epoch, interpreting between hearing and deaf people did not exist as we know it today. However, in addition to the school's deaf director, it is known that some hearing staff members at the school for deaf children played an important role in serving as mediators of communication between deaf students and the hearing community. Some records from the early 20th century indicate that at least one staff member became known as an "expert interpreter" in judicial cases in which deaf people had been involved (Jullian, 2018a, 2018b). At that time, there was no formal interpreter training in existence. When a serious communication need was apparent, a deaf person would most likely go to the school to request interpreting support.

For some years, the Claretian Missionaries taught catechism for deaf people at the *San Hipolito* church; it is likely that this was done in sign language. Soon, mass for the deaf community became part of the church's services. Some of the services were "interpreted" by these missionaries. Because this was well known, when a need for interpreting came up in the community, deaf people began to come to the church requesting an interpreter. These historical documented events demonstrate some kind of "formal" interpreting that was done outside the realm of family members taking on the role of the interpreter (Cruz-Aldarete & Serrano, 2008).

During the following decades, the first associations of deaf people began to emerge, such as La Asociación Deportiva de silentes de México (Mexican Deaf Association of Sports; 1931), La Asociación Mexicana de Sordomudos (Mexican Association of the Deaf-Mute; 1939), and Club Deportivo de Sordomudos (Sports Club of the Deaf-Mute; 1944), to name just a few. Within the associations, there were hearing allies, but mostly family members who knew sign language performed the role of interpreters when necessary. Thus, for a while, the role of the interpreter was taken on by members of the school, church, or an ally of the deaf community.

Contrary to spoken language interpreting, SLI was not considered a profession or even a trade. The same people who served as interpreters saw themselves as altruistic service providers for the deaf community. This work fell on teachers, deaf people's relatives, or religious venues. Even with good intentions, this brought about a series of problems:

- Interpreting was done without any prior formal training in the interpreting process.
- Interpreting was done without any type of code of professional ethics, so interpreters did not have ethical or professional boundaries.
- Interpreters were unaware of visual languages or had little knowledge of deaf culture.
- Many interpreters had limited sign language skills or would sign some kind of Spanish signing system (e.g., signing exact Spanish signs).
- Interpreters were expected to adopt a philanthropic approach and help deaf people to resolve non-language issues.

First Attempts to Professionalize SLI

During the 1980s and 1990s, the fight for the rights of people with disabilities began. This led to the creation of various laws and the amendment of others, including laws such as Ley sobre Sistema Nacional de Asistencia Social (Law of the National Social Assistance; 1986), Ley General de Salud (General Health Law; 1984), and Ley General de Educación (General Education Law; 1993). Thanks to these new laws, people with disabilities, including deaf people, were more visible. In the 1980s, the educational governmental office, the Secretaría de Educación Pública, published a sign language dictionary. In addition to this, one of the most-watched news channels began to include a DI, Perla Moctezuma, a well-known leader and activist in the deaf community. At the time, some interpreters were also present at many public and governmental events. Interpreters for these events were mostly hearing heritage signers who had grown up with deaf parents, as well as religious interpreters.[4] Although they had no formal training and no code of ethics, these interpreters thought interpreting was their moral obligation and took it upon themselves to travel and work long hours voluntarily. They believed that as family members of deaf people or because of their strong spiritual convictions, they had a duty to interpret. These heritage signers and religious interpreters are recognized as being the ones who started to build the road to the professionalized field of SLI in Mexico—the "movers and shakers" of what was one day to become the SLI profession.

Toward the late 1980s and early 1990s, some interpreters who were living in northern Mexican cities alongside the border with the United States crossed over the border into the United States as students or visitors to take classes and workshops on SLI and also to attend deaf, sign language, and interpreters' events (Ramsey & Peña, 2009). With time, international conferences were held in different parts of Mexico, and deaf presenters from abroad brought their own interpreters, who worked with the seasoned local interpreters. This was an enriching opportunity for Mexican interpreters to observe the work of other professional conference sign language interpreters. The best part of this was that the professional interpreters from abroad were willing to work with the local interpreters. Some of the expert interpreters from abroad mentored, provided feedback, answered questions, and shared their journeys with regard to how they became professionals. These cross-border and foreign seasoned interpreters became additional stepping-stones toward the unofficial commencement of the interpreting training. Before this, some of the Mexican sign language interpreters thought that natural visual LSM was for social communication only, but consciously they began to understand the difference between meaning-based interpreting between LSM < > Spanish (or any other spoken language) and interpreting literally using a Mexican-Spanish signed system or using LSM signs in Spanish grammatical word order. Also, the visiting mentor interpreters from the United States, as well as Canada and Spain, helped with the understanding of various issues, including why team and relay interpreting were necessary, meaning-based interpreting, the use of sign language linguistic features in interpreting, and processing time, among other skills.

Years later, our SLI visitors also assisted with the importance of having a deontological code of professional conduct to help regulate the field of SLI in Mexico. Interpreters from different cities were duplicating the unofficial training and workshops received from the cross-border and seasoned foreign interpreters. This allowed the SLI interpreting field to informally put down roots and grow in Mexico. With time, more hearing signers began to take workshops given by the now-practicing LSM interpreters. Later, staff from the educational field also took an interest in these workshops. Thus, there were three groups of people aspiring to becoming sign language interpreters: heritage signers, religious practitioners, and educational staff.

In 1995, approximately 35 sign language interpreters from across the country were independently actively working (some with paid work and some volunteering), and about 20 of them gathered at a conference held in Mexico City that same year. On May 25, 1995, the Asociación Nacional de Intérpretes de Lengua de Signos (ANILS; National Association of Sign Language Interpreters) was formed and officially registered.[5] It is believed to be the first official national association of sign language interpreters in Mexico. The founding members of this organization voted in Fidel Montemayor Zetina, a heritage signer interpreter, as the president of the association. The mission and vision of this association were to provide training, create networking among colleagues, set guidelines on SLI, and eventually evaluate and qualify LSM interpreters. The long-term goal was to certify them through collaboration with an official educational institute. All members were expected to volunteer at least 8 hours of interpreting per year. ANILS had no funds and was constantly being challenged with regard to its motives and legal status, and because the original board of ANILS had not assembled to do any business meetings in years, this organization eventually ceased its activities. Other states established sign language interpreter associations that continue to function to this day. The new national sign language interpreters' association, Intérpretes y Traductores de la Lengua de Señas en la República Mexicana A.C. (AIT-LS), was founded and was recognized by the World Association of Sign Language Interpreters (WASLI) in 2014. It began with 14 members and now has more than 115 sign language interpreter members in five different states. There are dozens more practitioners who identify themselves as independent interpreters. These independent sign language interpreters do not belong to AIT-LS or to any specific organization.

During the first decade of the 21st century, Mexico's government signed various international agreements on the rights of persons with disabilities and began to create new laws and programs that benefited the deaf community, including the Ley General de Personas con Discapacidad (General Law of People With Disabilities; 2005), which officially recognizes the use of LSM. These laws and programs indicated the use of LSM and sign language interpreters as different forms of accessibility. The implementation of the law has taken some time, yet interpreters are more visible in a range of different settings. Some universities established educational programs and hired LSM interpreters for their deaf students, and public organizations, political organizations, and NGOs began to hire interpreters for their events. This growing need for interpreters in different fields meant that interpreters needed to seek a way to professionalize.

SIGN LANGUAGE INTERPRETER EDUCATION AND CERTIFICATION IN MEXICO

To date, Mexico has no formal SLI training or preparation programs in any higher education institutions at the degree level. However, because of the high demand for interpreters, some associations and higher education institutions, with the collaboration of sign language interpreters and both deaf and hearing heritage signers, established *diplomados* and SLI courses.[6] In Mexico, a diplomado is a nondegree diploma course or series of courses that focus on a specific area of knowledge. These tend to be completed in a set number of hours to be taken in a set number of months or up to a year. They are a popular choice for continuing education and professional development, allowing students to improve their skills and knowledge without needing to invest in a full degree program or when a degree program does not exist.

Evidence of how the different associations and schools set up the nondegree courses is not available. However, one of the cowriters and first instructors of a diplomado given by the Universidad Autónoma de Baja California, known as UABC, on the Tijuana campus under the School of Languages, shared with us information and documentation from El Departamento de Formación Profesional y Vincualción Universtaria (the Department of Vocational Training and University Qualification), which coordinated under the School of Languages the first SLI diploma conducted by this university. It began in September 2004 and ended in May 2005, with a duration of 160 hours divided up into quarters of four courses of 40 hours each. These courses were Spanish (40 hours), Deaf Culture/Deaf and SLI history (40 hours), Consecutive Interpreting (40 hours), and Simultaneous Interpreting (40 hours).[7] The second 160-hour diplomado began in January 2006 and ended in November 2007; a third intense fast-track 160-hour diplomado started in December 2007 and ended in February 2008. After this program, because of budgeting and a low number of registrations (many could not afford the tuition), the UABC stopped offering the SLI diplomados. In these 4 years, the university handed out about 60 SLI certificates of completion. To this date, diplomados from different organizations, some academic and some NGOs (e.g., SLI Associations and deaf associations), still offer them. Regardless, there are no standards, standardized programs, or a consistent curriculum for training. Each institution creates the teaching program as they see fit.

Toward the end of the first decade of the 21st century, LSM interpreters decided it was time for an official document to recognize their profession. The Consejo Nacional para el Desarrollo y la Inclusión de las Personas con Discapacidad (CONADIS), a governmental agency working for the benefits of people with disabilities, created a task force with seasoned specialists in SLI and leaders of the deaf community to develop Mexico's first official SLI certification process. This process was governed and approved by CONOCER the governmental national office of the development and accreditation of the nondegree, skilled, knowledge-based, specialization labor certifications that involve professional attitudes, values, and tasks. This specialized task force, governed by CONOCER and coordinated by CONADIS, developed the first official certification at the national level for SLI, titled Norma Técnica de Competencia Laboral de Prestación de servicios de Interpretación de la lengua de señas mexicana al español y viceversa (NUIPD001.01),[8] which later changed to Estándar de Competencia Laboral de Prestación de servicios de Interpretación de la lengua de señas mexicana al español y viceversa (EC0085).[9] At a later stage, some members of the original EC0085 task force collaborated with CONADIS in the creation of an official code of professional conduct for the EC0085-certified interpreters. This code of professional conduct was published in the federal bulletin on June 9, 2009, in the *Diario Oficial de la Federación* (DOF).

The EC0085 standard requires that when an interpreter passes the evaluation and becomes certified, the interpreter will be able to perform the following:

1. Elaborate a written contract with all the parties involved and create a physical setting for interpreting.
2. Interpret consecutively and simultaneously from to Spanish to LSM and vice versa.
3. Do a sight translation from written Spanish to LSM and vice versa.
4. Pass the written portion of a knowledge base test on interpreting and deaf culture.

The results were given as either being *COMPETENTE* (competent) or *TODAVIA NO COMPETENTE* (not yet competent) with a minimum passing score of 97.3 out of 100. Many candidates took the test, but very few received a passing score. A written social media communication sent by an official representative of CONOCER mentioned that as of January 31, 2020, only 82 interpreters had been certified nationwide. Since the EC085 went into a moratorium status because of a formal revision that started in September 2019, no additional interpreters were certified under this standard.[10] This is a problem because the ratio is only one certified interpreter per 15,365 deaf people.[11] In addition to the level of difficulty, many interpreters sent formal written complaints to the evaluation entities and shared with the media that the evaluation rubric was skewed.[12] The evaluation centers combined with the rater's fees became an additional problem. Quite a few interpreters expressed that they could not afford nor were they willing to pay for the test itself.[13] Interestingly, the EC0085 assessment had no curriculum to prepare or train aspiring sign language interpreters. The certification was developed with consideration of the existing SLI practitioners, and no training was developed.

Where We Are Now

Although Mexico's situation in the field of SLI has experienced many issues, there has been a breakthrough. Deaf people are no longer quiet when it comes to demanding their accessibility rights; they are involved in the creation of new national laws; and Mexico's government has signed international conventions for people with disabilities. WASLI has been more involved in training hearing interpreters and DIs; national and international spoken language interpreters' associations are collaborating with sign language interpreters; and some interpreters are even looking for additional professional development outside of Mexico. Although no formal training in SLI is available, there are some self-study programs and workshops that are provided with recent Mexican publications on sign language interpreting techniques (Peña & Magaña-Cabrera, 2015), a manual on Mexico's legal interpreting field with a chapter focusing on SLI (Carreón, Rosado, & Maya, 2017), and a book with medical knowledge references applied with an anecdotal approach to medical interpreting for SLI (Díaz de León González, 2020). Although there have been other publications about sign language and deaf people, these three books are the only ones to date that focus on SLI.

Some deaf and interpreting community members believed that the EC0085 certification was neither a transparent nor an accurate assessment. This led some deaf and interpreters' associations to start their own in-house assessment for accrediting SLI interpreters. Because in-house accreditation has no legal or academic recognition, the sign language interpreters, key members of the deaf community, and government entities decided it was time to revamp the EC0085 certification. On September 2019, Sistema Nacional del Desarrollo Integral de la Familia created a new task force to update the certification. The new task force included heritage signers, multilinguals (LSM, English, Spanish), one deaf person,[14] and a binational dual-certified interpreter (ASL and LSM). All task force members are LSM certified (EC0085), educated (at least to the Bachelor of Arts level), and seasoned, with an average of 20 years in the SLI field. In addition to interpreters, the task force included a signing lawyer, who assessed with the compliance portion of the standard and rating guidelines, and staff members of Sistema Nacional del Desarrollo Integral de la Familia. The task force successfully turned in the finished revision and revamped certification competency guidelines for the new certification in November 2020. The revision of the certification was approved by CONOCER with a new name and number, Interpretación de conferencia de lengua de señas mexicana <> español (LSM < > Spanish Conference Interpreting Competency Standards), the EC1319.[15] Although business practices and knowledge of the field are part of the evaluation, this new certification standard focuses more on interpreting skills than on the services provided by the interpreter. Nevertheless, there is still much work to do in the Mexican SLI field. In 2021, 25 interpreters passed CONOCER's new evaluation EC1319; in 2022, 101 had passed; and by the fall of 2023, another 90 had passed. This gives a total of 216 EC1319-certified sign language interpreters in the whole country, which happens to be a very low number compared with the number of deaf people who need access through sign language interpreters. The authors believe that this number is so low because of the lack of formal training in the field.

The Mexican Deaf Community Perspective

The growing communication access demands of the Mexican deaf community create accountability on interpreters for their performance when interpreting. Deaf signers have rights and expect to be part of the solution to the lack of qualified interpreters. The document *Nada sobre nosotros sin nosotros: La Convención de Naciones Unidas sobre discapacidad y la gestion civil de derechos* (Hernández Sánches & Fernández Vázquez, 2016) highlights the "nothing about us without us" movement, which sees discussions and decision-making for people with disabilities as unacceptable if people with disabilities have not partaken in the decision-making.[16] This phrase and its principle have been echoed around the deaf community. They have been adamant about their inclusion and access to communication in all decision-making. This includes how and where skilled sign language interpreters must be present. One of their accomplishments is that an interpreter must be televised for all presidential conferences like *Las mañaneras*.[17] This has meant more visibility for SLI and has allowed the deaf community to evaluate the LSM skills that interpreters might or might not have. Deaf people are now expecting and demanding that more skilled interpreters be available in additional areas, such as the medical field, the legal field, academia, cultural events, and the entertainment industry. Although needs and demands are expressed, no higher education institution has yet accepted the responsibility of developing and providing an SLI education program.

Sadly, because of the absence of formal training on SLI and how to work with interpreters, many deaf people outside large cities still lack understanding of the interpreter's role as a professional service provider. Many deaf people still lack the understanding that interpreters are entitled to receive some kind of monetary compensation for their interpreting services. They are also not aware that there is a code of professional conduct that govern the ethics of interpreting, which includes interpreters' having the right to charge for their service. Some deaf people still see the interpreter as the "helper" of deaf people. Others might think that it is acceptable for interpreters to charge for their services but that interpreters should provide discounts to deaf people for being the "owners" of LSM. Others, including some heritage signers, have adopted a mentality that "allowing" a hearing interpreter to use their LSM for their own monetary benefit is unethical when the interpreter refuses to volunteer his or her time or provide discounts for service bills. Nevertheless, more and more deaf community members have become aware of the highly skilled work involved in being a professional, skilled LSM < > Spanish interpreter.

Although it is true that some interpreters are growing professionally, given that there are limited formal pathways for education and training for sign language interpreters in Mexico, many interpreters remain without crucial competencies. There is hardly any formal accessible training in the academic field; there is a lack of classes in interpreting programs. Except for some northern border cities, the farther away from Mexico City you are, the more problematic it is. Most states in the country have either no sign language interpreters or unskilled ones.

Some deaf people have filed complaints in the social media, with the human rights department, and with other governmental offices because of the lack of interpreters or the use of unskilled ones. Some deaf people believe that it is better to have no interpreter than an unskilled one. However, many are still willing to look for "any" interpreter, regardless of the skill level, because of the need involved in everyday life events like job interviews, doctor visits, legal situations, and business transactions. The need to have a skilled interpreter in everyday life events has caused issues in hiring interpreters. Most skilled and seasoned interpreters have higher competitive fees. Unethically, some signers decide to compete by offering their "interpreting" services at very low cost. All this has hurt the Mexican deaf community and the professionalization of the SLI industry.

Allies

As more deaf people understand their rights and are empowered, interpreting settings are evolving in the following ways:

- Interpreters are starting to be viewed as stakeholders who provide a professional job or service and nonpaying community service.
- In the past, many deaf people would ask the interpreter for their opinion on a specific matter before, during, or after the interpreting job. Some interpreters would even take it upon themselves to become the adviser of deaf people or the hearing client. Now, interpreters no longer do this in interpreting assignments.
- Deaf people have realized that interpreters are mediators between two languages and two cultures.
- Many members of the deaf community now understand that even though heritage signers are highly skilled in LSM, interpreting is more than just having language skills. They now understand that for them to be skilled and professional, additional tools and some kind of professional training are required.

The deaf community and many LSM interpreters are reaching out to associations and NGOs to request collaboration in resolving the many existing issues; others approach different types of businesses and stakeholders. With the view that some interpreters lack skills that reflect natural usage of LSM, members of the deaf community have published LSM dictionaries with introductions to grammar and culture and have used social media to provide LSM signs and cultural knowledge. In the past few years, some government agencies have provided free workshops and training for interpreters in the legal field, and some SLI associations, in collaboration with leaders from the deaf community, have also offered training to their members. Increasingly, more deaf people speak up and publicly, through the news and social media, reprehend the signers who are taking on the role of interpreting without the needed skill set. However, deaf people have singled out not only these pseudo-interpreters but also the organizations that are hiring them. These complaints from the deaf community are endorsed by many professional sign language interpreters who wish to help the field to maintain and enhance competency standards and ethical interpreting.

This collaboration among some governmental offices, different NGO organizations, interpreters, and deaf members of the community gives hope that the SLI field, with time, can gain the acknowledgment and respect of other stakeholders and consumers of interpreting services. Even novice interpreters are starting to be seen as potential skilled interpreters and giving deaf people more hope for the future. The SLI field expects that one day these unseasoned interpreters might be able to start rendering services in non–high-risk settings.

The Impact of COVID-19 on SLI in Mexico

As a result of the COVID-19 lockdown that began in March 2020, all public and private events were closed and canceled; consequently, all scheduled interpreting was also rescinded. During lockdown, most sign language interpreters were without work. The following month, in April 2020, Mexico City's SLI association coordinated an initiative that invited LSM interpreters from around the country to join a social media messaging group and volunteer part time to do video remote interpreting for any remote medical appointments deaf people might have. About 40 interpreters nationwide joined the social media group to volunteer when interpreting was needed. We lack exact data on how many deaf people benefited from this service, but we are aware that the service was used. This list of volunteer interpreters was shared with federal government offices, which shared it with some state offices. Nevertheless, the states did very little to promote it; the interpreters and deaf people had to do their best to disseminate such available services.

Under the "new normal," interpreters had to start providing interpreting services in a remote way. The challenge was that regardless of experience, skills, or certifications, remote SLI interpreting was a new modality for most.[18] Educational and conference SLI had to be set up in home interpreting stations. Sign language interpreters had to find cameras, computers, backgrounds, and appropriate lighting to try to provide interpreting services. Because of the lack of training, many problems arose: issues with lighting (too dark, too light, shadows); issues with having the right camera; and problems with the focus, the background, or finding a place with the fewest visual distractions possible. Before the pandemic, professional team interpreting was still in a developmental stage, so to engage in teamwork from afar was an additional challenge. Regardless of all of this, national and international interpreters' organizations eventually shared some helpful guidelines on remote interpreting. Although it was a large investment, more and more LSM interpreters are adjusting to this new way of interpreting.

If one tries to look for blessings in disguise in Mexico's SLI field during these awful pandemic times, remote interpreting would be top of the list. More SLI is now offered for conferences and academic opportunities. Once the vaccinations were rolled out and lockdown restrictions were lessened, more schools and other community events continued to function in a hybrid status, with SLI being provided. With the limited number of skilled interpreters available to do in-person interpreting nationwide, remote interpreting, even with its challenges, has helped solve the problem of needing to rely only on the local interpreters available, who were in scarce supply. Even when Mexican deaf people have attended international events, they have been successful in obtaining an LSM remote interpreter.

This pandemic has caused a lot suffering, and we have lost friends and loved ones. Still, "every cloud has a silver lining." We have learned to adapt, and the field of SLI is resiliently surviving and continues to move ahead. We are grateful to scientific and technological advancements that have allowed us to provide SLI in our modest developing field to the deaf community.

The Road Ahead

At present, the main challenge faced by interpreters is the lack of professionalization. Although other Spanish-speaking countries have technical careers in interpreting, associate's degrees, accredited specialized certificate programs, and even bachelor's degrees in SLI, to date, Mexico has none of the above. As mentioned earlier, there are some nondegree diplomados and workshops available, but these do not fulfill the requirements of a degree for an interpreter training or preparation program. Regardless, it is acknowledged that there are some seasoned, experienced, self-taught practitioners who are proficient and capable of applying SLI expectations to jobs in the community. It is these interpreters who long to have formal training, professional degrees, professional development, and credits from educational institutions.

Lack of training leads to a second challenge: Many interpreters lack LSM proficiency. Some signers doing interpreting jobs consider their knowledge of LSM to be sufficient after having taken workshops or webinars on SLI and having learned the tools necessary to be interpreters. Some might have even passed an evaluation, like EC0085 or EC1319, because they had good test-taking abilities. There is no ongoing renewal of certification[19] or proof required of hours of continuing education. As such, some interpreters believe that being certified means there is no more work to be done; now they are professionals, and nothing else is needed. This has caused these interpreters to ignore the need to undertake any further training, and thus, their interpreting skills stagnate. Additionally, the lack of ethics training can have a negative impact on both the deaf community and the SLI profession.

In the absence of formal interpreting training programs, it is common for aspiring interpreters to attend LSM courses and receive a certificate of participation and then use it as proof of expertise in sign language. Some of these signers present the certificate of participation as a professional document in LSM and start self-advocating as being interpreters themselves; because there is a high demand for LSM interpreters, they are readily offered interpreting assignments. Both the entities that offer the work and the "pseudo"-interpreters think that this will suffice in meeting the high demands for interpreters. Some of these assignments are medical, and others are in legal settings, and as a result, the outcome could be worse than having no interpreter at all. Part of the problem here is related to the fact that society is still in continuing need of education on what the role of a sign language interpreter is.

Sadly, a large number of people in Mexican society still see deaf people from a medical perspective and not a linguistic and cultural one. The nonsigning community needs to have answers to questions such as: Who are Mexican deaf people? What is deaf culture? What is LSM? Why is it considered in the law an autochthonous Mexican language? What skills are necessary to become an interpreter? What is the difference between a skilled signer and a professional interpreter? Does being bilingual in LSM and Spanish qualify someone as an interpreter? Are family members, friends, church members, or school personnel qualified to be a "temporary" interpreter when there is no one else to interpret? Is it wrong to look for the least expensive "interpreter"? Until the answers to these questions become more embedded in general knowledge, how are those hiring interpreters supposed to know or understand how to hire the most appropriate person for an interpreting assignment? As it stands, with no academic degree training, who has the authority in deciding who interprets and who should not?

One more challenge we face as a community is in relation to the unethical attitude of many interpreter colleagues. Again, because of the lack of formal training, guidance, and appropriate leadership, many of these practitioners have contributed directly or indirectly, consciously or unconsciously, to a divided profession. Other interpreting stakeholders are not seen as collogues or healthy competitors but rather as rivals. Some follow the set standards (EC0085 and EC1319) only if it benefits them, so they end up working with double standards. Although deaf people have the right to state their preferences when requesting an interpreter, things can get out of hand when some of these "preferred interpreters" try to monopolize by campaigning for themselves and try to be endorsed by deaf people. This again has hurt the rights of the deaf community to have language accessibility, while the SLI profession continues to have unresolved issues.

Aside from the need to generally develop the SLI profession further and introduce formal training opportunities for hearing interpreters, it has been recognized that the field in Mexico needs to develop opportunities for DIs.

Deaf Interpreters

For some time now, Mexico has had events in which DIs provided what we term *hacer espejo* (mirroring),[20] such as tactile interpreting for deafblind people or when bilingual deaf people interpret between ASL < > LSM when American deaf visitors present in local events. However, on July 23–25, 2014, in Mexico City, the association AIT-LSM collaborated with local government and sponsored a WASLI North America regional conference. Presenters used International Sign (IS), and deaf and hearing interpreters were involved in rendering between

IS < > ASL < > Spanish < > LSM. A series of presentations and workshops for interpreters, including an introduction to the role of DIs, were presented. One of the visiting DIs offered a workshop in which deaf leaders of the community participated. This workshop included techniques and practice opportunities, which created an enthusiastic environment because of what might be the start of the concept of a more formal type of deaf interpreting in Mexico.

This event empowered more deaf leaders to take up the task of interpreting. DIs soon started to appear in important televised events. Although this has been a great breakthrough, the work of DIs is at an even earlier stage of professional development than is that of hearing sign language interpreters. Formal bilingual (LSM/Spanish) training for deaf people is keenly needed. Hearing interpreters have shared that many times, they are called to interpret for "semilingual" deaf people[21] and that they lack the experience or techniques needed to mediate communication with these people. With robust training, DIs are in the ideal position for this work. There is a great need and therefore a high demand for DIs in Mexico. The SLI field in Mexico has many questions on the role of the DI. Would DIs be required to be bilingual in only sign languages or sign systems? How is the second sign language proficiency evaluated? If Spanish becomes one of the working languages, what level of proficiency in Spanish would suffice? What about Spanish lipreading to LSM?[22] How would interpreting and language skill competencies be evaluated before accreditation or certification of a DI? Are DIs required to have hearing Mexican culture knowledge? How would this be taught? Would a specialized code of ethics for DIs be required? Do hearing sign language interpreters need special training to team with DIs? These and other similar questions are raised when the notion of a DI is considered. We will have to inquire about what other, more experienced countries are doing in this field. At present, Mexico is a member of WASLI, so it is likely it will be one of the main resources to guide Mexico toward professionalization for the DI field.

CONCLUSION

The SLI road in Mexico has been a bumpy one, but it has started to level out. We are hopeful that it will one day become a smooth highway. Even with all the challenges, the SLI field has begun to grow. Stakeholders are confident that although many issues still exist, these will eventually be resolved. It is a work in progress. As with any other profession, the SLI profession will require time to mature. Meanwhile, there are some key goals that need to be met. It is hoped that the SLI field in Mexico will:

• Understand the language accessibility needs of the deaf community.
• Educate private and public industries on the role of sign language interpreters.

- Educate members of society on why there are sign language interpreters in the community.
- Work on having hearing interpreters and the deaf community become allies.
- Encourage both hearing and deaf people to work together to become allies with the private and public sector.
- Establish a system whereby schools collaborate with specialized and seasoned interpreters, as well as the deaf community, to develop interpreter training programs.
- Establish some sort of governing board (hearing/deaf interpreters, members of the deaf community, and governmental representatives) that can regulate and mediate the professionalization of the interpreting field.
- Implement assessments, evaluation, and training of experts to obtain a more accurate reflection of the interpreting field.
- Require SLI third-party agencies to be more transparent and honest in how they offer interpreting jobs in the competitive market.
- Train the seasoned qualified interpreters to be mentors and trainers for novice interpreters.
- Show evidence of teamwork.
- Seek guidance from experts in the spoken language interpreting field.
- Reach out to collaborate and create a network with other countries that share similar needs in the field.
- Highly respect the deaf community and make them part of the preparation of the SLI field.
- Create high standards for interpreters and create a system that can make the interpreters accountable for their actions in the field.
- Require professional development to all who are out there in the community interpreting for deaf people.
- Create some kind of curriculum within an HEI and offer interpreting training preparation programs.

History has demonstrated that Mexico has resilient people. With this in mind, we strongly believe that the SLI field will conquer and will become a profession with professional stakeholders, collaborators, and allies with the Mexican deaf community. To attain this, we are hopeful that a higher education institution will start an interpreting training or preparation program for sign language interpreters.

NOTES

1. Italia Morayta is a well-known pioneer spoken language interpreter in Mexico. More on her professional story as an interpreter can be found on Liderazgo | CM Idiomas. http://www.cmidiomas.com/fundadora.html

2. See https://www.interpretesdeconferencias.mx/?fbclid=IwAR3m_ATkUVOlrGhTAuT6n-BfXz8AgM-HqvbOi82T527boV116dJVIqEHkUYY

3. For example, Sergio Peña, one of the authors, has a membership certificate from ATIP-BC dated 1998.

4. Catholics and Jehovah's Witnesses were the two main religions that, in addition to interpreting their religious services, were out in the community volunteering part of their time to interpreting.

5. *Memorias del segundo congreso de Intérpretes del Lengua de Signos de México, Formación desde el contexto educativo*, the unpublished conference proceedings (1997). Peña (2000) also narrates this in the video, *Development of Sign Language Interpretation: A Trilingual Discussion in English/LSM/Spanish* by the National Multilingual Interpreting Project (NMIP-2000).

6. Mexican education laws recognize only those professions, degrees, specializations, certifications, diplomados, and certificates of completion that are validated by the *Secretaría de Educación Pública* (SEP), the national office or secretary of public education.

7. UABC campus Tijuana is a graduate and undergraduate university located on the Mexican side of the United States–Mexico border that is south of the border from San Diego, California (United States). Sergio Peña, one of the coauthors of this chapter, collaborated in writing the teaching program, and he coordinated and participated in coteaching in the courses.

8. LSM to Spanish and Vice-Versa Interpreting Services' Technical Labor Norms.

9. LSM to Spanish and Vice-Versa Interpreting Services' Standards.

10. The authors did not have access to an official written document because of Mexican privacy laws, so Peña interviewed Cecilia Rojas privately via social media to obtain the information. Ms. Rojas is one of CONOCER's spokespersons, and she could share only what the privacy laws allowed. Date of interview: March 19, 2020.

11. In December 2019, INEGI, the governmental agency on demographics, reported that the number of people 5 years of age and older with a hearing disability (including deafened adults) was 15,366 (18.6% of 7.7 million people with disabilities).

12. Later, during a revision, the task force and some independent raters noted that the weighed point system on the rubric was not distributed correctly by not assigning enough points to the performance of the actual interpreting and assigning too much weight to non-interpreting areas. They also noted that the key answers of the written portion of the test did have some errors.

13. The cost of some advertised evaluation sites in combination with the raters' fees in 2018–2019 was an average of 10,000 Mexican pesos ($529.87 U.S. dollars; exchange rate at 18.8727 Mexican pesos to a U.S. dollar).

14. Several deaf interpreters were invited to be part of this task force, but only one turned in on the due date all of the preliminary documentation.

15. EC1319 was announced, released, and published on December 28, 2020 by DOF (https://www.dof.gob.mx/nota_detalle.php?codigo=5608949&fecha=28/12/2020).

16. Documented, printed, and released by the nonpartisan governmental organization, *Consejo Nacional para Prevenir la Discriminación* (CONAPRED; The National Council on Preventing Discrimination). https://www.conapred.org.mx/documentos_cedoc/Nada%20sobre%20nosotros%20sin%20nosotros-Ax.pdf

17. *Las mañaneras* (The Morning Ones), are daily morning talks, press conferences, and governmental updates given by Mexico's President Andrés Manuel López Obrador (2018–2024).

18. To this date, Mexico does not provide funded video remote interpreting or video relay services either in the public or the private sector.
19. The Código de conducta profesional (Code of Professional Conduct) of CONADIS does include professional development as one of its tenets. However, because they are not bylaws but a code of ethics, there is no way to enforce it.
20. *Hacer espejo*, which means "to mirror," is when a signer copies the signing of someone else to make the signing visible to everyone.
21. Peña & Magaña-Cabrera (2015) explain that in most Latin American countries, the term *semilingual* is defined more as deaf people who do not use any kind of a formal sign language because of language deprivation. They might be visual communicators, use home signs, or gesture with no linguistic conventions.
22. There are a few well-known deaf people in the community who are bilingual and interpret into LSM by lipreading from spoken Spanish.

REFERENCES

Adams, M. M. (2006). *The lives of deaf Mexicans: Struggle and success*. [DVD]. DawnSignPress.
Alfaro, R. A. (2019, August 13). México prehispánico: Las discapacidades y los dioses. Souvenir. https://revistasouvenir.com/mexico-prehispanico-las discapacidades-y-los-dioses/
ANILS. A.C. (1997). *Encuentro nacional: Memorias del segundo congreso de intérpretes de lengua de signos de México. Formación desde el contexto educativo*. [Unpublished conference proceedings].
BBC. (2019, January 31). Las Mañaneras. *BBC*. https://www.bbc.com/mundo/noticias-america-latina-47066862.
CATIE Center, St. Catherine University. (2017). Mexico's development of sign language interpretation: A trilingual discussion [Video archive]. https://grad2cert.org/mexicos-development-of-sign-language-interpretation-a-trilingual-discussion/
Carreón, M. C., Rosado T., & Maya D. (2017). *Manual of the judicial interpreter in Mexico*. Colegio Mexicano de Intérpretes. CMIC Colegio Mexicano de Interpretes de Conferencias.
Consejo Nacional para el Desarrollo y la Inclusión de las Personas con Discapacidad. (2009). *Código de conducta professional para los intérpretes de la Lengua de Señas Mexicana*. https://vdocuments.mx/codigo-de-conducta-profesional-para-los-interpretes-de-la-lengua-de-senas-mexicana.html
Cruz-Aldrete, A. (2008). *Gramática de la Lengua de Señas Mexicana*. [Unpublished doctoral dissertation]. Colegio de México, Mexico City. https://revistasouvenir.com/mexico-prehispanico-las-discapacidades-y-los-dioses/
Cruz-Aldrete, M. (2009). *La educación del sordo en México siglos XIX y XX: La Escuela Nacional de Sordomudos*. https://cultura-sorda.org/la-educacion-del-sordo-en-mexico-siglos-xix-y-xx-la-escuela-nacional-de-sordomudos/
Cruz-Aldrete, M. (2018). El modelo de evaluación de la educación bilingüe de la comunidad de sordos de México: Un problema sin voces. *Voces de la educación, 3*(5), 40–48.
Cruz-Aldrete, M. & Sanabria, E. (2006). *Algunos aspectos sociolingüísticos de la comunidad de sordos en México*. University of Sonora, Hermosillo.
Cruz-Aldrete, M., & Serrano, J. (2018). La Comunidad Sorda Mexicana: Vivir entre varias lenguas: LSM, ASL, LSM, español, inglés, maya. *Convergencias: Revista de Educación, 1*(2), 83–102.

Díaz de León González, F. J. (2020). *enSordécete para sanarlos. Libro especializado para la atención a sordos en los servicios de interpretación de lengua de señas en áreas médico-hospitalarias.* Editorial Letra Minúscula.

Dirección General de Planeación. (2019). *Programación y estadísticas de educación. Figuras principales del sistema nacional de educación.* 2018-2019 (Primera Edición), Government of México.

DOF Diario oficial de la federación. (2009, June 9). *Provisiones de servicios de interpretación de la lengua de señas mexicana al español y viceversa.* Norma Técnica de Competencia Laboral NUIPD001.01 Agreement SO/I-09/02-S.

DOF Diario oficial de la federación (2018). *Ley General para la Inclusión de las Personas con Discapacidad.* (2011; updated 2018). [General law for the inclusion of people with disabilities]. http://www.diputados.gob.mx/LeyesBiblio/pdf/LGIPD_120718.pdf

DOF Diario oficial de la federación (2020). *Breve historia del periódico oficial en México.* https://www.dof.gob.mx/historia.php

Hernández Sánchez, M., & Fernández Vázquez, M. T. (2016). *Nada sobre nosotros sin nosotros. La Convención de Naciones Unidas sobre discapacidad y la gestión civil de derechos.* Consejo Nacional para Prevenir la Discriminación. Secretaría de Gobernación. Nada_sobre_nosotros_sin_nosotros_Ax_pdf.pdf

INDEPEDI CDMX. (2017). La historia de la lengua de señas mexicana. In *Diccionario de la lengua de señas mexicana Ciudad de México* (pp. 41–52). CDMX Government.

INEGI. (2019, December 3). Estadística a propósitos del día internacional de las personas con discapacidad. Datos nacionales. Press Bulletin No. 638/19.

Jullian, C. (2018a). Haciendo "hablar" a una historia muda. Surgimiento y consolidación de la comunidad sorda de Morelia. *Relationships History and Society Studies, 39*(153), 261. doi:10.24901/rehs.v39i153.378

Jullian, C. (2018b). Inclusión antes de la Inclusión tres ejemplos notables en la historia de la Escuela Nacional de Sordomudos. *Revisita de administración pública, 53*(1), 191–203.

Oviedo, A. (2015). *México, atlas sordo.* https://cultura-sorda.org/mexico-atlas-sordo/#Geschichte

Peña S., & Magaña-Cabrera, J. L. (2015). *Lo que hace a un intérprete SER INTÉRPRETE. Técnicas y herramientas para intérpretes de lenguas señadas y español* (1st ed.). Independent.

Ramsey, C., & Peña, S. (2010). Sign language interpreting at the border of the two Californias. In R. L. McKee & J. E. Davis (Eds.), *Interpreting in multilingual, multicultural contexts* (pp. 3–27). Gallaudet University Press.

Secretaría de Educación Pública. (2012). *Orientaciones para la atención educative de alumnos sordos que cursan la educación básica, desde el modelo educativo bilingüe-bicultural.* CDMX Government.

Secretaría de Gobernación-SG. (2014, April 30). Programa nacional para el desarrollo y la inclusión de las personas con discapacidad, 2014-2018. http://dof.gob.mx/nota_detalle.php?codigo=5343100&fecha=30/04/2014

Segura-Malpica, L., & Autonomous University of the State of Morelos. (2005). *La educación de los sordos en México: controversia entre los métodos educativos, 1867–1902.* https://cultura-sorda.org/educacion-de-los-sordos-en-mexico-controversia-metodos-1867%E2%80%901902/

RACHEL MCKEE, GEORGE MAJOR, AND
SUSIE OVENS

15

*Thirty-Five Years of Sign Language
Interpreter Education and Professional
Practice in Aotearoa New Zealand*

New Zealand[1] has a diverse population of 5 million and is located in the South Pacific, with Australia and Pacific Island nations being its closest neighbors. It has a developed economy and a welfare state that provides public health, education, and social security benefits. Legal recognition of the indigenous Māori language in 1987 and processes of redress for colonization impacts since 1840 have contributed to an environment conducive to deaf claims to language and cultural recognition. The government's acknowledgment of a social model of disability and its legal commitment to accessibility and inclusion (e.g., ratification of the United Nations Convention on the Rights of Persons With Disabilities in 2008) have also been favorable to the growth of interpreting services.

The New Zealand Sign Language (NZSL) Act 2006[2] granted NZSL official language status, which was an unusually high-status form of recognition (McKee & Manning, 2019). However, the only practical measure created by this law is the right to use NZSL in legal proceedings, for which competent interpreters must be provided. *Competent* was defined as holding an NZSL interpreting qualification and having 2 years' experience after graduation. Apart from this requirement, the NZSL Act did not directly touch upon the regulation, training, provision, or employment conditions of interpreters. However, the recognition of NZSL has created moral leverage for the advancement of interpreting provision and language access by the deaf community. Consumer expectations about interpreters' skills and professional conduct have become more discerning, which partly reflects an increase in deaf professionals who have had access to higher education.

An indirect effect of NZSL recognition has been an increase in government and public bodies engaging NZSL interpreters to work at public events and in televised briefings by politicians on topics of high public interest (e.g., COVID-19 briefings, civil emergencies, or discussion of controversial proposed legislation). Another indirect outcome of the NZSL Act was the 2015 establishment of an NZSL Advisory Board,[3] which gives advice to government policymakers with regard to NZSL users and allocates an annual NZSL Fund that supports community projects and contracted work on strategic priorities for NZSL. The NZSL Fund has supported language documentation and other research that contributes to the resources available for teaching NZSL and interpreting (see, for example, Major et al., 2017).

Who Are We?

Rachel McKee, hearing, began learning sign language in the first New Zealand (NZ) training course for interpreters in 1985. After graduate study and interpreting experience in the United States of America (United States), she cofounded the NZSL interpreting program at Auckland University of Technology (AUT) in 1992 with husband David McKee, a deaf American academic. Rachel has collaborated with several generations of the NZ deaf community and interpreters in the development of training, NZSL teaching, research, and policy.

George Major is hearing and first learned NZSL as an undergraduate linguistics student. She qualified as an NZSL/English interpreter in 2004 and worked mainly as a community and tertiary interpreter. George's doctoral study in Australia explored the role of interpreters in facilitating rapport work in a health care setting. She was privileged to represent the Sign Language Interpreters Association of NZ (SLIANZ) as the Oceania regional representative for the World Association of Sign Language Interpreters (WASLI) from 2007 to 2011 and learned a lot about the profession through working with colleagues from many different countries at an international level. Since 2014, George has been program leader and lecturer on the NZSL/English interpreting and deaf studies programs at AUT.

Susie Ovens is a deaf NZSL lecturer who has taught generations of interpreters at AUT for more than 20 years. Susie was born deaf and attended the Kelston School for the Deaf as a child and then later attended a mainstream high school. Susie's journey in NZSL teaching began with a Certificate in Deaf Studies: Teaching NZSL to Adults from Victoria University of Wellington, followed by a master's degree in language teaching from AUT. Susie's upbringing in the deaf community, as well as international travel as a sportsperson, exposed her to a wide variety of signed languages and different generational styles of signing within the NZ deaf community. Susie now leads NZSL teaching at AUT and also contributes to interpreting teaching and assessment.

CONTEXTUALIZATION: TRANSLATION AND INTERPRETING IN NEW ZEALAND

Although NZ has an active professional association of translators and interpreters and a government-sponsored phone interpreting service, the regulation and infrastructure for provision of language services are relatively underdeveloped in NZ (Royal Society of New Zealand, 2013). Certification from the National Accreditation Authority for Translators and Interpreters (NAATI; administered in Australia for 160+ languages)[4] or a university degree/graduate diploma in Translation and Interpreting (T&I) are required for full membership in the New Zealand Society of Translators and Interpreters (NZSTI), which has about 200 members. The Māori Language Commission certifies Māori interpreters and translators.

Entry-level training courses are available for spoken language interpreters at AUT and Unitec.[5] In-service training and professional development are also offered within some community-based interpreting agencies, while postgraduate offerings in T&I are available at the University of Auckland, the University of Canterbury, and AUT.

PROFESSIONALIZATION OF SIGN LANGUAGE INTERPRETING IN NEW ZEALAND

The typical progression from voluntary interpreting to ad hoc training to formalized training was shortcut in NZ by training initiatives in 1985 and 1992 that accelerated the establishment of sign language interpreting (SLI) services in a deaf community that was accustomed to making do without interpreters or the visible use of sign language. The concept of a professional interpreter role, along with the American Sign Language (ASL) sign interpreter, arrived at the point of first training in 1985. An oralist deaf education system from 1880 to 1979 denied the existence of sign language, and a demand for interpreting was first articulated by the National Deaf Association in the late 1970s (Dugdale, 2001), around the time that the Signed English system was introduced into deaf education. Until then, deaf people had limited expectations for access to civic participation, higher education, and professional employment. Self-advocacy was constrained for the NZ deaf community before the linguistic validation of NZSL and the influence of "deaf pride" discourses during the 1980s. NZ's hosting of the World Games for the Deaf in 1989 brought sign language to public attention, spurred the teaching of NZSL to many volunteers, and demonstrated the value of interpreters in enabling deaf leaders to negotiate effectively with hearing world organizations (McKee, 2004).

Establishing an interpreting service was the primary goal that drove the formation of the New Zealand Association of the Deaf (NZAD) in 1977 (now called

Deaf Aotearoa), and accordingly, the training and employment of interpreters were initiated by them in 1985 (Dugdale, 2001). Training is now independent of Deaf Aotearoa, although they still host the largest interpreting service agency and are considered a key stakeholder.

SLIANZ was incorporated in 1997 as the professional body that represents sign language interpreters. SLIANZ does not have a regional branch structure, but local networks of interpreters are active in several areas. SLIANZ holds regular conferences, supports professional development workshops, promotes the use of qualified interpreters, maintains a code of ethics and practice, facilitates mentoring, and is a representative voice for interpreters in consultation with external organizations. SLIANZ maintains links with SLI organizations overseas and has served as the Oceania regional representative for WASLI.

Although NAATI certification is recognized as a professional standard for spoken language interpreters in New Zealand, NAATI's sign language certification is designed for Australian Sign Language (Auslan), which differs from NZSL (and has a different training context). For this reason, NAATI certification has not been applied to NZSL interpreters. The bachelor's (BA) degree in NZSL/English interpreting is the minimum requirement for qualification and entry to the profession.

SLIANZ has approximately 100 qualified members; about two thirds of these are based in Auckland, as the largest population center with the largest deaf community. Although the government funds interpreting in the employment, health, tertiary education, and justice sectors, the supply of interpreters does not meet demand, ensuring that a range of work is readily available for qualified interpreters. Undersupply means that unqualified interpreters are still engaged in some situations, and qualified interpreters might be pressured to work in contexts for which they are not ideally skilled.

RESEARCH ON SLI IN NEW ZEALAND

Interpreter education in NZ has drawn strongly on the international research literature on interpreting, with language and cultural studies supported by descriptive and sociolinguistic research on NZSL undertaken since the late 1980s. Research on interpreting in NZ has been slower to develop within a practice profession. Topics that have been investigated and that contribute to learning in the SLI education program include the following: interpreting as a factor in social change in the deaf community (McKee, 2004), effects of sign language recognition (McKee, 2010; McKee & Nilsson, 2023), role construction and trilingual language mediation in Māori settings (McKee & Awheto, 2010), practices and effects of untrained interpreters in classrooms (McKee & Smith, 2003), dealing with lexical variation in interpreting (McKee et al., 2008), media interpreting in natural disasters (McKee, 2014), interpreting and access in health care settings

(Major, 2022; Major et al., 2020; Witko et al., 2017), and interpreting multiparty meetings (Henley & McKee, 2020).

Sign Language Interpreter Education in New Zealand

The first training course, of 4 months' duration, was held in 1985 under the auspices of NZAD, which obtained government and philanthropic funding to engage an interpreter trainer from California State University, Northridge. The local sign language (not documented at that time) was learned by recruiting groups of deaf volunteers as language models. Their signs were recorded by the teacher and students throughout the course and published as a first dictionary. Although the first course had few materials to draw upon, there were reciprocal benefits from this direct collaboration with the community: Deaf participants gained critical awareness of their language and learned about the goals of interpreter training. The trainees formed relationships with community members through visiting homes, clubs, and activities as part of their curriculum—experiences that tend to diminish once sign language resources are available and training becomes more institutionalized (Cokely, 2005).

After the 1985 course, the NZAD employed three of the graduates to serve three regions of the country. Until 1994, this service was sometimes augmented by interpreters contracted from Australia and the United Kingdom, who brought new influences into NZSL and exposure to overseas professional practices. The next major development was the establishment of a permanent education program, which began as a 2-year diploma and later expanded into a BA degree, as we outline in the following sections.

Diploma in SLI

In 1992, an undergraduate Diploma in Sign Language Interpreting (DipSLI) began at AUT and became the required qualification to work as a sign language interpreter in NZ. The program had deaf–hearing coleadership, which helped secure strong engagement with the NZ deaf community. Collaborative teaching also mentored deaf people who did not have teaching backgrounds to take on teaching roles. The original diploma curriculum drew on North American models of interpreting and curricula that were current in the late 1980s and 1990s, developed by pioneers in the field such as Sharon Neumann-Solow, Betty Colonomos, Dennis Cokely, Nancy Frishberg, Charlotte Baker-Shenk, and Anna Witter-Merithew.[6] The DipSLI was a 2-year, full-time course with an entry requirement of beginner-level NZSL proficiency.

Bachelor of Arts (NZSL/English Interpreting)

In 2011, a 3-year BA (NZSL/English Interpreting) program replaced the DipSLI and became the required qualification to practice.[7] The BA degree remains at AUT, and the curriculum retains the key elements of the DipSLI. The first year focuses on intensive NZSL acquisition and gaining familiarity with deaf community and culture. The second year focuses on more advanced NZSL skills, including comparative analysis of NZSL and English structures, introduction of interpreting models, basic dialogic interpreting techniques, contextual knowledge of settings, and ethical decision-making skills. The third year is focused almost entirely on more advanced practical interpreting skills.

A key change was that the bachelor's program enrolls students with no prior NZSL skills and thus teaches introductory language skills. However, most students who enter the program have already learned some NZSL, often at community classes or in deaf families, so the early NZSL courses have mixed proficiency levels. The first-year NZSL courses are also open to students from other degrees who take NZSL as an elective or minor subject. This is good for building numbers and the profile of NZSL at the university, but it can be a challenge for teachers because students learning the language as an elective have different motivations and priorities from those in the interpreting program. Interpreting students are also required to take core courses, standard across all bachelor's degrees at AUT, including academic writing, intercultural competence in the NZ context, and research skills.

The open-entry policy means that there is little opportunity to assess the suitability of applicants for interpreting, and applicants who are new to NZSL and the deaf community cannot themselves accurately predict whether interpreting is something that they will enjoy or in which they will succeed. Thus, although first-year NZSL classes are quite large, attrition means that the practical interpreting courses starting in Year 2 are much smaller. Students need to achieve a B grade average or above in the NZSL courses in Year 1 to continue with the interpreting major in Year 2 and reach a required grade level in Year 2 interpreting skills courses to progress to Year 3. Those who do not, or who decide that interpreting is not for them, can change track to the "NZSL and Deaf Studies" major.

Several courses are co-taught with the spoken language interpreting program in "language-neutral" delivery. This has benefits as well as constraints. Students learn introductory-level ethical decision-making alongside others from diverse linguistic and cultural backgrounds, broadening their understanding of different worldviews and the challenges faced by interpreters of other languages, especially those of other minority languages. In the language-neutral health and legal interpreting courses (of which students select one or the other, but generally not both), NZSL students acquire a more detailed understanding of these topics than was previously possible in the DipSLI. However, co-enrollment limits opportunity to develop practical language and culture-specific interpreting competencies in these specialist areas, so the key outcomes are higher-level knowledge-based skills. The majority of NZSL interpreting students choose the health stream upon advice from NZSL staff, as the knowledge developed here can be more directly useful in the early years of interpreting.

BA Practicum

Graduates report that the practicum in the final year is a vital component of the BA course, designed to give students field experience and to develop reflective analysis skills. The practicum consists of 30 to 40 hours of observation of qualified interpreters and 30 to 40 hours of work experience, usually beginning in jobs teamed with qualified interpreters and then progressing to teaming with another student or working solo where appropriate. The lecturer running this course is responsible for coordinating assignments for students, liaising with agencies, and liaising directly with interpreters and interpreting users. For each field experience, students write a guided online journal entry, reflecting on features of language and translation, contextual factors, professional behavior, teaming strategies, and issues relating to roles and ethics.

In addition to fieldwork, students have taught sessions to introduce the practicum, develop more advanced ethical decision-making skills, and address aspects of workplace readiness, including professional appearance, self-care, prevention of occupational overuse syndrome, coworking and positioning, and assignment preparation. There are visits to class from interpreting agencies, as well as from SLIANZ, who introduce students to the mentoring system. Mentoring is available to students from their third and final year through to 2 years after graduation and entails the pairing of a less experienced interpreter with a more experienced interpreter for peer reflection and guidance.

Generally speaking, professional interpreters (from very experienced to new graduates) are generous in the time that they give to students observing and working with them for practicum, often debriefing with them at length afterward when their schedules allow. As more interpreted events are formally or informally livestreamed, students and interpreter mentors need to be aware of protecting students doing practicum work from being livestreamed, as trainee interpreters. Appropriately managing personal social media use while developing a professional persona as an interpreter is also an issue that is now explicitly addressed as part of preparation for professional practice.

Learning Technologies

Although in-class learning remains the basis of program delivery, advances in video technology and online interfaces allow interpreting students to independently access resources and tasks online in a more flexible and autonomous manner. Online learning management platforms (e.g., GoReact, designed specifically for analyzing and giving feedback on SLI)[8] have improved assessment formats and feedback possibilities for both teachers and students. More experience in using technology-mediated NZSL during study also helps to prepare students for future video interpreting work, which is a growing mode of practice. At the time of writing, two theory courses (deaf community and culture) are livestreamed to allow students from other parts of the country to access classes online.

It has been widely anticipated that online learning modes can eventually resolve the geographic constraint of a single training program and the uneven distribution of qualified interpreters across the country. However, our experience of adapting to remote delivery mode during the COVID-19 pandemic in 2020 to 2021 showed that face-to-face learning can be replaced only to a certain degree in foundation-level NZSL learning and practical interpreter skill development, as also noted elsewhere (Halley et al., 2022). There remain additional unresolved challenges with distance delivery modes in terms of likely enrollment numbers and the workload associated with delivering an alternative delivery mode within the same staffing capacity.

The COVID-19 pandemic forced an increasing reliance on online teaching during repeated lockdowns beginning in early 2020. This led to an enhanced use of technology that will benefit the program beyond the pandemic, including more sophisticated use of GoReact for learning and assessment and better use of Zoom to connect students with interpreters in other centers. At the same time, however, many students struggled with motivation during isolated online learning, and disparities in internet quality made online tasks more accessible to some students than to others. The experience has only reinforced for both staff and students that face-to-face learning is at the heart of the program, and fully switching to online learning should be only a temporary measure (McKee & Pivac Alexander, 2023).

THE ROAD AHEAD

Although the SLI profession in NZ is unified by a single training and qualification pathway, most interpreters do not enter the profession as heritage signers, and each cohort includes a variety of academic backgrounds and a range of NZSL knowledge, and thus the exit competency levels of graduates vary. Over time, it has become clear that a professional level of interpreting competence is difficult to achieve in a 3-year bachelor's degree. Even with a 3-year degree, most graduates still have "developing" NZSL proficiency and interpreting skills and need to learn a lot more on the job to cope with the range of work they typically face. Compared with 10 years ago, however, the larger workforce means that new graduates are (generally, depending on their location) under less pressure to accept high-consequence interpreting assignments than was the case in the past.

An institutional change from a more vocational training orientation to a university structure, as well as increased costs, have reduced the amount of contact teaching time. When the course was established in 1992, it was an intensive program, with approximately 25 class contact hours per week for 32 weeks per year; class contact is now reduced to approximately 12 to 15 hours per week for 24 weeks per year, with students expected to engage in independent learning activities, including online components. Although the trend toward greater learner autonomy is sound in principle, it is rather difficult (and time consuming in other ways for teachers) to implement in a language that has limited availability of high-quality resources to support independent study and interpreting skill development.

Sustaining an adequate number of students of suitable caliber to run a viable program in a small population is difficult, especially with the increasing fiscal pressures that face tertiary education institutions. Administrative demand to maintain student numbers can compromise entry standards or progression between years of the program, which in turn affect exit standards. Although entry to the degree does not require prior NZSL skills, the availability and quality of NZSL classes outside the course affect the profile of entering students. Only one other university offers NZSL and deaf studies courses (Victoria University Wellington), from which some students transfer into the interpreting program; most entering students have learned introductory NZSL in community adult education classes that vary in quality.

Achieving demographic balance in entering and graduating cohorts is a challenge shared by many countries; women students far outnumber men, and increasing course completions by Māori students is an ongoing goal being addressed through various initiatives. The availability of an NZSL curriculum for mainstream high-schools and the growing visibility of NZSL in the public domain seem to be increasing the number of young people who are interested in studying interpreting, and the age of entering students has dropped over time to include more school-leavers than in the past. Younger students often do well academically and acquire NZSL readily, but on the other hand, they might lack the breadth of life experience that supports interpreting practice skills. Social oversight and personal guidance are also considerations to ensure the safety and preparedness of younger students in their extracurricular interactions with the deaf community, where they might encounter unwanted attention or situations that are difficult for them to negotiate as young, mostly female, newcomers to the language and community.

Recruiting and maintaining academically qualified teachers of interpreting and NZSL remain challenging in a small country and in a field with a relatively short professional history. There are no SLI courses available above bachelor's level, as a specialist postgraduate program in a small professional population is considered financially unsustainable in the current university funding conditions. Deaf NZSL teachers are trained in an undergraduate certificate in teaching NZSL,[9] so current teaching staff have pursued postgraduate study in the allied fields of applied linguistics or linguistics. A strength of the program is having experienced deaf teachers who embrace the use of new technology to enhance learning experiences for students. Deaf lecturers maintain relationships with the local deaf community to secure their participation in course-related activities with students, which provides invaluable exposure to authentic language and cultural experience. A variety of interpreting practitioners contribute to teaching and practicum guidance on the course, which exposes students to professional models and networks beyond the two interpreting lecturers.

A Changing Target-Language Population

The training and employment of interpreters are challenged by the rapidly changing demographics and language profiles of the deaf community. Over the past 30 years, 90% of deaf children in NZ have attended mainstream schools, where the conditions for acquisition of NZSL vary greatly, compared with the more collective language socialization experience of older generations who attended residential schools up until the 1980s. With free public health provision, NZ has high rates of bilateral infant cochlear implantation. The extent to which the normalization of cochlear implants and associated use of spoken English as a first or parallel language could alter demand for interpreting services has not been forecast in NZ, but change seems inevitable. The decline of collective deaf education and growing demographic diversity (including more migrants and refugees) in the deaf population predict more variation in the forms of NZSL that interpreters will encounter in the community. Global influences on NZSL are also apparent as a result of more mobility and online exposure to other sign languages, which is manifesting as variation and change in linguistic repertoires of deaf signers (McKee et al., 2022).

Deaf Community Social Opportunities

As evidenced in other parts of the world, changes in the ways that contemporary deaf communities socialize mean that it is significantly harder now for interpreting students to gain NZSL exposure in deaf spaces, although this is what they need to develop confidence using the language. Auckland hosts the largest deaf community in NZ, and the program is thus well situated for extracurricular involvement in deaf events—for example, attending deaf club and volunteering at community events. However, compared with previous decades, there are significantly fewer face-to-face deaf events and spaces; for example, participation in deaf sports events has declined, and the deaf club is attended by fewer deaf people than previously, so it is accordingly more noticeable if a large group of hearing students attend. Furthermore, students are under increasing financial stress as study fees and living costs rise, and most need to work in their spare time. Employment commitments compete with their availability to attend community events, which is a barrier to creating the strong social connections in the community on which interpreting students relied in earlier times.

These contextual changes require that interpreter educators organize more social NZSL opportunities for students at or through the university, in ways that benefit the deaf community equally. An example is an annual "AUT NZSL Day" at the Auckland Deaf Society, in which students, staff, and community members spend an intensive day together in an NZSL medium, sharing food and engaging in language activities. On the flip side of decreasing community "events," there is an expanding volume of prepared and spontaneous NZSL texts on diverse topics available to students in the digital landscape of YouTube, websites, vlogs, and social media. These community-generated sources are valuable resources for language and cultural learning, to supplement pedagogical resources.

Māori Language and NZSL Interpreting

As the Māori language has become increasingly visible in NZ society since the 1990s, there has been a growing, though not well quantified, call for sign language interpreters who can interpret trilingually between Māori, NZSL, and English in Māori cultural settings and at public events where Māori is used as one of the languages of proceedings or formalities. The availability of trilingual interpreters is important for Māori deaf people who want to participate in Māori-speaking contexts and to access knowledge of their cultural heritage (Smiler, 2004). The desire for more Māori-speaking interpreters and the coinage of signs to express Māori concepts are partly about gaining access to hearing Māori domains and partly about the representation of ethnic identity within the deaf community (Simchowitz, 2023; McKee et al., 2007). The BA program affirmatively recruits students who are speakers of Māori, but this remains quite challenging because less than a quarter of the population who identify as Māori can speak the language to any degree, and very few of these know or choose to learn NZSL. Furthermore, Māori individuals who are fluent speakers of Māori (e.g., graduates of Māori-medium schools) have a variety of career opportunities open to them as a result of their bilingualism. The BA program does not have capacity to teach or assess interpretation between Māori and NZSL but supports Māori-speaking interpreters to apply their knowledge of interpreting principles and techniques to their use of Māori as an additional working language. In addition, most students in the degree program now elect to take an introductory course in Māori language to acquire at least basic familiarity with the language, which is increasingly present in public contexts.

Deaf Interpreters

Although deaf people with informally recognized interpreting skills work with hearing interpreters in some situations, demand is unquantified, and practice is ad hoc because NZ does not yet have specific training or employment protocols for deaf people working in interpreting roles. Because of geographic isolation, interlingual interpreting between different sign languages is a rare demand in NZ, and there is no local opportunity for deaf people to work in transnational conference contexts, as is seen internationally. The main call for deaf interpreters (DIs) occurs with individuals who lack fluency in NZSL, have "fund of information" deficits (Pollard & Barnett, 2009), or are in complex situations such as mental health or court proceedings. There is no established tradition of deafblind interpreting provided by DIs, as exists in other countries (e.g., Australia, the United States). Setting up a system of training and certification for DIs is challenged by small scale and lack of expert practitioner role models. An advocacy organization, Deaf Interpreters New Zealand, has advocated for the development of this pathway, with support from SLIANZ and the AUT interpreting program.

Deaf people produce translation of written texts into NZSL—usually public or institutional information that is posted online to make it accessible to the community. One deaf-led translation agency exists, and a deaf team within Deaf Aotearoa also regularly produces translated information in NZSL. Several deaf people have worked in theater interpreting teams in recent years. As yet, deaf individuals undertaking translation work are not trained or certified. Although interpreters are sometimes seen in television news clips of media briefings by public figures, there is no regular television programming in NZSL, so this is not an arena in which deaf (or hearing) translators and interpreters have been employed.

Conclusions

Since 1985, SLI and SLI education in NZ have developed from nothing to a field of academically qualified interpreters who work in diverse community settings, including political and public contexts, and in a national video interpreting service. Legal recognition of NZSL in 2006 has increased awareness of NZSL and accessibility, but the law did not create more rights or resources in the provision of interpreting. Although professional unity is enhanced by all interpreters qualifying through a single bachelor's degree program, there is still scope to ensure more consistency in practice standards beyond entry-level qualification. Gaps remain in quantifying demand for training, certification, and employment of interpreters and for Māori-speaking NZSL interpreters.

The standard of SLI education and professional practice in NZ is robust in relation to international best practice, but challenges and opportunities to maintain excellence are ever present. The need to generate original learning resources is now greatly assisted by the plethora of video applications available to teachers, students, and the community, which are harnessed to support the learning, teaching, and assessment of NZSL and interpreting. Technological developments, on the other hand, require constant adaptation of teaching and learning approaches. In a small country, few professional leaders have the necessary combination of practitioner experience and advanced academic qualification to teach interpreting, so capacity to expand alternative modes of delivery and to innovate new specializations or a postgraduate pathway is constrained.

The move to a bachelor's degree has increased the status and depth of training but has also reduced teaching contact time in favor of more student learning outside the classroom. At the same time, we see a reduction of traditional community social spaces, an increase of NZSL in the digital language landscape, and increasing diversity in the linguistic profiles of NZSL users. These environmental changes challenge interpreter educators to plan opportunities for authentic language and cultural exposure, which is vital to readiness to work as an interpreter.

Notes

1. Some of the text from the original chapter on New Zealand (McKee et al., 2009) in the *International Perspectives on Sign Language Interpreter Education* volume (Napier, 2009) features in this chapter in the second volume where the information has not changed.
2. NZSL Act 2006: www.legislation.govt.nz/act/public/2006/0018/latest/DLM372754. html?src=qs
3. NZSL Advisory Board: www.odi.govt.nz/nzsl/about-board/
4. National Accreditation Authority for Translators and Interpreters (www.naati.com.au); see Australia chapter in this volume for more information.
5. Unitec is part of Te Pūkenga, New Zealand's national network of polytechnics, industry training organizations, and institutes of technology. See: https://www.unitec.ac.nz/about-us
6. Coauthor of the United States of America chapter in this volume.
7. Bachelor of NZSL/English Interpreting: https://www.aut.ac.nz/courses/bachelor-of-arts/new-zealand-sign-language-english-interpreting-major
8. See https://get.goreact.com
9. Certificate in Deaf Studies: Teaching NZSL: www.wgtn.ac.nz/explore/degrees/certificate-in-deaf-studies-teaching-new-zealand-sign-language/overview

References

Cokely, D. (2005). Shifting positionality: A critical examination of the turning point in the relationship of interpreters and the deaf community. In M. Marschark, R. Peterson & E. Winston (Eds.), *Sign language interpreting and interpreter education* (pp. 208–234). Oxford University Press.

Dugdale, P. (2001). *Talking hands, listening eyes: The history of the Deaf Association of New Zealand.* The Deaf Association of New Zealand.

Halley, M. A., Wessling, D. M., & Sargent, S. N. (2022). Virtual and viral: Shifts in signed language interpreter education during the COVID-19 pandemic. *Journal of Interpretation, 30*(1), Article 5. https://digitalcommons.unf.edu/joi/vol30/iss1/5

Henley, R., & McKee, R. (2020). Going through the motions: Participation in interpreter-mediated meeting interaction under a deaf and a hearing chairperson. *International Journal of Interpreter Education, 12*(1), 5–23.

Major, G. (2022, November 25–26). *Not a one-size-fits-all: The complexity of interpreter role* [keynote presentation]. Australian Institute of Interpreters and Translators 2022 Conference, Brisbane, QLD, Australia.

Major, G., McKee, R., McGregor, K., & Pivac, L. (2020). Deaf women's health vocabulary: Challenges for interpreters working in a language of limited diffusion. *International Journal of Interpreter Education, 12*(2), 4–20.

Major, G., Pivac, L., & Ovens, S. (2017). *Deaf health stories in NZSL* [YouTube video]. https://www.youtube.com/watch?v=bZ_mQWB64bk

McKee, R. (2004). Signs of change: Interpreting as a tool for empowerment in the New Zealand deaf community. In S. Fenton (Ed.), *For better or for worse: Translation as a tool for change in the Pacific* (pp. 89–132). St. Jerome.

McKee, R. (2010). Action pending: Four years on from the NZSL Act 2006. *VUW Law Review, 42,* 277–97.

McKee, R. (2014). Breaking news: Sign language interpreters on television during natural disasters. *Interpreting, 16*(1), 107–130.

McKee, R., & Awheto, S. (2010). Constructing roles in a Māori deaf trilingual context. In R.L. McKee & J.E. Davis (Eds.), *Interpreting in multilingual, multicultural contexts* (pp. 85–118). Gallaudet University Press.

McKee, R., Major, G., & McKee, D. (2008). Lexical variation and interpreting in New Zealand Sign Language. In C. Roy (Ed.), *Diversity and community in the worldwide sign language interpreting profession: Proceedings of the second WASLI Conference* (pp. 89–106). Douglas McLean Publishing.

McKee, R., & Manning, V. (2019). Implementing recognition of New Zealand Sign Language 2006–2018. In M. De Meulder, J. Murray, & R. L. Mckee (Eds.), *The legal recognition of sign languages: Advocacy and outcomes around the world* (pp. 224–237). Multilingual Matters.

McKee, R., & Nilsson, A. (2023). Interpreters as agents of language planning. *Journal of Translation and Interpreting, 17*(3), 429–454.

McKee, R., & Pivac Alexander, S. (2023). Teaching sign language remotely in the COVID-19 pandemic. *The Language Learning Journal,* 1–17. https://doi.org/10.1080/09571736.2023.2293010

McKee, R., & Smith, E. (2003). Report on a survey of teacher aides of "high" and "very high needs" deaf students in mainstream schools. Deaf Studies Research Report, No.3; Deaf Studies Research Unit, School of Linguistics and Applied Language Studies, Victoria University of Wellington. http://www.Vuw.Ac.Nz/Lals/Research/Deafstudies/DSRU

McKee, R. L., McKee, D., Smiler, K., & Pointon, K. (2007). Māori signs: The construction of indigenous deaf identity in New Zealand Sign Language. In D. Quinto-Pozos (Ed.), *Sign languages in contact* (pp. 31–81). Gallaudet University Press.

McKee, R., Vale, M., Alexander, S. P., & McKee, D. (2022). Signs of globalization: ASL influence in the lexicon of New Zealand Sign Language. *Sign Language Studies, 22*(2), 283–319.

Pollard, R. Q., & Barnett, S. (2009). Health-related vocabulary knowledge among deaf adults. *Rehabilitation Psychology, 54*(2), 182–185.

Royal Society of New Zealand. (2013). Languages in Aotearoa New Zealand. *RSNZ* (March), 1–8. http://royalsociety.org.nz/media/Languages-in-Aotearoa-New-Zealand.pdf

Simchowitz, M. (2023). *Language practices of Māori Deaf New Zealand Sign Language users for identity expression* [Unpublished master's thesis]. Te Herenga Waka-Victoria University of Wellington. https://doi.org/10.26686/wgtn.22798976

Smiler, K. (2004). *Māori Deaf: Perceptions of cultural and linguistic identity of Māori members of the New Zealand Deaf community* [Unpublished master's thesis]. Victoria University of Wellington.

Witko, J., Boyles, P., Smiler, K., & McKee, R. (2017). Deaf New Zealand Sign Language users' access to healthcare. *New Zealand Medical Journal 130*(1466), 53–61.

HILDE HAUALAND AND
ANNA-LENA NILSSON

16

Sign Language Interpreting

Education and Professionalization in Norway

Sign language interpreting (SLI) has come a relatively long way toward professionalization in Norway, in comparison with both spoken language interpreting in Norway and SLI in many countries around the world. Deaf, deafblind, deafened, and hard of hearing people have a legal individual right to SLI services free of charge. The provision of these services is well-regulated. University-level education is mandatory for sign language interpreters, a code of professional ethics exists, and many sign language interpreters are members of a union branch that specifically targets sign language interpreters. Also, Norwegian Sign Language (*norsk tegnspråk* [NTS]) interpreters are relatively homogenous in that almost all have completed a 3-year bachelor education program that is a prerequisite to working for the public SLI services. The Norwegian Labour and Welfare Organization (NAV) has an almost monopolistic role in both assigning interpreters and paying their salaries, and nearly all interpreters work for NAV. This organization of the provision of SLI services is indicative of Norway's position as a state in which the government is responsible for providing a wide range of services to the population (Esping-Andersen, 1990; Ozolins, 2010). Norway shares borders with Sweden and Finland and is one of the Nordic welfare states.

On the one hand, the homogeneity of and limited variation in SLI services secure deaf people relative freedom to request SLI services when they consider an interpreter to be necessary. The current organization of SLI service provision also prevents unskilled interpreters from taking assignments from qualified interpreters. On the other hand, the lack of diversity in interpreters' competencies and their being part of a bureaucratic organization like NAV entails some challenges for both deaf people and interpreters.

In this chapter, we will discuss both the positive features and some of the drawbacks of the current organization of SLI education and services in Norway.

WHO ARE WE?

Hilde, deaf, is a social anthropologist and professor at the Department of International Studies and Interpreting at Oslo Metropolitan University (OsloMet—storbyuniversitetet), Norway, where she is a member of the Interpreting, Language, and Communication research group. She is a teacher and researcher in deaf studies, SLI as a profession and a social institution, and language ideologies. She has been a guest researcher at Gallaudet University and has researched the politics and ideologies behind video interpreting services. Her publications include articles on sign language interpreters and professionalism, SLI services and their impact on service provisions, the politics of video interpreting, disability, identity, and marginalization, deaf people and transnational connections, and sign language ideologies. Except for a few ad hoc interpreting assignments and teaching deaf studies and professional theory to sign language interpreters, Hilde has been mostly on the receiving end of SLI services.

Anna-Lena, hearing, is a professor of signed language and interpreting in the Department of Language and Literature at Norwegian University of Science and Technology (NTNU—Norges teknisk-naturvitenskapelige universitet) in Trondheim, where she is a member of the Language and Communication in Organizations and Professions research group. She has a doctor of philosophy (PhD) degree in signed language linguistics from the Department of Linguistics at Stockholm University, and is a trained Swedish Sign Language/Swedish/English interpreter with longstanding experience in Swedish and international settings. She has trained interpreters since 1994, contributed to establishing the bachelor of arts (BA) program in sign language interpreting at Stockholm University in 2013. She was also involved in setting up a national accreditation system for Swedish Sign Language/Swedish interpreters. Anna-Lena only occasionally has taken assignments for the Norwegian SLI services.

The reader will notice that there is not much information about sign language interpreters' work conditions and salaries in this chapter, but there is more emphasis on the organization of services and education of interpreters, which are the two aspects of SLI of which the authors have the most experience and knowledge.

CONTEXTUALIZATION: TRANSLATION AND INTERPRETING IN NORWAY

SLI and public sector interpreting (PSI, between two spoken languages) differ in terms of regulation, the organization of service provision, and the qualifications required. Two distinct reasons for these differences are disability legislation and the (historical) linguistic demography in Norway. During the 1970s, an increased focus on inclusion and participation of disabled people in society paved the way for the establishment of professional SLI services in Norway. At the same time, there was growing scientific recognition that sign languages were legitimate languages, which probably also fueled the argument for establishing (sign language) interpreting education and services (deWit, 2016; Haualand, Nilsson, & Raanes, 2018; Ozolins, 2010; Pöchhacker, 2016).

Traditionally, Norway has been considered a monolingual country, and the public language debate has concerned mainly the dispersion and use of the two standard variants of written Norwegian. The Sami population, however, represents a considerable linguistic minority in Norway (about 40,000 people out of a total of approximately 5.4 million inhabitants), but the Norwegian government did not endorse or protect their languages until the 1980s (Duolljá & Gaski, 2021). In 2021, a language act was passed, stating that the two variants of written Norwegian, Sami, Kven (a language of Finnish descent), Romani, Romanes, and NTS are the Norwegian languages that the government has a particular responsibility to endorse and protect. An official report overseeing the status of NTS assumes there are about 10,500 users of NTS, including deaf, hard of hearing, and hearing people (Kultur- og likestillingsdepartementet, 2023).

Despite steady migration to Norway, especially since the 1970s, it has taken the Norwegian government a long time to publicly acknowledge that Norway is a multilingual country. Public and health service legislation now forces service providers to ensure that their clients are informed and heard, which indirectly is also considered an obligation to engage interpreters when needed. The training and certification of spoken language interpreters are, however, much more varied than for sign language interpreters. Service providers were not obliged to hire *qualified* interpreters until the implementation of the Interpreting Act, effective from January 1, 2022, which mandates public service providers to use qualified interpreters when serving people who do not speak Norwegian. Currently, the minimum qualification for spoken language interpreters is, however, considerably lower than that for sign language interpreters. Spoken language interpreters have only to successfully complete a bilingual test and a 3-day course about the responsibilities of interpreters. The national registry of interpreters does, however, have several levels of qualification, with a BA in interpreting *and* a government authorization as the highest level. The heterogeneity among spoken language interpreters is thus much larger than among sign language interpreters. Sign language interpreters are now included in this registry, and there is currently (2023) ongoing work to adapt the state authorization test for NTS interpreters to make it possible for them to be authorized at the highest level.

Sign language translation has so far not been considered a separate skill in Norway, and there is consequently no training focusing on this skill. In the following section, we will give an overview of the professionalization processes for interpreting, with an emphasis on SLI.

The Professionalization of SLI in Norway

During the 1960s and 1970s, *Norges Døveforbund* (Norwegian National Association of the Deaf, NDF), like associations of the deaf in several other countries, took on an active role in lobbying the government to take responsibility for training sign language interpreters and paying them for their work. This action was inspired partially by the success in establishing such services in the neighboring country Sweden (Lundström, n.d.).

Within a relatively short time span, from the 1970s to the early 2000s, SLI in Norway went from being a charity-based volunteer service to a profession that meets both organizational and performative criteria for professions. There is an organized labor market; there is mandatory and specialized higher education; interpreting is considered a specialized skill that requires training in an institute of higher education; performance is based on both practice and theoretical knowledge; and professional performance is regulated by a code of ethics (Molander & Terum, 2008; Parsons, 1968; Skaaden, 2019). Comparing some of the major milestones in terms of legislation and service development with the length and scope of education, it is evident that they mutually reinforced the professionalization process in Norway (see Table 1).

Table 1. Some Major Milestones in the Professionalization Process in Norway

Year	Legislation and Organization of SLI services	Year	SLI Education
1972	Interpreters paid to interpret in hospitals	1974	One-week course
		1978	First course approved by the Ministry of Education (2 + 3 weeks).
1981	Right to free interpreting services for deaf, deafblind, and deafened persons stipulated in the National Insurance Act	1982–1988	Courses continue (3 + 3 weeks)
1989	Trial period offering public services	1989	1-year university-level interpreter education in Oslo
1994	National public interpreting services established, located at regional centers for assistive technology	1994	Interpreter education extended to 2 years, now also in Trondheim
2003	Cap removed on annual interpreting hours provided for each person	2002	3-year BA programs in interpreting, now also in Bergen

As can be seen in Table 1, deaf people were granted the individual right to receive SLI services in 1981, not long after the first courses for interpreters were offered. Another step toward professionalization was the establishment of the Norwegian Association of Interpreters (*Tolkeforbundet*) in 1978. During 1989, when interpreter education became a 1-year university-level program, a trial period of offering public interpreting services was also initiated. This was an important step toward a regulated labor market for sign language interpreters.

The Organization of SLI Services

In Norway, SLI services are an individual right for deaf people. This means they enjoy relative freedom to decide when they consider there to be a need for interpreting. When entering higher education or applying for jobs, they do not have to burden universities or employers with the cost of interpreting. Also, deaf people can request interpreters for private festivities and to attend courses and meetings without having to ask family, friends, or private organizations or businesses to pay. The organization of SLI services is an example of Ozolin's assertion that Scandinavian countries stand out with their emphasis on "explicit public provision or close public supervision of delegated services" (Ozolins, 2010, p. 198). Costs are mostly covered by NAV, which contrasts with countries where public interpreting services (among other services) are provided mainly by or through private companies, nongovernmental organizations, charities, foundations, or voluntary associations. As Norway is one of the Scandinavian "welfare states," and NAV has a virtual monopoly on providing interpreting services, we will next briefly describe what this means for the provision of and payment for interpreting services.

Although there is no cap on hours, the availability of interpreters and the capacity of regional NAV offices to coordinate requests for SLI services do, however, impose limits on the actual provision of services. Nearly all sign language interpreters are employed by NAV, either as full-time employees or on a freelance basis.[1] In 2021, there were 220 employed interpreters and 400 freelance interpreters who worked for NAV (L. Stadshaug, personal communication, June 2, 2021). Interpreters who are employees work mainly during "office hours," which are normally approximately from 8:00 a.m. to 4:00 p.m. in Norway. Because freelance interpreters have no duty to take assignments, the office hour work schedule among employees as well as service coordinators means that it can be difficult to find interpreters who are available for assignments in the evenings or during weekends. Since the interpreting services provided at no charge by NAV are part of the Norwegian Labour and Welfare Administration, workplace interpreting and health care interpreting are prioritized.

In most other countries, video interpreting services are provided by institutions or companies other than those that provide on-site services, but NAV also provides video interpreting services, which operate on weekdays from 8:00 a.m. to 8:00 p.m. The video interpreting services also are offered to provide services for shorter and more spontaneous assignments, including telephone calls, and they are provided by sign language interpreters who work in studios dedicated to this (Haualand, 2011, 2014). During the COVID-19 pandemic, interpreters did, however, also provide services from their homes, thus extending the services beyond the studios and times set by NAV's ordinary operating hours for video interpreting.

Educational interpreting in primary and secondary education, however, is organized and paid for by local educational authorities. Deaf children in Norway have a legal right to receive education in and about NTS, regardless of which school they attend. According to the regulations, primary education in NTS should not be conducted via interpreters. Nevertheless, as a consequence of a lack of qualified NTS teachers, local schools with one or more deaf pupils are currently hiring sign language interpreters as (unqualified) sign language teachers or assistants. In addition, there are five upper secondary schools spread over the country that provide some classes in NTS but also hire interpreters for some classes. There are no reliable statistics on the number of sign language interpreters working in primary or secondary education, and schools do not always require the interpreters they hire to have actually passed all of the exams in an interpreter education program.

At the performance level, interpreters are expected to work according to the principles of impartiality and accuracy. The labor market is thoroughly regulated, with opportunities for both permanent employment and contract assignments, and the payments for sign language interpreters' work are standardized, albeit low, compared with salaries for other professions with an education of similar length. Since 1983, the professional association of sign language interpreters, Tolkeforbundet, has had a code of professional ethics that members must follow. However, membership in Tolkeforbundet has never been mandatory. In 2019, a subgroup of interpreters was established in the Union of University and College Graduates (*Akademikerforbundet*), and Tolkeforbundet was dismantled in 2020. The subgroup of interpreters is now the only labor union unit that works specifically for interpreters, but many interpreters are organized in other labor unions.

With increased diversity among deaf people, requests for deaf interpreters have increased. Thus far, fewer than five deaf interpreters have graduated from a BA program in SLI, but NAV has paid ad hoc deaf interpreters for quite some time. This has especially been the case for assignments with deaf asylum seekers who do not know NTS but must be interviewed for legal assessment of their cases (Olsen, 2018). In 2023, NAV hired the first deaf interpreter in a permanent position.

Sign Language Interpreter Education
in Norway

As Table 1 shows, both the rights to interpreting services and the length of the interpreter education expanded gradually from 1978. In 1989, it became a 1-year university-level program, which was extended to 2 years in 1994, and from 2002 the interpreter education became a 3-year bachelor program, with the first year devoted to learning NTS. Since then, the education has remained a 3-year bachelor program offered at OsloMet in Oslo, at the Western Norway University of Applied Sciences (HVL; Høgskulen på Vestlandet [HVL]) in Bergen, and at NTNU in Trondheim. No substantial new rights or regulations have changed the rights of deaf people, the level of interpreting services offered, or the labor market for interpreters, except for the establishment of video interpreting. NAV hires predominantly sign language interpreters[2] who have graduated from one of the 3-year BA programs in sign language and interpreting (or an education of equal length from a foreign university, if the interpreter knows NTS and Norwegian). With only one major employer, which hires only interpreters with a degree from one of three BA programs, the market for nonprofessional sign language interpreters is virtually nonexistent.

A few interpreters have also completed a master's of arts (MA) degree, but NAV does not currently differentiate between interpreters who have a BA and interpreters with a MA or other types of continuing professional development (CPD), so the incentives for sign language interpreters to specialize or engage in CPD are few.

Until the SLI education program in Oslo introduced a test to document basic sign language skills before entrance to the program in 2022, students in the programs were not required to know NTS when they entered their program. The latter is still the case for students entering the programs in Bergen and Trondheim. Upon graduation, they are expected to have the skills to provide interpreting between Norwegian and NTS, interpreting and guidance for deafblind individuals, interpreting between Norwegian and "sign-supported Norwegian," and speech-to-text interpreting (real-time captioning). The two latter methods are used mostly for deafened or hearing-impaired adults who know Norwegian well but need interpreters to access spoken Norwegian. Teaching and exams include all these interpreting methods in all three programs. This very broad approach to training is related to the current labor market. In general, all sign language interpreters in Norway are expected to meet the needs and requests of a wide range of deaf, deafblind, hard of hearing, and deafened people, in all walks of life.

For public sector spoken language interpreters, the situation is quite different. A 1-year course has been offered at OsloMet since 2007 and at HVL in Bergen since 2020. A 3-year BA program for PSI started in Oslo in 2018. This new program for PSI between two spoken languages is currently offered only at OsloMet, and as the name indicates, the program is tailored to interpreting in the public sector. Whereas sign language interpreters are required to have completed a BA in SLI, having completed the BA in PSI is not mandatory to carry out PSI assignments. A major difference between the BA in PSI and a BA in SLI has been that PSI students must pass a bilingual test *before* they enter the program, whereas students did not need any qualifications in NTS (or any other sign language) before entering their program. As the program in Oslo now requires basic sign language skills before students enter the program, this could be considered a step toward additional harmonization between spoken and signed language interpreting programs.

Structure and Content of the SLI BA Program

In Trondheim and Bergen, the first year of the BA programs in SLI focuses on students' learning NTS and sign language linguistics, as well as learning about the history and culture of deaf people. Oslo also offers such a 1-year course; it is not part of the BA program, but students passing this course with a C grade or better do not need to take the entrance test for the BA program in SLI. All students are admitted on the basis of their grade points from secondary education, and they are required to present a certificate from the police authorities indicating that they are fit to practice, as do students who want to become nurses, teachers, etc. The number of applicants generally exceeds the number of students who are admitted to the programs.

The number of students in the first year of the program has been larger than the number of students who continue for the second and third years. Some students, for a variety of reasons, might want to study NTS for only 1 year. Another, smaller, group of students realize during the first or second year that they do not want to become interpreters. They might still continue their studies and combine their newly acquired sign language skills with some other program of study. On a national level, approximately 150 students begin their studies every year (including those who study NTS for only 1 year), and every year about 25–35 students graduate from the programs. In Oslo, the prerequisite of students' having basic sign language skills before entering the program is motivated partially by an aim to reduce the dropout rate, which is influenced by unrealistic expectations among students.

The three BA programs (in Oslo, Bergen, and Trondheim) are organized differently, but all students are expected to develop the practical and theoretical skills needed to work as interpreters upon graduation. The theoretical subjects they study are, for example, interpreting theory, professional theory (such as ethics, division of labor, legal issues), linguistics, and deaf studies. When students know enough sign language to make translation work meaningful, they will gradually work their way from translation exercises to consecutive interpreting. Finally, during the third year, they are expected to master simultaneous interpreting. They also practice techniques for team interpreting and peer support. As mentioned, students must also learn the basics of speech-to-text interpreting, interpreting and guidance for deaf-blind people, and interpreting into sign-supported Norwegian. Traditionally, the focus has been on interpreting into/from NTS and interpreting and guidance for deafblind people, whereas comparatively less time has been dedicated to interpreting into sign-supported Norwegian and speech-to text interpreting. More recently, there have been indications from employers that the demand for speech-to-text interpreting is rapidly increasing. In addition, employers have stated a need for students to learn video interpreting.

At all three universities, programs include a number of periods of practical training under the guidance of both internal and external supervisors (such as experienced sign language interpreters). The total number of weeks spent on periods of required practical training varies between the programs, from 12 to 14 weeks.

When students start their studies in SLI with no previous knowledge of sign language, the programs are too short for most of them to be skilled interpreters when they graduate. This is another reason Oslo now requires students to have basic sign language skills before entering the program. Students will nevertheless be trained to an "entry-to-practice" level and will have to continue to develop their skills after graduating. There are, however, no organized pathways to secure the desired CPD. It is also not possible for them to specialize in any of the skills they are expected to learn during the program. Therefore, meta-knowledge, ability, and routines for professional reflection and awareness of their position as interpreters are embedded into the training throughout the programs (Erlenkamp et al., 2011).

SLI education in Norway is by and large research based. An increasing number of interpreter educators are now researchers themselves, having completed PhDs in, for example, linguistics, social anthropology, and applied linguistics. Although many educators also publish internationally, the edited volume *Tolking— Språkarbeid og profesjonsutøvelse (Interpreting—Language work and professional practice)* (Haualand et al., 2018), with chapters in both Norwegian and Swedish, was a much-needed update of interpreting research in a Nordic context. The volume is currently read by students in all three programs, thus creating a shared knowledge basis for future interpreters. A corpus and a dictionary for NTS are also under way and are expected to become important resources for the programs.[3]

Certification

There is currently no external certification or accreditation system for sign langauge interpreters in Norway, which means that all testing of sign language interpreters takes place within the respective BA programs. The government authorization for interpreters is not open for asssessment of sign language interpreters yet, and therefore graduating from one of the BA programs is the only means of certification available to sign language interpreters. There are both theoretical and practical exams in the programs, and when a student has passed all exams, they are formally entitled to work as an interpreter. The official title is *Offentlig godkjent tolk for døve, døvblinde og hørselshemmede* (publicly approved interpreter for the deaf, deafblind, and hard of hearing). There is, however, ongoing work to adapt the state authorization test for sign language interpreters, possibly from 2024.

Challenges for Sign Language Interpreter Education

Though the education has gradually improved, with more trainers having attended higher education and an increase in research-based curricula, there are still some challenges. One major challenge is the fact that there are currently no programs training sign language teachers, leading to a severe lack of qualified sign language teachers (Raanes, 2019).[4] With the revision of the program in Oslo in 2022, a sign language didactics strand was introduced, and students may choose between interpreting studies and sign language didactics topics in their second and third years. The sign language didactics strand in Oslo now offers tertiary-level courses about NTS and signed language linguistics directed at students who are already fluent signers. It is also possible to combine parts of the program in Trondheim with studying pedagogy, instead of becoming an interpreter.

Although programs are open to deaf people, they generally receive the same education as hearing students, with some adaptations to the practical training and work requirements. This has made programs less attractive to potential deaf interpreters. It is hoped that the program in Oslo will be more attractive to deaf students because they will not have to spend the first year learning a language and about a culture they already know well.

There is currently no MA program in SLI offered in Norway. As potential student numbers are relatively low, the national regulations for MA programs (requiring groups of a certain size for the program to be considered sustainable) will make it difficult to start a separate MA program in SLI. The Centre for Academic and Professional Communication at NTNU started a master's program in Academic and Professional Communication in the fall of 2019, and several sign language interpreters have registered in the first cohorts. It is hoped that this program will eventually offer specialized modules for such students. Taking a master's degree is costly, however, and as was described previously, there are currently no financial incentives for interpreters to obtain an MA.

The Road Ahead

The labor market related to SLI in Norway is thoroughly regulated, and there are hardly any untrained sign language interpreters working, but there are few incentives or opportunities for sign language interpreters to specialize in any particular field of interpreting or to seek education beyond their BA level. As in the other Nordic countries, there are no formal requirements for CPD (Nilsson, 2018), and further education or specialized qualifications will not lead to higher payment or other benefits from the main employer NAV. Some interpreters voluntarily participate in short training courses or seminars provided by the European Forum of Sign Language Interpreters (efsli) or other interpreter trainers. As NAV currently neither requires nor encourages interpreters to participate in CPD activities, there has been very little focus on developing formal CPD activities, such as courses in institutes of higher education.

Because opportunities to work for other employers are very limited, interpreters with specialized knowledge or qualifications beyond a BA degree in interpreting cannot seek out other employment to get a higher salary, either. Given that hourly wages and work conditions offered to freelance interpreters are currently not competitive, it can be difficult to find interpreters outside of office hours, despite the relatively high number of interpreters compared with the number of deaf people in Norway. With broad, generalist programs and the lack of opportunities to specialize later, it is probably not totally unfounded to say that on a group level, NTS interpreters are "jacks of all trades," with only very few interpreters being masters of any.

For more than a decade, the NDF has expressed its frustration with the absence of deaf community involvement in the public services. They are concerned about the limited access to SLI outside of office hours, the unreliable emergency preparedness, and a cumbersome booking system. In light of an increasing professional and linguistic heterogeneity among deaf people, they also express their concern about the lack of professional development among sign language interpreters.

The interpreters, on their side, have expressed frustration with low salaries (especially for freelance interpreters), lack of opportunities (and incentives) for CPD, and limited possibilities to influence the development and organization of NAV's interpreting services—something that in turn affects the working conditions of interpreters. Although the SLI programs are to a large extent still designed and run by persons who are themselves sign language interpreters, NAV's SLI services are organized under regional centers for assistive technology, none of which are led by a sign language interpreter. Hence, sign language interpreters rely on non-interpreters for the organization of their labor market and on non-interpreters' definitions of what their tasks and institutional responsibilities are.

Combined with the lack of deaf community involvement in the SLI service provision, this lack of professional control over the services means that neither deaf people nor sign language interpreters have much influence over the current system for provision of SLI services. A number of evaluation reports since 2008 (Agenda Kaupang, 2016; Hjort, 2011; Tolkeutredningen, 2008) have suggested reorganizing SLI services for increased cost control, more deaf community involvement, and more CPD and specialization opportunities, but few substantial changes have been implemented, mainly because of cost issues. The now-dismantled professional association of interpreters and the NDF had signed a cooperation agreement (resembling the agreements signed by the World Association of Sign Language Interpreters–World Federation of the Deaf and the European Forum of Sign Language Interpreters–European Union of the Deaf). One of the unions has taken over some of the work previously conducted by the professional association and is currently cooperating with NDF to lobby both the Norwegian Parliament and the Ministry for Labor and Social Affairs to change how services are organized. Partly as a consequence of the critique expressed in evaluation reports, NAV employed two consultants in 2020. They are trained sign language interpreters themselves and will work on management issues related to NAV's services and to improve communication between NAV and both the SLI education programs and the deaf community. It is, however, too early to say what will come out of this.

NOTES

1. Interpreters who work in primary or secondary education are hired by local educational authorities. There are also some workplaces that have hired in-house interpreters, and some interpreters work for the national broadcasting company *Norsk rikskringkasting AS* (NRK; Norwegian Broadcasting Corporation). However, interpreters hired by other institutions generally also take freelance assignments for NAV, so there are probably very few, if any, sign language interpreters who do not work for NAV at all.
2. NAV also hires speech-to-text reporters, some of whom might not have a BA in SLI.
3. More information can be found here: https://www.ntnu.edu/isl/nts-language-ecology
4. This situation is a national problem that affects not only the SLI programs but also deaf children and their families, as their rights to learn NTS are compromised by the lack of qualified teachers.

REFERENCES

Agenda Kaupang. (2016). *Helhetlig gjennomgang av tolkeområdet*. https://www.regjeringen.no/no/dokumenter/helhetlig-gjennomgang-av-tolkeomradet/id2483538/

Duolljá, S.-E. K., & Gaski, H. (2021). Samisk. In *Store norske leksikon*.

Erlenkamp, S., Amundsen, G., Berge, S. S., Grande, T., Mjøen, O. M., & Raanes, E. (2011). Becoming the ears, eyes, voice & hands of someone else. In L. Leeson, S. Wurm, & M. Vermeerbergen (Eds.), *Signed language interpreting: Preparation, practice and performance* (pp. 12–36). Routledge.

Esping-Andersen, G. (1990). *The three worlds of welfare capitalism*. Polity Press.

Haualand, H. (2011). Interpreted ideals and relayed rights—Video interpreting services as objects of politics. *Disability Studies Quarterly*, *31*:4. https://dsq-sds.org/index.php/dsq/article/view/1721

Haualand, H. (2014). Video interpreting services: Calls for inclusion or redialling exclusion? *Ethnos*, *79*, 287–305.

Haualand, H., Nilsson, A.-L., & Raanes, E. (2018). *Tolking: språkarbeid og profesjonsutøvelse.* Gyldendal.

Hjort, P. (2011). *Fornying av Tolketjenesten Del 1: Organisering og fagutvikling, tjenester og lønns- og arbeidsvilkår.* NAV Hjelpemidler og tilrettelegging.

Kultur-og likestillingsdepartementet. (2023). *Tegnspråk for livet : forslag til en helhetlig politikk for norsk tegnspråk, 2023*(20). Ministry of Culture.

Lundström, B. (n.d). *Teckenspråket är grunden i vår profession. En bok om Sveriges Teckenspråk-stolkars Förening.* Sveriges Teckenspråkstolkars Förening.

Molander, A., & Terum, L. I. (2008). *Profesjonsstudier.* Universitetsforlaget.

Nilsson, A.-L. (2018). Continuing Professional Development (CPD) – Continuing to develop your skills. In S. Coster (Ed.), *Proceedings. Nordic Seminar Umeå February 2018. Theory in practice – Practice in theory* (pp. 11–32). Sveriges Teckenspråkstolkars Förening.

Olsen, E. T. (2018). Deaf and refugee—A different situation. *Border Crossing, 8*(1), 237–254. https://bordercrossing.uk/bc/article/view/737

Ozolins, U. (2010). Factors that determine the provision of public service interpreting: comparative perspectives on government motivation and language service implementation. *The Journal of Specialised Translation, 14*, 194–215.

Parsons, T. (1968). Professions. In D. L. Sills (Ed.), *International encyclopedia of the social sciences* (Vol. 12, pp. 536–547). The Free Press.

Pöchhacker, F. (2016). *Introducing interpreting studies* (2nd ed.). Routledge.

Raanes, E. (2019). Tegnspråklæreres bakgrunn, kompetanse og erfaringer med ulike utdanningsprogram. *NOA norsk som andrespråk, 35*(1), 63–92.

Skaaden, H. (2019). Ethics and profession. In M. Phelan, M. Rudvin, H. Skaaden, & P. Kermit (Eds.), *Ethics in public service interpreting* (pp. 147–201). Routledge.

Tolkeutredningen. (2008). *Framtidens tolke- og kommunikasjonstjenester for døve, døvblinde og hørselshemmede.* Arbeids- og velferdsdirektoratet.

Wit, M. de. (2016). *A comprehensive guide to sign language interpreting in Europe.* CreateSpace.

ANNA KOMAROVA, TATIANA DAVIDENKO,
VALERIA VINOGRADOVA, AND BENCIE WOLL

17

Development of Sign Language Interpreters' Professional Training in Russia

As of 2024, Russia is the largest country in the world, nearly twice the size of Canada. Forty percent of the land is located in Europe, and the rest, to the east of the Urals, is in Asia. It occupies 11% of the world's land but has a population of around 146 million people, which places Russia in ninth place among other countries in terms of population size. There are at least 120,000 people in Russia who communicate in Russian Sign Language (RSL). There are approximately 280 different languages with different statuses in the country, and RSL is officially recognized as a separate language that, according to the 2010 census, occupies 38th place among other languages. The Russian Empire (1721–1917) and then the Union of Soviet Socialist Republics (USSR; 1922–1991) existed in an even bigger territory, which took in other countries, including Armenia, Azerbaijan, Belarus, Georgia, Estonia, Kazakhstan, Kyrgyzstan, Latvia, Lithuania, Tajikistan, Turkmenistan, Ukraine, and Uzbekistan. The focus of this chapter is primarily on Russia, but we do give a brief review in relation to the former States of the Soviet Union, and more information about the neighboring countries can be seen in Komorova (2022).

WHO ARE WE?

The late Anna Komarova and Tatiana Davidenko were prominent figures in the field of sign language interpreting (SLI) in Russia. Anna, a hearing heritage signer, grew up surrounded by influential members of the deaf community, including her stepfather, who was the chair of the Moscow City branch of the All-Russian Society of the Deaf (VOG—Vserossiskoye Obshchestvo Glukhikh). She worked at VOG as an assistant to its president and as a Russian > English > RSL interpreter for international issues in the late 1980s and 1990s. Throughout her work as the director of the Galina Zaitseva Center for Deaf Studies and Bilingual Education, she insisted on the provision of sign language teaching by deaf instructors and greater involvement of deaf people in policymaking and education related to sign language teaching and interpreting. Anna was also a member of the board of the Russian Association of Sign Language Interpreters (RASLI) and regional representative for Transcaucasia on the board of the World Association of Sign Language Interpreters (WASLI) from 2005 to 2019 and in the World Federation of the Deaf expert group on deaf education from 2007 to 2015. Anna began working with Tatiana in the 1990s, when both became involved with deaf education and sign language teaching and research.

Tatiana was born deaf into a large deaf family in 1953 in Leningrad (now Saint Petersburg). Members of her family died during the siege of Leningrad in World War II, while others managed to escape on a "deaf boat" (Snoddon, 2014). Tatiana and her mother moved to Moscow in 1958, and both were active members of the Moscow deaf community. Tatiana's mother worked at a factory that employed large numbers of deaf people, while Tatiana first worked at a toy factory and then became an artist working with the oldest deaf theater in the region, the Mimika (Sign Language) and Gesture Theater, which opened in 1963. In 1990, Tatiana started to work with Galina Zaitseva, who had a great influence on Anna and Tatiana's interest in and work on sign language linguistics and deaf education. Tatiana became an essential representative of the deaf community among educators at universities that provide RSL as part of their curricula. She regularly led courses for sign language interpreters.

Anna and Tatiana's work was essential in the creation of the first full-time SLI degree at Moscow State Linguistic University (MSLU). They also participated in the process of preparing and providing assessment and certification of sign language interpreters and served on the committee of the regional Association of Sign Language Interpreters, as well as being members of the review board for sign language interpreters.

Tatiana passed away on June 28, 2020; Anna passed away on October 10, 2022. Their loss has been felt deeply by the deaf community in Russia and by colleagues internationally. Their service to the deaf community is regularly remembered at events and talks dedicated to research on sign language and deafness. This chapter, which both began as coauthors, was unfinished at the time of their deaths; Valeria Vinogradova and Bencie Woll were asked to complete the text, given their familiarity with the history of SLI in Russia and having been Anna and Tatiana's colleagues for many years.

Valeria is a hearing linguist and a cognitive neuroscientist. She is a graduate of the first cohort of students who received a full-time bachelor's degree in SLI in Russia in 2016. Tatiana and Anna were her teachers at the Galina Zaitseva Center for Deaf Studies and Bilingual Education and MSLU.

Bencie Woll is a hearing sign language linguist, and the founder and former director of the Deafness Cognition and Language Research Centre (DCAL) at University College London. She collaborated with both Tatiana and Anna on a number of
projects, including the 1990s sign language teacher training programs in Bristol and
Moscow and research on the acquisition of a second sign language by hearing and
deaf signers.

CONTEXTUALIZATION: TRANSLATION AND INTERPRETING IN RUSSIA

Translation and interpreting (T&I) training (primarily for spoken and written languages) is offered at more than 50 universities in Russia, and more than 300 professional simultaneous interpreters and several thousand consecutive interpreters work
in the country (Matyushin & Buzadzhi, 2021). The first training attempts focused
on translation, with consecutive interpreting introduced at the Translation Department of the Maurice Thorez Institute (now MSLU) in the 1950s (Chernov, 1999).
Currently, T&I often fall under a more general degree in linguistics (for example, at
Moscow State University or MSLU), and the interpreting qualification is specified
in addition in the diplomas and degrees awarded.

SLI degrees offered in Russia are not separated from spoken language interpreting
degrees; rather, they are based on interpreting programs for English/Russian interpreters, with the curriculum modified to add sign languages as a second "foreign"
language, together with other subjects related to sign language, sign language linguistics, and relevant aspects of deaf studies.

PROFESSIONALIZATION OF SLI IN RUSSIA

VOG was established in 1926. The postrevolutionary period was a time of intense
industrialization, and one of the main aims of VOG and other deaf associations in
the USSR was to concentrate the deaf population in big cities and provide basic
training for work in factories and power plants. Most deaf people worked either in
groups in state factories alongside hearing workers or at special factories for deaf
people, owned by VOG, with between 50 and 300 workers. Articles written in the
deaf monthly magazine *The Life of Deaf-Mutes* between 1930 and 1940 demonstrate that issues related to interpreter training and provision were always of high
importance in VOG. Interpreters were much needed in workshops and factories,
in branches of VOG, for evening classes, and in universities, where groups of deaf
students attended from 1931 onward.

Galina Zaitseva (1934–2005) was the first person to introduce the term RSL
in 1991; before that, for more than 20 years, she had studied both theoretically
and experimentally what she called then "conversational sign speech." Galina

was an outstanding personality, originally a teacher of the deaf and a philologist, who conducted many research studies on RSL linguistics and RSL in education. Many deaf people recognize her as "the one who woke us up so we stopped treating our language as jargon or something not valuable" (Komarova & Palenny, 2014).

The British project, or "Bristol" project as it was also known, though modest in scale, was a turning point in the whole movement for sign language recognition and deaf people's rights in Russia. It started with Bencie Woll, Jim Kyle, and Galina Zaitseva (all hearing) and Gloria Pullen (deaf) who collaborated on developing a new approach to RSL teaching. A new curriculum was developed, initially for RSL level 1, and a group of deaf teachers were trained as RSL teachers both in Bristol and in Moscow. In autumn 1991, the first group of hearing people studied RSL with the newly trained deaf teachers, and in 1992, the first four deaf teachers who had been trained in Bristol also trained a new group of RSL deaf teachers/instructors. Of these trainees, only four to five stayed in the profession because of low pay and lack of regular employment. There were only about one or two groups of hearing learners per year, plus annual groups of parents of deaf children, teachers of the deaf from various schools, and short intensive continuing professional training courses for interpreters, organized in collaboration with the Moscow branch of VOG. Interpreters' upskilling courses usually consisted of 18 to 24 hours of instruction and included a short lecture on RSL linguistics, as well as practical classes, generally with the aim of "converting" them from signed Russian to RSL. The success of this program varied from group to group and depended greatly on individual attitudes and skills.

The Center for Deaf Studies and Bilingual Education grew out of the British project. It was established in 1998 and renamed in Zaitseva's honor after her death (the Zaitseva Center for Deaf Studies and Bilingual Education). After finding long-term premises, the center began to offer regular sign language classes. Gradually, teaching was expanded to levels 2 and 3 with 46 to 52 hours of RSL teaching for each level. The center's courses were never directed at the training of interpreters; however, some level 3 graduates started working as interpreters after gaining practical work experience.

The Period After the Collapse of the Soviet Union

With the end of the existence of the Soviet Union, the collapse of the socialist economy put an end to VOG factories and their interpreters. Large state factories substantially reduced the numbers of their workers and were no longer required to provide interpreters. Salaries for staff in local VOG organizations or in educational settings were extremely low. By 1998, the number of sign language interpreters in Russia had decreased from 5,500 to about 520. VOG data published in 2004 identified around 800 interpreters, which included many workers, such as secretaries, accountants, and even those in more senior management positions, who also served as interpreters (Palenny, 2005). The situation was similar in most of the former Soviet countries.

In March 2005, the first conference on SLI was organized as an initiative of VOG Vice President Nikolai Chaushian and the Zaitseva Center. Interpreters from 31 local branches of VOG and from neighboring countries took part in the conference. Signed Russian interpreters who had trained at the Interregional Center for Rehabilitation of Individuals with Hearing Impairments, or the Pavlovsk college for the deaf (previously called, and mostly known as, the Leningrad Rehabilitation Center, LRC), and who are still influential and who continue to criticize and correct the signing of young deaf people, and qualified deaf teachers of RSL (including those from deaf families) also attended the 2005 conference. Their perspective was expressed by one of the longest-serving teachers from LRC at the conference: "We, interpreters, cannot go down to the level of deaf people; we must pull them up to our level." These attitudes were strongly attacked by the deaf conference participants, but outside major cities, many deaf people still express the view that interpreters "are hearing, are trained, and know better" than deaf people, although these interpreters are unable to understand and interpret from RSL into Russian.

Data about interpreters' careers were collected from the Russian delegates at the conference by means of questionnaires. Interpreters' salaries had been gradually improving, as deaf people received a guaranteed annual personal provision of 40 hours of free interpreting, with payment covered by the state. Numbers of interpreters varied widely; although there was an average ratio of 1 interpreter to 149 deaf people, in Moscow the ratio was 1:274; in Pskov, 1:200, and in Krasnodar, 1:288. The number of interpreters who were heritage signers ranged from 20% to 100% across regions. Only 14% of interpreters had university-level training, with 22% having received their associate's degrees, and 31% having attended VOG intensive courses (Antipov, Chaushian, & Komarova, 2005). Shocked by these figures, VOG increased its sponsorship of interpreter training courses in the Russian regions and invited the Zaitseva Center's deaf teachers to run these courses, which were usually delivered by a hearing trainer and two deaf RSL teachers, with student groups split by language level. The hearing and deaf trainers taught together, discussing RSL linguistics topics and offering practical assignments; the hearing teacher checked on the quality of interpreting into spoken Russian. Attitudes to the courses varied from complete rejection to the euphoric "It was an eye-opening experience!"

There is limited availability of more recent figures, and the VOG data include only interpreters working in VOG offices and clubs. The 2018 Russian survey data identified 703 interpreters, of whom 93% were women, 73% were more than 40 years of age, 29% had university-level education, 47% had a college-level education, and 24% had a secondary school education only. Interpreters working in educational settings or as freelancers are not included in these data (Larionov, 2019; Ionichevskaya, 2014).

The RASLI was established in 2010; it started as a small-scale organization in Moscow but now includes 14 regions of Russia, with 135 interpreters, including 24 deaf interpreters (22 qualified to work with deafblind people and two International Sign interpreters with no official qualification). RASLI joined WASLI in 2015, and the European Forum of Sign Language Interpreters (EFSLI) in 2019.

In the early 2000s, the Moscow branch of VOG and the Zaitseva Center initiated accreditation on demand for interpreters in Moscow, with exam commissions having a majority of deaf experts. By 2013, the accreditation process had been formally developed and approved by VOG. Renewed accreditation is obligatory for working interpreters every 5 years. At present, there is an exam in five parts, which can be taken either in the Zaitseva Center or in the RASLI offices: (1) a test on professional ethics; (2) and (3) consecutive interpreting of a short text from Russian into RSL and a written Russian translation of an RSL video text; and (4) and (5) simultaneous interpreting from spoken Russian into RSL and from an RSL video text into spoken Russian (Komarova, Chaushian, & Egorova, 2006).

In 2003–2004, VOG, with strong pressure from the Moscow deaf community, started taking steps toward influencing a change in legislation with regard to sign language, which at that time had the legal status of "a means of interpersonal communication." The resolutions from the 2005 conference and the 2007 international conference on "Linguistic Rights of the Deaf" included urgent recommendations to change sign language legislation and provide official status to RSL. A draft law of 2005 had put RSL on a par with other minority languages of the Russian Federation, but it had never been signed. The amendments to the law were finally signed by the Russian president on December 30, 2012. The new law officially recognized RSL and envisaged a number of positive steps, including professional interpreter training at both the vocational and university levels (Komarova & Palenny, 2014; Komorova, 2022).

Thus, in 2012, RSL was officially recognized. Recognition led to the creation of 4-year interpreter training programs at two universities: MSLU (2012) and Novosibirsk Technological University (2013). Each has an annual intake of hearing students with no prior knowledge of RSL. Four deaf teachers from the Zaitseva Center provide teaching of RSL in Moscow; there is only one deaf teacher in Novosibirsk. These new programs are creating a new generation of interpreters, who are not always accepted by older colleagues or clients. Major changes in attitudes toward RSL have taken place, especially among young urban deaf people, but there is still little understanding of and knowledge about deaf studies and sign language in general in either the deaf or hearing communities.

SIGN LANGUAGE INTERPRETER EDUCATION IN RUSSIA

Principles of SLI in Russia were first discussed in two chapters of Victor Fleury's book *Glukhonemye* (Deaf-mutes), published in 1835 (see Zaitseva & Komarova, 1998; Zaitseva, 2006). He described differences between the grammar of RSL and that of Russian, with one chapter giving a detailed analysis of the interpreting of prayers from Russian to RSL.

There is limited information available about SLI in the small number of publications about deaf people in the second half of the 19th century and the early 20th century. One striking exception is the set of minutes and documents from the first All-Russian Congress of Deaf-Mutes (1917). Discussions and arguments related to interpreting and interpreters were among the most prominent topics of the meeting. At an earlier time, when sign language had been used in deaf education, teachers had served as interpreters, and they had maintained this function even when schools no longer used sign language and teachers were not fluent in RSL. The deaf delegates were angry that teachers from oral schools, who often had no knowledge of sign language, influenced the lives of deaf people through their negative attitudes—for example, in legal settings, with the consequence that courts often found deaf defendants guilty. Teachers received payment for interpreting despite deaf people often being victims of inaccurate interpreting. Hearing children of deaf parents did help but often had limited general knowledge and poor Russian literacy skills. For these and other reasons, the 1917 Congress emphasized that only organizations of the deaf should evaluate interpreters' competence (Komarova, 2001; Palenny, 2005).

The development of RSL/Russian interpreting, interpreter education, and training in Russia is tightly bound up with the dramatic changes in government from the early 20th century onward, specifically the creation of the Soviet Union after the Revolution in 1917 and its collapse in 1991. One of VOG's leaders, Semyon Ivanov, developed a program for interpreter training, initially in Moscow and then throughout Russia. From the early 1930s, the Moscow branch of VOG organized 2-month training courses for interpreters, initially for those from Moscow and later for those from other towns of central Russia. The courses comprised 200 hours of "Mimika" (the term used at that time for sign language), 40 hours of "political literacy," and 40 hours of organizational work.

Both deaf leaders and interpreters regularly raised concerns about long working hours and pressure on interpreters working alone. Courses to improve literacy among deaf people were widespread from 1929 onward, and interpreters worked 6- to 7-hour days on these courses with limited breaks; both deaf people and interpreters reported exhaustion and an inability to perform their other duties. It is worth mentioning that the first group of deaf students with a full-time interpreter was admitted to the chemistry faculty of Moscow State University in 1932, with a second group starting 2 years later at the Moscow State Technological School (now University), where there have been regular groups of deaf students ever since.

Ivanov's training program manual was published in 1951; during his career, he trained more than 800 interpreters (Komarova, 2001; Komarova & Pursglove, 2003). The manual represents a mixture of modern ideas and misunderstandings about sign language. On the one hand, he wrote that "if you transfer the meaning of the word or the phrase but do not use face mimika [RSL], you have done only half of the task . . . not only the hands but also the face and, partially, the body, should move." On the other hand, he stated, "there is no grammar in mimika [RSL]," and "there are many thousands of words in Russian, but we can interpret only two or three thousand into signing and the gaps should be filled by fingerspelling" (Palenny, 2005). He did note, however, that it is not possible to become a professional interpreter with just 2 months of training, that much contact with the deaf community is needed, and that it is harder to understand deaf people than to produce signing.

The situation with regard to SLI training changed in the 1950s. The curriculum developed by Semyon Ivanov began to be considered as teaching "ungrammatical" signing (i.e., RSL rather than signed Russian) and was replaced by longer courses run by hearing interpreters, with the main goal of teaching signed Russian. The main ideologist of this new approach was Joseph Geilman, later one of the authors of Gestuno[1] (World Federation of the Deaf, 1975). Geilman, a hearing son of well-educated deaf parents, was born in Leningrad (now Saint Petersburg), and from a very young age he began to interpret for his parents and their friends. His parents died in the famine during the siege of Leningrad in World War II. In their memory, he decided to work for the deaf organization and soon became a recognized authority in signing and interpreting. In 1957, he published an article titled "The Interpreter and the Culture of Interpreting" in which he severely criticized Semyon Ivanov's courses and proposed a new approach to interpreter training. His program included economics, the organization of socialist competition, legislation, labor safety in relation to deaf people and interpreters, and pedagogy. He also discussed adding new signs to the lexicon and the standardization of signs: "It would help to unify the 'mimika' of deaf-mutes throughout the Soviet Union" (Palenny, 2005). In the same year, he also published the first RSL dictionary, which included photographs; in the 1970s, he expanded this dictionary into four volumes with 1,660 signs (Geilman, 1975). In 1960, Geilman's program to teach signing to beginners was approved. It comprised 368 teaching hours, including 288 hours for teaching signs and fingerspelling. His views differed radically from those espoused by VOG:

> The main task is to improve "mimika" by making it closer and closer to the spoken language . . . . signing does not help the development of abstract thinking in deaf people, does not provide development of their personalities . . . . The expressive possibilities of sign language compared to spoken language are very limited, and the sign cannot convey the intense meaning and subtleties of the word . . . . Sign vocabulary should be expanded

by creating new signs . . . . Interpreting should be accompanied by articulation of spoken words and the order of words in spoken Russian should be maintained. (Palenny, 2005)

Geilman believed that through this approach, the level of literacy among deaf people would improve.

In 1965, under his initiative, a special college for deaf students, the LVC, was opened in Pavlovsk, the site of the first school for deaf children that had been established in 1806. The college trained accountants, club workers, artists, and sculptors and attracted deaf students from all parts of the Soviet Union. In 1976, LRC opened an interpreting faculty that offered full-time 3-year courses, as well as various intensive courses for applicants from all parts of the USSR (Palenny, 2005). This program trained interpreters of signed Russian and perpetuated an attitude of superiority over what was considered to be the "illiterate signing" of deaf people. This training program is still functioning under the title, "Organization for Surdocommunication" [Deaf communication] at the LRC. It is mainly a distance learning course, with signed Russian taught by hearing interpreters. There are other college courses with the same title in Moscow (College for Preparation of Social Workers), Saint Petersburg (National Open Institute), Siberia (e.g., Tyumen College of Industrial and Social Technologies), and other regions (e.g., Chelyabinsk Socio-Professional College, Tambov Pedagogical College). The courses typically offer approximately 2 years of distance learning studies. Similar in-person programs are offered from time to time at the LRC, the Russian State Social University (Moscow), and Kazan Federal University. All of these programs usually focus on the learning of individual signs, with training in consecutive and simultaneous interpreting of Russian-language texts into signed Russian. Other subjects, such as deaf special education, deaf psychology, legislation, and social services, are also included. Such approaches to interpreter training reinforce paternalistic attitudes toward deaf people, their culture, and their language, and they diminish the status of the national sign language.

In addition to the emphasis on signed Russian, the period from the 1930s to the collapse of the Soviet Union was also marked by an act taken by VOG, and its consequences are still felt in everyday life in Russia. In 1932, the VOG chairman, Pavel Saveliev, wrote in the federation magazine about those interpreters who had higher levels of education or more work experience in the deaf organization:

> there exists the wrong and unacceptable practice of keeping interpreters just for interpreting without providing them with any other occupation, without giving them other responsible missions . . . . We do not follow Comrade Stalin's guidelines to provide career growth within the collective group . . . . We must provide interpreters with better working conditions, and, wherever possible, not misuse their service as interpreters. We must eliminate the position of interpreter and combine these functions with other technical or important duties, depending on abilities, in the VOG section, club or factory. (Palenny, 2005)

This position, that interpreters should not just interpret but should have leading roles in the deaf community, still affects work and the relationship between deaf people and interpreters; even a few years ago, interpreters still occupied top positions in local deaf organization branches and dominated deaf individuals and groups in factories, educational settings, and local deaf clubs.

The Chicken or the Egg? The Role of RSL Teachers in Interpreter Training

All discussions about RSL teaching and interpreter training have encountered the question of who should teach. For some time, this was an ongoing problem—how to start change without a sufficient cohort of RSL teachers, given that only two experienced deaf RSL teachers continued teaching throughout the 1990s.

In 2000, renewed interest among Moscow-based deaf people triggered the opening of RSL teacher training programs at the Zaitseva Center. The program included lectures and workshops on RSL linguistics and teaching, but only small numbers were trained. In 2013, the Moscow branch of VOG set up similar courses under their own auspices in the Zaitseva Center. Selection of candidates for the course was very strict; ultimately, 16 people (15 from Moscow and one from Nizhni Novgorod) were accepted into the course, mostly deaf people from deaf families. These courses emphasized applied RSL linguistics and practical teaching (Davidenko & Komarova, 2006), and most of those who completed the course became, and continue to be, RSL teachers. There has continued to be a pipeline of deaf RSL teachers trained at the Zaitseva Center, with, for example, 10 deaf teachers of RSL qualified in 2019, but most of these are based in Moscow. However, as neither the Moscow VOG nor the Zaitseva Center is an officially recognized educational institution, graduates' certificates have not been recognized everywhere (Komarova & Palenny, 2014).

One interesting project stands out from other attempts to develop successful interpreter training programs. It was initiated by the Finnish University of Applied Sciences in Kuopio and the Karelian State Pedagogical University in Russia, with the Zaitseva Center as a partner organization. Sixteen students from the Department of Special Education and Psychology in Petrozavodsk, in addition to being trained as teachers in special education, were offered an additional program to train as RSL interpreters. Even with the expertise of deaf and hearing specialists from Finland and the experience of the Zaitseva Center teachers, there was doubt that this program would be successful. The skeptical attitude was based on the lack of RSL teachers in Karelia, which is about 1,000 km northwest of Moscow, and the limited numbers of deaf people with whom the students could interact. However, enthusiasm and the impressive diligence of the students, together with the joint efforts of the team members from Moscow and Kuopio, had impressive outcomes. Students had lectures and classes given by Finnish trainers, 1 week of experience in Finland, and eight intensive 1-week courses delivered by the team from Moscow. Between sessions, the students practiced signing with mirrors and video cameras and through interaction with local hearing heritage signers and deaf children and adults. Follow-up data indicated that half of the group had retained very good signing skills, and two were working as interpreters part time (there were limited employment opportunities for interpreters in Karelia) (Komarova & Palenny, 2014).

The most recent development in this field has been a 1-year RSL teacher training program that was successfully delivered in 2018–2019 by MSLU. The group comprised 10 students (all female, eight deaf and two hard of hearing, eight from deaf families and two from hearing families) who either had already obtained bachelor's degrees or had completed at least 3 years of a bachelor's program. One of the original aims of the program was to provide qualified RSL teachers for other parts of Russia, where there are substantial teacher shortages. However, this aim was not achieved: One student from Kazakhstan returned to Almaty but had serious difficulties in getting a job; one teacher returned to her hometown of Tula; while students from Ivanovo and Krasnodar preferred to remain in Moscow after the training.

The program consisted of five 32-hour modules (Russian language, linguistics, educational psychology, methodology, deaf history) and 224 hours of practical teaching skills: RSL, applied RSL linguistics, and methods and principles of L1 and L2 teaching, delivered by the first two authors of this chapter. At the end of the course, the students were required to give a minimum of three RSL lessons themselves to obtain their qualification. At the time of writing, there are 10 qualified RSL teachers who hold state university diplomas.

Programs to Train Special Education Teachers/Interpreters

In 2001, the Moscow State City Pedagogical University decided to include RSL as a language in their training of teachers of special education. The courses included one RSL lesson per week throughout all 5 years of study, with a state final exam in RSL. The University declared that course graduates would receive diplomas in two professions: teacher of the deaf and sign language interpreter. However, the first two authors of the present chapter insisted that the students should not receive an interpreter qualification because the dominance of the pedagogical content, insufficient hours of instruction in RSL, and lack of other important curriculum content would fail to ensure good interpreting skills. Although not successful in its aim of producing teachers who were also qualified as interpreters, this course offered an interesting and useful experience, as three groups of future teachers of the deaf became relatively fluent in RSL, had the opportunity to study deaf culture and deaf history, and became well qualified for work in a bilingual setting (Komarova, 2006).

Linguistics-Based Education for RSL Interpreting

In 2009, the Moscow State Pedagogical University invited the first two authors of this chapter to teach a 1-year interpreter training program as a higher education qualification. Applicants could have any university degree and some interpreting experience. Two groups of interpreters completed this program in 2010 and 2011, but the results were not satisfactory. There were insufficient hours allocated to enable coverage of RSL linguistics, theory of interpreting, and deaf history and culture. The students' levels of RSL and motivation varied widely; although some were fully invested in the program, others were just interested in obtaining a university diploma.

The year 2012 marked a new era of interpreter training, as MSLU recruited a group of 11 students (all female, 10 of whom had no knowledge of RSL) to an undergraduate interpreter training program. The program has continued since 2012, with an annual intake, and in 2017, a master's degree program was added.

There are no preliminary interviews with applicants. However, general communication skills are reviewed before formal acceptance into the program. Applicants must demonstrate a good level of English as a second language, plus good results on high school graduation exams. RSL is taught like any other second language (French, German, or Spanish). In the bachelor's program, students are introduced to RSL in the second term, and then they have 8 or 10 hours of practical RSL per week. Most of the RSL hours are taught by six deaf teachers; one hearing teacher teaches applied RSL linguistics and interpreting into Russian, and students also receive instruction in sign-supported Russian from a second hearing teacher. It is hoped that signed Russian might be offered in the future as a standalone module during the final year of studies or in the master's program, as its current inclusion in the RSL interpreting program is confusing to students. Two deaf teachers give lectures on interpreting and the deaf community, including some content related to deaf history. During Years 3 and 4, students have work experience, including observation and active practice, but this part of the program is not well organized, and in the opinion of the authors of the present chapter, should extend over more hours. The first group of students was fortunate to have the opportunity to experience two attachments of several weeks each at DCAL in University College London; a second group had the opportunity to work as volunteers at the Deaf Olympics in Khanty-Mansijsk (Russia) (Komarova & Palenny, 2014). The students have had a variety of different experiences to support their learning—for example, attendance at efsli conferences and workshops, "deaf weeks," deaf theater, museum visits, and other excursions involving RSL, either interpreted or guided by deaf people. Of the groups, each consisting of 40 graduates, about half work with RSL, and most of those who have become interpreters hold other jobs, as well. For example, one graduate is involved with teaching/researching linguistics, while others work as interpreters between Russian and English, while others are English teachers or work in theaters, museums, or sports activities. Ten of the BA students have since completed or are currently studying in the MA program.

The creation of the interpreter training program at MSLU was followed in 2013 by the establishment of a second program at the Novosibirsk State Technological University (NSTU), in the Faculty of Humanities Education. This program is also designed for students with English as their first foreign language and RSL as their second foreign language. The situation in Siberia is slightly different from that in Moscow, as NSTU has many deaf students in different faculties, in associate's degree and BA programs (180 deaf students in 2024). There is also the Laboratory of Russian Sign Language (established in 1995), the original aim of which was to provide interpreting services to the deaf students. After receiving brief intensive training in the summer of 2011 at the Zaitseva Center, the laboratory set up RSL courses for any interested students at levels 1 and 2. The laboratory's two deaf and three hearing teachers/interpreters also provide training to potential RSL interpreters who can either join the associate's degree program (3 years after high school graduation; as of 2024, the program lasts 4 years for those who have finished only 9 years of school education) or the university's 4-year BA program. The groups of students in Novosibirsk are much larger than those in Moscow: In 2020, 19 students were enrolled in the associate's degree program (as of 2024, 31 students in total across the first 3 years of the 4-year program) and 149 in the BA program (as of 2024, 83 students across the 4 years of the program); out of 172 graduates to date (60 in 2019, 30 in 2020, 25 in 2021, 30 in 2022, 27 in 2023), approximately 20% work with sign language in Russia and Kazakhstan. Deaf and hearing students work together on many projects; they also live together in the halls of residence. An opportunity to meet and interact with deaf students at the university campus on a daily basis is one very positive feature for the Novosibirsk RSL interpreting students.

In addition to the two existing university training programs, the official recognition of RSL in 2012 has led a number of universities and other educational organizations to consider offering initial training or further professional developments, but they have had little success in establishing these to date.

Russia's Neighbors: Former Member Countries of the USSR

The following section gives a brief overview of training and provision in the former member countries of the Soviet Union. As mentioned previously, deaf organizations were established in the 15 Soviet countries that were part of the USSR (for example, Lithuania, Latvia, Uzbekistan, Georgia, Armenia, Belarus) between 1920 and 1940. Apart from Ukraine, there had been no interpreter training in any of those countries.

In Ukraine in 1975, courses affiliated with the Ukrainian Deaf Organization (UTOG) were established, and between that date and 1993, nearly 600 interpreters received initial training and continuing education. Heritage signers and hearing individuals who worked in deaf clubs in these countries and had sign language skills were sent for training to the Leningrad Rehabilitation Center, to VOG in Moscow, or to UTOG intensive training courses in Kiev. Those who received training in Russia and Ukraine often returned to their native countries as indisputable authorities on SLI.

The collapse of the Soviet Union in 1991 resulted in economic instability, and the number of interpreters decreased dramatically in all 15 countries. In 2000 to 2008, the Finnish Association of the Deaf (FAD), with the Zaitseva Center as a partner, ran a development project in the countries of the former Soviet Union, including workshops for interpreter training. The FAD project provided a better understanding of the situation in each country. Although it is impossible within the scope of this chapter to write about each country in detail, Komarova (2019, 2022) provides information about nine of these countries, which later joined WASLI as a single region (Armenia, Azerbaijan, Belarus, Georgia, Kyrgyzstan, Russia, Tajikistan, Ukraine, and Uzbekistan), plus three other countries, which became representatives in the WASLI regions of Transcaucasia, Central Asia, and the Caucasus. It is important to note that from a political point of view, the term *national sign language* (e.g., Armenian Sign Language, Kyrgyz Sign Language) is used, but whereas the spoken/written languages in these countries belong to different language families, with different cultures and religions, there is just one sign language (RSL) with regional dialects, because of the history of deaf education and deaf culture within the Soviet Union (Komarova, 2019, 2022), where the Soviet past is a common experience for all (Davidenko & Komarova, 2014).

Between 2000 and 2008, short training workshops (1–6 days in length) were run in various locations in Finland and Russia for representatives from one or more of these countries. Participants included interpreters and deaf participants, with training provided by both Russian and international interpreter trainers.

At the time of that project, the provision of interpreters varied enormously across the countries involved. Some countries (Tajikistan, Kyrgyzstan) had fewer than five interpreters; others had no official interpreting provision because of lack of funding to pay interpreters (Armenia, Uzbekistan); in other countries, those providing interpreting had very limited signing skills. Since then, there have been further changes. Some countries have, with an emphasis on their regional RSL dialect, organized their own interpreter training—provided, for example, by Japanese and South Korean trainers in Uzbekistan and Kyrgyzstan, by French and American trainers in Armenia and Moldova, and by Norwegians and Americans in Georgia. Georgia stands in contrast to these other countries: As a result of legislation and the provision of regular payments to interpreters, the number of interpreters in Georgia increased from 5 in 2005 to 35 in 2016. Almost all of the interpreters in Georgia are heritage signers and are employed in schools and colleges (including mainstream educational settings for deaf learners), emergency call centers, or the national television network.

The situation in the Baltic countries is somewhat different, as Lithuanian (1995), Latvian (2000), and Estonian (2007) Sign Languages are officially recognized. The University of Tartu (Estonia) provides a 3-year interpreter training program, and a similar course has been offered by the Linguistics College in Vilnius (Lithuania) since 2001. Most sign language interpreters in Lithuania have college or university education, with around 90 interpreters serving 3,400 deaf people.

Interpreter training and provision in Belarus and Ukraine differ from the other countries. In Belarus, the national deaf organization is responsible for both interpreter services and training. Month-long courses are provided by the Ministry of Social Welfare. In 2008, the Belarussian State Pedagogical University started initial training and further professional development for interpreters. Four groups of 80 people have received diplomas as sign language teachers/interpreters, including one deaf person. Around 70 of these work as interpreters for the 9,000 deaf Belarussians. In addition to working in factories and branches of the deaf organizations, interpreters also work in 24/7 interpreter call centers in Minsk, Gomel, Grodno, and Brest.

In Ukraine, the sign language was officially recognized in legislation in 2011. The SLI Council is linked to UTOG, and in 2019, it became a WASLI member organization. UTOG runs interpreter training courses and, from 2007, has been training interpreters in Ukrainian Sign Language (USL) rather than signed Ukrainian. The courses are 2 months long, and in addition to language teaching, they include topics related to deaf people, the deaf community, and deaf organizations. Deaf teachers are employed on the courses, as well as heritage signers. All are accredited by the Ukraine Accreditation Commission. The most recent data (Deafsign, n.d.) report 324 interpreters, including 40 working in factories, serving 40,000 deaf people in the country; there is also regular interpreting on national television (Trikin, n.d.).

The Road Ahead

The Ministry of Health and Social Development in 2011 calculated an estimated shortage of 7,600 interpreters. In March of that year, the government doubled the number of free hours of interpreting to 84 hours per year. Although the various training programs have increased the number of interpreters, as of 2021, 70% of interpreters were children of deaf adults, and VOG estimated that 4,000 more sign language interpreters were still needed in the country (Korinenko, 2021). At the time of writing of this chapter, university degrees in SLI are provided only by MSLU, NSTU (Novosibirsk State Technical University), and Kazan Federal University (which accepted its first cohort of students in 2022). In Moscow, interpreters have other opportunities for skills development, such as attending free practical workshops on interpreting from RSL into Russian at the GES-2 House of Culture, an art space that hosts regular events in RSL. The situation in major cities, such as Moscow, Saint Petersburg, and Novosibirsk, is markedly different from that in the rest of Russia. In Tatarstan, for example, there are 35 sign language interpreters (mostly hearing heritage signers) for the 4,000 members of the deaf community.

With a more or less adequate pipeline of good-quality training for interpreters in the larger population centers, the major challenges are in the provinces: to change attitudes about RSL vis-a-vis signed Russian in both the hearing and deaf communities and to create appropriate training programs. In recent years, there has been substantial growth in the number of researchers working on the linguistics of RSL, but this has yet to translate into applied outcomes in relation to interpreter training. With the passing of Anna Komarova and Tatiana Davidenko, Russia lost two of the most important innovators and leaders in sign language interpreter and translator training.

NOTE

1. Gestuno was a vocabulary of signs designed to be used for international communication at WFD events.

REFERENCES

Antipov, V., Chaushian, N., & Komarova, A. (Eds.) (2005). *Mezhdunarodnaia konferentsiia perevodchikov zhestovogo yazyka* [Proceedings of the international conference of sign language interpreters]. VOG.

Chernov, G. V. (1999). Simultaneous interpretation in Russia: Development of research and training. *Interpreting, 4*(1), 41–54.

Davidenko, T., & Komarova, A. (2006). Kratkii ocherk po lingvistike russkovo zhestovovo yazyka [A brief essay on the linguistics of Russian Sign Language]. In *Sovremennye aspekty zhestovogo yazyka* [Modern Aspects of Sign Language]. VOG.

Davidenko, T., &, Komarova, A. (2014). *Berech' raznobrazie* [Keep diversity]. In *Za zhestovyi yazyk!* [For Sign Language!]. VOG.

Deafsign. (n.d.). *Perevodchiki zhestovo yazika v Evrope: sukhie tzifri – neozhdaniye fakti* [Sign language interpreters in Europe: Numbers and unexpected facts] http://deafsign.ulcraft.com/news/zagholovok_stat_i012345678

Fleury, V. (1835). *Glukhonemye* [Deaf-mutes]. Pluchart's Publishing House.

Geilman, J. (1975). *Specificheskie sredstva obshchenija gluxix. Daktilologija i mimika.* [Specific means of communication for the deaf: Fingerspelling and signs]. VOG.

Komarova, A. (Ed.). (1998) *Deaf children and bilingual education.* Zagrei.

Komarova, A. (2001). *Nekotorye fakty iz istorii russkogo zhestovogo yazyka* [Some facts from the history of Russian Sign Language]. Zagrei.

Komarova, A. (2006) *Programmy spetsializatsii zhestovyi yazyk* [New curricula for specialization in sign language] (14 programs).

Komarova, A. (2018) *Sign language interpreting: Underwater hazards* (A report to EFSLI at the international conference on sign language interpreting). https://efsli.org/efsliblu/wp-content/uploads/2018/10/Conf-in-Moscow-AK.pdf

Komarova, A. (2019). *Transcaucasia* (A summary report to WASLI).

Komarova, A. (2022). Sign language interpreting in Russia and its neighbouring countries in the EECAC. In C. Stone, C., R. Adam, R. M. de Quadros & C. Rathmann (Eds.), *The Routledge handbook of sign language translation and interpreting* (pp. 536–551). Routledge.

Komarova, A., & Palenny, V. (Eds.) (2014). *Za zhestovyi yazyk!* [For sign language!].

Komarova, A., & Pursglove, M. (2003). The changing world of the Russian deaf community. In L. Monaghan, C. Schmaling, K. Nakamura & G. H. Turner, G. (Eds.), *Many ways to be Deaf: International variation in deaf communities* (pp. 249–259). Gallaudet University Press.

Komarova, A., Chaushian, N., & Egorova, I. (2006). *Materials for accreditation of sign language interpreters.* VOG.

Korinenko, E. (2021). *Pochemu v Rossii ne khvatayem sudoperevodchikov i shto s etim delat'.* [Why there are not enough sign language interpreters in Russia and what to do about it]. https://iz.ru/1231494/ekaterina-korinenko/v-tri-goda-ia-osoznala-chto-radi-roditelei-nado-vyuchit-zhestovyi-iazyk.

Larionov, M. (2019). I vnov' o perevodchikakh [And again about interpreters]. *VES (V edinom stroju,* 7 [United we stand]).

Matyushin, I., & Buzadzhi, D. (2021). Conference interpreting in Russia. In M. Albl-Mikasa & E. Tiseliu (Eds.) *The Routledge handbook of conference interpreting* (pp. 140–149). Routledge.

Palenny, V. (2005) Istoriia podgotovki perevodchikov v Rossii [History of interpreter training in Russia]. In O. Antipov (Ed.), *Mezhdunarodnaia konferentsiia perevodchikov zhestovogo yazyka* [Proceedings of the international conference of sign language interpreters] (pp. 36–56). Avtorskie prava.

Snoddon, K. (2014). *Telling deaf lives: Agents of change.* Gallaudet University Press.

Trikin O. (n.d). *Stan perekladatskoi diyalnosti v Ukraini* [Become a translator in Ukraine].

World Federation of the Deaf. (1975). *Gestuno: International sign language of the deaf. The revised and enlarged book of signs agreed and adopted by the Unification of Signs Commission of the World Federation of the Deaf. Carlise:* British Deaf Association [for] the World Federation of the Deaf.

Ionichevskaya, L. (2014). Zakon i problemy perevodcheskikh uslug [Law and problems of translation services]. In *Za zhestovyi yazyk!* [For sign language!].

Zaitseva, G. (1991). *Daktilologija i zhestovaya rech* [Fingerspelling and sign language]. Prosveshcheniye.

Zaitseva, G., & Komarova, A. (1998). *Deaf people and sign language in the book "Deaf-mutes" by V. I. Fleury.* Zagrei.

Zaitseva, G. (2006). *Zhest i slovo: Nauchnye i metodicheskie stat'i* [Sign and word: Scientific and methodological articles].

Zaitseva, G., Braudo, T., & Komarova, A. (1998). The beginnings of bilingual education for deaf children in Russia. *Deafness and Education, 22*(2), 1–34.

Zavaritskii, D. (2019). *Victor Ivanovich Fleury.* Polytech-Press.

NATASHA PARKINS-MALIKO AND
RAZAQ FAKIR

18

Interpreting Andragogy Through Blended Teaching and Learning

The South African Context

This chapter sets out to document the historical training practice of South African Sign Language (SASL) interpreters and current trends. It further aims to posit a reformed approach to the pedagogical practice of interpreter training, testing, and accreditation. The unique characteristics of the plurilingual linguistic repertoires of language practitioners (interpreters) are acknowledged, both in epistemic and ontological approaches to knowledge creation in interpreting studies and practice. This chapter focuses on a profound awareness of language self-representation as it relates to deaf interpreters (DIs). It frames the benefits of "mother tongue" and cultural identity as it relates to language practice training. Further to this, Ubuntu translanguaging realities within linguistic superdiversity, as presented in South African communities, are explored to inform and frame a responsive, domesticated language practice curriculum for the training of deaf and hearing SASL interpreters.

WHO ARE WE?

Natasha Parkins-Maliko, hearing, is a lecturer at the University of the Witwatersrand (WITS), Johannesburg, and heads the Interpreting Department in the School of Languages, Literature, and Media. She holds a master of arts (MA) in linguistics (University of the Free State), a European Master in Sign Language Interpreting (EUMASLI; Humak University, Finland), and a doctor of philosophy (PhD) degree in translation and interpreting (WITS).

Natasha's research interest is in the scholarship of teaching and learning (SOTL), toward realignment of the translation and interpreting (T&I) studies curriculum in

higher education. She is also a sign language interpreting (SLI) practitioner, specializing in communication access for deaf and deafblind persons in a variety of
settings, mostly educational, conference, and media. She has 22 years of interpreting
experience, and her expertise focuses on three strands, namely: T&I and professional development through research.

Razaq Fakir, deaf, is a DI and translator. His experience encompasses project
management and coordination, language teaching, research, and development.
He holds a bachelor's degree from the University of Malawi, a BA with honors
in SASL linguistics from WITS, and an interpreting certificate from the WITS
Language School. His professional interest is grounded in deaf interpreting,
linguistics, translation, and language practice. Razaq actively pursues excellence
in interpreting and translation through advocacy for equitable access to information for deaf people.

The South African Context

To appreciate the position of language practitioners in South Africa, it is imperative
to understand the language policy environment and how this dynamically impacts
the academic credentialing of SASL interpreters. Sign language is mentioned in
four South African laws, namely the South African Constitution, the Use of Official
Languages Act, the South African Schools Act, and the Pan South African Language
Board (PANSALB) Act.

The 1996 South African Constitution contains specific provisions that refer to
the protection of languages and rights relating to language. The most important of
these is Section 6, which recognizes only 11 languages as official languages: isiNde-
bele, Northern Sotho, Sesotho, Siswati, XiTsonga, Setswana, Tshivenda, isiXhosa,
isiZulu, Afrikaans, and English. Other nonofficial spoken languages in South Africa
include, but are not limited to, Khoekhoegowab, !Orakobab, Xirikobab, Nǀuuki,
Phuthi, Hlubi, Bhaca, Lala, Nhlangwini, Nrebele, Mpondro, !Xunthali, Khwedam,
KheLobedu, SePulana, HiPai, SeKutswe, SeṮokwa, Thonga, LaNgomane,
SheKgalagari, and XiRonga. Various stakeholders, including deaf organizations,
interpreters, and allies, lobbied for the official status of SASL, which culminated
in the recognition of SASL as the 12th official language in May 2023 by the
South African National Parliament.

The PANSALB is an organization in South Africa established through Act 59 of
1995 to promote multilingualism, develop the official languages, and protect language rights in South Africa. This organization focuses, among other things, on the
status of language planning, T&I, and language rights and mediation. PANSALB
promoted the SASL Charter to be approved in terms of Section 234 of the Constitution, Act 108 of 1996.

Pledge 8 of the charter refers specifically to SASL interpreting and interpreters in Sections 3.6, 3.7, 3.10, and 3.14:

- 3.6. A national interpreting resource center must be established to assist in the training, regulation, monitoring, and maintenance of databases of accredited, qualified, and experienced professional SASL interpreters.
- 3.7. SASL trainers and interpreters must be accredited and be in possession of qualifications that are accredited by the South African Qualifications Authority (SAQA).
- 3.10. SASL interpreters should undergo refresher training for a week every 6 months.
- 3.14. Higher education institutions (HEIs), technical colleges, and other skill development centers must provide SASL interpreting services for deaf students, trainers, apprentices, etc.

One of the aims of the Use of Official Languages Act 12 (2012) is to regulate and monitor official languages and to require the adoption of a language policy by a national department, national public entity, and national public enterprise. In this regard, in the 2020 State of the Nation address, the South African president stated:

> Following the recognition by the Department of Basic Education (DoBE) in 2018 of SASL as a home language and the recommendation by the Parliamentary Constitutional Review Committee (PCRV) that it be the 12th official language, we are now poised to finalize the matter. (State of the Nation, 2020)

South Africa became a state party to the United Nations Convention on the Rights of Persons With Disabilities (UNCRPD) on November 30, 2007. As noted by the parliamentary monitoring group during a consultative meeting (February 28, 2011), the University of the Western Cape Centre for Disability Law and Policy briefed the Committee on South Africa's compliance with the UNCRPD. It is documented that since its ratification in 2007, "South Africa had not adequately incorporated the Convention into its own legal framework, which weakened the effect of the Convention in South Africa."

Article 9.2 (e) of the UNCRPD states that state parties shall take appropriate measures "to provide forms of live assistance and intermediaries, including guides, readers, and professional sign language interpreters, to facilitate accessibility to buildings and other facilities open to the public."

To support the views on professionalization of sign language interpreters (Stone, 2013), it is imperative that stakeholders ensure that progressive policies and practice are maintained with regard to the training and services of SASL interpreters. In addition to this policy environment, according to the South African Census (2011), 0.5% of the population use SASL. This percentage reflects and confirms the linguistic minority status of SASL.

Despite South Africa's approval of the UNCRPD, the conditions for language access and language practice have yet to be operationalized. Public service access for deaf citizens has not seen a major change for the better of the citizenry.

Given the lack of enforcement of the South African Language Practitioners' Council (SALPC) Act, it is clear that SASL interpreters work with a minority language that was recently declared an official language. Despite the official status of SASL, interpreters do not have equal professional status with practitioners who work with languages that have had official status since 1994. Despite this disempowered status, there are legally binding instruments to advocate for professional SLI services, where a "professional" is understood to be an adequately trained, educated, and certified practitioner holding the relevant qualifications, experience, and accreditation to operate as an interpreter.

Contextualization: Translation and Interpreting in South Africa

Interpreting as a language practice profession is widely practiced in South Africa, with freelance practitioners, various agencies, and deaf organizations providing interpreting services. This scenario dictates the development of ontological knowledge related to SLI practice.

In 2014, the South African Parliament passed the SALPC Act (Act No. 8, 2014), which is aimed at regulating the language practitioner industry through the SALPC, which acts as an advisory body to the Minister of Arts and Culture on issues affecting the language profession. The regulation of language practitioners aims to set the bar for the quality and professionalization of language practitioners; thus, it is regrettable that to date (since 2014), the SALPC has not been operationalized.

Within this legislated language practice environment, HEIs seek to provide language practice graduates with professional degrees, credited through the Council of Higher Education and in line with the SAQA National Qualifications Framework (NQF). Qualifications are offered nationally through technical and vocational education and training colleges and universities, pitched at levels 5 to 10. The NQF is aimed at the alignment of certificates, diplomas, and degrees on the various levels.

The professionalization of translators and interpreters in South Africa leans strongly on licensing through accreditation by the South African Translators' Institute (SATI). SATI, founded in 1956, is the largest language practitioner association in South Africa, with a membership of 800, representing professional, academic, and amateur translators, interpreters, editors, proofreaders, text reviewers, terminologists, copywriters, and others involved in the language practice profession. With the hiatus in operationalizing the SALPC, SATI accredits hearing SASL interpreters in simultaneous interpreting in SASL and their spoken language combination.

Providing guidance on certification of interpreting skills on the basis of test administration is done by educational institutions and professional organizations, but the validity and reliability of testing remain underexplored in the South African context (Waddington, 2004). Pragmatic validity and normative testing are issues that should be reviewed with a lens of equitable assessment practice in the context of a translanguaging environment (Parkins-Maliko, 2015).[1] Strides are being made within higher education, where language practice studies are offered to design equitable assessment tools and procedures in advancing fair testing (including for SASL interpreters) to ensure that "a reliable assessment instrument is one that gives the same result for people of similar skill levels regardless of who administers the test, who rates the test, when the test is given or what version of the test is applied" (Roat, 2006, p. 9). Despite the slow pace of development of the epistemology of SASL, it is evident that SASL as a language practice profession is flourishing. SASL interpreters continue to deliver interpreting services, with only a handful accessing higher education to obtain professional qualifications.

Professionalization of SLI in South Africa

Napier (2004) emphasizes the importance of discussion, reviewing the past and present situations of interpreter training to make it possible to place the development of the SLI profession within a historical context and to make predictions for the future of the profession. The philippic colonial education system of apartheid South Africa is reflected in the training and education of language practitioners. In working toward nation-building and reconciliation, the transformative government legislated various legal instruments aimed at the restoration of the linguistic and cultural pride of its people. The operationalization of this restoration is through shrewd education and training, domesticated in a linguistically and culturally diverse South Africa. In addressing the epistemic foundations of interpreting studies, we acknowledge the contribution made by European scholars in this field but with cautious acceptance of its applicability in ontological language practice within the frame of a minority language, SASL. The disjunction is evident in the interpreting models posited by various scholars, which lack a unique lens on the realities of the Global South. The contributing factors of plurilingualism, a Third World context, and the slow pace of development and recognition of SASL as an official language contribute to the mismatch between classroom teaching (epistemology) and interpreting practice in the field (ontology). Akach (2006) mentions the colonization of sign languages and extends its effect to sign language interpreters. With this lens, the historical overview of SASL interpreter training is written.

The earlier education and training of SASL interpreters present a model of informal, ad hoc training offered by various deaf structures through experienced practitioner-facilitators in the form of workshops, seminars, and on-the-job training.

This model formed the early foundation of SASL interpreter training and gave birth to a limited scope for language practice advancement in a minority language sphere. The lack of South African interpreting scholars affected the development of mainstream academic interpreting programs, where SASL was incorporated into the curricula with other spoken language interpreting programs only from the year 2000. As a guiding document for this discussion, we refer to the SAQA NQF. The following section provides the context of current language practice qualifications for SASL interpreters with reference to the NQF.

The move toward professionalization of SLI is enacted through the SALPC Act. The impact of legislation and social change has shifted the landscape, and the increased opportunities for deaf people have changed the nature of the profession. It has been suggested, however, that with such rapid growth and change, the SLI field in the United States of America and various other countries has entered a state of market disorder (Witter-Merithew & Johnson, 2004), which is also evident in South Africa. Demand is outstripping supply so fast that it is leading to inappropriate practice in the field, such as inadequately skilled practitioners gaining regular employment, often interpreting for deaf children in schools and national events. Because of the erosion of hard-fought standards and the lack of a solid foundation as a profession, the field does not have the necessary "teeth" to censure poor practice, to control admission to the profession, or to dictate employment standards, and for this reason, there is a risk of being relegated to the status of a semi-profession.

SIGN LANGUAGE INTERPRETER EDUCATION IN SOUTH AFRICA

The past two decades saw a turn in the tide of SLI education in South Africa. SASL interpreters are increasingly enrolling in formal language practice programs offered by HEIs. Training varies on the basis of the institutional curriculum and is offered through face-to-face contact or online platforms. The recycled approach, termed *blended learning*, provides a conducive teaching and learning space where SASL interpreting students are able to continue learning while still keeping their practice as interpreters in the field.

The Department of Higher Education states in their mission that the aim of higher education must be to "develop capable, well-educated and skilled citizens who are able to compete in a sustainable, diversified and knowledge-intensive international economy, which meets the development goals of the country." In line with the Department of Higher Education's mission is an adapted curriculum that must be at the heart of the academic project. According to Maphosa et al. (2014), a review of the curriculum must have the following components: identifying what is working well and identifying issues and concerns. Thus, it is crucial that the interpreting studies curriculum be reviewed specifically for SLI education and for DIs.

Education and training of interpreters should be constructed and delivered with both hearing interpreters and DIs, with a constructionist approach aiming to prepare the team to work together in real-life assignments. Working toward a revised curriculum should bring in new knowledge of interpreting in multilanguage contexts. This much-needed redress will pave the way for the training of market-relevant interpreters who can function optimally in plurilingual settings, delivering an accessible interpreting product.

The development of a curriculum underpinned by andragogy is an important consideration in the African context because most interpreters who enroll for formal interpreter training are adults. *Andragogy* is derived from the Greek terms *aner* (genitive *andros*), meaning "man," and *agein*, meaning "to lead"; thus, andragogy means "leading men or adults." The Netherlands led the establishment of the andragogy approach in sociology and psychology (van Enckevort, 1971; Have, 1973). Knowles et al. (2014, p. 175), acknowledged the factors that influence andragogy design and teaching methodology by stating, "The various effects of adult experience on instruction are that it creates a wider range of individual differences; provides rich resources for learning; creates biases that can inhibit new learning; and provides grounding for adults' self-identity." It is these factors on which the training model was envisioned. Ferreira and Maclean (2017) highlighted the need for an adapted training model specifically in the online space.

The andragogical curriculum is increasingly filling the epistemic gaps in addressing the decolonization of the curriculum. Through inclusion of plurilingual assessment opportunities, innovative teaching and learning practices have been documented as informed by adult interpreting students. The diverse linguistic repertoires of SASL interpreting students are acknowledged and incorporated into establishing grounded language practitioners.

Language practice qualifications with an English/SASL language combination are offered by the University of the Free State, North-West University, the University of Pretoria, the Durban University of Technology, the University of South Africa, and WITS. The School of Languages, Literature, and Media at WITS offers postgraduate qualifications (postgraduate diploma, honors, master's, and PhD degrees) based on andragogical curriculum design principles.

Complementing the online method of teaching with andragogical principles is a novel approach taken by the WITS Department of Translation and Interpreting, where a specialist translation module for interpreters is offered. When enrolling for interpreting studies, students must also take a compulsory module in translation as part of their interpreting degree. In this module, SASL interpreters are trained on text analysis, reformulation, and translation strategies. This educational practice has resulted in increasing SASL interpreting graduates' awareness and successful application of translation strategies and principles, mostly in consecutive interpreting settings. Furthermore, it advances the understanding of "interpreting for meaning" through delivering a coherent and cohesive interpreting product into and from SASL. The development of new courses in the interpreting studies track at WITS goes through a rigorous quality assurance process, overseen by the Quality and Academic Planning Office, to ensure that the academic developments meet required quality standards.

In line with online learning, the migration of a fully online mode of delivery for interpreting studies modules was necessitated by COVID-19 health protocols. Some modules and assessments that had been done face to face were adjusted to complement the online learning space. Furthermore, preassessment for the interpreting studies program is done remotely via online interviews and online assessment tests. COVID-19 has effectively demanded an adapted level of online teaching and presence for both interpreting students and educators. Online content delivery has quickened the awareness of the diversity of learning needs and learners' experiences, and thus an adapted offering of interpreting modules is presented during this time. Central to the online learning space is the application of adult learning principles, in which consideration is made of the realities of working from home and studying from home in a developing context. This context brings to the fore the massive digital poverty divide evident in most Global South settings, with students not having access to electronic devices, reliable internet connectivity, or funds for the purchase of additional data. Despite advocating for training migration, institutions have also been exposed as having no reliable tools, platforms, staff expertise, or funds to support this new education setup. Training in the online space is transforming daily, with new lessons learned as we continue in the "new normal." The principle of andragogy, however, is a solid groundwork for understanding learning trends in the online space, where students operate on an unsupervised adult level.

SLI education is informed by theoretical approaches and equally strong tenets in ontological approaches based on informed practice-situated learning. There is a consistent evolution of the SASL interpreter profile and role identity, shifting from practitioners to researchers informed by ontological experience. These "practi-searchers" (Napier, 2006) are steadily providing seminal scholarly works toward the epistemic development of SASL interpreting as a specialized interpreting model. Various postgraduate dissertations and theses have been produced by postgraduate, graduate, and honors undergraduate students on a range of interpreting topics.

A feeder system to SASL interpreting provision is also in practice through eDeaf—Employ and Empower. eDeaf was established in 2007 as a leading provider of (deaf) skills development training in South Africa. This organization provides training, recruitment, ongoing support services, and interpreter services. Since 2018, eDeaf has piloted an SASL interpreter internship program that aims to provide grassroots SASL interpreters with foundational knowledge, both practical and theoretical, to function as trained interpreters. Grassroots interpreters are those who have a high proficiency level in SASL, less than 5 years' experience in interpreting, and no formal interpreter training. In addition, this skills program intends to provide interpreter interns an opportunity to enroll at an HEI, given that the certificate issued is on NQF Level 4.

SASL Interpreter Testing and Accreditation

In earlier years, SASL interpreters practiced in a non-legislated environment in which a license was not required. In 2004, SATI accredited the first group of four SASL interpreters with English/SASL language combinations. SATI continues to accredit SASL interpreters despite critique of its mandate and its provision of SASL accreditation, given that matters of language practice, such as accreditation, lie squarely with the SALPC (Parkins-Maliko, 2015).

To date (2021), SATI has accredited 12 SASL interpreters, as reflected in their database. Unverified databases from the Deaf Federation of South Africa (DeafSA) and the South African National Interpreting Centre, as well as the South African Government Central Supplier procurement database, list a total of 738 SASL interpreters. This number does not reflect categorization by professional or nonprofessional status, nor does it categorize interpreters according to provincial, national, and international skills categories. The paradox of SATI accreditation is that it has been a toothless tool because interpreters operate in an environment with no regulation, and interpreters do not see SATI accreditation as a goal to attain.

Progress is being made within higher education institutions where language practice studies are offered to design equitable assessment tools and procedures in advancing fair testing for SASL interpreters. Accreditation of SASL interpreters must follow a normative test approach to ensure fair testing with the aim of accreditation. The specialization of DIs has given rise to the need to construct an assessment tool that is sufficient to measure the skill level of DIs for accreditation to practice on par with accredited hearing interpreters.

Deaf Interpreters

The inherent nature of DIs' linguistic and cultural identity provides plenty of opportunities toward realizing professional interpreting services through self-representation. Bontempo (2015) posits that DIs often specialize in interpreting between signed language pairs and bring an innate understanding of signed language and deaf culture to the work as deaf people themselves. The phenomenon of DIs in the South African language practice landscape is an evolving concept, given the practice of language brokering as practiced by deaf people in communicative events that require brokering between SASL and other sign language forms. The DIs in South Africa operate in a broad semiotic repertoire of translanguaging, affected by several factors, such as the multilingual environment, the colonial history of deaf schools, and also South Africa's position as a destination for deaf immigrants from other African countries due its status as an economic hub. This on its own provides a rich field ripe for research to provide a lens on how DIs navigate this repertoire.

The term DI itself is very enigmatic in a country that labels interpreters on a spectrum of language interpreting and translation, with various terms loosely used to describe interpreters, such as *deaf interpreter, relay interpreter, signed hand interpreter, hand language interpreter, sign language translator, translator for the deaf,* or simply *translator.* This range of terms does not define whether interpreters are either deaf or hearing and does not consider DIs as a distinct group based on their skill set.

Historically, there has been no label applied to deaf individuals who have provided language brokering services except "relay interpreter." This term is still used and has found its way into the SASL vocabulary as an established sign and concept of reference to the interpreting space of a DI. The lack of understanding of the definition and role of a DI cannot be regarded in isolation, given that the same has been recorded in other countries, such as by Boudreault (2005) in North America. On that basis, it can be said that the status and progress of DIs in South Africa are still in their infancy.

Before university entities accepted enrollment from deaf interpreting students, training of DIs was primarily association led. Between 2009 and 2010, DeafSA decided to train three DIs as part of a Level 1 interpreting training certificate program offered through North-West University, but this program presented epistemic and ontological curriculum gaps. The certification was supposed to come not from the university but from the Department of Social Development. DeafSA also partnered with SATI in 2009 for a certificate of attendance training focusing on medical interpreting. In 2017, another organization, Childline South Africa, organized a 3-day certificate of attendance training focusing on court interpreting. In addition, there have been scattered informal workshops organized by deaf associations and small deaf-owned businesses, but documentation in terms of the dates and duration of training, topics covered, numbers in attendance, database, and subsequent tracking of the progress of attendees is nonexistent, which presents a major setback. No documented data are currently available as to how many DIs have been enrolled and received certification. In 2020–2021, DeafSA was involved in training 10 DIs online, with classes occurring hourly each week, and students were given practice opportunities in interpreting in internal organization meetings under the watch of a hearing interpreter mentor. The training listed here is anecdotal at best, as there is no documented evidence. This represents a missed opportunity to garner recognition for DIs by showcasing the DIs trained through these cohorts, which in turn could have led to streams of funding for training and establishment of formal courses and degree programs in deaf interpreting. These measures would subsequently lead to professionalism and standing as a leader in sub-Saharan Africa, given that Africa as a whole is lagging behind in terms of training.

An example of academic training that is well documented was carried out by the authors using external funding obtained after vigorous mobilization. In 2017–2018, through the Education, Training, and Development Practices Sector Education and Training Authority (ETDP SETA), a skills program was developed in which hearing and deaf interpreting students were trained on a program called Professional Development for South African Language Practitioners. In this program, 25 current and budding DIs were trained on various topics to lay a foundation for follow-up degreed training. The first-of-its-kind pilot DI training was carried out in Johannesburg and Cape Town. This training was hosted at the WITS Education campus independent of the WITS Language School and the T&I Department because the training emphasized a multilingual approach. Interpreting students in separate classes came together for combined classes for critical parts of the training covering teamwork, support and "feed" strategies, and general interpreting strategies for hearing–deaf interpreting teams. Although this was a pilot phase necessitating a second full-fledged phase, funding constraints and internal university bureaucracy have prevented the inception of the next stage of this training.

Training opportunities for DIs have largely been limited in comparison to those for hearing interpreters. In instances in which DIs were trained, it was documented that they are non-native signers usually labeled as "hard of hearing." The effect of this echoes Cokely's (as cited in Bontempo, 2015) misgivings over the increased social distance between non-native users of signed languages and deaf communities because many non-native users do not associate with the deaf community and find it difficult to assimilate cultural norms and to become truly fluent in SASL, which affects their competence and performance as interpreters. Mainstream interpreting programs offered by the South African universities have not attracted DIs or aspiring deaf students mainly because of lecturer apathy, audism, lack of awareness, absence of skilled and knowledgeable trainers, and lack of relevant training material and resources. Razaq, the second author of this chapter, applied to the WITS postgraduate interpreting and translation program and was rejected on the basis of the department's lack of readiness for deaf students and was given the suggestion to take up a translation course as an elective instead. When he enrolled for introductory studies in interpreting, he had to source his own interpreter because the language unit did not have one, nor did it have a budget to recruit one. His lived experience is an example of the limited academic training opportunities for DIs.

Generally, universities are ill equipped to handle and accommodate deaf students aspiring to enroll for language practice qualifications. This situation is not entirely the fault of universities, but the number of deaf students entering tertiary education is at best low, and there is also minuscule interest in pursuing language practice (interpreting) as a degree qualification. Negative societal attitudes are another factor that renders universities not yet open to embracing DIs, which in itself discourages aspiring deaf students from considering interpreting or translation as a career. South African universities have not done much to reach out to potential high school students with the goal of encouraging them to aspire to language practice as a career. The specialized Translation for Interpreters course at the WITS Department of T&I is one of the programs that needs to be marketed intensively. It is hoped that more deaf students will enroll to pursue translation as a field in the coming years. Since the program's inception, only two deaf students have taken a translation course; they are currently doing translation for international companies in this field, which is in itself a good indicator of the efficacy and relevance of the skills in the job market. The evidence of the need for deaf translators is glaring, and we hope to be able to progress to a space in which all translation work for SASL is given to deaf professionals with mother tongue proficiency.

Herein lies a missed opportunity, as students, specifically those from deaf schools, do not always have a world of knowledge of the opportunities available. Hosting symposia and inviting DIs working in various platforms offers deaf learners a wider lens into the field of work. It is worth noting that DIs based in the country are more visible on the international sign language stage than on the local one. DIs are important in any societal engagement, whether public or private. As is happening in most countries that have advanced interpreter training, the ideal, as noted by Napier (2004), would be to have interpreter education carried out in universities. This ideal presents a challenge in South Africa that needs to be overcome with recognition and elevation of deaf interpreting as a field.

Despite the fact that the SALPC and SATI recognize SASL as one of the languages available for interpreters' and translators' accreditation, it is somewhat surprising that it is actually harder for DIs to achieve accreditation. This highlights the necessity of introducing DI training courses into HEIs, which would subsequently enable discussion and review of the accreditation process to incorporate DIs. For the most part, DIs have been working in community settings, such as health care and police contexts. Community interpreting is largely viewed as being low status on the interpreting scale—an amateur undertaking.

Consequently, community DIs secure few assignments and limited opportunities for developing their professional skills. The COVID-19 situation has brought mixed results with regard to opportunities for DIs. Given that modes of interpreting have varied from live to video remote interpreting,[2] glaring gaps have been exposed in digital literacy and remote coworking, resulting in DIs not being offered opportunities. This is exacerbated by the decrease in the number of interpreting assignments available, leaving the few hearing interpreters to scramble for jobs that they prefer doing on their own. In 2021, during a presidential briefing on COVID-19 lockdown regulations, a DI made a premier appearance, which was greatly welcomed in the deaf community and in interpreting circles. This is but a mere drop in the ocean of possibilities for the provision of deaf-led interpreting services.

The Road Ahead

Given the available legislative framework (SALPC Act), the recognition of SASL as an official language, and the provision of academic language practice qualifications, it is anticipated that the training and provision of qualified SASL interpreters will increasingly become the norm. In the case of DI training, more awareness and advocacy are still needed to pursue equal recognition, opportunity, and working conditions. An African proverb states, "The sun does not forget a village just because it is small." Thus, deaf interpreting as an emerging profession in South Africa must advocate for access to HEI language practice programs and subsequent interpreting opportunities.

Continued effort is made to embrace the multilingual repertoires of interpreters to allow for epistemic acculturation in addressing superdiversity. The various interpreter training models in South Africa have not exhausted their scope for delivering better interpreting opportunities. Herein lies a dormant opportunity for exchange programs with other countries with established programs (e.g., in Europe) in developing a domesticated SLI and sign language translation degree program for both deaf and hearing interpreting students. The future of SASL interpreting and translation and other language practice professions relies on the operationalization of the SALPC to enable equitable recognition of SASL interpreters in the field of language practice.

Conclusion

It is now an opportune time for a turnaround in the training practice of SASL interpreters, in particular DIs. "*Moleta ngwedi o leta lefifi.*" (One who waits for the moon, waits for darkness.) In bearing the light, it is imperative that deaf and hearing interpreting scholars and practitioners collaboratively pursue equitable training, education, and accreditation of SASL interpreters.

This collaboration calls for key stakeholders, such as the South African Government (Department of Arts and Culture; Department of Women, Youth, and Persons with Disabilities), HEIs, structures mandated to advocate for the rights of deaf people, interpreter associations, and practitioners, to draft and enact a clear legal instrument that is aimed at ensuring training and credentialing of professional language practitioners, specifically SASL interpreters, with no exception to the law.

Notes

1. Makalela (2018, p. 191) defines *translanguaging* in the context of the plurilingual environment: "In African situations of linguistic confluence, the notion of alternation is complex in that alternation within and between languages could involve more than two languages in the same communicative event."
2. Braun (2015) and Napier (2012) adequately describe *video remote interpreting* as an advancement in communication technologies such as telephony, videoconferencing, and webconferencing where interpreter-mediated communication is contracted as an official interpreting service.

References

Akach, P. (2006). Colonization of sign languages and the effect on sign language interpreters. In R. Mc Kee (Ed.), *Proceedings of the Inaugural Conference of World Association of Sign Language Interpreters* (pp. 32–43). Douglas McLean.

Bontempo, K. (2015). Signed language interpreting. In H. Mikkelson & R. Jourdenais (Eds.), *Routledge handbook of interpreting* (pp. 112–128). Routledge.

Boudreault, P. (2005). Deaf interpreters. In T. Janzen (Ed.), *Topics in signed language interpreting: Theory and practice* (pp. 323–355). John Benjamins.

Braun, S. (2015). Remote interpreting. In H. Mikkelson & R. Jourdenais, R. (Eds.), *Routledge handbook of interpreting* (pp. 352–367). Routledge.

Ferreira, D., & Maclean, G. (2017). Andragogy in the 21st century: Applying the assumptions of adult learning online. *Language Research Bulletin, 32*, 10–19.

Have, T. (1973, June 12–14). On andragogy. *Scutrea Papers from the Third Annual Conference*, Grantly Hall, Leeds, University of Leeds.

Knowles M., Holton, E., Swanson, R., & Robinson, P. (2005). *The adult learner: The definitive classic in adult education and human resource development* (6th ed.). Elsevier.

Loeng, S. (2018). Various ways of understanding the concept of andragogy. *Cogent Education, 5*(1), 1496643. https://doi.org/10.1080/2331186X.2018.1496643

Makalela, L. (2014). Teaching indigenous African languages to speakers of other African languages: The effects of translanguaging for multilingual development. In L. Hibbert & C. van der Walt (Eds.), *Multilingual universities in South Africa: Reflecting society in higher education* (pp. 88–104). Multilingual Matters.

Maphosa, C., Mudzielwana, N., & Netshifhefhe, L. (2014). Curriculum development in South African higher education institutions: Key considerations. *Mediterranean Journal of Social Sciences. 5*. https://doi.org/10.5901/mjss.2014.v5n7p355

Department of Women, Youth, and Persons with Disabilities. (2011, February 28). Meeting minutes: South Africa's compliance with UN Conventions on Rights of Persons With Disabilities and Rights of the Child: Input by Civil Society. https://pmg.org.za/committee-meeting/12656/

Napier, J. (2004). Sign language interpreter training, testing, and accreditation: An international comparison. *American Annals of the Deaf, 149*(4), 350–359.

National Qualifications Framework. (n.d.). Pretoria, South Africa. https://www.rscnetwork.co.za/national-qualification-framework/

Parkins-Maliko, N. (2015). *Accreditation reform for South African Sign Language Interpreters: An action research study* [Unpublished master's thesis]. Humak University, Finland.

Roat, C. (2006). *Certification of health care interpreters in the United States: A primer. A status report and considerations for national certification.* The California Endowment.

South African Constitution. (n.d.). Pretoria, South Africa. https://www.justice.gov.za/legisla tion/constitution/SAConstitution-web-eng.pdf

South African Sign Language Charter. (n.d.). Pretoria, South Africa. https://www.gov.za/sites/ default/files/gcis_document/201910/42739gon1273.pdf

State of the Nation Address. (2020, February 13). South Africa. https://www.gov.za/ state-nation-address#2020

Stone, C. (2013). The UNCRPD and "professional" sign language interpreter provision. In C. Schäffner, K. Kredens, & Y. Fowler (Eds.), *Interpreting in a changing landscape* (pp. 83–100). John Benjamins.

Use of Official Languages Act. (n.d.). Pretoria, South Africa. https://www.gov.za/documents/ use-official-languages-act

Van Enckevort, G. (1971). Andragology: A new science. *Aontas Newsletter, 1,* 1.

Vertovec, S. (2007). Super-diversity and its implications. *Ethnic and Racial Studies 30*(6), 1024–1054.

Waddington, C. (2001). Different methods of evaluating student translations: The question of validity. *Meta: Translators' Journal, 46*(2), 311–325.

Witter-Merithew, A., & Johnson, L. (2004). Market disorder within the field of sign language interpreting: Professionalization implications. *Journal of Interpretation*, 19–55.

MALIN TESFAZION, ELISABET TISELIUS,
AND JOHANNA MESCH

19

Sign Language Interpreter Education in Sweden

Stretching over the northernmost parts of Europe, with Norway, Finland, and Denmark as its closest neighbors, Sweden remains a sparsely populated (10.5 million inhabitants) and linguistically a fairly uniform country. It is the cradle of the world-famous social-democratic "welfare state," which emerged over the course of the 20th century and is characterized by a strong vision of full inclusion for all members of society (Haualand & Holmström, 2018). Over the same period, Sweden also transformed from a monolingual and homogenous society to a much more multilingual and culturally diverse society; of Sweden's approximately 10.5 million inhabitants, about 20% were born abroad (SCB, 2022). The deaf population consists of about 10,000 individuals (SDR, 2021), and in addition there are approximately 2,000 people who are deafblind (NKCDB, 2021).

The Language Act states that the public society shall protect and promote Swedish Sign Language (svenskt teckenspråk [STS]) and that deaf people have the right to learn, develop, and use STS. This means that deaf people have the same legislated rights as other minority groups (Sami, Meänkieli, Finnish, Romani Chib, and Yiddish) or allophone language speakers to have access to interpreting services. Deaf people's right to interpreters was affirmed in the 1994 Disability Reform (Swedish Government Official Reports [Statens offentliga utredningar; SOU], 2004:64). The right to use interpreters is also codified in several other Swedish laws. For example, the following laws all directly refer to interpreters: the Language Act (Swedish Code of Statutes [Svensk författningssamling; SFS], 2009:600); the Health and Medical Services Act (SFS, 2017:30); the Support and Service for Persons With Certain Functional Impairments Act (SFS, 1993:387); the Administrative Procedure Act (SFS, 2017:900); the Code of Juridical Procedure (SFS, 1942:740); and the Administrative Court Procedure Act (SFS, 1971:201).

Interpreting services are also codified, though more indirectly, in the Patient Act (SFS, 2014:821).

We begin by contextualizing translation and interpreting of both signed and spoken languages in Sweden. We then talk about the status of STS and the professionalization of sign language interpreting (SLI) and discuss the development of interpreter education, with reference to deaf and hearing interpreters alike. We discuss the issue of readiness to work after formal education, as well as continuing professional development. Finally, we reflect on the status of STS/Swedish interpreting in the present day and on the current state of research into SLI and interpreter education.

Who Are We?

Malin Tesfazion is the director of studies for the SLI program at the Institute for Interpreting and Translation studies, Stockholm University. Malin was born in southern Sweden. She is a new signer (De Meulder, 2018).[1] When she was 20, she moved from her hometown to Stockholm (the capital of Sweden) to learn sign language. Her motivation for learning sign language and eventually becoming a sign language interpreter was her desire to combine head and hands in her work life. In Stockholm, Malin engaged with the deaf community and started the very first SLI program in Stockholm (Edsvikens vårdgymnasium, which later moved to Väddö folkhögskola). She engaged with the deaf community through her interest in board games and cofounded Spelgänget (literally "the game gang"). Malin has been an active sign language interpreter for 25 years, working mainly for the SLI unit at Stockholm University. When Stockholm University was looking to establish a SLI program, she became involved in the setup and opening of the program. Currently, she teaches SLI in the bachelor of arts (BA) program, both theoretical and practical courses. She gives lectures on sign language interpreting to the spoken language programs. As Malin did her interpreter training in the folk high school system (discussed later), she did not have an academic degree. This meant that while starting to teach in the BA program, she also did her own BA in SLI. Malin is currently finishing her master of arts (MA) thesis at Stockholm University on interpreting for hearing signers.

Elisabet Tiselius, a nonsigner, is an associate professor in interpreting studies and teaches in the programs for public service interpreting, conference interpreting, and SLI at Stockholm University. Elisabet was born and raised in Stockholm, where she still lives. Before starting her doctor of philosophy (PhD) degree, she did not have any experience with SLI. Elisabet trained to be a conference interpreter in Swedish, English, and French, and after 20 years of interpreting for the European Union (EU), she pursued a PhD. While doing her doctoral studies in Bergen, Norway, she met Ingeborg Skaten, a sign language interpreter and teacher who was very engaged in the deaf community in Bergen. Ingeborg introduced Elisabet to sign language and to the deaf community in Bergen. They then started a small research project together with Gro Hege Saltnes Urdal on teaching SLI to deaf students, and Elisabet also started teaching interpreting theory to SLI students in Bergen.

Back in Stockholm, fresh out of her PhD studies, Elisabet started at Stockholm University at the same time that the SLI program started. Her teaching is mainly in the spoken language interpreting programs, but she also teaches interpreting theory to the SLI students. She still does research on SLI and supervises student theses at all levels. She is still an active interpreter for spoken French, English, and Danish into Swedish, is a Swedish state-authorized public service interpreter, is accredited with the EU, and is a member of the International Association of Conference Interpreters (*Association Internationale des Interprètes de Conférence* [AIIC]). Her research interests involve cognitive processes of interpreting, interpreting in health care, depiction in SLI, and training of (deaf) interpreters.

Johanna Mesch is a full professor of sign language in the Sign Language Section within the Department of Linguistics at Stockholm University. Originally from Finland, she moved to Sweden at age 24 and became the first deaf professor in the Nordic countries. She is a deaf linguist who has been active in initiating a variety of new directions in the study of sign language and tactile sign language. Johanna earned her PhD in sign language linguistics in 1998, making her the first scholar worldwide to examine deafblind communication strictly from a linguistic perspective. Her research primarily focuses on sign language linguistics and the corpora in STS, which includes the learner corpus and the tactile sign language corpus. Notably, both Johanna's mother and sister worked as sign language interpreters, and her son has embarked on his journey as a sign language interpreter.

CONTEXTUALIZATION: TRANSLATION AND INTERPRETING IN SWEDEN

Historically, Sweden has been a country with a strong translation industry—many works of fiction and nonfiction are translated into Swedish from other languages. At the same time, spoken language interpreting has not been a large industry; Swedish civil servants and politicians working in international settings are generally fluent in multiple languages, thus lessening reliance on interpreters.

In the 1960s, actions were taken to strengthen interpreter training and standards, for the benefit of deaf people and migrant populations (which can, of course, also include deaf people). These actions led to interpreter training programs and eventually the creation of a state-level authorization for interpreters (a public certification procedure, discussed later). The first course aimed at SLI was founded in 1969 (Lemhagen & Almqvist, 2013). To support and supervise training for both signed and spoken language interpreters, the Swedish Parliament passed a regulation to establish the

Institute for Interpreting and Translation Studies, which was founded in 1986. The institute was founded as an independent body located at Stockholm University with a special responsibility for promoting and monitoring translation and interpreting education in Sweden (Lemhagen & Almqvist, 2013). The first conference interpreting training course was founded in 1993, just before Sweden joined the EU (Almqvist, 2016).

As in many other countries, signed and spoken language interpreting have not historically had common ground or aligned goals. The right to an interpreter and funding of interpreting services for each group are, to some extent, based on different laws. In addition, sign language interpreters generally serve populations that, while often marginalized, are primarily native to Sweden, whereas spoken language interpreters generally serve immigrant populations.

As noted previously, Sweden has a strong legislative framework affirming individuals' right to an interpreter. The existence of this legal right does not, however, mean that interpreters are always called on when needed (Haualand & Holmström, 2018). As such, there are interactions that take place without language mediation and others in which ad hoc or temporary solutions are used, a situation that arises mainly from a failure to request interpreters. Underlying reasons for this failure have, to the best of our knowledge, not been investigated.

Training for both spoken and signed language interpreters is currently offered at the university level, as well as at the postsecondary folk high schools.[2] Folk high school programs for STS/Swedish interpreters (*n* = 2) are 4 years long (Hein, 2009), and the university-level education (*n* = 1) is a 3-year BA program.

PROFESSIONALIZATION OF SLI IN SWEDEN

In 1981, the Swedish Parliament recognized STS as the first language of Swedish deaf people. The professionalization of sign language interpreters in Sweden has gone hand in hand with the recognition of STS as a first language for deaf people and the development of sign language interpreter programs. The first sign language dictionary was published in 1968, and one of the driving forces behind dictionaries was for the benefit of sign language students and sign language interpreters (Bergman & Nilsson, 1999). Interpreting services for deaf people were made free of charge in 1968, and the first SLI education program in Sweden was founded in 1969 (Persson Bergvall & Sjöberg, 2012). Before the institution of training programs and the legislated right to interpreters, deaf people depended on relatives, teachers in deaf schools, the church, and the Salvation Army for interpreting.

In the 1900s, government-designated "social workers for the deaf" provided interpreting, as part of efforts to improve deaf people's access to the labor market (SOU, 1937, p. 34). The first training program established in the late 1960s was only 6 weeks long, but by 1980 it had developed into a 1-year course. In the early training programs, language instruction, per se, was not a part of the course of study; rather, candidates were required to provide a certificate of STS proficiency from local deaf clubs as a prerequisite to entering the training program (Landström, 2004). The Swedish Sign Language Interpreters' Association (STTF) was founded in 1969 and has since then worked systematically to professionalize the sign language interpreter profession through education, development of ethics guidelines, and demands for working conditions.

Hein (2009) described how great efforts were made by the Swedish National Association for the Deaf (Sveriges Dövas Riksförbund [SDR]) and the STTF to develop and lengthen SLI training. The fact that, in 1991, the Institute for Interpreting and Translation Studies (TÖI) was given monitoring responsibility for the education of sign language interpreters also contributed to the professionalization of SLI, as TÖI was charged with developing a common curriculum for interpreter education, in addition to supervising programs.

In 2004, the possibility of being state authorized was made available to sign language interpreters. Currently, the state authorization is offered in 67 languages, including STS. State authorization requires the candidate to pass both a written test of specialized knowledge of Swedish civil society and an interpreting test between Swedish and STS. The state authorization is administered by the Swedish Legal, Financial, and Administrative Services Agency (in Swedish, Kammarkollegiet). Today, 235 sign language interpreters are authorized in Sweden. The authorization exists both on a general level and as a specialization in law or health care. At the time of writing, there are nine state-authorized sign language interpreters specializing in health care and five in law. The state authorization is a professional exam separate from the training courses, and in order to pass, advanced interpreting skills and long experience are necessary. Kammarkollegiet is also responsible for a national registry of all interpreters (signed and spoken) who have graduated from an interpreting program. A trained interpreter can register in the registry. Currently, 21 trained sign language interpreters are registered, but the actual figure is considerably higher. For most sign language interpreters, there is no clear incentive for registering, as they are employees and would not have been employed without an SLI education.

Sign language interpreters in Sweden are normally employed by government administrative regions or by private companies. There are also freelancers working for both bodies. Furthermore, some private and public employers employ in-house interpreters who work on site (e.g., Swedish television, Riksteatern Crea [theater in sign language], and Stockholm University). As previously noted, costs for interpreting services are, in general, covered by public funds with no charge directly to deaf people. Deaf people can get sign language interpreters for community services such as health care, family occasions (e.g., weddings and funerals), leisure, and some specific work-related instances. The access to SLI services is unlimited in theory (except for work, discussed later). However, the access depends on availability. A system for allocation of interpreters is in place in every county. Health care interpreting is highly prioritized, whereas leisure interpreting is less prioritized. Consequently, prioritization of requests creates challenges for accessing interpreters in some situations or contexts. The prioritization is done by the regional interpreting provider (organized by the county) and is supposed to follow the Health and Medical Services Act (SFS, 2017:30). There are no systematic studies on how this prioritization procedure is done.

Deaf people have access to interpreters in educational contexts, including higher education. In compulsory education, deaf children either attend a school for deaf children or are integrated into a mainstream classroom. Deaf children integrated into a mainstream classroom have access to student assistants with at least some STS knowledge (Holmström, 2013) and sometimes also to interpreters. No specific statistics are available on the actual numbers of deaf students in mainstream compulsory education, and the situation of these students has, to date, been the subject of only one study, carried out by Holmström (2013). In higher education, students have the right to interpreters for everything related to university activities (i.e., lectures, group work, and tutorials), as well as for social activities, such as student union activities and breaks (Stockholm University, 2018). The number of deaf and hard of hearing students receiving educational SLI and speech-to-text interpreting has increased steadily at Stockholm University and at other universities in Sweden, rising from 104 students in 2016 to 108 students in 2017, 117 students in 2018 and 2019, 146 students in 2020, 179 students in 2021, and a total of 197 (149 female and 48 male) students in 2022. In 2022, about 15 students used speech-to-text interpreting[3]; of those, some students choose SLI for some classes and speech-to-text interpreting for others. The three universities with the largest community of deaf students in 2022 were Stockholm University (44), Örebro University (25), and Gothenburg University (14). Stockholm University is the only university with employed interpreters on staff, but all universities are required to provide interpreters if needed.

One area in which access to an interpreter could be a challenge is in the workplace. The number of interpreting hours made available is often limited because of economic issues. Interpreters are typically not directly employed by the company that employs the deaf worker, and responsibility for providing interpreters may be unclear. This often leads to limited inclusion for deaf employees.

Despite the well-established interpreting services and the strong legal base for the right to interpreters, the interpreting market and the working conditions for interpreters have shifted over the past decade. Salaries have stagnated at comparatively low levels, and working conditions have deteriorated, with a higher demand for video relay interpreting and for providing services during inconvenient working hours. Furthermore, as in many European countries, the deaf population is experiencing changes related to issues such as increasing rollout of cochlear implants in young deaf children and mainstream (nonsigning) education for deaf children. This means that the SLI profession will continue to change, and it could potentially result in the only available sign language role model for children being less fluent users (Skaten et al., 2021). As we are in the midst of these changes, more detailed discussion of such issues is outside the scope of this chapter.

Sign Language Interpreter Education in Sweden

Formal education of STS/Swedish interpreters dates to 1969, when a 6-week short course was organized by the SDR and the Swedish National Board of Education. This course began as a direct response to the increased need for interpreters because of the legislation from 1968 affirming the right to interpreters (discussed previously). Participants in the course were expected to be fluent in STS before enrolling, and as a consequence, most candidates had strong links to the deaf community. By 1980, the short course had expanded into a yearlong program and was offered at different folk high schools. Candidates were still required to have knowledge of STS before starting the program.

Sweden also has a long tradition of education for tactile SLI. The first training, started in 1975, was a 2-week-long session organized by the Salvation Army and focused on interpreting for people with deafblindness (Landström, 2004). In 1987, a yearlong tactile SLI course was extended to 2 years. In 1989, the two separate strands of sign language interpreter training and tactile sign language interpreter training were merged, and they have been offered as a joint program at folk high schools since then. The Disability Reform of 1994 established county councils' responsibility for offering interpreting services, thus increasing pressure on the education system to provide training in tactile SLI for deafblind people.

TÖI's original mandate of monitoring the education of translators and interpreters of spoken languages was expanded to include the education of sign language interpreters in 1991. By this time, the sign language interpreter program had developed into a 2-year-long program. During this time period, there was a significant shortage of trained interpreters in Sweden. TÖI and STTF undertook a joint mission to further develop sign language interpreter education, with the goal of increasing the number of trained interpreters to result in a solid group of dedicated professionals. However, it was not until the Disability Reform (1994), and its guarantee of interpreting services provided by the county councils (which meant that the number of interpreted hours increased greatly), that this group had a natural way to build a career.

Hein's (2009) chapter in the first edition of this volume on SLI education stated that there were seven 3- to 4-year training programs at folk high schools but none at the university level. The folk high schools provided a solid interpreter education; however, folk high schools are not linked to university programs, and therefore, further professionalization was limited in Sweden. The situation in Sweden was also unique within the Nordic countries, as both Finland and Norway had university-level programs.

The collaboration between SDR, the Swedish Association for the Deafblind (Förbundet Sveriges Dövblinda [FSDB]), and the STTF continued to develop sign language interpreter training. These organizations were working actively to create an SLI program at the university level. In 2009, these stakeholder groups lobbied the Ministry of Education to respond to the demand for higher education opportunities for interpreters, and funding was allocated for this purpose in 2011. TÖI at Stockholm University was asked by the Ministry of Education to start to plan a university-level program at the BA level for SLI education (Lemhagen & Almqvist, 2013). The first students were admitted to the new program in 2013. The program was a joint effort between the Department of Linguistics and TÖI. The first cohort graduated in 2016.

Interpreter education currently takes place in folk high schools and at the university level (at TÖI). Both types of programs lead to similar work opportunities in SLI, and both programs are publicly funded and free of charge for the students. Students are also eligible for subsidized student loans. The following sections describe the two programs, starting with the university program.

Sign Language Interpreter Education at University

The university program is a full-time BA program consisting of 180 European Credit Transfer and Accumulation System (ECTS) credits over 3 years. The entry requirement for the program is a high school diploma (with English and Social Sciences). Unlike the early days of interpreter education, there is no prerequisite for previous knowledge of sign language and no entrance test. Stockholm University also offers theory-focused MA- and PhD-level degrees in Translation Studies with a focus on SLI.

Since 2023, both deaf and hearing candidates can apply for the program. There are two different tracks differentiated by whether the student has sign language as their first language (L1) or is learning STS as a second language (L2). The two tracks have some different courses and some of the same courses (which are taught to both tracks together). Sign language learners start with a 1-year focus on sign language education (37.5 ECTS credits in sign language acquisition, 17.5 ECTS credits in sign language–related courses, and 5 ECTS credits in language variation in spoken Swedish), and L1 students start with a 1-year focus on sign language as a topic (50 ECTS credits in STS, 10 ECTS credits in International Sign[4]). In the second year, students from both tracks start interpreting exercises and take theoretical courses on interpreting (22.5 ECTS credits in interpreting exercises, 17.5 ECTS credits in theoretical courses). For L2 students, the sign language training continues parallel to interpreting exercises (20 ECTS credits in sign language learning). L1 students focus on deaf studies, specialized interpreting, and STS second-language acquisition (20 ECTS credits). During the second year, the interpreting exercises introduces 5 ECTS credits in tactile sign language (added in 2019). In the third and final year, students take 40 ECTS credits in interpreting (including internship and tactile SLI) and 20 ECTS credits in theoretical courses (including a BA thesis; Lindström et al., 2018).

The teaching faculty consists of staff members (nine with PhDs and six with BAs or MAs). The eight deaf teachers (both PhDs and MAs/BAs) are employed full time at the Department of Linguistics (Stockholm University) and teach in the interpreter education program for part of their time. The seven hearing teachers (both PhDs and MAs/BAs) are employed at the Institute for Interpreting and Translation Studies, but not all of them are employed full time. Employment varies (55% and up). Those who are not employed full time (n = 3) are active sign language interpreters the rest of their professionally active time. In addition, we also have one deaf teaching assistant (20%) and a number of invited guest teachers.

At the university program, the beginner's course in STS is taught mainly by deaf teachers. Hearing teachers teach STS in parallel with the deaf teachers (i.e., not coteaching) but with a slightly different focus. Hearing teachers share the experience with the students of learning STS as a second language, whereas deaf teachers teach STS as native speakers. In a study of SLI students at Stockholm University by Holmström and Balkstam (reported by Holmström, 2018), the first 6 weeks of STS language acquisition were compared between two groups, one taught by a deaf teacher and one taught by a hearing teacher. Differences were found mainly in communication with deaf persons, which was better for the group taught by a deaf teacher, and metalinguistic knowledge, which was better for the group taught by a hearing teacher. However, after the first year, there were no significant differences between the two groups (Holmström, 2018).

Students with STS as L1 are taught mainly by teachers with STS as L1. The first year, the focus is on grammar, linguistics, and translation (Swedish–STS, as well as International Sign). The curriculum is currently undergoing changes. One course is shared with the L2 students focusing on contrastive linguistics (STS and Swedish).

The interpreting exercises are taught by hearing sign language interpreter teachers, and about one third of the classes are cotaught with or taught by deaf sign language teachers and deaf sign language interpreter teachers. The course on tactile SLI is co-taught with teachers with deafblindness. Interpreting theory courses and literature seminars are taught by hearing SLI teachers, and the sign language theory courses are taught by deaf teachers. Occasionally, 20 ECTS credits of the interpreting theory courses are taught by hearing interpreting teachers who are not signers but have a solid understanding of SLI. The BA thesis course is taught by hearing interpreting teachers. All BA thesis supervisors hold a doctoral degree.

The internship portion of the program consists of 1 week of observations during the second year and 5 weeks of internship at interpreting agencies during the third year. Students observe supervisors as they carry out their daily work and have opportunities to interpret when appropriate. After the program, students might also complete additional shorter internship courses (from 7.5 ECTS credits [5 weeks] to 30 ECTS credits [one term]). This course is not part of the diploma but is meant to increase the opportunity to practice professionally to alleviate the entrance into the job market. Approximately 20% of the students take this opportunity. During these courses, students work as interpreters but are closely supervised by experienced interpreters. They also write reports and participate in debriefing seminars. Internship supervisors are active, experienced sign language interpreters. They can, but do not have to, complete a specific university-provided training related to supervision.

A university education faces three main challenges. First, providing a natural sign language environment in a hearing-dominated university is difficult. To address this, the Sign Language Unit and Department of Linguistics are striving to create sign language–only zones on campus, currently in the form of language cafés. Second, there is a varying level of interest among students to enroll in the program. The exact reason for this has not been researched. As a remedy, publicity campaigns have been made to attract new students.

Another challenge is the graduation rates of students in the program. It is a long and challenging program, in which students have to master STS, learn to interpret, and also write a BA thesis. Personal contact with university programs in the Nordic countries shows the same trend in the other Nordic countries. Statistics from the four past cohorts (2016, 2018, 2019, and 2020) show that there is a graduation rate of between 10% and 30% of students who enrolled in the first year. These low figures might be attributed to, among other things, the fact that students must acquire a new language from scratch to a level at which interpreting is possible, as STS is only very rarely offered in high school, and most students come without previous knowledge of STS. Furthermore, they also learn to interpret at the same time, and both of these tasks require very intensive studies.

The COVID-19 pandemic had impacts at different levels. Swedish authorities did not impose a full lockdown, but recommended working from home as of March 16, 2020. The rectorate at Stockholm University urged all teaching to be moved online as of March 16, 2020. This meant that all teaching, including SLI exercises, was moved online. Online teaching was provided through Zoom via a university license. After initial fumbling for effective teaching practices, we also found advantages in using online platforms. For example, students could easily turn off their sound and thereby create more effective decoding exercises from STS, and organization in smaller groups for groupwork became more time efficient when breakout rooms were used. For the autumn term of 2020, practical programs could get an exemption to move back on site, provided that groups were small and a safe distance was maintained. The SLI program got permission to go back to campus. During this period, seminars and theoretical courses were taught online, and classes focusing on practice moved back to campus. Students in the program are required to be present for a minimum of 80% of their classes, but during the COVID-19 pandemic, people were urged to stay at home if they experienced COVID symptoms. Thus, the teaching staff had to be more lenient with regard to the 80% rule. As Sweden never imposed compulsory face mask use, face masks were not an issue for the SLI program. Almost 4 years later, we have kept the habit of easily moving into teaching on the digital platform if necessary. We also have classes for which the guest lecturer is present remotely, which was never the case before the COVID-19 pandemic. One of the on-site practicum events has stayed online after the pandemic. On a side note, part of the job description of interpreters is video remote interpreting, and our students have thus gotten a lot of practice in this setting.

Sign Language Interpreter Education at Folk High Schools

The first 4-year folk high school program was introduced in 1996. In 2006, all seven of the folk high schools offering sign language interpreter education introduced 4-year programs and adopted a joint curriculum created by TÖI. Today there are two remaining folk high schools still offering sign language interpreter education. Since 2012, they have jointly developed a new curriculum, though each one of them is free to design its own syllabus, which means that each has a slightly different program. The Swedish National Agency for Higher Vocational Education (Myndigheten för yrkeshögskolan [MYH]) is currently responsible for the programs, oversees the budget, and allocates funding.

The joint curriculum prescribes the length of the program (currently 160 weeks, i.e., 4 years), the scope (full time and at least 20 contact hours per week), the number of internship weeks, the content, and the goal of the program. The joint curriculum also prescribes entrance requirements, which are a high school diploma or similar, as well as satisfactory hearing and eyesight. The folk high schools used to have an entrance test (see Hein, 2009), which consisted of both practical and theoretical elements, as well as an interview; currently, they do placement interviews with students with previous sign language knowledge.

The first year of the folk high school program consists of teaching STS exercises that prepare students for interpreting. The second year continues with STS classes and interpreting classes that focus on interpreting into spoken Swedish, as well as mobility guidance for deafblind people. In the third year, interpreting in STS is introduced and taught parallel with advanced STS classes and classes that focus on tactile interpreting. The fourth year continues to focus on SLI in both directions, tactile interpreting, and continued language acquisition. During Years

3 and 4, the students also participate in different internships with a of minimum of 8 weeks in total.

At the folk high schools, STS is taught mainly by deaf teachers, whereas hearing SLI teachers teach mainly interpreting exercises. Teachers at folk high schools are, in general, employed staff, as far as we have been able to establish. One of the folk high school teachers has a PhD. One folk high school also employs a teacher who is deafblind, but for tactile interpreting, guest lecturers who are deafblind are invited to all schools. Teaching of interpreting theory is incorporated into all courses rather than being taught separately, and these courses are taught by both deaf and hearing teachers. Important topics included in these courses include interpreter ethics and codes of practice.

The folk high schools work closely with interpreting agencies, and students are offered internships in collaboration with these agencies. Interpreters who supervise the students at the agencies are trained to become supervisors by the folk high schools. Students first observe working interpreters, and then they have the chance to interpret under the supervision of the experienced supervisor. Folk high schools and local deaf organizations work closely together, mainly by organizing activities to strengthen language acquisition and fluency in a natural environment.

The challenges faced by folk high school interpreting programs are similar to those faced by the university, including decreasing student interest and variable graduation rates. A challenge specific to folk high schools is access to trained teachers, both for interpreting and for STS. There is only one interpreter teacher training program available (offered at TÖI), and currently very few potential SLI teachers have taken it.

As far as we have been able to establish, the COVID-19 pandemic hit hard for the folk high schools, as they had a long period when staff and students were not permitted on site.

Finally, it is important to note the differences between the two educational systems. On the surface, they might seem similar, and they are certainly producing interpreters with at least basic interpreting skills. They differ in terms of approach to curriculum and syllabus. The university program is less flexible, as it is firmly anchored in the academic tradition and offers an academic degree, which can be used for purposes other than working as a professional sign language interpreter, whereas the folk high schools are more independent and freer to adapt curricula and syllabi to individual students and to adapt to quickly changing market requirements. Our aim in this chapter has not been to highlight one type of program at the expense of the other but rather to give a comprehensive overview of the two systems.

Work-Readiness and Support From the Deaf Community

In terms of readiness for work as a sign language interpreter, very few students from either of the two types of educational programs are completely ready to work upon graduation. This is attributable to many different factors. Students aspiring to become sign language interpreters who are not already fluent in STS need to acquire a high level of fluency in the language and become familiar with the deaf community. Both processes are time consuming and might require more than the 3 or 4 years spent in the training program. Another important factor is the need to acquire skills in simultaneous interpreting, a complex cognitive task that also requires time to master (and that might not be possible for everyone to master). It is not possible to predict at the outset of training how much time an individual will need in order to acquire simultaneous interpreting skill (Timarová & Ungoed-Thomas, 2008). Both the university and the folk high schools attempt to ease the transition into the workforce through contact with deaf and deafblind communities, interpreting agencies, and last but certainly not least, more experienced sign language interpreters. This process requires ongoing effort and engagement with the community and stakeholders.

SDR, FSDB, and the Swedish Association of Hard-of-Hearing People (Hörselska-dades Riksförbund [HRF]) have been strong supporters of sign language interpreter education, both in terms of setting policy and lobbying for improvements. SDR is the administrator of one of the folk high schools (Västanvik folkhögskola), though it is not responsible for the interpreter training program at that location. At the same time, these organizations are, at present, more focused on access to interpreting services than on training of interpreters. Local deaf and deafblind organizations, as well as deaf and deafblind individuals, are involved to varying extents in all interpreter training programs. Students also participate in activities and study visits at local deaf and deafblind organizations. On the whole, the SLI programs in Sweden are well established and trusted by the community.

Sign Language Interpreter Teacher Training

Traditionally, future sign language interpreters have been taught by active sign language interpreters (similar to the situation of spoken language interpreting). In the late 1990s and early 2000s, occasional courses for interpreter educators were organized at TÖI and at Linköping University. The course in Linköping was particularly aimed at educators of sign language interpreters (Lemhagen & Almqvist, 2013). Since 2018, TÖI has organized a training course for interpreter educators of both signed and spoken languages.

Interpreter Education for Deaf Interpreters and Translators

Since 2015 deaf people had the opportunity to attend interpreting courses designed for deaf interpreters. The courses are offered through the folk high school system and aim to train deaf people in interpreting. Approximately 40 people have graduated from the course, and about 10 to 15 deaf people work regularly as interpreters.

The first two classes who graduated from the program were also trained in sign language translation, in numbers that correspond to approximately 20 trained sign language translators. Since 2023, deaf people have been able to apply to the university program, as described previously. Deaf interpreters work in the same context as hearing interpreters.

Another developing area is sign language translation, as it is established and demanded in Sweden, and the European accessibility directive has further increased the demand (2018/1808). However, there are currently not enough trained sign language translators available, thus many lack training when they take up a position. Major users of sign language translators are news channels, the sign language department at the Swedish television station, and schools.

The Road Ahead

SLI education and the provision of interpreters in Sweden have been the focus of several green papers and reports over recent decades (SOU, 2022:11; Statskontoret, 2015:25; SOU, 2011:83; SOU, 2004:64), which has led to the current developments in sign language interpreter education. The SLI education at folk high schools will probably persist for the foreseeable future. A growing area is speech-to-text interpreting. One of the folk high schools that used to have an interpreter program (*Södertörns folkhögskola*) has discontinued their interpreting program but kept their popular yearlong speech-to-text interpreting course. It is open both to sign language interpreters wishing to broaden their competencies and to candidates wishing to work exclusively as speech-to-text interpreters.

One result of the green papers is the drive to integrate SLI education into higher education programs. A consequence of the integration has been that students are required to write a BA thesis to obtain their degree. To facilitate the completion of student theses, the researchers at TÖI and the Department of Linguistics opened their resources and research projects to BA students. For instance, the *Invisible Process* project (Tiselius, 2017) compares students and experienced professional interpreters; this project has generated three BA theses. Another example is the *Simultaneous Sign Language Interpreting Corpus* (Nilsson, 2014), which is a corpus of simultaneous interpreting that generated one BA thesis.

The MA program in interpreting is not focused solely on SLI; one MA student is currently writing a thesis on SLI in workplace meetings and interpreting for hearing signers. Another MA thesis with students from Stockholm University as participants focused on SLI students' profiles.

As SLI education was integrated into the university level, the program had to be designed so that it would fulfill basic university requirements, comprising 180 ECTS credits and a BA thesis. Since the program started, we have noted gaps with regard to certain skills and have adjusted the curriculum as a result. For example, deafblind interpreting was not part of the initial program, but it has now been integrated. Furthermore, as a response to the demand from active interpreters to get access to the theoretical courses in the program, the theoretical introductory course was opened up for other students. As a result, hearing interpreters and deaf interpreters who are active professionals have had the opportunity to participate in these courses alongside prospective interpreters who are enrolled in the university course. Another issue currently being discussed is whether the university course should be extended to 4 years to integrate more practicum and more skills-based courses.

When the earlier chapter was published by Hein (2009), there was still no doctoral work on SLI in Sweden. In 2010, the first Swedish PhD in SLI was completed (Nilsson, 2010). The next PhD investigating SLI was by Warnicke (2017) on video relay interpreting. Today, there is a PhD program in translation studies with a focus on interpreting. SLI is thus represented at all academic levels.

Research into both SLI and sign language as a second language has grown along with the university-level SLI program. The research community includes hearing and deaf researchers, as well as signers and nonsigners. One example of a research project linked to the SLI program is Holmström (2018), discussed previously. Furthermore, research has been initiated on the use and structure of tactile STS (e.g., Mesch, 1998). Research on tactile interpreting in STS is ongoing, and a first report has been published (Gabarró-López & Mesch, 2020).

Other important research is Mesch and Schönström's learner's corpus *Swedish Sign Language as a Second Language STSC-L2* (Mesch & Schönström, 2018, 2021, 2023; Schönström, 2021; Schönström & Mesch, 2022). The corpus consists of a dataset with longitudinal data collected from 38 adult hearing L2 learners of STS, the majority of whom are students from the sign language interpreter program. The project deals with the acquisition of sign language as a second language and the process of learning a new language through a new modality (i.e., the gestural–visual modality as opposed to the vocal–aural modality). One study is about overuse of mouthing (borrowing elements from their L1 spoken Swedish). Other studies investigate the use of viewpoint shifts and sign fluency. The results will benefit SLI education, as they will shed light on L2 learners' early STS language acquisition stages and contribute to understanding the underlying reasons for different challenges that are typical in this context. This type of documentation has not been done previously.

The unit for educational interpreting at Stockholm University has seen an increase in demand for speech-to-text interpreting, and from that demand, a joint project was run on speech-to-text interpreting (Pedersen & Norberg, 2018).

In terms of international cooperation, the training programs in Sweden are active in the Nordic Seminar, a collaborative conference series organized by the Nordic Sign Language Interpreter organizations. Through the Swedish STTF, there is also a close and active cooperation with the European Forum for Sign Language Interpreters (efsli) and the World Association of Sign Language Interpreters. A concrete result of this collaboration was the efsli 2019 conference, which was organized by STTF in Malmö and involved many teachers and trainers of the STS programs as presenters, student volunteers, organizers, and members of the scientific committee.

Conclusions

As shown in our overview, SLI education in Sweden has undergone major changes over the past decade. We assume that changes over the coming years will not be as dramatic, although we suspect more changes will occur in the educational programs before the change settles. We hope for more MA theses focusing on SLI. In particular, it would be ideal to encourage more scholarly works that focus on the interpreter education program itself. Interestingly, there are very few continuing professional development opportunities in Sweden, and continuing professional development is not compulsory. This is, thus, an area where change would be welcome.

Just as we see changes in the increased demand for speech-to-text interpreting and new technical developments in terms of speech recognition, we also expect to see changes in the different skills that sign language interpreters need to master. We have also noted that there are not enough statistics about students' careers after completion of the interpreter training programs. This is an area in which more research is needed. However, we believe that sign language interpreter education will be stable for the foreseeable future.

Notes

1. *New signers* are people who learn a sign language later in life and often outside traditional contexts and then choose to use that language on an everyday basis for personal and professional reasons.
2. *Folk high schools* provide postsecondary education and are common in the Nordic countries (Finland, Sweden, Norway, and Denmark) and northern Europe (Germany, Austria, and Switzerland). They are publicly funded and based on the Danish philosopher Grundtvig's pedagogical ideas on education as universal and common (Frímansson, 2006). Folk high schools do not grant academic degrees, though they might teach academic topics. Based on the principle of universal and common education, they are open to all kinds of students, both those with and without secondary education. However, individual programs such as the interpreting program might require a secondary education degree.
3. *Speech-to-text interpreting* is performed in real time by interpreters who use a (specially adapted or standard) keyboard connected to a screen to produce subtitles (Norberg et al., 2015).
4. *International Sign* is what Whynot (2016) defines as a form of contact signing used in international settings in which people who are deaf attempt to communicate with others who do not share the same conventional, native signed language. It has been broadly used to refer to a range of semiotic strategies of interlocutors in multilingual signed language situations, whether in pairs or in small- or large-group communications. See also Hou and Kusters (2019) for a further discussion on issues with International Sign.

REFERENCES

Almqvist, I. (2016). *Tolkutbildning i Sverige: ett kritiskt vägval*. [Interpreter education in Sweden: a crucial decision] Stockholms universitet. http://www.diva-portal.org/smash/get/diva2:917045/FULLTEXT02

Bergman, B., & Nilsson, A-L. (1999). Teckenspråket [The Sign Language]. In K. Hyltenstam (Ed.), *Sveriges sju inhemska språk - ett minoritetsspråksperspektiv* [Sweden's seven indigenous languages – A minority language perspective]. *Studentlitteratur*, 329–351.

De Meulder, M. (2018). "So, why do you sign?" Deaf and hearing new signers, their motivation, and revitalisation policies for sign languages. *Applied Linguistics Review, 10*(4), 705–724.

European Union. (2018, November 14). Directive 2018/1808 of the European Parliament and of the Council of 14 November 2018 amending Directive 2010/13/EU on the coordination of certain provisions laid down by law, regulation or administrative action in Member States concerning the provision of audiovisual media services (Audiovisual Media Services Directive) in view of changing market realities. https://eur-lex.europa.eu/eli/dir/2018/1808/oj

Frímannsson, G. H. (2006). Introduction: Is there a Nordic model in education? *Scandinavian Journal of Educational Research, 50*(3), 223–228.

Gabarró-López, S., & Mesch, J. (2020). Conveying environmental context to deafblind people: a study of tactile sign language interpreting. *Frontiers Education, 5*, 1–12.

Haualand, H., & Holmström, I. (2019). When language recognition and language shaming go hand in hand–sign language ideologies in Sweden and Norway. *Deafness & Education International, 21*(2–3), 99–115.

Hein, A. (2009). Interpreter education in Sweden: A uniform approach to spoken and signed language interpreting. In J. Napier (Ed.), *International perspectives on sign language interpreter education* (pp. 124–145). Gallaudet University.

Holmström, I. (2019). Teaching a language in another modality: A case study from Swedish Sign Language L2 instruction. *Journal of Language Teaching and Research, 10*(4), 659–672.

Holmström, I. (2018). Teaching Swedish Sign Language as a second language to interpreter students. In S. Costner (Ed.), *Proceedings: Nordic Seminar Umeå February 2018: Theory in practice - Practice in theory* (pp. 80–91). Sveriges teckenspråkstolkars förening.

Holmström, I. (2013). *Learning by hearing? Technological framings for participation* [Unpublished doctoral dissertation]. Örebro University.

Holmström, I. & Schönström, K. (2017). Resources for deaf and hard-of-hearing students in mainstream schools in Sweden—A survey. *Deafness & Education International, 19*(1), 29–39.

Hou, L. & Kusters, A. (2019). Sign languages. In K. Tusting (Ed.), *The Routledge handbook of linguistic ethnography* (pp. 340–355). Routledge.

Landström, I. (2004). *Mellan samtid och tradition – folkhögskolans identitet i kursutbudets yrkesinriktning* [Between contemporary and tradition – the identity of the folk high schools reflected in the professional profile of the course selection] [Doctoral dissertation]. Linköping Studies in Education and Psychology 99. Linköping University. http://www.diva-portal.org/smash/get/diva2:244480/FULLTEXT01.pdf

Lemhagen, G., & Almqvist, I. (2013). *Tolk- och översättarinstitutet. En särskild inrättning 1986–2012*. [Institute for Interpreting and Translation Studies. A special organ 1986–2012]. Stockholm, Sweden: Tolk- och översättarinstitutet. http://www.diva-portal.org/smash/get/diva2:636681/FULLTEXT01.pdf

Lindström, J., Tesfazion, M., & Tiselius, E. (2018). Making theory work in practice: Theory and practice: intertwined and inseparable at TÖI, Stockholm University. In S. Costner (Ed.), *Proceedings Nordic Seminar Umeå February 2018—Theory in practice—Practice in theory* (pp. 68–80). STTF.

Mesch, J. (2001). *Tactile sign language: Turn taking and questions in signed conversations of deafblind people.* [Doctoral dissertation]. Signum Verlag.

Mesch, J. (1998). *Teckenspråk i taktil form - turtagning och frågor i dövblindas samtal på teckenspråk* [Unpublished doctoral dissertation]. Stockholm University.

Mesch, J., & Schönström, K. (2023). Self-repair in hearing L2 learners' spontaneous signing: A development study. *Language Learning, 73,* S1.

Mesch, J., & Schönström, K. (2021). Use and acquisition of mouth actions in L2 sign language, learners: A corpus-based approach. *Sign Language Linguistics, 24*(1), 33–59.

Mesch, J., & Schönström, K. (2018, May 12). From design and collection to annotation of a learner corpus of sign language. In M. Bono, E. Efthimiou, E. Fotinea, T. Hanke, J. Hochgesang, J. Kristoffersen, J. Mesch & Y. Osugi (Eds.), *Proceedings of the 8th Workshop on the Representation and Processing of Sign Languages: Involving the language community [Language Resources and Evaluation Conference (LREC)]*, Miyazaki, Japan (pp. 121–126). European Language Resources Association.

Nationellt Kunskapscenter för Dövblindfrågor (NKCDB). 2021. *Fakta om dövblindhet* [Facts about deafblindness]. https://nkcdb.se/dovblindhet/fakta-om-dovblindhet/kort-fakta/

Nilsson, A-L. (2014). *Datamängd. Projektet Teckenspråkets rumsliga dimension vid simultantolkning.* [Dataset. Project for the space dimension of sign language in simultaneous interpreting]. Avdelningen för teckenspråk, Institutionen för lingvistik, Stockholms universitet.

Nilsson, A.-L. (2010). *Studies in Swedish Sign Language: Reference, real space blending, and interpretation* [Unpublished doctoral dissertation]. Stockholm University.

Norberg, U., & Pedersen, J. (2018, October 17). *Say it again, Sam: nyskapande skrivtolkning för döva studenter.* [Innovative speech-to-text interpreting for deaf students] [Presentation]. Higher Seminar at the Institute for Translation and Interpreting Studies. Stockholm.

Norberg, U., Stachl-Peier, U., & Tiittula, L. (2015). Speech-to-text interpreting in Finland, Sweden and Austria. *International Journal of Translation and Interpreting Research, 7*(3), 36–49.

Persson Bergvall, I., & Sjöberg, M. (2012). *Årtal – ur handikapphistorien. Handikapphistoriska föreningen.* [Years – in the history of disability. The Association for disability history]. https://www.likaunika.org/Filer/Wordfiler(1)/Rapporter/Aratal-ur-Handikapphistorien.pdf

Roy, C. B., & Napier, J. (Eds). (2015). *The sign language interpreting studies reader.* John Benjamins.

Schönström, K. (2021). Sign languages and second language acquisition research: An introduction. *Journal of the European Second Language Association, 5*(1), 30–43.

Schönström, K., & Mesch, J. (2022). Second language acquisition of depicting signs: A corpus-based account. *Language, Interaction and Acquisition, 13*(2), 199–230.

SFS. (1942:740). Code of Juridical Procedure.

SFS. (1971:201). Administrative Court Procedure Act.

SFS. (1993.387). Support and Services for Person With Certain Functional Impairments.

SFS. (2009:600). The Language Act.

SFS. (2014:821). Patient Act.

SFS. (2017:740). Code of Juridical Procedure Act.

SFS. (2017:900). Administrative Procedure Act.

SFS (1993). Support and Service for Persons with Certain Functional Impairments Act.

Skaten, I., Urdal, G. H. S., & Tiselius, E. (2021). Exploring deaf sign language interpreting students' experiences from joint sign language interpreting programs for deaf and hearing students in Finland. *Translation and Interpreting Studies, 16*(3), 147–167.

Swedish Government Official Reports (SOU). (1937:34). *Betänkande med förslag till åtgärder för förbättrande av de blindas och de dövstummas arbetsförhållanden och förvärvsmöjligheter avgivet av särskilt tillkallade utredningsmän* [Public inquiry with proposal created by specially appointed investigators for action to improve the blind and the deaf-dumbs working conditions and access to work]. https://lagen.nu/sou/1937:34#US22

Swedish Government Official Reports. (2011:83). *En samlad tolktjänst – samordning och utveckling av tolktjänst för barndomsdöva, vuxendöva, hörselskadade och personer med dövblindhet* [A united interpreting service—coordination and development of the interpreting services for adult deaf, hard of hearing and people with deafblindness]. https://www.regeringen.se/49b6a0/contentassets/8c5b259fe9aa46668d881d89d3a19631/en-samlad-tolktjanst-sou-201183

Swedish Government Official Reports (SOU). (2022:11). *Handlingsplan för en långsiktig utveckling av tolktjänsten för döva, hörselskadade och personer med dövblindhet* [Action plan for a long-term development of the interpreting services for deaf, hard of hearing and people with deafblindness]. https://www.regeringen.se/rattsliga-dokument/statens-offentliga-utredningar/2022/03/sou-202211/

Swedish Government Official Reports (2004). (SOU). (2004:64). *Teckenspråk och teckenspråkiga. Översyn av teckenspråkets ställning* [Sign language and signers. An inventory of the status of Swedish Sign Language]. https://www.regeringen.se/49b6aa/contentassets/ee1ffc35f75e4ffe83d85fd800b585ca/teckensprak-och-teckensprakiga.-oversyn-av-teckensprakets-stallning-hela-dokumentet-sou-200654

Statistics Sweden. (2022). *Sveriges befolkning* [The population of Sweden]. https://www.scb.se/hitta-statistik/sverige-i-siffror/manniskorna-i-sverige/sveriges-befolkning/

Statskontoret. (2015). *Det framtida behovet av teckenspråks- och skrivtolkar. En översyn av tolkutbildningarna vid folkhögskolorna* [The future need for sign language and speech-to-text interpreting. An inventory of the interpreter educations at the folk high schools]. https://www.statskontoret.se/siteassets/publikationer/2015/201525.pdf

Sveriges Dövas Riksförbund (SDR). (2021). *Hur många döva finns det i Sverige?* [How many deaf people are there in Sweden]. https://sdr.org/question/hur-manga-dova-finns-det-i-sverige/

Timarová, Š. & Ungoed-Thomas, H. (2008). Admission testing for interpreting courses. *The Interpreter and Translator Trainer, 2*(1), 29–46.

Tiselius, E. (2016). *Invisible process: Cognition and working memory of dialogue interpreting.* http://tanken.se/wp-content/uploads/2015/10/VR-Informationsunderlag-projekt.pdf

Warnicke, C. (2017). *Tolkning vid förmedlade samtal via Bildtelefoni.net – Interaktion och gemensamt meningsskapande* [Interpreting in mediated conversations through Bildtelefoni.net – Interaction and co-creation of meaning]. Doctoral dissertation. Studies from the Swedish Institute for Disability Research 85. Linköping: Linköpings Universitet. https://oru.diva-portal.org/smash/get/diva2:1089956/FULLTEXT01.pdf

Whynot, L. A. (2017). *Understanding International Sign: A sociolinguistic study.* Gallaudet University Press.

SAM LUTALO-KIINGI, GOEDELE A. M. DE
CLERCK, DOROTHY LULE, JOHN BUYINZA,
AND GRAHAM H. TURNER

20

Sign Language Interpreter Education in Uganda

Uganda is located in East Africa and bordered by the Democratic Republic of Congo to the west, South Sudan to the north, Kenya to the East, Tanzania to the south, and Rwanda to the southwest. Uganda became a British protectorate at the end of the 19th century and gained independence from Britain on October 9, 1962. when its economic revival, structural reforms, human rights ambitions, formation of organizations for women and disabled people, and its joining of international development programs in the light of The United Decade of Disabled Persons (1983–1992) were internationally lauded. Between 1992 and 2006, the Ugandan deaf community benefited from a series of North–South partnerships with the Danish Deaf Association (*Danske Døves Landsforbund* [DDL]), which were cooperative and sustainable and resulted in building capacity of Ugandan deaf leaders and Ugandan Sign Language (UgSL) instructors, interpreters, and researchers (Lutalo-Kiingi & De Clerck, 2015, 2017; De Clerck & Lutalo-Kiingi, 2018). Uganda's political reforms, cooperation with stakeholders and disability organizations, and collegial consultancy enabled Uganda to become the first African country to have its sign language (constitutionally) recognized.

However, in recent decades, the well-being of Ugandan citizens and engagement in human rights advocacy on the part of nongovernmental organizations (NGOs) have been overshadowed by challenges of democratic governance and human rights implementation, as well as (donor) concerns about governmental strategy planning, elite corruption, and increased suppression of political criticism (Dicklitch & Lwanga, 2003; Tangri & Mwenda, 2006).[1]

The current Ugandan population is approximately 42,368,800, according to the Ugandan Bureau of Statistics (UBOS) and United Nations Development Program

(UNDP) estimate (UBOS, 2020; UNDP, 2020). According to the 2019 UNDP indicators, 65% of the employed population older than 15 years earns less than $3.20 a day. Uganda has one of the youngest and most rapidly growing populations in the world. Unfortunately, many youths struggle to access decent and gainful employment; the few who are employed often work in vulnerable employment circumstances, characterized by low pay and job insecurity (Kanyamurwa, 2020). Uganda has a low Human Capital Index, which means that Ugandan children are less likely to be able to access full and high-quality education and to be in good health; rates of school completion and literacy are lower than those of countries in the region. The Ministry of Gender, Labour, and Social Development notes a prevalence of persons with disabilities of 12.4% in the adult population, adding up to 5,194,360 people, of whom deaf and hard of hearing people constitute 3.6%, estimated at 187,000. When this is compared with an estimate based on membership in regional deaf associations as documented during research for the UgSL dictionary (Wallin et al., 2006), it is likely that there are now more than 50,000 culturally and linguistically deaf people living in Uganda.

More than 40 spoken languages are used in Uganda, with the most commonly used being English, Luganda, and Swahili (Nakayiza, 2013). Hence, it is appropriate to understand Ugandan society as multiethnic, multicultural, and multilingual, as is the case in most African countries (e.g., Altmayer & Wolff, 2013; Barmgbose, 2014). The status of these languages is defined by the Uganda's constitution, as well as by the daily use of the languages. The Constitution of the Republic of Uganda (1995; 2015, Article 6, p. 32) recognizes English and Swahili, respectively, as "the official" and "the second official language of Uganda." Article 6 refers to cultural recognition of the use of indigenous languages among members of the same ethnolinguistic group, mentioning that "any other language (than the official languages) may be used as a medium of instruction in schools or other educational institutions, or for legislative, administrative or judicial purposes" (pp. 32–33). The constitution aims to "encourage the development, preservation and enrichment of all Ugandan languages" (Constitution of the Republic of Uganda, 1995; 2015, p. 27).

The Constitution's cultural and language policy also aims to "promote the development of a sign language for the deaf" (Constitution of the Republic of Uganda, 1995; 2015, p. 27). UgSL is considered the first language of deaf Ugandans. It is considered a national sign language of deaf people living in different parts of the country with varying norms, beliefs, and customs. There is regional variation in UgSL, as well as sociolinguistic variation related to age, gender, and ethnolinguistic background (Lutalo-Kiingi & De Clerck, 2015a; Lutalo-Kiingi, 2016).

Uganda, being a multilingual society, hosts conflicting aims and prejudices from differing perspectives, different interests on the part of politicians, mixed language philosophies, and mixed political beliefs; thus, linguistic rights and the freedom to use mother tongues continue to elude Ugandans (Namyalo & Nakayiza, 2015). Most Ugandans have a local language as their first language and are familiar with English as a second language (Namyalo & Nakayiza, 2015). For example, Uganda has more than 5,000,000 users of Luganda, which is spoken in the Central region. Even though Luganda is not recognized as an official language, the historical, political, economic, and social significance of the language has provided Ugandans with opportunities to access justice, education, religion, and media through Luganda (Namyalo & Nakayiza, 2015). Wolff (2013) used the term "language factor" to refer to the historical relationship of colonialism and the higher status of official status, which tend to be used in distinguished realms of life, such as politics and education. Wolff argues that, in the multilingual and multicultural realities of daily life in sub-Saharan Africa, this hidden language factor is a drawback to the realization of the United Nations Sustainable Development Goals.

Drawing on Wolff's perspective, Lutalo-Kiingi & De Clerck (2016, 2017) have used the term "sign language factor" to highlight the hidden higher status of spoken languages versus signed languages, as well as related symbolic violence within the community, which devalues the language and cultural knowledge of deaf native signers, influences UgSL interpreting practice, and poses risks to the sustainability of UgSL. Because of Uganda's long period of civil war and its deprivation of development cooperation in the period before linguistic research documented the linguistic uniqueness of each signed language, UgSL has known only limited structural exposure to Western signed languages.

Who Are We?

Sam is deaf and a senior lecturer in UgSL at the Department of Hearing Impairment and Sign Language Interpretation Studies, head of the Department of Hearing Impairment and Sign Language Interpretation Studies at Kyambogo University (KyU) in Uganda. With more than 28 years of experience in UgSL teaching, he has been involved in the establishment of training programs in UgSL instruction (since 1994) and interpreting (since 2002). His doctoral thesis was titled "A Descriptive Grammar of Morpho-Syntactic Constructions in Ugandan Sign Language (UgSL)" (2014, iSLanDS, UCLan, United Kingdom). He also works as a deaf interpreter (DI).

Goedele is deaf and holds a doctor of philosophy degree in comparative sciences of culture and master's degrees in languages and literature and in psychology. She conducted anthropological research on the emancipation processes in and sustainable development of the Ugandan deaf community in cooperation with Sam Lutalo-Kiingi, after which she has continued to support further academic research and documentation in Uganda, including the study of UgSL interpreting. Goedele runs a private counseling practice for hard of hearing, deaf, and deafblind youth, adults, and elders in Flanders, Belgium.

Dorothy is hearing and holds a bachelor's degree in deaf studies, Bristol University; United Kingdom, and a master's degree in special needs, Maseno University, Kenya.

She was involved in the establishment of the UgSL diploma course in the Department of Hearing Impairment and Sign Language Interpretation Studies, Kyambogo University, where she taught until her official retirement from active academic services.

John is hearing and holds a diploma in UgSL interpreting, a degree in social work and community development, Kyambogo University, and a master's in public health-health promotion, Uganda Martyrs University. He works as a UgSL interpreter/part-time lecturer at the Department of Hearing Impairment and Sign Language Interpretation Studies at KyU in Uganda. He is a member of the Uganda National Association of Sign Language Interpreters (UNASLI).

Graham H. Turner is hearing and an emeritus professor in the Centre for Translation and Interpreting Studies at Heriot-Watt University (HWU) in Scotland. He hosted Sam Lutalo-Kiingi's Visiting Fellowship Award by the British Academy, which supported research into sign language interpreting (SLI) education in Uganda. He recently retired from active academic service.

CONTEXTUALIZATION: TRANSLATION AND INTERPRETING IN UGANDA

Translation and interpreting (T&I) studies in multilingual sub-Saharan Africa are an emerging field. Since the 1990s, Makerere University's Departments of Foreign Languages (French, German, Spanish, Arabic, and Chinese), African Languages (Luganda, Swahili, and Runyakitara), and General Linguistics (a combination of the former languages) have organized training in interpreting and translation as a module within the bachelor of arts (BA) programs. Research in interpreting and translation in the aforementioned languages is also limited (personal communication, January 26, 2021, Dr. David Enoch Ssebuyungo). The only other institution of advanced education providing training in interpreting and translation is KyU, which organizes the UgSL interpreting training program.

Makerere's Center for Languages and Communication provides interpreting and translation services at the community level; the lack of degree programs in interpreting and translation is a drawback for services at the academic level and for the registration of a professional association of interpreters and translators. Qualified language and linguistics graduates who completed interpreting and translated modules provide services primarily in the legal, administrative, medical, conferencing, and educational settings. Some Ugandans have studied in Kenya and obtained academic qualifications in interpreting or translation studies (D. E. Ssebuyungo, personal communication, January 26, 2021).

Given Uganda's multilingual and multicultural context (Clyne, 2017), and the large number of Ugandan citizens growing up with knowledge of more than one language and participating in multiple official and unofficial realms of life, it is understandable that T&I services in Uganda are not limited to the aforementioned graduates. It is common for fluent users of the spoken local languages to provide T&I services as long as the need arises. As such, it is not unusual for a court to ask a Master in Law who is fluent in Luganda to interpret or for a nurse who is fluent in spoken Luganda to interpret in the hospital (Namyalo & Nakayiza, 2015). This has been evidenced in different settings, including the political setting, though it has a blended approach of professionally trained translators or interpreters and bilingual communicators who have acquired the Ugandan local languages naturally. These kinds of settings (e.g., religious settings, social-cultural settings, and personal communication in one-to-one meetings) have particularly fronted and provided a platform for T&I services. However, it is worth noting that not every person can provide quality translation or interpreting services, and there is some social control on the quality of interpreting, conflicts of interests, etc. Nonetheless, it is important to acknowledge that translation and interpreting services are being offered in all areas of life, given the multilingual and multicultural nature of Ugandan society and sub-Saharan Africa in general (Orem et al., 2014).

Professionalization of SLI in Uganda

The seeds for UgSL interpreting training were planted during the Regional Sign Language Conferences in Eastern and Southern Africa, which were held during the 1980s and 1990s by the World Federation of the Deaf (WFD) in cooperation with national deaf organizations and donors from the Nordic countries (see also Lutalo-Kiingi & De Clerck, 2015b).

In the 1980s, a period characterized by the civil wars, the Kampala deaf community used to meet in the capital to share ideas. It was in these meetings that many deaf people expressed that they saw a need for interpreters. However, it was only in post-war Uganda that NGOs and organizations of people with disabilities became more active in Kampala. For example, the Kampala Welfare Association of the Deaf and the Deaf Development Association (DDA), along with deaf elders[2] and deaf youth,[3] came together to explore solutions to communication barriers. During these meetings, they opted to train family and friends as volunteer interpreters (Lutalo-Kiingi & De Clerck, in press a, b). From there, deaf Ugandans participated in Regional Sign Language Conferences, increasing their encounters with deaf professionals and sign language interpreters. Such experiences were eye-openers in their understanding of the profession of SLI and the role of a sign language interpreter in facilitating communication among community members and mainstream society.

In the early 1990s, deaf Ugandans were increasingly exposed to sign language interpreters and the importance of their work in facilitating communication. In 1990, Edreke Ssendagire and Florence Mukasa, members of the Uganda National Association of the Deaf (UNAD), were invited to attend the second sign language conference in Ethiopia (Lutalo-Kiingi & De Clerck, 2015c). During this conference, they experienced barriers during meetings with officials, and then-president of the WFD, Lisa Kauppinen, asked them why they had not brought an interpreter, a question that raised their awareness about the need and use of sign language interpreters.

Best practices in using sign language interpreters were also shown to deaf Ugandans when deaf leader Gloria Pullen, a deaf project development worker from the United Kingdom, attended a funders' meeting with Action on Disability Development (ADD) in Kampala in Uganda (Pullen, 2001). The meeting was mediated by British Sign Language (BSL)/English interpreters and gave deaf Ugandans much to think about in terms of their own access to sign language interpreters. Furthermore, the initial visit of Asger Bergmann, former DDL president, and Lilly Krarup, former chairperson of the Third World Committee of DDL in 1992, which was intended to gain a broad understanding of the needs of deaf Ugandans and explore partnership opportunities, was another impactful moment in exposing meeting participants to sign language interpreters, as they brought a Danish Sign Language interpreter to mediate the communication during official meetings.

During this period, Sam Lutalo-Kiingi, who had been exposed to SLI during meetings at the Kenyan Deaf Association, started to informally train UgSL interpreters[4] because he needed SLI for his meetings with people at the DDA, a deaf organization in Kampala, as well as for accessing his college courses when he was training as an electrician.

In 1992, the third regional sign language conference took place in Kenya. Interpreters from other African nations were present, and the conference was attended by several deaf Ugandans. During this conference, Florence Mukasa reached out to Liz Scott Gibson, a BSL/English and International Sign interpreter from Scotland in the United Kingdom. Through this meeting, Liz Scott Gibson volunteered to provide a 1-week interpreting training course in Kampala in 1993.

The first project between the DDL and UNAD, funded by the Danish International Development and Cooperation Agency (DANIDA) (1992–1994) and the Danish Ministry of Foreign Affairs, was coordinated by the late Raija Moutgaard, a Finnish Sign Language interpreter, who worked in Uganda from 1993 onward. Moutgaard also knew UgSL and International Sign and interpreted during official meetings or presentations of the UNAD and the DDA, and she supported the aforementioned training by Liz Scott Gibson. During this project, two weekly short courses were organized, with the aim of providing basic UgSL lessons to teachers, interpreter trainees, and parents and relatives of deaf children and deaf adults so they could learn some UgSL, including practical and theoretical elements and aspects of deaf culture. In addition, trainee interpreters were taught basic interpreting theory and practical skills. Liz Scott Gibson also contributed to another short course on interpreting in preparation for the fourth regional conference, which Uganda hosted in 1994. This training contributed to further understanding and practice of the professional role of a sign language interpreter and the need for professional training.

During the fourth regional conference, which was on SLI, contributions by international interpreters, interpreter trainers, and linguists were made. They explored various topics in relation to the field of interpreting, including theoretical lectures, history of SLI, ethics in interpreting, linguistics, interpreter training curriculum and organization, interpreting provision, and linguistics of interpreting (Skjoldan & Glad, 1994). This conference provided valuable information to the participants. It also drew the attention of policymakers and emphasized the need for recognition of UgSL as a legitimate medium of communication for deaf citizens.

Increased need for quality SLI provision led to further strengthening of qualifications among interpreter trainees. The Regional Sign Language Project (RSLP II) in 1998 responded to the need to train sign language interpreter trainers and sign language instructors. This project funded an advanced training course in Denmark and included 12 deaf instructor trainees and 12 hearing interpreter trainees from each of the four East African countries (Uganda, Kenya, Tanzania, and Zambia). As a result, deaf instructors and hearing interpreter students were trained to develop signing and interpreting skills in their respective regional countries (see also Lutalo-Kiingi & De Clerck, 2015b; Lutalo-Kiingi et al., 2022).

In Uganda, extensive training through a series of courses and practice over 12 weeks in 3 years (2000–2003) saw the birth of the national certification for UgSL interpreters and deaf instructors. Assessment and evaluation of students to determine their interpreting skills and linguistic competence were done by the Uganda National Institute of Special Education (UNISE), which merged in 2001 with other institutions to form KyU, under the memorandum of understanding with DDL (supported by the Danish government through DANIDA; Lutalo-Kiingi, 2015b). The certificate in interpreting was crucial, as it was the first official credential for sign language interpreters; later, this credential served as a minimum entry requirement for the diploma-level interpreting program.

To promote the recognition of SLI as a profession, attempts were made to provide systematic training in the field (Baker, 1992). A partnership between KyU and DDL in collaboration with DANIDA, called the Sign Language project (2002–2006), took place and resulted in scientific research on UgSL being conducted, as well as the 2-year UgSL diploma program. Project highlights included curriculum development and its validation through university systems and processes; identifying project staff members (both deaf and hearing); identifying hearing interpreters to be trained by consultants from the Center for Sign Language and Sign-Supported Communication; organizing the management of sign language research and interpreter education at the university level; and ensuring the availability of relevant training equipment and materials, including books and resources, in the library. The trainers selected were identified as experts in sign language linguistics, and trainers of interpreters were also consulted to ensure that the program was underpinned by research in interpreter education. In 2006, the project was completed and handed over to KyU to take on full responsibility for its formal implementation and program sustainability (also see Wallin et al., 2006; Lutalo-Kiingi & De Clerck, 2015b, 2016; Lutalo-Kiingi, 2016, 2019). Nearly 22 years later, professional SLI education is still ongoing. The project staff were able to continue to deliver the program and work at KyU by taking supplementary training and professional development, which was done enthusiastically. More than 270 professional sign language interpreters have graduated from the diploma program and have successfully served the community.

WHERE WE ARE TODAY

Although an initial idea to create an association of UgSL interpreters was first conceptualized in 1993, because of lack of funds and leadership gaps, it was not until the first UgSL interpreters graduated from the Diploma in UgSL Interpreting program in 2003 that the UNASLI was established as a professional body. Because of financial constraints, the secretariat desk was housed under the UNAD from 2003 to 2018. This was not without conflicts of interest, which were a drawback in terms of the professionalism of the organization. In 2019, the UNASLI was legally recognized and registered with the Ugandan Non-Governmental Organization Board.

To date, the main activities of the UNASLI have been limited to the organization of general assemblies and elections of office bearers, which contribute to the monitoring of its day-to-day operation. It is hoped that its recently achieved status as an independent NGO will contribute to an expansion of its activities to further support continuous professional development through training activities, dissemination of updated information about UgSL interpreting, responses to support and counseling inquiries of UgSL interpreters, and the publication of newsletters. Therefore, it is important for the association to make known the way it works and the possibilities it can offer.

There is increasing demand from courts for UgSL interpreters to be members of an accredited body for UgSL interpreting. As there has only been the diploma degree, recognition has not been possible. Courts currently accept UgSL interpreters after receiving a letter from the UNASLI. However, the establishment of the bachelor's and master's programs in UgSL interpreting and translation (discussed later) is likely to enable the UNASLI to receive full accreditation by the government, which will make a change in the recognition of the profession.

The use of SLI services to facilitate communication is a human right, recognized by international legislation such as the United Nations Convention on the Rights of Persons With Disabilities (UNCRPD), ratified by Uganda in 2008. The need for professionally trained and qualified UgSL interpreters is also supported by Ugandan national legislation and policy statements in relation to professionals working with persons with disabilities. The Persons With Disabilities Act (PWDs Act, 2006), Article 4, states that under general obligations, the state shall "Promote the training of professional and staff working with [persons with disabilities] in rights recognized in this convention so as to better provide the assistance and services guaranteed by those rights." In addition, the revised PWDs Act (2020) mandates the National Council for Persons With Disabilities under function (g) "to regulate the human support services for [persons with disabilities] including [sign language interpreters]." Meanwhile, Article 15 on access to justice, information, and training says that it is the state's obligation to "promote the development, training and use of sign language, . . . and [sign language interpreters] in all public institutions at all government functions" (PWDs Act, 2019). Enhanced quality interpretation in public institutions is supported in many document guidelines issued by the Ugandan parliament and by local governments (e.g., Kampala City Council Authorities) to support the sign language interpreters working with the Ugandan deaf member of parliament and with deaf councilors under political employment bodies.

Despite the legal and policy provisions in support of qualified UgSL interpreters in public institutions, the profession of UgSL T&I has no legal protection. Although in practice, UgSL translation is being done in the community and is also increasingly being done by DIs (e.g., for translating policy reports), it is not yet recognized as a task separate from UgSL interpreting. However, recent discussions in stakeholder meetings related to the bachelor and master of science (MSc) UgSL training programs have contributed to raising awareness among professionals. Certain interpreting services are seen as less important than others, and recognition and protection vary among different realms of life. The remuneration of some UgSL interpreters is the state's obligation, whereas for other UgSL interpreters, it is the obligation of the consumers (both deaf and hearing) who use the interpreting services. For example, in education, the law in Subsection 5 of the PWDs Act (2019) states that "an institution of learning which is owned or aided by Government that enrolls a learner with a disability, shall provide sign language services for that learner, learning instructional materials and assistive devices, suitable for the learner and required for examinations by the learner." This statement does not specifically mention working with qualified interpreters, nor does it mention work fees. Although government institutions must provide sign language services, there is no quality control. In practice, this often results in UgSL interpreters working without a professional job status, legal backup, or any compensation for their work. It also means that people, in other professions who do not have a degree in UgSL interpreting often do the work of an interpreter (e.g., teachers with limited knowledge of UgSL doing interpreting assignments in educational settings). Salaries of UgSL interpreters with diploma qualifications working in educational settings tend to be lower than salaries of teachers with diploma degrees in the same settings. These low salaries are due to a lack of policies around UgSL interpreting, as well as the fact that interpreters tend to be paid by parent–teacher associations. There are also differences in the payment of interpreters with the same qualifications in government settings, such as the Ugandan parliament or ministries, and there are differences in the payment of UgSL interpreters working for broadcasters and national television. Therefore, advocacy for appropriate legislation and policy on the remuneration of UgSL interpreting and maintaining professional standards in various interpreting settings, such as the education, health services, legal, religious, social, and community domains, is vital for further professionalization and for facilitating official recruitment of UgSL interpreters in the public service systems.

Currently, the national association is limited in capacity to oversee the practices of spoken or signed language translators. The identification of Ugandan language translators to offer their services is entirely about the closeness of an individual translator to those who require the services and references from other people or organizations for whom the translator had worked previously. Finally, we should add that, unlike the UgSL interpreters, who have at least some form of protection through clauses within the Acts, spoken language interpreters and translators do not have any policies or legislation that back up the provision of translation services. As we mentioned earlier, the lack of degree programs and professional qualifications for interpreters and translators is a drawback in terms of policy and legislative recognition. Therefore, there is a lot to be done in the country to attain the quality provision of interpreting and translating services.

Sign Language Interpreter Education in Uganda

The current educational pathway to a career in SLI requires interpreters to take a 2-year study program at the diploma level in UgSL interpreting offered at the Department of Special Needs Studies, Faculty of Special Needs and Rehabilitation (formerly known as the Uganda National Institute of Special Education [UNISE]), at KyU. Currently, the diploma accreditation provides sign language interpreters with career opportunities. The certified diploma qualification in interpreting, which is university based, provides the common standard for employment and advancement for further studies.

Because this program is the only available formal diploma interpreter training program, to be admitted, interested candidates must obtain the minimum academic qualification equivalent to the requirement for admission at the university level. An additional requirement for enrollment is that one needs to have a good command of both English and UgSL. Also, applicants must have satisfactory eyesight and hearing abilities (these criteria are changing and are described later). Having a strong upper motor stature, which is needed for the production of sign language when standing/sitting, is also a requirement.

Generally, the key objective is for trainees to become fluent in both UgSL and English so as to demonstrate the ability to interpret between languages at the end of the training. In so doing, students develop the capabilities to understand the meaning given in the source language and convey its equivalent meaning in the target language. Once the formal education has been completed, trained interpreters are advised to continue to build their body of knowledge further through professional development. Higher education is encouraged, and membership in UNASLI is expected for all the trained interpreters.

As in many countries without formal training programs for DIs (Bartlett & Anderson, 2011; Stone & West, 2012), Uganda also has a few DIs who are working in a range of settings (e.g., judicial, medical, family, and community settings). Although these DIs have been trained as sign language instructors, there have been no opportunities for them to train as interpreters. Certainly, the lack of professional training for DIs has been a drawback to the professionalization of the field. Admission of DIs into the Diploma in UgSL Interpreting program was not considered when the program was established in the 1990s. Since this time, Uganda has seen an increasing number of deaf persons conferred with academic awards (certificates and bachelor's and master's degrees) in different academic fields at the college and university levels. Recognizing the need to train DIs, the university has a new 5-year strategy that will enable DIs to become professionally trained and qualified (see later).

As of the writing of this chapter, there are seven educators (two deaf, five hearing) in the program at KyU: Senior Lecturer Sam Lutalo-Kiingi, UgSL Senior Technician Bonnie Busingye, Assistant Lecturer Dorothy Lule (retired; part time), and Lecturer Julius Patrick Omguru. Unfortunately, Lecturer Proscovia Ssuubi Nantongo passed away in July 2021, and at the time of writing, KyU was still looking into possibilities for replacement. Nancy Katumba Muwangala and John Buyinza are employed by KyU on short-term contracts as interpreters and part-time lecturers currently teaching the core courses of interpreting in the UgSL interpreting diploma course.

Sam Lutalo-Kiingi and Bonnie Busingye are deaf persons who are tasked with the responsibility of training and overseeing UgSL acquisition skills, deaf culture, and sign linguistics. Dorothy Lule, the late Proscovia Suubi Nantongo, John Buyinza, and Julius Patrick Omugur are tasked with the responsibility of the expressive and receptive skills training, which includes processes of interpreting, bimodal interpreting, and professionalism, among others. Dorothy Lule, who also taught UgSL interpreting in the diploma course as an assistant lecturer, retired in 2020. Dorothy Lule, the late Proscovia Ssuubi Nantongo, and Sam Lutalo-Kiingi were trained in interpreting education during the DDL project. Although opportunities for staff members to obtain advanced academic degrees have been supported by KyU, they have also depended on international donors and funding. Continued capacity building of educators in the UgSL interpreting programs is vital to secure the quality and sustainability of interpreter education at KyU.

KyU is the only academic institution that offers the diploma program in UgSL Interpreting, which has existed for more than 22 years now. The training is offered on a full-time basis within the four semesters of the 2 years, where each academic year consists of two semesters of 17 weeks, of which 15 weeks are for teaching and 2 weeks are for examinations at the end of the semester. According to the revised and amended curriculum, the courses are modular, with each module having specific university credit unit value. The obligatory course contents offered are divided in two parts, one being sign language and the other interpreting. We will outline these generally, without profiling each module unit it comprises.

The sign language component makes up a larger part of the curriculum, where UgSL is taught intensively. The course modules were designed to enable students develop sign language skills (expressive and receptive fluency) to be able to communicate freely with deaf people. As a result, UgSL is used for instruction and conversation in the lecture rooms right from the first day to the end of the training. Occasionally, a staff interpreter might provide an interpretation if needed to ensure that both the interpreter trainees and the lecturer understand each other. These modules provide trainees with linguistic knowledge of UgSL and include topics such as phonology, morphology, syntax, and semantics. Particular attention is paid to linguistic knowledge and acquisition of UgSL features—for instance, nonmanual features, constructed action and dialogue, placement, productivity of signs, and use of classifiers, to mention but a few. High priority is given to practical exercises, as required by the course modules, to raise the level of the students' performance. Considerable time is allocated to practical activities for independent and individual studies, as well as for working in groups. Examples include watching and discussing recorded signed videos or DVDs that show stories told by deaf adult fluent users of UgSL, followed by students' recording their own retelling of the stories and comparing their signing to that of the deaf signer. In addition, other course module units taught help trainees to understand the deaf community and culture, deaf history, sociopsychology of the deaf, deafness and development, and sign linguistics and sociolinguistics.

The interpreting training part, on the other hand, is taught intensively during the second year. For example, the modules on interpreting from UgSL to English or from English to UgSL are taught with the purpose of helping students to convey accurately the meaning of what is rendered in UgSL/English through the interpreter's interpretation. Emphasis is on developing their bilingual and bimodal ability to concentrate in a focused manner to understand the structure of and derive meaning from the full accessed signed UgSL/spoken English. Students learn to pay particular attention to and analyze the detailed visual information on the signer's face (facial expressions) to improve the perception of visual information. In addition, students practice to become fluent UgSL signers and English speakers. They practice the use of simple and correct English/UgSL sentence structures, focusing on vocal elements such as tone, inflection, rate, pauses, emphasis, sentence endings, and other paralinguistic features called for in UgSL. Students also learn the "dos and don'ts" of interpreting into and from UgSL and English. For example, students learn how to manage their voices, practice breathing techniques, and sit comfortably to avoid tension.

Other interpreting module courses include theories of interpreting ethics and professionalism, processes of interpreting, and psychology of interpreting. Time is allocated to students' individual or group work to improve their skills through making use of the audio resources to practice UgSL interpreting. They also make use of signed videos of deaf adults signing fluently in different signing styles to widen their knowledge of UgSL variations and vocabularies.

The curriculum requires written and practical examinations on the course units taught at the end of each semester. Some assignments and examinations, both theoretical and practical, are used to assess and evaluate student progress. Examinations done practically are submitted in UgSL on video/laptops and flash drives. The students are obliged to pass all the coursework and examinations. Additionally, students undertake a practicum in simultaneous interpreting in the community, which is monitored and assessed during recess periods in both the first and second years. Students also undertake one independent project on a specific topic taken from an area of the students' choice related to the practice of interpreting. Successful students should demonstrate a grasp of issues through independent reading and evidence of analytical skills in the chosen areas. These too count toward the students' successful final assessment before they qualify and graduate as professional qualified UgSL interpreters.

The team has encountered major challenges in human resources and in financial and material resources for UgSL interpreting and translation teaching and research. Lecturers have improvised by creating and using their own resources to facilitate teaching, aiming to compensate for outdated resources such as analog television screens, projectors, video recorders, and videotapes that were provided by our Danish donors. Lecturers have also tried to advocate through the department by requisitioning new technologies such as video recorders, voice recorders, and laptops; the installation of a sign language lab; and the provision of technical support. Action needs to be taken to optimize these resources so the bachelor's and master's programs in UgSL interpreting and translation can be successful. The university also has to provide resources (academic books and journals) to support research on UgSL, the Ugandan deaf community, and UgSL interpreting and translation, and educators and students need to be able to access these resources via the library or other online platforms.

Research on UgSL interpreter education has begun only recently. The development of the UgSL training programs was first documented during Sam Lutalo-Kiingi's doctoral studies (e.g., Lutalo-Kiingi, 2014) and was further documented as a part of an anthropological research project on the sustainability of the Ugandan deaf community (Lutalo-Kiingi & De Clerck, 2015, 2017, 2018). In addition, Bonnie Busingye completed a master's dissertation on "Evaluating Teaching and Learning Processes for the Diploma in Ugandan Sign language Interpreting program" (Busingye, 2016) during her studies in pedagogy at KyU, which included suggestions for improvement of the program. She recommended improved time management by staff and students, increased interaction with the Ugandan deaf community, and more diverse contacts with deaf role models.

In collaboration with HWU in Edinburgh, Scotland, in the United Kingdom, and supported by a Visiting Fellowship Award from the British Academy (2018–2019), Sam Lutalo-Kiingi conducted a research study on UgSL interpreting and interpreting education to inspire a revision of academic degree programs at the university (this revision is discussed further). This study included qualitative in-depth interviews with deaf clients and UgSL interpreters, as well as focus groups with the respective target groups, to identify challenges and gaps in UgSL interpreting services across different domains of life. As part of this study, the existing UgSL interpreting diploma course was evaluated and compared with training programs at HWU and others in the United Kingdom. During the fellowship, draft curricula for a bachelor's degree program in UgSL interpreting and translation were developed and discussed with staff members at KyU in Uganda and HWU. Today, this program is in the last stage of seeking approval for accreditation from the National Council for Higher Education. After returning to Uganda, in response to a strong need for further capacity building, Sam also worked with KyU staff members on a master's degree program. The master's program in UgSL interpreting and translation has already received accreditation.

Although the profession of UgSL interpreting in Uganda is similar to SLI in other parts of the world, the developing world context continues to provide unique challenges for UgSL interpreters and service users. As mentioned earlier, UgSL interpreters will find themselves working in a wide variety of multilingual settings. They also face renumeration challenges because of the absence of governmental funding for interpreting services in domains such as health care, employment in private workplaces, and family and community settings. As such, deaf services users need to pay for UgSL interpreting services in these domains, or UgSL interpreters need to work voluntarily. Although UgSL interpreting services are well respected in some domains (e.g., in the operations of NGOs), the status of the academic degree (diploma) might not equate to appropriate payment by the government in educational and political contexts.

The lack of an independent agency for the provision of UgSL interpreting services also creates ethical risks for deaf service users, deaf professionals, and UgSL interpreters. Some of these challenges can be addressed through a bachelor's degree program aimed to teach the Ugandan context and train interpreters to work in a diverse range of professional settings, including the noted multilingual settings. Having a BA program will also enhance the working relationships between UgSL interpreters and deaf community members, and importantly, it will meet the conditions for recognition of the profession of UgSL interpreting, which in turn can generate opportunities for governmentally supported interpreting services.

A research dissemination workshop held at KyU on March 12, 2019, with a panel discussion raised awareness among all stakeholders about the need for advanced academic training in UgSL interpreting. It highlighted the changed socioeconomic environment, with a strong emphasis on the importance of academic qualifications and the increased number of deaf people seeking access to academic training in interpreting and translation. During this workshop, deaf community members gained further understanding of the profession of UgSL interpreters, and UgSL interpreters learned what a BA program would provide them, particularly the training they need to navigate the challenges they are experiencing. NGOs became more aware of the working circumstances of UgSL interpreters.

Academic degrees in UgSL interpreting and translation are also needed to improve the socioeconomic welfare of UgSL interpreters, who will receive appropriate payment for their services, and and the welfare of Ugandan deaf community members, who will have better access to and better opportunities for education, employment, and inclusion in Ugandan society. Against the background of limited academic opportunities for training in interpreting and translation in Uganda, the establishment of a degree program in UgSL is quite remarkable.

The Road Ahead

In 2017, legal and policy reforms of the Ugandan government encouraged public universities to revise their academic educational structures to concentrate on the organization of bachelor's, master's, and PhD programs. Certificate and diploma courses were to be transferred to other institutions of higher education. To meet these challenges, KyU undertook a review and restructuring of its educational programs, which resulted in a 5-year strategy plan (2020–2025) that has received approval from the Ugandan government. The establishment of the bachelor's and master's degrees in UgSL Interpreting and Translation is part of this strategic plan and will receive internal funding for capacity building to train and hire (additional) staff members. The BA and MSc programs have received approval by the Department and Faculty and are currently being discussed at the level of the University Senate and Council,[5] after which they will ultimately be submitted to the National Council for Higher Education in Uganda for accreditation. To meet the aforementioned challenges of capacity building, knowledge exchange, and resources, the university is also actively networking and exploring cooperation with international partners, who are offering SLI and sign language translation programs.

These university-level qualifications will improve the prospects of UgSL interpreters, boosting interpreters' earning potential and allowing them to pursue work across sectors, in national and international settings. Furthermore, it is expected that the training program will support ongoing advocacy for the recognition of UgSL interpreting as a profession by the Ugandan government and, ultimately, for the governmental and private sector provision of UgSL T&I services in sub-Saharan Africa.

The availability of qualified UgSL interpreters and translators across Uganda, including DIs and deaf translators, is vital to enabling deaf people's participation in all domains of public life, providing them with better access to education and employment, and enhancing their opportunities for inclusion (Lutalo-Kiingi, 2019). It is envisaged that the development of partnerships in Uganda and internationally will continue in post–COVID-19 times to enable the programs to generate sufficient resources and to continue with capacity building. We also hope to be able to continue to develop further research on UgSL interpreting, especially because there is a strong need to learn more about SLI and SLI education in multilingual settings in sub-Saharan Africa.

Acknowledgments

We write this in memory of our colleague, Proscovia Ssuubi Nantongo, who passed away during the writing of this chapter. Her passing was a big loss for the UgSL community and the UgSL interpreting program at KyU. We thank the British Academy for the Visiting Fellowship Award to fund the "Professional Ugandan Sign Language (UgSL) Interpreting Services: Evaluating an Academic Training Program and Identifying Challenges in Practice" research project and the Centre for Translation and Interpreting Studies (CTISS) at HWU in Scotland for hosting Sam Lutalo-Kiingi as a visiting fellow. Looking back on the historical developments of the UgSL interpreting education programs, the authors owe much appreciation to all the international experts and professionals who have generously supported capacity building and knowledge exchange in the country over the past three decades. This international support has enabled KyU to continue to train UgSL interpreters and translators and to upgrade their training programs to meet academic standards.

Notes

1. For a discussion of Uganda's political ambivalence, its influence on Ugandan deaf community leadership, and risks related to research with the Ugandan deaf community, see De Clerck & Lutalo-Kiingi, 2018.

2. *Deaf elders* refers to the first and second generations of deaf Ugandans who joined Uganda School for the Deaf during its establishment in the 1950s and contributed to the emergence and development of UgSL. This group of deaf Ugandans interacted with deaf adults working at the school.

3. *Deaf youth* refers to the third and fourth generations of deaf Ugandans who attained education at the Uganda School for the Deaf, were fluent UgSL signers, and often pursued higher or advanced education in Kenya (for further information on the history of deaf education in Uganda and the development and emergence of UgSL, see Lutalo-Kiingi & De Clerck, in press).

4. The first sign language interpreters whom Sam Lutalo-Kiingi began to train were Barbara Magezi and the late Proscovia Ssuubi Nantongo.

5. The MSc has already been accredited in 2023 and will be implemented next year in 2024. The BA is awaiting accreditation.

REFERENCES

Akach, P. A. O., Mweri, G., & Hempel, L. (1992). *Third East African sign language seminar: Sign language in education of the Deaf.* Karen, Nairobi.

Altmayer, C., & E. Wolff. (2013). *Africa: Challenges of multilingualism.* Peter Lang.

Awoii, P. M. (2011). A glimpse at the development of sign language interpretation in Uganda. In B. Costello, M. Thumann, & R. Shaw (Eds.), *Conference proceedings of the World Association of Sign Language Interpreters, Durban, South Africa* (pp. 29–38). World Association of Sign Language Interpreters.

Baker, M. (1992). *In other words: A course book on translation.* Routledge.

Baker, W. G. (2001). *Uganda: The marginalization of minorities.* Minority Rights Group International.

Bamgbose, A. (2014). The language factor in development goals. *Journal of Multilingual and Multicultural Development, 35*(7), 646–657.

Bartlett, P., & Anderson, S. (2011). Developing deaf interpreting training and assessment frameworks. In B. Costello, M. Thumann, & R. Shaw (Eds.), *Conference proceedings of the World Association of Sign Language Interpreters, Durban, South* (pp. 39–49). World Association of Sign Language Interpreters.

Busingye, B. (2016). *Evaluating teaching and learning processes for the Diploma in Ugandan Sign Language Interpreting program: A case study of the Department of Special Needs Studies, Kyambogo University* [Unpublished master's thesis]. Kyambogo University.

Clyne, M. (2017). Multilingualism. In F. Coulmas (Ed.), *The handbook of sociolinguistics* (pp. 301–314). Blackwell Publishing Ltd.

De Clerck, G. A. M., & Lutalo-Kiingi, S. (2018). Ethical and methodological responses to risks in fieldwork with Deaf Ugandans. *Contemporary Social Science.* https://doi.org/10.1080/21582041.2017.1347273

Dicklitch, S., & Lwanga, D. (2003). The politics of being non-political: Human rights organization and the creation of a positive human rights culture in Uganda. *Human Rights Quarterly, 25,* 482–509.

Kanyamurwa, J. M. (2020). The political economy of globalization and employment returns to youth in Uganda. In S. O. Oloruntoba & T. Falola (Eds.), *The Palgrave handbook of African political economy* (pp. 375–398). Palgrave Macmillan.

Lutalo-Kiingi, S. (2016). A descriptive grammar of morphosyntactic constructions in Ugandan Sign Language (UgSL). *Sign Language & Linguistics, 19*(1), 132–141.

Lutalo-Kiingi, S. (2019*). Professional Ugandan Sign Language interpreting services and training programs: Views of UgSL interpreters and deaf service users.* [Paper presentation]. World Conference of the World Association of Sign Language Interpreters, Paris, France.

Lutalo-Kiingi, S., & De Clerck, G. A. M. (2015a). Ugandan Sign Language. In J. B. Hansen, G. A. M. De Clerck, S. Lutalo-Kiingi, & W. B. McGregor (Eds.), *Sign languages of the world: A comparative handbook* (pp. 811–840). De Gruyter Mouton.

Lutalo-Kiingi, S., & De Clerck, G. A. M. (2015b). Deaf citizenship and sign language diversity in sub-Saharan Africa: Promoting partnership between sign language communities, academia, and NGO's in development in Uganda and Cameroon. In A. C. Cooper & K. K. Rashid (Eds.), *Citizenship, politics, difference: Perspectives from sub-Saharan signed language communities* (pp. 29–63). Gallaudet University Press.

Lutalo-Kiingi, S., & De Clerck, G. A. M. (2015c, September 29). *Developing sustainably? The Ugandan deaf community looking back and forward: 1992–2006 Partnership of DDL, UNAD, and Kyambogo University funded by DANIDA.* [Poster presentation]. Kyambogo University.

Lutalo-Kiingi, S., & De Clerck, G. A. M. (2016). Perspectives on the sign language factor in Sub-Saharan Africa: Challenges of sustainability. In G. A. M. De Clerck and P. V. Paul (Eds.), *Sign language, sustainable development, and equal opportunities. Envisioning the future for deaf students* (pp. 134–160). Gallaudet University Press.

Lutalo-Kiingi, S., & De Clerck, G. A. M. (2017). Perspectives on the sign language factor in Sub-Saharan Africa: Challenges of sustainability. *American Annals of the Deaf, 162*(1), 47–56.

Lutalo-Kiingi, S., Buyinza, J., De Clerck, G. A. M., & Turner, G. H. (2022). Challenges in the professionalization of sign language interpreting in Uganda. In C. Stone, R. Adam, R. M. De Quadros, & C. Rathmann (Eds.), *The Routledge handbook of sign language translation and interpreting* (pp. 283–295). Routledge.

Lutalo-Kiingi, S., & De Clerck, G. A. M. (In press a). *Developing sustainably? The Ugandan deaf community looking back and forward.* Fountain Publishers.

Lutalo-Kiingi, S., & De Clerck, G. A. M. (In press b). The Ugandan deaf community and its history of UgSL development: Challenges in the on-going colonialism of African deaf communities. In B. Carty & S. Lutalo-Kiingi (Ed.), *Colonialism in deaf history. The Proceedings of the 10th Deaf History International Conference (DHI), UTS Function Centre University, July 18–21, 2018.*

Nakayiza, J. (2013). *The sociolinguistics of multilingualism in Uganda: A case study of the official and non-official language policy, planning and management of Luruuri-Lunyara and Luganda.* [Unpublished doctoral dissertation]. University of London, London, England.

Namyalo, S., & J. Nakayiza. (2015). Dilemmas in implementing language rights in multilingual Uganda. *Current Issues in Language Planning, 16*(4), 409–424.

Okombo, O. D. (2001). *Language policy: The forgotten parameter in African development and governance strategies.* [Unpublished inaugural lecture]. University of Nairobi, Nairobi.

Orem, J. N., Mafigiri, D. K., Nabudere, H., & Criel, B. (2014). Improving knowledge translation in Uganda: More needs to be done. *The Pan African Medical Journal, 17*(1), 1–14.

Pullen, G. (2001). *Deaf development programme in Uganda.* In A. Callaway (Ed.), *Deafness and development: Learning from projects with deaf children and deaf adults in developing countries* (pp. 21–25). University of Bristol Print Services.

Skjoldan, H., & Glad, P. (1994). *Fourth East and Southern African Sign language seminar: Sign language interpreting for the Deaf.* Kampala, Uganda, Danish Deaf Association.

Stone, C., & West, D. (2012). Translation, representation, and the Deaf "voice." *Qualitative Research*, *12*(6), 645–665.

Tangri, R., & Mwanda, A.M. (2006). Politics, donors, and the ineffectiveness of anti-corruption institutions in Uganda. *The Journal of Modern African Studies*, *44*, 101–124.

The Republic of Uganda. (1995). Constitution of the Republic of Uganda. Law Development Centre.

The Republic of Uganda. (2006). The Persons With Disabilities Act. Uganda Government Printing & Publishing Corporation.

The Republic of Uganda. (2015). Constitution of the Republic of Uganda: With Amendments. Uganda Government Printing & Publishing Corporation.

The Republic of Uganda. (2020). The Persons With Disabilities Act. Uganda Government Printing & Publishing Corporation.

UBOS. (2020). Population & Censuses: Statistical abstract. Enhancing Data Quality and Use. *Uganda Bureau of Statistics*. https://www.ubos.org/explore-statistics/20/

UNDP. (2020). Human Development Reports: Uganda total population. *United Nations Development Program*. http://hdr.undp.org/en/indicators/44206

UNDP Human Development Reports. (2019). *Working poor at PPP$3.20 a day (% of total employment)*. http://hdr.undp.org/en/indicators/153706

Wallin, L., Lule, D., Lutalo-Kiingi, S., & Busingye, B. (2006). *Ugandan Sign Language dictionary*. Kyambogo University.

ROBERT ADAM, JEMINA NAPIER, AND
STACEY WEBB

21

How Far We Have Come, and How Much Further Do We Have to Go?

Sign Language Translation and Interpreting
in the United Kingdom

From a national perspective, the United Kingdom (UK) is made up of four nations: England, Scotland, Wales, and Northern Ireland, with an estimated total population of 66.4 million people.[1] According to the Office of National Statistics (ONS) census (2021), 17.1% (880,000) declared that they feel they could speak English well, and 3.1% (161,000) stated that they could not speak English at all.

It is difficult to estimate the exact number of deaf signers throughout the UK, but on the basis of an analysis of the 2011 Scottish census results, Turner (2020) estimated between 40,000 and 70,000 deaf British Sign Language (BSL) users. The ONS 2021 census, however, stated that 22,000 have BSL as their *first* language.

There is a well-documented history of sign language use and sign language interpreting (SLI) within the British isles over the centuries. The first mention of a signing deaf person was Princess Joanna Stuart of Scotland (1428–1486); the first school for deaf children was established in Edinburgh in 1760 (Jackson, 2001); and the first record of a sign language interpreter was in the Old Bailey, the central criminal court, in 1771, when a hearing person was sworn to interpret for a deaf person convicted of stealing (Stone & Woll, 2008). The membership organization representing deaf people, the British Deaf Association (BDA), was established in 1890 by deaf people and has continued to be active to the present period. Over the years, BDA has maintained strong relationships with SLI organizations in the UK.

BSL as we would recognize it now was particularly fostered through the various deaf residential schools established in the 18th century, and the regional dialectical variation that is notable in BSL is often associated with the locations of those schools

(Quinn, 2010). In Northern Ireland, deaf people use both Irish Sign Language (ISL) and BSL, typically depending on the religious affiliation of the school they attended. The UK also has many settled sign language communities from various parts of the world, but particularly from Lithuania, Poland, and Czechia (Stone, 2010), and more recently from Ukraine. These deaf people migrate to the UK as refugees, as asylum seekers, or for marriage or employment (Emery & Iyer, 2022) and typically will learn BSL over time.

The British Sign Language Act (UK) was proclaimed in 2022. Other pieces of legislation in and around the UK also refer to using professional sign language interpreters, placing the onus on public bodies to provide accessibility in BSL: the Police and Criminal Evidence Act (1984), the Human Rights Act (1998), the Communications Act (2003), the Equality Act (2010), the BSL (Scotland) Act (2015), and the National Health Service Accessible Information Standards (2017).

Additionally, the 2007 United Nations Convention on the Rights of Persons with Disabilities (UNCRPD) refers to sign language seven times across five articles, relating to definitions, recognition, and promotion of sign language, education, and SLI, and reference is also made to deaf culture (De Meulder, 2014). Stone (2013) indicates that all these provisions and items of legislation meet the UK obligations of ratification of the UNCRPD, although policy and practice can diverge widely worldwide, as found by Haualand and Allen (2009).

Consequently, government funding is available for BSL interpreting services (and other accommodations) for deaf BSL users in schools, further education colleges and universities (through Disabled Student Support Schemes), the workplace (through the UK Government Access to Work scheme), and the legal and health care systems (devolved to public services).

There has been a historical tendency for England, Wales, and Northern Ireland to form one professional SLI organization and for Scotland to form another, so at international interpreting conferences, the UK has often been represented by two different organizations. The first regulatory body for BSL interpreters was established in 1980 (the Council for the Advancement of Communication with Deaf People [CACDP]), and the first association of sign language interpreters was established in Scotland in 1981 (the Scottish Association of Interpreters for the Deaf, which became the Scottish Association of Sign Language Interpreters [SASLI] in 1988), followed by the Association of Sign Language Interpreters UK (ASLI) in 1987.

Early sign language researchers, such as Brennan (1975), Deuchar (1984), Kyle and Woll (1985), and Brien (1992), demonstrated that BSL was and is a full language with its own grammar and vocabulary. This development took place in parallel to the genesis of the BSL interpreting profession. SLI and sign language translation (SLT) researchers such as (but not limited to) Llewellyn-Jones (1981), Steiner (1998), Napier (1998), Stone (2005), Dickinson (2010), and Skinner (2020) and deaf researchers such as Collins (2005), Allsop (2008), and Adam (2011) have all contributed to the scholarly activity in this field.

WHO ARE WE?

As authors of this chapter, we have all been practitioners and researchers involved in the training of deaf and hearing sign language translators and interpreters for many years, as outlined in our positionality statements in the Introduction chapter. With respect to the UK specifically, we all work at Heriot-Watt University, where we teach in undergraduate and postgraduate education programs and conduct research on SLT and SLI practices and pedagogy. We have been (and continue to be) involved in various advisory groups, boards, and networks at the national and international levels that influence the development of the profession and training/education.

CONTEXTUALIZATION: TRANSLATION AND INTERPRETING IN THE UK

Translation and interpreting (T&I) in the UK is not a regulated profession like others such as nursing, teaching, and social work; and it has perceived lower status than these other professions, which leads to constant issues with procurement and quality of T&I services. Signed and spoken language T&I are mapped to the same professional standards, but the provision of training and education tends to take place separately (similar to Australia; see Bontempo et al., in this volume). Registration (license to practice) is also carried out separately, and although neither is a regulated profession, there is a strong expectation that sign language interpreters and translators should be registered in order to practice. In fact, the SLI profession is often considered to have led the way in the development of professional standards in community interpreting practice (Napier, 2015).

Procurement of all interpreters and translators is carried out by the respective authorities (e.g., the Ministry of Justice for court and legal interpreting, the National Health Service for hospital, medical, and emergency services), and there is usually no representation from deaf communities or the T&I profession during those processes. For the spoken language interpreting profession, the National Register of Public Service Interpreters (NRPSI) is an independent and voluntary regulator of professional interpreters that was established in 1994 on the recommendation of a Royal Commission on Criminal Justice that a register should be established "using only interpreters with proven competence and skills, who are governed by a nationally recognized code of conduct." A register has the functions of maintaining a register, recognizing the necessary qualifications, ensuring standards, and investigating complaints, as well as promotion of the importance of the register. The register has

1,800 registrants covering 100 languages for the entire UK. There are many universities in the UK at which people can train at the undergraduate and postgraduate levels to become interpreters and translators in spoken languages.

Interpreters are also represented by professional membership associations; for example the Chartered Institute of Linguistics (CIOL) and the Institute of Translation and Interpreting (ITI). The CIOL offers qualifications in T&I in house, which leads to an applicant becoming a member of a chartered professional body. The ITI has corporate education members, which are universities all around the UK that offer postgraduate qualifications in T&I. All these organizations generally act as membership bodies for practicing professionals who work in language T&I, and they work toward the promotion of high standards in each of these professions through the endorsement of the appropriate training programs. In the UK, there is also the Association of Police and Court Interpreters (ACPI), which represents freelance interpreters working in the criminal justice system in the UK and which operates a call center for locating interpreters for assignments.

In the UK, all qualifications for T&I, both for signed and spoken languages, are mapped against the National Occupational Standards (NoS) in T&I. These are a set of standards that describe the knowledge, skills, and understanding an individual needs in order to be considered competent at a job that covers a wide range of occupations across different business sectors.[2] These standards apply to all professionals and are reviewed on a regular basis by representatives of the profession, industry awarding organizations (of language and T&I qualifications), and training bodies. Currently, the NoS for interpreting, for example, are:

- Assess your ability to undertake interpreting assignments.
- Prepare for interpreting assignments.
- Interpret one way as a professional interpreter.
- Interpret two ways as a professional interpreter.
- Evaluate and develop your professional practice as an interpreter.
- Produce sight translations within interpreting assignments.
- Produce immediate translations within interpreting assignments.
- Work with other interpreters.
- Undertake remote interpreting assignments. (https://www.ukstandards.org.uk)

All courses in the higher or further education sectors therefore need to be mapped against these NoS. A qualification specification has been developed by Signature[3] for a Level 6 Diploma in Sign Language Interpreting and Translation, outlining the understanding and knowledge in four different streams required to become qualified in an area of practice:

- Spoken/signed interpreting (targeted at hearing interpreters)
- Signed/signed interpreting (targeted at deaf interpreters)

- Relay (intralingual) interpreting (targeted at deaf interpreters)
- Written/signed translation (targeted at deaf translators)

This qualification is unique in that it brings all the work done by deaf and hearing practitioners under the same qualification as general T&I practitioners, and all sign language interpreters and translators, whether interlingual or intralingual, are considered to be equal in terms of qualification levels. As such, it is more common now in the UK to talk about the sign language translation and interpreting (SLTI) field, rather than just the SLI field. In addition, there is an advanced level (Level 6) certificate in working with deafblind people.

PROFESSIONALIZATION OF SIGN LANGUAGE INTERPRETERS IN THE UK

Over the millennia, deaf people have met to talk in sign language, and Greek, Roman, and Jewish writings (Woll & Adam, 2012; Woll & Ladd, 2003), have mentioned deaf people and sign languages. It has followed that there is a need for SLI, and the earliest known instance of SLI in the UK (Leahy, 2016) took place in 1324 in England in the case of John de Orleton, whose hearing sister Isabella seems to have been his interpreter during a meeting with representatives the court of King Edward II, when he was interviewed by the King's representatives and was considered to have willingly given his consent "by signs." This is, as Leahy indicated, a unique case because during medieval times, deaf people were not allowed to have much legal or financial independence (see also Woll & Adam, 2012, for a short review of how deaf people were considered in antiquity). Stone and Woll (2008) discussed the use of interpreters during Victorian times in the Old Bailey, the English central criminal court, where hearing people were sworn into court proceedings to act as interpreters; these people were often associates or family members of deaf people.

The role of sign language interpreters in the UK was historically performed by family members, colleagues, missioners (members of the clergy), friends, and acquaintances (Corfmat, 1990; Scott-Gibson, 1991). The professionalization of SLTI can be traced back to when SASLI began accrediting interpreters in 1980 and the BDA set up the Communication Skills Project funded through the former UK Government's Department of Health and Social Security (1977–1981). SLI became an independent profession in the UK with the establishment of the interpreter registration panel by the CACDP in 1982. Nine interpreters who had passed a new assessment, and 112 people who had the Deaf Welfare Examination Board (DWEB) qualification (for missioners who were able to interpret), joined the register (Simpson, 2007). Although there were deaf people in the first few intakes, they were a small minority, and deaf people did not rejoin the register until 35 years later when sign language/sign language and SLT qualifications were offered (Napier, 1998). Originally, entry to the CACDP register was approved by passing a full-day examination with five different components that assessed skills in BSL-to-English simultaneous interpreting, English-to-BSL simultaneous interpreting, BSL < > English dialogic interpreting, BSL-to-English translation, and an ethical/theoretical viva. Candidates who passed the exam were eligible to register. Before that, people who had attained their Stage 3 (advanced level) BSL qualification could register as a trainee interpreter. The examination was scrapped when the new vocational qualification system was introduced in the early 2000s (see below, and Napier, 2004, for a detailed overview). By the 2000s, the UK saw a move away from *traditional* interpreters who were heritage signers,[4] that is, hearing and deaf people from deaf families, to new signers[5] who were attracted to learning BSL as a second language (Stone, 2012).

Currently, the SLTI profession is represented in the UK by ASLI and the Visual Language Professionals (VLP). In Scotland, the Scottish Collaborative of Sign Language Interpreters (SCOSLI; formerly SASLI) represents BSL interpreters based in Scotland, though some interpreters are affiliated with ASLI or both ASLI and SCOSLI. ASLI also hosts a Deaf Interpreter Network (DIN), an initiative that was established in the mid-2000s and has provided deaf practitioners with space within the organization. These membership organizations seek to represent the interests of sign language interpreters and translators in the UK, and they increasingly organize continuing professional development (CPD) opportunities for their members.

The UK is unique in that there are independent registration bodies that act as independent regulators of SLTI: the National Registers of Communication Professionals working with Deaf and Deafblind People (NRCPD) and the Regulatory Body of BSL Interpreters and Translators (RBSLI). In Scotland, this function is taken up by the Scottish Register for Language Professionals with the Deaf Community (SRLPDC; formerly SASLI[6]). Registration with these bodies is contingent on having the appropriate SLTI qualification, demonstration of the minimum number of hours of CPD completed annually, liability insurance, and background checks in order to be "safe" to practice. There are also two union bodies in the UK that lobby for working conditions and pay rates for interpreters: the Scottish Union of Public Service Interpreters (primarily for spoken language interpreters) and the National Union of British Sign Language Interpreters (NUBSLI).

In the late 1990s and early 2000s, Black sign language interpreters joined Black deaf activists in their journeys to America to connect with other more established Black self-organized groups in both the American Black Deaf community and the Black American SLI profession. The London Ethnic Minority Deaf Association (LEMDA) and the Black and Asian Sign Language Interpreters Network (BASLIN) were two organizations that emerged around the same time (Obasi, 2013). From these initiatives, the first-ever directory of interpreters from ethnic minorities was produced. Both organizations folded, but in the wake of the #BlackLivesMatter movement, interest was resurrected, and support was established through the now very active Interpreters of Colour Network (IOCN) and the Muslim BSL Interpreters Network (MBSLIN).

At the time of writing, the number of BSL interpreters and translators who are voluntarily registered with a professional regulatory body is approximately 1,600. Through a survey of working BSL interpreters, Brien, Brown, and Collins (2002, 2004) identified deaf, male, ethnic minority, and disabled people as being underrepresented in the profession. As a result of ongoing concerns about the lack of diversity and equality of opportunities in the profession, ASLI commissioned a census of the SLTI profession in the UK in 2021, with the aim of taking a snapshot of the profession. A consortium of universities led by Heriot-Watt University with the University of Wolverhampton and the University of the West of Scotland carried out this work to examine the demographic profile of the profession, using a census-style questionnaire that was circulated online. The data were collated from 690 completed responses (Napier et al., 2021, 2022).

The census found that the mean age of SLTI practitioners was 44 years (with a range of 18 years of age to 76 years of age). The profession was 82.02% female, 16.81% male, 0.43% nonbinary/genderqueer, and 0.28% transgender. In the deaf SLTI profession, the gender balance is 60% female and 40% male. With respect to ethnicity, 89.56% of respondents identify as white, and 8.84% identify as Black or minority ethnic background. The largest single ethnic group was Black Caribbean, followed by Black African/Caribbean and then Southeast Asian. It was found that the SLTI profession does not reflect the diversity in the populace, although there are more interpreters who identify as Black than Asian. There is also a higher proportion of LGBTQIA+ SLTI practitioners (14.49%) than that in the UK population, which has 2.2% of people identifying as such.

The census report listed 20 recommendations for stakeholder and training organizations for the promotion of SLTI as a profession and recruitment of more diverse groups into teaching teams and student cohorts, with a call for more collaboration across key organizations to improve the diversity and representation in the SLTI profession. One popular initiative is the Going Pro conference hosted by ASLI every year, which targets SLTI students who are about to graduate or trainees to encourage them to establish their professional networks. Likewise, ASLI also hosts an "Early Career Interpreter Network," providing newly qualified SLTI practitioners an opportunity to discuss their experiences.

Although there have been many advances in the professionalization of SLTI in the UK, Webb and Best (2020) argued that the profession is actually at risk of not professionalizing further because of the many regulatory bodies and professional associations, the varied pathways to becoming an interpreter, and the lack of legislation and understanding around who is qualified to work as an interpreter.

Sign Language Translator and Interpreter Education in the UK

SLI training was originally done in house by deaf organizations and service providers and consisted of short courses taken by participants who were already fluent in BSL (Scott-Gibson, 1991). Much of the traditional interpreting for deafblind people and those needing "relay" interpreters was still undertaken by deaf interpreters, though with little recognition or professional standing outside of their networks (Adam et al., 2011; Adam et al., 2014; Morgan and Adam 2012).

The first university courses were offered by the University of Durham and the University of Bristol in the early 1990s, and currently courses are offered at Heriot-Watt University, the University of Wolverhampton, and the University of Central Lancashire, with post-registration training at Queen Margaret University (Napier et al., 2021). Leeds University, the University of Middlesex, and Queens University Belfast also previously offered interpreter training, but those (along with Durham and Bristol) all closed down to lack of university support for small numbers of enrollees.

The current educational pathways to a career in SLTI are through the academic route, the vocational route, or a combination of both. The academic qualification route is based in universities and usually takes 3–4 years to complete; it typically does not have a minimum level of BSL skill as a prerequisite. A vocational qualification route, on the other hand, involves studying at an assessment center that has been approved by Signature, the awarding body for BSL and interpreting qualifications, and undertaking a course that covers both the theoretical and practical aspects of the course, with assessment being through the production of a portfolio of work after approximately 12–18 months of study. Students are required to hold a BSL qualification at the same level—i.e., Level 6, which is mapped against the national qualification standards for languages.

As noted earlier, interpreting qualifications were initially given only for BSL/English interpreting, but in recent years, sign language < > sign language qualifications, sign language translator qualifications, and intralingual/relay interpreting qualifications have been added to the complement of qualifications available and endorsed through the NRCPD, which are mapped against the NoS. Each of the standards in the document relates to the various aspects of T&I: assessment of skills, preparation for assignments, interpreting one way, interpreting two ways, evaluation of professional practice, and production of sight translations.

On completion of these qualifications, students can apply for registration with the registration bodies. For instance, one could apply for registration with the NRCPD as a trainee sign language interpreter (TSLI) or trainee sign language translator (TSLT) or as a registered sign language interpreter (RSLI) or registered sign language translator (RSLT) after having met the requirements of registration (which include a commitment to CPD, background checks, and liability insurance, as well as the requisite qualifications). In 2021, "relay interpreting" was added to the RSLT qualification by Signature, and a group of deaf people were also assessed for inclusion on the NRCPD register as intralingual relay interpreters. To progress from TSLI and TSLT to RSLT and RSLI, practitioners need to demonstrate that they have met the threshold through further training and evidence of work experience.

Napier et al. (2021) found that the pathway to registration was mainly a combination of academic and vocational (39.7%), followed by vocational (38.8%) and academic (21.5%), and that 61% of respondents have completed some academic education before completing the course. There are fewer academic courses available for deaf interpreters and translators, so 64% of deaf practitioners completed a vocational course and 16% had done an academic course.

Currently, there are only four university programs throughout the UK that lead to RSLI or RSLT status (two undergraduate courses at Heriot-Watt University and the University of Wolverhampton, two postgraduate courses at the University of Central Lancashire and the University of Wolverhampton), as well as seven vocational programs throughout the country (Napier et al., 2021). At universities, there are both deaf and hearing academic staff who teach on SLTI courses, and there are usually two main areas of study: BSL and SLTI, supplemented by studies in the culture, politics, and history of deaf communities. Many vocational courses are led by deaf and hearing people teaching together, but there is often a tendency for deaf trainers to teach on vocabulary and content in BSL and for hearing trainers to teach interpreting theory and practice (though this is not always the case). There is also a post-qualifying postgraduate course at the Queen Margaret University for students to study specialist modules in the legal, medical, mental health, education, employment, and arts and theater fields. Heriot-Watt University is the only university that offers students the opportunity to study BSL alongside another spoken language (French, Spanish, German, or Chinese). Heriot-Watt University also offers a Master of Science (MSc) in Sign Language Interpreting, which is part of the European Master in Sign Language Interpreting (EUMASLI)[7] in collaboration with Humak University of Applied Sciences in Finland and Magdeburg-Stendal University of Applied Sciences in Germany. This program has been running since 2009 and is an innovative international program that is intended to contribute to the development of the professional field of interpreting between deaf and hearing people by bringing together sign language translators and interpreters from across the world. It aims to prepare participants for research, development, and leadership functions in their respective countries or internationally.

It is possible to identify potential training priorities in the UK by investigating the domains of work performed by SLTI practitioners in their everyday work. The census (Napier et al., 2022) found that the main domains of work were:

- Workplaces (with Access to Work funding) (33.88%)
- Medical appointments (20.6%)
- Education both further and higher (11.59%)
- Remote interpreting (10.97%)
- Small ad hoc meetings (7.83%)
- Mental health appointments (7.65%)
- Children's education (5.55%)
- Theater (3.39%)
- Training events, conferences/seminars, legal (2.04%)
- Religious events

The least desirable domains were found to be in-vision television work and legal domains (particularly court, followed by policing), as well as political and musical events. This would indicate two things: that there is a need for training in workplace, medical, and educational interpreting because these seem to take up a large proportion of the work done by BSL interpreters, but also that training in the other less desirable domains is needed because interpreters might not feel as confident in accepting television or legal assignments, even though legal interpreting can be life-critical for deaf people.

The census also found that male interpreters were more prepared to take on high-profile work such as television in-vision and political and legal work and that fewer female interpreters who responded were willing to take on high-status work (which the team defined as in-vision television work, conferences, mental health, and court work), and it was recommended that courses in future ensure there are greater opportunities for training and mentoring in these specialist areas to ensure that supply meets demand.

The Impact of the COVID-19 Pandemic

It is worth noting how the SLTI profession has been impacted by the COVID-19 pandemic. The provision of BSL interpreting for public health announcements during the pandemic across the UK was disparate (Napier & Adam, 2022). The Scottish and Welsh announcements had interpreters in the press briefing room broadcast on all television channels, whereas the UK Government relied on provision through the BBC News channel, which was often inaccessible to people who did not have broadband television packages or who were using various devices.

Despite historical resistance from the profession to working online, the pandemic forced many BSL interpreters and translators to switch to online service delivery, as noted by De Meulder, Pouliot, and Gebreurs (2021) in their surveys of SLI across Europe over three periods during the pandemic. With the shift to online working, the census results (Napier, et al., 2021, 2022) noted that SLTI practitioners are more likely to work online, more likely to have a remote working setup at home, and less likely to return to full-time in-person work. Furthermore, the pandemic enabled more choice for deaf professionals, who could secure interpreting services from their preferred interpreters even if they lived in a different part of the country. It also meant that interpreters could choose to work with deaf people in different contexts that did not require lengthy travel times. As such, the SLTI profession in the UK, as with most countries, faces an interesting time ahead in navigating a post-pandemic world. Anecdotal reports confirm that deaf people are finding it harder to secure interpreters locally for face-to-face appointments, as interpreters would prefer to continue to work from home.

In response to the rapid changes in the SLTI profession brought about by the COVID-19 pandemic, educators have faced the imperative task of adapting their curricula to equip future interpreters with the necessary skills and knowledge. The shift to online service delivery has underscored the importance of integrating technology into the training of sign language interpreters. Educators must now consider not only the traditional skills of face-to-face interpretating but also the nuances and challenges posed by remote interpreting. This includes imparting proficiency in the use of relevant technological tools and platforms that facilitate effective communication in virtual settings.

The pandemic also highlighted the need to prepare interpreters for both individual and team-based remote work. Educators must address the unique dynamics of virtual collaboration, emphasizing skills such as clear communication through digital channels, the effective use of videoconferencing platforms, and the ability to navigate potential technical challenges. Teamwork, which has been a cornerstone of interpreting practice, now extends beyond physical proximity, requiring interpreters to collaborate seamlessly in a virtual environment.

The Road Ahead

In terms of the road ahead, there is an increasing amount of research being conducted on SLTI in the UK. Research is still conducted predominantly by hearing practitioners, but more deaf practitioners/scholars are becoming involved in SLTI research and coauthorship. Since the first doctor of philosophy thesis on SLI in the UK was completed (Stone, 2005), there have been at least 18 more PhDs focusing on SLTI, with several more currently in progress.

Furthermore, with postgraduate training options, there are also more master of arts theses being completed, so the professional interpreting association conferences often feature academic, research-based presentations as well as practical CPD workshops. The groundswell in SLTI research provides a bedrock to underpin and inform best practices in SLTI, and the UK is at the forefront of many of these developments.

A number of developments will have an impact on the SLTI profession in the UK. First, education authorities in England, Wales, and Scotland are taking steps to offer BSL as a language to be studied in schools. This raises the possibility for school-aged children to consider SLI (and for deaf school children to consider SLT or SLI) as a potential career. The opportunity for school-aged children to study BSL could mean that it would be possible to require students to have studied some BSL before applying for a university-level SLTI course. Additionally, this increased profile of BSL in schools can only have a positive impact on numbers of applicants for SLTI courses.

Since 2021, the primary awarding body for BSL T&I qualifications (NRCPD) has offered a suite of new qualifications, which include intralingual/relay interpreting. This will for the first time put deaf relay interpreters (or intralingual interpreters) on a par with their professional hearing peers, and this opens up potential opportunities for new training courses. As seen in the ASLI census, deaf SLTI practitioners are underrepresented in the profession and are also trained mostly through the vocational route. Although there has been more uptake in the Wolverhampton MA and EUMASLI programs of deaf students who are already working as translators and interpreters, there are currently no specific courses for deaf practitioners through the academic route. Although it is possible for them to join a generic SLTI academic course at the undergraduate level, very few deaf people have taken up this option thus far. Anecdotally, it is thought this might be due to the lack of sufficient work opportunities after graduation to justify studying full time for 3–4 years. It is hoped that this will change in the future. There is also more potential for CPD courses tailored to deaf practitioners.

Additionally, the ASLI census highlighted underrepresentation in the following communities: South Asian practitioners, SLTI practitioners of different faiths, and women of all backgrounds are underrepresented in high-status work. As noted earlier, the census report flagged strong recommendations for future action by making an "extensive list of 20 recommendations across five categories concerning (1) diversity/representation in the SLTI profession, (2) marketing/promotion of the SLTI profession, (3) training/education of SLTI practitioners, (4) SLTI practice, and (5) ongoing review. These recommendations include various actions, such as targeting BSL classes for recruitment into interpreter education programs, establishing an SLTI education network, ensuring diverse representation in any marketing materials, promoting SLTI to deaf children as a career option, and requiring SLTI practitioners to engage with equality and diversity topics as part of their CPD, as well as administering the census every 5 years" (Napier, et al., 2022, p. 10). A concerted effort will be required from the various stakeholders to improve representation of minoritized communities in the

SLTI profession. Practitioners, training centers, registration bodies, awarding bodies, membership organizations, and importantly, representatives of the diverse deaf community organizations will need to work closely together to improve this representation within the community. The census report also recommended the establishment of a Sign Language Interpreter and Translator Education Network (equivalent to the Conference of Interpreter Trainers [CIT] in the United States) to enable researchers and educators to exchange information, monitor demands, and collaborate on recruitment strategies.

In Australia, sign language interpreters are accredited for specializations in conference, medical, and legal interpreting.[7] At the time of writing, NRCPD has initiated a working group to explore the possibility of a specialized registration category for legal interpreting. It could well be that mirroring Australia by having a range of specialized options for SLTI available in the UK is the way forward, now that a suite of SLTI qualifications have been developed and released. These "streams" could then lead to relevant specializations in these areas of work, especially as the census identified the domains of work for an SLTI practitioner in the UK.

Sign language legislation, such the British Sign Language Act (UK) in 2022[8] and the BSL (Scotland) Act 2015,[9] which both put the onus on public bodies and publicly funded authorities to plan for BSL access across a variety of domains, means that there could be an increase in demand for SLTI. The aim of the UK BSL Act (2022) is to recognize BSL as a language of England, Wales, and Scotland; to require the Secretary of State to report on the promotion and facilitation of the use of BSL by ministerial government departments; and to require guidance to be issued in relation to BSL. At the time of writing, a BSL advisory board has recently been established with representatives of British deaf communities to advise public services and to increase the number of SLTI practitioners in the profession.

NOTES

1. https://www.ons.gov.uk/peoplepopulationandcommunity/populationandmigration/populati.onestimates/articles/overviewoftheukpopulation/august2019
2. https://www.ukstandards.org.uk
3. https://www.signature.org.uk/wp-content/uploads/2021/10/INTRA6-Sept-2021.pdf
4. We use Napier's (2021) definition of *heritage signers* as deaf or hearing people who have grown up with one or two deaf parents and used sign language at home as their primary language.
5. *New signers* learn a sign language later in life and often outside traditional contexts and then choose to use that language on an everyday basis for personal and professional reasons. These can be deaf or hearing people (De Meulder, 2018).
6. Previously SASLI had two functions—as a membership organization and also as a regulatory body. In 2020, it was decided to split the two functions and form two new organizations:: SRLPDC and SCOSLI.

7. See the Australian chapter in this volume for a discussion of interpreter accreditation by the National Accreditation Authority for Translators and Interpreters (NAATI).
8. https://bills.parliament.uk/bills/2915
9. http://bslscotlandact2015.scot
10. https://www.eumasli.eu

References

Adam, R. Carty, B., & Stone, C. (2011). Ghost writing: Deaf translators within the deaf community. *Babel, 57*(3), 375–393.

Adam, R., Aro, M., Druetta, J. C., Dunne, S., & af Klintberg, J. (2014). Deaf interpreters: An introduction. In R. Adam, C. Stone, S. D. Collins, & M. Metzger (Eds.), *Deaf interpreters at work: International insights* (pp. 1–18). Gallaudet University Press.

Allsop, L., & Kyle, J. (2008). Translating the news: A deaf translator's experience. In C. J. Kellett Bidoli & E. Ochse (Eds.), *English in International Deaf communication* (p. 444). Peter Lang.

Brennan, M. (1975). Can deaf children acquire language? *American Annals of the Deaf, 120*(5), 463–479.

Brien, D. (1992). *Dictionary of British Sign Language/English*. Faber and Faber.

Brien, D., Brown, R., & Collins, J. (2002). *The organization and provision of British Sign Language/English interpreters in England, Scotland and Wales. A study carried out on behalf of the Department for Work and Pensions*. Unpublished research report, University of Durham, UK.

Brien, D., Brown, R., & Collins, J. (2004). Some recommendations regarding the provision and organization of British Sign Language/English interpreters in England, Scotland and Wales. *Deaf Worlds, 20*(1), 6–60.

Collins, J., & Walker, J. (2005). *Deaf interpreter, What is it?* [Paper presentation]. Inaugural Conference of the World Association of Sign Language Interpreters, Worcester, South Africa.

Corfmat, P. (1990). *Please sign here: Insights into the world of the deaf*. Churchman Publishing.

Deuchar, M. (1984). *British Sign Language*. Routledge & Kegan Paul.

De Meulder, M. (2018). "So, why do you sign?" Deaf and hearing new signers, their motivation, and revitalisation policies for sign languages. *Applied Linguistics Review, 10*(4), 705–724.

De Meulder, M., Pouliot, O., & Gebruers, K. (2021). *Remote sign language interpreting in times of Covid–19*. [Unpublished research report]. Utrecht University of Applied Sciences, the Netherlands.

Dickinson, J. (2010). *Interpreting in a community of practice A sociolinguistic study of the signed language interpreter's role in workplace discourse*. [Unpublished doctoral dissertation]. Heriot-Watt University, Edinburgh, Scotland.

Emery, S. & Iyer, S. (2022). Deaf migration through an intersectionality lens. *Disability & Society, 37*(1), 89–110.

Jackson, P. (2001). *A pictorial history of deaf Britain*. Deafprint.

Kyle, J. & Woll, B. (1985). *Sign language: the study of deaf people and their language*. Cambridge University Press.

Leahy, A. (2016). The history of interpreting. *British Deaf News*.

Llewellyn-Jones, P. (1981). Simultaneous Interpreting. In B. Woll, J. Kyle, & M. Deuchar (Eds.), *Perspectives on British Sign Language and Deafness*. Croom Helm.

Morgan, P., & Adam, R. (2012). Deaf interpreters in mental health settings – some reflections and thoughts for deaf interpreter education. In K. Malcolm & L. Swabey (Eds.), *In our hands: Educating healthcare interpreters* (pp. 190–208). Gallaudet University Press.

Napier, J. (1998). Free your mind—the rest will follow. *Deaf Worlds, 14*(3), 15–22.

Napier, J. (2004). Sign language interpreter training, testing and accreditation: An international comparison. *American Annals of the Deaf, 149*(4), 350–359.

Napier, J. (2015). Comparing spoken and signed language interpreting. In H. Mikkelson & R. Jourdenais (Eds.), *Routledge handbook of interpreting studies* (pp. 129–143). Routledge.

Napier, J. & Adam, R. (2022). Prophylactic language use: The case of deaf signers in England and their (lack of) access to government information during the COVID-19 pandemic. In P. Blumczynski & S. Wilson (Eds.), *The languages of COVID-19: Transnational and multilingual perspectives on global healthcare* (pp. 161–177). Routledge.

Napier, J., Skinner, R., Adam, R., Stone, C., Pratt, S., & Obasi, C. (2021). *A demographic snapshot of the profession: The 2021 Census of sign language translators & interpreters in the UK. Research report.* https://asli.org.uk/census-report-2021/

Napier, J. Skinner, R., Adam, R., Stone, C., Pratt, S., Hinton, D. P., & Obasi, C. (2022). Representation and diversity in the sign language translation & interpreting profession in the United Kingdom. *Interpreting and Society: An Interdisciplinary Journal, 2*(2), 119–130.

Obasi, C. (2013). Race and ethnicity in sign language interpreter education, training and practice. *Race Ethnicity and Education, 16*(1), 103–120.

Quinn, G. A. (2010). Schoolization: An account of the origins of regional variation in British Sign Language. *Sign Language Studies, 10*(4), 476–501.

Scott-Gibson, L. (1991). Sign language interpreting: An emerging profession. In S. Gregory & G. Hartley (Eds.), *Constructing deafness* (pp. 253–258). Pinter in association with the Open University.

Simpson, S. (2007). *Advance to an ideal: The fight to raise the standard of communication between Deaf and hearing people*. Scottish Workshop Publications.

Skinner, R. (2020). *Approximately there—positioning video-mediated interpreting in frontline police services* [Unpiblished doctoral dissertation]. Heriot-Watt University, Edinburgh, Scotland.

Steiner, B. (1998). Signs from the void: The comprehension and production of sign language on television. *Interpreting, 3*(2), 99–146.

Stone, C. (2005). *Towards a deaf translation norm* [Unpublished doctoral thesis]. University of Bristol, Bristol.

Stone, C. (2010). Access all areas: Is sign language interpreting that special? *Journal of Specialised Translation, 14*, 41–54.

Stone, C. (2012). Interpreting. In R. Pfau, M. Steinbach & B. Woll (Eds.), *Sign language: An international handbook*. (pp. 980–997). De Gruyter.

Stone, C., & Woll, B. (2008). Dumb O Jemmy and others: Deaf people, interpreters and the London courts in the eighteenth and nineteenth centuries. *Sign Language Studies, 8*(3), 226–240. https://doi.org/10.1353/sls.2008.0009

Turner, G. H. (2020). How many people use British Sign Language? Scotland's 2011 census and the demographic politics of disability and linguistic identity. In J. Kopaczyk, & R. McColl Millar (Eds.), *Language on the move across domains and communities. Selected papers from the 12th Triennial Forum for Research on the Languages of Scotland and Ulster, Glasgow 2018*, (pp. 37–70). FRLSU.

Webb, S., & Best, B. (2020). The most important cog in the system: A case for legislative change to drive professionalisation. *Journal of Interpretation*, *28*(1), Article 6. https://digitalcommons.unf.edu/joi/vol28/iss1/6

Woll, B., & Adam, R. (2012). Sign language and the politics of deafness. In M. Martin-Jones, A. Blackledge, & A. Creese (Eds.), *The Routledge handbook of multilingualism* (pp. 100–115). Routledge.

Woll, B., & Ladd, P. (2003). Deaf communities. In M. Marschark & P. Spencer (Eds.), *The handbook of deaf studies, language and education* (pp. 151–163). Oxford University Press.

CHRISTOPHER TESTER AND
ANNA WITTER-MERITHEW

22

History Is a Relentless Master

The State of Interpreter Education in the
United States of America

This chapter describes the status of sign language interpreting (SLI) education in the United States (U.S.) by providing an overview of the current landscape, prevailing issues, and emerging trends. Such an undertaking requires recognition of the ongoing demographic changes within the signing deaf population and the implications for new generations of deaf children as they enter the public education system and society in general (Schafer & Cokely, 2015). These individuals' complex and variable communication needs provide the most essential source of insight and curricular guidance for SLI education programs. Before we explore interpreter education, we will provide a brief overview of the language and sociopolitical climate of the deaf community in the United States.

Within the United States, the de facto languages of the deaf community are American Sign Language (ASL) and English (Fenlon & Wilkinson, 2015; Hill, 2015; Quinto-Pozos & Adam, 2015). Spoken Spanish is the most common second language in the United States. Within ASL, variations emerged, including Black ASL (BASL), as the result of the history of racial segregation in U.S. deaf schools (Hill, 2021; McCaskill et al., 2011). However, until recently, BASL was not researched because of its minority status within ASL (Hill, 2015). Further research on linguistic diversity is needed, deaf community members have long promoted the value of sign language. In 1880, the National Association of the Deaf (NAD) was founded, and sign language was promoted as the core value of the deaf community. It was not until 1960 that linguist William Stokoe identified ASL as a language (Fenlon & Wilkinson, 2015; Stokoe, 1960).

According to the 2021 American Community Survey (ACS) through Cornell University, about 3.6% of the U.S. population reported a hearing disability

(Disabilitystatistics.org, accessed November 3, 2023). Although there are no clear statistics on how many deaf and hard of hearing individuals report using ASL as their primary language, it is often suggested that it is about 500,000 people to 1 million, on the basis of a 2006 study (Mitchell et al., 2006). Despite the challenges in acquiring data on the signing deaf population, there has been a significant shift in recognizing that not all deaf community members agree, perceive themselves to have the same shared experience, or share the same use of ASL (Hill, 2021; Kusters et al., 2020; Ruiz-Williams et al., 2015), which leads to challenges in developing SLI education to meet the needs of the diverse deaf and signing community (Cokely, 2015).

Who Are We?

Christopher is deaf and is an actor, consultant, educator, and interpreter. As a seasoned presenter, he specializes in workshop and seminar facilitation on topics such as disability rights and laws, deaf and hard of hearing awareness, and interpreting. He is a former assistant professor at Gallaudet University and a former adjunct instructor for the City University of New York (CUNY)'s ASL/English interpreter education program (IEP). Additionally, he has interpreted for several off- and on-Broadway shows, national and international conferences, and the United Nations, and he specializes in legal interpreting. His recent research focuses on the work of deaf interpreters (DIs) within the court of law.

Christopher is a member of the International Association for Conference Interpreters (Association Internationale des Interprètes de Conférence [AIIC]) and is an accredited international sign interpreter with the World Federation of the Deaf–World Association of Sign Language Interpreters (WFD-WASLI). He is fluent in American, British, and International Sign languages. He received his doctor of philosophy (PhD) degree and his European Master in Sign Language Interpreting (EUMASLI) through Heriot-Watt University in Edinburgh, Scotland, and his bachelor's degree at the College of the Holy Cross. Additionally, he received a professional certificate from CUNY's ASL/English IEP. After having lived in Edinburgh and Berlin for nearly 4 years, he returned to private practice and resides in New York City.

Through invitation, sponsorship, and supervision by the U.S. deaf community, Anna initially entered the field of interpreting in 1972. As a 75-year-old, white female who is a hearing, heritage signer, having always lived within the United States, she acknowledges her privileged access to certain systems, networks, and resources. She strives to be aware of her own biases and to recognize how they shape her perspectives, assumptions, practice, teaching, and research. Her academic credentials include a bachelor's degree in professional studies focused on linguistics and interpreting and a master's degree in education. Additionally, she has graduate certificates in distributed learning (distance education) and teaching ASL and interpreting. As a nationally certified and state-licensed interpreter, she worked primarily in community, legal, and postsecondary settings. For much of her career, she specialized as a certified legal interpreter.

Throughout her career, Anna has been mentored and supervised by deaf individuals in leadership roles and/or hearing individuals rooted within the deaf community, and this guidance has been central to all of her endeavors. Early in her career, while engaged in freelance interpreting, she also coordinated interpreting services for government agencies in Georgia and later in postsecondary settings at the National Technical Institute for the Deaf (NTID), in Rochester, New York. She began teaching as an interpreter educator in 1975, also at NTID. As an educator, she taught in a 2-year degree program in North Carolina and a 4-year degree program and graduate certificate programs in Colorado; she also engaged in program design, curricular development, and program administration, and for 16 years designed, developed, and administered in-service training grants funded by the U.S. Department of Education Rehabilitation Services Administration (RSA).

In 2016, Anna retired from the University of Northern Colorado. She continues to engage in SLI education program consultation and curricular development, diagnostic assessment, and mentoring services. She had the privilege of serving in executive leadership roles within the professional associations of interpreters and interpreter educators in the United States, the Registry of Interpreters for the Deaf (RID) and the Conference of Interpreter Trainers (CIT). This service includes cofounding the CIT, serving two terms as vice president of the CIT and RID, serving one term as president of RID, serving a two-and-a-half-year term as the interim executive director of the RID (during which time the Center for Assessment of Sign Language Interpretation [CASLI] was established and implemented), and serving as the project coordinator assisting the CIT in establishing the U.S. IEP accrediting body, the Commission on Collegiate Interpreter Education.

CONTEXTUALIZATION: TRANSLATION AND INTERPRETING IN THE UNITED STATES

Historically, the SLI profession has had limited interaction with the greater translation and interpreting field within the United States. Most of the involvement has occurred as individual researchers, scholars, and practitioners in interpreting and/or interpreter education have sought participation in conferences and organizations focused on spoken languages, such as the American Translators Association (ATA), founded in 1959, and the National Association of Judiciary Interpreters (NAJIT). Dr. Brenda Nicodemus, former director of the Gallaudet University Center for Advancement of Interpreting and Translation Research, offered a few highlights related to engagement between spoken language and signed language organizations (personal communication, January 24, 2022).

- In 2012, conference sign language interpreters were admitted to the AIIC. The AIIC Sign Language Network (SLN) brings together AIIC members to act as contact people for conference interpreters working with one or more sign languages.
- In 2015, Gallaudet University's Department of Interpreting and Translation hosted a Summer Research Institute in collaboration with the University of Maryland interpreting program. The Institute was funded by the European Society for Translation Studies and drew researchers, scholars, and practitioners from spoken and sign language fields.
- With increasing frequency, journals and conferences traditionally focused on spoken languages are accepting articles and presentations about signed language interpreting research.

This increase in collaboration between spoken and sign language interpreters corresponds, in part, with the implementation of U.S. Executive Order 13166, which requires improving access to services for persons with limited English proficiency (Department of Justice, 2000). This is the first legally binding guidance for the provision of different languages (other than ASL) within the United States. The Americans With Disabilities Act (ADA), which provides similar and comprehensive legally binding guidance for the provision of access to individuals who have disabilities became law in 1990. One key difference between these regulations is that the ADA requires all programs and services, both public and private, regardless of whether they receive federal funding or not, to provide accommodations (with some exemptions), whereas, for other languages, accommodations are required only if the programs or services receive federal funds.

PROFESSIONALIZATION OF SLI IN THE UNITED STATES

In 1964, the RID, the first national professional sign language interpreting organization, was founded (Cokely & Winston, 2009). In 1972, RID introduced the first national certification and assessment system. In 1981, the *Journal of Interpreting* was established under the RID to disseminate current research to advance the academic study of interpreting. Meanwhile, various federal laws (e.g., Section 504 under the Rehabilitation Act of 1973, Public Law 142, U.S. Statutes at Large 89 [1975], both of which predate the aforementioned U.S. Executive Order 13166), and the ADA) established the right to communicative access for people with disabilities, including the use of ASL interpreters as reasonable access for the deaf population. These laws, in turn, enabled the SLI profession. The federal government supported the right to communicative access through federally funded grant initiatives. Several grants that promoted specialist training in addition to the IEPs will be described in the section "Specialist Practice."

Where We are Today

Since the founding of RID, other professional interpreter organizations have been formed in response to the needs that different portions of the interpreting community felt RID did not adequately address. One such group was SLI educators, who met to begin the establishment of an organization—the CIT—in 1979.[1] In 1985, RID attempted to recognize the unique needs of its individual members by establishing Special Interest Groups (SIGS) that would provide a structure for members to organize around common issues. The first approved SIG was the Deaf Caucus. Today, RID has eleven member sections (no longer called SIGS).[2]

However, since its founding of RID, the RID membership demographics have failed to mirror the diverse pool of working professionals and community ASL/English interpreters. Those who experienced underrepresentation, marginalization, and even blatant ostracism formed collective organizations in response to the gaps RID did not adequately or accurately address—three in particular (S. Hill, personal communication 2022):

1. The National Alliance of Black Interpreters (NAOBI) was founded and birthed by the activism of the Black deaf community. Efforts to formalize the establishment of NAOBI began in 1986. The goal of the organization is to promote excellence and empowerment among African American/Black sign language interpreters (Mooney et al., 2001);
2. Mano a Mano, whose mission is to provide an infrastructure for access to trilingual interpreters, was established in 2003 (Annarino et al., 2014); and
3. National Deaf Interpreters (NDI) was formed in 2017, which supports a biennial DI conference and is the central organization to promote DI.

In 2016, RID created a separate entity responsible for developing and administering the interpreter certification, the Center of the Assessment of Sign Language Interpreters (CASLI). Several different credentials were suspended because of the weakened reliability of the exams. In 2021, CASLI released a newly designed performance exam for certified DIs after the CDI exam was suspended for 6 years. Generalist exams for certified hearing interpreters were released in the autumn of 2022. The RID continues to confer certification on candidates who pass the CASLI exams and meet academic and experiential requirements. RID's interpreter certifications are recognized throughout the United States and within the court systems despite there not being a federal law requiring certification. However, CASLI is not the only credentialing body in the United States.

Many states within the United States have developed their own qualifications or licensures for SLI. For example, in Texas, there is a Board of Evaluation of Interpreters (BEI) that provides certification, which has been adopted in several other states. These states allow for state qualification or RID certification, and some states require both. For interpreters working within the K–12 educational system,[3] 41 states require interpreters to be assessed through the Educational Interpreter Performance Assessment (EIPA; NAIE, 2021). Most state educational agencies use scores from the EIPA, administered through the Diagnostic Center at Boys Town National Research Hospital in Boys Town, Nebraska, to set the state standard for sign language interpreters to work in K–12 settings. The scoring is distributed on a 5-point Likert scale across four performance domains (involving 36–38 skill areas), and the final score is based on the average score across all domains. The EIPA score used by each state varies. Currently, a 3.0 is the minimum standard in nine states; 3.5 is the minimum standard in 23 states; and 4.0 is the minimum standard in 11 states (Johnson et al., 2018, p. 73). Boys Town currently recommends a 4.0 skill level for K–12 interpreters (p. 74).

SLI Education in the United States

There are more than 150 IEPs nationwide (Hunt & Nicodemus, 2014). Sixty-five percent of the programs are established at local community colleges, where an associate's degree (2-year program; Associate of Arts [AA]/Associate of Science [AS]) is granted. Such programs are housed under various administrative structures, including vocational training, human services, and behavioral sciences (Cogen & Cokely, 2015). RID's mandate in 2012 that sign language interpreters must possess a bachelor's degree to take the certification exam has fostered a shift toward the availability of more baccalaureate programs (Cogen & Cokely, 2015). Fifty-four percent of AA/AS degree programs have partnered with 4-year institutions to allow students to transfer and complete a bachelor's degree. Currently, the curriculum for SLI education is inconsistent nationwide. Instead, each university can create and develop its own curriculum with some guidance from different certification requirements and consideration of pedagogy studies. Some programs include ASL instruction, where the students can apply without any knowledge of ASL. Few programs have a prerequisite that candidates have some minimum ASL skills before applying for the interpreter degree program.

As a result of the COVID-19 pandemic, many programs shifted to an online format using videoconferencing and learning platforms for the classes (Department of Education, 2021; Shaw & Halley, 2021). A government study demonstrated that COVID-19 had a disparate effect on students' academic growth, mental health, and access to the internet, which affected access to education, particularly for students of color, LGBTQI students, students with disabilities, and students from low-income backgrounds (Department of Education, 2021). One study explored SLI students' service learning during the COVID-19 pandemic and found that the service could be somewhat adaptive through online learning (Shaw & Halley, 2021). However, further and ongoing studies are needed to understand the impact of the transition from in-person classes to online learning for IEPs.

Slow progress in modifying SLI education programs in response to the changes within signing deaf communities is one of the consequences associated with the diminished role of deaf people in guiding the preparation of interpreters (see Ball, 2013; Cokely, 2011, 2012; Colonomos, 2013; Mathers & Witter-Merithew, 2014; Suggs, 2012; L. Taylor, 2013; Williamson, 2012). Limited published data have highlighted the shift in the needs of deaf signers and the implications for SLI education and delivery of SLI services. Nevertheless, since the beginning of the 21st century, advances in technology and medicine have led to significant increases in the use of technology in communication. For example, cochlear implants and the use of video technology for communication, the widespread use of hearing screenings for newborn infants, the increase in early intervention programs, and the proliferation of mainstream education policy all converged. It is estimated that more than 75% of all deaf children attend public mainstream classrooms (Antia, 2013). As a result, the complexity of language use within the deaf population has increased and is impacted by the highly variable nature of language acquisition by most deaf children (Schembri et al., 2018). In today's U.S. society, deaf people learn ASL at various ages and achieve varying degrees of competence.

In 2015, the National Interpreter Education Center (NIEC), housed at Northeastern University, was charged by its funding source, the U.S. Department of Education RSA, with conducting a study to assess the demographic and technological changes of recent years that impact the population of deaf individuals and the interpreters who work with them (Cogen & Cokely, 2015). The study, referred to as the Trends Report, had the goal of identifying areas for improvement and opportunities for aligning current practices with future needs (p. 1).

The Trends Report documented shifts in the demographics of the signing population, which also suggests shifts in needs. These shifts are attributable to factors associated with medical changes, aging, globalization, and advances in education. For example, the number of newborns and children who are deaf and have co-occurring conditions has significantly increased (Van Naarden Braun et al., 2015). These children present a wide range of unique language and communication needs. The number of deaf senior citizens has also grown because of increases in life longevity and the spike in the number of deaf individuals with congenital rubella syndrome born during the 1960s, who are now entering their 60s. The older deaf population is experiencing changed abilities and communication needs as part of the aging process (Cogen & Cokely, 2015), and as communication shifts online, they are also being impacted (see Roberson et al., 2011). Furthermore, minority and immigrant populations have increased, and deaf individuals within these populations also have unique, complex, and diverse communication needs. On the other end of the spectrum is the increasing number of deaf individuals who are pursuing advanced study and holding professional positions in which they apply highly technical expertise, such as in the fields of real estate, contemporary art, medicine, law, business administration, education, mental health, filmmaking, and information technology (Hauser et al., 2008). These individuals' communication needs involve language and discourse patterns that are specialized and discipline specific.

The result of these demographic changes is that interpreters face a complex and diverse range of language and communication needs, requiring interpreters to have higher levels of competence and the ability to adapt their work to various variables. Language use within the U.S. deaf community is more complex than it was previously because of this wide range of variables. The NIEC 2015 report underscores the need to increase the competence of interpreting practitioners and recruit and expand the practice of DIs to address these demands.

Persistent Issues in the Preparation of Interpreters

When the variables identified in the Trends Report are considered in their totality, they compound the significant challenges historically associated with preparing sign language interpreters in the United States. The most notable challenge is the persistent struggle of second-language learners to attain native-like competency in ASL and the ensuing implication for acquiring interpreting competence (Witter-Merithew et al., 2022). This struggle is manifested in "the gap" between graduation and certification or work-readiness. For several decades, the field of SLI education has been working to address the school-to-work-readiness gap for most IEP graduates.

The gap in work-readiness was first discussed by Anderson and Stauffer (1990), and it has continued to be debated by other authors for the past three decades (e.g., Bozeman & Williamson, 2014; Cogen & Cokely, 2016; Godfrey, 2011; Maroney & Smith, 2010; Patrie, 1994; Ruiz, 2013; Stauffer, 1994; Schafer & Cokely, 2016; Volk, 2014; Witter-Merithew & Johnson, 2004). This gap has been tied to a range of influencing factors, but at its root is insufficient mastery of ASL before the acquisition of interpreting skills (Witter-Merithew et al., 2022). The gap results in many new interpreters having a minimal ability to practice, which is more concerning at a time when greater degrees of competence and specialization are needed to meet the diverse needs of the deaf population. Furthermore, there are few formal, structured postgraduation pathways for induction through which graduates can gain experience and supervision with minimal risk to themselves and their consumers (Cogen & Cokely, 2015; Witter-Merithew et al., 2014).

Progress Toward Competent Practice

In the face of these persistent challenges, incremental progress has been made. In 2006, the RID began requiring a baccalaureate degree as a prerequisite to sitting for the national certification performance exam. In 2010, the NIEC prepared an Interpreter Education Needs Assessment Trends Report (Cokely & Winston, 2010) that examined the findings of the 2006 and 2009 IEP surveys. In the 2009 survey, one measurement explored the graduation–to–RID certification rate for the responding baccalaureate programs. The results showed that 22% achieved the national certification within 6–12 months after graduation, 28% within 12–18 months after graduation, 17% within 18–24 months after graduation, and 6% more than 24 months after graduation. Twenty-eight percent (28%) of the responding programs indicated that they did not track certification rates of graduates.

A few years later, Godfrey (2011) also explored the amount of time needed for graduates to achieve national certification as one aspect of the characteristics of effective IEPs. The data she collected showed improvement from the NIEC's 2009 survey. She reported that baccalaureate programs responded that 50% of graduates required 6–12 months after graduation to earn national-level credentials. Eighty percent (80%) had RID national credentials within 13–18 months after graduation, 20% required 19–24 months, and no program reported requiring longer than 24 months. This suggests that the generalist competence of graduates from baccalaureate IEPs is improving. This information has not been updated since.

Specialist Practice

In further response to the shifting demographic trends impacting the signing deaf population in the United States and the emphasis the NIEC Trends Report placed on the need for increasing the number of DIs to function as language and interpreting specialists (Cogen & Cokely, 2015), the 2017–2021 RSA federally funded interpreter education cycle changed its focus. A significant shift toward expanding specialized interpreting practice began about two decades ago in the United States, primarily because of funding made available by the federal government. Within the U.S. Department of Education, two different sources of funding have benefited aspiring and working interpreter practitioners: the Office of Special Education Programs (OSEP), which has provided grants for the preparation of K–12 interpreters to work with deaf youth, and the RSA, which has been providing funding for more than 30 years for the preparation of interpreters who work with deaf adults. Grant funding from both sources is currently awarded to postsecondary institutions with baccalaureate education programs for interpreters that have achieved program accreditation from the CCIE. Funding was awarded to universities that committed to developing programming that included recruiting and expanding the skills and practice of DIs, explicitly related to working with deafblind individuals, deaf individuals with atypical language use, and deaf individuals within the U.S. legal system.

OSEP Grants for Preparing K–12 Interpreters

The OSEP grants help address state-identified needs for highly qualified personnel working with children in K–12 settings and help ensure that personnel have the necessary skills and knowledge, as defined through evidence-based practices, to successfully serve those children (Johnson et al., 2018). The funding is designated primarily as financial support for SLI students engaged in baccalaureate studies and covers costs, inclusive of tuition and other education provisions within the United States.

Students receiving the funding are referred to as OSEP scholars. In exchange for this financial support, OSEP scholars, upon graduation, agree to work in a related position within a K–12 setting for 2 years for each year of support they received. For example, if they received grant funding for 2 years of their university study, they have a 4-year service obligation to fulfill. If they successfully fulfill this service obligation, they are not required to pay back the funds to the federal government. The federal government has occasionally offered similar programs in the United States to recruit and train personnel for other essential but difficult-to-fill positions within public systems, such as teachers and nurses.

Postsecondary programs preparing sign language interpreters who apply for and receive these funds must have a scope and sequence of curriculum that prepares interpreting OSEP scholars to work in K–12 settings. The cycle and programs vary. An illustration of an OSEP-funded baccalaureate program is the ASL/English Interpreting Program at the University of Northern Colorado. This program consists of 120 credits, 80 of which comprise the major in interpreting. The remaining 40 credits focus on eight areas of liberal arts requirements. Eighteen of the 80 significant credits are specific to the concentration in K–12 interpreting. This 18-credit concentration includes the following types of courses (Johnson et al., 2018, p. 130).

1. Three knowledge courses that explore the education system, classroom environment, classroom discourse, and the communication needs of students who are deaf and hard of hearing;
2. Two skills-based courses specifically focused on interpreting content and discourse specific to the K–12 environment; and
3. Two leadership courses focused on working within the educational system as part of the educational team, ethical decision-making, roles and responsibilities, professionalism, supervision of interpreting systems, conflict resolution, and other related topics.

The other 62 credits in the major constitute the general foundation of competence required for all ASL/English interpreters based on entry-to-practice competencies recognized in SLI and SLI education in the United States (Witter-Merithew & Johnson, 2005). On completion of the OSEP-funded program, learners are expected to complete the EIPA.

As a result of increased specialized training and performance requirements set by state standards, there has been impressive improvement in the performance of K–12 interpreters on the EIPA. Several studies provide detailed analysis of the EIPA performance outcomes of interpreters over time (see Johnson et al., 2015; Johnson et al., 2018, Chapter 5, pp. 65–81; and Johnson & Witter-Merithew, 2004). Additionally, primarily through leadership efforts by administrators within the field of interpreter education in partnership with other stakeholders, state education standards continue to evolve. Such changes help to ensure that deaf children receive appropriate interpreting services and help create meaningful access and inclusion.

RSA-Funded Specialized Training

Various expert workgroups explored specialist competence in interpreting within the National Consortium of Interpreter Education Centers (NCIEC) during the 2005–2016 funding cycle (Witter-Merithew, 2010). These efforts defined competencies and documented best and effective practices in specialized settings, such as the legal, medical/health care, substance abuse/mental health, and vocational rehabilitation (employment) settings. The NCIEC also defined competencies associated with interpreting via technology, trilingual interpreting, and DIs—these competency documents are available at www.interpretereducation.org.

In the United States, a dynamic model of classifying specialization was adopted by the fields of interpreter education and interpreting. This model acknowledges specialization according to setting, function, or population served. *Setting* refers to the time, place, and circumstance in which interpreting is set and all the context surrounding it, including the backgrounds and characteristics of the consumers— e.g., a classroom, medical, or legal setting. *Function* refers to the unique role or activities of the interpreter during the provision of interpreting services—e.g., an interpreter using technology while providing interpreting services, an interpreter serving as a designated interpreter,[4] an interpreter serving as a trilingual interpreter,[5] or a DI serving as a language specialist. *Population served* refers to a specific group of individuals within the deaf population to whom interpreting services are provided—e.g., deafblind individuals or individuals who are "deaf+" (deaf with additional disabilities) (Witter-Merithew, 2010).

Through this approach to specialization, the NCIEC developed a curriculum for preparing legal interpreters, health care interpreters, interpreters working in vocational rehabilitation (employment) settings, DIs, and trilingual interpreters. Annotated bibliographies based on a literature review, best-practices documents, and other resources are also available for use in the field of interpreter education.[6]

THE ROAD AHEAD

Federally funded Department of Education grants are implementing promising developments. In addition, new graduate degree programs in interpreting and interpreting pedagogy offer opportunities for rigorous study and practice, teacher education, and research. In the remaining sections of this chapter, four specific areas of progress in the field of SLI education in the United States will be discussed: (1) increased preparation of and reliance on DIs, (2) preparation of specialist practitioners, (3) the accreditation of IEPs, and (4) graduate education for interpreter practitioners and interpreter educators. Of these four areas of progress, it is the opinion of the present authors that it is the preparation of and reliance on DIs and their expertise as language specialists that will make the most significant contribution to addressing the increasing needs of deaf individuals with atypical use of sign language.

Increased Reliance on DIs

Deaf individuals have served as language and communication brokers for centuries, whether as mediators for family members (Napier, 2021), community ghost-writers (Adam et al., 2011), or translators (Cole, 2019; Stone, 2009); in deaf schools in the classroom with teachers who are not fluent in ASL (Adam et al., 2011; Boudreault, 2005; Forestal, 2005); or in courtrooms writing back and forth with the judge (Leahy, 2020). In the most recent two decades, through training and practice, the work of DIs has evolved into professional practice (Adam et al., 2014). The SLI profession recognizes the innate value of the lived experience of deaf language brokers.

Although research on DIs is still relatively new, a growing body of literature addresses aspects of DI practices. The selected few represent research within the U.S. context: describing DIs' translation and interpreting processes (Forestal, 2011; Sforza, 2014; Tester, 2019); DIs' professionalization and ethical decision-making (Forestal, 2005; Sheneman, 2016); DIs' perceptions of their role (Adam et al., 2014; Cole, 2020; Cole, 2019; NCIEC Deaf Interpreter Work Team, 2010); curriculum development and training of and by DIs (McDermid, 2010; NCIEC Deaf Interpreter Work Team, 2010); identification of fundamental characteristics and functions required of DIs (Bienvenu & Colonomos, 1992; Boudreault, 2005; NCIEC Deaf Interpreter Work Team, 2010); co-working between DIs and non-deaf interpreters (Nicodemus & Taylor, 2014; Reinhardt, 2015; Ressler, 1999; Smith, 2015; Stone & Russell, 2014);

and the practices of DIs in specific settings (Tester, 2018, 2021) or with specific populations, such as deafblind individuals (Collins, 2014; Sforza, 2014).

In 2007, the NCIEC, which was coordinated by the NIEC from 2006–2016 through federal interpreter training grant funds from the RSA, established a Deaf Interpreter Work Team to survey and develop training materials for DIs.[7] Although non-deaf interpreters have interpreter training programs designed explicitly for ASL/English interpreting, Forestal (2005) surveyed experienced DIs and found that most DIs did not have consistent or reliable interpreter education or training. Furthermore, resources designed specifically for DIs were lacking. These findings propelled the NCIEC Deaf Interpreter Work Team to develop a Deaf Interpreter Curriculum intended for delivery as an in-service training program.

The development of the Deaf Interpreter Curriculum began with national surveys of working DIs, focus groups with DIs, and interpreter educators within the United States. The data collected led to identifying and defining a set of DI competencies. These competencies were then translated into six modules following a sequential approach for preparing DIs to work within the community. The curriculum does not address conference interpreting or interpreting in legal settings.

The NCIEC released its Deaf Interpreter Curriculum in 2015. As part of this release, the NCIEC trained a pool of deaf individuals from regions across the United States to serve as trainers and to help infuse the curriculum into in-service training initiatives. These trainers have taken the lead in advancing training opportunities for DIs. The curriculum is also available for download and use by other interpreter educators and trainers. These resources, the results of the survey, and the curriculum are available via a designated website.[8]

Only two pre-service programs explicitly designed for deaf individuals have been established. The Road to Deaf Interpreting,[9] a 2-year, 16-weekend program for deaf individuals interested in becoming interpreters, is based in Massachusetts. The second program is through the National Technical Institute for the Deaf (NTID), which established a noncredit Certificate in Deaf Interpreting program for 2022–2023.

Preparation of Specialist Practitioners

In the 2021–2026 cycle of federal funding for interpreter education, the RSA continued a shift in focus from the NCIEC collaborative to funding fewer programs with increased awards to focus specifically on the shifts in demographics of the deaf population that were highlighted in the 2015 Trends Report (Cogen & Cokely, 2015). Currently, four programs are being implemented in universities that offer baccalaureate education to aspiring ASL/English interpreters, all of which were members of the NCIEC during the 2005–2016 funding cycle and offered

RSA-funded programs during the 2017–2021 cycle. All continue to be accredited by the CCIE.

1. Center for Atypical Language Interpreting (CALI) within Northeastern University's ASL Program addresses the growing demand for interpreters with specialized skills to serve deaf and deafblind persons with atypical language. Curricular materials and other resources are available at the program's website (https://www.northeastern.edu/cali/).

2. CATIE Center, located at St. Catherine University, was awarded two grants to advance interpreter education during the 2021–2026 cycle.

   a. Ways to Work: CATIE Center will design, offer, and evaluate two self-directed tracks offering the educational material used in the cohort tracks, including structure, modules, and resources, for use by novice interpreters across the United States—for replication in an IEP or as a self-directed learning commitment—to prepare novice interpreters to achieve the credentials required by their locations in order to serve the community (https://www.stkate.edu/newswire/news/st-catherine-university-awarded-two-department-education-grants-catie-center).

   b. Project Level Up Advancing Healthcare Interpreter Competencies aims to increase the number of working interpreters trained and qualified to interpret in health care settings, thereby reducing the gaps in equity in health care communication for deaf, hard of hearing, and deafblind individuals. Over the 5-year project, 175 interpreters will complete the Cohort Track, and it is anticipated that more than 3,000 working interpreters will participate in the self-directed track. A community of practice will be available to all participants to foster ongoing discussion, reflection, and learning (https://www.stkate.edu/newswire/news/st-catherine-university-awarded-two-department-education-grants-catie-center).

3. The Deafblind Interpreting National Training and Resource Center at Western Oregon University. On the basis of a determination of the core competencies for interpreting for deafblind individuals through surveys, interviews, focus groups, and a review of the literature that exists in the field of deafblind interpreting, the Center designed the program delivery of online modules as well as an on-site experience. Deafblind individuals are a part of this training, serving as leaders and mentors to the interpreters, advising and supporting their ProTactile ASL skill development and fluency. An online repository of deafblind resources is available. See http://www.dbinterpreting.org for more information.

4. University of Northern Colorado's Improving Rural Interpreter Skills (IRIS) project will serve individuals who work as ASL/English interpreters in rural areas around the country and commonly lack the comprehensive knowledge and skill sets required to provide equal communication access to the deaf, hard of hearing,

and deafblind communities. They are generally overlooked by training entities and professional organizations. It will focus on improving the skills of 80 working interpreters and 20 mentors/facilitators in designated rural areas across the United States.[10]

These grant-funded programs continue to advance specialized practice for SLI in the United States significantly. They also offer ongoing resources for interpreter educators and mentors that support the advancement of both generalist and specialized interpreting practice. Advancement of both is needed to respond to the changing demographic trends within the deaf population.

Accreditation of IEPs

Another area of continuing progress in interpreter education is the accreditation of IEPs. The accreditation of IEPs is under the purview of the CCIE. CCIE was founded in 2006 to promote professionalism in interpreter education, resulting from leadership and development led primarily by the CIT over nearly two decades. Standards were developed, reviewed, and approved, and options evolved for establishing a separate and autonomous accreditation body. The overarching goal of accreditation of IEPs is to help ensure that graduates from bachelor's degree programs are qualified to enter the workforce and work successfully as practitioners.

The CCIE accreditation process requires programs to evidence compliance with a robust set of standards. The standards address policies on entry requirements, curricular goals, faculty selection, teaching methods, assessment, and projected student outcomes. At the time of this writing, 15 baccalaureate degree and three associate degree interpreting programs have been accredited.[11] This is approximately 13.5% of the 150 programs currently offered in the United States. Thus, although national standards exist and have been adopted, the accreditation system is still in an emergent stage as an oversight body helping to regulate IEPs (Witter-Merithew, 2018). After nearly 15 years of applying the standards to the accreditation process, the standards are undergoing a national review and revision process to understand the cause behind the low accreditation rate.

Increasing Research and Scholarship

A final area of progress in interpreter education in the United States is the increase in graduate-level SLI and interpreter pedagogy programs. Gallaudet University established the first master's program in SLI in 1988 (Metzger et al., 2019). Since 2010, four additional graduate-level programs in interpreting and pedagogy have opened and are thriving, and one PhD program has opened (Cogen & Cokely, 2015).

With the increase of graduates and PhD programs, there has been a marked increase in research and scholarship. The development and introduction of Dean and Pollard's (2013) *Demand Control Schema: Interpreting as a Practice Profession* is an example of how research has shifted interpreter education and practice to align with practice professions. Their scholarship has also deepened the exploration of ethics and interpreter decision-making (Dean, 2014; Dean & Pollard, 2013). Research in the United States still focuses heavily on the education and practice of SLI. There has been little attention to the resulting demand and impact on the public service institutions and public schools where deaf students receive interpreting services in order to access their education, which would inform the education and training of interpreters (Cogen & Cokely, 2015; Nicodemus & Swabey, 2011; Swabey & Nicodemus, 2011).

Despite the limited attention to the demand, there is a growing number of deaf non-interpreting scholars who are contributing to further analysis of the profession, bringing more critical "deaf eyes" on interpreting issues, ranging from the impact of interpreters on deaf academics to deaf patients in health care to interpreting in education and its impact on deaf learners (see Holcomb & Smith, 2018). In another volume, deaf professionals and professional interpreters published strategies for working together as partners in the interpreting event, specifically when interpreters become designated to deaf professionals (see Hauser et al., 2008). Several researchers have challenged the principle of whether SLI fosters a false sense of inclusion (e.g., Robinson et al., 2020) or might actively cause language deprivation in deaf children in public school settings (e.g., Caselli et al., 2020).

Another notable shift in the research is attention to increasing representation and recruiting diverse community members within SLI education programs, whether as faculty or as students. Diverse representation within the faculty encourages cultural competence, leading to active recruitment and retention of African American interpreting students within the IEP (Oyedele, 2015). Furthermore, IEPs that include ASL instruction often are not a good fit for heritage ASL users, both deaf and hearing, which in turn reduces their opportunity to receive formal interpreter training and professional recognition within the profession (Cogen & Cokely, 2015; Isakson, 2018; Williamson, 2016). There is also a small case study of a DI instructor teaching the interpreting process (Tester et al., 2018), which reported a positive reaction from non-deaf students in learning and discussing advanced interpreting theory in ASL. These studies are a part of the shift for interpreter education to become more attentive to the demographic shifts within the deaf population and to encourage alternative approaches to better reflect their needs by recruiting and training more fluent heritage ASL users, interpreters of color, and DIs.

However, studies have also shown that the higher education structure is causing IEPs to be overstretched, and the job demands for interpreter educators are high

(Cogen & Cokely, 2015; Webb & Napier, 2015). Given that many educators are employed casually on an ad hoc/adjunct basis, or not yet in or on a tenure track position, there needs to be greater investment into programs by some of the institutions at large. In the study by Webb & Napier (2015), they identified that educators had a large workload, showcasing 19 tasks that interpreter educators were expected to manage. These findings were based on data collected from educators working in four countries, one of which was the United States. The majority are tasks that are the result of working in an academic institution (e.g., administrative tasks, committee participation) versus the teaching of interpreting and direct contact with students. They also highlighted that educators focus on developing community partnerships and seeking funding to support resource development. Webb (2017) posited that these factors were perceived by interpreter educators as impacting student work-readiness, noting that further exploration is needed to see how these factors impact learners and the ability of the university to function effectively as the gatekeepers for the profession.

CONCLUSION

In the past decade, progress has been made in advancing interpreter education in the United States in several ways: an increase in baccalaureate pre-service programs; the accreditation of IEPs; the shift to more specialized training; the recruitment of, training of, and reliance on DIs; and the availability of more graduate programs in interpreting and interpreting pedagogy. There has also been a slow but steady improvement in closing the gap between graduation and certification. Moreover, recently, greater attention has been given to expanding the recruitment and training of interpreters of color and heritage signers, both deaf and hearing. However, much more still needs to be achieved, particularly as it pertains to research to determine the effectiveness of the progress that has been made and to find consistent and creative ways to ensure that deaf consumers have an active role in gatekeeping.

De Meulder and Haualand (2019, p. 13) argued that "the provision of sign language interpreting services has become the institutionally normative, often unquestioned, solution to grant deaf people access to education and public services." Although we have seen improvements in the pre-service and in-service training options for aspiring and working interpreters, we need more research on the impact of specialist practice and the quality of access received by deaf consumers (e.g., Kurz, Schick, & Hauser, 2015). Ultimately, we must strive to ensure that as we seek to advance, the needs and interests of the deaf population guide our decisions and actions.

Notes

1. https://cit-asl.org/about/
2. https://rid.org/membership/benefits/member-sections/
3. In the United States, *K–12* refers to kindergarten and first through 12th grades. K–12 is a short form for public and private education before college and university.
4. *Designated interpreters* are collaborative partners on staff who work at the direction of a deaf professional (Hall et al., 2019).
5. A *trilingual interpreter* is someone who interprets between English, Spanish, and ASL.
6. See www.interpretereducation.org under the Specialization section.
7. See Cokely & Winston, 2009, for the complete history of NCIEC.
8. See www.diinstitute.org
9. See: https://roadtodeafinterpreting.webs.com/
10. See https://www.unco.edu/irisproject/
11. See http://www.ccie-accreditation.org/accredited-programs.html

References

Adam, R., Carty, B., & Stone, C. (2011). Ghostwriting: Deaf translators within the Deaf community. *Babel, 57*(4), 375–393.

Adam, R., Stone, C., Collins, S. D., & Metzger, M. (Eds.). (2014). *Deaf interpreters at work: International insights.* Gallaudet University Press.

Anderson, C., & Stauffer, L. (1990). *Identifying standards for the training of interpreters for deaf people.* University of Arkansas Rehabilitation Research and Training Center on Deafness and Hearing Impairment.

Annarino, P., Aponte-Samalot, M., & Quinto-Pozos, D. (Eds.) (2014). *Towards effective practice: Interpreting in Spanish-influenced settings.* National Consortium of Interpreter Education Centers.

Antia, S. (2013). *Raising and educating deaf children: Foundations for policy, practice and outcomes.* http://www.raisingandeducatingdeafchildren.org/2014/01/01/deaf-and-hard-of-hearing-students-in-the-mainstream/

Ball, C. (2013). *Legacies and legends: History of interpreter education from 1800 to the 21st century.* Interpreting Consolidated.

Bienvenu, M., & Colonomos, B. (1992). Relay interpreting in the '90s. In L. Swabey (Ed.), *Proceedings of the Eighth National Convention of the Conference of Interpreter Trainers* (pp. 69–80). Conference of Interpreter Trainers.

Blackorby, J., & Knokey, A. M. (2006). *A national profile of students with hearing impairments in elementary and middle school: A special topic report from the Special Education Elementary Longitudinal Study.* SRI International.

Boudreault, P. (2005). Deaf interpreters. In T. Janzen (Ed.), *Topics in signed language interpreting: Theory and practice* (pp. 323–355). John Benjamins.

Bozeman, L., & Williamson, M. (2014). Roots: Engaging the deaf community as language mentors. In *Our roots: The essence of our future: Proceedings of the Conference of Interpreter Trainers.* Conference of Interpreter Trainers.

Caselli, N. K., Hall, W. C., & Henner, J. (2020). American Sign Language interpreters in public schools: An illusion of inclusion that perpetuates language deprivation. *Maternal and Child Health Journal* (24). https://doi.org/10.1007/s10995-020-02975-7

Cogen, C., & Cokely, D. (2015). *Preparing interpreters for tomorrow: Report on a study of emerging trends in interpreting and implications for interpreter education.* National Interpreter Education Center (NIEC), Northeastern University.

Cokely, D. (2005). Shifting positionality: A critical examination of the turning point in the relationship of interpreters and the deaf community. In M. Marschark, R. Peterson, & E. A. Winston (Eds.), *Sign language interpreting and interpreter education* (pp. 3–28). Oxford University Press.

Cokely, D. (2011). Sign language interpreters—Complicit in a devil's bargain? Paper presented at Street Leverage. http://www.streetleverage.com/2011/12/sign-language-interpreters-complicit-in-a-devils-bargain/

Cokely, D. (2012). Vanquished native voices—A sign language interpreting crisis? Paper presented at Street Leverage. http://www.streetleverage.com/2012/01/vanquished-native-voices-a-sign-language-interpreting-crisis/

Cokely, D., & Winston, B. (2009). The National Consortium of Interpreter Education Centers in the United States of America. In J. Napier (Ed.), *International perspectives on sign language interpreter education* (pp. 267–293). Gallaudet University Press.

Cole, J. (2020). Deaf translators: What are they thinking? *Journal of Interpretation, 28*(1), 23.

Cole, J. (2019). *Storied realities: An examination of the lived experiences of deaf translators.* Unpublished doctoral dissertation, Gallaudet University.

Collins, S. D. (2014). Adverbial morphemes in Tactile Sign Language: Deaf-blind interpreting. In R. Adam, C. Stone, S. D. Collins, & M. Metzger (Eds.), *Deaf interpreters at work: International insights* (pp. 117–139). Gallaudet University Press.

Colonomos, B. (2013). *Sign language interpreters and the quest for a Deaf heart.* Paper presented at Street Leverage. http://www.streetleverage.com/2013/02/sign-language-interpreters-and-the-quest-for-a-deaf-heart/

De Meulder, M., & Haualand, H. (2019). Sign language interpreting services: A quick fix for inclusion? *Translation and Interpreting Studies.* https://doi.org/10.1075/tis.18008.dem

Dean, R. K. (2014). Condemned to repetition? An analysis of problem-setting and problem-solving in sign language interpreting ethics. *The International Journal of Translation and Interpreting Research, 6*(1), 60–75. https://doi.org/10.12807/ti.106201.2014.a04

Dean, R. K., & Pollard Jr., R. Q. (2013). *The demand control schema: Interpreting as a practice profession.* Create-Space Independent Publishing Platform.

Department of Education. (2021). Education in a pandemic: The disparate impacts of COVID-19 on America's students. Department of Education: Office of Civil Rights. https://www2.ed.gov/about/offices/list/ocr/docs/20210608-impacts-of-covid19.pdf

Forestal, E. (2005). The emerging professionals: Deaf interpreters and their views and experiences on training. In M. Marschark, R. Peterson, & E. A. Winston (Eds.), *Sign language interpreting and interpreter education* (pp. 235–258). Oxford University Press. https://doi.org/10.1093/acprof/9780195176940.001.0001

Forestal, E. (2011). *Deaf interpreters: Exploring their processes of interpreting.* Unpublished PhD Dissertation, Capella University.

Godfrey, L. (2011). Characteristics of effective interpreter education programs in the United States. *International Journal of Interpreter Education, 3*, 88–105.

Hauser, A., Hauser, P. & Finch, K. (Eds.) (2008). *Deaf professionals and designated interpreters: A new paradigm.* Gallaudet University Press.

Holcomb, T. K., & Smith, D. H. (Eds.). (2018). *Deaf eyes on interpreting.* Gallaudet University Press.

Hunt, D. I. J., & Nicodemus, B. (2014). *Gatekeeping in ASL-English interpreter education programs: Assessing the suitability of students for professional practice.* 18.

Isakson, S. K. (2018). The case for heritage ASL instruction for hearing heritage signers. *Sign Language Studies, 18*(3), 385–411.

Johnson, L., Schick, B., & Bolster, L. (2015). *EIPA data analysis: K–12 patterns of practice.* CIT Poster Session.

Johnson, L., Taylor, M. M., Schick, B., Brown, S., Bolster, L. (2018). *Complexities in educational interpreting: An investigation into patterns of practice.* Interpreting Consolidated.

Johnson, L., & Witter-Merithew, A. (2004). Interpreting skills acquired at a distance: Results of a data-driven study. *Journal of Interpretation,* 95–115.

Kurz, K., Schick, B., & Hauser, P. (2015). Deaf children's science content learning in direct instruction versus interpreted instruction. *Journal of Science Education for Students with Disabilities, 18*(1), 23–37. https://doi.org/10.14448/jsesd.07.0003

Leahy, A. (2020). *Paths to signed language interpreting in Great Britain and America, 1150–1900.* Unpiublished dooctoral dissertation, University of Birmingham.

Maroney, E., & Smith, A. R. (2010). Defining the nature of the "gap" between interpreter education, certification and readiness-to-work: A research study of bachelor's degree graduates. *Views, 27,* 35–37.

Mathers, C., & Witter-Merithew, A. (2014). The contribution of deaf interpreters to gatekeeping within the interpreting profession: Connecting to our roots. In D. Hunt & S. Hafer (Eds.), *Our roots: The essence of our future conference proceedings.* CIT Publications.

McDermid, C. (2010). Culture brokers, advocates, or conduits: Pedagogical considerations for deaf interpreter education. *International Journal of Interpreter Education, 2* (1), Article 8. https://tigerprints.clemson.edu/ijie/vol2/iss1/8 26

Metzger, M., Cagle, K., & Hunt, D. (2019). Undergraduate and graduate level interpreter education: Pedagogical considerations. In Sawyer, D., Austermühl, F., & Raído, E. (Eds.), *The evolving curriculum in interpreter and translator education. Stakeholder perspectives and voices.* John Benjamins.

Mitchell, R., Young, T., Bachleda, B, & Karchmer, M., (2006). How many deaf people are there in the United States? Estimates from the Survey of Income and Program Participation. *Journal of Deaf Studies and Deaf Education, 11*(1),112–9.

Mooney, M., Aramburo, A., Davis, J., Dunbar, T., Roth, A., & Nishimura, J. (2001). *National multicultural interpreting project curriculum.* El Paso Community College. https://stkate.app.box.com/s/g4nrnppvc7rof1oa4s6b1z5ff8c4jjca

Napier, J. (2021). *Sign language brokering in deaf-hearing families.* London: Palgrave.

National Association of Interpreters in Education (2021). *State requirements for educational interpreters.* naiedu.org/state-standards/

NCIEC Deaf Interpreter Work Team. (2010). *Towards effective practice: Competencies of the deaf interpreter* (p. 15). NCIEC: The National Consortium of Interpreter Education Centers. http://www.diinstitute.org/wp-content/uploads/2012/07/DC_Final_Final.pdf

Nicodemus, B., & Swabey, L. (Eds.). (2011). *Advances in interpreting research: Inquiry in action.* John Benjamins.

Nicodemus, B., & Taylor, M. (2014). Deaf and hearing interpreting team preparation: A study using conversation analysis. In R. Adam, M. Metzger, C. Stone, & S. D. Collins (Eds.), *Deaf interpreters at work: International insights* (pp. 90–116). Gallaudet University Press.

Oyedele, E. W. (2015). *Persistence of African-American/black signed language interpreters in the United States: The importance of culture and capital.* [Master's thesis]. Western Oregon University. https://digitalcommons.wou.edu/theses/19?utm_source=digitalcommons.wou.edu/theses/19

Patrie, C. J. (1994). The readiness-to-work gap. In E. A. Winston (Ed.), *Mapping our course: A collaborative venture: Proceedings of the 10th National Conference of Interpreter Trainers* (pp. 53–56).

Reinhardt, L. R. (2015). *Deaf-hearing interpreter teams: Navigating trust in shared space.* Thesis, Western Oregon University. https://digitalcommons.wou.edu/theses/21

Ressler, C. I. (1999). A comparative analysis of a direct interpretation and an intermediary interpretation in American Sign Language. *Journal of Interpretation*, 71–97.

Road to Deaf Interpreting. (n.d.). Retrieved June 26, 2020, from https://roadtodeafinterpreting.webs.com/

Roberson, L., Russell, D., & Shaw, R. (2011). American Sign Language/English interpreting in legal settings: Current practices in North America. *Journal of Interpretation*, *21*(1), 64–79.

Robinson, O., Sheneman, N., & Henner, J. (2020). *Toxic ableism among interpreters: Impeding deaf people's linguistic rights through pathological posturing.* Conference Proceedings of the 2019 WASLI conference. Paris, France.

Ruiz, M. J. (2013). *Professional project curriculum development: Experiential learning in interpreter education programs.* [Master's thesis]. Western Oregon University, Monmouth, OR. https://digitalcommons.wou.edu/theses/9

Schafer, T. & Cokely, D. (2016). *Understanding the challenges of deaf interpreters: Needs assessment report.* National Interpreter Education Center, Northeastern University. http://www.interpretereducation.org/wp-content/uploads/2014/02/Final-Deaf-Interpreter-FG-Report-12-16.pdf

Schembri, A., Fenlon, J., Cormier, K., and Johnston, T. (2018). Sociolinguistic typology and sign languages. *Frontiers in Psychology*, *9*, Article 200.

Sforza, S. (2014). DI(2) Team Interpreting. In R. Adam, S. D. Collins, M. Metzger, & C. Stone (Eds.), *Deaf interpreters at work: International insights* (pp. 19–28). Gallaudet University Press.

Shaw, S., & Halley, M. (2021). Service learning during the COVID-19 pandemic: A model of temporal, spatial, and cultural adaptability, *Journal of Interpretation*, *29*(1), Article 3.

Sheneman, N. (2016). Deaf interpreters' ethics: Reflections on training and decision-making. *Journal of Interpretation*, *25*(1), Article 8.

Smith, A. (2015). *Signposting: Neutral channel communications in deaf-hearing interpreting teams.* [Unpublished master's thesis], The University of Applied Sciences Magdeburg-Stendal, Magdeburg, Germany.

Stauffer, L. (1994). A response to the "readiness-to-work gap." In E. A. Winston (Ed.), *Mapping our course: A collaborative venture: Proceedings of the 10th National Conference of Interpreter Trainers* (pp. 57–59). CIT.

Stone, C., & Russell, D. (2014). Conference interpreting and interpreting teams. In R. Adam, C. A. Stone, S. D. Collins, & M. Metzger (Eds.), *Deaf interpreters at work: International insights* (pp.140–156). Gallaudet University Press.

Swabey, L., & Nicodemus, B. (2011). Bimodal bilingual interpreting in the U.S. healthcare system: A critical linguistic activity in need of investigation. In B. Nicodemus & L. Swabey (Eds.), *Advances in interpreting research: Inquiry in action* (pp. 241–259). John Benjamins.

Suggs, T. (2012). A Deaf perspective: Cultural respect in sign language interpreting. *Street Leverage*. http://www.streetleverage.com/2012/08/a-deaf-perspective-cultural-respect-in-sign-language-interpreting/

Taylor, L. (2013). Modern questor: Connecting the past to the future of the field. *Street Leverage*. http://www.streetleverage.com/2013/02/modern-questor-connecting-the-past-to-the-future-of-the-field/

Tester, C. (2018). How American Sign Language–English interpreters who can hear determine need for a deaf interpreter for court proceedings. *Journal of Interpretation, 26*(1), 28.

Tester, C. (2019). *Scoping study: What is the Deaf interpreter's perception of their interpreting process in the courts.* [Unpublished manuscript]. Heriot Watt University.

Tester, C. (2021). *Intralingual interpreting in the courtroom: An ethnographic study of Deaf interpreters' perceptions of their role and positioning.* [Unpublished doctoral dissertation]. Heriot Watt University, Edinburgh, Scotland.

Tester, C., Olsen, D., & Hills, R. (2018). A case study of a deaf interpreter teaching interpreting process courses. In *Reaching new heights in interpreter education—Mentoring, teaching and leadership: Proceedings of the 2018 Conference of Interpreter Trainers.* CIT. https://citsl.org/a-case-study-of-a-deaf-interpreter-teaching-interpreting-process-courses/

Van Naarden Braun, K., Christensen, D., Doernberg, N., Schieve, L., Rice, C., Wiggins, L., Schendel, D., & Yeargin-Allsopp, M. (2015). Trends in the prevalence of autism spectrum disorder, cerebral palsy, hearing loss, intellectual disability, and vision impairment: Metropolitan Atlanta, 1991–2010. *PLoS ONE* 10(4): e0124120. https://doi.org/10.1371/journal.pone.0124120.

Volk, C. (2014). Sign language interpreter education: Time for a national call to action. Paper presented at Street Leverage. http://www.streetleverage.com/2014/10/sign-language-interpreter-education-time-for-a-national-call-to-action/

Webb, S. (2017). *Job demands, job resources, wellbeing, and student outcomes: A study of sign language interpreter educators' perceptions.* [Unpublished doctoral dissertation]. Heriot Watt University.

Webb, S., & Napier, J. (2015). Job demands and resources: An exploration. *International Journal of Interpreter Education, 7*(1), 23–50.

Williamson, A. (2012). The cost of invisibility: Codas and the sign language interpreting profession. Paper presented at Street Leverage. http://www.streetleverage.com/2012/11/the-cost-of-invisibility-codas-and-the-sign-language-interpreting-profession/.

Williamson, A. (2016). Lost in the shuffle: Deaf-parented interpreters and their paths to interpreting careers. *International Journal of Interpreter Education* 8(1), 4–22.

Witter-Merithew, A. (2010). *Conceptualizing a framework for specialization in ASL-English interpreting: A report of project findings and recommendations.* Mid-America Regional Interpreter Education Center of the NCIEC. http://www.interpretereducation.org/specialization/

Witter-Merithew, A. (2018). Certification, licensure, and specialty endorsements: The credentialing of sign language interpreters. In L. Roberson & S. Shaw (Eds.) *Signed language interpreting in the 21st century: Foundations and practice.* Gallaudet University Press.

Witter-Merithew, A., & Johnson, L. (2004). Market disorder within the field of sign language interpreting: Professionalization implications. *Journal of Interpretation,* 19–56.

Witter-Merithew, A., & Johnson, L. (2005). *Toward competent practice: Conversations with stakeholders.* RID Publications.

Witter-Merithew, A., Laurion, R., Gordon, P., & Mathers, C. (2014). Field-based induction: Creating the essential elements for building competence in specialized settings. In
Our roots—the essence of our future: Proceedings of the 2014 Conference of Interpreter Trainers
(pp. 187–201). http://www.cit-asl.org/new/past- conferences/proceedings/2014-proceedings/
Witter-Merithew, A., Taylor, M. M., Johnson, L., & Bonni, E. (2022). Deaf language mentoring: Case studies, outcomes, and looking forward. In Swabey, L. & Herring, R. (Eds.),
*Insights and innovations in signed language interpreting pedagogy: Celebrating forty years of the
conference of interpreter trainers.* Gallaudet University Press.

STACEY WEBB, JEMINA NAPIER, AND
ROBERT ADAM

Conclusion

By learning about sign language translation and interpreting (SLTI) education in other contexts than our own, we can develop perspective on where we are, how far we have come, and how far we have to go, and we can provide ideas in how to get there.

The aim of this volume has been to share insights and expertise on SLTI education within both established programs and the ad hoc training world. The diverse content within each chapter highlights varying degrees of advancement in SLTI training across countries. Nevertheless, a common thread unites them all—a shared commitment to the pursuit of professionalism and the professionalization of this vital field.

Throughout the chapters, several recurring themes have emerged. First, the changing dynamics within contemporary deaf communities have made it increasingly challenging for interpreting students to gain authentic sign language exposure in deaf spaces. Many programs admit students with no prior sign language knowledge, requiring them to simultaneously learn sign language and interpreting skills over the typical 3- to 4-year program duration, leading to a readiness-to-work gap. While some programs incorporate work placements or internships in sign language environments or shadowing working interpreters, such practices are inconsistent.

Additionally, it is important to note that SLTI educational programs cater to predominantly hearing nonsigning students. In many countries, opportunities for deaf interpreter/translator training, accreditation, or work are still in the early stages of development. Some countries have yet to recognize the potential for deaf interpreters and translators. Only a few countries have separate deaf interpreter qualifications, and only one country at the time of publication has a specific deaf translator qualification.

Looking ahead, several consistent themes about the future of the field of SLTI also emerged across the chapters. These include exploring strategies to encourage both deaf and hearing heritage signers to pursue careers in the profession and how to grow and support the development of the deaf SLTI profession.

The growing importance of online learning, particularly in a post–COVID-19 world, prompts discussions on how to expand training reach through digital platforms. Furthermore, in anticipation of the evolving landscape of SLTI, considerations involve identifying the future soft and hard skills necessary to work as a sign language interpreting (SLI) or sign language translation (SLT) practitioner, given the increasing number of individuals joining the deaf community as new signers.[1] These considerations raise further questions about how to diversify the profession, not only in terms of representativeness (e.g., race, gender, disability, sexuality) but also potentially teaching SLTI students a range of skills, such as subtitling, respeaking, and notetaking, to work with a wider spectrum of deaf people with diverse language access needs.

Finally, discussions centered around the role of SLT in SLTI and whether it should be taught as a separate discipline and to whom it should be taught. These ongoing conversations aim to shape the future of SLTI education and practice, ensuring it remains responsive to the evolving needs of both deaf people and interpreting professionals.

Throughout these chapters, we have delved into the complexities of SLTI education worldwide. We hope that, like us, you have found the mix of similarities and differences intriguing. As we explore the experiences of fellow educators and witness the evolution of our profession, we gain insights into our own journeys. Learning about SLTI education in diverse contexts not only provides perspective on our progress but also sparks questions about the future for ourselves, our profession, and our pedagogy. We believe that these questions are the seeds of meaningful discussions, the quest for answers, and the catalysts for positive change. We encourage you to ponder, "What's next for me? What's next for my profession? What is the best way to train deaf and hearing practitioners in my country?" Let these inquiries propel you forward.

In the ever-evolving landscape of the SLTI profession and SLTI education, it is through these inquiries and dialogues that we continue to shape a profession that is not only responsive to the needs of deaf communities but also adaptable to the challenges and opportunities of our dynamic world. Embracing the questions that lie ahead, we embark on a journey of continuous improvement and innovation, ensuring that SLTI connects languages, cultures, and, most importantly, people.

Although it was not possible for this volume to provide an exhaustive overview of SLTI education worldwide, it has offered an assorted range of examples that can offer key insights into SLTI education across international contexts. We envisage that the chapters in this volume will provide readers with a broader global perspective on the state of SLTI education and training across nations and what lessons we can learn from one another. Furthermore, we aspire to support the many countries that still lack formalized SLTI education programs in their pursuit of further professionalization of SLTI.

NOTE

1. *New signers* are defined as people who learn a sign language later in life and can include both deaf and hearing people: De Meulder, M. (2018) "So, why do you sign?" Deaf and hearing new signers, their motivation, and revitalisation policies for sign languages. *Applied Linguistics Review, 10*(4), 705–724.

CONTRIBUTORS

Note: Asterisks denote contributors who are now deceased.

Robert Adam
  Heriot-Watt University
  Edinburgh, United Kingdom

Washington Akaranga
  University of Nairobi
  Nairobi, Kenya

Alejandra Álvarez
  National Autonomous
  University of Mexico
  Mexico City, Mexico

Karen Bontempo
  Macquarie University
  Sydney, Australia

John Buyinza
  Kyambogo University
  Kampala, Uganda

José Luís Magaña Cabrera
  Interpreter, Translator, and Educator
  Mexico City, Mexico

Tatiana Davidenko*
  Galina Zaitseva Centre for Deaf Studies
  and Bilingual Education
  Moscow, Russia

Goedele De Clerck
  Independent Researcher and Counselor
  Flanders, Belgium

Kristof De Weerdt
  KU Leuven
  Antwerp, Belgium

Nad'a Hynková Dingová*
  Charles University
  Prague, Czechia

Razaq Fakir
  Overseas Interpreting
  Valencia, Spain

Daniel Fobi
  University of Education
  Winneba, Ghana

Karolien Gebruers
  Heriot-Watt University
  Edinburgh,
  United Kingdom

Nadja Grbić
  University of Graz
  Graz, Austria

Timothy Mac Hadjah
  Leiden University
  Leiden, The Netherlands

Liisa Halkosaari
  Humak University of
  Applied Sciences
  Helsinki, Finland

Hilde Haualand
 Oslo Metropolitan University
 Oslo, Norway

Selman Hoti
 Kosovar Association of the Deaf
 Prishtina, Kosovo

Nigel Howard
 University of British Columbia and
 University of Victoria
 Vancouver, Canada

Kristy Jonckers
 KU Leuven
 Antwerp, Belgium

Leonida Tausi Kaula
 Center for Sign Language Interpreting
 Services
 Nairobi, Kenya

Harumi Kimura
 College of the National Rehabilitation
 Center for Persons with Disabilities
 Tokorozawa City, Japan

Anna Komarova*
 Galina Zaitseva Centre for Deaf Studies
 and Bilingual Education
 Moscow State Linguistic University
 Moscow, Russia

Denisa Lachmanová
 Charles University
 Prague, Czechia

Lorraine Leeson
 Trinity College Dublin
 Dublin, Ireland

Patricia Levitzke-Gray
 Shenton College Deaf Education Centre
 Perth, Australia

Arttu Liikamaa
 Humak University of Applied
 Sciences
 Helsinki, Finland

Stephanie Linder
 Danish Deaf Association
 Copenhagen, Denmark

Wei Lu
 Zhejiang Vocational College of
 Special Education China
 Zhejiang, China

Dorothy Lule
 Kyambogo University
 Kampala, Uganda

Sam Lutalo-Kiingi
 Kyambogo University
 Kampala, Uganda

Teresa Lynch
 Trinity College Dublin
 Dublin, Ireland

George Major
 Auckland University of
 Technology
 Auckland, New Zealand

Juha Manunen
 Humak University of Applied
 Sciences
 Kuopio, Finland

Elisa Maroney
 Western Oregon University
 Monmouth, OR, United States of
 America

Rachel McKee
 Victoria University of Wellington
 Wellington, New Zealand

Johanna Mesch
　Stockholm University
　Stockholm, Sweden

Noriko Miyazawa
　National Research Association for Sign
　Language Interpretation
　Kyoto, Japan

Ronice Müller de Quadros
　Federal University of Santa
　Catarina
　Florianópolis, Brazil

Jefwa G. Mweri
　University of Nairobi
　Nairobi, Kenya

Jemina Napier
　Heriot-Watt University
　Edinburgh, United Kingdom

Jeanette Nicholson
　Asign
　Toronto, Canada

Anna-Lena Nilsson
　Norwegian University of
　Science and technology
　Trondheim, Norway

Marco Stanley Nyarko
　Kwame Nkrumah University of
　Science and Technology
　Kumasi, Ghana

Radka Nováková
　Charles University
　Prague, Czechia

Susie Ovens
　Auckland University of Technology
　Auckland, New Zealand

Natasha Parkins-Maliko
　University of the Witwatersrand
　Johannesburg, South Africa

Sergio Peña
　Independent Interpreter and Educator
　Mexico City, Mexico

Debra Russell
　University of Alberta
　Edmonton, Canada

Sarah Sheridan
　Trinity College Dublin
　Dublin, Ireland

Christian Stalzer
　University of Graz
　Graz, Austria

Marianne Rossi Stumpf
　Federal University of Santa Catarina
　Florianópolis, Brazil

Malin Tesfazion
　Stockholm University
　Stockholm, Sweden

Christopher Tester
　Independent Interpreter and Educator
　New York, NY, United States of America

Elisabet Tiselius
　Stockholm University
　Stockholm, Sweden

Graham H. Turner
　Heriot-Watt University
　Edinburgh, United Kingdom

Myriam Vermeerbergen
　KU Leuven
　Antwerp, Belgium

Valeria Vinogradova
   Center for Language and Brain
   HSE University
   Moscow, Russia

Stacey Webb
   Heriot-Watt University
   Edinburgh, United Kingdom

Anna Witter-Merithew
   Interpreter Educator and Consultant
   North Carolina, United States of
   America

Bencie Woll
   University College London
   London, United Kingdom

Xiaoyan Xiao
   Xiamen University
   Xiamen, China

Xiao Zhao
   Xiamen University
   Xiamen, China

INDEX

Figures and tables are indicated by "f" and "t" following page numbers.